The Complete One-Week Preparation for the CISCO CCENT/CCNA ICND1 Exam 640-822

A Certification Guide with over 2000 Sample Questions and Answers with Explanations Second Edition (March 2011)

Thaar AL_Taiey
MSNE, MSSE, BSEE, IWWHS

The Complete One-Week Preparation for the CISCO CCENT/CCNA ICND1 Exam 640-822 A Certification Guide with over 2000 Sample Questions and Answers with Explanations Second Edition (March 2011)

Thaar AL_Taiey

iUniverse publishing

The Complete One-Week Preparation for the CISCO CCENT/CCNA ICND1 Exam 640-822
A Certification Guide with over 2000 Sample Questions and Answers with Explanations Second Edition (March 2011)

This book is designed to provide information about Cisco Official topics for the ICND1 Exam for the CCENT certification. Every effort has been made to make this book as complete and accurate as possible, but no warranty or fitness is implied. The information is provided on an "as is" basis. The author and the publisher shall have neither liability nor responsibility to any person or entity with respect to any loss or damages arising from the information contained in this book. The opinions expressed in this book belong to the author.

If you have any comments regarding how we could improve the quality of this book, or otherwise alter it to better suit your needs, you can contact us through an e-mail at feedback@thaartechnologies.com. Please be sure to include the book's title and ISBN in your message. We greatly appreciate your assistance.

TRADEMARKS
CISCO, CCNA, ICND1, ICND2 and CCENT are registered trademarks of CISCO Systems, Inc. and/or its affiliates in the US and certain other countries. All other trademarks are the property of their respective owners.

iUniverse books may be ordered through booksellers or by contacting:

iUniverse
1663 Liberty Drive
Bloomington, IN 47403
www.iuniverse.com
1-800-Authors (1-800-288-4677)

Because of the dynamic nature of the Internet, any Web addresses or links contained in this book may have changed since publication and may no longer be valid. The views expressed in this work are solely those of the author and do not necessarily reflect the views of the publisher, and the publisher hereby disclaims any responsibility for them.

Any people depicted in stock imagery provided by Thinkstock are models, and such images are being used for illustrative purposes only.

Certain stock imagery © Thinkstock.

ISBN: 978-1-4620-0934-3 (pbk)
ISBN: 978-1-4620-0935-0 (ebk)

Library of Congress Control Number: 2011905022

Printed in the United States of America

iUniverse rev. date: 4/1/2011

Designer and Editor:
Thaar AL_Taiey and iUniverse teams
Technical reviewer:
Thaar AL_Taiey

Comments

The following reviews are received for the previous books of the author:

kirkusreviews
"http://www.kirkusreviews.com/book-reviews/non-fiction/thaar-al_taiey/complete-one-week-preparation-cisco-ccentccna-icnd/"
Editor Review (reviewed on November 23, 2010)
An ambitious collection of 2,000 practice questions and answers that attempts to familiarize the reader with the first CISCO networking exam, the CCENT.
Through the device of questions and answers, AL_Taiey encourages students to carefully read about the concepts essential to an understanding of how computer networks function and the process by which they are designed. By formatting the book into sections that map to critical concepts in the CISCO curriculum, AL_Taiey aids the student in concentrating on the areas in which they may feel they need to improve. The questions are direct even if the language is sometimes awkward. On several of AL_Taiey's "check all that apply" style of questions, all the listed answers are correct, which forces the reader to carefully read all of the foils. This is a valuable skill if one is preparing for any CCNA exam. While the book may prepare someone for the written parts of the exams, tackling the entire book in one week, as suggested by the title, would be a daunting task. AL_Taiey describes the step-by-step processes by which one configures routers and switches, and this provides a good base of technical knowledge, but the lab experiences, simulations and practical knowledge required to pass this particular exam will have to come from somewhere else. For a student who has worked in the field or someone who has had access to the CISCO Academy curriculum, this book would function well as additional study guide/test prep material. But without this foundation, the most likely outcome would be an improved score on the written portion of the test; what is commonly referred to as a "paper certification."
Addresses the written aspect of the CISCO Certification process but the reader will need to fill in the practical portion from other sources, or better yet from work experience, before attempting the CCENT Exam.

Great CCENT Preparation, October 6, 2010
By J_Williams (Boston, MA) Amazon.com
This book was very instrumental in preparing me for the CCENT exam. After going through every chapter and answering all the questions, I had a strong grasp of the objectives. It took me longer than a week, but persistence and perseverance paid off. I can't wait for his ICND 2 book to become available.

Read This Book, October 1, 2010
By Edward (USA) Amazon.com
Thanks to this book and the CCENT boson simulation, I completely understand the CISCO CCENT in one week. This is the first book I have read that uses this way of writing. It simply describes all CCENT topics by more than 2000 questions and answers. Each section of the book is written in the form of questions and answers, which makes the preparation of the CCENT certification very easy. Also, I found it a complete guide and it helped me as a beginner in the CISCO networking.

Name: Joel Philip, Dec 2009
Thank you for writing your CCNA ICND1 study guide book. I really appreciate the way you presented the content and this is how all books concerning technology should be written, I hope that I can experience one of your other books in the future. Thank you again.

About the Author

Thaar Al_Taiey holds a Master degree (MSc) in Nuclear Engineering (MSNE) specialist in Software Engineering (MSSE) and Bachelor of Science degree (BSc) in Electrical Engineering (BSEE). He has more than nineteen years of experience in the Automated System fields. His experience is in the Distributed Control Systems based VME, Internetworking based CISCO, UNIX Operating Systems (Ultrix-32, OSF-1, SCO, Solaris, and Linux), Oracle ORDBMs, and Windows OSs. In these areas, he works as a Data Center Manager, IT Consultant and Supervisor, Network Architect and Network Manager, Senior Network Engineer, UNIX System Administrator, Oracle DBA, Windows Server Administrator, and Technical Support Engineer. For the past 15 years, AL_Taiey has been closely involved with the computer and networking systems development. In the field of training, he has instructed and developed several technical courses including the CISCO CCNA/CCENT ICND1 640-822 courses. Mr. AL_Taiey is the leading scientist for many thoughts and ideas in many fields of technologies. He is the author of a number of technical papers and books. He is currently the Chairman of ThaarTechnologies and is a member of the IWWHS.

Author Books

In addition to this book, Mr. Thaar AL_Taiey has several other books in the field of technology:

1. 4 in 1: The Complete One-Week Preparation for the CISCO CCENT/CCNA ICND1 Exam 640-822 with Three CISCO Simulated Exams A Certification Guide with over 2160 Sample Questions and Answers with Comprehensive Explanations First Edition (Jan 2011), ISBN: 978-0-9831212-4-4 (pbk), ISBN: 978-0-9831212-5-1 (ebk).
2. 4 in 1: The Complete One-Week Preparation for the CISCO CCENT/CCNA ICND1 Exam 640-822 with Three CISCO Simulated Exams A Certification Guide Based over 2160 Sample Questions and Answers with Comprehensive Explanations Third Edition (Dec 2010), ISBN: 978-0-9831212-2-0 (pbk), ISBN: 978-0-9831212-3-7 (ebk).
3. 3 in 1: The Complete Simulated Three CISCO Exams for the CISCO CCNA/CCENT ICND1 Certification Exam 640-822 with 160 Most Difficult Questions and Answers with Comprehensive Explanations (First Edition Nov 2010), ISBN: 978-0-9831212-0-6 (pbk), ISBN: 978-0-9831212-1-3 (ebk).
4. The Complete One-Week Preparation for the CISCO CCENT/CCNA ICND1 Exam 640-822: A Certification Guide Based over 2000 Sample Questions and Answers with Explanations Second Edition (July 2010), ISBN-13: 978-1450237055, ISBN: 978-1-4502-3706-2 (ebk).
5. CCNA ICND1 640-822 CCENT Study Guide and Examination Guide Q&A, First Edition Sept 2008, ISBN-13: 978-1419667589.

Table of Content
TABLE OF CONTENT
CONTENTS
LIST OF FIGURES
LIST OF TABLES
INTRODUCTION
CHAPTER 1 INTRODUCTORY: IS ESSENTIAL
CHAPTER 2 INTERNETWORKING PROTOCOLS AND IP ADDRESSING
CHAPTER 3 SUBNETTING
CHAPTER 4 INTERNETWORKING DEVICES
CHAPTER 5 INTERNETWORKING ROUTING PROTOCOLS
CONCLUSION
APPENDIX A ANSWERS TO THE CHAPTER'S LEARNING QUESTIONS
INDEX

To all my family and iUniverse team!
All my thanks!

Table of Content

Contents

viii

List of Figures

List of Tables

CISCO Icons Used in This Book

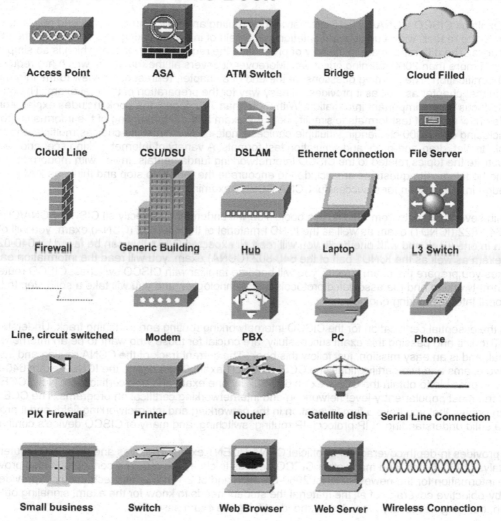

Access Point   ASA   ATM Switch   Bridge   Cloud Filled

Cloud Line   CSU/DSU   DSLAM   Ethernet Connection   File Server

Firewall   Generic Building   Hub   Laptop   L3 Switch

Line, circuit switched   Modem   PBX   PC   Phone

PIX Firewall   Printer   Router   Satellite dish   Serial Line Connection

Small business   Switch   Web Browser   Web Server   Wireless Connection

Command Syntax Conventions

The CISCO IOS Command Reference conventions are used in this book to present command's syntax. These conventions are described as follows:

- **Bold** indicates commands and keywords that are entered literally by the user.
- Italic indicates arguments for which actual values are supplied.
- Vertical bars (|) separate alternative, mutually exclusive elements.
- Square brackets ([ ]) indicate an optional element.
- Braces ({ }) indicate a required choice.
- Braces within brackets ([{ }]) indicate a required choice within an optional element.

Introduction:

This book explains CISCO CCNA/CCENT internetworking routing and switching concepts and guarantees the certification to the reader, with a unique presentation in the field of internetworking. It is written like the other usual textbooks. The differences are in the way of presenting the required information, which is so simple, and in the addition of more than 2000 learning questions. Moreover, it covers all the materials, which are required by the CISCO certification. The learning questions, at the end of a chapter, represent a review to the information presented in that chapter as well as it provides an easy way for the preparation of the real exam. The questions are made to focus on the important information. With more than 740 pages, the book includes explanatory text and provides new types of test formats to simplify both the exam and the presenting of the information to the readers, including over 2000 challenging multiple-choices-single-answer, multiple-choices-multiple-answers, fill-in-the-blank, testlet, drag-and-drop, and simulation test formats. A variety of internetworking scenarios are also used to illustrate the topics related to the CISCO internetworking fundamentals. In line with modern training and teaching methodology, the questions are included to encourage the reader to stop and think, as well as to test his knowledge in preparation for a successful CCNA CCENT examination.

You will gain several benefits from reading this book. You will understand perfectly all CISCO CCNA/CCENT topics for 640-822 (ICND1) exam as well as the ICND1 material of the 640-802 (CCNA) exam, you will obtain the certification in one week and with one book, you will read all expected Q&As that can be faced by 640-822 (CCENT) exam as well as the ICND1 part of the 640-802 (CCNA) exam, you will read the information easily, which makes you prepare the exam directly, you will become familiar with CISCO switches, CISCO routers, CISCO internetworking and the associated protocols and technologies, and you will take a solid step to become a professional Internetworking engineer.

CCENT is the essential certification for the CISCO internetworking routing and switching track. Understanding the CCENT topics and passing this exam successfully, are crucial for those who want to be an Internetworking professional, and is an easy mission, just follow this book. The current track of the CCNA routing and switching contains two exams and two certifications, the CCENT/ICND1 exam 640-822 and the ICND2 exam 640-816. However, it is possible to obtain the CCNA exam 640-802 by one exam and one certification. Now, CCENT and CCNA are the most popular entry-level networking and internetworking certification programs. The CCENT certification proves that you have a firm foundation in the networking and internetworking field, and it proves that you have a solid understanding of IP protocol, IP routing, switching, and many of CISCO device's configurations.

The book provides in-depth coverage of all official CCNA CCENT exam objectives and uses 2800 router, 1841 router, catalyst 2960 switch, and many other CISCO devices to clarify the required concepts. It also provides an up-to-date information for the newest catalyst 2960-S switch and 802.11n wireless technology. It provides objective-by-objective coverage of all the material the student needs to know for the exam, signaling out critical information, outlining necessary procedures, and identifying the exam essentials.

The book is composed of ten chapters. Each chapter treats each internetworking entity with clear, simple, easy-to-follow sections, text boxes and numerous conceptual figures. The book contains more than 313 Figures, 150 Tables, and hundreds of CISCO Switches' and Routers' Configurations. At the end of each chapter, a number of learning questions and a list of the commands, which are used in that chapter, are given. To make the reader/student more familiar with the CISCO exam, which is not requiring explaining the answer, some of the answers are not provided with explanations. However, explanations for these answers can be obtained easily from their questions. This will preserve the reader time by eliminating all the repeated information and it will not waste his/her time by extra statements. To encourage the reader to stop and think as well as to test his knowledge, the answers are not given directly after the learning questions; instead, the answers are listed in Appendix A with complementary discussions. In contrast, an interactive e-book edition of this book is underdevelopment now, to provide a test engine, an online simulation engine access, and an easy way to find the answers for the readers. Adding reader comments will also be possible with this new edition.

This book uses mainly the passive voice way of writing to give the reader strong-straightforward information without confusing the reader by extra-not required statements. This way of writing is also used by CISCO for devices' configurations, and by several computer technical books and operating systems; hence, the reader will be more familiar with CISCO devices' configurations while he/she reads this book.

The 2000 questions are distributed across the book as shown below:

Chapter 1: Internetworking Essentials	312
Chapter 2: Internetworking IP Protocol and IP Addressing	280
Chapter 3: Subnetting IP Network and VLSMs	85
Chapter 4: Internetworking OS CISCO Devices	239
Chapter 5: Internetworking Routing Protocols	228
Chapter 6: Internetworking Switching	219
Chapter 7: Internetworking OS Management Facilities	216
Chapter 8: Internetworking WAN Technologies	188
Chapter 9: Internetworking Wireless Technology: an Introduction	139
Chapter 10: Internetworking Security: an Introduction	94

This book is a unique one that is designed to offer both the CCNA/CCENT study guide and examination guide. The book covers essential topics on the Internetworking and security that can be understood, even if the students do not have a technical background. The book is necessary for any CISCO Internetworking and security related certifications. It is designed and organized for absolute beginners as well as for professional in CISCO internetworking. For beginners to be able to follow the train of thought and to ease the presenting of the technical information to them, the book gradually presents the information by highly organized only ten chapters, and then each chapter is decomposed into a number of sections and subsections. The TRUE/FALSE and Correct/Incorrect types of questions are used to review the important information easily to the beginners. For those who have a good technical background and ready for certification, the book can be used as an additional technological certification guide, and the learning questions can be used as a refresher for their information before taking the exam. Moreover, Questions like "Try to decide which option gets in which blank" and "Match ... etc." are used to simulate "Drag-and-drop" types of questions in the exam. Therefore, the book knowledge is what the student needs to be a successful networking professional, and it is a valuable technological resource for those on the job with internetworking.

By understanding perfectly the information presented in this book, internetworking-engineering basics and answering the CCNA CCENT exam related questions would be guaranteed. The main questions herein are intended to reflect the type of questions presented on the CCNA and CCENT tests.

This book was developed and written not just to tell you the topics of the internetworking, but to make you professional in this field and to help you learn how to apply the topics. No matter what your experience level in this field, the book will help you overtake the exams successfully with full scores. The book is designed to make you pass the CCENT/CCNA certification in a straightforward-easy way with extreme confidence and total marks from the first time, in one week. Moreover, you can use the CISCO key terms, which are found on "www.chahada.com/docs/glossary.doc ", as a glossary for this book.

The following CISCO CCNA/CCENT topics are described carefully in this book:

FIRST.	Describing the operation of computer data networks
SECOND.	Describing the required CISCO Devices for CCENT
THIRD.	Operating CISCO Switches and Routers
FOURTH.	Implementing small switched CISCO networks
FIFTH.	Implementing an IP addressing scheme and IP services to meet the network requirements for small and large offices
SIXTH.	Implementing a small and a large routed network
SEVENTH.	Managing and verifying CISCO switches and routers

EIGHTH.	Explaining and selecting the appropriate administrative tasks required for a WLAN
NINTH.	Implementing and verifying several WAN links
TENTH.	Identifying security threats to a network and describing general methods to mitigate those threats
ELEVENTH.	Describing Wireless technology

The book covers all the CISCO CCNA/CCENT ICND1 exam objectives and provides the following features:

- More than 2000 Q&A with explanations and examples
- Hundreds of CISCO Switches' and Routers' Configurations
- Easy to read
- Easy to understand
- Easy to pass the exam in one week and from the first time
- No waste of time
- All expected Q&A
- Up to date testing techniques
- Enjoyment of CCNA/CCENT Learning
- Guaranteed the CCNA/CCENT Examination
- Presenting all types of the CISCO Exam Q&As
  - Multiple-choice single answer
  - Multiple-choice multiple answer
  - Drag-and-drop
  - Fill-in-the-blank
  - Testlet
  - Simulations

The book is supported by the complete training materials including Test Books, Q&A Flashes, and Video Training founded on www.ThaarTechnologies.com.

Goals of the Book

The following are the main goals of this book:

1. Providing a self-study guide and a self-examination guide resource that covers all the CISCO CCNA/CCENT topics for 640-822 (ICND1) exam as well as the ICND1 material of the 640-802 (CCNA) exam.
2. Helping examinees obtain certification in one week and with one book
3. Providing all expected Q&As that can be faced in the 640-822 (ICND1) exam as well as the ICND1 part of the 640-802 (CCNA) exam.
4. Presenting the information in an easy way that makes the examinees prepare the exam directly while they are reading the book.
5. Helping network engineers to become familiar with CISCO switches, CISCO routers, CISCO internetworking and the associated protocols and technologies.

How to Use the Book

To read and understand the concepts behind this book easily, it is better to follow the guidelines below:

1. Read the book chapter by chapter from chapter one until chapter ten.
2. Read each chapter section by section.
3. Read and understand each section separately.
4. Read and answer the learning questions, at the end of each chapter.

By doing so, you will obtain the following:

- Easily reading the whole book
- Easily understanding the subjects one by one
- Easily passing the exam
- No waste of time
- Enjoyment of CCENT Learning

This book covers all the CISCO CCENT/CCNA exams topics carefully compiled and written by Thaar AL_Taiey. Try to understand the concepts very well, and then answer the learning questions at the end of each chapter. These questions provide a review of the information presented in that chapter, as well as an easy way to prepare for the real exam. The questions are made to focus on the important information.

To complete the book and take the exam successfully in one week, the following timetable can be followed: However, if you do not already have one year of experience, using a Network Simulator software while you are reading this book is recommended.

Day 1: Chapter 1, and Chapter 2. Mark the points that you need to repeat
Day 2: Chapter 3, and Chapter 4. Mark the points that you need to repeat.
Day 3: Chapter 5, and Chapter 6. Mark the points that you need to repeat.
Day 4: Chapter 7, and Chapter 8. Mark the points that you need to repeat.
Day 5: Chapter 9, and Chapter 10. Mark the points that you need to repeat. Then, Test yourself using the three CISCO simulated exams, which are founded in the *3 in 1* book.
Day 6: Review to the points that you marked to be repeated. Then, test yourself again using the three CISCO simulated exams, which are founded in the *3 in 1* book.
Day 7: Take the real exam.

The Differences Between this Book and the other CCENT/CCNA Books by the Author Thaar AL_Taiey

To cover the readers' needs, author Thaar AL_Taiey wrote the CCENT/CCNA certification guides using two different ways. The first way is based on the questions and answers, which means that the book is not a usual textbook, instead, each section of the book is written in the form of questions and answers. The second way is a usual textbook and the questions are put at the end of each chapter. Therefore, you need only to buy the book(s), which is/are suitable to you.

Based Questions and Answers Books

- 4 in 1: The Complete One-Week Preparation for the CISCO CCENT/CCNA ICND1 Exam 640-822 with Three CISCO Simulated Exams A Certification Guide Based over 2160 Sample Questions and Answers with Comprehensive Explanations Third Edition (Dec 2010), ISBN: 978-0-9831212-2-0 (pbk), ISBN: 978-0-9831212-3-7 (ebk)
- The Complete One-Week Preparation for the CISCO CCENT/CCNA ICND1 Exam 640-822: A Certification Guide Based over 2000 Sample Questions and Answers with Explanations Second Edition (July 2010), ISBN-13: 978-1450237055, ISBN: 978-1-4502-3706-2 (ebk).
- CCNA ICND1 640-822 CCENT Study Guide and Examination Guide Q&A, First Edition Sept 2008, ISBN-13: 978-1419667589.

Usual TextBooks

- 4 in 1: The Complete One-Week Preparation for the CISCO CCENT/CCNA ICND1 Exam 640-822 with Three CISCO Simulated Exams A Certification Guide with over 2160 Sample Questions and Answers with Comprehensive Explanations First Edition (Jan 2011), ISBN: 978-0-9831212-4-4 (pbk), ISBN: 978-0-9831212-5-1 (ebk)

- The Complete One-Week Preparation for the CISCO CCENT/CCNA ICND1 Exam 640-822: A Certification Guide with over 2000 Sample Questions and Answers with Explanations Second Edition (March 2011), to be published by iUniverse Inc (this book).

CHAPTER 1
INTERNETWORKING
ESSENTIALS

In this chapter, some fundamental concepts and terms that can be used in the internetworking are described.

This chapter summarizes some common themes presented throughout the remainder of this book. The chapter focuses mainly on mapping the Open System Interconnection (OSI) model to networking and internetworking functions; OSI model represents the building blocks for internetworks. The advantages of networking models are also stated in this chapter. Understanding the conceptual model helps understanding the complex pieces that make up an internetwork. This chapter also describes in details the concepts of Networking, Internetworking, Physical and Logical Network Topologies, and Ethernet LAN.

The following topics are emphasized in this chapter:

- Networking essentials
- Internetworking essentials
- Internetworking evolving
- Internetworking models
- OSI reference model
- OSI encapsulation and de-encapsulation terminologies
- Ethernet LANs
- Data transmission types
- CSMA/CD algorithm
- Ethernet addressing
- Ethernet connection and cabling

By understanding perfectly the information presented in this chapter and answering the 312 learning questions at the end of this chapter, understanding OSI reference model, understanding Ethernet LAN, and answering the CCNA/CCENT exam related questions will be guaranteed. The main questions herein are intended to reflect the type of questions presented on the CCENT Test.

Networking Essentials

In this section, networking essentials are presented and the types of networking topologies are described.

A network is a collection of connection devices (NICs-Network Interface Cards, routers, switches, firewalls) and end system machines (PCs, servers) interconnected together by some means. Networks carry data in many types of environments, including homes, and up to large enterprises. Networks also carry data in many types of media, including wired and wireless. To accomplish it tasks, network uses many types of connection devices such as NICs, hubs, bridges, switches and routers. These devices will be discussed deeply throughout this book.

Network Functions and Benefits

Today, the main function of computer networks, in addition to share and exchange information between computer machines, it provides communication. In business, networks play a major role. It simplifies and streamlines business processes through the use of data, application and hardware sharing.

Networks make rapidly data and information exchanging. Therefore, business's resources can be used more efficiently. However, several types of resources can be shared by computer networks. This includes but is not limited to: Data and applications, Physical resources, Network storage, Backup devices and of course networking devices and media. Furthermore, users of the network can use many types of networking applications, such as, E-mail, Web browsers, Internet talk, instant messaging, Download application, Broadcasting alerter, RSS feeds, Books reader, Collaboration and Database.

Generally, network applications can be one of the following types; system-to-system batch applications, user interactive applications, and user real-time applications.

Note: The terms above and several other terms in this chapter are given without further discussion because they are out of the scope of CCENT exam and this book does not want to confuse the reader by extra-information. However, more detail can be found from www.google.com.

Networks can be described and compared according to network performance and structured. This includes: Speed, Cost, Security, Availability, Scalability, Reliability, Manageability, and Topology. Today, cost of the network becomes less affecting factor when selecting the network and factors such as speed, security and easily managed network become the main factors for selecting the network. However, this depends on the importance of the network to the business process.

Physical and Logical Network Topologies

Topology defines the interconnection method used between devices, including the layout of the cabling and all paths used in data transmissions. Networks have two types of topologies; the physical and logical topologies. The physical topology is the arrangement of the network (nodes) devices, end systems (laptops, PCs and servers) and the network cables in wired networks. The logical topology, on the other hand, is the mapping of the data flows between the nodes in the network that forming the physical topology.

Physical Network Topology

As stated above, the physical topology is the arrangement of the network devices, end systems (laptops, PCs and servers) and the network cables in wired networks. Some of these topologies depend on the type of cabling that will be installed. Types of cables that are used in the network will be described in the following sections. However, the three basic categories of physical topologies are: Bus, Ring and Star. Figure 1-1 shows the basic physical topologies used in networking.

Figure 1-1 The Basic Physical Topologies

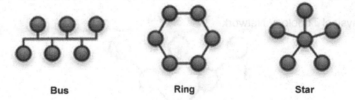

| Bus | Ring | Star |

Bus Topology

In this topology, all network devices and automated machines are cabled together in a line. Each machine is connected to the single bus cable through some kind of connector. The main cable segment must end with a terminator that absorbs the electrical signal when it reaches the end of the cable. Since only one cable is utilized, it can be the single point of failure. If the network cable breaks, the entire network will be down, since there is only one cable. This is the main disadvantage of the bus network. Using only one cable, on the other hand, will make the transfer speed between the computers on the network is faster. The bus topology includes both linear bus and distributed bus topologies. An example of this topology is a Thicknet Ethernet cable.

Ring Topology

In this topology, all network devices and automated machines are cabled together with the first device connected to the last to form a ring. This means that each machine is connected to the network in a closed loop or ring. In the ring topology, data is transmitted within a "token". Token travels around the ring. If a machine wants to transmit data, it adds that data and the destination address to the token. The token move around the ring until it finds the destination device, which takes the data out of the token. The primary advantage of this topology is that no token collisions occur. On the other hand, the primary disadvantage of ring topology is the failure of one machine will cause the entire network to fail. Two types of ring topology exist: single-ring and dual-ring. As names imply, the first one uses one ring, whereas the second one uses two rings to transmit the token. The dual-ring uses two rings to allow token to be sent in both directions. This design provides redundancy as compared with the single-ring design, meaning that if one ring fails, token can be transmitted on the second ring.

Star Topology

In this topology, all network devices and automated machines are connected together by a central cabling device. In local area networks where the star topology is used, each machine is connected to a central hub/switch. This will provide each machine on the network a dedicated, point to point connection to the central hub/switch. An advantage of the star topology is the simplicity of adding other machines. Another advantage of using such a topology is that when a cable connected one machine to a central hub/switch is broken, only that one machine is affected and disconnected from the network, and the rest of the network remains operational. This advantage is important and it is the reason why almost every newly designed Ethernet LAN based on a physical star topology. The primary disadvantage of the star topology is the hub/switch represents a single point of failure. If the hub/switch were to fail the entire network would fail as a result of the hub/switch being connected to every machine on the network. The star topology includes both extended-star and distributed-star topologies. When a network is expanded to include an additional network device that is connected to the main network devices, the topology is referred to as an extended-star topology. A common deployment of this topology is in a hierarchical (Tree) design network such as a Campus LAN or an Enterprise or a WAN. Figure 1-2 shows the tree physical topology.

Today, most extended-star networks employ a redundant connection to a separate set of connection devices to prevent isolation in the event of a device failure, especially the central node (core switch, router, and firewall), since if one of these devices fails, a large portion of the network can become isolated. Distributed-star topology is composed of individual networks that are based upon the physical star topology connected together in a linear fashion, i.e., 'daisy-chained'. Therefore, the distributed-star topology has no central connection.

Figure 1-2 The Tree Physical Topology Network

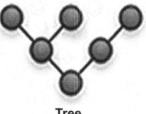

Tree

Mesh Topology

In addition to the basic physical topologies discussed above there is a mesh topology. Mesh topology is similar to star topology. It provides redundancy between machines in a star topology. A network can be fully meshed or partial meshed depending on the level of redundancy required. Figure 1-3 shows these types of physical topology. The mesh topology increases the overall network cost, but it improves network availability and reliability. Full-meshed network connects each machine to all other machines with a point-to-point link for redundancy and fault tolerance– this makes it possible for data to be simultaneously transmitted from any single node to all the other nodes. This topology provides the highest fault tolerant capabilities because the failure of any single link does not affect connectivity in the network. On the other hand, full-meshed network is expensive and complex for practical networks, although the topology is used when there are only a small number of nodes to be interconnected. In a partial-meshed topology, at least one machine maintains to multiply connections to all other machines (meshed) using a point-to-point link. The most important machines should be meshed. This topology trades off the cost of meshing all machines by meshing only the most important machines. By taking some of the advantages of the physical fully mesh topology, such as, the redundancy, the expense and complexity required for a connection between every machine in the network, is not required. All the data that is transmitted between nodes in the partially meshed networks takes the shortest path between nodes, except in the case of a failure in one of the links. When one link is failed, the data must take an alternate path to the destination node.

Figure 1-3 The Fully Connected and Partial Connected Mesh Topologies

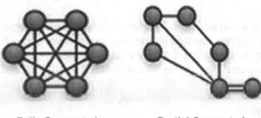

Fully Connected Mesh   **Partial Connected Mesh**

Logical Network Topology

The logical topology is the mapping of the data flows between the nodes in the network that forming the physical topology-that is, the way in which data accesses the network media and transmits bits across it. Logical topologies are often closely related to media access control (MAC) methods and protocols. The logical topologies are generally determined by the used network protocols, not by the physical layout of the network. Logical topologies can be dynamically reconfigured by special types of equipment such as routers, switches and firewalls.

The physical and logical topologies may or may not be identical in any particular network. For example; in a linear bus physical network topology, the data travels along the length of the bus. Therefore, the network has both a physical bus topology and a logical bus topology. On the other hand; in a star physical topology, the data may travels in a ring logical topology.

The most common implementation of LANs today is a star topology. In either a physical bus or a physical star, Ethernet uses a logical bus topology.

Internetworking Essentials

In this section, internetworking history is presented as well as the types of internetworking are described.

The CCNA exams, and particularly the CCENT (640-822) exam, focus on the concepts, protocols, and devices of two major networking types: enterprise networking and the Small Office/Home Office or SOHO networking. An enterprise network is a network created by one corporation, or enterprise, for allowing its employees to communicate and to provide services to the outside customers. A SOHO networking allows a user to connect to the Internet using a PC or laptop or mobile and any Internet connection, such as the high-speed cable Internet connection or wireless connection. This type of networking uses the same concepts, protocols, and devices used to create enterprise networks, but both are differing by some features, which are required by that type. Because most enterprise networks also connect to the Internet, the SOHO user can sit at home, or in a small office, and communicate with servers at the enterprise network, as well as with other hosts in the Internet.

In fact, the term "Internet" itself is formed by shortening the phrase "interconnected networks." The Internet consists of most every enterprise network in the world, plus billions of devices connecting to the Internet directly through Internet service providers (ISPs). Basically, The ISP role is to provide internet services to others. Therefore, to create the Internet, ISPs offer Internet access, using a cable TV line, a phone line or a wireless connection. Each enterprise typically connects to at least one ISP, using permanent connections generally called wide-area network (WAN) links. Finally, the ISPs of the world also connect to each other. These interconnected networks—from the smallest PC based home network, to cellular phones and automated devices, to enterprise networks with thousands of devices—all connect to the global Internet.

Internetwork

An **internetwork** is a collection of individual networks, which function as a single large network, connected by intermediate networking devices (routers, switches, bridges). Internetworking refers to the industry, products, and procedures that meet the challenge of creating and administering internetworks. Figure 1-4 depicts some different kinds of network technologies that can be interconnected by routers and other networking devices to create an internetwork.

Figure 1-4 Internetworking Creation

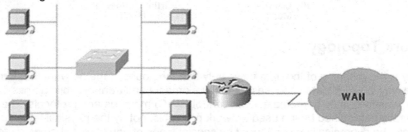

The term internetwork is used in this book and in many other resources to refer generally to a network made up of routers, switches, bridges, cables, and other networking equipment, and the word **network** is used to refer to the more specific concept of an IP network.

History of the Internetworking

The first networks used mainframes and attached dummy terminals. These are time-sharing networks. Such environments were implemented by both IBM's Systems Network Architecture (SNA) and Digital's network architecture. Networks and networking have grown exponentially over the last 20 years.

Local-area networks (LANs) developed around the PC revolution in 1980's. LANs connected multiple users in a relatively small geographical area to exchange files and messages, as well as access shared resources such as file servers and printers.

Wide-area networks (WANs) interconnect LANs with geographically dispersed users to create connectivity. Some of the technologies used for connecting LANs include T1, T3, ATM, ISDN, ADSL, Frame Relay, Radio links, Wireless and others.

Nowadays, high-speed LANs and switched internetworks are becoming widely used, largely because they operate at very high speeds and support high-bandwidth applications such as, multimedia, TV and videoconferencing.

Types of networking

A basic LAN network is shown in Figure 1-5. This LAN connects three PCs together using a simple (now) networking device called a hub. This network is actually one collision domain and one broadcast domain, and these are the major weaknesses of this type of networking. As this network is growth, the problems such as network speed degradation will appear.

Figure 1-5 Hub Based Network

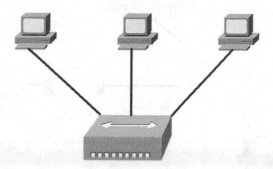

The above problem can be solved by using *network segmentation*, i.e. breaking up the large network into many smaller LANs. This is done by using devices like *bridges, switches*, and *routers*. Figure 1-6 displays a segmented network. By using a switch in this network, each segment/LAN connected to the switch is now a separate collision domain. However, this network is still one large broadcast domain.

Figure 1-6 Switched Based Network

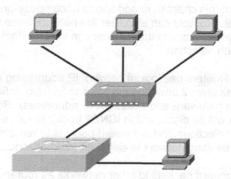

To connect networks together and to route packets of data from one network to another, routers must be used. Routers, by default, break up the network *broadcast domain* into many smaller ones. The broadcast domain is a set of all automated machines on a network segment that listen to all the broadcasts sent on that network segment. Figure 1-7 shows the using of the router that creates an internetwork and breaks up broadcast domains as well as collision domains.

Figure 1-7 Router Based Network

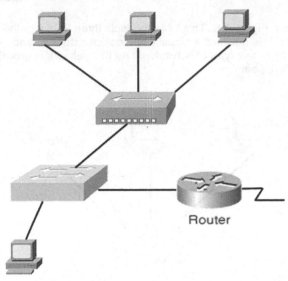

Router

Routers Vs Switches

Routers are used to break up **broadcast domains**. When an automated machine (IP network host) sends a broadcast message, every device on the network must listen, read and process that broadcast—unless there is a router in the network. When the router's interface receives this broadcast, it can discard the broadcast without forwarding it on to other networks, depending on the type of broadcast. Types of broadcast messages will be discussed in the following sections of this chapter. In addition to decompose broadcast domains, routers decompose collision domains as well. Routers can also filter the network based on layer 3 (Network layer) information (e.g., IP address). Router functions in the network can include Packet switching, Packet filtering, Internetwork communication and Path selection.

Routers are really layer 3 switches. Routers use logical network IP addressing and provide packet switching throughout the internetwork, whereas layer 2 switches are used to forward or filter frames (network Layer 2 concept) and switches are based on hardware addresses (MAC addresses). Routers can also provide packet filtering by using access lists (which will be discussed in ICND2 book). Routers use a routing table-a map of the Internetwork-to make network path selections and to forward packets to remote networks. When routers are used throughout the networks, the resulting network is called an internetwork.

Switches on the other hand, don't forward packets to other networks as routers do. Switches only switch frames from one port to another within the switched network. However, CISCO switches have other functionalities, such as, Port security and Power Over Ethernet (PoE). The main purpose of a switch is to optimize network performance and to provide more bandwidth for the LAN's users. This will be discussed in the following sections of this chapter.

By default, switches break up *collision domains*. Each port on a switch represents its own collision domain. Collision domain is an Ethernet network terminology used to describe how hosts within an Ethernet network must be conducted. When one particular host sends a packet on Ethernet segment, all other devices on that same segment must receive this frame. If at the same time, a different host transmits a frame on the same Ethernet segment, a collision will occur. Hence, no one of the transmitted frames will be understood. Therefore, both sending hosts must retransmit, one at a time. Usually collisions do not occur in the switched network since each interface on a switch represents its own collision domain. Hubs represent a real medium for collisions since all host segments connect to a hub represent only one collision domain and only one broadcast domain. Hence, Hubs create only one collision domain and only one broadcast domain and switches create multiple collision domains (one per interface) but a single broadcast domain, whereas, routers provide multiple collision domains (one per interface) and a separate broadcast domain for each interface (Ports in L3 switch).

Bridges and switches break up collision domains on a LAN. Switch is basically just a multiple-port bridge with more intelligent functions. Both bridges and switches cannot be used to isolate broadcast or multicast packets.

Obviously, there are several designs for each network but the best network design is one that's correctly configured to meet the business requirements of the organization it designs. Today, LAN switches with routers, is the best network design.

Let's take a look to Figure 1-8. How many collision domains and broadcast domains are in this network? It is found there are seven collision domains and two broadcast domains. Since, only the router breaks up broadcast domains by default. And since there are three connections for this router (one for WAN), that gives two broadcast domains. Now, how many collision domains in this network? The bridge network equals three collision domains. Adding the switch network of four collision domains—one for each switch port—and it is found the total number of collision domains in this network are seven.

Figure 1 8 Using Hub and Bridges

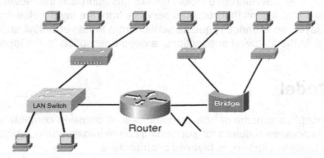

In Figure 1-9, each port on the switch is a separate collision domain and each VLAN (explanation of the VLAN can be found in chapter 6 of this book and ICND2 book in more details) is a separate broadcast domain. Router is still required for routing between VLANs. Now, how many collision domains are in this network? It is clear there are 14th collisions domains in this network—remember that connection between the switches is considered a collision domain The broadcast domain is still two as in the previous Figure 1-8 without using the VLAN.

Figure 1-9 Typical Internetworks

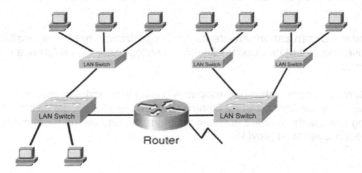

Internetworking Reference Models

In the late 1970's, to make computers from different venders communicate to each other, the International Standard Organization (ISO) introduced a reference model called Open Systems Interconnection (OSI). OSI is introduced to break the barrier of only one type of computers can communicate to each other. For example, companies ran DECnet propriety protocol (from Digital Equipment Corporation (DEC) company) can communicate with an IBM propriety protocol only if their devices depend on OSI model, otherwise, these devices will not be able to communicate to each other.

OSI is the Open System Interconnection reference model for communications. OSI Model is an abstract description for layered communications and computer network protocol design. The OSI model facilitates an understanding of how information travels throughout a network. The OSI model was introduced in 1984 to help vendors create interoperable network devices and software in the form of protocols and rules so that different vendor networks could work with each other. As compared with other reference models, the OSI model is considered as the primary architectural model for networking today. It describes how data and network information are communicated from an application on one computer through the network media to an application on another computer. Although some of the original protocols that comprised the OSI model are still used, the OSI as a whole never succeeded in the marketplace since several de facto protocols (such as TCP/IP) and their models are dominant in the marketplace. Now, the OSI model is mainly used as a point of reference for discussing other protocol specifications and especially the TCP/IP protocol. That is why it is required in CCNA/CCENT examinations. The OSI reference model breaks this approach into seven layers. A layer is a collection of conceptually similar functions that receives services from the layer below it and provides services to the layer above it. On each layer, an *instance* requests service from the layer below and provides services to the instances at the layer above. In the following subsections, a deep description to the layered approach will be given.

OSI Reference Model

A **reference model** is a conceptual scheme of how communications between computerized devices should be happened. It divides all the processes required for successful communication into logical groupings called **layers**. This type of system design is known as **layered architecture**.

To overtake the CCENT exam, the OSI reference model must be understood. OSI is the Open System Interconnection reference model for communications. The OSI model now is mainly used as a point of reference for discussing other protocol specifications.

To develop a network based software; developers use a reference model to find and understand the required communication processes and to see what types of functions need to be done on any one layer. To develop a network protocol for a certain layer, only the specific functions of that layer should be taken into account, not those of any other layer.

ISO-International Standard Organization: An international organization that is responsible for a wide range of standards, including those relevant to networking. The ISO developed the OSI reference model, a popular networking reference model.

OSI-Open Systems Interconnection reference model: A conceptual model defined by ISO to describe how any combination of devices can be connected for communication. The OSI model divides the task into seven functional layers, forming a hierarchy with the applications at the top and the physical medium at the bottom, and it defines the functions each layer must provide.

The Advantages of the layered approach

Too Many benefits can be obtained from adopting the layered approach (hierarchical). Layered approach is the process of breaking up the functions or tasks of networking into smaller pieces, called layers, and defining standard interfaces between these layers. The layers break a large, complex set of concepts and protocols into smaller pieces, making it easier to develop, easier to implement with hardware and software, and easier to troubleshoot. The most important benefit of the OSI model is to allow different vendors' networks to interoperate.

Example 1-1: A ftp software (like cuteftp) does not need to think about what the network topology looks like, the Ethernet card in the PC does not need to think about the contents of the files to be transferred by cuteftp, and a router that connected to the network does not need to think about the contents of the files as well. Each one of those is specified, implemented and operated in a separate layer.

The following list shows the benefits of layered specifications:

Interoperability: Computerized devices from multiple vendors can work the same network; this is by creating products to meet the same networking standards (standardization). It encourages industry standardization by defining what functions occur at each layer of the model.

Easy development and learning: Breaking the software into pieces allows easier program changes and faster product evolution. It divides the network communication process into smaller and simpler components, thus helping component development, design, and troubleshooting. It also prevents changes in one layer from affecting other layers. Clearly small pieces are easy to learn and understand.

Modularity: Several venders can participate in developing the same Software. One vendor can write software that implements higher layers programs (ex., web browser) and another vendor can write software that implements the lower layers (TCP/IP protocol).

OSI Layers

As stated previously, the OSI is used to describe how any combination of devices can be connected for communication. It also provides a framework for creating and implementing networking devices, standards and internetworking strategies.

The OSI can be divided into two groups. The upper layers of the OSI (application, presentation, and session) define functions focused on the application (how the applications within the hosts will communicate with each other and with end users). The bottom four layers (transport, network, data link, and physical) define how data is transmitted end-to-end (focused on end-to-end delivery of the data). Figure 1-10 shows the three upper layers and the four lower layers and their functions.

As shown in Figure 1-10, the OSI reference model consists of seven layers:

- Application layer (layer 7)
- Presentation layer (layer 6)
- Session layer (layer 5)
- Transport layer (layer 4)
- Network layer (layer 3)
- Data Link layer (layer 2)
- Physical layer (layer 1)

Figure 1-10 clears that the computer user interfaces at the Application layer. It is also clear that the upper layers are dedicated for user applications communicating between hosts. Physical network characteristics, networking type, hardware addresses, routing or logical addresses are not related to these upper layers. These are the responsibilities of the four bottom layers.

Figure 1-10 The OSI Upper and Lower Layers

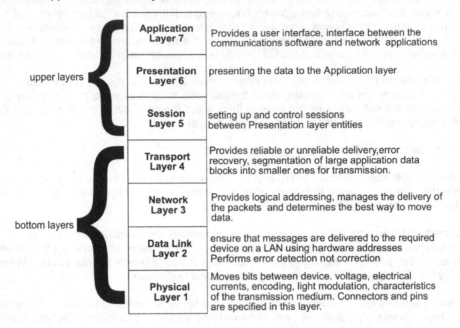

Figure 1-10 clears the four bottom layers that define how data is transferred through a physical medium. All data transmission functions between hosts are dedicated in these bottom layers.

Each layer defines a set of typical networking functions. The OSI model can be used as a standard of comparison to other networking models. Figure 1-11 shows OSI as compared with TCP/IP and Novell NetWare.

Figure 1-11 TCP/IP and Netware Protocol Stacks as Compared with OSI

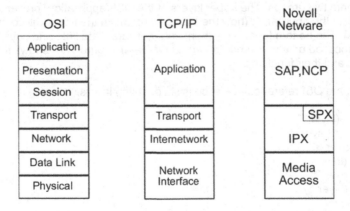

As an example, TCP/IP's internetwork layer, as implemented by IP, equates most directly to the OSI network layer. So, it is widely known that IP is a network layer, or Layer 3 protocol, using OSI terminology and numbers

for the layer.

Both the CCENT and ICND2 exams focus on issues in the lower layers—in particular, with Layer 2 and Layer 3, where switching and routing technologies are implemented respectively.

Too many protocols are implemented on the OSI layers. Table 1-1 lists typical protocols considered to be comparable to the OSI layers.

Table 1-1 Typical Protocols, Devices and the OSI.

OSI Layer	Protocol Examples	Devices
7	Telnet, HTTP, FTP, internet browsers, SMTP gateways , SNMP, VoIP	Firewall, intrusion detection and preventation systems
6	JPEG, ASCII, EBCDIC, TIFF, GIF, PICT, encryption, decryption, MPEG, MIDI.	Encryption systems, decryption systems
5	RPC, SQL, NFS, NetBIOS names, AppleTalk ASP, DECnet, SCP	RPC Servers, SQL Servers, NFS Servers, NetBIOS names Servers, WINS servers
4	TCP, UDP, SPX	Layer 4 switch
3	IP, IPX, AppleTalk DDP, ARP, RARP	Router
2	IEEE 802.3/802.2, 802.11, HDLC, Frame Relay, PPP, FDDI, ATM	LAN switch, Bridges, wireless access point, cable modem, DSL modem
1	EIA/TIA-232, V.35, EIA/TIA-449, RJ-45, Ethernet, 802.3, 802.5	LAN hub, repeater

Figure 1-12 shows a summary of the main functions defined at each layer of the OSI model.

Now, let us describe each layer in more details.

The application layer: This layer is the closest OSI layers to the end user, which means that both the OSI application layer and the user interact directly with the software application. This layer defines the interface between the communications software and any applications that need to communicate outside the computer on which the application resides. Some examples of application layer implementations include Telnet, Hypertext Transfer Protocol (HTTP), File Transfer Protocol (FTP), Secure FTP (SFTP) and Simple Mail Transfer Protocol (SMTP). For example, a Cuteftp is an application on a computer. The Cuteftp needs to obtain the file; OSI Layer 7 defines the protocols used on behalf of the application to obtain the file.

The presentation layer: This layer establishes a context between different application layer entities. This makes the higher-layer entities use different syntax and semantics, as long as the presentation service understands both and the mapping between them. The purpose of this layer is presenting the data to the Application layer. Furthermore, this layer is responsible for data translation and code formatting. This layer is a translator and provides coding and conversion functions. Functions like data compression, decompression, encryption, and decryption are dedicated in this layer. Some multimedia functions are also implemented in this layer.

The Session layer: This layer is responsible for setting up and control conversations (called sessions) between Presentation layer entities. This layer also provides dialogue (connection) control between devices, or nodes. It establishes, manages and terminates the connections between the local and remote application. It organizes the system's communications by offering three different modes: simplex, half duplex, and full duplex. Moreover, it establishes a check pointing, adjournment, termination, and restart procedures. The Session Layer is commonly implemented explicitly in application environments that use remote procedure calls.

Figure 1-12 The Main Functions of the OSI

Application Layer 7	File, print, message, databae, multimedia and application services
Presentation Layer 6	data encryption, compression, translation services and code formatting.
Session Layer 5	dialogue control between devices, or nodes
Transport Layer 4	end-to-end connection, virtual circuits
Network Layer 3	routing, path determination
Data Link Layer 2	framing, performs error detection not correction
Physical Layer 1	physical topology,sending bits and receiving bits

The transport layer: Layer 4 protocols focus on issues related to data delivery to the other computers—for instance, error recovery, segmentation of large application data blocks into smaller ones for transmission, and reassembly of those blocks of data on the receiving computer. The transport protocols provide end-to-end data transport services. Function like establishing a logical connection between end-to-end hosts on an internetwork is also implemented in this layer. This layer is dedicated for providing mechanisms for multiplexing upper layer applications, establishing sessions, and controlling virtual circuits. This layer also hides details of any specific network information from the higher layers by providing transparent data transfer. The term reliable networking is used at the Transport layer. It means that acknowledgments, sequencing, and flow control functions can be used. The Transport layer can be connectionless or connection-oriented. Some protocols are state and connection oriented. The connection-oriented means that the Transport Layer can keep track of the segments and retransmit those that fail. Although developed under the TCP/IP Model and not strictly conforming to the OSI definition of the Transport Layer, typical examples of Layer 4 protocols are the Transmission Control Protocol (TCP) and User Datagram Protocol (UDP). Tunneling protocols operate at the Transport Layer, such as carrying non-IP protocols such as IBM's SNA or Novell's IPX over an IP network, or end-to-end encryption with IPSec. L2TP carries PPP frames inside transport packet.

The Network layer: This layer provides the functional and procedural means of transferring variable length data sequences from a source to a destination via one or more networks, while maintaining the quality of service requested by the Layer 4. This layer (also called layer 3) manages the delivery of the packets (end-to-end communication) and determines the best way to move data. To accomplish this task this layer defines the Logical addressing so that any endpoint can be identified. The values of these addresses are chosen by the network engineer or defined automatically using DHCP server. This layer also defines how routing works and how routes are learnt so that the packets can be delivered. Routers (layer 3 devices) are specified at the Network layer and provide the routing services within an internetwork. This layer might also perform fragmentation and reassembly, and report delivery errors. The following duties are defined by the IP, which operate at this layer:

- Examining the destination IP address of a packet.
- Comparing that address to the IP routing table.
- Fragmenting the packet if the outgoing interface requires smaller packets.
- Queuing the packet to be sent out to the interface.

Two types of packets are used at the Network layer: data and route updates.

Internet Protocol (IP) in the TCP/IP is an example of layer 3 protocols. It manages the connectionless transfer of the data one hop at a time, from the end system to the ingress router, router to router, and from the egress router to the destination end system. It is only responsible for the detection of incorrect packets, so they may be discarded. Therefore, IP is not responsible for reliable delivery to a next hop. When the medium of the next hop cannot accept a packet in its current length, IP is responsible for **fragmenting** the packet into sufficiently small packets that the medium can accept.

Example 1-2: Router Main functions. When a packet is received on a router interface, the destination IP address is checked. If the packet isn't destined for that particular router, it will look up the destination network address In the routing table. Once the router chooses an exIt Interface, the packet wIll be sent to that Interface to be framed and cent out on the local network. If the router can't find an entry for the packet's destination network in the routing table, the router drops the packet.

The data link layer: This layer (Layer 2) provides the physical transmission of the data and handles error notification, network topology, and flow control. This means that this layer will ensure that messages are delivered to the required device on a LAN using hardware addresses and translates messages from the Network layer into bits for the Physical layer to transmit. Data link layer also defines the format of a header and trailer that allows devices attached to the medium to send and receive data successfully. The data link trailer, which follows the encapsulated data, typically defines a Frame Check Sequence (FCS) field, which allows the receiving device to detect transmission errors. Examples of the specifications that work in this layer include the Ethernet IEEE 802.3 and 802.2 and –High Level Data Link Control (HDLC) for a point-to-point WAN link.

The physical layer: Typically, this layer refers to standards from other organizations. This layer deals with the physical characteristics of the transmission medium, which include the specification of connectors, pins, electrical currents, encoding, and light modulation. In particular, it defines the relationship between a device and a physical medium. This includes the layout of pins, voltages, cable specifications, Hubs, repeaters, network adapters, Host Bus Adapters (HBAs used in Storage Area Networks) and more. Multiple specifications sometimes are used to complete all details of the physical layer. The main duties of this layer are: sending bits and receiving bits

As a final comment in the OSI layer, some of the networking devices operate at all seven layers of the OSI model. The following is a list of some of these devices:

- Network hosts.
- Gateways.
- Web and application servers.
- Network management stations

OSI Encapsulation and De-encapsulation Terminologies

Data Encapsulation is a process of adding a header to wrap the data that flows down the OSI model. OSI like TCP/IP defines processes by which a higher layer asks for services from the next lower layer. This is done by encapsulating the higher layer's data behind a header by the lower layer.

OSI uses what is called a *protocol data unit*, or *PDU*. A PDU represents the message that includes the headers and trailers for that layer, as well as the encapsulated data. A PDU for a specific layer has a specific format that implements the specifications and requirements of that layer. Layers 7 to 2 are communicated logically. The only hardware connection is at the physical layer or layer 1. Thus, in order for a layer to communicate across the network, it must pass down its PDU to the next lower layer for transmission. OSI refers to the PDU of each layer in the form of "Layer N PDU," with "N" referring to the number of the layer being discussed. As an example, a segment is a *Layer 4 PDU*. The term *L4PDU* is a shorter version of the phrase *Layer 4 PDU*.

When layer N PDU wants to go down the model to Layer N-1, it becomes the data that the layer N-1 protocol is **service**. Therefore, the layer N PDU is called the layer N-1 *service data unit (SDU)*. Now, layer N-1 adds its own PDU format, preceding the SDU with its own headers and appending trailers as necessary and the result will be N-1 PDU. This process is called *data encapsulation*, because the entire contents of the higher-layer message are encapsulated as the data payload of the message at the lower layer.

The process continues, all the way down the model to the physical layer. In the theoretical model, the whole encapsulation process ends up with a PDU at layer 1 that consists of application-layer data that is encapsulated with headers and trailers (as necessary) from each of layers 7 through 2 in turn, as shown in Figure 1-13.

Layers 7 through Layer 3 of the OSI define only a header, with the data from the next higher layer being encapsulated behind the header. The data link layer defines both a header and a trailer and places the L3PDU between the header and trailer. The L2 header contains the source and destination MAC address and the trailer contains the Frame check sequence (FCS) used for verifying the data integrity.

Figure 1-13 represents the typical encapsulation process, with the top of the figure showing the application data and application layer header, and the bottom of the figure showing the L2PDU that is transmitted onto the physical link.

Figure 1-13 The Typical Encapsulation Process

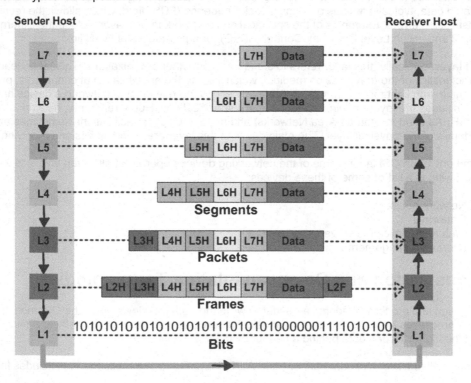

A reverse to encapsulation process is implemented in the recipient (remote) machine to interpret the data; this process is called *De-encapsulation*. When the recipient machine receives a sequence of bits, the layer 1 passes the bits to the layer 2 for manipulation. The layer 2 at the recipient machine checks the layer 2 trailer (the FCS) to see if the data is in error to be discarded, otherwise if the data is not in error, the layer 2 reads and interprets the control information in the layer 2 header. Then it strips the header and trailer and passes the remaining data up to layer 3 based on the control information in the data link header. The remaining layers perform similar de-encapsulation processes as necessary to deliver the actual data to the end user at the recipient machine.

The encapsulation and de-encapsulation processes at the source and destination machines produce a type of logical communication between peer layers in the OSI model. This form of communication is called *peer-to-peer communication*. During this communication, the protocols at each layer exchange PDU between peer layers, as shown in Figure 1-13.

Figure 1-13, depicts that segments, packets and frames are generated in layer 4, layer 3 and layer 2 respectively. These are TCP/IP terms and it will be discussed in details in the upcoming chapters of this book.

Ethernet LANs

Computers send bits to each other over a particular type of physical networking medium using physical and data link layers protocols. The OSI physical layer defines how to physically send bits over a particular physical networking medium. The OSI data link layer defines some rules about the data that is physically transmitted, including hardware (H/W) addresses of the sending device and recipient device, and rules that organize the sending time to prevent data collisions.

A LAN is a common type of network found in homes, small business offices, and large enterprise networks. It is considered as a basic part of large enterprise networks. An Enterprise network consists of several sites; each site can be made of several LANs. A LAN connects the end-user devices together, which allows the local computers to communicate with each other. LANs are connected by switches and other connecting devices, whereas sites are connected by routers. Routers are used to connect both the LAN and a wide-area network (WAN). This will provide connectivity between the various sites of the large enterprise network. With routers and a WAN, the computers at different sites can also communicate.

Understanding the LAN functions, network components, network topologies and standards, frames, Ethernet addresses, and network operational characteristics are important for an overall knowledge of the internetworking technologies.

This section explains some of the basics of the local-area networks (LAN). The term LAN refers to a set of Layer 1 and 2 standards designed to work together for implementing geographically small networks. Further Ethernet LAN explanations will be found in the upcoming chapters of this book.

Ethernet LAN Definition

A data communications system that operates at high speed over short distances (up to a few thousand meters), has a specific user group, and is not a public switched telecommunications network, but may be connected to one. A LAN is usually managed and owned by a single organization. A LAN permits users to exchange data, share a common printer or master a common computer (server), or execute a shared application. A LAN can vary widely in their sizes (from two computers up to hundreds of computers).

An interconnection of LANs within a limited geographical area, such as a government base, is commonly referred to as a *campus area network*. An interconnection of LANs over a city-wide geographical area is commonly called a *metropolitan area network* (MAN). An interconnection of LANs over large geographical areas, such as nationwide, is commonly called a *wide area network* (WAN). Furthermore, LANs are not subject to public telecommunications regulations.

Ethernet Network Components

Ethernet LANs consist of several automated machines called network nodes and several types of interconnecting media. The network nodes can be one of two major classes:

- **Data terminal equipment (DTE)**—Devices that are either the source or the destination of data. DTEs are typically devices such as computers and network servers that often referred to as end stations.
- **Data communication equipment (DCE)**—Intermediate network devices that receive and forward data across the network. DCEs may be both standalone devices such as repeaters, network switches, network bridges and routers, or communications interface units such as network interface cards (NIC) and modems.

The current Ethernet media options include two general types of copper cable: unshielded twisted-pair (UTP) and shielded twisted-pair (STP), plus several types of optical fiber cable. However, the wireless network has no physical media.

In addition to the above components, Ethernet LANs require some software that working in the network nodes (including IOS in CISCO devices) and make LAN useful plus some protocols that manage its working, such as Ethernet protocols, TCP/IP suite and DHCP.

Ethernet History

From decades the most common type of LAN is Ethernet. Like many inventions, Ethernet began inside a corporation that was looking for a solution to a specific problem "**The need is the mother of the invention**". Xerox needed an effective way to network the personal computer in its offices. From that, Ethernet was born. (See http://patft.uspto.gov/netacgi/nph-Parser?u=%2Fnetahtml%2Fsrchnum.htm&Sect1=PTO1&Sect2=HITOFF&p=1&r=1&l=50&f=G&d=PALL&s1=4063220.PN.&OS=PN/4063220&RS=PN/4063220 and http://inventors.about.com/library/weekly/aa111598.htm for more details on the history of Ethernet.) Xerox was developed the original Ethernet as an experimental coaxial cable network in the 1970s to operate with a data rate of 3 Mbps using a carrier sense multiple access with collision detection (CSMA/CD) protocol (which will be discussed in the next subsections of this chapter). Success with Xerox network led to the 1970s joint development of the 10-Mbps Ethernet Version 1.0 specification by the three-company consortium: Digital Equipment Corporation (DEC), Intel Corporation, and Xerox Corporation. This Ethernet became known as *DIX Ethernet*, referring to DEC, Intel, and Xerox. It is called thicknet (because of the thickness of the coaxial cable used in this network). In 1980s this standard of Ethernet was updated to add more capabilities, and it was referred to as Ethernet Version 2.0 (Ethernet II). The first standard draft was published on September 30, 1980 within IEEE.

The Institute of Electrical and Electronics Engineers (IEEE) is a professional organization that defines network standards. The IEEE formed two committees that worked directly on Ethernet based on the CSMA/CD—the IEEE 802.3 committee and the IEEE 802.2 committee. The 802.3 committee worked on physical layer standards as well on a sublayer of the data link layer called *Media Access Control (MAC)*. The IEEE assigned the other functions of the data link layer to the 802.2 committee. This upper part of the data link layer was called the *Logical Link Control (LLC)* sublayer. Notice that, the 802.2 standard applied to Ethernet as well as to other IEEE standards LANs such as Token Ring (See, http://tools.ietf.org/html/rfc1042 for modern LLC RFC.) This set of standards is most often referred to as simply "Ethernet". The original IEEE 802.3 standard was based on Ethernet II specifications, and it was very similar to the Ethernet Version 1.0 specifications. The draft standard was approved by the 802.3 working group in 1983 and was subsequently published as an official standard in 1985 (ANSI/IEEE Std. 802.3-1985). To take advantage of improvements and developments in the networking technologies, a number of supplements to the standard have been defined yet.

Ethernet Network Topologies and Structures

Regardless of LANs size or complexity, all will be a combination of only three basic interconnection structures or networking building blocks. The point-to-point interconnection is the simplest structure as shown in Figure 1-14. In this network only two network units are involved, and the connection may be DTE-to-DTE, DCE-to-DCE, or DTE-to-DCE. The cable in point-to-point interconnections is known as a network link. Depending on the type of cable and the transmission method that is used, the maximum allowable length of the link is set.

Figure 1-14 Point-to-Point Interconnections

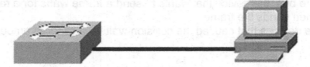

The original Ethernet networks were implemented with a coaxial bus topology, as shown in Figure 1-15. The physical Ethernet consists of the coaxial cabling, which is a bus topology, and collective Ethernet NICs in the computers (nodes). The bus is shared among all nodes on the Ethernet. When a node wants to send some bits to another node on the bus, it sends an electrical signal, and the electricity propagates to all nodes on the Ethernet.

10BASE5 and 10BASE2 are types of old Ethernets. The 10 represents the maximum transmission speed, which is 10Mbps. The *BASE* stands for baseband signaling. The 5 in 10BASE5 represents the maximum length of cable, which is 500 m. Whereas, the 2 in 10BASE2 represents the maximum length of cable which is 200 m. 10BASE5 also known as thicknet, whereas, 10BASE2 known as thinnet. This is a simple description to these Ethernets. More detail will be found in this chapter.

Figure 1-15 shows a sample of 10BASE2 Ethernet, which uses a single bus, created with coaxial cable and Ethernet NICs.

Figure 1-15 Coaxial Bus Topologies

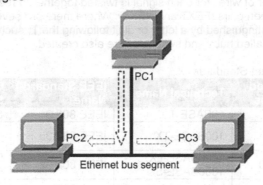

The solid lines in Figure 1-15 represent the physical network cabling. The dashed lines with arrows represent the path that it will be taken by PC1's transmitted frames. PC1 sends an electrical signal across its Ethernet NIC onto the cable, and PC2 and PC3 receive the signal since this is a bus topology which means that the transmitted signal is received by all stations on the LAN.

Ethernets that use a single bus need another logic/protocol to manage the network. Imagine what happened if two or more electrical signals were sent at the same time on a single bus. Of course, they would overlap and collide, making both signals unintelligible. So to ensure that only one device sends traffic on the Ethernet at one time, Ethernet defined an algorithm, known as the *carrier sense multiple access with collision detection* (*CSMA/CD*) algorithm. Otherwise, the Ethernet would have been unusable. This algorithm, manages how the bus is accessed. This is similar to what happened in a room with many people. It's hard to understand what more than one person are saying at the same time, so usually, one-person talks, and the rest listen.

The CSMA/CD algorithm, which is applied for both 10BASE5 and 10BASE2 Ethernets, can be summarized as follows:

- A device that wants to send a frame checks the LAN before sending a frame to ensure that the LAN is silent—in other words, no frames are currently being sent.
- If there is a frame on the bus, the device that wants to send a frame waits for a random amount of time until the LAN is silent and then sends the frame.
- If a collision occurs, the devices that caused the collision wait for a random amount of time and then try again.

A collision occurs in these Ethernets because the transmitted electrical signal travels along the entire length of the bus and when two stations send a frame at the same time, their frames overlap, causing a collision. So, all devices on a 10BASE5 or 10BASE2 Ethernet need to use CSMA/CD to make a LAN useful by avoiding collisions and recovering a LAN when collisions occur.

Common Ethernet Standards

10BASE5 and 10BASE2 Ethernet networks used coaxial cable for physical layer connectivity. From 1990, the use of twisted pair cables was begun. **Ethernet over twisted pair** refers to the use of cables that contain insulated copper wires twisted together in pairs for the physical layer of an Ethernet network. IEEE defined several Ethernet standards for twisted pair cables. The most widely used are **10BASE-T** (1990), **100BASE-TX** (1995), and **1000BASE-T** (1999), running at 10Mbps, 100Mbps, and 1000Mbps (1Gbps) respectively. Table 1-2 lists the most commonly used IEEE Ethernet standards. The **number** (10, 100, or 1000) in the beginning of the standard name refers to the theoretical maximum transmission speed in megabits per second (Mbps). The **BASE** is short for baseband signaling, meaning that there is no frequency-division multiplexing (FDM) or other frequency shifting modulation in use; each signal has full control of wire, on a single frequency. The **T** designates twisted pair cable, where the pair of wires for each signal is twisted together to reduce radio frequency interference and crosstalk between pairs (FEXT and NEXT). Where there are several standards for the same transmission speed, they are distinguished by a letter or digit following the T, such as *TX*. To support these new standards, networking devices called hubs and switches were also created.

Table 1-2 Most Common Ethernet Standards

Network Name	Speed Mbps	Technical Name	IEEE Standard Name	Cable Type, Maximum Length
Ethernet	10	10BASE-T	IEEE 802.3	Copper, 100 m
Fast Ethernet	100	100BASE-TX	IEEE 802.3u	Copper, 100 m
Gigabit Ethernet	1000	1000BASE-LX, 1000BASE-SX	IEEE 802.3z	Fiber, 5 km (LX), 550 m (SX)
Gigabit Ethernet	1000	1000BASE-T	IEEE 802.3ab	Copper, 100 m

Repeaters

Because of many reasons such as the *Attenuation*, 10BASE5 and 10BASE2 had limitations on the total length of a cable. With 10BASE5, the limit was 500 m; with 10BASE2, it was 185 m (approximately 200 m). The number of DTEs did not exceed 1024 in 10BASE5. To overcome these limitations a *repeater* is used.

Attenuation means that electrical signals pass over a cable, suffer from weaknesses in the strength of the signal as it travels farther along the cable.

As shown in Figure 1-5, repeater (hub) connects multiple cable segments, receives the electrical signal from one cable, interprets the electrical signals (bits), and generates clean (without noise), strong (amplification) signals out the other cable. Repeater only examines and generates electrical signals and does not interpret what the bits mean. Therefore, a repeater is considered to operate at Layer 1 of the OSI model.

Hubs

Hubs are basically multiport repeaters. That means, the hub simply regenerates the electrical signal that comes in one port and sends the clean, strong generated signal out every other port. That also means, the hub generates several electrical buses (but internally, Hub creates One Shared Electrical Bus), as shown in Figure 1-5, just like 10BASE2 and 10BASE5. One bus for each LAN connected to a specific hub port. Therefore, the use of CSMA/CD algorithm will still be required since collisions can still occur in 10BASE-T.

The use of hubs in network design solved some big problems with 10BASE5 and 10BASE2 networks. One of the biggest problems is the availability. In 10BASE5 and 10BASE2 LANs any single cable problem could, and probably did, take down the whole network. Whereas in the 10BASE-T network, a cable connects each device to the hub, so a single cable problem affects only one device/one LAN. This means that 10BASE-T networks are much higher availability than 10BASE5 and 10BASE2 networks. Furthermore, the use of twisted pair cables, in a star topology, lowered the cost of purchasing and installing the cabling.

Today, switches are more likely to be used instead of hubs.

Switches

Switches are intelligent devices and therefore, switches can perform much more functions than hubs and can play much better than hubs (See the datasheet for CAT2.96K switch on www.cisco.com.) LAN switches increase the available bandwidth of the Ethernet network and significantly reduce, or even eliminate, the number of collisions on a LAN. Unlike hubs, switches do not create a single shared electrical bus, forward received electrical signals out all other ports. Instead, switches do the following:

- Switches interpret the bits in the received frame so that they can typically send the frame out to the required port, rather than all other ports of the switch.
- Switches can forward one frame at a time, buffering other frames in memory when they need to forward multiple frames out the same port, thereby avoiding collisions.

LAN switches increase the available bandwidth of the Ethernet network as compared with hubs. In particular:

- No collisions can occur when only one device is connected to each port of a switch.
- Each port of the switch has its own separate bandwidth, which is not shared with devices connected to another switch port. This means that a switch with 1000-Mbps ports has 1000 Mbps of bandwidth *per port* (2000 Mbps full-duplex). This is the real difference between *shared Ethernet* and *switched Ethernet*. Hub is a shared Ethernet network where all ports share the same hub bandwidth, whereas the switch is a switched Ethernet where each port has a separate bandwidth.

Since, the switch's logic requires that the switch look at the Ethernet frame header, which is considered a Layer 2 feature. Therefore, switches are considered to operate as a Layer 2 device, whereas hubs are Layer 1 devices.

As a final comment in this section, since the early 1990s, the cabled network design of choice has been the star-connected topology, shown in Figure 1-16. The central network device is either a hub or a network switch. All connections in a star network are point-to-point links implemented with either twisted-pair or optical fiber cable.

These networks are still suffering from collision and broadcast problems. However, collision cannot be occurred, and broadcast can be stopped, in switches based networks. More details about the use of switches in the network will be found in this book.

Figure 1-16 Switched Star-Connected Topology

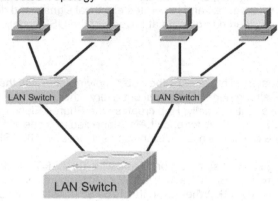

Ethernet LAN standards

Ethernet LAN standards specify cabling and signaling at both the physical and data link layers of the OSI model. This section describes the Ethernet data-link protocols. It covers Ethernet standards, CSMA/CD algorithm, Ethernet addressing, framing, and error detection. Figure 1-17 shows how LAN protocols are mapped to the OSI mode.

Figure 1-17 Mapping Ethernet LAN Protocols to the OSI Model

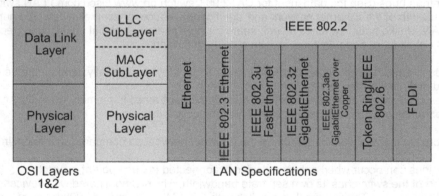

As with all IEEE 802 protocols, the OSI data link layer is divided into two IEEE 802 sublayers, the *Media Access Control* (MAC) sublayer and the *Logical Link Control* (*LLC*) sublayer. The IEEE 802.3 physical layer corresponds to the OSI physical layer.

All Ethernet standards use the same small set of data-link standards. From 10BASE5 and up to 10-Gbps Ethernet networks, the Ethernet addressing works the same on all the types of Ethernet. Furthermore, the CSMA/CD algorithm is applying to most types of Ethernet, unless it has been disabled. These are the most significant strengths of the Ethernet family of standards.

LLC Sublayer

The *Logical Link Control* (*LLC*) sublayer of the data link layer manages communications between devices over a single link of a network. IEEE 802.2 specifications defined LLC to support both connectionless and connection-oriented services used by higher-layer protocols. LLC is created to allow part of the data link layer to function independently from existing technologies. IEEE 802.2 defines a number of fields in data link layer frames that enable multiple higher-layer protocols to share a single physical data link. It also participates in the encapsulation process.

MAC Sublayer

The *Media Access Control* (*MAC*) sublayer of the data link layer manages protocol access to the physical network medium. The IEEE 802.3 MAC specification defines MAC addresses, which enable multiple devices to uniquely identify one another at the data link layer. A device to be networked must have a unique MAC address. This identification is made by using MAC table of physical addresses of devices. The MAC table is maintained by LLC sublayer.

The MAC sublayer has two primary functions:

- Data encapsulation, including frame assembly before transmission, and frame parsing/error detection during and after reception
- Media access control, including initiation of frame transmission and recovery from transmission failure

Data Transmission Types: Simplex, Half-Duplex, and Full-Duplex

Before studying the CSMA/CD algorithm, it is better to review who is vulnerable to collisions in the networking. This depends on the type of data transmission used. Some types of data transmission are virtually invulnerable to collisions- while others are vulnerable to collisions.

Simplex data transmission is a connection in which data will always flow in one direction. Therefore, it will not suffer collisions. Since data flows in one direction, there is no mutual communication between the sending and receiving stations- therefore, simplex transmission will not be seen in everyday networks. Simplex transmissions, however, are using in broadcasting companies when they want to send a video in a one-way data transmission to a home television, as shown in Figure 1-18.

Figure 1-18 Simplex Transmission

Half-duplex data transmission allows mutual communication between the sending and receiving stations, as shown in Figure 1-19. A device either sends or receives data at any point in time, but never both at the same time. Half-Duplex is where almost all collisions will happen: since each device may not know the other is transmitting. If a collision occurs, the data collides over the bus, and the data is corrupted.

For a practical example, the phones can be taken here as a reference. When two persons talk at the same time in the same phone call, their taking will collide and will not be understood to both persons, and they must repeat their talking, one person in one direction at a time.

Full-duplex data transmission allows devices to send and receive data at any point in time, as shown in Figure

1-20. Virtually, no collisions take place on a full-duplex transmission, so there is no need for CSMA/CD. Full-duplex increases the overall throughput- since sending and receiving are taken place on two different channels. Theoretically, Full-duplex doubles the data transfer rate.

Figure 1-19 Half-Duplex Transmission

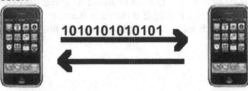

Figure 1-20 Full-Duplex Transmission

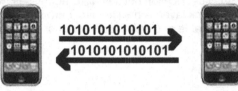

The collisions will be eliminated when the Full-duplex and switches are used. However, collisions may still occur when a Full-duplex transmission is configured for a network that operates under a hub. This is because switches forward data only to nodes that need it using *micro segmentation* technology, while hubs forward incoming data to all computers connected to it. Thus, the fault lies within the collision-prone characteristics of the hub. CSMA/CD must be deployed whenever collisions could occur, in hub networks of course.

Moreover, switches can buffer frames in memory. Switches can completely eliminate collisions on switch ports that connect to a single host. In such network collisions cannot occur, since this network connects the switch to one host per port, which allows the use of full-duplex operation.

To implement full duplex in a switched network, CSMA/CD logic on the devices on both ends of the cable must be disabled. As a result, the performance of such a switched Ethernet on that cable has been doubled by allowed simultaneous transmission in both directions.

CSMA/CD Algorithm

Carrier Sense Multiple Access with Collision Detection (CSMA/CD), is a layer 2 protocol in the OSI model. It is used in the networking as a control protocol in which a carrier sensing and collision detection algorithms are used. The CSMA/CD protocol was originally developed as a means by which two or more stations could share a common medium in a switch-less environment. Each Ethernet MAC determines for itself when it will be allowed to send a frame.

The CSMA/CD access rules are summarized by the protocol's acronym:

- **Carrier Sense (CS)**—each station continuously listens for signal (carrier) on the medium to determine when the medium is idle. Carrier sense, as shown in Figure 1-21, is the ability of a NIC to check the network for any communication. The NIC will attempt to transmit the data, if there is no traffic on the network, otherwise, the NIC should not attempt to transmit data. However, by carrier sense only, it is impossible to be sure that data isn't in the process of being sent by other computers and therefore, collision may occur.

Figure 1-21 Carrier Sense

Is any PC Transmitting Data

| Yes | No |
| Do not Transmit Data | Transmit Data |

- **Multiple Access (MA)**—Stations may begin transmitting any time they detect that the network is idle (there is no traffic). The MA, as shown in Figure 1-22, provides the ability to multiple devices to access the network with the same priority, which is the perfect environment. This, of course, means that collisions are more possible to occur.

Figure 1-22 Multiple Access

- **Collision Detect (CD)**—if two or more devices in the same CSMA/CD network (collision domain), listen for network traffic, hear nothing, and begin transmitting at the same time, the data streams from the transmitting stations will collide with each other as shown in Figure 1-23, and both transmissions will be destroyed. Therefore, each transmitting device must be capable of detecting that a collision has occurred before sending its frame. Each transmitting device must stop transmitting as soon as it has detected the collision, transmits a jam signal, and then must wait for a random time interval (determined by a back-off algorithm) before attempting to retransmit the frame, as shown in Figure 1-24. Collisions are normally resolved in microseconds.

Figure 1-23 Collision Detection

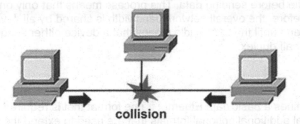

collision

CSMA/CD is a modification of pure CSMA. CD is used to improve CSMA performance by terminating transmission as soon as a collision is detected, and reducing the probability of a second collision on retry.

There are several methods for CD. CD methods are media dependent. On an electrical bus such as Ethernet, collisions can be detected by comparing transmitted data with received data. If they are not identical, another transmitter is overlaying the first transmitter's signal, collision is occurred, and transmission terminates immediately. A jam signal is sent, which will cause all transmitters to back off by backoff delay, reducing the probability of a collision when the first retry is attempted. Ethernet is the classic CSMA/CD protocol. However, in Full Duplex Ethernet, collisions are impossible since data is transmitted and received on different wires, and each segment is connected directly to a specific switch port. Therefore, CSMA/CD is not used on Full Duplex Ethernet networks. In addition, CSMA/CD is no longer used in the 10 Gigabit Ethernet specifications, due to the requirement of switching based network. Similarly, few implementations support CSMA/CD (half duplex) in the Gigabit Ethernet and in practice it is nonexistent.

Figure 1-24 Collision Detection with Backoff Algorithm

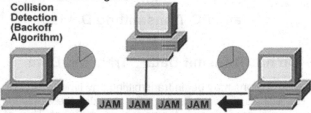

The CSMA/CD algorithm is implemented in the following steps:

Step 1 A device that wants to send a frame listens until the Ethernet is idle.

Step 2 The transmitter station(s) start(s) sending the frame, if the Ethernet is idle.

Step 3 After sending the frame, the transmitter station (s) listen(s) again to make sure that no collision has occurred in the network.

Step 4 If a collision occurs; devices involved in the collision keep transmitting (jamming signal) for a short period of time, to make sure all devices on the network see the collision.

Step 5 Each device sees the jamming signal, and invokes the back-off algorithm. Each device will have a random timer that determines when it can transmit again.

Step 6 When each random timer expires, the process starts again with Step 1.

CSMA/CD does not completely prevent collisions, but it does ensure that the Ethernet work sufficiently if collisions may occur. However, the CSMA/CD algorithm has several impacts on network performance. The CD algorithm adds a delay to the network which degrades the overall performance. Furthermore, CS causes devices to wait until the Ethernet is idle before sending data. This process means that only one device can send data at any one instant in time. Therefore, the overall network bandwidth is shared by all devices connected to the same hub. Notice that, waiting to send until the LAN is idle means that a device either sends or receives data at any point in time, which is called half duplex.

Ethernet Frames

The IEEE 802.3 standard defines a basic data Ethernet frame format that is required for all MAC implementations, plus several additional optional formats that are used to extend the protocol's basic capability. The framing used for Ethernet has changed a couple of times over the years. The recent changes to Ethernet framing are made by IEEE in 1997. It includes some of the features of the original Xerox Ethernet framing (1970s), along with the framing defined by the IEEE (1980s).

One of the most significant strengths of the all Ethernet family of protocols is that these protocols use the same small set of data-link standards. First, the CSMA/CD algorithm is applying to most types of Ethernet, unless it has been disabled. Clearly, CSMA/CD is technically a part of the data link layer. Second, Ethernet addressing works the same on all the types of Ethernet, from 10BASE5 and up to 10Gbps Ethernet. However, framing has changed several times over the years as stated above.

Framing defines how a string of bits is interpreted in the Data-link protocols. In other words, framing defines the meaning of the bits transmitted and received over a network through the physical layers of the sending and receiving devices. Frame can also be defined as a "container" into which data is placed for transmission in Ethernet LAN network. The frame contains the actual data that is being transmitted in addition to header and trailer information.

The basic MAC sublayer data frame format contains the seven fields shown in Figure 1-25.

Figure 1-25 LAN MAC Frame Format

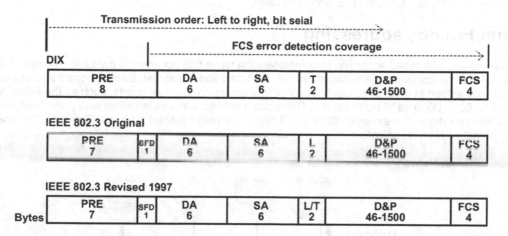

Ethernet Frame consists of the following fields:

- **Preamble (PRE)**: This field consists of 7 bytes. The PRE is an alternating pattern of 1s and 0s that tells receiving stations that a frame is coming, and that provides a means to **synchronize** the frame-reception portions of receiving physical layers with the incoming bit stream.
- **Start-of-frame delimiter (SFD)**: This field consists of 1 byte. The SFD is an alternating pattern of 1s and 0s. It tells the receiving computer that the transmission of the actual frame is about to start. SFD ends with two consecutive 1-bits indicating that the next bit is the left-most bit in the left-most byte of the destination MAC address.
- **Destination address (DA)**: This field consists of 6 bytes, which contains the MAC address of NIC on the local network to which the frame is being sent. The DA field identifies which station(s) should receive the frame. The left-most bit in the DA field indicates whether the address is an individual address (indicated by a 0) or a group address (indicated by a 1). The second bit from the left indicates whether the DA is globally unique (indicated by a 0) or locally administered (indicated by a 1). The remaining 46 bits are a uniquely assigned value that identifies a single station, a defined group of stations, or all stations on the network.
- **Source addresses (SA)**: This field consists of 6 bytes. The SA field identifies the frame sending station. The SA is always an individual address and the left-most bit in the SA field is always 0.
- **Length/Type (L/T)**: This field consists of 2 bytes. This field indicates either the number of data bytes that are contained in the data field of the frame, or the frame type ID (the type of protocol listed inside the frame) if the frame is assembled using an optional format. Either length or type is presented in the frame, but not both. If the Length/Type field value is less than or equal to 1500, the number of LLC bytes in the Data field is equal to the Length/Type field value. If the Length/Type field value is greater than 1536, the frame is an optional type frame, and the Length/Type field value identifies the particular type of frame being sent or received.
- **Data and Pad (D&P)**: This field consists of the packet (L3 PDU) that is received by receiving station from layer 3 on the transmitting station. This field is basically, a sequence of n bytes of any value, where n is less than or equal to 1500. If the length of the Data field is less than 46 (too short), the

Data field must be extended by adding a filler (a pad) sufficient to bring the Data field length to 46 bytes. Notice that, the IEEE 802.3 specification limits the data portion of the 802.3 frame to a maximum of 1500 bytes. The Data field was designed to hold Layer 3 packets, which must be confirmed with the maximum transmission unit (MTU) that defines the maximum Layer 3 packet that can be sent over a medium. The largest IP MTU allowed over an Ethernet is 1500 bytes.

- **Frame check sequence (FCS)**: This field consists of 4 bytes. This sequence contains a 32-bit cyclic redundancy check (CRC) value, which is created by the sending MAC and is recalculated by the receiving MAC to ensure that the frame has transmitted without corruption. The FCS is generated over the DA, SA, Length/Type, and Data fields.

Ethernet Frames addressing

Ethernet frames are addressed according to communication types that occurred in the LAN. In general, there are three types of communication in the network: unicast, multicast and broadcast. Each Ethernet address is 6 bytes long. It is usually written in a hexadecimal format that is organized in pairs or quads, such as the following: 00:00:1d:34:bc:00 or 0000:1d34:bc00. In CISCO devices, the MAC address is written with periods separating each set of four hex digits. For example, 0000.0C12.1A3E is a valid Ethernet address. Figure 1-26 indicates the forms of Ethernet LAN communications.

Figure 1-26 Ethernet Network Communication

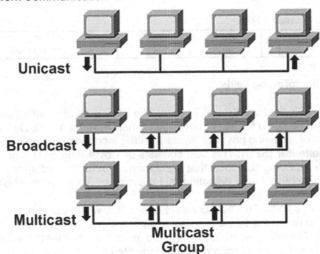

The IEEE defines the following types of communication for the Ethernet:

- **Unicast:** It is used to identify a single NIC on the Ethernet. This type of network communication sends a frame from one sender node and addressed to one destination node. Nodes use unicast addresses to identify the sender and receiver nodes of an Ethernet frame. This type of communication is the predominant form of communication on LANs and within the internet.

For Group addresses, which identify more than one NIC in the LAN, the IEEE defines two more categories:

- **Multicast:** It is used to identify a group of NICs on the Ethernet. This type of network communication sends a frame from one sender node and addressed to a group of destination nodes. This type allows a group of nodes on a LAN to communicate. Nodes must be members of a multicast group to receive the information. To use IP multicasts over an Ethernet, the multicast MAC addresses used by IP must follow this format: 0100.5e*xx.xxxx*. Any value can be used instead of the *x's*.

- **Broadcast:** It is used to identify all NICs on the Ethernet. This type of network communication sends a frame from one sender node and addressed to all destination nodes. This type allows all nodes on a LAN to communicate and to process the same frame. Broadcast address is the most often used of the IEEE group MAC addresses. It has a value of FFFF.FFFF.FFFF (hexadecimal notation).

When a host needs to provide information to all the hosts on the network or when the location of special services/devices for which the address is not known, broadcast transmission is used.

Here are examples for the using of broadcast transmission:

- Requesting unknown host address
- Mapping upper layer addresses to lower layer addresses
- Exchanging routing information by routing protocols (routing updates)

Broadcast packets are usually restricted to the local network by routers, whereas unicast packets can be routed throughout the internetwork. This restriction is dependent on the configuration of the router that borders the network and the type of broadcast. There are two types of broadcasts:

Directed Broadcast

A directed broadcast is sent to all hosts on a specific network (non-local network). For example, for a host outside of the 172.16.2.0 /24 network to communicate with the hosts within this network, the destination address of the packet would be 172.16.2.255. Although the routers do not forward directed broadcasts by default, they may be configured to do so.

Limited Broadcast

This type of broadcast is used for communication that is limited to the hosts on the local network (not to host on the non-local network). These packets use a destination address 255.255.255.255. Routers do not forward this broadcast. Packets addressed to the limited broadcast address will only appear on the local network. For this reason, an IPv4 network is also referred to as a *broadcast domain* where the router forms the boundary for this broadcast domain. As an example, a host within the 172.16.2.0 /24 network would broadcast to all the hosts in its network using a packet with a destination address of 255.255.255.255.

Ethernet Addressing

Ethernet address, MAC address, NIC address, hardware address, physical address, LAN address, universally administered address (UAA) and burned-in address, all are names of the same thing that is Ethernet address. It is the means by which data is addressed and directed to the proper receiving node in the network. Because, the MAC sublayer protocols in the Data Link layer such as IEEE 802.3 define the addressing details, the IEEE calls these addresses the "MAC addresses". The IEEE defines the format and assignment of Ethernet addresses. Each NIC on the network must have a unique unicast MAC address according to the IEEE specification so that it is possible to identify that NIC globally. This address is often referred to as the burned-in address (BIA) that is burned into the ROM chip on the card by Ethernet card manufacturers and cannot be changed, and to meet some private needs, some vendors allow the modification of this address. Because the IEEE universally regulates the address assignment of Ethernet addresses, BIAs sometimes are called *universally administered addresses (UAA)*.

A MAC address can be decomposed into two parts:

- The first half– IEEE Assigned (24-bit) of the address uniquely identifies the manufacturer of the card which is assigned by the IEEE to each manufacturer, is called the *organizationally unique identifier (OUI)*. Within the OUI, the first two bits have the following meaning only when used in the destination MAC address:

  - **Broadcast or multicast bit:** The left-most bit indicates whether the address is an individual address (indicated by a 0) or a group address (indicated by a 1).
  - **Locally administered address bit:** The second bit from the left indicates whether the MAC address is globally unique (indicated by a 0) or locally administered (indicated by a 1).

- The second half–Vendor Assigned (24-bit) of the address uniquely identifies the NICs for one manufacturer so that one MAC address must not be used on another card of the same manufacturer.

Each manufacturer assigns a MAC address with its own OUI as the first half of the address, with the second half of the address. Figure 1-27 shows the structure of Ethernet address.

Figure 1-27 Structure of Ethernet Addresses

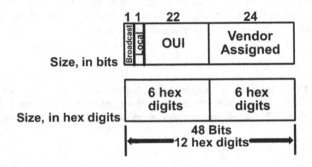

The use of Length/Type Field in the Ethernet Frames

To identify the different network layer (Layer 3) protocols from different vendors on the Ethernet, the protocol Type field is added in the frame, so that the receiving node knows what type of L3 PDU is in the Ethernet frame. For example, to make the receiving node knows that an IP packet is inside an Ethernet frame, the Type field (as shown in Figure 1-25) would have a value of 0800 hexadecimal (2048 decimal).

Because of the changes to Ethernet framing over the years, the protocol Type field can be identified by another option in the frame, particularly when sending IP packet and in this case the original Type field is used as a Length field for that frame, identifying the length of the entire Ethernet frame. If the 802.3 Type/Length field (in Figure 1-25) has a value less than 0600 hexadecimal (1536 decimal), the Type/Length field is used as a Length field for that frame. Therefore, another field (Type field) is needed to identify the type of L3 protocol inside the frame.

To create a Type field for frames that use the Type/Length field as a Length field, either one or two additional headers are added after the Ethernet 802.3 header but before the L3 PDU. For example, when sending IP packets, the Ethernet frame has two additional headers:

- An IEEE 802.2 Logical Link Control (LLC) header
- An IEEE Subnetwork Access Protocol (SNAP) header

Both the SNAP header Type field and Ethernet Type/Length field have the same purpose, with the same reserved values. Figure 1-28 shows an Ethernet frame with these additional headers.

Figure 1-28 The 802.2 SNAP Headers

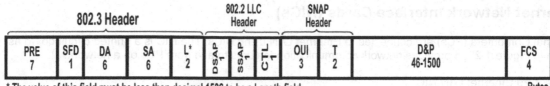

* The value of this field must be less than decimal 1536 to be a Length field

Bytes

Error Detection in Ethernet Frames

As stated previously, Ethernet defines a trailer at the end of each frame, with the trailer containing a FCS field used for the purpose of error detection. Error detection is the process of discovering if a frame's bits incorrect as a result of transmission over the network. Generally such errors may occur as a result of some kind of signal interference during frames transmission.

To detect an error, the sending machine calculates a complex mathematical function, with the frame contents as input, putting the result into the frame's FCS field. The receiving device does the same mathematical function on the receiving frame; if its calculation doesn't match the FCS field, an error occurred, the frame is discarded and retransmission is required (retransmission occurs by Layer 4 TCP protocol as part of error recovery procedures), otherwise, nothing will be happened.

Ethernet Frames Reception

Clearly, Frame reception is the reverse of frame transmission. For both half-duplex and full-duplex transmissions, Ethernet frame reception is essentially the same, except that full-duplex MACs must have separate frame buffers and data paths to allow for simultaneous frame transmission and reception.

When the frame is received, the destination address of the received frame is checked and matched against the machine's address list (its MAC address, its group addresses, and the broadcast address) to determine whether the frame is destined for that machine. If an address match is found, the frame length is checked, and the received FCS is compared to the FCS that was generated during frame reception. If the frame length is the same and there is an FCS match, the frame type is determined by the contents of the Length/Type field. The frame is then parsed and forwarded to the appropriate upper layer in the destination machine.

Ethernet Connection and Cabling

Some of Ethernet cable standards use coaxial cable or optical fiber; others are using **Ethernet over twisted pair.** There are several different standards for this copper-based physical medium. The most widely used are **10BASE-T** (Ethernet), **100BASE-TX** (Fast Ethernet; FE), and **1000BASE-T** (Gigabit Ethernet; GE). Ethernet over twisted pair refers to the use of cables that contain insulated copper wires twisted together in pairs for the physical layer of an Ethernet network—that is, a network in which the Ethernet standard protocol provides the data link layer. All these three standards use the same RJ45 connectors. Generally, different generations of Ethernet equipments can be freely mixed, since higher speed implementations always support the lower speeds. These standards always use eight positions modular connectors, usually called RJ45. The cables are four-pairs of twisted cable. Each of the three standards support both full-duplex and half-duplex communication. All these standards operate over distances of up to 100 meters. Some key differences however exist, particularly with the number of wire pairs needed in each case, and in the type (category) of cabling. Moreover, Power over Ethernet (PoE) technique can be implemented over UTP cables.

Understanding the Ethernet connection components is important in the CCENT studying. This section describes the use of UTP cabling in Ethernet network with a sufficient detail.

Ethernet Network Interface Cards (NICs)

Personal Computers (PCs) are connected to Ethernet LAN using NICs. The NIC is a printed circuit board as shown in Figure 1-29. It provides network communication features to and from PCs on a network.

Figure 1-29 Ethernet LAN NIC

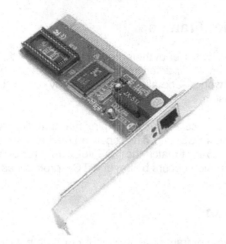

The NIC implements the electronic circuitry required to communicate using a specific physical layer and data link layer standard such as Ethernet or token ring. The protocols used in the NIC provides a base for a full network protocol suite, allowing communication on the same LAN for small groups of computers as well as communication on a large-scale network (WAN, Internet) through routable protocols, such as IP.

The NIC can be plugged into a motherboard PCI expansion slots, in this case it's called LAN adapter, and it can be built within a motherboard as a build-in Ethernet port. It provides the PC an interface to the LAN and it has a MAC address which is burned and stored in ROM by manufacture. To make the NIC work efficiently with the PC, it has some requirements. These are: IRQ line, I/O address, a memory space, and drivers. Sometimes the word *controller* is used to refer to the NIC.

Ethernet Connection Media

EIA/TIA standards body defined the Ethernet cables and connectors specifications. This means that RJ-45 connector and Ethernet cabling categories are derived from the EIA/TIA specifications. Several types of connection media can be used in a LAN deployment. Figure 1-30 presents the typical connection media types.

The RJ-45 connector represents the most common type of connection media, where the letters "RJ" stands for registered jack and the number "45" refers to a specific physical connector that has eight conductors. Another type of connection media is presented in Figure 1-31.

In addition to the popular RJ-45 connectors and ports, CISCO LAN switches have a few interfaces that use either Gigabit Interface Converters (GBIC) or Small-Form Pluggables (SFP). Figure 1-32 shows a 1000BASE-T GBIC. A GBIC is a hot-swappable I/O device that plugs into a Gigabit Ethernet switch port; this means that physical ports can be changed without having to purchase a whole new switch. A GBIC is interchangeable, which gives the flexibility to deploy other 1000BASE-X technology without having to change the physical interface or the model of the router or switch. Using a different kind of GBIC or SFP, CISCO switch can use a variety of cable connectors and types of cabling and support different cable lengths. GBICs are typically used for Uplinks of the LAN backbone.

Figure 1-30 Types of Connection Media

RJ-45   AUI
Connector Connector

Figure 1-31 Fiber Optical Connector

Figure 1-32 1000BASE-T GBIC

GBICs support copper UTP and fiber-optic media for Gigabit Ethernet transmission. There are several types of the fiber-optic GBICs, as shown in Figure 1-33. These types are:

- Short wavelength (1000BASE-SX)
- Long wavelength (1000BASE-LX/LH)
- Extended distance (1000BASE-ZX)

Figure 1-33 Fiber GBIC

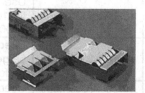

Fiber-Optic GBIC   GBIC Fiber Optic
                                     Shields

The fiber-optic GBIC is a transceiver that converts serial electric currents to optical signals and vice versa.

Twisted-Pair Cables and RJ-45 Connectors

Twisted-Pair (TP) cable is a copper wire-based that can be either unshielded (UTP) or shielded (STP). The most popular Ethernet standards are using UTP cabling, which include either two or four pairs of wires. The wires inside the cable have an outer jacket of flexible plastic to protect the wires since these wires are thin and subtle. To prevent the wire from breaking, a thin plastic coating (insulation material) covers each individual copper wire and to make it easy to look at the ends of the cable and identify the ends of an individual wire, the plastic coating on each wire has a different color.

The wires in each pair are twisted around each other as shown in Figure 1-34. This will give one of the advantages of TP cables, which is the ability to cancel interferences from Electro-Magnetic Interference (EMI) and Radio Interference (RFI). An electro-magnetic field is created outside the wire when the current passes over any wire. The magnetic field can in turn cause electrical noise on other wires in the cable. By twisting together the wires in the same pair, with the current running in opposite directions on each wire, the magnetic field created by one wire mostly cancels out the magnetic field created by the other wire. Moreover, to reduce crosstalk between the pairs, the number of twists varies. The permitted number of twists per meter must follow accurate specifications defined in ANSI/TIA/EIA-568-A (for CAT 5). Because of its small size and lightweight, TP cables can be installed easily.

Figure 1-34 TP Cable

There are several categories of UTP cable. Table 1-3 lists these categories. The most commonly used categories in the network today are Cat. 1, 5, 5e, and 6.

Table 1-3 UTP Categories

Type	Speed	Description
Cat. 1	Up to 20KHz	Used for telephone communication.
Cat. 2	Up to 4Mbps	Used for data transfer at speed up to 4 Mbps.
Cat. 3	Up to 10Mbps	Used in 10BASE-T Ethernet networks.
Cat. 4	Up to 16Mbps	Used in Token Ring networks.
Cat. 5	10/100/1000Mbps	Used in FastEthernet networks. It can be used for 10Mbps Ethernet. It can also be used for 1000Mbps for 10 meters.
Cat. 5e	10/100/1000Mbps	Used in Ethernet up to Gigabit networks. Cat. 5e generally provides the best price for performance.
Cat. 6	10/100/1000Mbps 10Gbps	Used in Ethernet up to Gigabit networks and 10Gbps over shorter distances.
Cat. 6a	10/100/1000Mbps	Used in network up to 10 Gigabit data transfer

	10GbE		for 100 meters.
Cat. 7	10/100/1000Mbps 10Gbps/100Gbps		Used in network up to 10 Gigabit data transfer and it may support the upcoming 100Gbps standard
Cat. 7a	Unknown		Upcoming standard that supports Ethernet bandwidths have not been defined.

Figure 1-35 shows Cat. 6, Cat. 5e, Cat. 5, and a standard telephone cable for comparison.

Figure 1-35 Types of UTP Categories.

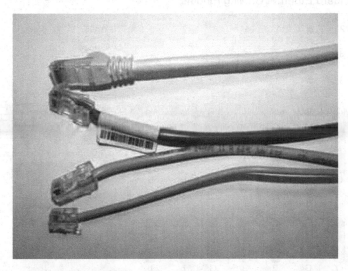

The RJ-45 connector is used at the end of UTP cable with the ends of the wires inserted into the connector. The RJ-45 connector has eight specific physical locations, called *pins,* into which the eight wires of the cable can be inserted into the correct positions. The RJ-45 connector needs to be inserted into an *RJ-45 port* in the switch or any other networking device. Figure 1-36 shows the UTP cables, and RJ-45 connectors. Figure 1-30 shows an RJ-45 port.

Figure 1-36 RJ-45 Connectors and Cables

 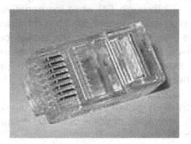

UTP Cabling Pinouts Implementation

To implement UTP cable in a LAN, the connection type i.e., straight-through or crossover cable and the EIA/TIA type of cable must be determined at first. The wires in the UTP cable must be connected to the correct pin positions in the RJ-45 connectors in order for communication between two end points to work correctly. The RJ-45 connector has eight *pins*, into which the eight copper wires of the UTP cable are inserted. The wiring *pinouts* must conform to the EIA/TIA Ethernet cabling standards described in this section.

The Telecommunications Industry Association (TIA) and the Electronics Industry Alliance (EIA) groups (not IEEE), define standards for UTP cabling, color coding for wires, and standard pinouts on the cables. (For more details, see http://www.tiaonline.org and http://www.eia.org). Figure 1-37 shows two pinout standards from the EIA/TIA, with the color coding and pair numbers listed.

Figure 1-37 EIA/TIA Standard Ethernet Cabling Pinouts

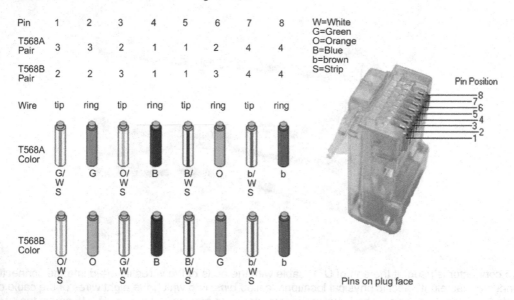

Figure 1-37 shows that the eight wires in a UTP cable have either a solid color (green, orange, blue, or brown) or a striped color scheme using white and one of the other four colors. Furthermore, a single-wire pair uses the same base color. For example, the green wire and the green/white striped wire are paired and twisted. For example, in Figure 1-37, the notation's G/W refers to the green-and white striped wire and so on.

Four of the wires (two pairs) carry the positive voltage, and the other four wires carry the negative voltage. The positive are called "tip" (T1 through T4) while the negative are called "ring" (R1 through R4). At the end of the UTP cable, the RJ-45 plug is connected, which is the male component. The male component is inserted into a female component (the jack, i.e., a socket). The jack is found in a network device, wall, patch panel or cubicle portion outlet. Figure 1-36 shows the male component whereas Figure 1-29 shows the female component. The front view of the male component, shown in Figure 1-37, identifies the pin locations which are numbered from 8 on the left to 1 on the right.

Correct wiring pinout on each end of the cable is required to build a working Ethernet LAN. For 10BASE-T and 100BASE-TX networks, two pairs of wires of the UTP cable are required, whereas four pairs of wires are required for 1000BASE-T.

In 10BASE-T and 100BASE-TX Ethernets, one pair should be used to send data in one direction, and the other pair should be used to receive data. Two wires are used for full-duplex networks. Ethernet NICs should send data using pair 3 according to the T568A pinout standard (the pair connected to pins 1 and 2). While, Ethernet NICs should receive data using pair 2 according to the T568A standard (the pair at pins 3 and 6). On the other hand, hubs and switches do the opposite—they receive on the pair 3 according to the T568A pinout standard (the pair at pins 1, 2), and they send on the pair 2 according to the T568A pinout standard (the pair at pins 3, 6). Therefore, to create a straight-through LAN cable, both ends of the cable must use the same EIA/TIA pinout standard on each end of the cable. This means that the pin number of the wire must be the same at both end of the wire when an Ethernet straight-through cable is used. To be more clarify, wire at pin 1 on one end of the cable must be connected to pin 1 at the other end of the cable; the wire at pin 2 must be connected to pin 2 on the other end of the cable; and so on. Figure 1-38 shows how to use the straight-through cable.

Figure 1-38 The Use of Straight-Through Cable

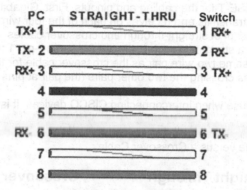

From the above description, clearly that, devices on the ends of the cable use opposite pins when they transmit/receive data. For such cases (connecting PC_NIC to a hub, switch …etc.) a straight-through cable is used. On the other hand, there are some cases that require connecting PC_NIC to PC_NIC or router to a router or switch to switch or switch to a router …etc. These cases require connecting two devices that both ends of the cable use the same pins to transmit and the same pins to receive. Therefore, the pinouts of the cable must be set up to swap/cross the wire pair. This type of cable is called a *crossover cable*. For example, when connecting two switches directly, both switches send on the pair at pins 3,6, and receive on the pair at pins 1,2, the cable must cross the pairs. Figure 1-39 shows the connection of a switch to a switch using a crossover cable.

Figure 1-39 A Switch to Switch Connection Using a Crossover Ethernet Cable

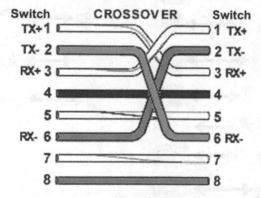

As a summary, devices on opposite ends of a cable that use the same pair of pins to transmit need a crossover cable (T568A at one end; T568B at the other). Devices that use an opposite pair of pins to transmit need a straight-through cable (either T568A or T568B at each end). Table 1-4 lists the network devices and the pin pairs they use for 10BASE-T and 100BASE-TX Ethernets.

Table 1-4 The Used Pin Pairs for the devices in 10BASE-T and 100BASE-TX

Devices That Use 1,2 for Transmitting and 3,6 for Receiving	Devices That Use 3,6 for Transmitting and 1,2 for Receiving
PC NICs	Hubs
Wireless Access Point	Bridges
Networked printers	Switches
Routers	Firewalls

The logic above differs in 1000BASE-T for the cabling and pinouts. First, Gigabit Ethernet requires four wire pairs. Secondly, Gigabit Ethernet transmits and receives on each of the four wire pairs simultaneously. However, Gigabit Ethernet does have a concept of straight-through and crossover cables, with a minor difference in the crossover cables. The pinouts for a straight-through cable are the same—pin 1 to pin 1, pin 2 to pin 2, and so on. The crossover cable crosses the same two-wire pair as the crossover cable for the other types of Ethernet—the pair at pins 1,2 and 3,6—as well as crossing the two other pairs (the pair at pins 4,5 with the pair at pins 7,8).

To choose which type of cable to use when interconnecting CISCO devices, it is better to follow Figure 1-40 for different type of interconnections.

Figure 1-40 Straight-through Cable versus a Crossover Cable

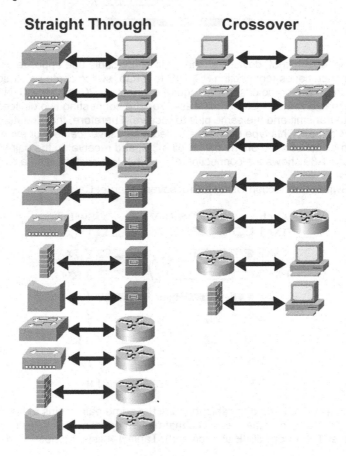

Now, there is no need to take care about which type (crossover or straight-through) to be used in the LAN, all are working. The current CISCO switches have a feature called auto-mdix that notices when the wrong cabling pinouts are used. This feature makes the cable work in spite of its type by readjusting the switch's logic.

To know how an enterprise network can be interconnected with different types of UTP cable, see Figure 1-41.

Figure 1-41 Different Types of UTP Cables in the Enterprise Network.

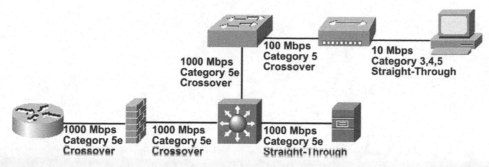

Summary

In this chapter, a strong foundation for networking and internetworking are presented. The background presented here is essential for understanding the rest of the book and undertaking the examination. A solid foundation to build a comprehensive knowledge of the networking technology is provided in this chapter. The following subjects are covered:

- Networking essentials
- Internetworking essentials
- Internetworking evolving
- Internetworking models
- OSI reference model
- OSI encapsulation and de-encapsulation terminologies
- Ethernet LANs
- Data transmission types
- CSMA/CD algorithm
- Ethernet addressing
- Ethernet connection and cabling

At the end of the chapter, several learning questions are given to evaluate the learning level from this chapter. The correct answers and solutions with complementary discussions are found in appendix A, "Answers to Chapters Learning Questions."

Chapter 1 Learning Questions

1-1.   Try to decide which option gets in which blank.

A network is a collection of _____ (NICs-Network Interface Cards, routers, switches, firewalls) and _____ (PCs, servers) interconnected together by some means.

    A.   end systems machines
    B.   connection devices

1-2.   Try to decide which option gets in which blank.

Networks carry data in many types of environments, including _____, and up to _____.

    A.   homes
    B.   large enterprises

1-3.   Try to decide which option gets in which blank.

Networks also carry data in many types of media including _____ and _____. To accomplish it tasks, networks use many types of connection devices such as NICs, hubs, bridges, switches and routers.

    A.   wired
    B.   wireless

1-4.   Which of the following statements are correct about networks? (Select all that apply)

    A.   A main office usually has one large enterprise network to connect all users and employees.
    B.   A main office with a large enterprise network can have thousands of employees and users who depend on this network to do their jobs and business, By network, employees and users have access to all information and resources that are accessible by the network.
    C.   A network is a connected of several types of devices that can communicate with each other.
    D.   Networks carry data in many types of environments, including homes, and up to large enterprises.
    E.   Remote users can connect to a main office through internet or WAN networks.
    F.   Networks can be wired or wireless.

1-5.   Try to decide which options get in the blank.
Today, the main function of computer networks, in addition to share and exchange information between computer machines, it provides _____.

    A.   transportation
    B.   communication
    C.   assistance

1-6.   TRUE/FALSE: In business, networks play a major role; it simplifies and streamlines business processes using data, application, and hardware sharing.

    A.   TRUE
    B.   FALSE

1-7.   TRUE/FALSE: Networks make rapidly data and information exchanging. Therefore, business's resources can be used more efficiently. However, several types of resources can be shared by computer networks.

    A.   TRUE
    B.   FALSE

1-8.   Which of the following resources can be shared by the networks? (Select all that apply)

    A.   Data and applications
    B.   Physical resources
    C.   Network storage
    D.   Backup devices
    E.   Networking devices and media

1-9.   Users of the network can use many types of networking applications. This includes but is not limited to: (Select all that apply)

    A.   E-mail
    B.   Web browsers
    C.   Internet talk
    D.   instant messaging
    E.   Download application
    F.   Broadcasting alerter
    G.   RSS feeds
    H.   Books' reader
    I.   Collaboration
    J.   Database

1-10.   There are several types of application interaction using the network. These are: (Select all that apply)

    A.   system-to-system batch applications
    B.   user interactive applications
    C.   user real-time applications

1-11.   Networks can be described and compared according to the network performance and structured. This includes: (Select all that apply)

    A.   Speed
    B.   Cost
    C.   Security
    D.   Availability
    E.   Scalability
    F.   Reliability
    G.   Manageability
    H.   Topology

1-12.   TRUE/FALSE: Today, cost of the network becomes less affecting factor when selecting the network and factors such as speed, security and easily managed network become the main factors for selecting the network. However, this depends on the importance of the network to the business process.

    A.   TRUE
    B.   FALSE

1-13. Which of the following resources are not sharable on the network? (Select all that apply)

A. applications
B. peripherals
C. memory
D. storage devices
E. data
F. processors
G. graphic adapter
H. mother board

1-14. Which of the following is a common network application? (Select all that apply)

A. e-mail
B. Internet talk
C. instant messaging
D. collaboration
E. Download application
F. Broadcasting alerter
G. graphics creation
H. RSS feeds
I. Book's reader
J. databases
K. word processing
L. spreadsheets
M. Web browsers

1-15. Match the following network characteristics to their suitable definitions.

1. speed
2. security
3. manageability
4. availability
5. scalability
6. reliability
7. cost
8. topology

A. The protection-ability level for all network resources
B. The administer-ability level to all network resources
C. The expandability of the network to accommodate the future expansion, such as more users or more data transmission
D. The dependability of the network
E. The easy-ability to access the network by users
F. The overall price of network components: This includes installation, and maintenance.
G. The physical and logical structure of the network
H. The fast-ability of transmitting data over the network

1-16. Try to decide which option gets in which blank.

Topology defines the _____ method used between devices including the layout of the _____ and all paths used in_____.

    A.   Interconnection
    B.   cabling
    C.   data transmissions

1-17. Try to decide which option gets in which blank.
Networks have two types of topologies. These are the _____ and the _____.

    A.   logical topology
    B.   physical topology

1-18. Match each of the following network's topologies to its suitable definition.

    1.   physical topology
    2.   logical topology

    A.   It is the arrangement of the network (nodes) devices, end systems (laptops, PCs and servers) and the network cables in wired networks.
    B.   It is, on the other hand, the mapping of the data flows between the nodes in the network that forming the physical topology.

1-19. TRUE/FALSE: The three basic categories of physical topologies are Bus, Ring, and Star.

    A.   TRUE
    B.   FALSE

1-20. TRUE/FALSE: In bus topology, all network devices and automated machines are cabled together in a line. Each machine is connected to the single bus cable through some kind of connector. The main cable segment must end with a terminator that absorbs the electrical signal when it reaches the end of the cable.

    A.   TRUE
    B.   FALSE

1-21. Which of the following is an advantage/disadvantage of the bus topology?

    A.   Since only one cable is utilized, it can be the single point of failure. If the network cable breaks, the entire network will be down.
    B.   Using only one cable will make the transfer speed between the computers on the network is faster.

    1.   Advantage
    2.   Disadvantage

1-22. Try to decide which option gets in which blank.

The bus topology includes both _____ and _____topologies. An example of this topology is a _____ Ethernet cable.

    A.   linear bus
    B.   distributed bus
    C.   Thinnet
    D.   Thicknet

1-23. TRUE/FALSE: In ring topology, all network devices and automated machines are cabled together with the first device connected to the last to form a ring. This means that each machine is connected to the network in a closed loop or ring.

    A.   TRUE
    B.   FALSE

1-24.   TRUE/FALSE: In a ring topology, data is transmitted within a "token." Token travels around the ring. If a machine wants to transmit data, it adds that data and the destination address to the token. The token move around the ring until it finds the destination device, which takes the data out of the token.

    A.   TRUE
    B.   FALSE

1-25. Which of the following is an advantage/disadvantage of the ring topology?

    A.   In this topology, there are no token collisions occur.
    B.   The failure of one machine will cause the entire network to fail.

    1.   Advantage
    2.   Disadvantage

1-26. Try to decide which option gets in which blank.

Two types of ring topology exist: _____ and_____. As names imply, the first one uses one ring, whereas the second one uses two rings to transmit the token. The dual-ring uses two rings to allow token to be sent in_____. This design provides _____as compared with single-ring design, meaning that if one ring fails, token can be transmitted on the second ring.

    A.   single-ring
    B.   dual-ring
    C.   both directions
    D.   redundancy

1-27.   TRUE/FALSE: In star topology, all network devices and automated machines are connected together by a central cabling device. In local area networks where the star topology is used, each machine is connected to a hub/switch.

    A.   TRUE
    B.   FALSE

1-28.   TRUE/FALSE: Star topology will provide each machine on the network a dedicated, point-to-point connection to the central hub/switch.

    A.   TRUE
    B.   FALSE

1-29. Which of the following is an advantage/disadvantage of the star topology?

    A.   In star topology, there is simplicity of adding other machines.
    B.   In star topology when a cable, which connects one machine to a central hub/switch, is broken, only that one machine is affected and disconnected from the network, and the rest of the network remains operational. This is important and it is the reason why almost every newly designed Ethernet LAN based on a physical star topology.
    C.   In star topology, there is a central hub/switch, which represents a single point of failure. If the

hub/switch were to fail, the entire network would fail because of the hub/switch being connected to every machine on the network.

1.   Advantage
2.   Disadvantage

1-30.   TRUE/FALSE: Almost every newly designed Ethernet LAN is based on a physical star topology.

A.   TRUE
B.   FALSE

1-31.   TRUE/FALSE: In star topology, if the hub/switch were to fail the entire network would fail because of the hub/switch being connected to every machine on the network.

A.   TRUE
B.   FALSE

1-32.   Which of the following is a type of the star topology? (Select all that apply)

A.   extended-star topology
B.   distributed-star topology

1-33.   Which of the following is true about extended-star topology? (Select all that apply)

A.   When a network is expanded to include an additional network device that is connected to the main network devices, the topology is referred to as an extended-star topology.
B.   A common deployment of this topology is in a hierarchical (Tree) design network such as a Campus LAN or an Enterprise or a WAN.
C.   Today, most extended-star networks employ a redundant connection to a separate set of connection devices to prevent isolation in the event of a device failure, especially the central node (Core switch, router, and firewall), since if one of these devices fails, a large portion of the network can become isolated.
D.   Distributed-star topology is composed of individual networks that are based upon the physical star topology connected together in a linear fashion, i.e., 'daisy-chained'. Therefore, the distributed-star topology has no central connection.

1-34.   Which of the following is true about distributed-star topology? (Select all that apply)

A.   When a network is expanded to include an additional network device that is connected to the main network devices, the topology is referred to as an extended-star topology.
B.   A common deployment of this topology is in a hierarchical (Tree) design network such as a Campus LAN or an Enterprise or a WAN.
C.   Today, most extended-star networks employ a redundant connection to a separate set of connection devices to prevent isolation in the event of a device failure, especially the central node (Core switch, router, and firewall), since if one of these devices fails, a large portion of the network can become isolated.
D.   Distributed-star topology is composed of individual networks that are based upon the physical star topology connected together in a linear fashion – i.e., 'daisy-chained' – with no central or top level connection point (e.g., two or more 'stacked' hub/switch s, along with their associated star connected nodes).

1-35.   Which of the following is true about mesh topology? (Select all that apply)

A.   Mesh topology is similar to star topology.
B.   It provides redundancy between machines in a star topology.
C.   A network can be fully meshed or partial meshed depending on the level of redundancy required.
D.   The mesh topology increases the overall network cost, but it improves network availability and reliability.

1-36.   Which of the following is a type of the mesh topology? (Select all that apply)

A.   fully meshed topology
B.   partial meshed topology
C.   star meshed topology

1-37.   Which of the following is true about Full-meshed topology? (Select all that apply)

A.   Full-meshed network connects each machine to all other machines with a point-to-point link for redundancy and fault tolerance– this makes it possible for data to be simultaneously transmitted from any single node to all the other nodes.
B.   This topology provides the highest fault tolerant capabilities because the failure of any single link does not affect connectivity in the network.
C.   On the other hand, full-meshed network is expensive and complex for practical networks, although the topology is used when there are only a small number of nodes to be interconnected.
D.   In a partial-meshed topology, at least one machine maintains multiply connections to all other machines (meshed) using a point-to-point link.
E.   The most important machines should be meshed.
F.   This topology trades off the cost of meshing all machines by meshing only the most important machines.
G.   By taking, some of the advantages of the physical fully mesh topology, such as, the redundancy, the expense and complexity required for a connection between every machine in the network, is not required.

1-38.   Which of the following is true about Partial-meshed topology? (Select all that apply)

A.   Full-meshed network connects all machines to one another with a point-to-point link for redundancy and fault tolerance– this makes it possible for data to be simultaneously transmitted from any single node to all the other nodes.
B.   This topology is the highest fault tolerant topology because the failure of any single link does not affect connectivity in the network.
C.   On the other hand, full-meshed network is expensive and complex for practical networks, although the topology is used when there are only a small number of nodes to be interconnected.
D.   In a partial-meshed topology, at least one machine maintains multiply connections to all other machines (meshed) using a point-to-point link.
E.   The most important machines should be meshed.
F.   This topology trades off the cost of meshing all machines by meshing only the most important machines.
G.   This topology makes it possible to take advantage of some of the redundancy that is provided by a physical fully mesh topology without the expense and complexity required for a connection between every machine in the network.

1-39. TRUE/FALSE: All the data that is transmitted between nodes in the partially meshed networks takes the shortest path between nodes, except in the case of a failure in one of the links. When one link is failed, the data must take an alternate path to the destination node.

A.   TRUE

B.   FALSE

1-40.   Match the following topologies to their correct descriptions.

1.   A common deployment of this topology is in a hierarchical (Tree) design network such as a Campus LAN or an Enterprise or a WAN.
2.   All machines are connected to one another with a point-to-point link for redundancy and fault tolerance.
3.   All network devices and automated machines are cabled together in a line. Each machine is connected to the single cable through some kind of connector.
4.   This topology uses two central connection circles to allow token to be sent in both directions. This design provides redundancy as compared with single central connection circle design.
5.   All network devices and automated machines are cabled together with the first device connected to the last to form a circle.
6.   All network devices and automated machines are connected together by a central cabling device, with no other connections between them.
7.   Each machine has a connection to all the other devices.
8.   At least one machine maintains multiply connections to all other machines (meshed) using a point-to-point link.

A.   extended-star topology
B.   star
C.   partial-mesh
D.   bus
E.   ring
F.   mesh/fully mesh
G.   dual-ring

1-41.   Which of the following is true about logical topology? (Select all that apply)

A.   The logical topology is the mapping of the data flows between the nodes in the network that forming the physical topology-that is, the way in which data accesses the network media and transmits bits across it.
B.   It is the way where data passes through the network from one device to the next without regard to the physical interconnection of the devices.
C.   Logical topologies are often closely related to media access control (MAC) methods and protocols.
D.   The logical topologies are generally determined by the used network protocols, not by the physical layout of the network.
E.   Logical topologies can be dynamically reconfigured by special types of equipment such as routers, switches, and firewalls.

1-42.   TRUE/FALSE: The physical and logical topologies may or may not be identical in any particular network. For example; in a linear bus physical network topology, the data travels along the length of the bus. Therefore, the network has both a physical bus topology and a logical bus topology. On the other hand; in a star physical topology, the data may travels in a ring logical topology.

A.   TRUE
B.   FALSE

1-43.   TRUE/FALSE: In a linear bus physical network topology, the data travels along the length of the bus. Therefore, the network has both a physical bus topology and a logical bus topology.

A.   TRUE

B.   FALSE

1-44.   TRUE/FALSE: The most common implementation of LANs today is a star topology. In either a physical bus or a physical star, Ethernet uses a logical bus topology.
A.   TRUE
B.   FALSE

1-45.   Which of the following statements are accurate about logical topologies? (Select all that apply)

A.   The logical topology is the mapping of the data flows between the nodes in the network that forming the physical topology.
B.   It is, the way in which data accesses the network media and transmits bits across it.
C.   It depends only on the type of computers to be connected in the network.
D.   It defines the way in which the automated devices are connected to each other.
E.   A network can have similar logical and physical topologies.

1-46.   Match the following types of networks to their correct descriptions.

1.   This network is created by one corporation, or enterprise to allow its employees to communicate and to provide services to the outside customers.
2.   This network allows a user to connect to the Internet using a PC or laptop or mobile and any Internet connection, such as the high-speed cable Internet connection or wireless connection.

A.   Enterprise network
B.   SOHO network

1-47.   Which of the following statements is accurate about SOHO network? (Select all that apply)

A.   This type of networking uses the same concepts, protocols, and devices used to create enterprise networks, but both are differing by some features, which are required by that type.
B.   Because most enterprise networks also connect to the Internet, the SOHO user can sit at home, or in a small office, and communicate with servers at the enterprise network, as well as with other hosts in the Internet.

1-48.   TRUE/FALSE: In fact, the term "Internet" itself is formed by shortening the phrase "Interconnected networks." The Internet consists of most every enterprise network in the world, plus billions of devices connecting to the Internet directly through Internet service providers (ISPs). The ISP role is to provide internet services to others.

A.   TRUE
B.   FALSE

1-49.   TRUE/FALSE: To create the Internet, ISPs offer Internet access, using a cable TV line, a phone line, or a wireless connection. Each enterprise typically connects to at least one ISP, using permanent connections generally called wide-area network (WAN) links. Finally, the ISPs of the world also connect to each other. These interconnected networks—from the smallest PC based home network, to cellular phones and automated devices, to enterprise networks with thousands of devices—all connect to the global Internet.

A.   TRUE
B.   FALSE

1-50.   TRUE/FALSE: An **internetwork** is a collection of individual networks, which function as a single large network, connected by intermediate networking devices (routers, switches, bridges). Internetworking refers to the industry, products, and procedures that meet the challenge of creating and administering internetworks.

    A.   TRUE
    B.   FALSE

1-51.   TRUE/FALSE: The term **internetwork** is used in this book and in many other resources to refer generally to a network made up of routers, switches, bridges, cables, and other networking equipment, and the **network** term is used to refer to the more specific concept of an IP network.

    A.   TRUE
    B.   FALSE

1-52.   TRUE/FALSE: The first networks used mainframes and attached dummy terminals. These are time-sharing networks. Such environments were implemented by both IBM's Systems Network Architecture (SNA) and Digital's network architecture. Networks and networking have grown exponentially over the last 30 years.

    A.   TRUE
    B.   FALSE

1-53.   Try to decide which option gets in which blank.

Local-area networks (LANs) developed around the _____ revolution in 1980's. LANs connected multiple users in a relatively _____ geographical area to exchange files and messages, as well as access shared resources such as file servers and printers.

    A.   PC
    B.   Mobile
    C.   small

1-54.   Try to decide which option gets in which blank.

Wide-area networks (WANs) interconnect _____ with geographically _____ to create connectivity. Some of the technologies used for connecting LANs include T1, T3, ATM, ISDN, ADSL, Frame Relay, Radio links, Wireless, and others.

    A.   LANs
    B.   dispersed users

1-55.   TRUE/FALSE: Nowadays, high-speed LANs and switched internetworks are becoming widely used, largely because they operate at very high speeds and support high-bandwidth applications such as, multimedia, TV, and videoconferencing.

    A.   TRUE
    B.   FALSE

1-56.   Try to decide which option gets in which blank.

A basic **LAN** network is shown in Figure 1-5. This LAN connects three PCs together using a simple (now) networking device called_____. This network is actually _____ and _____ and these are the major weaknesses of this type of networking. As this network is growth, the problems such as network speed _____ will appear.

    A.   hub

B.   one collision domain
C.   one broadcast domain
D.   degradation

1-57.   Try to decide which option gets in which blank.

The above problem can be solved by using network segmentation, i.e. _____ the large network into many smaller LANs. This is done by using devices like bridges, _____, and routers. Figure 1-6 displays a segmented network. By using a switch in this network, each segment/LAN connected to the switch is now a _____. However, this network is still one large broadcast domain.

A.   breaking up
B.   switches
C.   separate collision domain

1-58.   Try to decide which option gets in which blank.

To _____ networks together and to _____ packets of data from one network to another, routers must be used. Routers, by default, _____ the network broadcast domain into many smaller ones. The broadcast domain is a set of all automated machines on a network segment that listen to all the broadcasts sent on that network segment. Figure 1-7 shows the using of the router that creates an internetwork and breaks up broadcast domains as well as _____.

A.   connect
B.   route
C.   break up
D.   collision domains

1-59.   Try to decide if the following paragraph correctly depicts the Routers.

A.   Correct
B.   Incorrect

"Routers are used to break up **broadcast domains**. When an automated machine (IP network host) sends a broadcast message, every device on the network must listen, read and process that broadcast—unless there is a router in the network. When the router's interface receives this broadcast, it can discard the broadcast without forwarding it on to other networks, depending on the type of broadcast. Types of broadcast messages will be discussed in the following sections of this chapter. In addition to decompose broadcast domains, routers decompose collision domains as well."

1-60.   What is the function of a router in the network? (Select all that apply)

A.   providing the connection points for the media
B.   breaking up broadcast domain
C.   breaking up collision domain
D.   sending and receiving data-endpoint in the network
E.   providing the means by which the signals are transmitted from one networked automated device to another
F.   interconnecting networks and choose the best paths between them
G.   filtering the traffic over interconnected networks so that the data is transmitted through the most efficient route

1-61.   What is the function of a switch in the network? (Select all that apply)

A.   breaking up collision domain
B.   choosing the path over which data is sent to its destination
C.   sending and receiving data-endpoint in the network
D.   providing network attachment to the end systems and intelligent switching of the data within the local network
E.   connecting separate networks and filter the traffic over those networks so that the data is transmitted through the most efficient route
F.   breaking up broadcast domain

1-62.   What is the function of the network interconnections in the network?

A.   connecting separate networks and filter the traffic over those networks so that the data is transmitted through the most efficient route
B.   choosing the path over which data is sent to its destination
C.   providing a means for data to travel from one point to another in the network
D.   providing network attachment to the end systems and intelligent switching of the data within the local network
E.   breaking up collision domain
F.   breaking up broadcast domain

1-63.   Try to decide which option gets in which blank.

In addition to the breaking up broadcast domain by default, routers can filter the network based on layer 3 (Network layer) information (e.g., IP address). Router functions in the network can include _____, _____, _____ and _____.

A.   Packet switching
B.   Packet filtering
C.   Internetwork connection
D.   Path selection

1-64.   Try to decide which option gets in which blank.

Routers are really layer 3 switches. Routers use _____ and provide packet switching throughout the internetwork, whereas layer 2 switches are used to forward or _____ (network Layer 2 concept) and switches are based on hardware addresses (MAC addresses). Routers can also provide packet filtering by using _____ (which will be discussed in ICND2 book). Routers use a _____ -a map of the Internetwork-to make network path selections and to forward packets to remote networks. When routers are used throughout the networks, the resulting network is called an _____.

A.   logical network IP addressing
B.   filter frames
C.   access control lists
D.   internetwork
E.   routing table

1-65.   Try to decide which option gets in which blank.

Switches, on the other hand, do not forward packets to other networks like those that routers do. Switches only _____ frames from one port to another within the switched network. However, CISCO switches have other functionalists such as, Port security and Power Over Ethernet (PoE). The main purpose of a switch is to _____ network performance and to provide _____ for the LAN's users. This will be discussed in the following sections of this chapter.

A. switch
B. optimize
C. more bandwidth

1-66.   Try to decide which option gets in which blank.

By default, switches break up **collision domains**. Each port on a switch represents its own collision domain. Collision domain is an Ethernet network terminology used to describe how hosts within an Ethernet network must be conducted. When one particular host sends a packet on Ethernet segment, all other device _____must receive this frame. If at the same time, a different host transmits a frame on the same Ethernet segment, a _____ will occur. Hence, no one of the transmitted frames will be understood. Therefore, both sending hosts must _____, one at a time. Usually collisions do not occur in the switched network since each interface on a switch represents its own collision domain. Hubs represent a real medium for collisions since all host segments connect to a hub represents only one, collision domain and broadcast domain.

A. on that same segment
B. collision
C. retransmit

1-67.   Match each of the following devices to its operation

1. Hub
2. Switch
3. Router

A. It creates only one, collision domain and broadcast domain.
B. It creates multiple collision domains (one per interface) but a single broadcast domain.
C. It creates multiple collision domains (one per interface) and a separate broadcast domain for each interface.

1-68.   Try to decide if the following paragraph correctly depicts the bridges.

A. Correct
B. Incorrect

"Bridges and switches break up collision domains on a LAN. Switch is basically, just a multiple-port bridge with more intelligent functions. Both bridges and switches cannot be used to isolate broadcast or multicast packets."

1-69.   TRUE/FALSE: Obviously, there are several designs for each network but the best network design is one that is correctly configured to meet the business requirements of the organization it designs.

A. TRUE
B. FALSE

1-70.   TRUE/FALSE: LAN switches with routers, is the best network design.

A. TRUE
B. FALSE

1-71.   Look to Figure 1-8, how many collision domains and broadcast domains are in this network? (Select all that apply)

A. Only the router breaks up broadcast domains by default. In addition, since there are three connections for this router (one for WAN), that gives two broadcast domains.

   B.   The bridge network equals three collision domains. Adding the switch network of four collision domains—one for each switch port. Therefore, it is found that the total numbers of collision domains in this network are seven.

1-72.   TRUE/FALSE: In Figure 1-9, each port on the switch is a separate collision domain and each VLAN is a separate broadcast domain. Router is still required for routing between VLANs. Now, how many collision domains are in this network? It is clear there are 14th collisions domains in this network—remember that connection between the switches is considered a collision domain. The broadcast domain is still two as in Figure 1-8 without using the VLAN.

   A.   TRUE
   B.   FALSE

1-73.   TRUE/FALSE: OSI is introduced to break the barrier of only one type of computers can communicate to each other. For example, companies ran DECnet propriety protocol
(from the Digital Equipment Corporation (DEC) company) can communicate with an IBM propriety protocol only if their devices are depending on OSI model, otherwise, these devices will not be able to communicate to each other.

   A.   TRUE
   B.   FALSE

1-74.   Which of the following statements is true about OSI model? (Select all that apply)

   A.   OSI is the Open System Interconnection reference model for communications.
   B.   OSI Model is an abstract description for layered communications, and it is a design for computer network protocol.
   C.   The OSI model facilitates an understanding of how information travels throughout a network
   D.   The OSI model was introduced in 1984 to help vendors create interoperable network devices and software in the form of protocols and rules so that different vendor networks could work with each other.
   E.   As compared with other reference models, the OSI model is considered as the primary architectural model for networking today. It describes how data and network information are communicated from an application on one computer through the network media to an application on another computer.
   F.   Although some of the original protocols that comprised the OSI model are still used, the OSI as a whole never succeeded in the marketplace since several de facto protocols (such as TCP/IP) and their models are dominant in the marketplace.
   G.   Now, the OSI model is mainly used as a point of reference for discussing other protocol specifications and especially the TCP/IP protocol. That is why it is required in CCNA/CCENT examinations.

1-75.   TRUE/FALSE: The OSI reference model breaks network approach into seven layers.

   A.   TRUE
   B.   FALSE

1-76.   Which of the following statements are accurate about OSI layers? (Select all that apply)

   A.   A layer is a collection of conceptually similar functions that receive services from the layer below it and provide services to the layer above it.
   B.   On each layer, there is an instance, which requests service from the layer below and provides services to the instances at the layer above.

1-77. Try to decide which option gets in which blank.

A **reference model** is a _____ of how _____ between computerized devices should be happened. It divides all the processes required for successful communication into logical groupings called _____. This type of system design is known as **layered architecture**.

    A.   communications
    B.   conceptual scheme
    C.   **layers**

1-78. Try to decide which option gets in which blank.

To develop network-based software, developers use a _____ to find and _____ the required communication processes and to see what types of functions need to be done on any one layer. To develop a network protocol for a certain layer, only the specific functions of that layer should be taken into account, _____ of any other layer.

    A.   reference model
    B.   understand
    C.   not those

1-79. Try to decide if the following paragraph correctly depicts the **ISO**.

    A.   Correct
    B.   Incorrect

"**ISO-International Standard Organization**: An international organization that is responsible for a wide range of standards, including those relevant to networking. The ISO developed the OSI reference model, a popular networking reference model."

1-80. Try to decide if the following paragraph correctly depicts the **OSI reference model**.

    A.   Correct
    B.   Incorrect

"**OSI-Open Systems Interconnection reference model**: A conceptual model defined by ISO to describe how any combination of devices can be connected for communication. The OSI model divides the task into seven functional layers, forming a hierarchy with the applications at the top and the physical medium at the bottom, and it defines the functions each layer must provide."

1-81. Try to decide which option gets in which blank.

Too Many benefits can be obtained from adopting the layered approach (hierarchical). Layered approach is the process of _____ the functions or tasks of networking into _____, called layers, and defining standard interfaces between these layers. The layers break a large, complex set of concepts, and protocols into smaller pieces, making it easier _____, easier _____ with hardware and software, and easier _____. The most important benefit of the OSI model is to allow different vendors' networks to _____.

    A.   breaking up
    B.   smaller pieces
    C.   to develop
    D.   to implement
    E.   to troubleshoot

F.   interoperate

1-82.   Which of the following is an advantage of the layered model? (Select all that apply)

A.   Interoperability
B.   Easy development and learning
C.   Modularity

1-83.   Try to decide which option gets in which blank.

Interoperability: It computerized devices from multiple vendors' _____ work the same network; this is by creating products to meet the same networking standards (standardization). It encourages industry _____ by defining what functions occur at each layer of the model and making standard interface definitions between each layer.

A.   can not
B.   can
C.   standardization

1-84.   Try to decide which option gets in which blank.

Easy development and learning: Breaking the software into _____ allows easier program changes and faster product development. It divides the network communication process into smaller and simpler components, thus helping component development, design, and troubleshooting. It also _____ changes in one layer from affecting other layers. Clearly small pieces are easy to learn and understand.

A.   pieces
B.   prevents

1-85.   Try to decide which option gets in which blank.

Modularity: Several venders can _____ in developing the same Software. One vendor can write software that implements _____ programs (ex., web browser) and another vendor can write software that implements the lower layers (TCP/IP protocol).

A.   participate
B.   higher layers

1-86.   Try to decide which option gets in which blank.

As stated previously, the OSI is used to describe how any combination of devices can be _____ for the purpose of_____. It also provides a framework for creating and implementing_____, standards and internetworking strategies.

A.   communication
B.   connected
C.   networking devices

1-87.   Which of the following statements is true about OSI model? (Select all that apply)

A.   The OSI can be divided into two groups.
B.   The upper layers of the OSI (application, presentation, and session) define functions focused on the

application (how the applications within the hosts will communicate with each other and with end users).

C. The bottom four layers (transport, network, data link, and physical) define how data is transmitted end-to-end (focused on end-to-end delivery of the data).

1-88. TRUE/FALSE: As shown in Figure 1-10, the OSI reference model consists of seven layers. These are:

- Application layer (layer 7)
- Presentation layer (layer 6)
- Session layer (layer 5)
- Transport layer (layer 4)
- Network layer (layer 3)
- Data Link layer (layer 2)
- Physical layer (layer 1)

A. TRUE
B. FALSE

1-89. Which of the following is true regarding Figure 1-10? (Select all that apply)

A. Figure 1-10 shows the three upper layers, the four lower layers, and their functions.
B. Figure 1-10 clears that the computer user interfaces at the Application layer. It is also clear that the upper layers are dedicated for user applications communicating between hosts. Physical network characteristics, networking type, hardware addresses, routing or logical addresses are not related to these upper layers, these are the responsibilities of the four bottom layers.
C. Figure 1-10 clears the four bottom layers that define how data is transferred through physical media. All data transmission functions between hosts are dedicated in these bottom layers.

1-90. Match each OSI layer to its function.

1. application
2. presentation
3. session
4. transport
5. network
6. data link
7. physical

A. Providing a user interface, interface between the communications software and network applications
B. Presenting the data to the Application layer
C. Setting up and controlling sessions between Presentation layer entities.
D. Providing reliable or unreliable delivery, error recovery, and segmentation of large application data blocks into smaller ones for transmission
E. Providing a logical addressing, managing the delivery of the packets and determining the best way to move data
F. Ensuring that messages are delivered to the required device on a LAN using hardware addresses and performing error detection not correction
G. Moving bits between devices and voltage, electrical currents, encoding, light modulation, characteristics of the transmission medium, connectors, and pins are specified in this layer.

1-91. Which of the following is true about OSI model? (Select all that apply)

    A.   Each layer defines a set of typical networking functions.

    B.   The OSI model can be used as a standard of comparison to other networking models.

1-92.   TRUE/FALSE: TCP/IP's internetwork layer, as implemented by IP, equates most directly to the OSI network layer. Therefore, it is widely known that IP is a network layer, or Layer 3 protocol, using OSI terminology and numbers for the layer.

    A.   TRUE
    B.   FALSE

1-93.   Which of the following protocols are implemented in the OSI layer 7? (Select all that apply)

    A.   Telnet
    B.   HTTP
    C.   FTP
    D.   internet browsers
    E.   SMTP gateways
    F.   SNMP
    G.   VoIP
    H.   Video Over IP

1-94.   Which of the following protocols are implemented in the OSI layer 6? (Select all that apply)

    A.   JPEG
    B.   ASCII
    C.   EBCDIC
    D.   TIFF
    E.   GIF
    F.   PICT
    G.   Encryption
    H.   Decryption
    I.   MPEG
    J.   MIDI

1-95.   Which of the following protocols are implemented in the OSI layer 5? (Select all that apply)

    A.   RPC
    B.   SQL
    C.   NFS
    D.   NetBIOS names
    E.   AppleTalk ASP
    F.   DECnet
    G.   SCP

1-96.   Which of the following protocols are implemented in the OSI layer 4? (Select all that apply)

    A.   TCP
    B.   UDP
    C.   SPX

1-97.   Which of the following protocols are implemented in the OSI layer 3? (Select all that apply)

    A.   IP

B.   IPX
C.   AppleTalk DDP
D.   ARP
E.   RARP

1-98.   Which of the following protocols are implemented in the OSI layer 2? (Select all that apply)

A.   IEEE 802.3
B.   IEEE 802.2
C.   HDLC
D.   Frame Relay
E.   PPP
F.   FDDI
G.   ATM

1-99.   Which of the following protocols are implemented in the OSI layer 1? (Select all that apply)

A.   FIA/TIA-232
B.   V.35
C.   EIA/TIA-449
D.   RJ-45
E.   Ethernet
F.   802.3
G.   802.5

1-100.   Which of the following devices are implemented in the OSI layer 7? (Select all that apply)

A.   Firewall
B.   intrusion detection systems
C.   intrusion preventation systems

1-101.   Which of the following devices are implemented in the OSI layer 6? (Select all that apply)

A.   Encryption systems
B.   Decryption systems

1-102.   Which of the following devices are implemented in the OSI layer 5? (Select all that apply)

A.   RPC Servers
B.   SQL Servers
C.   NFS Servers
D.   NetBIOS names Servers
E.   WINS servers

1-103.   Which of the following devices are implemented in the OSI layer 3? (Select all that apply)

A.   Router
B.   LAN switch
C.   Bridges
D.   Wireless access point
E.   Cable modem
F.   DSL modem

1-104.   Which of the following devices are implemented in the OSI layer 2? (Select all that apply)

    A.   Router
    B.   LAN switch
    C.   Bridges
    D.   Wireless access point
    E.   Cable modem
    F.   DSL modem

1-105.   Which of the following devices are implemented in the OSI layer 1? (Select all that apply)

    A.   LAN hub
    B.   Repeater
    C.   LAN Switch

1-106.   Try to decide which option gets in which blank.

The application layer: This layer is the closest OSI layers to the _____, which means that both the OSI application layer and the user interact directly with the software application. This layer defines the _____ between the communications software and any applications that need to communicate _____ the computer on which the application resides. Some examples of application layer implementations include Telnet, Hypertext Transfer Protocol (HTTP), File Transfer Protocol (FTP), Secure FTP (SFTP), and Simple Mail Transfer Protocol (SMTP). For example, a Cuteftp is an application on a computer. The Cuteftp needs to obtain the file; OSI Layer 7 defines the protocols used on behalf of the application to obtain the file.

    A.   end user
    B.   Interface
    C.   outside

1-107.   Try to decide which option gets in which blank.

The presentation layer: This layer establishes a context between different application layer entities. This makes the higher-layer entities use different syntax and semantics, as long as the presentation service understands both and the mapping between them. The purpose of this layer is _____ the data to the application layer. In addition, this layer is responsible for data _____ and code formatting. This layer is a translator and provides coding and conversion functions. Functions like data _____, decompression, encryption, and _____ are dedicated in this layer. Some multimedia functions are also implemented in this layer.

    A.   presenting
    B.   translation
    C.   compression
    D.   decryption

1-108.   Try to decide which option gets in which blank.

The Session layer: This layer is responsible for _____ and _____conversations (called sessions) between presentation layer entities. This layer also provides dialogue (connection) control between devices, or nodes. It establishes, manages, and terminates the connections between the local and remote application. It organizes the system's communications by offering three different modes: simplex, half duplex, and _____. Moreover, it establishes a check pointing, adjournment, termination, and restart procedures. The Session Layer is commonly implemented explicitly in application environments that use remote procedure calls.

    A.   setting up
    B.   control
    C.   full duplex

1-109.   Try to decide which option gets in which blank.

The transport layer: Layer 4 protocols focus on issues related to _____ to the other computers—for instance, error recovery, segmentation of large application data blocks into smaller ones for transmission, and reassembly/desegmentation those blocks of data on the receiving computer. The transport protocols provide end-to-end data transport services. Function like establishing a _____ between end-to-end hosts on an internetwork is also implemented in this layer. This layer is dedicated for providing mechanisms for multiplexing upper layer applications, establishing sessions, and controlling _____. This layer also hides details of any specific network information from the higher layers by providing transparent data transfer. The term _____ networking is used at the Transport layer. It means that acknowledgments, sequencing, and flow control functions can be used. The Transport layer can be _____ or connection-oriented. Some protocols are stating and connection oriented. The connection-oriented means that the Transport Layer can keep track of the segments and retransmit those that fail. Although developed under the TCP/IP Model and not strictly conforming to the OSI definition of the Transport Layer, typical examples of Layer 4 protocols are the Transmission Control Protocol (TCP) and User Datagram Protocol (UDP). Tunneling protocols operate at the Transport Layer, such as carrying non IP protocols such as IBM's SNA or Novell's IPX over an IP network, or end-to-end encryption with IPSec. L2TP carries PPP frames inside transport packet.

    A.   data delivery
    B.   logical connection
    C.   virtual circuits
    D.   reliable
    E.   connectionless

1-110.   Try to decide which option gets in which blank.

The Network layer: This layer provides the functional and procedural means of transferring variable length data sequences from a source to a destination via one or more networks, while maintaining the quality of service requested by the Layer 4. This layer (also called layer 3) manages the delivery of the _____ (end-to-end communication) and determines the best way to move data. To accomplish this task this layer defines the _____ so that any endpoint can be identified. The values of these addresses are chosen by the network engineer or defined automatically using DHCP server. This layer also defines how _____ (forwarding) works and how routes are learned so that the packets can be delivered (path determination). Routers (layer 3 devices) are specified at the Network layer and are used to provide the routing services within an internetwork. This layer might also perform fragmentation and reassembly, and report delivery errors.

    A.   packets
    B.   logical addressing
    C.   routing

1-111.   Which of the following duties are defined and operated by the IP layer? (Select all that apply)

    A.   Examining the destination IP address of a packet
    B.   Comparing that address to the IP routing table
    C.   Fragmenting the packet if the outgoing interface requires smaller packets
    D.   Queuing the packet to be sent out to the interface

1-112.   Which of the following types of packets are used at the Network layer? (Select all that apply)

    A.   Data
    B.   Route updates
    C.   Frames
    D.   Bits

1-113.   TRUE/FALSE: Internet Protocol (IP) in the TCP/IP is an example of layer 3 protocols. It manages the connectionless transfer of the data, one hop at a time, from the end system to the ingress router, router to router, and from the egress router to the destination end system. It is only responsible for the detection of incorrect packets, so they may be discarded. Therefore, IP is not responsible for reliable delivery to a next hop. When the medium of the next hop cannot accept a packet in its current length, IP is responsible for **fragmenting** the packet into sufficiently small packets that the medium can accept.

    A.   TRUE
    B.   FALSE

Example 1-2, Router Main functions: When a packet is received on a router interface, the destination IP address is checked. If the packet is not destined for that particular router, it will look up the destination network address in the routing table. Once the router chooses an exit interface, the packet will be sent to that interface to be framed and sent out on the local network. If the router cannot find an entry for the packet's destination network in the routing table, the router drops the packet.

1-114.   Try to decide which option gets in which blank.

The data link layer: This layer (Layer 2) duties are provides the _____ of the data and handles_____, network topology, and flow control. It detects and possibly corrects errors that may occur in the Physical Layer. This means that this layer will ensure that messages are delivered to the required device on a LAN using _____ and translates messages from the Network layer into bits for the Physical layer to transmit. Data link layer also defines the format of a header and trailer that allows devices attached to the medium to send and receive data successfully. The data link trailer, which follows the encapsulated data, typically defines a Frame Check Sequence (FCS) field, which allows the receiving device to detect transmission errors. Examples of the specifications that work in this layer include the Ethernet IEEE 802.3 and 802.2 and –High Level Data Link Control (HDLC) for a point-to-point WAN link.

    A.   physical transmission
    B.   error notification
    C.   hardware addresses

1-115.   Which of the following is a function of the OSI Layer 2 protocols? (Select all that apply)

    A.   Delivery of bits from one device to another
    B.   Defining the type of NIC
    C.   Error recovery
    D.   Framing
    E.   Error detection

1-116.   Try to decide which option gets in which blank.

The physical layer: Typically, this layer refers to standards from other organizations. This layer deals with the _____ of the transmission medium. Connectors, pins, electrical currents, _____, and light modulation. In particular, it defines the relationship between a device and a physical medium. This includes the layout of pins, voltages, cable specifications, hubs, repeaters, network adapters, Host Bus Adapters (HBAs used in Storage Area Networks) and more. Multiple specifications sometimes are used to complete all details of the physical layer. The main duties of this layer are sending bits and receiving bits.

A.   physical characteristics
B.   encoding

1-117.   TRUE/FALSE: Some of the networking devices operate at all seven layers of the OSI model.

A.   TRUE
B.   FALSE

1-118.   Which OSI layer defines the logical network-wide addressing and routing functions?

A.   Layer 1
B.   Layer 2
C.   Layer 3
D.   Layer 4
E.   Layer 5
F.   Layer 6
G.   Layer 7

1-119.   Which OSI layer defines the standards for cabling and connectors?

A.   Layer 1
B.   Layer 2
C.   Layer 3
D.   Layer 4
E.   Layer 5
F.   Layer 6
G.   Layer 7

1-120.   Which OSI layer defines the standards for data formats and encryption?

A.   Layer 1
B.   Layer 2
C.   Layer 3
D.   Layer 4
E.   Layer 5
F.   Layer 6
G.   Layer 7

1-121.   Match each OSI layer to its function.

1.   application
2.   presentation
3.   session
4.   transport
5.   network
6.   data link
7.   physical

A.   Defining the electrical, mechanical, procedural, and functional specifications for network media
B.   Managing the delivery of the packet (end-to-end communication) and determines the best way to move data.
C.   Providing the physical transmission of the data and handling error notification, network topology,

and flow control
D.   Translating data and code formatting and it ensures that the information send at the application layer of one system is readable by the application layer of another system.
E.   Establishing, managing, and terminating sessions between two communicating hosts
F.   Segmenting data from the system of the sending host and reassembling the data into a data stream on the system of the receiving host
G.   Providing network services to the applications of the user, such as e-mail, file transfer, and terminal emulation.

1-122.   Which layer of the OSI and the TCP/IP protocols is the most multifarious?

A.   application
B.   presentation
C.   session
D.   transport
E.   network
F.   data link
G.   physical

1-123.   Which of the following statements is true about OSI encapsulation? (Select all that apply)

A.   Data Encapsulation is a process of adding a header to wrap the data that flows down the OSI model.
B.   OSI like TCP/IP defines processes by which a higher layer asks for services from the next lower layer. This is done by encapsulating the higher layer's data behind a header by the lower layer.

1-124.   Which of the following statements is true about OSI PDU? (Select all that apply)

A.   OSI uses what is called a protocol data unit, or PDU.
B.   A PDU represents the message that includes the headers and trailers for that layer, as well as the encapsulated data.
C.   A PDU for a specific layer has a specific format that implements the specifications and requirements of that layer.
D.   Layers 7 to 2 are communicated logically, the only hardware connection is at the physical layer or layer 1. Thus, in order for a layer to communicate across the network, it must pass down its PDU to the next lower layer for transmission.

1-125.   TRUE/FALSE: OSI refers to the PDU of each layer in the form of "Layer N PDU," with "N" referring to the number of the layer being discussed. As an example, a segment is a Layer 4 PDU. The term L4PDU is a shorter version of the phrase Layer 4 PDU.

A.   TRUE
B.   FALSE

1-126.   TRUE/FALSE: When layer N PDU wants to go down the model to Layer N-1, it becomes the data that the layer N-1 protocol is **service**. Therefore, the layer N PDU is called the layer N-1 service data unit (SDU). Now, layer N-1 adds its own PDU format, preceding the SDU with its own headers and appending trailers as necessary and the result will be N-1 PDU. This process is called data encapsulation, because the entire contents of the higher-layer message are encapsulated as the data payload of the message at the lower layer. The process continues, all the way down the model to the physical layer. In the theoretical model, the whole encapsulation process ends up with a PDU at layer 1 that consists of application-layer data that is encapsulated with headers and trailers (as necessary) from each of layers 7 through 2 in turn.

A.   TRUE
B.   FALSE

1-127.   Which of the following statements is true about OSI PDU? (Select all that apply)

A.   Layers 7 through Layer 3 of the OSI define only a header, with the data from the next higher layer being encapsulated behind the header.
B.   The data link layer defines both a header and a trailer and places the L3PDU between the header and trailer.
C.   The L2 header contains the source and destination MAC address and the trailer contains the Frame check sequence (FCS) used for verifying the data integrity.

1-128.   Which of the following statements is true about OSI de-encapsulation? (Select all that apply)

A.   A reverse to encapsulation process is implemented in the recipient (remote) machine to interpret the data; this process is called *De-encapsulation*.
B.   Whenever the recipient machine receives a sequence of bits, the layer 1 passes the bits to the layer 2 for manipulation.
C.   The layer 2 at the recipient machine checks the layer 2 trailer (the FCS) to see if the data is in error to be discarded, otherwise if the data is not in error, the layer 2 reads and interprets the control information in the layer 2 header.
D.   Then L2 strips the header and trailer and passes the remaining data up to layer 3 based on the control information in the data link header.
E.   The remaining layers perform similar de-encapsulation processes as necessary to deliver the actual data to the end user at the recipient machine.

1-129.   TRUE/FALSE: The encapsulation and de-encapsulation processes at the source and destination machines produce a type of logical communication between peer layers in the OSI model. This form of communication is called peer-to-peer communication. During this communication, the protocols at each layer exchange PDU between peer layers.

A.   TRUE
B.   FALSE

1-130.   The process of adding a TCP header followed by adding an IP header, and then a data link header and trailer, is an example of what?

A.   same-layer interaction
B.   data encapsulation
C.   data de-encapsulation
D.   none of the above answers

1-131.   Which of the following terms are used to identify the data that is transmitted by L1?
A.   Bit
B.   Data
C.   Segment
D.   Frame
E.   Packet
F.   Chunk

1-132.   Which of the following terms are used to identify the PDU that is created when encapsulating data inside L2?

A.   Bit
B.   Data
C.   Segment
D.   Frame
E.   Packet
F.   Chunk

1-133.   Which of the following terms are used to identify the PDU that is created when encapsulating data inside L3?

A.   Bit
B.   Data
C.   Segment
D.   Frame
E.   Packet
F.   Chunk

1-134.   Which of the following terms are used to identify the PDU that is created when encapsulating data inside L4?

A.   Bit
B.   Data
C.   Segment
D.   Frame
E.   Packet
F.   Chunk

1-135.   Arrange the steps of the data encapsulation process in the correct order.

1.   Step 1
2.   Step 2
3.   Step 3
4.   Step 4
5.   Step 5
6.   Step 6
7.   Step 7
8.   Step 8

A.   The user data is sent from an application to the application layer.
B.   The application layer adds the application layer header to the user data to produce L7PDU. The L7PDU becomes the data that is passed down to the presentation layer.
C.   The presentation layer adds the presentation layer header to the data to produce L6PDU. The L6PDU becomes the data that is passed down to the session layer.
D.   The session layer adds the session layer header to the data to produce L5PDU. The L5PDU becomes the data that is passed down to the transport layer.
E.   The transport layer adds the transport layer header to the data to produce L4PDU. The L4PDU becomes the data that is passed down to the network layer.
F.   The network layer adds the network layer header to the data to produce L3PDU. The L3PDU becomes the data that is passed down to the data link layer.
G.   The data link layer adds the header of the data link layer and trailer to the data to produce L2PDU. The L2PDU becomes the data that is passed down to the physical layer.
H.   The physical layer then transmits the bits onto the network media.

1-136. Complete the following statement: de-encapsulation does first occur in _____layer.

    A.   data link
    B.   application
    C.   transport
    D.   network
    E.   presentation

1-137. Match each layer with the function it performs in peer-to-peer communication.

    1.   transport
    2.   network layer
    3.   data link layer
    4.   physical layer

        A.   It encodes the data link frame into a pattern of 1s and 0s (bits) for transmission on the network media.
        B.   It encapsulates the network layer packet in a frame.
        C.   It encapsulates the session layer PDU in a segment.
        D.   It moves the data through the internetwork by encapsulating the data and adding a header to create a packet.

1-138. TRUE/FALSE: Computers send bits to each other over a particular type of physical networking medium using physical and data link layers protocols. The OSI physical layer defines how to send bits physically over a particular networking medium. The OSI data link layer defines some rules about the data that is physically transmitted, including hardware (H/W) addresses of the sending device and recipient device, and rules that organize the sending time to prevent data collisions.

    A.   TRUE
    B.   FALSE

1-139. Which of the following is true about LAN? (Select all that apply)

    A.   A LAN is a common type of network found in homes, small business offices, and large enterprise networks.
    B.   A LAN is considered as a basic part of large enterprise networks. An Enterprise network consists of a number of each site can be made of several LANs.
    C.   A LAN connects the end-user devices together, which allows the local computers to communicate with each other.
    D.   LANs are connected by switches and other connecting devices, whereas sites are connected by routers.
    E.   Routers are used to connect both the LAN and a wide-area network (WAN). This will provide connectivity between the various sites of the large enterprise network. With routers and a WAN, the computers at different sites can also communicate.

1-140. Which of the following statements is true about Ethernet LAN? (Select all that apply)

    A.   A data communications system that operates at high speed over short distances (up to a few thousand meters)
    B.   It has a specific user group.
    C.   It is not a public switched telecommunications network, but may be connected to one.
    D.   A LAN is usually managed and owned by a single organization.
    E.   A LAN permits users to exchange data, share a common printer or master a common computer

(server), or execute a shared application.

F.   A LAN can vary widely in their sizes (from two computers up to hundreds of computers).

1-141.   Which of the following statements is true about Ethernet LAN? (Select all that apply)

A.   An interconnection of LANs within a limited geographical area, such as a government base, is commonly referred to as a campus area network.

B.   An interconnection of LANs over a citywide geographical area is commonly called a metropolitan area network (MAN).

C.   An interconnection of LANs over large geographical areas, such as nationwide, is commonly called a wide area network (WAN).

D.   LANs are not subject to public telecommunications regulations.

1-142.   TRUE/FALSE: Ethernet LANs consist of a number of automated machines called network nodes and several types of interconnecting media.

A.   TRUE

B.   FALSE

1-143.   Network nodes can be one of two major classes. Which of the following is a type of the network node? (Select all that apply)

A.   Data Terminal Equipment (DTE)

B.   Data Communication Equipment (DCE)

1-144.   TRUE/FALSE: **Data terminal equipment (DTE)**—Devices that are either the source or the destination of data. DTEs are typically devices such as computers and network servers that all often referred to as end stations.

A.   TRUE

B.   FALSE

1-145.   TRUE/FALSE: **Data communication equipment (DCE)**—Intermediate network devices that receive and forward data across the network. DCEs may be both standalone devices such as repeaters, network switches, network bridges and routers, or communications interface units such as network interface cards (NIC) and modems.

A.   TRUE

B.   FALSE

1-146.   TRUE/FALSE: The current Ethernet media options include two general types of copper cable: unshielded twisted-pair (UTP) and shielded twisted-pair (STP), plus several types of optical fiber cable. However, the wireless network has no physical media.

A.   TRUE

B.   FALSE

1-147.   TRUE/FALSE: In addition to the above components, Ethernet LANs require some software that working in the network nodes (including IOS in CISCO devices) and make LAN useful plus protocols that manage its working, such as Ethernet protocols, TCP/IP suite, and DHCP.

A.   TRUE

B.   FALSE

1-148.   Which of the following is true about Ethernet history? (Select all that apply)

A.   From decades, the most common type of LAN is Ethernet.

B.   Like many inventions, Ethernet began inside a corporation that was looking for a solution to a specific problem **"The need is the mother of the invention."**

C.   Xerox needed an effective way to network the personal computer in its offices. From that, Ethernet was born.

D.   Xerox was developed the original Ethernet as an experimental coaxial cable network in the 1970s to operate with a data rate of 3 Mbps using a carrier sense multiple access with collision detection (CSMA/CD) protocol (which will be discussed in the next subsections of this chapter).

E.   Success with Xerox network led to the 1970s joint development of the 10-Mbps Ethernet Version 1.0 specification by the three-company consortium: Digital Equipment Corporation (DEC), Intel Corporation, and Xerox Corporation. This Ethernet became known as DIX Ethernet, referring to DEC, Intel, and Xerox. It is called thicknet (because of the thickness of the coaxial cable used in this network).

F.   In 1980s, this standard of Ethernet was updated to add more capabilities, and it was referred to as Ethernet Version 2.0 (Ethernet II). The first standard draft was first published on September 30, 1980 within IEEE.

1-149.   TRUE/FALSE: The Institute of Electrical and Electronics Engineers (IEEE) is a professional organization that defines network standards. The IEEE formed two committees that worked directly on Ethernet based on the CSMA/CD—the IEEE 802.3 committee and the IEEE 802.2 committee. The 802.3 committee worked on physical layer standards as well on a sublayer of the data link layer called Media Access Control (MAC). The IEEE assigned the other functions of the data link layer to the 802.2 committee. This upper part of the data link layer was called the Logical Link Control (LLC) sublayer. Notice that, the 802.2 standard applied to Ethernet as well as to other IEEE standards LANs such as Token Ring (See, http://tools.ietf.org/html/rfc1042 for modern LLC RFC.) This set of standards is most often referred to as simply "Ethernet." The original IEEE 802.3 standard was based on Ethernet II specifications, and it was very similar to the Ethernet Version 1.0 specifications. The draft standard was approved by the 802.3 working group in 1983 and was subsequently published as an official standard in 1985 (ANSI/IEEE Std. 802.3-1985). To take advantage of improvements and developments in the networking technologies, a number of supplements to the standard have been defined yet.

A.   TRUE

B.   FALSE

1-150.   What organization is responsible for the Ethernet standards?

A.   EIII

B.   ISO

C.   TIA

D.   EIA

E.   IEC

F.   IEEE

1-151.   TRUE/FALSE: Regardless of LANs size or complexity, all will be a combination of only three basic interconnection structures or networking building blocks. The point-to-point interconnection is the simplest structure as shown in Figure 1-14. In this network, only two network units are involved, and the connection may be DTE-to-DTE, DCE-to-DCE, or DTE-to-DCE. The cable in point-to-point interconnections is known as a network link. Depending on the type of cable and the transmission method that is used, the maximum allowable length of the link is set.

    A.   TRUE
    B.   FALSE

1-152.   Which of the following statements is true about original Ethernet LAN? (Select all that apply)

    A.   The original Ethernet networks were implemented with a coaxial bus topology, as shown in Figure 1-15.
    B.   The physical Ethernet consists of the coaxial cabling, which is a bus topology, and collective Ethernet NICs in the computers (nodes).
    C.   The bus is shared among all nodes on the Ethernet.
    D.   When a node wants to send some bits to another node on the bus, it sends an electrical signal, which propagates to all nodes on the Ethernet.

1-153.   TRUE/FALSE: 10BASE5 and 10BASE2 are types of old Ethernet. The 10 represents the maximum transmission speed, which is 10Mbps. The BASE stands for baseband signaling. The 5 in 10BASE5 represents the maximum length of cable, which is 500 m and the 2 in 10BASE2 represents the maximum length of cable, which is 200 m. 10BASE5 also known as thicknet, whereas, 10BASE2 known as thinnet. This is a simple description to these Ethernets.

    A.   TRUE
    B.   FALSE

1-154.   In 10BASE2, what does the number 10 represent?

    A.   the maximum transmission speed
    B.   for baseband signaling
    C.   the maximum length of cable

1-155.   In 10BASE2, what does the term BASE represent?

    A.   the maximum transmission speed
    B.   for baseband signaling
    C.   the maximum length of cable

1-156.   What does the number 2 represent in 10BASE2?

    A.   the maximum transmission speed
    B.   for baseband signaling
    C.   the maximum length of cable

1-157.   TRUE/FALSE: The solid lines in Figure 1-15 represent the physical network cabling. The dashed lines with arrows represent the path that it will be taken by PC1's transmitted frames. PC1 sends an electrical signal across its Ethernet NIC onto the cable, and PC2 and PC3 receive the signal since this is bus topology, which means that the transmitted signal is received by all stations on the LAN.

    A.   TRUE
    B.   FALSE

1-158.   TRUE/FALSE: Ethernets that use a single bus need another logic/protocol to manage the network. Imagine what happened if two or more electrical signals were sent at the same time on a single bus. Of course, they would overlap and collide, making both signals unintelligible. Therefore, to ensure that only one device sends traffic on the Ethernet at one time, Ethernet defined an algorithm, known as the carrier sense multiple access with collision detection (CSMA/CD) algorithm. Otherwise, the Ethernet would have been unusable. This algorithm, manages how the bus is accessed.

A. TRUE
B. FALSE

1-159. What is the purpose of CSMA/CD in the Ethernet?

A. To ensure that multiply device sends traffic on the Ethernet at one time.
B. To ensure that only one device sends traffic on the Ethernet at one time.
C. To ensure that any device does not send traffic on the Ethernet at anytime.

1-160. TRUE/FALSE: The CSMA/CD algorithm, which is applied for both 10BASE5 and 10BASE2 Ethernets, can be summarized as follows:

- A device that wants to send a frame checks the LAN before sending a frame to ensure that the LAN is silent—in other words, no frames are currently being sent.
- If there is a frame on the bus, the device that wants to send a frame waits for a random amount of time until the LAN is silent and then sends the frame.
- If a collision occurs, the devices that caused the collision wait for a random amount of time and then try again.

A. TRUE
B. FALSE

1-161. Which of the following statements is true about original Ethernet CSMA/CD? (Select all that apply)

A. A device that wants to send a frame does not check the LAN before sending a frame.
B. A device that wants to send a frame checks the LAN before sending a frame to ensure that the LAN is silent—in other words, no frames are currently being sent.
C. A device that wants to send a frame sends the frame to LAN immediately.

1-162. Which of the following statements is true about original Ethernet CSMA/CD? (Select all that apply)

A. If there is a frame on the bus, the device that wants to send a frame waits for a random amount of time until the LAN is silent.
B. If there is a frame on the bus, the device that wants to send a frame deletes its frame.
C. If there is a frame on the bus, the device that wants to send a frame waits for a random amount of time until the LAN is not silent.

1-163. Which of the following statements is true about original Ethernet CSMA/CD? (Select all that apply)

A. If a collision occurs, the devices that caused the collision try immediately to resend.
B. If a collision occurs, the devices that caused the collision wait for a random amount of time and then do not try again.
C. If a collision occurs, the devices that caused the collision wait for a random amount of time and then try again.

1-164. TRUE/FALSE: A collision occurs in these Ethernets because the transmitted electrical signal travels along the entire length of the bus and when two stations send a frame at the same time, their frames overlap, causing a collision. Therefore, all devices on a 10BASE5 or 10BASE2 Ethernet need to use CSMA/CD to make a LAN useful by avoiding collisions and recovering a LAN when collisions occur.

A. TRUE

B.　FALSE

1-165.　Which of the following statements is true about original Ethernet CSMA/CD? (Select all that apply)

A.　All devices on a 10BASE5 or 10BASE2 Ethernet does not need to use CSMA/CD to make a LAN useful by avoiding collisions and recovering a LAN when collisions occur.

B.　All devices on a 10BASE5 or 10BASE2 Ethernet need to use CSAM/CD to make a LAN useful by avoiding collisions and recovering a LAN when collisions occur

C.　All devices on a 10BASE5 or 10BASE2 Ethernet need to use CSMA/CD to make a LAN useful by avoiding collisions and recovering a LAN when collisions occur

1-166.　TRUE/FALSE: 10BASE5 and 10BASE2 Ethernet networks used coaxial cable for physical layer connectivity. From 1990, the use of twisted pair cables was begun.

A.　TRUE

B.　FALSE

1-167.　Which of the following statements is true about Ethernet over the twisted pair? (Select all that apply)

A.　**Ethernet over the twisted pair** refers to the use of cables that contain insulated copper wires twisted together in pairs for the physical layer of an Ethernet network.

B.　**Ethernet over the twisted pair** refers to the use of cables that contain insulated fiber wires twisted together in pairs for the physical layer of an Ethernet network.

C.　**Ethernet over the twisted pair** refers to the use of cables that contain insulated coaxial wires twisted together in pairs for the physical layer of an Ethernet network.

1-168.　TRUE/FALSE: IEEE defined several Ethernet standards for twisted pair cables. The most widely used are 10BASE-T (1990), 100BASE-TX (1995), and 1000BASE-T (1999), running at 10Mbps, 100Mbps, and 1000Mbps (1Gbps) respectively.

A.　TRUE

B.　FALSE

1-169.　Match each Ethernet standard to its speed.

1.　10BASE-T
2.　100BASE-TX
3.　1000BASE-T

A.　1000Mbps
B.　100Mbps
C.　10Mbps

1-170.　Which of the following is true regarding Table 1-2? (Select all that apply)

A.　Table 1-2 lists the most commonly used IEEE Ethernet standards.

B.　The **number** (10, 100, or 1000) in the beginning of the standard name refers to the theoretical maximum transmission speed in megabits per second (Mbps).

C.　The **BASE** is a short of the baseband signaling, meaning that there are no frequency-division multiplexing (FDM) or other frequency shifting modulation in use, each signal has full control of wire, on a single frequency.

D.　The **T** designates twisted pair cable, where the pair of wires for each signal is twisted together to reduce radio frequency interference and crosstalk between pairs (FEXT and NEXT).

E. Where there are several standards for the same transmission speed, they are distinguished by a letter or digit following the T, such as TX. To support these new standards, networking devices called hubs and switches were created.

1-171. Match each Ethernet standard symbol to its meaning.

1. **number** (10, 100, or 1000)
2. **BASE**
3. **T**

    A. It is a short of the baseband signaling, meaning that there are no frequency-division multiplexing (FDM) or other frequency shifting modulation in use, each signal has full control of wire, on a single frequency.
    B. It refers to the theoretical maximum transmission speed in megabits per second (Mbps).
    C. It designates for the twisted pair cable, where the pair of wires for each signal is twisted together to reduce radio frequency interference and crosstalk between pairs (FEXT and NEXT).

1-172. Match each Ethernet standard name to its maximum speed.

1. Ethernet
2. Fast Ethernet
3. Gigabit Ethernet

    A. 1000Mbps
    B. 100Mbps
    C. 10Mbps

1-173. Match each Ethernet standard name to its technical name.

1. Ethernet
2. Fast Ethernet
3. Gigabit Ethernet

    A. 1000BASE-T
    B. 100BASE-TX
    C. 1000BASE-LX
    D. 10BASE-T
    E. 1000BASE-SX

1-174. Match each Ethernet standard name to its IEEE standard name.

1. Ethernet
2. Fast Ethernet
3. Gigabit Ethernet

    A. IEEE 802.3
    B. IEEE 802.3u
    C. IEEE 802.3z
    D. IEEE 802.3ab

1-175. Match each Ethernet standard name to its cable type.

1. Ethernet

2.   Fast Ethernet
3.   Gigabit Ethernet

A.   Copper
B.   Fiber

1-176.   Match each Ethernet standard name to its maximum length.

1.   1000BASE-T
2.   100BASE-TX
3.   1000BASE-LX
4.   10BASE-T
5.   1000BASE-SX

A.   100 m
B.   5 km
C.   550 m

1-177.   TRUE/FALSE: Because of many reasons such as the **Attenuation**, 10BASE5 and 10BASE2 had limitations on the total length of a cable. With 10BASE5, the limit was 500 m; with 10BASE2, it was 185 m (approximately 200 m). The number of DTEs did not exceed 1024 in 10BASE5. To overcome these limitations a repeater is used.

A.   TRUE
B.   FALSE

1-178.   What is the maximum total length of a cable in the 10BASE5 networks?

A.   1500m
B.   2500m
C.   100m
D.   500m

1-179.   What is the maximum total length of a cable in the 10BASE2 networks?

A.   185 m
B.   285 m
C.   85 m
D.   385 m

1-180.   What is the maximum number of PCs that can be connected in the 10BASE5 networks and without using a repeater?

A.   124
B.   1024
C.   2024
D.   24

1-181.   TRUE/FALSE: To overcome the maximum number of PCs and cable length limitations in 10BASE5 and 10BASE2 a repeater is used.

A.   TRUE
B.   FALSE

1-182.   TRUE/FALSE: **Attenuation** means that electrical signals pass over a cable, suffer from weaknesses in the strength of the signal as it travels farther along the cable.

    A.   TRUE
    B.   FALSE

1-183.   TRUE/FALSE: As shown in Figure 1-5, the repeater (hub) connects multiple cable segments, receives the electrical signal from one cable, interprets the electrical signals (bits), and generates clean (without noise), strong (amplification) signals out the other cable. Repeater only examines and generates electrical signals and does not interpret what the bits mean. Therefore, a repeater is considered to operate at Layer 1 of the OSI model.

    A.   TRUE
    B.   FALSE

1-184.   What is the function of the repeater? (Select all that apply)

    A.   It connects multiple cable segments.
    B.   It extends cable length
    C.   It increases the number of PCs that can be connected on Ethernet.
    D.   It receives the electrical signal from one cable, interprets the electrical signals (bits), and generates clean (without noise), strong (amplification) signals out the other cable.

1-185.   Why a repeater is considered to operate at Layer 1 of the OSI model?

    A.   Because it only examines and generates electrical signals and does not interpret, what the bits mean.
    B.   Because it only examines and generates electrical signals and does interpret, what the bits mean.
    C.   Because it does not examine nor generate electrical signals and does not interpret, what the bits mean.

1-186.   TRUE/FALSE: Basically, hubs are multiport repeaters. That means, the hub simply regenerates the electrical signal that comes in one port and sends the clean, strong generated signal out every other port. That also means, the hub generates several electrical buses (but internally, Hub creates One Shared Electrical Bus), as shown in Figure 1-5, just like 10BASE2 and 10BASE5. One bus for each LAN connected to a specific hub port. Therefore, the use of CSMA/CD algorithm will still be required since collisions can occur in 10BASE-T.

    A.   TRUE
    B.   FALSE

1-187.   Which of the following statements are true about hub? (Select all that apply)

    A.   Hubs are multiport repeaters.
    B.   Hub simply regenerates the electrical signal that comes in one port and sends the clean, strong generated signal out every other port.
    C.   Hub generates several electrical buses.
    D.   Internally, Hub creates One Shared Electrical Bus.

1-188.   Why CSMA/CD is still being required in 10BASE-T?

    A.   since collisions cannot occur
    B.   since collisions can still occur
    C.   since broadcasts can still occur

1-189.   TRUE/FALSE: The use of hubs in network design solved some big problems with 10BASE5 and 10BASE2 networks. One of the biggest problems is the availability. In 10BASE5 and 10BASE2 LANs any single cable problem could, and probably did, take down the whole network. Whereas in the 10BASE-T network, a cable connects each device to the hub, so a single cable problem affects only one device/one LAN. This means that 10BASE-T networks are much higher availability than 10BASE5 and 10BASE2 networks. In addition, the use of twisted pair cables, in a star topology, lowered the cost of purchasing and installing the cabling.

    A.   TRUE
    B.   FALSE

1-190.   Which of the following problems are solved by using the hub in the Ethernet? (Select all that apply)

    A.   In the 10BASE-T network, a cable connects each device to the hub, so a single cable problem affects all devices connected to the hub.
    B.   In the 10BASE-T network, a cable connects each device to the hub, so a single cable problem affects only one device/one LAN.
    C.   The use of twisted pair cables, in a star topology, lowered the cost of purchasing and installing the cabling.

1-191.   Which of the following is true about switches? (Select all that apply)

    A.   Switches are intelligent devices and therefore, switches can perform much more functions than hubs and can play much better than hubs (See the datasheet for CAT2.96K switch on www.cisco.com.)
    B.   LAN switches increase the available bandwidth of the Ethernet network and significantly reduce, or even eliminate, the number of collisions on a LAN.
    C.   Unlike hubs, switches do not create a single shared electrical bus, forwarding received electrical signals out all other ports. Instead, switches do the following:
        ▪   Switches interpret the bits in the received frame so that they can typically send the frame out to the required port, rather than all other ports of the switch.
        ▪   Switches can forward one frame at a time, buffering other frames in memory when they need to forward multiple frames out the same port, thereby avoiding collisions.

1-192.   Which of the following statements are true about switches? (Select all that apply)

    A.   Switches are intelligent devices.
    B.   Switches can perform much more functions than hubs and can play much better than hubs.
    C.   Switches increase the available bandwidth of the Ethernet network.
    D.   Switches reduce, or even eliminate, the number of collisions on a LAN.
    E.   Switches do not create a single shared electrical bus like hubs.

1-193.   Which of the following statements describe the function of the switches? (Select all that apply)

    A.   Switches interpret the bits in the received frame so that they can typically send the frame out to the required port, rather than all other ports of the switch.
    B.   Switches can forward one frame at a time, buffering other frames in memory when they need to forward multiple frames out the same port, thereby avoiding collisions.

1-194.   TRUE/FALSE: LAN switches increase available bandwidth of the Ethernet network as compared with hubs. In particular:

    ▪   No collisions can occur when only one device is connected to each port of a switch.
    ▪   Each port of the switch has its own separate bandwidth, which is not shared with devices connected

to another switch port. This means, that a switch with 1000-Mbps ports has 1000 Mbps of bandwidth per port (2000 Mbps full-duplex.) This is the real difference between shared Ethernet and switched Ethernet. Hub is a shared Ethernet network where all ports share the same hub bandwidth, whereas the switch is a switched Ethernet where each port has a separate bandwidth.

A.   TRUE
B.   FALSE

1-195.   TRUE/FALSE: Since, the switch's logic requires that the switch look at the Ethernet frame header, which is considered a Layer 2 feature. Therefore, switches are considered to operate as a Layer 2 device, whereas hubs are Layer 1 devices.

A.   TRUE
B.   FALSE

1-196.   Which of the following types of networks cannot be considered as media for collision?

A.   Hub based network
B.   Switch based network, only one device is connected to each port of a switch.
C.   Switch based network, multiply devices are connected to each port of a switch.

1-197.   TRUE/FALSE: Since the early 1990s, the cabled network design of choice has been the star-connected topology, shown in Figure 1-16. The central network device is either a hub or a network switch. All connections in a star network are point-to-point links implemented with either twisted-pair or optical fiber cable. These networks are still suffering from collision and broadcast problems. However, collision cannot be occurred, and broadcast can be stopped, in switches based networks.

A.   TRUE
B.   FALSE

1-198.   Which of the following statements are true about modern Ethernet networks? (Select all that apply)

A.   It is a star-connected topology.
B.   The central network device is either a hub or a network switch.
C.   All connections in a star network are point-to-point links implemented with either twisted-pair or optical fiber cable.

1-199.   Which of the following is true about 10BASE2 cabling?

A.   Each device is connected to a centralized hub using UTP cabling.
B.   Each device is connected to a centralized switch using UTP cabling.
C.   Each device is connected in series using UTP cabling.
D.   Each device is connected in series using coaxial cabling.

1-200.   TRUE/FALSE: Ethernet LAN standards specify cabling and signaling at both the physical and data link layers of the OSI model.

A.   TRUE
B.   FALSE

1-201.   TRUE/FALSE: As with all IEEE 802 protocols, the OSI data link layer is divided into two IEEE 802 sublayers, the Media Access Control (MAC) sublayer and the Logical Link Control (LLC) sublayer. The IEEE 802.3 physical layer corresponds to the OSI physical layer.

    A.   TRUE
    B.   FALSE

1-202.   TRUE/FALSE: All Ethernet standards use the same small set of data-link standards. From 10BASE5 and up to 10-Gbps Ethernet networks, the Ethernet addressing works the same on all the types of Ethernet. In addition, the CSMA/CD algorithm is applying to most types of Ethernet, unless it has been disabled. These are the most significant strengths of the Ethernet family of standards.

    A.   TRUE
    B.   FALSE

1-203.   Which of the following is true about Ethernet LAN standards? (Select all that apply)

    A.   It specifies cabling and signaling at both the physical and data link layers of the OSI model.
    B.   The OSI data link layer is divided into two IEEE 802 sublayers.
    C.   All Ethernet standards use the same small set of data-link standards.

1-204.   Which of the following is a sublayer of the OSI data link layer? (Select all that apply)

    A.   Media Access Control (MAC) sublayer
    B.   Logical Link Control (LLC) sublayer
    C.   Media Link Control (MLC) sublayer
    D.   Logical Access Control (LAC) sublayer

1-205.   TRUE/FALSE: The Logical Link Control (LLC) sublayer of the data link layer manages communications between devices over a single link of a network. IEEE 802.2 specifications defined LLC to support both connectionless and connection-oriented services used by higher-layer protocols. LLC is created to allow part of the data link layer to function independently from existing technologies. IEEE 802.2 defines a number of fields in the frames of the data link layer, which enables multiple higher-layer protocols to share a single physical data link. It also participates in the encapsulation process.

    A.   TRUE
    B.   FALSE

1-206.   Which of the following is true about IEEE 802.2? (Select all that apply)

    A.   It is a sublayer of L2.
    B.   It manages communications between devices over a single link of a network.
    C.   It defined by IEEE to support both connectionless and connection-oriented services used by higher-layer protocols.
    D.   LLC is created to allow part of the data link layer to function independently from existing technologies.
    E.   IEEE 802.2 defines a number of fields in the frames of the data link layer, which enables multiple higher-layer protocols to share a single physical data link.
    F.   It also participates in the encapsulation process.
    G.   It maintains the MAC table.

1-207.   TRUE/FALSE: The Media Access Control (MAC) sublayer of the data link layer manages protocol access to the physical network medium. The IEEE 802.3 MAC specification defines MAC addresses, which enable multiple devices to identify uniquely one another at the data link layer. A device to be networked must have a unique MAC address. This identification is made by using MAC table of physical addresses of devices.

The MAC table is maintained by LLC sublayer.

    A.   TRUE
    B.   FALSE

1-208.   Which of the following is true about IEEE 802.3 MAC specification? (Select all that apply)

    A.   It is a sublayer of L2.
    B.   It manages protocol access to the physical network medium.
    C.   It defines MAC addresses.
    D.   It is based on the CSMA/CD process.
    E.   It specifies the physical layer (Layer 1).
    F.   It specifies the MAC portion of the data link layer (Layer 2).

1-209.   TRUE/FALSE: The MAC sublayer has two primary functions:

- Data encapsulation, including frame assembly before transmission, and frame parsing/error detection during and after reception
- Media access control, including initiation of frame transmission and recovery from transmission failure

    A.   TRUE
    B.   FALSE

1-210.   TRUE/FALSE: Before studying the CSMA/CD algorithm, it is better to review who is vulnerable to collisions in the networking. This depends on the type of data transmission used. Some types of data transmission are virtually invulnerable to collisions- while others are vulnerable to collisions.

    A.   TRUE
    B.   FALSE

1-211.   TRUE/FALSE: Collisions in the networking depend on the type of data transmission used. Some types of data transmission are virtually invulnerable to collisions- while others are vulnerable to collisions.

    A.   TRUE
    B.   FALSE

1-212.   Which of the following is a type of data transmission in the networking? (Select all that apply)

    A.   Simplex
    B.   Half-duplex
    C.   Full-duplex

1-213.   TRUE/FALSE: **Simplex** data transmission is a connection in which data will always flow in one direction. Therefore, it will not suffer collisions. Since data flows in one direction, there is no mutual communication between the sending and receiving stations- therefore, simplex transmission will not be seen in everyday networks. Simplex transmissions, however, are using in broadcasting companies when they want to send a video in a one-way data transmission to a home television, as shown in Figure 1-18.

    A.   TRUE
    B.   FALSE

1-214.   TRUE/FALSE: **Half-duplex** data transmission allows mutual communication between the sending and receiving stations, as shown in Figure 1-19. A device either sends or receives data at any point in time, but never both at the same time. Half-Duplex is the media for almost all collisions could happen: since each device may not know, the other is transmitting. If a collision occurs, the data collides over the bus and the data is corrupted.

A.   TRUE
B.   FALSE

1-215.   TRUE/FALSE: **Full-duplex** data transmission allows devices to send and receive data at any point in time, as shown in Figure 1-20. Virtually, no collisions take place on a full-duplex transmission, so there is no need for CSMA/CD. Full-duplex increases the overall throughput- since sending and receiving are taken place on two different channels. Theoretically, Full-duplex doubles the data transfer rate.

A.   TRUE
B.   FALSE

1-216.   Which of the following is true about Full-Duplex? (Select all that apply)

A.   Collisions will be eliminated when Full-duplex and switches are used.
B.   Collisions may still occur when a Full-duplex transmission is configured for a network that operates under a hub.
C.   This is because switches forward data only to nodes that need it using micro segmentation technology, while hubs forward incoming data to all computers connected to it.
D.   Thus, the fault lies within the collision-prone characteristics of the hub. CSMA/CD must be deployed whenever collisions could occur, in hub networks of course.

1-217.   TRUE/FALSE: Moreover, switches can buffer frames in memory, switches can eliminate collisions completely on switch ports that connect to a single host. In such network collisions cannot occur, since this network connects the switch to one host per port, which allows the use of full-duplex operation.

A.   TRUE
B.   FALSE

1-218.   TRUE/FALSE: To implement full duplex in a switched network, CSMA/CD logic on the devices on both ends of the cable must be disabled. As a result, the performance of such a switched Ethernet on that cable has been doubled by allowed simultaneous transmission in both directions.

A.   TRUE
B.   FALSE

1-219.   Match each data transmission type to its characteristics.

1.   Simplex
2.   Half-duplex
3.   Full-duplex

A.   It is a connection where data will always flow in one direction.
B.   It is not suffering collisions at all.
C.   There is no mutual communication between the sending and receiving stations.
D.   It is used in broadcasting companies when they want to send a video in a one-way data, transmission to a home television.
E.   It allows mutual communication between the sending and receiving stations.
F.   A device either sends or receives data at any point in time, but never both at the same time.
G.   It is where almost all collisions will happen: since each device may not know, the other is

transmitting.

H.   Phones used this type.
I.   It allows devices to send and receive data at any point in time.
J.   Virtually, no collisions take place on it.
K.   It increases the overall throughput-since sending and receiving are taken place on two different channels.
L.   It doubles the data transfer rate.
M.   To implement it in a switched network, CSMA/CD logic on the devices on both ends of the cable must be disabled.

1-220.   Which of the following data transmission types allows collision to occur? (Select all that apply)

A.   Simplex
B.   Half-duplex
C.   Full-duplex

1-221.   Which of the following is true about full-duplex? (Select all that apply)

A.   Collisions will not occur when a Full-duplex transmission is configured for a network that operates under a hub.
B.   Collisions may still occur when a Full-duplex transmission is configured for a network that operates under a hub.
C.   Collisions will occur on switched based network with multi-PCs connected on one switch port.
D.   Collisions will not occur on switched based network with multi-PCs connected on one switch port.
E.   To implement full duplex in a switched network, CSMA/CD logic on the devices on both ends of the cable must be disabled.

1-222.   TRUE/FALSE: **Carrier Sense Multiple Access with Collision Detection (CSMA/CD)**, is a layer 2 protocol in the OSI model. It is used in the networking as a control protocol in which a carrier sensing and collision detection algorithms are used.

A.   TRUE
B.   FALSE

1-223.   TRUE/FALSE: The CSMA/CD protocol was originally developed as a means by which two or more stations could share common media in a switch-less environment. Each Ethernet MAC determines for itself when it will be allowed to send a frame.

A.   TRUE
B.   FALSE

1-224.   TRUE/FALSE: CSMA/CD is a modification of pure CSMA. CD is used to improve CSMA performance by terminating transmission as soon as a collision is detected, and reducing the probability of a second collision on retry.

A.   TRUE
B.   FALSE

1-225.   TRUE/FALSE: There are several methods for CD. CD methods are media dependent. On an electrical bus such as Ethernet, collisions can be detected by comparing transmitted data with received data. If they are not identical, another transmitter is overlaying the first transmitter's signal, collision is occurred, and transmission terminates immediately. A jam signal is sent, which will cause all transmitters to back off by backoff delay, reducing the probability of a collision when the first retry is attempted. Ethernet is the classic CSMA/CD protocol.

However, in Full Duplex Ethernet, collisions are impossible since data is transmitted and received on different wires, and each segment is connected directly to a specific switch port. Therefore, CSMA/CD is not used on Full Duplex Ethernet networks. In addition, CSMA/CD is no longer used in the 10 Gigabit Ethernet specifications, due to the requirement of switching based network. Similarly, few implementations support CSMA/CD (half duplex) in the Gigabit Ethernet and in practice it is nonexistent.

A. TRUE
B. FALSE

1-226. Which of the following protocols is part of the CSMA/CD? (Select all that apply)

A. Carrier Sense
B. Multiple Access
C. Collision Detection

1-227. Match each protocol of CSMA/CD to its definitions.

1. Carrier Sense
2. Multiple Access
3. Collision Detection

A. Each station continuously listens for signal on the medium to determine when the medium is idle.
B. It is the ability of a NIC to check the network for any communication.
C. By this protocol only, it is impossible to be sure, that data is not in the process of being sent by other computers- so this is one possible beginning of a collision.
D. It provides the ability to multiple devices to access the network with the same priority.
E. By using this protocol, collisions are more possible to occur.
F. It provides each transmitting device the capability of detecting that a collision has occurred before sending its frame.
G. By this protocol, each transmitting device must stop transmitting as soon as it has detected the collision, transmits a jam signal, and then must wait for a random time interval (determined by a back-off algorithm) before attempting to retransmit the frame.

1-228. TRUE/FALSE: On an electrical bus such as Ethernet, collisions can be detected by comparing transmitted data with received data. If they are not identical, another transmitter is overlaying the first transmitter's signal, collision is occurred, and transmission terminates immediately. A jam signal is sent, which will cause all transmitters to back off by backoff delay, reducing the probability of a collision when the first retry is attempted.

A. TRUE
B. FALSE

1-229. Which of following steps is implemented as part of the CSMA/CD algorithm? (Select all that apply)

A. **Step 1** A device that wants to send a frame listens until the Ethernet is idle.
B. **Step 2** The transmitter station(s) start(s) sending the frame, if the Ethernet is idle.
C. **Step 3** After sending the frame, the transmitter station (s) listen(s) again to make sure that no collision has occurred in the network.
D. **Step 4** If a collision occurs; devices involved in the collision keep transmitting (jamming signal) for a short period, to make sure all devices on the network see the collision.
E. **Step 5** Each device sees the jamming signal, and invokes the back-off algorithm. Each device will have a random timer that determines when it can transmit again.
F. **Step 6** When each random timer expires, the process starts again with Step 1.

1-230.   Which of the following is true about CSMA/CD algorithm? (Select all that apply)

A.   It does not completely prevent collisions, but it does ensure that Ethernet works sufficiently if collisions may occur and the algorithm defines how the computers should notice a collision and how to recover.
B.   The CD algorithm adds a delay to the network, which degrades the overall performance.
C.   The algorithm never allows collisions to occur.
D.   When only two devices on the same Ethernet, this algorithm can work
E.   CS causes devices to wait until the Ethernet is idle before sending data.

1-231.   TRUE/FALSE: CS causes devices to wait until the Ethernet is idle before sending data. This process means that only one device can send data at any one instant in time. Therefore, the overall network bandwidth is shared by all devices connected to the same hub. Notice that, waiting to send until the LAN is an idle means that a device either sends or receives data at any point in time, which is called half-duplex.

A.   TRUE
B.   FALSE

1-232.   TRUE/FALSE: The IEEE 802.3 standard defines a basic data Ethernet frame format that is required for all MAC implementations, plus several additional optional formats that are used to extend the protocol's basic capability. The framing used for Ethernet has changed a couple of times over the years. The recent changes to Ethernet framing are made by IEEE in 1997. It includes some of the features of the original Xerox Ethernet framing (1970s), along with the framing defined by the IEEE (1980s).

A.   TRUE
B.   FALSE

1-233.   TRUE/FALSE: One of the most significant strengths of all Ethernet family of protocols is that these protocols use the same small set of data-link standards. First, the CSMA/CD algorithm is applying to most types of Ethernet, unless it has been disabled. Clearly, CSMA/CD is technically a part of the data link layer. Second, Ethernet addressing works the same on all the types of Ethernet, from 10BASE5 and up to 10Gbps Ethernet. However, framing has changed several times over the years as stated above.

A.   TRUE
B.   FALSE

1-234.   Which of the following is true about Ethernet? (Select all that apply)

A.   The CSMA/CD algorithm is applying to most types of Ethernet, unless it has been disabled.
B.   Ethernet addressing works the same on all the types of Ethernet, from 10BASE5 and up to 10Gbps Ethernet
C.   Framing has changed several times over the years.

1-235.   TRUE/FALSE: **Framing** defines how strings of bits are interpreted in the Data-link protocols. In other words, framing defines the meaning of the bits transmitted and received over a network through the physical layers of the sending and receiving devices. Frame can also be defined as a "container" into which data is placed for transmission in Ethernet LAN network. The frame contains the actual data that is being transmitted in addition to header and trailer information.

A.   TRUE
B.   FALSE

1-236.   Which of the following is true about Ethernet Framing? (Select all that apply)

A.   It defines how strings of bits are interpreted in the Data-link protocols.
B.   It defines the meaning of the bits transmitted and received over a network through the physical layers of the sending and receiving devices.
C.   It can be defined as a "container" into which data is placed for transmission in Ethernet LAN network.
D.   The frame contains the actual data that is being transmitted in addition to header and trailer information.

1-237.   Which of the following is a field in the Ethernet frame? (Select all that apply)

A.   PRE
B.   SFD
C.   DA
D.   SA
E.   L/T
F.   D&P
G.   FCS

1-238.   Match each frame field to its size.

1.   PRE
2.   SFD
3.   DA
4.   SA
5.   L/T
6.   D&P
7.   FCS

A.   7 bytes
B.   1 byte
C.   6 bytes
D.   2 bytes
E.   46-1500 bytes
F.   4 bytes

1-239.   Match each frame field to its function.

1.   PRE
2.   SFD
3.   DA
4.   SA
5.   L/T
6.   D&P
7.   FCS

A.   It provides a means to synchronize the frame-reception portions of receiving physical layers with the incoming bit stream.
B.   It tells the receiving computer that the transmission of the actual frame is about to start.
C.   It contains the MAC address of NIC on the local network to which the frame is being sent.
D.   It identifies the frame sending station.
E.   It indicates either the number of data bytes that are contained in the data field of the frame, or the frame type ID.
F.   It consists of the packet (L3 PDU) that is received by receiving station from layer 3 on the transmitting station.

G.   It contains a 32-bit cyclic redundancy check (CRC) value.

1-240.   TRUE/FALSE: Ethernet frames are addressed according to communication types that occurred in the LAN. In general, there are three types of communication in the network; these are unicast, multicast, and broadcast. Each Ethernet address is 6 bytes long. It is usually written in the hexadecimal format that is organized in pairs or quads, such as the following: 00:00:1d:34:bc:00 or 0000:1d34:bc00. In CISCO devices, the MAC address is written with periods separating each set of four hex digits. For example, 0000.0C12.1A3E is a valid Ethernet address.

A.   TRUE
B.   FALSE

1-241.   Which of the following is a type of communication in the network? (Select all that apply)

A.   Unicast
B.   Multicast
C.   Broadcast
D.   Castmulti

1-242.   Match each type of communication to its function.

1.   Unicast
2.   Multicast
3.   Broadcast

A.   It is used to identify a single NIC on the Ethernet.
B.   This type of network communication sends a frame from one sender node and addressed to one destination node.
C.   This type of communication is the predominant form of communication on LANs and within the internet.
D.   It is used to identify a group of NICs on the Ethernet.
E.   This type of network communication sends a frame from one sender node and addressed to a group of destination nodes.
F.   It is used to identify all NICs on the Ethernet.
G.   This type of network communication sends a frame from one sender node and addressed to all destination nodes.

1-243.   Which of the following types of communication can be used to communicate with more than one device at a time?

A.   Unicast
B.   Multicast
C.   Broadcast
D.   Castmulti

1-244.   TRUE/FALSE: When a host needs to provide information to all the hosts on the network or when the location of special services/devices for which the address is not known, broadcast transmission is used.

A.   TRUE
B.   FALSE

1-245.   When broadcast transmission is used? (Select all that apply)

A.   When a host needs to provide information to more than 1000 hosts on the network
B.   When a host needs to provide information to all the hosts on the network
C.   When the location of special services/devices for which the address is not known
D.   When the location of special services/devices for which the address is known

1-246.   Which of the following transmissions uses broadcast? (Select all that apply)

A.   Requesting unknown host address
B.   Mapping lower layer addresses to upper layer addresses.
C.   Mapping upper layer addresses to lower layer addresses.
D.   Routing updates

1-247.   Which of the following is true about Ethernet transmission? (Select all that apply)

A.   Broadcast packets are usually restricted to the local network by routers. This restriction is dependent on the configuration of the router that borders the network and the type of broadcast.
B.   Unicast packets can be routed throughout the internetwork.

1-248.   TRUE/FALSE: A directed broadcast is sent to all hosts on a specific network (non-local network). For example, for a host outside of the 172.16.2.0 /24 network to communicate with the hosts within this network, the destination address of the packet would be 172.16.2.255. Although the routers do not forward directed broadcasts by default, they may be configured to do so.

A.   TRUE
B.   FALSE

1-249.   TRUE/FALSE: This type of broadcast is used for communication that is limited to the hosts on the local network (not to host on the non-local network). These packets use a destination address 255.255.255.255. Routers do not forward this broadcast. Packets addressed to the limited broadcast address will only appear on the local network. For this reason, an IPv4 network is also referred to as a *broadcast domain* where the router forms the boundary for this broadcast domain.

A.   TRUE
B.   FALSE

1-250.   Match each type of broadcast to its using.

1.   Directed Broadcast
2.   Limited Broadcast

A.   It is sent to all hosts on a specific network (non-local network).
B.   Although routers do not forward these broadcasts by default, they may be configured to do so.
C.   The destination address of the packet would be w.x.y.255.
D.   This type of broadcast is used for communication that is limited to the hosts on the local network (not to host on the non-local network).
E.   Routers do not forward this broadcast. Routers act as a boundary for this broadcast.
F.   These packets use a destination address 255.255.255.255.
G.   Packets addressed by this type of broadcast will only appear on the local network.

1-251.   TRUE/FALSE: Ethernet address, MAC address, NIC address, hardware address, physical address, LAN address, universally administered address (UAA), and burned-in address, all are names of the same thing that is Ethernet address.

A.   TRUE
B.   FALSE

1-252.   TRUE/FALSE: Ethernet address is the means by which data is addressed and directed to the proper receiving node in the network.

A.   TRUE
B.   FALSE

1-253.   TRUE/FALSE: Because, the MAC sublayer protocols in the Data Link layer such as IEEE 802.3 define the addressing details, the IEEE calls these addresses the "MAC addresses." The IEEE defines the format and assignment of Ethernet addresses. Each NIC on the network must have a unique unicast MAC address according to the IEEE specification so that it is possible to identify that NIC globally. This address is often referred as the burned-in address (BIA), which means it is burned into the ROM chip on the card by Ethernet card manufacturers, and it cannot be changed. However, to meet some private needs, some vendors allow the modification of this address. Because the IEEE universally regulates the assignment of the Ethernet addresses, BIAs sometimes are called universally administered addresses (UAA).

A   TRUE
B.   FALSE

1-254.   Match each Ethernet address name to the reason of such naming.

1.   MAC addresses
2.   Burned-In Address (BIA)
3.   Universally Administered Addresses (UAA)

A.   Because, the MAC sublayer protocols in the Data Link layer such as IEEE 802.3 define the addressing details.
B.   Because, it is burned into the ROM chip on the card
C.   Because, the IEEE universally regulates the assignment of the Ethernet addresses.

1-255.   TRUE/FALSE: Each NIC on the network must have a unique unicast MAC address according to the IEEE specification so that it is possible to identify that NIC globally.

A.   TRUE
B.   FALSE

1-256.   Which of the following is a synonym to the Ethernet address? (Select all that apply)

A.   MAC address
B.   NIC address
C.   burned-on address
D.   hardware address
E.   physical address
F.   LAN address
G.   software address
H.   universally administered address (UAA)
I.   burned-in address

1-257.   TRUE/FALSE: Each manufacturer assigns a MAC address with its own OUI as the first half of the address, with the second half of the address.

    A.   TRUE
    B.   FALSE

1-258. What is the size of the MAC address?

    A.   48 bytes
    B.   48 bits
    C.   24 bits
    D.   24 byes

1-259. Which of the following is a part of the MAC address? (Select all that apply)

    A.   Original unique identifier (OUI) 24-bit
    B.   Organizationally unique identifier (OUI) 24-bit
    C.   Vendor Assigned (24-bit)
    D.   End-user Assigned (24-bit)

1-260. How many hex digits are in the MAC address?

    A.   6 hex digits
    B.   12 hex digits
    C.   24 hex digits
    D.   48 hex digits

1-261. Which of the following is true about Ethernet addresses? (Select all that apply)

    A.   MAC is the name of the part of the address that holds the manufacturer's code.
    B.   OUI is the name of the part of the address that holds the manufacturer's code.
    C.   A unique code into the first half of the address is assigned uniquely by the manufacturer.
    D.   First 2 bytes of the address are assigned uniquely by the manufacturer.
    E.   First 3 bytes of the address are assigned uniquely by the manufacturer.

1-262. Which of the following is accurate about an Ethernet address? (Select all that apply)

    A.   It is used in an Ethernet LAN, directs data to the proper receiving host.
    B.   Both the destination and source addresses consist of a 6-byte hex-decimal number.
    C.   It is the 4-byte hexadecimal address of the NIC on the sending computer.
    D.   It is the 4-byte hexadecimal address of the NIC on the receiving computer.

1-263. Which of the following is accurate about an Ethernet address? (Select all that apply)

    A.   The Ethernet address can never be changed.
    B.   To participate in the network, it is necessary for a host to have a unique MAC address.
    C.   It is represented by binary codes that are organized in pairs.
    D.   To participate in the network, it is not necessary for a host to have a unique MAC address.
    E.   It is physically located on the NIC of a host as a number in the hexadecimal format.

1-264. TRUE/FALSE: To identify the different network layer (Layer 3) protocols from different vendors on the Ethernet, the protocol Type field is added in the frame, so that the receiving node knows what type of L3 PDU is in the Ethernet frame. For example, to make the receiving node knows that an IP packet is inside an Ethernet frame, the Type field (as shown in Figure 1-25) would have a value of 0800 hexadecimal (2048 decimal).

    A.   TRUE

B.   FALSE

1-265.   TRUE/FALSE: Because of the changes to Ethernet framing over the years, the protocol Type field can be identified by another part in the frame, particularly when sending IP packet, and in this case, the original Type field is used as a Length field for that frame, identifying the length of the entire Ethernet frame. If the 802.3 Type/Length field (shown in Figure 1-25) has a value less than 0600 hexadecimal (1536 decimal), the Type/Length field is used as a Length field for that frame. Therefore, another field (Type field) is needed to identify the type of L3 protocol inside the frame.

A.   TRUE
B.   FALSE

1-266.   TRUE/FALSE: A Type field for frames that use the Type/Length field as a Length field can be created by adding, either one or two additional headers after the Ethernet 802.3 header but before the L3 PDU. For example, when sending IP packets, the Ethernet frame has two additional headers:

- An IEEE 802.2 Logical Link Control (LLC) header
- An IEEE Subnetwork Access Protocol (SNAP) header

Both the SNAP header Type field and Ethernet Type/Length field have the same purpose, with the same reserved values.

A.   TRUE
B.   FALSE

1-267.   Which of the following is true about Type field?

A.   It is used to identify the different network layer (Layer 3) protocols from different vendors on the Ethernet.
B.   Type field is added in the frame.
C.   Type field is added in the Packet.
D.   It is used to identify the different transport layer (Layer 4) protocols from different vendors on the Ethernet.

1-268.   Try to decide which option gets in the blank.

To make the receiving node knows that an IP packet is inside an Ethernet frame, the Type field would have a value of _____.

A.   0700 hexadecimal (1792 decimal)
B.   0800 hexadecimal (2048 decimal)
C.   0600 hexadecimal (1536 decimal)

1-269.   TRUE/FALSE: The protocol Type field can be identified by another part in the frame, particularly when sending IP packet and in this case, the original Type field is used as an origin field for that frame, identifying the origin of the entire Ethernet frame.

A.   TRUE
B.   FALSE

1-270.   TRUE/FALSE: When sending IP packets, the Ethernet frame has two additional headers:

- An IEEE 802.2 Logical Link Control (LLC) header

▪   An IEEE Subnetwork Access Protocol (SNAP) header

A.   TRUE
B.   FALSE

1-271.   TRUE/FALSE: Error detection is the process of discovering if the frame's bits are incorrect because of the transmission over the network.

A.   TRUE
B.   FALSE

1-272.   TRUE/FALSE: In network communication, errors may occur because of some kind of signal interference during frame transmission.

A.   TRUE
B.   FALSE

1-273.   TRUE/FALSE: To detect an error, the sending machine calculates a complex mathematical function, with the frame contents as input, putting the result into the frame's FCS field. The receiving device does the same mathematical function on the receiving frame.

A.   TRUE
B.   FALSE

1-274.   Which of the following cases requires error recovery?

A.   The sending machine calculates a complex mathematical function, with the frame contents as input, putting the result into the frame's FCS field. The receiving device does the same mathematical function on the receiving frame. The calculation equals to the value of FCS field.
B.   The sending machine calculates a complex mathematical function, with the frame contents as input, putting the result into the frame's FCS field. The receiving device does the same mathematical function on the receiving frame. The calculation does not equal to the value of FCS field.

1-275.   What will happen to the frame, if the receiving machine discovers an error in the frame transmission?

A.   The frame is discarded and retransmission is required.
B.   The frame is considered and retransmission is required.
C.   The frame is discarded and retransmission is not required.

1-276.   Which layer is responsible for error recovery?

A.   Layer 1
B.   Layer 2
C.   Layer 3
D.   Layer 4

1-277.   Which layer is responsible for error detection?

A.   Layer 1
B.   Layer 2
C.   Layer 3
D.   Layer 4

1-278. Which of the following is accurate about FCS field? (Select all that apply)

A.   It is part of the Ethernet trailer, not the Ethernet header.
B.   It is used for error removing.
C.   It is 1 byte long.
D.   It is used for error detection.

1-279. TRUE/FALSE: Clearly, Frame reception is the reverse of frame transmission. For both half-duplex and full-duplex transmissions, Ethernet frame reception is essentially the same, except that full-duplex MACs must have separate frame buffers and data paths to allow for simultaneous frame transmission and reception.

A.   TRUE
B.   FALSE

1-280. TRUE/FALSE: When the frame is received, the destination address of the received frame is checked and matched against the machine's address list (its MAC address, its group addresses, and the broadcast address) to determine whether the frame is destined for that machine. If an address match is found, the frame length is checked and the received FCS is compared to the FCS that was generated during frame reception. If the frame length is the same and there is an FCS match, the frame type is determined by the contents of the Length/Type field. The frame is then parsed and forwarded to the appropriate upper layer in the destination machine.

A.   TRUE
B.   FALSE

1-281. Arrange the following steps in the correct order.

A.   The frame is then parsed and forwarded to the appropriate upper layer in the destination machine.
B.   The frame length is checked and the received FCS is compared to the FCS that was generated during frame reception.
C.   The destination address of the received frame is checked and matched against the machine's address list.
D.   The frame type is determined by the contents of the Length/Type field.

1-282. Which of the following is true about Ethernet cabling and connections? (Select all that apply)

A.   Some of Ethernet cable standards use coaxial cable or optical fiber; others are used **Ethernet over the twisted pair**.
B.   There are several different standards for the twisted pair -based physical medium. The most widely used are 10BASE-T (Ethernet), 100BASE-TX (Fast Ethernet; FE), and 1000BASE-T (Gigabit Ethernet; GE).
C.   Ethernet over the twisted pair refers to the use of cables that contain insulated copper wires twisted together in pairs for the physical layer of an Ethernet network—that is, a network in which the Ethernet standard protocol provides the data link layer. All these three standards use the same RJ45 connectors.
D.   Generally, different generations of Ethernet equipments can be freely mixed, since higher speed implementations always support the lower speeds.
E.   These standards always use 8 positions modular connectors, usually called RJ45.
F.   The cables usually used are four-pairs of twisted cable.
G.   Each of the three standards (in B) supports both full-duplex and half-duplex communication
H.   All these standards (in B) operate over distances of up to 100 meters. Some key differences, however, exist, particularly with the number of wire pairs needed in each case, and in the type (category) of cabling. Moreover, Power over Ethernet (PoE) technique can be implemented over UTP

cables.

1-283. TRUE/FALSE: Personal Computers (PCs) are connected to Ethernet LAN using NICs. The NIC is a printed circuit board as shown in Figure 1-29. It provides network communication features to and from PCs on a network.

    A.   TRUE
    B.   FALSE

1-284. Which of the following is true about NIC? (Select all that apply)

    A.   The NIC implements the electronic circuitry required to communicate using a specific physical layer and data link layer standards such as Ethernet or token ring.
    B.   The protocols used in NIC provides a base for a full network protocol suite, allowing communication on the same LAN for small groups of computers as well as communication on a large-scale network (WAN, Internet) through routable protocols, such as IP.
    C.   The NIC can be plugged into a motherboard PCI expansion slots, in this case it is called LAN adapter, and it can be built within a motherboard as a build-in Ethernet port.
    D.   The NIC provides the PC an interface to the LAN.
    E.   The NIC has a MAC address, which is burned and stored in ROM by manufacture.
    F.   To make the NIC works efficiently with the PC, it has some requirements. These are IRQ line, I/O address, a memory space, and drivers. Sometimes the word controller is used to refer to the NIC.

1-285. Which of the following is true about NICs?

    A.   The NIC uses a serial connection to communicate with the network.
    B.   The NIC uses a serial connection to communicate with the computer.
    C.   The NIC uses a parallel connection to communicate with the computer.
    D.   The NIC uses a serial connection to communicate with the computer.

1-286. TRUE/FALSE: EIA/TIA standards body defined the Ethernet cables and connectors specifications. This means that RJ-45 connector and Ethernet cabling categories are derived from the EIA/TIA specifications. Several types of connection media can be used in a LAN deployment.

    A.   TRUE
    B.   FALSE

1-287. Which of the following organizations defined the Ethernet cables and connectors specifications?

    A.   IEEE
    B.   IEE
    C.   EIA/TIA
    D.   AIE
    E.   AIT

1-288. TRUE/FALSE: The RJ-45 connector represents the most common type of connection media, where the letters "RJ" stands for registered jack and the number "45" refers to a specific physical connector that has 8 conductors.

    A.   TRUE
    B.   FALSE

1-289. TRUE/FALSE: In addition to the popular RJ-45 connectors and ports, CISCO LAN switches have a few interfaces that use either Gigabit Interface Converters (GBIC) or Small-Form Pluggable (SFP). Figure 1-32 shows a 1000BASE-T GBIC. A GBIC is a hot-swappable I/O device that plugs into a Gigabit Ethernet switch port; this means that physical ports can be changed without having to purchase a completely new switch. A GBIC is interchangeable, which gives the flexibility to deploy other 1000BASE-X technology without having to change the physical interface or the model of the router or switch. Using a different kind of GBIC or SFP, the CISCO switch can use a variety of cable connectors and types of cabling and support different cable lengths. GBICs are typically used for Uplinks of the LAN backbone.

    A.   TRUE
    B.   FALSE

1-290.   TRUE/FALSE: GBICs support copper UTP and fiber-optic media for Gigabit Ethernet transmission. There are several types of the fiber-optic GBICs, as shown in Figure 1-33. These types are:

    ▪   Short wavelength (1000BASE-SX)
    ▪   Long wavelength (1000BASE-LX/LH)
    ▪   Extended distance (1000BASE-ZX)

    A.   TRUE
    B.   FALSE

1-291.   Which of the following interfaces is used in the CISCO devices?

    A.   RJ-45
    B.   Gigabit Interface Converters (GBIC)
    C.   Small-Form Pluggables (SFP)

1-292.   Which of the following is true about GBIC? (Select all that apply)

    A.   A GBIC is a hot-swappable I/O device that plugs into a Gigabit Ethernet switch port.
    B.   A GBIC is interchangeable, which gives the flexibility to deploy other 1000BASE-X technology without having to change the physical interface or the model of the router or switch.
    C.   It gives the possibility to use a variety of cable connectors and types of cabling and support different cable lengths.
    D.   GBICs are typically used for Uplinks.

1-293.   TRUE/FALSE: Twisted-Pair (TP) cable is a copper wire-based that can be either unshielded (UTP) or shielded (STP). The most popular Ethernet standards are using UTP cabling, which include either two or four pairs of wires. The wires inside the cable have an outer jacket of flexible plastic to protect the wires since these wires are thin and subtile. To prevent the wire from breaking, a thin plastic coating (insulation material) covers each individual copper wire and to make it easy to look at the ends of the cable and identify the ends of an individual wire, the plastic coating on each wire has a different color.

    A.   TRUE
    B.   FALSE

1-294.   TRUE/FALSE: The wires in each pair are twisted around each other as shown in Figure 1-34. This will give one of the advantages of TP cables, which is the ability to cancel interferences from Electro-Magnetic Interference (EMI) and Radio Interference (RFI). An electro-magnetic field is created outside the wire when the current passes over any wire. The magnetic field can in turn cause electrical noise on other wires in the cable. By twisting together the wires in the same pair, with the current running in opposite directions on each wire, the magnetic field created by one wire mostly cancels out the magnetic field created by the other wire. Moreover, to reduce crosstalk between the pairs, the number of twists varies. The permitted number of twists per meter must follow accurate specifications defined in ANSI/TIA/EIA-568-A (for CAT 5). Because of its small size and lightweight, TP cables can be installed easily.

A.   TRUE
B.   FALSE

1-295.   Why the wires in each pair of the TP cables are twisted around each other?

A.   To cancel interferences from animals
B.   To cancel interferences from Electro-Magnetic Interference (EMI) and Radio Interference (RFI)

1-296.   TRUE/FALSE: The magnetic field can in turn cause electrical noise on other wires in the cable. By twisting together the wires in the same pair, with the current running in opposite directions on each wire, the magnetic field created by one wire mostly cancels out the magnetic field created by the other wire.

A.   TRUE
B.   FALSE

1-297.   Which of the following is a category of the UTP cable? (Select all that apply)

A.   Cat 1
B.   Cat 2
C.   Cat 3
D.   Cat 4
E.   Cat 5
F.   Cat 5e
G.   Cat 6
H.   Cat 6a
I.   Cat 7
J.   Cat 7a

1-298.   Match each UTP category to its suitable speed.

1.   Cat 1
2.   Cat 2
3.   Cat 3
4.   Cat 4
5.   Cat 5
6.   Cat 5e
7.   Cat 6
8.   Cat 6a
9.   Cat 7

A.   Up to 20KHz
B.   Up to 4Mbps
C.   Up to 10Mbps
D.   Up to 16Mbps
E.   10/100/1000Mbps
F.   10/100/1000Mbps
G.   10/100/1000Mbps 10Gbps
H.   10/100/1000Mbps 10GbE
I.   10/100/1000Mbps 10Gbps/100Gbps

1-299.   TRUE/FALSE: The RJ-45 connector is used at the end of UTP cable with the ends of the wires inserted into the connector. The RJ-45 connector has eight specific physical locations, called pins, into which the eight wires of the cable can be inserted into the correct positions. The RJ-45 connector needs to be inserted into an RJ-45 port in the switch or any other networking device. Figure 1-36 shows the UTP cables and RJ-45 connectors, whereas, Figure 1-30 shows RJ-45 ports.

    A.   TRUE
    B.   FALSE

1-300.   Which of the following is true about UTP cabling? (Select all that apply)

    A.   To implement UTP cable in a LAN, the connection type i.e., straight through or crossover cable and the EIA/TIA type of cable must be determined at first.
    B.   The wires in the UTP cable must be connected to the correct pin positions in the RJ-45 connectors, in order for communication between two ends to work correctly.
    C.   The RJ-45 connector has eight pins, into which the eight copper wires of the UTP cable are inserted.
    D.   The wiring pinouts must conform to the EIA/TIA Ethernet cabling standards.
    E.   The Telecommunications Industry Association (TIA) and the Electronics Industry Alliance (EIA) groups (not IEEE), define standards for UTP cabling, color-coding for wires, and standard pinouts on the cables.

1-301.   Which of the following is true about UTP cabling? (Select all that apply)

    A.   Figure 1-37 shows that the eight wires in a UTP cable have either a solid color (green, orange, blue, or brown) or a striped color scheme using white and one of the other four colors.
    B.   In addition, a single-wire pair uses the same base color. For example, the green wire and the green/white striped wire are paired and twisted. For example, in Figure 1-37, the notations' G/W refers to the green-and white striped wire and so on.
    C.   Four of the wires (two pairs) carry the positive voltage and the other four wires carry the negative voltage.
    D.   The positive are called "tip" (T1 through T4) while the negative are called "ring" (R1 through R4).
    E.   At the end of the UTP cable, the RJ-45 plug is connected, which is the male component.
    F.   The male component is inserted into a female component (the jack i.e., a socket).
    G.   The jack is found in a network device, wall, patch panel, or cubicle portion outlet.

1-302.   TRUE/FALSE: Correct wiring pinout on each end of the cable is required to build a working Ethernet LAN. For 10BASE-T and 100BASE-TX networks, two pairs of wires of the UTP cable are required, whereas four pairs of wires are required for 1000BASE-T.

    A.   TRUE
    B.   FALSE

1-303.   Which of the following is true about UTP cabling? (Select all that apply)

    A.   In 10BASE-T and 100BASE-TX Ethernets, one pair should be used to send data in one direction and the other pair should be used to receive data.
    B.   Two wires are used for full-duplex networks.
    C.   Ethernet NICs should send data using pair 3 according to the T568A pinout standard (the pair connected to pins 1 and 2). While, Ethernet NICs should receive data using pair 2 according to the T568A standard (the pair at pins 3 and 6).
    D.   On the other hand, hubs and switches do the opposite—they receive on the pair 3 according to the T568A pinout standard (the pair at pins 1, 2), and they send on the pair 2 according to the T568A pinout standard (the pair at pins 3, 6).

E.   Therefore, to create a straight-through LAN cable, both ends of the cable must use the same EIA/TIA pinout standard on each end of the cable. This means that the pin number of the wire must be the same at both end of the wire when an Ethernet straight-through cable is used. To be more clarify, wire at pin 1 on one end of the cable must be connected to pin 1 at the other end of the cable; the wire at pin 2 must be connected to pin 2 on the other end of the cable; and so on.

1-304.   TRUE/FALSE: From the above description, clearly that, devices on the ends of the cable use opposite pins when they transmit/receive data. For such cases (connecting PC_NIC to a hub, switch …etc.), a straight-through cable is used. On the other hand, some cases require connecting PC_NIC to PC_NIC or router to a router or switch to a switch or switch to a router …etc. These cases require connecting two devices that both ends of the cable use the same pins to transmit and the same pins to receive. Therefore, the pinouts of the cable must be set up to swap/cross the wire pair. This type of cable is called a *crossover cable*. For example, when connecting two switches directly, both switches send on the pair at pins 3, 6, and receive on the pair at pins 1, 2, the cable must cross the pairs. Figure 1-39 shows the connection of a switch to a switch using a crossover cable.

A.   TRUE
B.   FALSE

1-305.   TRUE/FALSE: As a summary, devices on opposite ends of a cable that use the same pair of pins to transmit, need a crossover cable (T568A at one end; T568B at the other). Devices that use an opposite pair of pins to transmit need a straight-through cable (either T568A or T568B at each end). Table 1-4 lists, the network devices and the pin pairs they use for 10BASE-T and 100BASE-TX Ethernets.
A.   TRUE
B.   FALSE

1-306.   What is the minimum category number of a UTP cable for the Ethernet 1000BASE-T networks?

A.   Cat 1
B.   Cat 3
C.   Cat 4
D.   Cat 5
E.   Cat 5e

1-307.   Which of the following is a characteristic of the UTP? (Select all that apply)

A.   Each of the individual copper wires in UTP cable is insulated by cover material.
B.   UTP cable is a four-pair wire.
C.   It is saved from EMI and RFI.
D.   The RJ-45 connector is used at the end of UTP cable with the ends of the wires inserted into the connector.
E.   The wires in each pair are twisted around each other.
F.   There are seven categories for UTP.

1-308.   Match each UTP category to its characteristics.

1.   Cat 1
2.   Cat 2
3.   Cat 3
4.   Cat 4
5.   Cat 5
6.   Cat 5e
7.   Cat 6

A. Used in Ethernet up to Gigabit networks. It consists of 4 pairs of 24-gauge copper wires.
B. Used in Token Ring networks
C. Used in Gigabit Ethernets (1 Gbps)
D. Used for data transfer at speed up to 4 Mbps
E. Used in 10BASE-T Ethernet networks
F. Used for telephone communications; not used for transmitting data.
G. Used in FastEthernet networks.

1-309.   Which of the following is true about Gigabit Ethernet? (Select all that apply)

A. The logic above differs in 1000BASE-T for the cabling and pinouts. First, Gigabit Ethernet requires four wire pairs. Secondly, Gigabit Ethernet transmits and receives on each of the four wire pairs simultaneously.
B. However, Gigabit Ethernet does have a concept of straight through and crossover cables, with a minor difference in the crossover cables. The pinouts for a straight-through cable are the same—pin 1 to pin 1, pin 2 to pin 2, and so on. The crossover cable crosses the same two-wire pair as the crossover cable for the other types of Ethernet—the pair at pins 1,2 and 3,6—as well as crossing the two other pairs (the pair at pins 4,5 with the pair at pins 7,8).

1-310.   Which of the following is correct about Ethernet crossover cables? (Select all that apply)

A. Pins 1 and 2 on one end of the cable connect to pins 3 and 6 on the other end of the cable.
B. Pins 1 and 2 on one end of the cable connect to pins 1 and 2 on the other end of the cable.
C. Pins 4 and 5 on one end of the cable connect to pins 7 and 8 on the other end of the cable.
D. Pins 4 and 5 on one end of the cable connect to pins 4 and 5 on the other end of the cable.

1-311.   Which of the following pairs of devices would require a straight-through cable?

A. PC and PC
B. PC and router
C. PC and switch
D. Hub and switch
E. Hub and Hub
F. Router and hub
G. Wireless access point (Ethernet port) and switch
H. Router and switch

1-312.   TRUE/FALSE: Now, there is no need to take care about which type (crossover or straight through) to be used in the LAN, all are working. CISCO switches have a feature called auto-mdix that notices when the wrong cabling pinouts are used. This feature makes the cable work in spite of its type by readjusting the switch's logic.

A. TRUE
B. FALSE

CHAPTER 2
INTERNETWORKING IP PROTOCOL AND IP ADDRESSING

In this chapter, the network language that is required to make network devices talk to each other will be described. Transmission Control Protocol/Internet Protocol (TCP/IP) protocol and its origin will be detailed. The Department of Defense (DoD) created the TCP/IP suite to maintain communications in the event of catastrophic war. In this chapter, TCP/IP protocol will be emphasized and throughout this book, creating TCP/IP network using CISCO devices will be studied.

The following topics are emphasized in this chapter:

- TCP/IP and the DoD model.
- TCP/IP protocols suite.
- IP addressing and network classes.

By understanding perfectly the information presented in this chapter and answering the 280 learning questions at the end of this chapter; designing network using TCP/IP protocol, assigning the right IP addressing to the network and answering the CCNA/CCENT exam related questions would be guaranteed. The questions herein are intended to reflect the type of questions presented on the CCENT Test.

The DoD Model

In this section, DoD definition will be given firstly. Secondly, a comparison between DoD model and OSI model will be outlined. Thirdly, a comparison between DoD model and TCP/IP protocol will be discussed. Finally, TCP/IP protocols suite will be detailed.

The DoD model is a concentrated/ suppressor version of the OSI model. It is comprised of four layers, instead of seven layers in the OSI model: the process/application layer, The Host-to-Host layer, The Internet layer and the Network access layer. A vast array of protocols combines at each layer of the DoD model to integrate the various activities and duties.

In the **Process/Application layer** all user-related functions are implemented. This layer defines protocols for machine-to-machine application communication. It manages user-interface specifications.

The **Host-to-Host layer** is an intermediate layer between the process/application layer and the internet layer. This layer defines protocols for controlling the level of transmission services for applications. It handles issues like creating reliable end-to-end communication and ensuring the error-free delivery of data. Controlling data segment sequencing and maintaining data integrity are the responsibility of this layer.

In the **Internet layer,** all network communication related-functions are implemented in this layer. This layer defines protocols relating to the logical transmission of packets over the network. It addresses the hosts by giving them an IP address. It handles the routing of packets among multiple networks. It also manages the communication flow between the hosts.

In the **Network access layer,** all physical hardware related-functions are implemented in this layer. This layer defines protocols for the physical transmission of data. It monitors the data exchange through the network. It oversees hardware addressing.

Figure 2-1 shows a comparison between DoD and OSI models.

Figure 2-1 The DoD and OSI Models

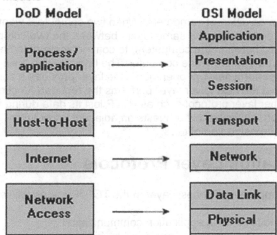

Clearly, In Figure 2-1 that both, DoD and OSI models have the same design concepts, and both have similar functions in similar places. By common-sense, both models are used to define network functions and the difference is how those functions occur. The top three layers in OSI mode correspond to process/application layer in DoD model. The Transport layer in OSI mode corresponds to Host-to-Host layer in DoD model. The network layer in OSI mode corresponds to Internet layer in DoD model. The bottom two layers in OSI mode correspond to Network access layer in DoD model. The network access layer is responsible for putting frames on the wire and pulling frames off the wire.

TCP/IP protocol suite can also be decomposed into four layers like DoD model. Figure 2-2 depicts the TCP/IP protocol suite and how its protocols are related to DoD model layers. In the figure, E refers to Ethernet, whereas, GBit refers to GigaBit.

Figure 2-2 The DoD Layers and the TCP/IP Protocol Suite

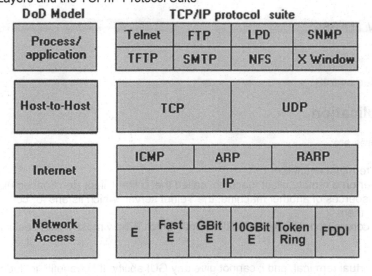

The Model concept introduces two types of interactions:

- **Same-layer interaction** on different computers: When two computers want to communicate, it creates an interaction between protocols on the same layers between the two computers. The protocol uses a header that is transmitted between the computers, to communicate data between computers.
- **Adjacent-layer interaction** on the same computer: The layers within a single computer interact between each other to perform network operation. One layer provides a service to a higher layer. The higher layer requests that the next lower layer performs the required function. An example to this type of interaction, when a higher layer protocol such as HTTP lost its data during transmission, HTTP would not take any direct action, but instead, it requests an adjacent lower layer (TCP) to provide error recovery and request retransmission of data.

The Process/Application Layer Protocols

The most common tasks of the application/Process layer in the TCP/IP are as follows:

- It defines protocols for node-to-node application communication.
- It controls user-interface specifications.
- It provides better Man Machine Interface (MMI).
- It provides data encryption/decryption.
- It provides data translation.

Typically, this layer implements/works several protocols/services. Most of them are user-oriented applications. These are:

- Telnet/SSH.
- FTP.
- TFTP.
- NFS.
- SNMP.
- SMTP.
- LDP.
- X window.
- HTTP, WWW, and SSL
- DNS.
- DHCP.
- BootP.
- VoIP and Video over IP

Telnet/SSH Application

The main Telnet features are:

- It is mainly a terminal emulation.
- It allows a user on a remote client machine, called the Telnet Client (terminal emulator), to access the resources of another machine, the Telnet server, which listens for commands and replies to them.
- Telnet name comes from "TELephone NETwork", which is how most Telnet sessions are occurred.

Telnet is a text-mode virtual terminal, and it cannot give any GUI ability. It is benefits include:

- Telnet emulated terminals are text-mode based and can execute procedures like displaying menus.
- It gives users the opportunity to access the applications on the remote server.
- It gives administrators the ability to manage the network remotely.

Telnet achieves its duty by making the client computer directly attached to the local telnet server through a virtual terminal image. It is mainly a terminal emulation to the remote server.

Secure Shell (SSH) on the other hand, does the same basic functions like Telnet, but in a more secure manner by encrypted all communications between the client and the server. SSH Like the Telnet application, its client software includes a terminal emulator. Furthermore, as with Telnet, the SSH server receives the text from each SSH client, processes the text as a command after pressing the ENTER key, and sends messages back to the client. The key difference between Telnet and SSH is that all the communications are encrypted and therefore, are private and less prone to a security risk.

File transfer Protocol (FTP)

FTP transfers files between any two networked machines using it. FTP cannot be used to execute remote files as programs. FTP is more than a protocol only; It Is also a program. Operating as a protocol, FTP is used by applications as an embedded tool. However, when it's used by clients to transfer files by hand, FTP is working as a program.

The main FTP benefits are:

- FTP is used to transfer files throughout the network.
- FTP provides accessing to both directories and files with certain operations.
- FTP is used to list and manipulate directories, type file contents, copy files between hosts, and other file operations.

Remote files can be transferred easily with low-latency using FTP. FTP duty is implemented in the network in the following scenario:

- Networking applications embedded FTP as a protocol to transfer files.
- Users can use FTP as a program to transfer files manually.
- FTP and Telnet can work together to virtually log the user into the FTP server and then allow transferring files.

FTP session begins by accessing the FTP server and then the user must supply an authenticated login to restrict access. Limited access into FTP server can be gained by logging using "anonymous" username. Secure FTP (SFTP) is a type of FTP that transfers files securely.

Trivial File Transfer Protocol (TFTP)

TFTP is used for transferring public files. It is a compact little protocol, which is used for transferring files throughout the network. It is not just a protocol; it is also a program. However, since there is no authentication for this protocol, it's considered as insecure protocol. Therefore, it's used for transferring public files. TFTP can do nothing but send and receive files. TFTP cannot be used to manipulate both files and directories.

TFTP is used to download a new IOS (Internetworking Operating System) to CISCO routers and switches. The differences between FTP and TFTP are:

- TFTP uses UDP whereas FTP uses TCP in the Host-to-Host layer.
- TFTP is only used to send and receive files, whereas, FTP can do more functions.

- TFTP transfers files with lowest-latency than FTP.
- TFTP does not require any authentication.
- TFTP has no directory-browsing abilities.
- TFTP can send much smaller blocks of data than FTP.

Network File System (NFS)

NFS is mainly used to provide file sharing between disparate file systems. It is the Sun Microsystems' created protocol. It allows remote file access across a network. NFS allows for a portion of the RAM on the NFS server machine to transparently store NFS client files.

Example 2-1, NFS Operation: To allow Windows 2008 Clients a portion on UNIX server, the NFS is used. NFS server must be installed on UNIX server and its client software must be installed on Windows 2008 clients. NFS allows for a portion of the RAM on the UNIX server to store Windows 2008 clients' files transparently. In spite of, both UNIX and Windows 2008 file systems are unlike-different case sensitivity, filename lengths, and security, users can access files in their normal ways by using NFS.

Simple Mail Transfer Protocol (SMTP)

SMTP uses a spooled, or queued, method of mail delivery on the internet. It is used to send e-mail. SMTP is working in the following sequences:

- At the sending site, the SMTP sends e-mail to the destination site(s).
- At the destination site(s), the message is spooled to a device.
- The server software at the destination site regularly checks the queue messages.
- The server software detects and then delivers any new messages.
- POP3 protocol is used to receive mail.

Line Printer Daemon (LPD)

LPD is one of the Daemons in the server that provide printer sharing. It is a server background process designed for printer sharing. Using LPD with the LPR (Line Printer) program, print jobs can be spooled and sent to the network's printers using TCP/IP. LPR program is used to manage printer jobs such as removing and applying jobs to the printer.

X Window

X window is designed to provide client/server applications based GUI. It allows a program, called an X window client, to run on one machine and have it display a program on another machine called X window server. X-window server must be installed and configured first, and then X-window client can be defined.

Simple Network Management Protocol (SNMP)

SNMP collects and manipulates valuable network information. It gathers data statistics about the network. It stands as a watchdog over the network, quickly notifying managers of any sudden events. SNMP can be adopted by stand-alone devices, and it can be embedded with Network Operation Systems (NOSs).

SNMP can be configured to prevent overloading the network. SNMP duty is implemented in the network in the following scenario:

- SNMP management station polls the devices on the network at fixed or random intervals to gather management data from these devices.

- When everything is OK, SNMP receives something called a **baseline**-a report delimiting the operational traits of a healthy network.
- When abnormal events occur, network watchdogs called **agents**, send an alert called a **trap** to the management station.

The World Wide Web (WWW), HTTP, and Secure Sockets Layer (SSL)

The internet is based mainly on the WWW which provides a way for better man machine interaction between servers called *Web servers* and client's *Web browsers*. The web servers store information in web page forms. The Web browsers' software installed on the client machine provides the means to connect to the web server and display the web pages stored on the web server. Several other application-layer functions must be worked between the server and the client, such as, identifying the web server using Universal Resource Locators (URLs), finding the Web Server Using DNS (DNS will be discussed in the following section) and transferring Files with HTTP. SSL must be used for accessing sensitive information, such as, electronic commerce (e-commerce) and other financial data, on public networks. SSL provides secure application layer features.

URL provides a way to easily identify the web server by defining the protocol used to transfer data, the name of the web server, and the particular web page on that server. For example: http://www.thaartechnologies.com/CCENT2010/CCENT2010.htm, where the protocol is Hypertext Transfer Protocol (HTTP), the hostname is www.thaartechnologies.com and the name of the web page is CCENT2010/CCENT2010.htm.

The HTTP application-layer protocol, defined in RFC 2616, defines how files can be transferred between the server and the client. The client begins requesting the required web page from the web server using HTTP after creating a TCP connection between the client's browser and the web server. When the client sends an HTTP GET request to the web server to obtain a specific web page, and if the web page is found on the web server and the server decides to send the web page, the server replies by an HTTP GET response, with a return code of 200 (OK), along with the file's contents. If the web page is not found on the web server, the server replies with return code of 404, which means "file not found."

Domain Name Service (DNS)

DNS is used to resolve host names, specifically Internet names, like www.thaartechnologies.com, automatically to its unique IP address on the Internet. It mainly resolves Fully Qualified Domain Names (FQDNs) which provides hierarchal-naming services.

DNS mainly makes possible using names like www.thaartechnologies.com instead of using www.thaartechnologies.com's IP address. The main benefits are:

- DNS resolves FQDNs. This makes accessing sites on a network and the Internet as well, much easier.
- It makes changing Internet sites to different ISP or changing their IP addresses possible without changing the FQDNs for these sites.
- It makes moving web pages to different service provider or changing their IP addresses possible without any differences appear to the users.

Example 2-2: The DNS processes. Figure 2-3 shows the DNS processes as initiated by a web browser. The user with IP address 213.188.87.93, enters the URL (http://www.thaartechnologies.com/CCENT2010/CCENT2010.htm), the DNS server 82.205.200.10 resolves the www.thaartechnologies.com name into the correct IP address (76.163.122.170), and the user starts sending packets to the web server.

Figure 2-3 Name Resolution Using DNS

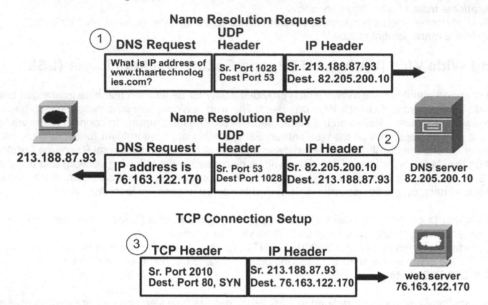

As a result of adopting DNS, Internet sites can be accessed using IP addresses, FQDNs like the www.thaartechnologies.com, and only host name if the domain name is configured on server or router. MAC addresses are not used. A FQDN is a hierarchy that can logically locate a name based on its domain identifier.

When **ip domain-name thaartechnologies.com** command is defined on the router, the suffix (thaartechnologies.com) will be appended to each request trying to access thaartechnologies.com domain. So, instead of typing "mail.thaartechnologies.com", it is possible to type "mail" only.

Bootstrap Protocol (BootP)

BootP is used by diskless workstation. It maps MAC address to its corresponding IP addresses. It is developed to become what is called Dynamic Host Configuration Protocol (DHCP).

Many benefits can be obtained by using BootP for diskless workstation, these include:

- BootP provides diskless workstation by its IP address.
- BootP provides diskless workstation by the host name of a server machine.
- BootP provides diskless workstation by the boot filename of a file that is to be loaded into memory and executed at boot-up.

Diskless workstation negotiates the server to find its IP address. A diskless workstation broadcasts a BootP request on the network when it is powered ON. A BootP server responds by telling the machine its IP address and the file-that should boot from, usually via the TFTP protocol. This is done by the server after looking up the client's MAC address in its BootP file.

Dynamic Host Configuration Protocol (DHCP)

DHCP has a great advantage in large networks (hundreds of users and more). It helps administrators in assigning IP addresses to clients by providing the IP addresses dynamically to hosts on a network. It works well in a small-to-even-very-large network. DHCP server software can be installed on dedicated machines, or it can be embedded in CISCO routers. It is developed from BootP, but it's different.

DHCP server can provide the host by a lot of information. It assigns an IP address, a subnet mask, a domain name, a default gateway (router), a DNS information, and a WINS information to host. However, DHCP server does not design to provide a Proxy information to a host.

Host registers its MAC address in the DHCP server database. When a host is powered ON, it broadcasts a DHCP request on the network. A DHCP server hears the DHCP request and looks up the client's scope fields. The DHCP server leased the host an IP address for the duration specified in the server by the administrator or by default.

The differences between BootP and DHCP are:

- BootP gives an IP a host, but the host's hardware address must be entered manually in a BootP table.
- DHCP can be considered as Dynamic BootP, since MAC addresses are entered automatically. Only IP addresses scopes are defined manually on the DHCP server.
- BootP is used to send an operating system that a host can boot from. DHCP does not perform this task.
- DHCP gives a lot of information to host.
- BootP is used by diskless workstation.

Simply, DHCP (dynamic BootP) EQUALS TO BootP (MAC addresses entered manually) PLUS a lot of information (Subnet mask, DNS, default gateway, WINS, …etc) MINUS OS booting abilities.

Typically, the DHCP process uses the following four set of messages between the DHCP server and the DHCP client to accomplish its task.

1. *DHCP Discover Message*: A LAN broadcast message sends from the DHCP client to the DHCP server in order to discover server.
2. *DHCP Offer Message*: A directed message sends from the DHCP server to the DHCP client in response to message 1 in order to offer the DHCP service.
3. *DHCP Request Message*: A directed message sends from the DHCP client to the DHCP server in order to request the DHCP network information.
4. *DHCP Acknowledgement message*: A directed message sends from the DHCP server to the DHCP client in order to acknowledge and to provide the required DHCP client network information such as, client IP address, client subnet mask, client gateway, … Etc.

VoIP, Video over IP and Quality of Service (QoS)

Today, most organizations begun to use Internet phone service or IP phones instead of using PBX based phone. IP Phone can pass voice traffic over the data network inside the IP packets using application protocol called Voice over IP (VoIP). Typically, a single VoIP call consumes less than 30 kbps of bandwidth. To convert normal speech voice to IP packet several steps must be followed as shown in Figure 2-4.

Video over IP, on the other hand, is an application protocol that can be used to pass video traffic over the data network inside IP packets. Video over IP requires more bandwidth (300 kbps to 10 Mbps) per video.

Both VoIP and Video over IP application layer protocols require specific network service needs. The term quality of service (QoS) is used to categorize the application needs from the network services. The application will work well if the network meets those application needs. The QoS tools must be used for a network to be able to support high-quality VoIP and video over IP. A wide variety of QoS tools can be configured on CISCO routers and switches to support the QoS needs of the various applications.

Figure 2-4 VoIP Steps

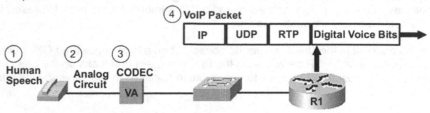

VoIP traffic has the following QoS demands on the network:

- **Low delay:** VoIP requires a very low delay—typically less than 200 milliseconds (.2 seconds).
- **Low jitter:** Jitter is the variation in the network traffic delay. VoIP requires—typically less than 30 milliseconds (.03 seconds).
- **Loss:** When a break in the sound of the VoIP call is occurred, that means an IP packet(s) is/are lost during transmission. Packets are lost because of errors or a router doesn't have enough room to store the packet while waiting to send it.

Table 2-1 summarizes some the needs of various types of applications for the four main QoS requirements.

Table 2-1 QoS Applications' Needs

Application	Bandwidth	Delay	Jitter	Loss
VoIP	Low	Low	Low	Low
One-way video over IP (space cameras)	Medium	Medium	Medium	Low
Two-way video over IP (video-conferencing)	Medium/high	Low	Low	Low
Interactive mission-critical data (web-based bank database)	Medium	Medium	High	High
Interactive business data (online support chat)	Low/medium	Medium	High	High
Non-business (checking a personal account)	Medium	High	High	High
File transfer (backing up information)	High	High	High	High

The Host-to-Host Layer Protocols

Host-to-Host layer in the TCP/IP shields the upper-layer applications from the complexities of the bottom layers and the network. It defines protocols for setting up the level of transmission service for applications. It handles issues like creating reliable end-to-end communication or unreliable communication and ensuring the error-free delivery of data. It also handles segment sequencing and maintains data integrity. As soon as Host-to-host layer receives the data stream from upper-layer, this layer processes it and makes it ready for suitable transmission type. Two protocols are implemented in Host-to-Host layer: TCP and UDP.

Transmission Control Protocol (TCP)

TCP is the core of the TCP/IP protocol. It takes large blocks of information from an application and breaks them into segments (Block → Segment), numbers and sequences each segment before transmission to the destination site, and then, it creates a **virtual circuit** with the destination site before transmitting data. TCP uses a **connection-oriented** communication type. TCP is a full-duplex, connection-oriented, reliable, and accurate protocol. TCP provides error-checking techniques. The reliability that has been added by TCP is often unnecessary in today's networks, since today's networks are much more reliable.

Before a transmitting site starts to send segments down the model; a virtual circuit is created between the sending host and the destination sites. Virtual circuit should be established before the sending host starts sending data. During the initial handshake, the two TCP layers (at the sending host and at the destination sites) also agree on the amount of information that's going to be sent before the recipient's TCP sends back an acknowledgment. With every-thing agreed upon in advance, the path is ready for reliable communication to take place between the sending host and the destination sites. When transmission begins, TCP numbers and sequences each segment so that the destination's TCP protocol can put the segments back into the order the application intended. After these segments are sent, TCP (on the transmitting host) waits for an acknowledgment of the receiving end's TCP virtual circuit session. The sending host will retransmit any segment that is not acknowledged.

TCP Segment Format

TCP (on the transmitting host) segments a data stream from upper layers and prepares it for the network layer which then routes the segments as packets through an internetwork. The data streams are rebuilt at the receiving host Transport Layer to upper-layer applications or protocols. The TCP segment format is shown in Figure 2-5. Furthermore, the complete TCP description can be found in RFC 793.

Figure 2-5 TCP Segment Format

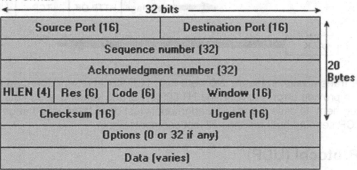

As shown in Figure 2-5, the TCP header is 20 bytes long. The TCP segment contains the following fields:

Source port: Source port is the port number of the host that sends the data.
Destination port: Destination port is the port number of the application that requests the data on the destination host.
Sequence number: Sequence number is a number that added to each data so that it can put the data back in the correct order or retransmit missing or damaged data.
Acknowledgment number: Acknowledgment number defines which TCP octet is expected to come next.
HLEN: HLEN is the header length, which defines the number of 32-bit words in the header.
Reserved: Reserved is always set to zero.
Code: Code bits are used to set up and terminate a session.
Window: Window is the window size the sending host is willing to accept, in octets.

Checksum: Checksum is the Cyclic Redundancy Check (CRC) used by TCP to check everything. It checks both the header filed and data field.
Urgent: Urgent pointer indicates the end of urgent data that used by some applications.
Option: Option sets the maximum TCP segment size to either 0 to 32 bits.
Data: Data includes the upper-layer data.

From the number of fields in the header of TCP, it clears that TCP has many overheads.

Example 2-3: TCP Services Provided to HTTP. Figure 2-6 shows how TCP works between Client and HTTP server. When the client tries to open explorer and fetch a home page, it sends a Get HTTP request to the HTTP server. HTTP usually, uses TCP to reliably, handle its messages. The HTTP server replies to the client by ACK and the required home page. When the client receives the home page, it acknowledges the HHTP server.

Figure 2-6 TCP Services Provided to HTTP

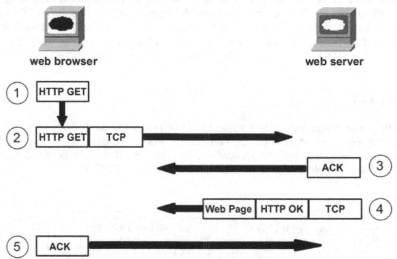

For any reason, if either transmission in Figure 2-6 were lost, TCP would resend the data and ensure that it was received successfully. To provide error recovery, the HTTP server (the sending host) sets a retransmission timer and waits for acknowledgment. In case the acknowledgment is lost or all transmitted segments are lost and when the timer expires, the TCP sending host resends all lost segments again.

User Datagram Protocol (UDP)

UDP takes large blocks of information from an application and breaks them into segments (Block → Segment). It numbers each segment before transmission to the destination site. UDP does not create a virtual circuit with the destination site before transmitting data. It is a **connectionless** communication. Therefore, it is an unreliable and inaccurate protocol, but it is efficient. It can be used in place of TCP depending on the application developer decision. UDP is a thin protocol which means, it does not take much bandwidth on a network. It is faster than TCP for data transferring. It also provides error-checking techniques.

UDP receives upper-layer blocks of information, and breaks them into segments. UDP gives each segment a number for reassemble into the intended block at the destination. After these segments are sent, UDP (on the destination host) rebuilds the blocks from the received segments according to their numbers. UDP only numbers the segments and not sequencing them, at the sending host UDP does not care in which order the segments arrive at the destination host. Furthermore, UDP does not allow for an acknowledgment to ensure the arrival. Because of this, it is referred to as unreliable protocol.

Examples of applications that use UDP instead of TCP are SNMP and NFS. On the hand, VoIP is an example of the application that uses and must use TCP because of its sequencing.

UDP Segment Format

UDP (on the transmitting host) segments a data stream from upper layers and prepares it for the network layer. The network layer then routes the segments as packets through an internetwork. The packets are handed to the receiving host's Transport layer protocol, which rebuilds the data block to hand to upper-layer applications or protocols.

Figure 2-7 shows the UDP segment format. The figure shows the different fields within the UDP header.

Figure 2-7 UDP Segment Format

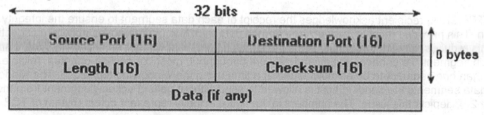

The UDP header is 8 bytes long. The UDP segment contains the following fields:

Source port: Source port is the port number of the host that sends the data.
Destination port: Destination port is the port number of the application that requests the data on the destination host.
Length: Length is the length of UDP header and UDP data. It is the length of the segment.
Checksum: Checksum is the Cyclic Redundancy Check (CRC). UDP checks everything, the header, and data fields.
Data: Data is handed down to the UDP protocol, which includes the upper-layer data.

From the number of fields in the header of UDP, it clears that UDP has very low overheads as compared with TCP.

Port Numbers for Host-to-Host protocols

Host-to-Host protocols must use port numbers to communicate with upper layers. Port numbers give away for different applications to cross the network simultaneously. At the sending host, the port numbers are dynamically assigned. The source port number must be any number between 1024 and 65534. Destination port numbers are assigned according to destination applications within the above range. 1023 and below are defined in RFC 1700 as well-known port numbers and cannot be used only by well-known applications (ex: ftp control: TCP 21, ftp data: TCP 20, SSH: TCP 22, telnet: TCP 23, smtp: TCP 25,dns: TCP/UDP 53, dhcp: UDP 67,68, tftp: UDP 69, www: TCP 80, POP3: TCP 110, snmp: UDP 161, SSL: TCP 443, RTP-based Voice (VoIP) and Video: UDP 16,384–32,767…etc).

Figure 2-8 shows the sample of the reserved, well-known port numbers with their corresponding TCP/IP protocols and services.

Figure 2-8 Ports for TCP/UDP Headers

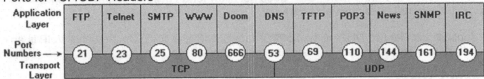

Flow Control Using TCP Windowing

Window field is used for flow control along with the Sequence and Acknowledgment fields in the TCP header. Window field sets the maximum number of unacknowledged bytes that are allowed at any instant in time. In another words, the TCP window controls the transmission rate at a level where receiving host congestion and data loss do not occur. Two types of windowing are discussed here:

Fixed Windowing

By default, TCP at the recipient acknowledges the receipt of each data segment to ensure the integrity of the transmission. This provides reliable, connection-oriented data transfers, and removes network congestion issues. However, this reduces network throughput since the sending host must wait for an acknowledgment after sending each segment. To enhance the overall network throughput, most connection-oriented, reliable protocols allow more than one segment to be acknowledged at a time using the windowing technique. The window is the number of data segments the sending host is allowed to send without getting acknowledgment from the receiving host. Figure 2-9, depicts this issue. The numbers in the figure actually represent octets (bytes) of TCP segments contents.

Figure 2-9 Fixed Windowing

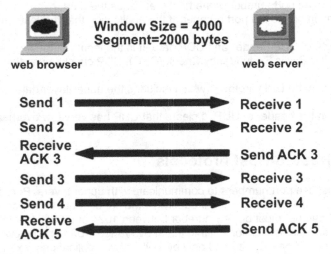

TCP Sliding Windowing

As shown in Figure 2-9, fixed windowing uses a window of fixed size, which does not change. In sliding windowing, the window size is negotiated at the beginning of the connection and can be changed dynamically during the TCP session. It is called a *sliding window*, since the actual sequence and acknowledgment numbers grow over time. Sometimes it is called a *dynamic window*, since the size of the window changes over time. To illustrate how the window is working, assume the example shown in Figure 2-10 with a current window size of 4000, and each TCP segment has 2000 bytes of data.

Figure 2-10 TCP Sliding Windowing

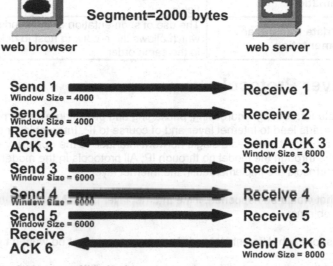

The following are the steps of this type of windowing:

- During the connection setup procedure, the sending host and the receiving host exchange their initial window size values (4000 in this example).
- The sending host machine starts sending segments.
- The sending host must wait after sending the second segment because the window is full. This provides a control to the flow of data.
- When the acknowledgment has been received from the receipt machine, a new window can be begun and sent by receipt machine.
- If no errors have occurred during transmission, the receipt machine grants the server (sending host) to send a larger window.
- Now, the size of the window is changed to 6000 bytes. This means that the server can now send 6000 bytes before it receives an acknowledgment.

The window starts small and then grows until errors occur. Windowing only provides flow control to number of bytes that can be transmitted before receiving an acknowledgment. It does not require that the sending host stop send in all cases. A sliding window enhances the overall network throughput and results in more efficient use of bandwidth. If a receiving host reduces the window size to 0, this effectively stops any further transmissions until a new window greater than 0 is sent.

As a summary, Table 2-2 lists the main features supported by TCP and/or UDP.

Table 2-2 Transport Layer Features

Transport Feature	Description
Multiplexing using ports	The use of port numbers at the receiving host to choose the correct application for which the data is destined.
Error recovery (reliability)	The use of numbering and acknowledging data.

Flow control using windowing	The use of (variable) window sizes to prevent cognitions at the receiving host which protects buffer space and routing devices.
Connection establishment and termination	The use of initialization process for Port Numbers and Sequence and Acknowledgment fields.
Ordered data transfer and data segmentation	The use of segmentation at the sending host which allows the receiving host to deliver bytes in the same order.

The Internet Layer Protocols

Internet layer is responsible for: routing, addressing, packaging and providing a single network interface to the upper layers. All network roads lead to Internet layer and of course to IP. Internet layer is the only layer in the model that dedicating for routing. It provides a single network interface to the upper-layer protocols. The core of this layer is IP and all paths through the model go through IP. All protocols in the model use IP in this layer. IP, ARP, RARP, and ICMP protocols are implemented in the Internet layer.

Now, let us investigate what would be happened, if the Internet layer is not found with the TCP/IP suite. The following are the major problems:

- Specific modules for each different Network Access protocol must be written by application developers.
- Applications would come in many different versions, one for Ethernet, another one for FDDI, and so on.
- Routing would be embedded within applications. This would cause difficulties in writing applications and degradation in network performance.

To prevent these problems, IP provides routing and one single network interface for upper-layer protocols.

Internet Protocol (IP)

IP is simply the core of TCP/IP. It receives segments from the Host-to-Host layer and fragments them into datagrams (packets), (Segment → Packet). It is essentially the Internet layer itself. The other protocols (ARP, RARP, ICMP ...etc.) found here to support it. It adds a software or logical address called IP address for both source and destination hosts in each packet.

IP breaks segments into smaller unit called packets suitable for transmission. It is aware of all the interconnected networks, since all machines on the network have an IP address. It adds IP addresses to packets and provides routing between disparate networks. Routing and IP addressing are the major benefits for this protocol.

After receiving the segments from the upper-layers and assembling the segments into packets, IP assigns each packet the IP addresses of the sending host and of the recipient. IP then, looks at each packet's address and uses a routing table to decide where a packet is to be sent next. IP chooses the best path. Each router (layer-3 device) that receives a datagram makes routing decisions based upon the packet's destination IP address and other factors. IP reassembles datagram's back into segments on the receiving host (Packet → Segment). However, the complete IP description can be found in RFC 791.

IP is a connectionless protocol, which means that IP does not exchange control information (called a handshake) to establish an end-to-end connection before transmitting data to the destination host. IP relies on protocols in other layers to establish the connection if connection-oriented services are required. IP also relies on protocols in another layer to provide error detection and error recovery. Because it contains no error detection or recovery code, IP is sometimes called an unreliable protocol.

IP Packet Format

IP (on the transmitting host) packets a segment from the Host-to-Host layer and prepares it for the Network access layer. IP (on the receiving host) rebuilds the segments to hand to the Transport layer protocols.

Figure 2-11 shows the IP Packet format. The figure shows the different fields within the IP header. It is so important to understand what each field in the IP Packet is.

Figure 2-11 IP Header Format

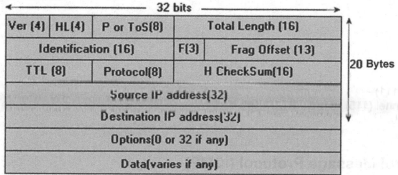

The IP Packet contains the following fields:

Version: Version is the IP version number. Mostly, IPv4 is used.
HLEN: HLEN or IP Header Length (IHL) is the header length, including optional fields, which defines the number of 32-bit words in the header.
Priority or ToS or Differentiated Services Field (DS Field): Priority defines the type of Service telling how the datagram should be handled for different class of application.
Total/Packet length: Total length is the length of the header and data or the length of the packet.
Identification: Identification is a unique IP-packet value that identifies each packet.
Flags: Flag provides a fragmentation indication.
Fragment offset: Fragment offset provides fragmentation and reassembly capabilities when the packet is too large to put in a frame.
TTL: TTL is the Time to Live, which is set into a packet at the source machine. It gives it a time to live. If it does not obtain the destination machine before the TTL expires, it's discarded. This prevents IP packets from continuously circling the network looking for a destination.
Protocol: Protocol is the port of upper-layer protocol (TCP is port 6 or UDP is port 17).
Header Checksum: Header Checksum is the Cyclic Redundancy Check (CRC) checks the header fields only.
Source IP address: Source IP address is the IP address of sending machine.
Destination IP address: Destination IP address is the IP address of destination machine.
IP Option: IP Option is used for special network services such as, network testing, debugging, and security.
Data: Data is handled down to the IP protocol, which includes the upper-layer data.

The Network layer sees the protocols at the Transport layer as numbers called (Protocol numbers). IP treats with other protocols using Protocol number. The protocol number is important, if the header did not carry the protocol information for the next layer, IP would not know what to do with the data carried in the packet.

Figure (2-12) depicts the relationship between the IP and Upper layer protocols. . IP can send the data to either TCP port 6 or UDP port 17 (both hex addresses).

Figure 2-12 The Protocol Field in an IP Header

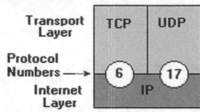

The following are some popular protocols that can be specified in the protocol type field of an IP header.

- ICMP (1).
- TCP (6).
- IGRP (9).
- UDP (17).
- IPv6 (41).
- GRE (47).
- IPX in IP (111).
- Layer-2 tunnel (115)
- EIGRP (88).
- OSPF (89)

Internet Control Message Protocol (ICMP)

ICMP works at the network layer and is found to support IP. It is a management protocol and messaging service provider for IP. Its messages are carried as IP datagrams. ICMP packets are encapsulated within IP datagrams.

Example 2-4, ICMP using: Router advertisements are announced over the internetwork using ICMP, reporting IP addresses for the router's network interfaces and some related information. Network hosts such as routers, uses these advertisements to update their routing tables with up-to-date routes information. A **router solicitation** is a request for immediate advertisements and may be sent by a host when it starts up using ICMP.

Example 2-5, ICMP events, and messages: The following are some of the common events and messages that use ICMP:

- **Buffer Full**: ICMP is used to send out this router message when its memory buffer for receiving incoming datagram's is full.
- **Destination Unreachable**: ICMP is used to send out this router message back to the sending host when the router cannot send the packet to unknown destination.
- **Hops**: ICMP is used by the executioner router to send a message, informing the sending machine of the demise of its datagram after deleting the packet when it reaches a maximum hop count or maximum number of routes that can be passed to reach its destination.
- **Ping**: ICMP echo messages are used by Ping utility to check the physical connectivity of the network.
- **Traceroute**: Traceroute uses ICMP timeouts to find a path a packet takes as it traverses an internetwork.

The following are the functions of ICMP:

- Discover subnet masks.
- Report TCP, time to exist exceeded.
- Redirect UDP messages.

- Transport SNMP Gets.
- Report routing failures.

Many different kinds of routing failures can be reported via the ICMP frame Destination Unreachable (type 3). Masks can be found using the Address Mask Request and Reply ICMP frames (type 17, 18). TTL (Time to live) and Redirection exist at the Network layer (IP) rather than the Transport layer (TCP, UDP).

Address Resolution Protocol (ARP)

ARP is important for IP communication. It is used by IP to convert software addresses to hardware addresses. ARP discovers the hardware address of a host from a known IP address (IP address → MAC address). It uses a destination broadcast MAC address to map its IP address to its real MAC address. It is found to support IP in the Internet layer. ARP broadcasts are carried as IP datagrams.

When IP has a datagram to send, it must inform a Network Access Protocol, such as Ethernet or Token Ring, of the destination's MAC address on the local network. IP tries to find the destination MAC address in the ARP cache; it uses ARP to find this information. If IP does not find the destination MAC address in the host ARP cache table, IP will discover if the destination host on local or on a remote network, using Network Mask calculation. If the destination MAC address is on the remote network, IP will send a datagram to the next default gateway. If the destination MAC address is on the local network, IP will send an ARP broadcast (with the destination address = FF: FF: FF: FF: FF: FF) on the local network asking the machine with the specified IP address to reply with its MAC address. Notice that, no communication on a local network can be taken place unless both the sending and receiving MAC addresses are known.

Figure 2-13 depicts the operation of ARP on a network.

Figure 2-13 Local ARP Broadcast

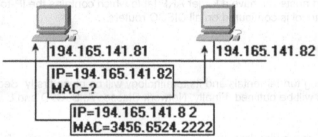

ARP (on the sending host) adds IP addresses of both source and destination hosts and only the MAC address of the source host before transmission the ARP broadcast packet on local network. It uses 00: 00: 00: 00: 00: 00 as Target hardware address and FF: FF: FF: FF: FF: FF (Ethernet broadcast) as Destination address in Ethernet header.

Reverse Address Resolution Protocol (RARP)

RARP discovers the IP address for a diskless workstation from its hardware address (MAC address → IP address). It is found to support IP in the Internet layer. RARP broadcasts are carried as IP datagrams. It works at the Network layer and it is important for IP communication. It is used by IP to convert hardware addresses to software addresses.

When a diskless workstation is powered UP, it sends a broadcast message containing its MAC address, to a configured RARP server asking for its IP address. RARP server responds to the broadcast message with the answer, giving the diskless workstation its IP address. RARP is a reveres to ARP operation.

Figure 2-14 depicts the operation of RARP on a local network.

Figure 2-14 RARP Broadcast

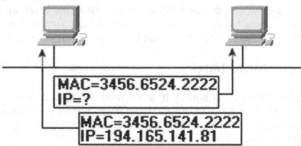

BootP is a process working in the Process/Application layer, whereas RARP is a protocol working in the Internet layer. BootP uses RARP to map MAC address → IP address. DHCP application uses RARP to map MAC address → IP address.

Proxy Address Resolution Protocol (Proxy ARP)

Proxy ARP isn't really a separate protocol. Proxy ARP is a service runs by servers or routers on behalf of other devices that are separated from their query by a router. Proxy ARP can actually help machines reach remote subnets. One advantage of using Proxy ARP is that it can be added to a single router on a network without making any changes to the routing tables of all the other routers that live in the same network. Another advantage of using Proxy ARP is that it can help the network when the default gateway goes down without the need to reconfigure the hosts. One disadvantage of using Proxy ARP is that it will increase the amount of traffic on the network subnet, and hosts will have a larger ARP table which contains the IP-to-MAC address mappings. By default, Proxy ARP protocol is configured on all CISCO routers.

IP Addressing

In this section, IP addressing fundamentals and its terminology will be given firstly. Secondly, Network addressing and its classes will be outlined. Finally, Network Classes A, B, C, D and E will be discussed. Here the focus will be on IPv4 only.

IP address is a software numeric identifier assigned to each host on an IP network. IP address allows a host on one network to communicate with another host on a different network, regardless of the type of LANs the hosts are associating with. IP address uniquely identifies hosts on the Internetwork and makes them communicate.

Here are the differences between IP address and MAC address:

- IP address is a software address, whereas MAC address is a hardware (hard-coded) or physical address.
- IP address is used for finding hosts on an Internetwork, whereas MAC address is used for finding hosts on a local network.
- An administrator assigns IP address (manually or dynamically) whereas MAC address is assigned by the manufacture.
- IPv4 address is 32-bit (4-byte) long, whereas MAC address is 48-bit (6-byte).

IP Terminology

Below, are few of the most important terminologies, which frequently used in the Internet Protocol.

Bit: One binary digit, either a 1 or 0
Byte: Always 8 bits
Octet: Always 8 bits
Network address: The designation used in routing to send packets to a remote network, for example, 20.0.0.0 (Class A), 172.17.0.0 (Class B), 194.165.141.0 (Class C).
Broadcast address: This refers to address that includes all nodes on a network. For example, 255.255.255.255 is the broadcast address for all networks and all nodes, 194.165.141.255 is the broadcast address for all subnets and nodes on network 194.165.141.0, 172.17.255.255 is the broadcast address for all subnets and nodes on network 172.17.0.0, 20.255.255.255 is the broadcast address for all subnets and nodes on network 20.0.0.0. It is used when sending information to all nodes on a subnet or all subnets on a network is an issue.

Hierarchical IP Addressing

IP address consists of 32 bits of information. These bits are divided into four sections, referred to as octets or bytes, each containing 1 byte (8 bits). IP address can be represented in one of the following forms:

- Dotted-decimal, as in 194.165.141.80.
- Binary, as in 11000010.10100101.10001101.01010000.
- Hexadecimal, as in C2.A5.8D.50.

Dotted-decimal or binary forms are often used in the IP addressing.

IP addressing is a 32-bit, structured or hierarchical address. It is not a flat or nonhierarchical, address. The main differences between flat and structured addressing are:

- Hierarchical scheme can handle a large number of addresses, namely (2^{32} or about 4.3 billion).
- Hierarchical can be structured into two- or three-level, i.e. into network and host, or network, sub-network, and host, whereas flat type cannot.
- Flat addressing uses all 32 bits as a unique identifier, whereas Hierarchical-addressing uses part of the address as network address and the other parts are used for subnet and host or just the node address.
- Hierarchical can be used for efficient routing, whereas flat cannot.

Efficient routing cannot be obtained when the flat addressing scheme is adopted, since all routers on the Internet must store the address of every single machine on the Internet. This would make routing tables very big.

Network Addressing

Network address is a number that uniquely identifies each network. Each machine on the same network shares the same network address as part of its IP address. An example of network address is 172.17 in the IP address 172.17.40.11.

Node address Is a number that uniquely identifies each machine on the network. It is sometimes called host address. It must be unique because it identifies a particular machine-an individual-as opposed to a network, which is a group of addresses. An example of node address is 40.11 in the IP address 172.17.40.11.

The internetwork professionals create classes of networks based on network size. So according to network size, Internetwork is divided into classes. Five valid network classes are available for dividing internetwork:

- Class A: This is used to create a small number of networks possessing a very large number of nodes.
- Class B: This is used to create a number of networks possessing a number of nodes.
- Class C: This is used to create a very large number of networks possessing a small number of nodes.
- Class D: This is used for multicast networking.
- Class E: This is used for research and experimental purposes.

Figure 2-15 depicts the configuration of network classes, which are used by networkers:

Figure 2-15 IP Network Classes

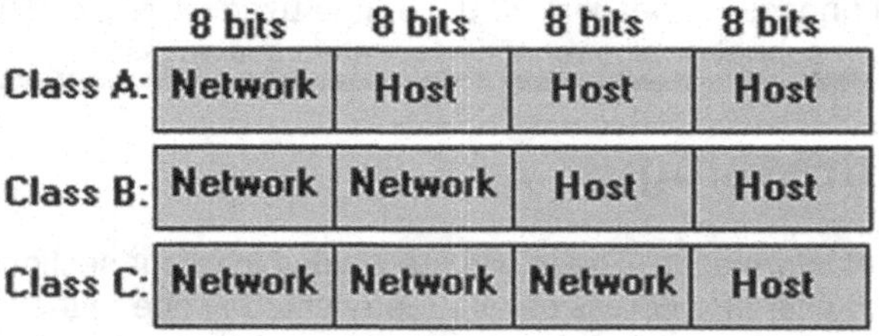

A mandate for the leading-bits section of the address is defined for each different network class. As follows:

- Class A leading-bit is 0.
- Class B leading-bits are 10.
- Class C leading-bits are 110.
- Class D leading-bits are 1110.
- Class E leading-bits are 1111.

Binary-to-Decimal conversion

Below, are few comments regarding the Binary-to-decimal Conversion, which is frequently required in the Internet Protocol. Binary numbers use 8 bits to define a decimal number. These bits are weighted from right to left in an increment that doubles in value.

The following is the bit weight in a byte.
128   64   32   16   8   4   2   1

The following is an example of a binary-to-decimal conversion:

128	64	32	16	8	4	2	1	Bits weight
1	1	0	0	0	0	1	0	Binary value

Add the value of the bits as follows:

1*128+1*64+0*32+0*16+0*8+0*4+1*2+0*1=194

> The following list is important for Subnetting and Network classes:
>
> 00000000=0
> 10000000=128
> 11000000=192
> 11100000=224
> 11110000=240
> 11111000=248
> 11111100=252
> 11111110=254
> 11111111=255

According to leading bits checking, the efficient routing is ensured. For example, since a router knows that a Class B network address always starts with a 10, the router could send a packet to the destination host after reading only the first two bits of its address.

Class A Addresses

Class A is used for very big networks like the Internet. For calculating the maximum number of hosts per each Class A network, the first address (all hosts bits are OFF) and the last address (all hosts bits are ON) are not considered. Other class A characteristics are:

- The first bit of the first byte must always be **OFF**, or **0**. This means a Class A address must be between 0 and 127.
- The first byte is assigned to the network address, and the three remaining bytes are used for the node addresses.
- The Class A networks format is Network.Node.Node.Node.
- The maximum number of networks in Class A is $2^7=128$. However, the actual maximum number of networks in Class A is $2^7-2=128-2=126$.
- The possible number of nodes for each Class A network is $2^{24}=16,777,216$. However, the actual number of nodes per each Class A network is $2^{24}-2=16,777,216-2=16,777,214$.

The range 0 to 127 for class A is obtained by the following operation:
00000000=0 (first bit must be OFF and other bits are set to 0).
01111111=127 (first bit must be OFF and other bits are set to 1).
The 127 of course, is an illegal address for Class A, as it will be cleared in the following subsections.

Example 2-6, Class A format: In the IP address 20.10.111.200, 20 is the network address, and 10.111.200 is the node address. Every machine on this particular network would have the distinctive network address of 20. The example clears the distinction between host and network octets in Class A address.

Example 2-7, Class A Valid host IDs: For network in example 2-6, the valid host IDs are in between the following: 20.0.0.0. All host bits OFF is the network address. All host bits ON is the broadcast address. Therefore, the valid hosts are the number in between the network address and the broadcast address: 20.0.0.1 through 20.255.255.254. As a rule when calculating the valid host IDs is that **the host bits cannot all be turned OFF or ON at the same time**. The example describes how valid hosts range is calculated for Class A addresses. Again, the host bits cannot all be turned OFF or ON at the same time.

Class B Addresses

Class B is used for medium-sized to large-sized networks. For calculating the maximum number of hosts per each Class B network, the first address (all hosts bits are OFF) and the last address (all hosts bits are ON) are not considered. Other class B characteristics are:

- The first bit of the first byte must always be **ON**, or **1** and the second bit of the first byte must always be turned **OFF**, or **0**. This means a Class B address must be between 128 and 191.
- The first and second bytes are assigned to the network address, and the remaining two bytes are used for the node addresses.
- The Class B networks format is Network.Network.Node.Node.
- The maximum number of networks in Class B is $2^{14}=16,384$.
- The possible number of nodes for each Class B network is $2^{16}=65,536$. However, the actual number of nodes per each Class B network is $2^{16}-2=65,536-2=65,534$.

The range 128 to 191 for class B is obtained by the following operation: **10**000000 = 128 (first bit must be ON, the second bit must be OFF, and other bits are set to 0).**10**111111=191 (first bit must be ON, the second bit must be OFF, and the other bits are set to 1).

Example 2-8, Class B format: In the IP address 172.17.10.100, 172.17 is the network address, and 10.100 is the node address. Every machine on this particular network would have the distinctive network address of 172.17. The example clears the distinction between host and network octets in Class B address.

Example 2-9, Class B Valid host IDs: For network in example 2-8, the valid host IDs are in between the following: All host bits OFF is the network address. All host bits ON is the broadcast address. Therefore, the valid hosts are the number in between the network address and the broadcast address: 172.17.0.1 through 172.17.255.254. The example describes how the hosts range is calculated for Class B addresses. However, the host bits cannot all be turned OFF or ON at the same time.

Class C Addresses

Class C is used for small networks. For calculating the maximum number of hosts per each Class C network, the first address (all hosts bits are OFF) and the last address (all hosts bits are ON) are not considered. Other class C characteristics are:

- The first and second bits of the first byte must always be **ON**, or **1** and the Third bit of the first byte must always be turned **OFF**, or **0**. This means a Class C address must be between 192 and 223.
- The first, second and third bytes are assigned to the network address, and the remaining byte is used for the node addresses.
- The Class C network format is Network.Network.Network.Node.
- The maximum number of networks in Class C is $2^{21}=2,097,152$.
- The possible number of nodes for each Class C network is $2^8=256$. However, the actual number of nodes per each Class B network is $2^8-2=256-2=254$.

The range 192 to 223 for class C is obtained by the following operation: **11**000000 =192 (the first and second bits must be ON, the third bit must be OFF, and other bits are set to 0). **11**011111=223 (the first and second bits must be ON, the third bit must be OFF, and other bits are set to 1.)

Example 2-10, Class C format: In the IP address 194.165.141.82, 194.165.141 is the network address, and 82 is the node address. Every machine on this particular network would have the distinctive network address of 194.165.141. The example clears the distinction between host and network octets in Class C address.

Example 2-11, Class C Valid host IDs: For network in example 2-10, the valid hosts IDs are in between the following: All host bits OFF is the network address.194.165.141.255, All host bits ON is the broadcast address. Therefore, the valid hosts are the number in between the network address and the broadcast address: 194.165.141.1 through 194.165.141.254. The example describes how the valid hosts range is calculated for Class C addresses. However, the host bits cannot all be turned OFF or ON at the same time.

Class D & E Addresses

In this section, IP classes D&E and the Reserved IP addresses will be discussed.

Special Network Classes and Reserved IP Addresses

Network Classes D and E are reserved for special requirements. Some IP addresses are also reserved for special purposes. Administrators should not assign these addresses to node. The following list summarized all these addresses.

- Network Class D (224-239) is reserved for Multicasting purposes.
- Network Class E (240-255) is reserved for Research and Scientific purposes.
- Network address of all 0s is interpreted to mean "this network or segment."
- Network address of all 1s is interpreted to mean "all networks and segments."
- Network 127 is reserved for loopback tests, and it cannot be used as Class A network address. It is reserved as loopback address of the node. It allows that node to send a test packet to itself without generating network traffic.
- Node's address of all 0s is interpreted to mean "this node."
- Node's address of all 1s is interpreted to mean "all nodes" on the specified network; for example, 194.165.141.255 means "all nodes" on network 194.165.141 (Class C).
- Routers to designate the default route use IP address 0.0.0.0.
- IP address 255.255.255.255 is considered as Broadcast to all nodes on the current network.

IP Version 6 Addressing (IPv6)

IPv6 is defined in the mid-1990s with a primary goal is to significantly increase the number of available IP addresses spaces. Table 2-3 summarizes the differences between IPv4 and IPv6. IPv6 details will be given in ICND2 book.

The migration from IPv4 to IPv6 has been rather slow since almost all the organizations are using IPv4 and there are several developments have been made to IPv4 to overcome the address space problem, such as the use of NAT, which will be discussed in more details in chapter 8 of this book.

The 128-bit IPv6 address is written in hexadecimal notation, with colons between each quartet of symbols. Even in hexadecimal, the addresses can be long. Therefore, IPv6 also allows for abbreviations, as is shown in Table 2-3.

Table 2-3 IPv4 Versus IPv6

Address Feature	IPv4	IPv6
Size of address	32 bits, 4 octets	128 bits, 16 octets
Example	126.1.1.100	0000:0000:0000:0000:FFFF:FFFF:7E01:0164
Same address, abbreviated	Not possible	::FFFF:FFFF:7E01:0164
Number of possible host addresses, ignoring reserved values	2^{32}, (More than 4 billion)	2^{128}, (roughly 3.4×10^{38})

Summary

In this chapter, a strong foundation for internetworking protocol (IP suite) is presented. The information presented here is essential for designing and configuring the IP networks. The IP consists of several protocols, such as TCP, UDP, and IP. These protocols are layered into four hierarchy levels depending on their functions. A unique IP address must be assigned to each node on the network. Some Internet addresses are reserved for special uses and cannot be used for host, Subnet, or network addresses. Several TCP/IP documentations list ranges of Internet addresses, and show, which addresses are reserved and those available for use. Several examples are used to clarify the ideas behind this chapter. The following topics are covered:

- TCP/IP and the DoD models
- TCP/IP protocols suite.
- IP addressing and network classes

At the end of the chapter, several learning questions are given to evaluate the learning level from this chapter. The correct answers and solutions with complementary discussions are found in appendix A, "Answers to Chapters Learning Questions."

Chapter 2 Learning Questions

2-1. TRUE/FALSE: The DoD model is a suppressor version of the OSI model.

    A. TRUE
    B. FALSE

2-2. How many layers do DoD model is comprised of?

    A. One
    B. Two
    C. Three
    D. Four

2-3. Which of the following is a layer for the DoD model? (Select all that apply)

    A. The Process/Application Layer
    B. The Host-to-Host layer
    C. The Internet layer
    D. The Network Access layer
    E. The Physical layer

2-4. TRUE/FALSE: A vast array of protocols combines at each layer of the DoD model.

    A. TRUE
    B. FALSE

2-5.
    1. What is the main function for the **Process/Application layer** in the DoD model? (Select all that apply)
    2. What is the main function for the **Host-to-Host layer** in the DoD model? (Select all that apply)
    3. What is the main function for the **Internet layer** in the DoD model? (Select all that apply)
    4. What is the main function for the **Network access layer** in the DoD model? (Select all that apply)

        A. It defines protocols for machine-to-machine application communication.
        B. It manages user-interface specifications.
        C. It defines protocols for controlling the level of transmission services for applications.
        D. It handles issues like creating reliable end-to-end communication and ensuring the error-free delivery of data.
        E. It controls data segment sequencing and maintains data integrity.
        F. It defines protocols relating to the logical transmission of packets over the entire network.
        G. It addresses the hosts by giving them an IP address.
        H. It handles the routing of packets among multiple networks.
        I. It manages the communication flow between the hosts.
        J. It defines protocols for the physical transmission of data.
        K. It monitors the data exchange through the network.
        L. It oversees hardware addressing.

2-6. Referring to Figure 2-1, which layer in the OSI model corresponds to the process/application layer in the DoD model? (Select all that apply)

    A. Application
    B. Presentation

C. Session
D. Transport
E. Network
F. Data Link
G. Physical

2-7.   Referring to Figure 2-1, which layer in the OSI model corresponds to the Host-to-Host layer in the DoD model? (Select all that apply)

A. Application
B. Presentation
C. Session
D. Transport
E. Network
F. Data Link
G. Physical

2-8.   Referring to Figure 2-1, which layer in the OSI model corresponds to the Internet layer in the DoD model? (Select all that apply)

A. Application
B. Presentation
C. Session
D. Transport
E. Network
F. Data Link
G. Physical

2-9.   Referring to Figure 2-1, which layer in the OSI model corresponds to the Network access layer in the DoD model? (Select all that apply)

A. Application
B. Presentation
C. Session
D. Transport
E. Network
F. Data Link
G. Physical

2-10.   Which of the following is true about DoD and OSI models?

A.   Both models are alike in design and concept and have identical functions.
B.   Both models are alike in design and concept and have not identical functions.
C.   Both models are alike in design and concept and have similar functions in similar places, but how those functions occur is different.
D.   Both models are unlike in design and concept and have not identical functions.

2-11.   TRUE/FALSE: The Model concept introduces two types of interactions. These are:

- **Same-layer interaction** on different computers: When two computers want to communicate, it creates an interaction between protocols on the same layers between the two computers. The protocol uses a header that is transmitted between the computers, to communicate data between computers.

- **Adjacent-layer interaction** on the same computer: The layers within a single computer interact between each other to perform network operation. One layer provides a service to a higher layer. The higher layer requests that the next lower layer performs the required function. An example to this type of interaction, when a higher layer protocol such as HTTP lost its data during transmission, HTTP would not take any direct action, but instead, it requests an adjacent lower layer (TCP) to provide error recovery and request retransmission of data.

    A.   TRUE
    B.   FALSE

2-12. What is the main purpose for the Application/Process layer in the TCP/IP? (Select all that apply)

    A. It defines protocols for node-to-node application communication.
    B. It controls user-interface specifications.
    C. It provides better Man Machine Interface (MMI).
    D. It provides data encryption/decryption.
    E. It provides data translation.

2-13. Which of the following services or protocols are typically implemented in the process/application layer? (Select all that apply)

    A. Telnet/SSH
    B. FTP
    C. TFTP
    D. NFS
    E. SNMP
    F. SMTP
    G. LDP
    H. X window
    I. HTTP, WWW, and SSL
    J. DNS
    K. DHCP
    L. BootP
    M. VoIP and Video over IP

2-14. Which of the following is true about **Telnet** application? (Select all that apply)

    A.   It is mainly a terminal emulation.
    B.   It allows a user on a remote client machine, called the Telnet Client (terminal emulator), to access the resources of another machine, the Telnet server, which listens for commands and replies to them.
    C.   Telnet is an abbreviation for "TELephone NETwork," which is how most Telnet sessions are occurred.

2-15. What is the benefit of the Telnet application? (Select all that apply)

    A.   Telnet emulated terminals are text-mode based, and it can execute procedures like displaying menus.
    B.   It gives users the opportunity to access the applications on the remote server.
    C.   It gives administrators the ability to manage the network remotely.
    D.   It gives users the ability to execute GUI applications on a remote network.

2-16. How Telnet application duty is implemented in the network?

    A.   Telnet achieves its duty by making the client computer directly attached to the local Telnet server through a virtual terminal image. It is mainly a terminal emulation to the remote server.

B.   Telnet achieves its duty by directly connected client computer to the local Telnet server network. This connection is a hardware connection and not a virtually connection to remote host.

2-17.   Which of the following is true about **SSH** application? (Select all that apply)

A.   **Secure Shell (SSH)** does the same basic things as Telnet do, but in a more secure manner by encrypted all communications between the client and the server.

B.   SSH Like the Telnet application, its client software includes a terminal emulator. In addition, as with Telnet, the SSH server receives the text from each SSH client, processes the text as a command after pressing the ENTER key, and sends messages back to the client. The key difference between Telnet and SSH is that all the communications are encrypted and therefore, are private and less prone to a security risk.

2-18.   Try to decide which option gets in which blank.

Users begin a Telnet session by running the _____ and then _____ to the Telnet server.

A.   logging on
B.   Telnet client software

2-19.   Which of the following is true about **FTP**? (Select all that apply)

A.   FTP transfers files between any two-networked machines using it.
B.   FTP cannot be used to execute remote files as programs.
C.   FTP is more than a protocol only; it is also a program.

2-20.   What is the benefit of the FTP? (Select all that apply)

A.   FTP is used to transfer files throughout the network.
B.   FTP provides accessing to both directories and files with certain operations.
C.   FTP is used to list and manipulate directories, type file contents, copy files between hosts, and other file operations.
D.   Secure FTP (SFTP) is a type of FTP that transfers files securely.

2-21.   How FTP duty is implemented in the network? (Select all that apply)

A.   Operating as a protocol, FTP is used by networked applications as an embedded tool.
B.   Operating as a program, when it is used by clients to transfer files by hand, FTP is working as a program.
C.   FTP and Telnet can work together to virtually log the user into the FTP server and then allow transferring files.

2-22.   Try to decide which option gets in which blank.

FTP session begins by accessing the FTP server and then the user must supply an _____ to restrict access by _____ and _____.

A.   an authenticated login
B.   usernames
C.   passwords

2-23.   TRUE/FALSE: Limited access into FTP server can be gained by logging using "anonymous" username.
A.   TRUE

B.   FALSE

2-24.   TRUE/FALSE: When adopting FTP as a program, remote files can be executed as programs.

A.   TRUE
B.   FALSE

2-25.   Which of the following is true about TFTP? (Select all that apply)

A.   It transfers files throughout the network.
B.   It is not just a protocol; it is also a program.
C.   It is insecure, not require any authentication to use it.
D.   It is a compact little protocol.

2-26.   What is the benefit of the TFTP? (Select all that apply)

A.   TFTP is used to send and receive files throughout the network.
B.   TFTP can be used to manipulate both files and directories.

2-27.   What is the difference between the FTP and TFTP protocols? (Select all that apply)

A.   TFTP uses UDP whereas FTP uses TCP in Host-to-Host layer.
B.   TFTP is only used to send and receive files, whereas FTP can do more functions.
C.   TFTP transferring files with lowest-latency than FTP.
D.   TFTP not requires any authentication.
E.   TFTP has no directory-browsing abilities.
F.   TFTP can send much smaller blocks of data than FTP.

2-28.   Which of the following is true about NFS? (Select all that apply)

A.   It is the Sun Microsystems' created protocol.
B.   NFS is mainly used to provide file sharing.
C.   It allows disparate file systems to interoperate.
D.   It allows remote file access across a network.

2-29.   How NFS duty is implemented in the network? (Select all that apply)

A.   NFS allows for a portion of the RAM on the NFS server machine to store NFS client files transparently.
B.   NFS allows for a portion of the RAM on the NFS client machine to store NFS server files transparently.

2-30.   TRUE/FALSE: NFS is mainly used to provide file-sharing facilities between machines have different file systems.

A.   TRUE
B.   FALSE

2-31.   TRUE/FALSE: NFS allows remote file access across a network.

A.   TRUE
B.   FALSE

2-32.   Which of the following is true about SMTP? (Select all that apply)

    A.   It is used to send e-mail.
    B.   It uses a spooled, or queued, method of mail delivery.

2-33.   How SMTP duty is implemented in the network? (Select all that apply)

    A.   At the sending site, the SMTP sends e-mail to the destination site(s).
    B.   At the destination site(s), the message is spooled to a device.
    C.   The server software at the destination site regularly checking the queue messages
    D.   The server software detects and then delivers any new messages.
    E.   POP3 protocol is used to receive mail.

2-34.   Which of the following protocols is used to send e-mail?
    A.   FTP
    B.   TFTP
    C.   SMTP
    D.   POP3

2-35.   Which of the following protocols is used to receive e-mail?

    A.   FTP
    B.   TFTP
    C.   SMTP
    D.   POP3

2-36.   TRUE/FALSE: SMTP uses a spooled, or queued, method of mail delivery.

    A.   TRUE
    B.   FALSE

2-37.   Try to decide which option gets in which blank.

POP3 is used by _____ e-mail applications for _____ of mail from a mail _____.

    A.   recovery
    B.   server
    C.   client

2-38.   Which of the following is true about LPD? (Select all that apply)

    A.   It is a server background process designed for printer sharing.
    B.   Using LPD with the LPR (Line Printer) program, print jobs can be spooled and sent to the network's printers using TCP/IP.

2-39.   TRUE/FALSE: LPD is used to remove and apply jobs to a printer.

    A.   TRUE
    B.   FALSE

2-40.   TRUE/FALSE: LPD is designed for printer sharing.
    A.   TRUE

B.   FALSE

2-41.   Which of the following is true about X window? (Select all that apply)

A.   It is designed to provide client/server applications based GUI.
B.   It allows a program, called X window client, to run on one machine and have it display a program on another machine called X window server.

2-42.   TRUE/FALSE: X window defines a protocol for the writing of graphical user interface-based client/server applications.

A.   TRUE
B.   FALSE

2-43.   Which of the following is true about SNMP? (Select all that apply)

A.   It collects and manipulates valuable network information.
B.   It gathers data statistics about the network.
C.   It stands as a watchdog over the network, quickly notifying managers of any sudden events

2-44.   How SNMP duty is implemented in the network? (Select all that apply)

A.   SNMP management station polls the devices on the network at fixed or random intervals to gather management data from these devices.
B.   When everything is OK, SNMP receives something called a **baseline**-a report delimiting the operational traits of a healthy network.
C.   When abnormal events occur, network watchdogs called **agents**, send an alert called a **trap** to the management station.

2-45.   Try to select the correct option to fill the blank.

When all is well, SNMP receives something called a _____. Which is a report delimiting the operational traits of a healthy network.

A.   Baseline
B.   Trap

2-46.   Try to select the correct option to fill the blank.
When abnormal events occur, agents send a _____ to the management station.

A.   Baseline
B.   Trap

2-47.   TRUE/FALSE: Internet is based mainly on the WWW, which provides a way for better man machine interaction between servers called web servers and client's web browsers. The web servers store information in web page forms. The Web browser's software installed on the client machine provides the means to connect to the web server and display the web pages stored on the web server.

A.   TRUE
B.   FALSE

2-48.   Which of the following application-layer functions must be worked between the web server and the client's web browser? (Select all that apply)

A.   Indentifying the web server using Universal Resource Locators (URLs)
B.   Finding the Web Server Using DNS
C.   Transferring Files with HTTP
D.   SSL must be used for accessing sensitive information, such as, electronic commerce (e-commerce) and other financial data, on public networks. SSL provides secure application layer features.

2-49.   TRUE/FALSE: URL provides a way to identify the web server easily by defining the protocol used to transfer data, the name of the web server, and the particular web page on that server. For example, http://www.thaartechnologies.com/CCENT2010/CCENT2010.htm, where the protocol is Hypertext Transfer Protocol (HTTP), the hostname is www.thaartechnologies.com, and the name of the web page is CCENT2010/CCENT2010.htm.

A.   TRUE
B.   FALSE

2-50.   TRUE/FALSE: The HTTP application-layer protocol, defined in RFC 2616, defines how files can be transferred between the server and the client.

A.   TRUE
B.   FALSE

2-51.   Which of the following is true about HTTP? (Select all that apply)

A.   The client begins requesting the required web page from the web server using HTTP after creating a TCP connection between the client's browser and the web server.
B.   When the client sends an HTTP GET request to the web server to obtain a specific web page, and if the web page is found on the web server and the server decides to send the web page, the server replies by an HTTP GET response, with a return code of 200 (OK), along with the file's contents.
C.   If the web page is not found on the web server, the server replies with return code of 404, which means, "file not found."

2-52.   Which of the following is true about DNS? (Select all that apply)

A.   DNS is used to resolve host names, specifically, the Internet names, like www.thaartechnologies.com, automatically to its unique IP address on the Internet.
B.   It mainly resolves Fully Qualified Domain Names (FQDNs).
C.   It provides hierarchal-naming services.

2-53.   What is the benefit of the DNS? (Select all that apply)

A.   DNS resolves FQDNs. This makes accessing sites on a network and the Internet as well, much easier.
B.   It makes changing Internet sites to different ISP or changing their IP addresses possible without changing the FQDNs for these sites.
C.   It makes moving web pages to different service provider or changing their IP addresses possible and without any differences appears to the users.

2-54.   How Internet sites are accessed with DNS? (Select all that apply)

A.   Using IP addresses
B.   Using FQDNs, like www.thaartechnologies.com
C.   Using the only host name if the domain name is configured on a server or a router

    D.   Using MAC address

2-55.   Try to decide which option gets in which blank.
A _____ is a _____ that can logically locate a system based on its _____.

    A.   domain identifier
    B.   FQDN
    C.   Hierarchy

2-56.   TRUE/FALSE: Because of adopting DNS, Internet sites can be accessed using IP addresses, FQDNs like the www.thaartechnologies.com, and only host name if the domain name is configured on server or router. MAC addresses are not used. A FQDN is a hierarchy that can logically locate a name based on its domain identifier.

    A.   TRUE
    B.   FALSE

2-57.   What does the following command mean? **ip domain-name** thaartechnologies.com.

    A.   It makes the thaartechnologies.com domain accessible.
    B.   It appends the domain name suffix (thaartechnologies.com) to each request. Therefore, instead of typing "mail.thaartechnologies.com", it is possible to type "mail" only.
    C.   It defines a router on thaartechnologies.com domain.

2-58.   Which of the following is true about BootP? (Select all that apply)

    A.   BootP is used by diskless workstation.
    B.   It maps MAC address to its corresponding IP addresses.
    C.   It is developed to become what is called Dynamic Host Configuration Protocol (DHCP).

2-59.   What is the benefit of the BootP for diskless workstation? (Select all that apply)

    A.   BootP provides diskless workstation by its IP address.
    B.   BootP provides diskless workstation by the host name of a server machine.
    C.   BootP provides diskless workstation by its MAC address.
    D.   BootP provides diskless workstation by the boot filename of a file that is to be loaded into memory and executed at boot-up.

2-60.   How BootP duty is implemented in the network? (Select all that apply)

    A.   Diskless workstation negotiates the server to find its IP address.
    B.   A diskless workstation broadcasts a BootP request on the network when it is powered ON.
    C.   A BootP server responds by telling the machine its IP address and the file-that should boot from, usually via the TFTP protocol. This is done by the server after looking up the client's MAC address in its BootP file.

2-61.   TRUE/FALSE: BootP provides diskless workstation by its MAC address.

    A.   TRUE
    B.   FALSE

2-62.   Which of the following is provided by BootP server as a response to BootP Client request? (Select all that apply)

    A.   Client IP address
    B.   Host name of a server machine
    C.   The boot filename of a file that is to be loaded into memory and executed at the Client boot-up
    D.   Client MAC address

2-63.   Which of the following protocols is used to carry the IP address of a BootP Client?

    A.   FTP
    B.   TFTP
    C.   UDP
    D.   TCP

2-64.   TRUE/FALSE: DHCP has a great advantage in large networks (hundreds of users and more).

    A.   TRUE
    B.   FALSE

2-65.   Which of the following is true about DHCP? (Select all that apply)

    A.   It gives an IP address to hosts.
    B.   It helps the administrators in assigning IP addresses.
    C.   It works well in small-to-even-very-large network environments.
    D.   DHCP server software can be installed on dedicated machines, or it can be embedded in CISCO routers.
    E.   It is developed from BootP, but it is different.

2-66.   What are the most common benefits of the DHCP? (Select all that apply)

    A.   It assigns an IP address to host.
    B.   It assigns a subnet mask to host.
    C.   It assigns a domain name to host.
    D.   It assigns a default gateway (router) to host.
    E.   It assigns the DNS information to host.
    F.   It assigns the WINS information to host.
    G.   It assigns the Proxy information to host.

2-67.   How DHCP duty is implemented in the network? (Select all that apply)

    A.   When a host is powered on, it broadcasts a DHCP request on the network.
    B.   A DHCP server hears the DHCP request and looks up the client's scope fields.
    C.   The DHCP server leased the host an IP address for a duration specified in the server by the administrator or by default.

2-68.   What is the difference between the BootP and DHCP? (Select all that apply)

    A.   BootP gives an IP a host, but the host's hardware address must be entered manually in a BootP table.
    B.   DHCP can be considered as Dynamic BootP, since MAC addresses are entered automatically. Only IP addresses scopes are defined manually on the DHCP server.
    C.   BootP is used to send an operating system, from which, a host can boot. DHCP not performs this task.
    D.   DHCP gives a lot of information to host.

E.   BootP is used by diskless workstation.

2-69.   TRUE/FALSE: DHCP provides a host by its MAC address.

A.   TRUE
B.   FALSE

2-70.   TRUE/FALSE: CISCO Router can operate as a DHCP server.

A.   TRUE
B.   FALSE

2-71.   TRUE/FALSE: Simply, DHCP (dynamic BootP) EQUALS TO BootP (MAC addresses entered manually) PLUS a lot of information (Subnet mask, DNS, default gateway, WINS, ...etc) MINUS OS booting abilities.

A.   TRUE
B.   FALSE

2-72.   Typically, the DHCP process uses the following four set of messages between the DHCP server and the DHCP client to accomplish its task. Which of the following messages are used in the DHCP task? (Select all that apply)

A.   DHCP Discover Message: A LAN broadcast message sends from the DHCP client to the DHCP server in order to discover server.
B.   DHCP Offer Message: A directed message sends from the DHCP server to the DHCP client in response to message A in order to offer the DHCP service.
C.   DHCP Response Message: A directed message sends from the DHCP server to the DHCP client in order to request the DHCP network information.
D.   DHCP Request Message: A directed message sends from the DHCP client to the DHCP server in order to request the DHCP network information.
E.   DHCP Acknowledgement message: A directed message sends from the DHCP server to the DHCP client in order to acknowledge and to provide the required DHCP client network information such as, client IP address, client subnet mask, client gateway, ... Etc.

2-73.   TRUE/FALSE: Today, most organizations begun to use Internet phone service or IP phones instead of using PBX based phone. IP Phone can pass voice traffic over the data network inside IP packets using application protocol called Voice over IP (VoIP). Typically, a single VoIP call consumes less than 30 kbps of bandwidth.

A.   TRUE
B.   FALSE

2-74.   TRUE/FALSE: Video over IP, on the other hand, is an application protocol that can be used to pass video traffic over the data network inside IP packets. Video over IP requires more bandwidth (300 kbps to 10 Mbps) per video.

A.   TRUE
B.   FALSE

2-75.   TRUE/FALSE: Both VoIP and Video over IP application layer protocols require specific network service needs. The term quality of service (QoS) is used to categorize the application needs from the network services. The application will work well if the network meets those application needs. The QoS tools must be used for a network to be able to support high-quality VoIP and video over IP. A wide variety of QoS tools can be configured on CISCO routers and switches to support the QoS needs of the various applications.

    A.   TRUE
    B.   FALSE

2-76.   Which of the following is a VoIP traffic QoS demand on the network? (Select all that apply)

    A.   **Low delay:** VoIP requires a very low delay—typically less than 200 milliseconds (.2 seconds).
    B.   **Low jitter:** Jitter is the variation in the network traffic delay. VoIP requires—typically less than 30 milliseconds (0.03 seconds).
    C.   **Loss:** When a break in the sound of the VoIP call is occurred, that means an IP packet(s) is/are lost during transmission. Packets are lost because of errors or a router does not have enough room to store the packet while waiting to send it.

2-77.   Match each of the following QoS VoIP parameters to its suitable need.

    1.   Bandwidth
    2.   Delay
    3.   Jitter
    4.   Loss

        A.   Low
        B.   Medium
        C.   High

2-78.   Match each of the following QoS One-way video over IP parameters to its suitable need.

    1.   Bandwidth
    2.   Delay
    3.   Jitter
    4.   Loss

        A.   Low
        B.   Medium
        C.   High

2-79.   Match each of the following QoS Two-way video over IP parameters to its suitable need.

    1.   Bandwidth
    2.   Delay
    3.   Jitter
    4.   Loss

        A.   Low
        B.   Medium
        C.   High

2-80.   Match each of the following QoS Interactive mission-critical data parameters to its suitable need.

    1.   Bandwidth
    2.   Delay
    3.   Jitter
    4.   Loss

     A.   Low
     B.   Medium
     C.   High

2-81.   Match each of the following QoS Interactive business data parameters to its suitable need.

     1.   Bandwidth
     2.   Delay
     3.   Jitter
     4.   Loss

     A.   Low
     B.   Medium
     C.   High

2-82.   Match each of the following QoS Non-business parameters to its suitable need.

     1.   Bandwidth
     2.   Delay
     3.   Jitter
     4.   Loss

     A.   Low
     B.   Medium
     C.   High

2-83.   Match each of the following QoS File Transfer parameters to its suitable need.

     1.   Bandwidth
     2.   Delay
     3.   Jitter
     4.   Loss

     A.   Low
     B.   Medium
     C.   High

2-84.   What is the main purpose for the Host-to-Host layer in the TCP/IP? (Select all that apply)

     A.   It shields the upper-layer applications from the complexities of the bottom layers and the network.
     B.   It defines protocols for setting up the level of transmission service for applications.
     C.   It handles issues like creating reliable end-to-end communication or unreliable communication and ensuring the error-free delivery of data.
     D.   It handles segment sequencing and maintains data integrity.
     E.   It processes the received data stream from upper layer, and makes it ready for sending through the network.

2-85.   Which of the following protocols are implemented in the Host-to-Host layer? (Select all that apply)

     A. TCP
     B. UDP
     C. TDP
     D. UCP

2-86.   Which of the following is true about TCP? (Select all that apply)

A.   It takes large blocks of information from an application and breaks them into segments. (Block →
       Segment)
B.   It numbers and sequences each segment before transmission to the destination site.
C.   It creates a **virtual circuit** with the destination site before transmitting data.
D.   It uses a **connection-oriented** communication type.
E.   It is a full-duplex, connection-oriented, reliable, and accurate protocol.
F.   It provides error-checking techniques.
G.   The reliability that has been added by TCP is often unnecessary in today's networks, since today's
       networks are much more reliable.

2-87.   What is the benefit of the TCP? (Select all that apply)

A.   It breaks block of data into small segments suitable for transmission.
B.   It guarantees data transmission.
C.   It provides error-checking techniques.

2-88.   Which of the following is true about **Virtual Circuit**?

A.   After a transmitting site starts to send segments down the model, the sender's TCP protocol contacts
       the destination's TCP protocol to establish a connection. What is created is known as a virtual circuit.
B.   Before a transmitting site starts to send segments down the model, the sender's TCP protocol
       contacts the destination's TCP protocol to establish a connection. What is created is known as a
       virtual circuit.

2-89.   How TCP duty is implemented in the network? (Select all that apply)

A.   Before a transmitting site starts to send segments down the model, a virtual circuit is created between
       the sender and the destination sites.
B.   During the initial handshake, the two TCP layers (at the sender and at the destination sites) also
       agree on the amount of information that is going to be sent before the recipient's TCP sends back an
       acknowledgment. With every-thing agreed upon in advance, the path is ready for reliable
       communication to take place between the sender and the destination sites.
C.   When transmission is beginning, TCP numbers and sequences each segment so that the
       destination's TCP protocol can put the segments back into the order the application intended.
D.   After these segments are sent, TCP (on the transmitting host) waits for an acknowledgment of the
       receiving end's TCP virtual circuit session.
E.   The sender will retransmit any segment that is not acknowledged.

2-90.   Try to decide which option gets in which blank.
Before a transmitting host starts to send segments down the model, the _____ TCP protocol contacts the
_____ TCP protocol to create a _____.

A.   Virtual circuit
B.   Destination's
C.   Sender's

2-91.   Try to select the correct option to fill the blank.

TCP breaks large blocks of information into _____.

A.   Frames

B.   Segments

2-92.   Try to select the correct option to fill the blank.

TCP receives information from upper-layer protocols in _____ form.

A.   Block
B.   Segment

2-93.   TRUE/FALSE: TCP (on the sender site) numbers and sequences each segment before transmission to the destination site.

A.   TRUE
B.   FALSE

2-94.   Which of the following depicts the TCP communication? (Select all that apply)

A.   It is unreliable communication.
B.   It is connection-oriented communication.
C.   It is full-duplex communication.
D.   It is reliable communication.
E.   It adds some overhead to the network.
F.   It is handshaking communication.

2-95.   Which of the following is a typical operational phase in a basic connection-oriented network service? (Select three)

A.   Data transfer
B.   ARP request
C.   ARP reply
D.   MAC address lookup
E.   Call termination
F.   Call setup
G.   Call prioritization
H.   Interrupt level

2-96.   Which protocol works at the Host-to-Host layer and creates a virtual circuit between hosts?

A.   TCP
B.   UDP
C.   IP
D.   TDP
E.   UCP

2-97.   Which layer of the OSI model creates a virtual circuit between hosts before transmitting data?

A.   Physical
B.   Data Link
C.   Network
D.   Transport
E.   Session
F.   Presentation
G.   Application

2-98.   TRUE/FALSE: TCP (on the transmitting host) segments a data stream from upper layers and prepares it for the network layer which then routes the segments as packets through an internetwork.

    A.   TRUE
    B.   FALSE

2-99.   TRUE/FALSE: The data streams are rebuilt at the receiving host Transport Layer to upper-layer applications or protocols.

    A.   TRUE
    B.   FALSE

2-100.   TRUE/FALSE: For any reason, if either transmission in Figure 2-6 were lost, TCP would resend the data and ensure that it was received successfully. To provide error recovery, the HTTP server (the sending host) sets a retransmission timer and waits for acknowledgment. In case the acknowledgment is lost or all transmitted segments are lost and when the timer expires, the TCP sending host resends all lost segments again.

    A.   TRUE
    B.   FALSE

2-101.   TRUE/FALSE: TCP segment has many overheads.

    A.   TRUE
    B.   FALSE

2-102.   Which of the following is true about UDP? (Select all that apply)

    A.   It takes large blocks of information from an application and breaks them into segments. (Block →
         Segment)
    B.   It numbers each segment before transmission to the destination site.
    C.   It does not create a virtual circuit with the destination site before transmitting data.
    D.   It is a **connectionless** communication.
    E.   It is an unreliable and inaccurate protocol, but it is efficient.
    F.   It can be used in place of TCP depending on the application developer decision.
    G.   It is a thin protocol, which mean does not take much of the bandwidth on a network.
    H.   It is faster than TCP for data transferring.
    I.   It provides error-checking techniques.

2-103.   What is the benefit of the UDP? (Select all that apply)

    A.   It breaks block of data into small segments suitable for transmission.
    B.   It transfers data faster.
    C.   It provides error-checking techniques.
    D.   It does not require reliable delivery-and it transfers data efficiently using far fewer network resources.

2-104.   How UDP duty is implemented in the network? (Select all that apply)

    A.   UDP receives upper-layer blocks of information, and breaks them into segments.
    B.   UDP gives each segment a number for reassemble into the intended block at the destination.
    C.   After these segments are sent, UDP (on the destination host) rebuilds the blocks from the received
         segments according to their numbers.

2-105.   Try to select the correct option to fill the blank.

UDP breaks large blocks of information into _____.

    A.   Segments
    B.   Packets

2-106.   Which of the following is true about UDP? (Select all that apply)

    A.   UDP receives upper-layer blocks of information, and breaks them into segments.
    B.   UDP gives each segment a number for reassemble into the intended block at the destination.
    C.   After these segments are sent, UDP (on the destination host) rebuilds the blocks from the received segments according to their numbers.
    D.   UDP only numbers the segments and not sequencing them, at the sending host UDP does not care in which order the segments arrive at the destination host.
    E.   UDP does not allow an acknowledgment to ensure the arrival. Because of this, it is referred to as unreliable protocol.

2-107.   Try to select the correct option to fill the blank.

UDP receives information from upper-layer protocols in _____ form.

    A.   Block
    B.   Segment

2-108.   TRUE/FALSE: UDP (on the sender site) contact the destination before delivering information to it.

    A.   TRUE
    B.   FALSE

2-109.   TRUE/FALSE: UDP (on the sender site) numbers and sequences each segment before transmission to the destination site.

    A.   TRUE
    B.   FALSE

2-110.   TRUE/FALSE: UDP assumes that the application will use its own reliability method.

    A.   TRUE
    B.   FALSE

2-111.   TRUE/FALSE: UDP is more reliable than TCP.

    A.   TRUE
    B.   FALSE

2-112.   Which of the following depicts the UDP communication? (Select all that apply)

    A.   It is unreliable communication.
    B.   It is connection-oriented communication.
    C.   It is connectionless communication.
    D.   It is reliable communication.
    E.   It adds a large amount of overheads to the network.
    F.   It is handshaking communication.

2-113.   Which protocol works at the Host-to-Host layer and does not create a virtual circuit between hosts?

    A.   TCP
    B.   UDP
    C.   IP
    D.   TDP
    E.   UCP

2-114.   Which layer of the OSI model uses unreliable, connectionless communication between hosts when transmitting data?

    A.   Physical
    B.   Data Link
    C.   Network
    D.   Transport
    E.   Session
    F.   Presentation
    G.   Application

2-115.   What is the difference between the TCP and UDP? (Select all that apply)

    A.   TCP is reliable, whereas UDP is unreliable.
    B.   TCP creates a virtual circuit, whereas UDP does not.
    C.   TCP sequences and numbers the segments before sending them, whereas UDP only numbers the segments before sending them (unsequenced protocol).
    D.   TCP is a connection-oriented communication, whereas UDP is a connectionless communication.
    E.   UDP sends data faster than TCP.
    F.   TCP is more accurate in data transmission than UDP.
    G.   UDP is a thin protocol, so it takes less of the network bandwidth than TCP.
    H.   UDP is a very low overhead protocol as compared with TCP.
    I.   TCP uses Acknowledgments (handshaking) whereas UDP does not.
    J.   TCP uses Windowing flow control whereas UDP does not.

2-116.   Try to decide which option gets in which blank.

Application developer uses TCP for _____ and UDP for _____.

    A.   Reliability
    B.   Faster transfers

2-117.   Which of the following is an example of an application that uses the UDP instead of the TCP? (Select all that apply)

    A.   SNMP
    B.   NFS
    C.   VoIP

2-118.   Which of the following is an example of application that uses the UDP instead of the TCP? (Select all that apply)

    A.   SNMP
    B.   NFS
    C.   VoIP

2-119.   TRUE/FALSE: UDP (on the transmitting host) segments the data blocks from upper layers and prepares them for the network layer.

    A.   TRUE
    B.   FALSE

2-120.   TRUE/FALSE: UDP (on the receiving host) rebuilds the data block to hand to upper-layer applications or protocols.

    A.   TRUE
    B.   FALSE

2-121.   TRUE/FALSE: UDP segment has many overheads as compared with TCP.

    A.   TRUE
    B.   FALSE

2-122.   Try to decide which option gets in which blank.

Host-to-Host protocols must use _____ to communicate with _____.

    A. Port numbers
    B. Upper layers

2-123.   Why TCP and UDP use port numbers?

    A.   Port numbers are useful for upper-layer working.
    B.   Port numbers give away for different applications to cross the network simultaneously.
    C.   Port numbers are useful for network layer working.
    D.   Port numbers keep track of different packets crossing the network simultaneously.

2-124.   TRUE/FALSE: At the sending host, the port numbers are dynamically assigned. The source port number must be any number between 1024 and 65534.

    A. TRUE
    B. FALSE

2-125.   TRUE/FALSE: Destination port numbers are assigned according to destination applications within the above range.

    A. TRUE
    B. FALSE

2-126.   Which range of the following is reserved for well-known port numbers that have been defined in RFC 1700?

    A. 1-1023
    B. 1024-2048
    C. 2049-4098
    D. 1-65534

2-127.   Which range of the following is used by upper layers to set up sessions with other hosts?

A. 1-1023
B. 1024-65534
C. 2049-4098
D. 1-65534

2-128. Which range of the following is used by TCP as source and destination addresses in the TCP segment?

A. 1-1023
B. 1024-65534
C. 2049-4098
D. 1-65534

2-129. TRUE/FALSE: The source host makes up the source port.

A. TRUE
B. FALSE

2-130. Which port does the echo process use?

A. 7/TCP/UDP
B. 9/TCP/UDP
C. 13/TCP/UDP
D. 21/TCP

2-131. Which port does the ftp control process use?

A. 7/TCP/UDP
B. 9/TCP/UDP
C. 13/TCP/UDP
D. 21/TCP

2-132. Which port does the ftp data use?

A. 7/TCP/UDP
B. 9/TCP/UDP
C. 13/TCP/UDP
D. 20/TCP

2-133. Which port does the Telnet process use?

A. 23/TCP
B. 25/TCP
C. 37/TCP/UDP
D. 42/TCP/UDP

2-134. Which port does the SSH process use?

A. 23/TCP
B. 22/TCP
C. 25/TCP/UDP
D. 42/TCP/UDP

2-135. Which port does the smtp process use?

A. 23/TCP
B. 25/TCP
C. 37/TCP/UDP
D. 42/TCP/UDP

2-136. Which port does the domain (DNS) process use?

A. 43/TCP/UDP
B. 53/TCP/UDP
C. 69/UDP
D. 70/TCP/UDP

2-137. Which port does the tftp process use?

A. 43/TCP/UDP
B. 53/TCP/UDP
C. 69/UDP
D. 70/TCP/UDP

2-138. Which port does the http (www) process use?

A. 79/TCP/UDP
B. 80/TCP
C. 101/TCP/UDP
D. 110/UDP

2-139. Which port does the POP3 process use?

A. 79/TCP/UDP
B. 80/TCP/UDP
C. 101/TCP/UDP
D. 110/UDP

2-140. Which port does the nntp process use?

A. 119/TCP/UDP
B. 144/TCP/UDP
C. 161/UDP
D. 179/TCP/UDP

2-141. Which port does the News process use?

A. 119/TCP/UDP
B. 144/TCP/UDP
C. 161/UDP
D. 179/TCP/UDP

2-142. Which port does the SNMP process use?

A. 119/TCP/UDP
B. 144/TCP/UDP
C. 161/UDP
D. 179/TCP/UDP

2-143.   Which port does the HTTPS process use?

    A. 443/TCP
    B. 543/TCP/UDP
    C. 444/TCP/UDP
    D. 417/TCP/UDP

2-144.   Which protocol does the DHCP service use at the Transport layer?

    A. UDP
    B. TCP
    C. IP
    D. ARP

2-145.   Which protocol does the BootP use at the Transport layer?

    A. UDP
    B. TCP
    C. IP
    D. ARP

2-146.   Which protocol does the NFS use at the Transport layer?

    A. UDP
    B. TCP
    C. IP
    D. ARP

2-147.   Which protocol does the RPC use at the Transport layer?

    A. UDP
    B. TCP
    C. IP
    D. ARP

2-148.   Which port does the RTP-based Voice (VoIP) and Video process use?

    A. 16,384–32,767/UDP
    B. 9/TCP/UDP
    C. 13/TCP/UDP
    D. 21/TCP

2-149.   Which of the following is true about TCP windowing? (Select all that apply)

    A.   Window field is used for flow control along with the Sequence and Acknowledgment fields in the TCP header.
    B.   Window field sets the maximum number of unacknowledged bytes that are allowed at any instant in time.
    C.   In other words, the TCP window controls the transmission rate at a level where receiving host congestion and data loss do not occur.

2-150.   Which of the following is a type of the windowing? (Select all that apply)

A.   Fixed Windowing
B.   TCP Sliding Windowing

2-151.   TRUE/FALSE: By default, TCP at the recipient acknowledges the receipt of each data segment to ensure the integrity of the transmission. This provides reliable, connection-oriented data transfers, and removes network congestion issues. However, this reduces network throughput since the sending host must wait for an acknowledgment after sending each segment. To enhance the overall network throughput, most connection-oriented, reliable protocols allow more than one segment to be acknowledged at a time using the windowing technique. The window is the number of data segments the sending host is allowed to send without getting acknowledgment from the receiving host. Figure 2-9, depicts this issue. The numbers in the figure actually represent octets (bytes) of TCP segment's contents.

A.   TRUE
B.   FALSE

2-152.   Assume that the fixed window size is 2000, the segment size is 1000 bytes, and no congestion is occurred at the receiving host. How many times the sending host can send before it receives an ACK?

A.   1
B.   2
C.   3
D.   4

2-153.   TRUE/FALSE: As shown in Figure 2-9, fixed windowing uses a window of fixed size, which does not change. In sliding windowing, the window size is negotiated at the beginning of the connection and can be changed dynamically during the TCP session. It is called a sliding window, since the actual sequence and acknowledgment numbers grow over time. Sometimes it is called a dynamic window, since the size of the window changes over time. To illustrate how the window is working, assume that the example in Figure 2-10 with a current window size of 4000 and each TCP segment has 2000 bytes of data.

A.   TRUE
B.   FALSE

2-154.   Which of the following can be considered as a step of the sliding windowing? (Select all that apply)

A.   During the connection setup procedure, the sending host, and the receiving host exchange, their initial window size values (4000 in this example).
B.   The sending host machine starts sending segments.
C.   The sending host must wait after sending the second segment because the window is full. This provides a control to the flow of data.
D.   When the acknowledgment has been received from the receipt machine, a new window can be begun and sent by the receipt machine.
E.   If no errors have occurred during transmission, the receipt machine grants the server (sending host) to send a larger window.
F.   Now, the size of the window is changed to 6000 bytes. This means that the server can send 6000 bytes before it receives an acknowledgment.

2-155.   Which of the following is true about sliding window? (Select all that apply)

A.   The window starts small and then grows until errors occur.
B.   Windowing only provides flow control to number of bytes that can be transmitted before receiving an acknowledgment.
C.   It does not require that the sending host stop send in all cases.

D.   A sliding window enhances the overall network throughput and this result from the more efficient use of the bandwidth.

2-156.   If a receiving host reduces the window size to 0, what does this mean?

A.   This effectively stops any further transmissions until a new window greater than 0 is sent.
B.   This effectively does not stop any transmissions until a new window greater than 0 is sent.

2-157.   PC1 sends six TCP segments to PC2 with 1000 bytes of data each and a window size of 6000, with sequence numbers 1000, 2000, 3000, 4000, 5000, and 6000. PC2 replies with an acknowledgment number of 6000. What should PC1 do next?

A.   Increase its window to 7000 or more segments
B.   Decrease its window to 5000 segments
C.   Resend all six previously sent segments.
D.   Resend the segment, with sequence number 6000
E.   Send the next segment, with sequence number 7000
F.   Stop sending segments.

2-158.   Match each of the following Transport layer features to its suitable description.

1.   Multiplexing using ports
2.   Error recovery (reliability)
3.   Flow control using windowing
4.   Connection establishment and termination
5.   Ordered data transfer and data segmentation

A.   The use of port numbers at the receiving host to choose the correct application for which the data is destined.
B.   The use of numbering and acknowledging data
C.   The use of (variable) window sizes to prevent cognitions at the receiving host, which protects buffer space and routing devices.
D.   The use of an initialization process for port numbers and Sequence and Acknowledgment fields.
E.   The use of segmentation at the sending host, which allows the receiving host to deliver bytes in the same order.

2-159.   Which of the following does the Internet layer provide? (Select all that apply)

A.   Routing
B.   Providing a single network interface to the upper layers
C.   Addressing
D.   Packaging

2-160.   Which of the following is true about Internet layer? (Select all that apply)

A. It is the only layer in the model that dedicating for routing.
B. It provides a single network interface to the upper-layer protocols.
C. The core of this layer is IP and all paths through the model go through IP.
D. All protocols in the model use IP in this layer.

2-161.   Which of the following protocols is implemented in the Internet layer? (Select all that apply)

A. IP

B. ARP
C. RARP
D. ICMP

2-162.   Try to investigate, what would be happened if the Internet layer were not found with the TCP/IP suite? (Select all that apply)

A.   Application developers must write specific modules for each different Network Access protocol.
B.   Applications would come in many different versions, one for Ethernet, another one for FDDI, and so on.
C.   Routing would be embedded within applications. This would cause difficulties in writing applications and degradation in network performance.

2-163.   Which of the following is true about IP? (Select all that apply)

A.   It receives segments from the Host-to-Host layer and fragments them into datagrams (packets). (Segment → Packet)
B.   It is essentially the Internet layer itself. The other protocols (ARP, RARP, ICMP …etc.) found here to support It.
C.   It adds a software or logical address called IP address for both source and destination hosts in each packet.

2-164.   What is the benefit of the IP? (Select all that apply)

A.   It breaks segments into smaller unit called packets suitable for transmission.
B.   It is aware of all the interconnected networks, since all machines on the network have an IP address.
C.   It adds IP addresses to packets.
D.   It provides routing between disparate networks.

2-165.   How IP duty is implemented in the network? (Select all that apply)

A.   After receiving the segments from upper-layers and assembling the segments into datagrams (packets), IP assigns each packet the IP addresses of the sending host and of the recipient.
B.   IP then, looks at each packet's address and uses a routing table to decide where a packet is to be sent next.
C.   IP chooses the best path. Each router (layer-3 device) that receives a datagram makes routing decisions based upon the packet's destination IP address and other factors.
D.   IP reassembles datagrams back into segments on the receiving host (Packet → Segment.)
E.   The complete IP description can be found in RFC 791.

2-166.   Which of the following depicts the IP communication? (Select all that apply)

A.   It is an unreliable communication.
B.   It is a connection-oriented communication.
C.   It is a reliable communication.
D.   It is a connection-less communication.

2-167.   Try to decide which option gets in which blank.
To identify devices on networks, _____ and _____ must be identified.

A.   Network Number
B.   Device ID

    C.   Segment no

2-168.   Try to select the correct option to fill the blank.
IP breaks segments from host-to-host layer into _____.

    A.   Frames
    B.   Packets

2-169.   Try to select the correct option to fill the blank.
IP receives information from Host-to-Host layer protocols in a _____ form.

    A.   Packet
    B.   Segment

2-170.   TRUE/FALSE: IP (on the sender site) adds IP addresses to each packet before transmission to the destination site.

    A.   TRUE
    B.   FALSE

2-171.   Which protocol works at the Internet layer and provides routing?

    A.   TCP
    B.   ICMP
    C.   IP
    D.   ARP
    E.   RARP

2-172.   Which layer of the OSI model adds IP source and IP destination addresses to the packets?

    A.   Physical
    B.   Data Link
    C.   Network
    D.   Transport
    E.   Session
    F.   Presentation
    G.   Application

2-173.   TRUE/FALSE: All hosts on a network have a logical ID called an IP address.

    A.   TRUE
    B.   FALSE

2-174.   TRUE/FALSE: IP (on the transmitting host) packets a segment from the Host-to-Host layer and prepares it for the Network access layer.

    A.   TRUE
    B.   FALSE

2-175.   TRUE/FALSE: IP (on the receiving host) rebuilds the segments to hand to the Transport layer protocols.

    A.   TRUE

B.   FALSE

2-176.   How does the Network layer see the protocols at the Transport layer?

A.   It sees as TCP protocol.
B.   It sees as UDP protocol.
C.   It sees as numbers called (Protocol numbers).

2-177.   Try to decide if Figure 2-12 correctly depicts the relationship between IP and Upper layer protocols.

A.   Correct
B.   Incorrect

2-178.   Which of the following protocols numbers are possible to be found in the protocol type field of an IP header?

A.   ICMP (1)
B.   TCP (6)
C.   IGRP (9)
D.   UDP (17)
E.   IPv6 (41)
F.   GRE (47)
G.   IPX in IP (111)
H.   Layer-2 tunnel (115)
I.   EIGRP (88)
J.   OSPF (89)

2-179.   Which protocol works at the Internet layer and provides a connection service between machines?

A.   ARP
B.   RARP
C.   IP
D.   ARPR

2-180.   What is the protocol number for the TCP?

A.   6
B.   11
C.   17
D.   27

2-181.   What is the protocol number for the UDP?

A.   6
B.   11
C.   17
D.   27

2-182.   Which of the following is true about ICMP? (Select all that apply)

A.   ICMP works at the network layer, and it is found to support IP.
B.   It is a management protocol and messaging service provider for IP.
C.   Its messages are carried as IP datagrams.

D.   ICMP packets are encapsulated within IP datagrams.
E.   It works at the Network layer.

2-183. Try to select the correct option to fill the blank.
ICMP messages are carried as _____.

A.   TCP segments
B.   IP datagrams

2-184.   Which protocol works at the Internet layer and provides messaging services for IP?

A.   TCP
B.   ICMP
C.   IP
D.   ARP
E.   RARP

2-185.   Which layer of the OSI model provides messaging services for IP?

A.   Physical
B.   Data Link
C.   Network
D.   Transport
E.   Session
F.   Presentation
G.   Application

2-186.   Which of the following is a function of the ICMP? (Select all that apply)

A.   Discover subnet masks
B.   Report TCP, time to exist exceeded
C.   Redirect UDP messages
D.   Transport SNMP Gets
E.   Report routing failures

2-187.   If a Router interface is congested, which protocol in the IP suite is used to tell neighbor routers?

A.   ARP
B.   RARP
C.   IP
D.   ICMP
E.   TCP

2-188.   Which protocol does the Ping utility use?

A.   ICMP
B.   ARP
C.   RARP
D.   TCP

2-189.   Which protocol is used to send a Destination Network Unknown message back to originating hosts?

A.   ARP

    B.   RARP
    C.   IP
    D.   ICMP

2-190.   Which of the following is true about ARP? (Select all that apply)

    A.   ARP is important for IP communication.
    B.   It is used by IP to convert software addresses to hardware addresses.
    C.   ARP discovers the hardware address of a host from a known IP address (IP address → MAC address.)
    D.   It uses a destination broadcast MAC address to map its IP address to its real MAC address. It is found to support IP in the Internet layer.
    E.   ARP broadcasts are carried as IP datagrams.

2-191.   How ARP duty is implemented in the network? (Select all that apply)

    A.   When IP has a datagram to send, it must inform a Network Access Protocol, such as Ethernet or Token Ring, of the destination's MAC address on the local network.
    B.   IP tries to find the destination MAC address in the ARP cache, it uses ARP to find this information.
    C.   If IP does not find the destination MAC address in the host ARP cache table, IP will discover if the destination host on local or on a remote network, using Network Mask calculation.
    D.   If the destination MAC address on a remote network, IP will send a datagram to the next default gateway.
    E.   If the destination MAC address on a local network, IP will send an ARP broadcast (with the destination address = FF: FF: FF: FF: FF: FF) on the local network asking the machine with the specified IP address to reply with its MAC address.

2-192.   Try to decide if Figure 2-13 correctly depicts the operation of ARP on a local network.

    A.   Correct
    B.   Incorrect

2-193.   Try to decide which option gets in which blank.

ARP resolves _____ to _____.

    A.   IP addresses
    B.   Network addresses
    C.   Ethernet addresses

2-194.   Try to select the correct option to fill the blank.
The media access control (MAC) address or physical address can be obtained by _____.

    A.   ARP
    B.   RARP

2-195.   Try to select the correct option to fill the blank.
ARP broadcasts are in _____ form.

    A.   Datagram
    B.   Segment

2-196.   TRUE/FALSE: ARP (on the sending host) adds IP addresses and MAC addresses of both source and destination hosts before transmission the ARP broadcast packet on the local network.

A.   TRUE
B.   FALSE

2-197.   Which protocol works at the Internet layer and provides "IP address → MAC address" mapping?

A.   TCP
B.   ICMP
C.   IP
D.   ARP
E.   RARP

2-198.   Which layer of the OSI model maps the IP address → MAC address?

A.   Physical
B.   Data Link
C.   Network
D.   Transport
E.   Session
F.   Presentation
G.   Application

2-199.   TRUE/FALSE: Before sending a packet to the destination host, its MAC address must be resolved.

A.   TRUE
B.   FALSE

2-200.   Which of the following protocols translates the software address to the hardware address on the same physical network?

A.   TCP
B.   ICMP
C.   IP
D.   ARP
E.   RARP

2-201.   Which of the following is true about RARP? (Select all that apply)

A.   It discovers the IP address for a diskless workstation from its hardware address. (MAC address → IP address)
B.   It is found to support IP in the Internet layer.
C.   RARP broadcasts are carried as IP datagrams.
D.   It works at the Network layer.

2-202.   How RARP duty is implemented in the network? (Select all that apply)

A.   When a diskless workstation is powered UP, it sends a broadcast message containing its MAC address, to a configured RARP server asking for its IP address.
B.   RARP server responds to the broadcast message with the answer, giving the diskless workstation its IP address.

2-203.   Try to decide if Figure 2-14 correctly depicts the operation of RARP on a local network.

A. Correct
B. Incorrect

2-204.   Try to decide which option gets in which blank.

RARP resolves _____ to _____.

A.   IP addresses
B.   Ethernet addresses
C.   Network addresses

2-205.   Try to select the correct option to fill the blank.

The IP address for diskless workstations can be found by _____.

A.   ARP
B.   RARP

2-206.   Try to select the correct option to fill the blank.

RARP broadcasts are in _____ form.

A.   Datagram
B.   Segment

2-207.   TRUE/FALSE: RARP (on a diskless workstation) adds IP addresses and MAC addresses of both source and destination hosts before transmission the RARP broadcast packet on the local network.

A.   TRUE
B.   FALSE

2-208.   Which protocol works at the Internet layer and provides "MAC address → IP address" mapping?

A.   TCP
B.   ICMP
C.   IP
D.   ARP
E.   RARP

2-209.   Which layer of the OSI model maps the MAC address → IP address?

A.   Physical
B.   Data Link
C.   Network
D.   Transport
E.   Session
F.   Presentation
G.   Application

2-210.   TRUE/FALSE: When an IP machine happens to be a diskless machine, it has no way of initially knowing its IP address, but it does know its MAC address.

A.   TRUE

    B.   FALSE

2-211.   Which of the following translates the hardware address to the software address?

    A.   TCP
    B.   ICMP
    C.   IP
    D.   ARP
    E.   RARP

2-212.   What is the difference between BootP and RARP? (Select all that apply)

    A. BootP is a process working in the Process/Application layer, whereas RARP is a protocol working in the Internet layer.
    B. BootP is a protocol working in the Internet, whereas RARP is a process working in the layer Process/Application layer.
    C. BootP uses RARP to map the MAC address → IP address.
    D. RARP uses BootP to map the MAC address → IP address.

2-213.   TRUE/FALSE: DHCP application uses RARP to map the MAC address → IP address.

    A.   TRUE
    B.   FALSE

2-214.   Which of the following is true about Proxy ARP? (Select all that apply)

    A.   Proxy ARP is a service runs by servers or routers on behalf of other devices that are separated from their query by a router.
    B.   Proxy ARP can actually help machines reach remote subnets.
    C.   One advantage of using Proxy ARP is that it can be added to a single router on a network without making any changes to the routing tables of all the other routers that live in the same network.
    D.   One advantage of using Proxy ARP is that it can help the network when the default gateway goes down without the need to reconfigure the hosts.
    E.   One disadvantage of using Proxy ARP is that it will increase the amount of traffic on the network subnet, and hosts will have a larger ARP table, which contains the IP-to-MAC address mappings.
    F.   By default, Proxy ARP protocol is configured on all CISCO routers.

2-215.   What is the IP address?

    A.   It is a software numeric identifier assigned to each host on an IP network.
    B.   It is a hardware numeric identifier assigned to each host by manufacture.

2-216.   What is the purpose of the IP address? (Select all that apply)

    A.   It allows a host on one network to communicate with another host on a different network, regardless of the type of LANs the hosts are associating with.
    B.   It uniquely identifies hosts on the Internetwork and makes them communicate.

2-217.   What is the difference between the IP and MAC addresses? (Select all that apply)

    A.   IP address is a software address, whereas MAC address is a hardware or physical address.
    B.   IP address is used for finding hosts on an Internetwork, whereas MAC address is used for finding hosts on a local network.

C.   An administrator assigns IP address (manually or dynamically) whereas MAC address is assigned by the manufacture.
D.   IPv4 address is 32-bit (4-byte) long, whereas MAC address is 48-bit (6-byte).

2-218.   How many bytes are Ethernet addresses?

A.   4 bytes
B.   6 bytes
C.   8 bytes
D.   16 bytes

2-219.   How many bytes are software addresses?

A.   4 bytes
B.   6 bytes
C.   8 bytes
D.   16 bytes

2-220.   TRUE/FALSE: An IP address consists of 32 bits of information.

A.   TRUE
B.   FALSE

2-221.   Which of the following is used to depict an IP address? (Select all that apply)

A.   Dotted-decimal, as in 194.165.141.80
B.   Binary, as in 11000010.10100101.10001101.01010000
C.   Hexadecimal, as in C2.A5.8D.50

2-222.   TRUE/FALSE: Dotted-decimal or binary forms are often used in the IP addressing.

A.   TRUE
B.   FALSE

2-223.   What type of addressing is used for the IP addressing?

A.   A flat or nonhierarchical, address
B.   A structured or hierarchical address

2-224.   What is the difference between flat and structured addressing? (Select all that apply)

A.   Hierarchical scheme can handle a large number of addresses, namely (2^{32} or about 4.3 billion).
B.   Hierarchical can be structured into two- or three-level, i.e. into network and host, or network, sub-network, and host, whereas flat type cannot.
C.   Flat addressing uses all 32 bits as a unique identifier, whereas Hierarchical-addressing use part of the address as network address and the other parts are used for subnet and host or just the node address.
D.   Hierarchical can be used for efficient routing, whereas flat cannot.

2-225.   What is true about network address? (Select all that apply)

A.   It is a number that uniquely identifies each network.
B.   Each machine on the same network shares the same network address as part of its IP address

C.   It is a number that uniquely identifies each machine on the network.

2-226.   What is true about node address? (Select all that apply)

A.   It is a number that uniquely identifies each machine on the network.
B.   It is sometimes called host address.
C.   It must be unique because it identifies a particular machine-an individual-as opposed to a network, which is a group of addresses.

2-227.   How Internetwork is divided?

A.   According to the network size, is divided into classes.
B.   According to the network using, is divided into families.
C.   According to the network using, is divided into groups.

2-228.   How many network classes are available in the IPv4?

A.   Three
B.   Four
C.   Five
D.   Six

2-229.   Which of the following is true about network classes? (Select all that apply)

A.   Class A: This is used to create a small number of networks possessing a very large number of nodes.
B.   Class B: This is used to create a number of networks possessing a number of nodes.
C.   Class C: This is used to create a very large number of networks possessing a small number of nodes.
D.   Class D: This is used for multicast networking.
E.   Class E: This is used for research and experimental purposes.

2-230.   Try to decide if Figure 2-15 correctly depicts the configuration of network classes.

A.   Correct
B.   Incorrect

2-231.   Which of the following is true about network classes?

A.   A mandate for the leading-bits section of the address is defined for each different network class. As follows:
- Class A leading-bit is 0.
- Class B leading-bits are 10.
- Class C leading-bits are 110.
- Class D leading-bits are 1110.
- Class E leading-bits are 1111.
B.   A mandate for the trailing-bits section of the address is defined for each different network class. As follows:
- Class A trailing -bit is 0.
- Class B trailing -bits are 10.
- Class C trailing -bits are 110.
- Class D trailing -bits are 1110.
- Class E trailing -bits are 1111.

2-232.   Which of the following is true regarding class A? (Select all that apply)

A. The first bit of the first byte must always be **OFF**, or **0**. This means a Class A address must be between 0 and 127.
B. The first byte is assigned to the network address, and the three remaining bytes are used for the node addresses.
C. The Class A network's formats are Network.Node.Node.Node.
D. The maximum number of networks in Class A is 2^7=128. However, the actual maximum number of networks in Class A is 2^7-2=128-2=126.
E. The possible number of nodes for each Class A network is 2^24=16,777,216. However, the actual number of nodes per each Class A network is 2^24-2=16,777,216-2=16,777,214.

2-233. What is the valid range of addresses that can be used in the first octet of a Class A network address?

A. 0-128
B. 1-126
C. 1-127
D. 128-191
E. 128-192
F. 192-223
G. 191-223
H. 224
I. 225

2-234. Which class of the IP address provides a maximum of only 16,777,214 host addresses per network ID?

A. Class A
B. Class B
C. Class C
D. Class D
E. Class E

2-235. Which of the following is true about first octet in the Class A addresses?

A. The first bit must always be ON only.
B. The first bit must always be OFF only.
C. The first bit must always be ON and the second bit must always be OFF.
D. The first bit must always be OFF and the second bit must always be ON.
E. The first and second bits must always be ON and the third bit must always be OFF.
F. The first and second bits must always be OFF and the third bit must always be ON.
G. The first, second and third bits must always be ON and the fourth bit must always be OFF.
H. The first, second, third and forth bits must always be ON.

2-236. Which of the following classes contains an IP address with first octet equal to 126?

A. Class A
B. Class B
C. Class C
D. Class D
E. Class E

2-237. Which of the following represents class A format?

A. Network.Network.Network.Network

B.   Network.Network.Network.Node
C.   Network.Network.Node.Node
D.   Network.Node.Node.Node
E.   Node.Node.Node.Node

2-238.   Which of the following IP addresses' classes provides a maximum of only 126 different network IDs?

A.   Class A
B.   Class B
C.   Class C
D.   Class D
E.   Class E

2-239.   Try to decide if 126.0.0.0 represents a Class A Valid host ID.

A.   Correct
B.   Incorrect

2-240.   Try to decide if 126.255.255.255 represents a Class A Valid host ID.

A.   Correct
B.   Incorrect

2-241.   Which of the following first octet values represents Class A network?

A.   255
B.   191
C.   172
D.   128
E.   127
F.   126

2-242.   Which of the following network classes can be used for the very large networks?

A.   Class A
B.   Class B
C.   Class C
D.   Class D
E.   Class E

2-243.   Which of the following network classes contains the very large node IDs per each Network ID?

A.   Class A
B.   Class B
C.   Class C
D.   Class D
E.   Class E

2-244.   Which of the following network classes contains the little network IDs?

A.   Class A
B.   Class B
C.   Class C

D.   Class D
E.   Class E

2-245.   Which of the following is true regarding class B? (Select all that apply)

A.   The first bit of the first byte must always be **ON**, or **1** and the second bit of the first byte must always be turned **OFF**, or **0**. This means a Class B address must be between 128 and 191.
B.   The first and second bytes are assigned to the network address, and the remaining two bytes are used for the node addresses.
C.   The Class B network's formats are Network.Network.Node.Node.
D.   The maximum number of networks in Class B is 2^14=16,384.
E.   The possible number of nodes for each Class B network is 2^16=65,536. However, the actual number of nodes per each Class B network is 2^16-2=65,536-2=65,534.

2-246.   What is the valid range of addresses that can be used in the first octet of a Class B network address?

A.   0-128
B.   1-126
C.   1-127
D.   128-101
E.   128-192
F.   192-223
G.   191-223
H.   224
I.   225

2-247.   Which class of the IP address provides a maximum of only 65,534 host addresses per network ID?

A.   Class A
B.   Class B
C.   Class C
D.   Class D
E.   Class E

2-248.   Which of the following is true about first octet in the Class B addresses?

A.   The first bit must always be ON only.
B.   The first bit must always be OFF only.
C.   The first bit must always be ON and the second bit must always be OFF.
D.   The first bit must always be OFF and the second bit must always be ON.
E.   The first and second bits must always be ON and the third bit must always be OFF.
F.   The first and second bits must always be OFF and the third bit must always be ON.
G.   The first, second and third bits must always be ON and the fourth bit must always be OFF.
H.   The first, second, third and forth bits must always be ON.

2-249.   Which of the following classes contains an IP address with the first octet equal to 172?

A.   Class A
B.   Class B
C.   Class C
D.   Class D
E.   Class E

2-250. Which of the following represents class B format?
- A. Network.Network.Network.Network
- B. Network.Network.Network.Node
- C. Network.Network.Node.Node
- D. Network.Node.Node.Node
- E. Node.Node.Node.Node

2-251. Which class of the IP address provides a maximum of only 16,384 different network IDs?

- A. Class A
- B. Class B
- C. Class C
- D. Class D
- E. Class E

2-252. Try to decide if 191.0.0.0 represents a Class B Valid host ID.

- A. Correct
- B. Incorrect

2-253. Try to decide if 191.255.255.255 represents a Class B Valid host ID.

- A. Correct
- B. Incorrect

2-254. Which of the following first octet values represents a Class B network? (Select all that apply)

- A. 255
- B. 191
- C. 172
- D. 128
- E. 127
- F. 126

2-255. Which of the following network classes can be used for the medium-sized to large-sized networks?

- A. Class A
- B. Class B
- C. Class C
- D. Class D
- E. Class E

2-256. Which of the following network classes contains the medium number of node IDs per each Network ID?
- A. Class A
- B. Class B
- C. Class C
- D. Class D
- E. Class E

2-257. Which of the following network classes contains the medium number of network IDs?

- A. Class A
- B. Class B

C.   Class C
D.   Class D
E.   Class E

2-258.   The IP address 172.17.0.0 is an example of what type of classes.

A.   Class A
B.   Class B
C.   Class C
D.   Class D

2-259.   Which of the following is true regarding class C? (Select all that apply)

A.   The first and second bits of the first byte must always be **ON**, or **1** and the Third bit of the first byte
     must always be turned **OFF**, or **0**. This means a Class C address must be between 192 and 223.
B.   The first, second and third bytes are assigned to the network address, and the remaining byte is used
     for the node addresses.
C.   The Class C network format is Network.Network.Network.Node
D.   The maximum number of networks in Class C is 2^21=2,097,152.
E.   The possible number of nodes for each Class C network is 2^8=256. However, the actual number of
     nodes per each Class B network is 2^8-2=256-2=254.

2-260.   What is the valid range of addresses that can be used in the first octet of a Class C network address?

A.   0-128
B.   1-126
C.   1-127
D.   128-191
E.   128-192
F.   192-223
G.   191-223
H.   224-239
I.   240-225

2-261.   Which class of the IP address provides a maximum of only 254 host addresses per network ID?

A.   Class A
B.   Class B
C.   Class C
D.   Class D
E.   Class E

2-262.   Which of the following is true about first octet in the Class C addresses?

A.   The first bit must always be ON only.
B.   The first bit must always be OFF only.
C.   The first bit must always be ON and the second bit must always be OFF.
D.   The first bit must always be OFF and the second bit must always be ON.
E.   The first and second bits must always be ON and the third bit must always be OFF.
F.   The first and second bits must always be OFF and the third bit must always be ON.
G.   The first, second and third bits must always be ON and the fourth bit must always be OFF.
H.   The first, second, third and forth bits must always be ON.

2-263. Which of the following classes contains an IP address with the first octet equal to 200?

    A.   Class A
    B.   Class B
    C.   Class C
    D.   Class D
    E.   Class E

2-264. Which of the following represents a class C format?

    A.   Network.Network.Network.Network
    B.   Network.Network.Network.Node
    C.   Network.Network.Node.Node
    D.   Network.Node.Node.Node
    E.   Node.Node.Node.Node

2-265. Which class of the IP address provides a maximum of only 2,097,152 different network IDs?

    A.   Class A
    B.   Class B
    C.   Class C
    D.   Class D
    E.   Class E

2-266. Try to decide if 194.0.0.0 represents a Class C Valid host ID.

    A.   Correct
    B.   Incorrect

2-267. Try to decide if 194.255.255.255 represents a Class C Valid host ID.

    A.   Correct
    B.   Incorrect

2-268. Which of the following first octet values represents class C network? (Select all that apply)

    A.   223
    B.   191
    C.   192
    D.   128
    E.   195
    F.   126

2-269. Which of the following network classes can be used for the small networks?

    A.   Class A
    B.   Class B
    C.   Class C
    D.   Class D
    E.   Class E

2-270. Which of the following network classes contains the little node IDs per each Network ID?

A. Class A
B. Class B
C. Class C
D. Class D
E. Class E

2-271.   Which of the following network classes contains too many networks' IDs?

A. Class A
B. Class B
C. Class C
D. Class D
E. Class E

2-272.   Which IP class has the most host addresses available by default?

A. Class A
B. Class B
C. Class C
D. Class D
E. Class E

2-273.   Which IP class has the most Network IDs available by default?
A. Class A
B. Class B
C. Class C
D. Class D
E. Class E

2-274.   Which IP class has the lowest Network IDs available by default?
A. Class A
B. Class B
C. Class C
D. Class D
E. Class E

2-275.   Which IP class has the lowest host IDs available by default?

A. Class A
B. Class B
C. Class C
D. Class D
E. Class E

2-276.   TRUE/FALSE: IP address starts with 127 octet, is a legal Class B address.

A. TRUE
B. FALSE

2-277.   Try to arrange the IP Classes shown below to correspond, the first octet values.

A. 244.   Class A.
B. 225.   Class B.

C.   222.   Class C.
D.   190.   Class D.
E.   125.   Class E.

2-278.   Which of the following is the valid class B addresses? (Select all that apply)

A.   10011111.01111000.01101101.11111000
B.   00011001.11001010.11100001.01100111
C.   10111101.11001000.00110111.01001100
D.   11011001.01001010.01101001.00110011
E.   10011001.01001011.00111111.00101011
F.   01111001.11001010.11100001.01100111

2-279.   TRUE/FALSE: IPv6 is defined in the mid-1990s with a primary goal is to increase the number of available IP addresses spaces, significantly.

A.   TRUE
B.   FALSE

2-280.   Match each version of IP address to its suitable details.

1.   IPv4
2.   IPv6
    A.   Size of address =32 bits
    B.   Size of address=4 octets
    C.   Size of address=128 bits
    D.   Size of address=16 octets
    E.   Address Example, 21.100.100.1
    F.   Address Example, 0000:0000:0000:0000:FFFF:FFFF:7AEA:010E
    G.   Address can be abbreviated.
    H.   It can support a number of possible host addresses, ignoring reserved values equal to 2^{32}
    I.   It can support a number of possible host addresses, ignoring reserved values equal to 2^{128}.

CHAPTER 3
INTERNETWORKING
SUBNETTING AND
VLSMs

In this chapter, IP addressing in the previous chapter will be continued by discussing the network subnetting that is used to decompose a large network into easy managed and high performance small networks. Variable Length Subnet Masks (VLSMs) will be described before giving some steps for IP network troubleshooting.

The following topics are emphasized in this chapter:

- Network Subnetting.
- Variable Length Subnet Masks (VLSMs).
- IP network troubleshooting.

By understanding perfectly the information presented in this chapter and answering the 85 learning questions at the end of this chapter; designing network using TCP/IP protocol, subnetting large networks, using VLSM's, troubleshooting IP network and answering the CCNA/CCENT exam related questions would be guaranteed. The questions herein are intended to reflect the type of questions presented on the CCENT Test.

Subnetting

In this section, breaking large networks into smaller networks in a process called Subnetting will be discussed. To create an efficient and easy manageable network, Subnetting strategies must be applied. Class A, B, C Subnetting techniques will be outlined in this section.

Subnetting refers to the technique, by which one large network is divided into many smaller networks. By Subnetting, one large network is divided into many smaller, easy manageable, more efficient networks. Subnetting strategy can be implemented for all network Classes, Class A, B, and C networks.

Several advantages can be obtained by applying Subnetting such as:

- Reducing network traffic.
- Optimizing network performance.
- Enhancing network reconfiguration and network fault tolerance.
- Simplifying network management.
- Providing spanning of large geographical distances.
- Creating many sub_networks from one large network.

However, the overall network cost is raised by adopting Subnetting strategy.

The Reasons for Using the Subnetting

There are many reasons for performing Subnetting. Below, are some of the benefits that can be obtained from applying Subnetting:

- Creating Sub_networks: Applying Subnetting creates many small sub_networks. Each small sub_network can be assigned to a specific administrative function.
- Reducing network traffic: Subnetting creates many smaller broadcast domains. Routers (Layer-3 Switches) are used to connect subnets or broadcast domains together. With routers, most traffic will stay on the local network, only packets forwarded to other networks will pass through the router. This will stop broadcast cancer from choking the entire network. The smaller broadcast domains, the less network traffic on that network subnet/segment.
- Optimizing network performance: As traffic is increased, network performance is degraded. Since

---

subnetting reduces traffic, network performance is optimized.

- Simplifying management: Creating smaller connected networks, makes isolating network problems and network troubleshooting easier.
- Tolerating network faults: Subnetting makes network more tolerant of network faults and makes network reconfiguration possible. Subnetting prevents the fault from propagating to all networks. Fault can be isolated within that faulty subnet. Redundant paths for packets can be guaranteed by subnetting. However, this can only be obtained by adopting a suitable subnetting strategy.
- Providing spanning of large geographical distances: Subnetting makes creating WAN networks more efficient. Since WAN links are considerably slower and more expensive than LAN links, a single large network that spans long distances can create performance problems. Creating smaller connected networks makes WAN network more efficient.
- Adding Routers or layer-3 devices: As nothing can be obtained without paying, Subnetting has a disadvantage, this is relating to the overall network cost. To connect subnets, a layer-3 device or router must be used. The number of routers that required depends on many factors. However, If VLANs is used to create subnets; the required number of routers can be reduced.

Subnetworks are created by taking bits from the host portion of the IP address and reserving them to define the subnet address. The more subnets per network, the fewer bits are available for defining hosts, the lowest number of host/subnet.

The following is the *General Subnetting Plan*, which is recommended to be followed:

General Subnetting Plan (GSP)

Below, is the recommended plan that should be followed for implementing Subnetting.

- State the required number of Network IDs.
A. One network ID for each subnet
B. One network ID for each WAN connection
- State the required number of host IDs per subnet.
A. One host ID for each TCP/IP node
B. One host ID for each router interface
- Design the network, by creating the following:
A. One subnet mask for the entire network
B. A unique subnet ID for each physical segment
C. A range of host IDs for each subnet

As shown in GSP, to calculate the best subnet mask and which IP address class to use, the number of hosts and subnets must be determined at first.

Subnet Masks

Subnet mask is a 32-bit value that allows the recipient of IP packets to distinguish the network ID portion from the host ID portion of the IP address. This allows every machine on the network to know which part of the host address will be used as the subnet address. Subnet mask is assigned on every machine in the network. Subnet mask is composed of 1s and 0s. The 1s in the subnet mask represents the portions that refer to the network or subnet addresses. Networks that do not need subnets, they use the default subnet mask. The 255.255.255.255 cannot be used. It is considered a broadcast address.

Default Subnet Mask

Below, are the default subnet masks for Class A, Class B, and Class C IP addresses. The default subnet mask cannot be changed.

- Class A: The default subnet mask is 255.0.0.0.
- Class B: The default subnet mask is 255.255.0.0.
- Class C: The default subnet mask is 255.255.255.0.

Default subnet masks cannot be changed. For example, subnet mask 255.255.0.0 cannot be used for Class C IP addresses. For a Class A network, the first byte in a subnet mask cannot be changed; it must read 255.0.0.0 at a minimum. For a Class B network, the first and second bytes in a subnet mask cannot be changed; it must read 255.255.0.0 at a minimum. For a Class C network, the first, second and third bytes in a subnet mask cannot be changed; it must read 255.255.255.0 at a minimum.

A non-subnetted class 'C' network that uses the default subnet mask has 8 bits available for host machines. Thus the total number of hosts that can be addressed on such a network is equal to 2^8; minus the network number (w.x.y.0.) and the broadcast address (w.x.y.255), for a total of 254 hosts.

To ease the implementation of the Subnetting, let us put it in the *General Subnetting Strategy*:

General Subnetting Strategy (GSS)

Below, is the recommended strategy that should be followed for implementing Subnetting. This strategy can be implemented for Class C, Class B and Class A IP addressing.
- State the IP addressing Class.
- State the available number of bits for defining the hosts. For example, there are only 8 bits available for defining the hosts in Class C.
- State the corresponding subnet masks by putting the masking 1s in the address. For example, Class C has the following subnet masks:
  - 10000000=128   Do not use, by RFC, not use one bit to define Subnetting. However, this mask is used by CISCO.
  - 11000000=192   2 bits are used for Subnetting.
  - 11100000=224   3 bits are used for Subnetting.
  - 11110000=240   4 bits are used for Subnetting.
  - 11111000=248   5 bits are used for Subnetting.
  - 11111100=252   6 bits are used for Subnetting.
  - 11111110=254   Do not use, because one bit cannot define a host.
  - 11111111=255   Do not use, because it is a broadcast address.

  Therefore, the first legal subnet mask for class C is 192 and the last one is 252.
- State the amount of subnets (2^x-2). X is the amount of masked bits, or the 1s. For example, 11100000 is $2^3-2=6$ subnets.
- State the amount of hosts per subnet (2^x-2). X is the amount of unmasked bits, or the 0s. For example, 11100000 is $2^5-2=30$ hosts per subnet.
- State the valid subnets (256-subnet mask = base subnet). For example, 256-224=32. This is the first subnet. The second subnet will be 64 by adding 32 and so on. These are the subnet addresses.
- State the valid hosts. Valid hosts are the numbers between the subnets, minus all 0s and all 1. For example, valid hosts between 32 and 64 subnets are (33, 34,

> 35,...62). 32 is considered the subnet address, and 63 is considered the subnet broadcast address.
> - State the broadcast address for each subnet. Broadcast address is all host bits turned ON, which is the number immediately preceding the next subnet.

Subnetting Class C IP Addresses

The valid Subnet masks for Class C are:

- 255.255.255.128.
- 255.255.255.192.
- 255.255.255.224.
- 255.255.255.240.
- 255.255.255.248.
- 255.255.255.252.

These are the valid subnet masks for class C IP addresses. Mask 255.255.255.255 is used for broadcast, and mask 255.255.255.254 is invalid, because using one bit to define hosts is incorrect.

Based on the GSS above, the following is some practice examples for Subnetting Class C IP addresses.

Example 3-1, Applying GSS for Class C IP address 194.165.141.0 and Subnet mask 255.255.255.192.

194.165.141.0	Network C address
255.255.255.192	Subnet mask

- State the amount of subnet bits. Since 192 in binary is equal to 11000000. This means there are two subnet bits.
- State the amount of subnets $(2^x-2) = 2^2-2=2$. Therefore, there are only two subnets for 192 masking.
- State the amount of hosts per subnet $(2^x-2) = 2^6-2=62$. Therefore, there are 62 hosts per each subnet, where 6 is the number of unmasked bits.
- State the valid subnets 256-192=64. Therefore, 64 is the value of the first subnet. Keep adding the base value to itself, until reaching the subnet mask. 64+64=128. 128+64=192. 192+64=256. The 192 is not used, because it is the subnet mask (all subnet bits turned ON). The 256 is invalid. Therefore, 64 and 128 are only the valid subnets.
- State the valid hosts. Valid hosts are the numbers between the subnets addresses exclusive the broadcast addresses. See the table below, please.
- State the broadcast address for each subnet. Broadcast address is the number immediately preceding the next subnet. See the table below, please.

Table 3-1 The 255.255.255.192 Subnets

Description	First Subnet	Second Subnet
The Subnet add. (first step)	194.165.141.64	194.165.141.128
First host add. (Third step)	194.165.141.65	194.165.141.129
Last host add. (fourth step)	194.165.141.126	194.165.141.190
Broadcast add. (second step)	194.165.141.127	194.165.141.191

As a conclusion, using mask 255.255.255.192 for Class C IP addresses will create 2 subnets and 62 valid hosts per subnet.

Example 3-2, Applying GSS for Class C IP address 194.165.141.0 and Subnet mask 255.255.255.224.

194.165.141.0   Network C address
255.255.255.224   Subnet mask

- State the amount of subnet bits. Since 224 in binary is equal to 11100000. This means there are three Subnet bits.
- State the amount of subnets (2^x-2) =2^3-2=6. Therefore, there are only six subnets for 224 masking.
- State the amount of hosts per subnet (2^x-2) =2^5-2=30. Therefore, there are 30 hosts per each subnet, where 5 is the number of unmasked bits.
- State the valid subnets 256-224=32. Therefore, 32 is the value of the first subnet. Keep adding the base value to itself until reaching the subnet mask. 32+32=64. 64+32=96. 96+32=128. 128+32=160. 160+32=192. 192+32=224. 224+32=256. The 224 is not used, because it is the subnet mask (all subnet bits turned ON). The 256 is invalid. The valid subnets are 32, 64, 96,128,160, and 192.
- State the valid hosts. Valid hosts are the numbers between the subnets addresses exclusive the broadcast addresses. See the table below, please.
- State the broadcast address for each subnet. Broadcast address is the number immediately preceding the next subnet. See the table below, please.

Table 3-2 The 255.255.255.224 Subnets

Description	Subnet 1	Subnet 2	Subnet 3	Subnet 4	Subnet 5	Subnet 6
The Subnet add.	32	64	96	128	160	192
First host add.	33	65	97	129	161	193
Last host add.	62	94	126	158	190	222
Broadcast add.	63	95	127	159	191	223

As a conclusion, using mask 255.255.255.224 for Class C IP addresses will create 6 subnets and 30 valid hosts per subnet.

Example 3-3, Applying GSS for Class C IP address 194.165.141.0 and Subnet mask 255.255.255.240.
194.165.141.0   Network C address
255.255.255.240   Subnet mask

- State the amount of subnet bits. Since 240 in binary is equal to 11110000. This means there are four subnet bits.
- State the amount of subnets (2^x-2) =2^4-2=14. Therefore, there are 14 subnets for 240 masking.
- State the amount of hosts per subnet (2^x-2) =2^4-2=14. Therefore, there are 14 hosts per each subnet, where 4 is the number of unmasked bits.
- State the valid subnets 256-240=16. Therefore, 16 is the value of the first subnet. Keep adding the base value to itself until reaching the subnet mask. The valid subnets are 16, 32, 48, 64, 80, 96, 112, 128, 144, 160, 176, 192, 208, and 224.
- State the valid hosts. Valid hosts are the numbers between the subnets addresses exclusive the broadcast addresses. See the table below, please.
- State the broadcast address for each subnet. Broadcast address is the number immediately preceding the next subnet. See the table below, please.

Table 3-3 The 255.255.255.240 Subnets

Subnet	16	32	48	64	80	96	112	128	144	160	176	192	208	224
First	17	33	49	65	81	97	113	129	145	161	177	193	209	225
Last	30	46	62	78	94	110	126	142	158	174	190	206	222	238
Broad.	31	47	63	79	95	111	127	143	159	175	191	207	223	239

As a conclusion, using mask 255.255.255.240 for Class C IP addresses will create 14 subnets and 14 valid hosts per subnet.

Example 3-4, Applying GSS for Class C IP address 194.165.141.0 and Subnet mask 255.255.255.248.

194.165.141.0   Network C address
255.255.255.248   Subnet mask

- 248=11111000. This means there are five subnet bits.
- 2^5-2=30 Subnets
- 2^3-2=6 hosts per each subnet
- 256-248=8. The valid subnets are 8, 16, 24, 32, 40, 48, 56, 64, 72, 80, 88, 96, 104, 112, 120, 128, 136, 144, 152, 160, 168, 176, 184, 192, 200, 208, 216, 224, 232, and 240.
- State the valid hosts. See the table below, please.
- State the broadcast address for each subnet. See the table below, please.

Table 3-4 The 255.255.255.248 Subnets. (First and last two subnets)

Subnet	8	16	232	240
First Host	9	17	233	241
Last Host	14	22	238	246
Broadcast	15	23	239	247

As a conclusion, using mask 255.255.255.248 for Class C IP addresses will create 30 subnets and 6 valid hosts per subnet.

Example 3-5, Applying GSS for Class C IP address 194.165.141.0 and Subnet mask 255.255.255.252.

194.165.142.0   Network C address
255.255.255.252   Subnet mask

- 252=11111100. This means there are six subnet bits.
- 2^6-2=62 Subnets
- 2^2-2=2 hosts per each subnet
- 256-252=4. The valid subnets are 4, 8, 12, 16, 20, …. and 248.
- State the valid hosts. See the table below, please.
- State the broadcast address for each subnet. See the table below, please.

Since the mask 252 creates only 2 hosts/subnet, it is usually used for a point-to-point communication, when planned subnetting is considered.

Table 3-5 The 255.255.255.252 Subnets. (First and last two subnets)

Subnet	4	8	244	248
First host	5	9	245	249
Last host	6	10	246	250
Broadcast	7	11	247	251

As a conclusion, using mask 255.255.255.252 for Class C IP addresses will create 62 subnets and 2 valid hosts per subnet.

Example 3-6, Subnetting Class C IP address 194.165.141.0 and Subnet mask 255.255.255.128.

194.165.141.0   Network C address

255.255.255.128   Subnet mask

- 128=10000000. This means there is only one subnet bit.
- One masked bit has two states either ON or OFF. Therefore, there are only two subnets 0 and 128.
- 2^7-2=126 hosts per each subnet
- State the valid hosts. See the table below, please.
- State the broadcast address for each subnet. See the table below, please.

Table 3-6 The 255.255.255.128 Subnets

Subnet	0	128
First Host	1	129
Last Host	126	254
Broadcast	127	255

As a conclusion, using mask 255.255.255.128 for Class C IP addresses will create 2 subnets and 126 valid hosts per subnet.

With 128 subnet mask, the GSS cannot be applied. The router must be configured to accept **subnet-zero** and to break the rules and use a 1-bit subnet mask. The command that must be issued on the Router is:

Configuration 3-1, Accepting subnet-zero by CISCO router:
THAAR(config)#ip subnet-zero

Using this command, the first and last subnet in your network design can be used. For example, the Class C mask of 192 provides subnets 64 and 128, but with the ip subnet-zero command, it is possible to use subnets 0, 64, 128, and 192. That is two more subnets for every subnet mask can be added.

To be familiar with this command, the following command line interface (CLI) shows this command, and it states that the command is enabled for host THAAR. CISCO has turned this command ON by default starting with CISCO IOS version 12.X.

Configuration 3-2, Running configuration showing the configuration of subnet-zero by CISCO router:

THAAR#sh running-config
Building configuration...
Current configuration: 928 bytes
!
hostname THAAR
!
ip subnet-zero
!

To answer the CISCO examination questions, the default ip subnet zero command is assumed to be configured. Therefore, the subnet zero, and the broadcast subnet must be used.

Subnetting Class C IP Addresses Summary
The following table concludes Class C Subnetting.

MASK	No. of Subnets without ip subnet-zero	No. of Subnets with ip subnet-zero	No. of hosts/subnet
128/25	N/A	2	126
192/26	2	4	62
224/27	6	8	30

240/28	14	16	14
248/29	30	32	6
252/30	62	64	2

The mask can be written using two notations, either 255.255.255.128 form or /25 form. The last notation represents the number of 1s in the first mask form. For example, the IP address 194.165.141.82 255.255.255.240 can be rewritten as 194.165.141.82/28. This notation is called **Classless Inter-Domain Routing (CIDR).** It is used by the ISP's (Internet Service providers) when allocating a block of addresses to the customer.

Simplified GSS for Class C IP Addresses

Below, is the simplified strategy that can be followed easily to implement the Subnetting.

- State the base subnet value using the 256-subnet mask = base subnet value
- State the subnet of the IP address by mixing the base value with itself until reaching the subnet that contains the required IP address.
- State the broadcast address.
- State the valid hosts

Example 3-7, Applying the simplified GSS for Class C IP address 194.165.141.20 and Subnet mask 255.255.255.240.

194.165.141.20   Network C address
255.255.255.240   Subnet mask

- 256-240=16
- 16+16=32, the IP address 20 falls between the two subnets and must be part of the 194.165.141.16 subnet.
- 31 is the broadcast address.
- 17-30 the valid hosts range.

As a conclusion, first start by using the 256 mask, which in this case is 256-240=16. The first subnet is 16; the second subnet is 32. The host (20) must be in the 16 subnet; the broadcast address is 31 and the valid host range is 194.165.141.17-194.165.141.30.

Subnetting Class B IP Addresses

The valid Subnet masks for Class B are:

- 255.255.128.0
- 255.255.192.0
- 255.255.224.0
- 255.255.240.0
- 255.255.248.0
- 255.255.252.0
- 255.255.254.0
- 255.255.255.0

- 255.255.255.128.
- 255.255.255.192.
- 255.255.255.224.
- 255.255.255.240.
- 255.255.255.248.
- 255.255.255.252.

These are the valid subnet masks for class B IP addresses. Mask 255.255.255.255 is used for broadcast, and mask 255.255.255.254 is invalid, because using one bit to define hosts is incorrect.

The Class B network address has 16 bits available for hosts addressing. This means that up to 14 bits can be used for subnetting since at least 2 bits must be left for host addressing. There are 14 different patterns can be used to subnet Class B address. The process of subnetting a Class B network is the same as for a Class C, except that, there are more host bits available for masking.

The same subnet numbers for Class C can be used for Class B, except a ZERO must be added to the network portion and a 255 to the broadcast section in the fourth octet. For example, 64.**0** is a Class B subnet address, and 127.**255** its broadcast address. The valid hosts range will be 64.1-127.254. This addition is only required, if the number of Subnetting bits less than 8.

Based on the GSS, the following is some practice examples for Subnetting Class B IP addresses.

Example 3-8, Applying GSS for Class B IP address 172.17.0.0 and Subnet mask 255.255.192.0.

172.17.0.0   Network B address
255.255.192.0   Subnet mask

- 192=11000000. This means there are two-Subnetting bits.
- 2^2-2=2 Subnets
- 2^14-2=16,382 hosts per each subnet
- 256-192=64. The valid subnets are 64 and 128.
- State the valid hosts. See the table below, please.
- State the broadcast address for each subnet. See the table below, please.

Table 3-7 The 255.255.192.0 Subnets

Description	First Subnet	Second Subnet
The Subnet	64.0	128.0
First Host	64.1	128.1
Last Host	127.254	191.254
Broadcast	127.255	191.255

From the table above, clearly, Class B Subnetting is like Class C subnetting; just the fourth octet's lowest and highest values are added. Using mask 255.255.192.0 for Class B IP addresses will create 2 subnets and 16,382 valid hosts per subnet.

Example 3-9, Applying GSS for Class B IP address 172.17.0.0 and Subnet mask 255.255.224.0.

172.17.0.0   Network B address
255.255.224.0   Subnet mask

- 224=11100000. This means there are three-Subnetting bits.
- 2^3-2=6 Subnets
- 2^13-2=8,190 hosts per each subnet

- 256-224=32. The valid subnets are 32, 64, 96, 128, 160, and 192.
- State the valid hosts. See the table below, please.
- State the broadcast address for each subnet. See the table below, please.

Table 3-8 The 255.255.224.0 Subnets

Descript.	Subnet 1	Subnet 2	Subnet 3	Subnet 4	Subnet 5	Subnet 6
Subnet	32.0	64.0	96.0	128.0	160.0	192.0
First host	32.1	64.1	96.1	128.1	160.1	192.1
Last host	63.254	95.254	127.254	159.254	191.254	223.254
Broadcast	63.255	95.255	127.255	159.255	191.255	223.255

As a conclusion, using mask 255.255.224.0 for Class B IP addresses will create 6 subnets and 8,190 valid hosts per subnet.

Example 3-10, Applying GSS for Class B IP address 172.17.0.0 and Subnet mask 255.255.240.0.

172.17.0.0   Network B address
255.255.240.0   Subnet mask

- 240=11110000. This means there are four-Subnetting bits.
- $2^4-2=14$ Subnets
- $2^{12}-2=4,094$ hosts per each subnet
- 256-240=16. The valid subnets are 16, 32, 48, 64, 80, 96, 112, 128, 144,160, 176, 192, 208, and 224.
- State the valid hosts. See the table below, please.
- State the broadcast address for each subnet. See the table below, please.

Table 3-9 The 255.255.240.0 Subnets. (First and last two subnets)

Subnet	16.0	32.0	208.0	224.0
First host	16.1	32.1	208.1	224.1
Last host	31.254	47.254	223.254	239.254
Broadcast	31.255	47.255	223.255	239.255

As a conclusion, using mask 255.255.240.0 for Class B IP addresses will create 14 subnets and 4,094 valid hosts per subnet.

Example 3-11, Applying GSS for Class B IP address 172.17.0.0 and Subnet mask 255.255.248.0.

172.17.0.0   Network B address
255.255.248.0   Subnet mask

- 248=11111000. This means there are five-Subnetting bits.
- $2^5-2=30$ Subnets
- $2^{11}-2=2,046$ hosts per each subnet
- 256-248=8. The valid subnets are 8, 16, 24, 32, 40, 48, 56, 64, 72, 80, 88, 96, 104, 112, 120, 128, 136, 144, 152, 160, 168, 176, 184, 192, 200, 208, 216, 224, 232, and 240.
- State the valid hosts. See the table below, please.
- State the broadcast address for each subnet. See the table below, please.

Table 3-10 The 255.255.248.0 Subnets. (First and last two subnets)

Subnet	8.0	16.0	232.0	240.0
First host	8.1	16.1	232.1	240.1
Last host	15.254	23.254	239.254	247.254

| Broadcast | 15.255 | 23.255 | 239.255 | 247.255 |

As a conclusion, using mask 255.255.248.0 for Class B IP addresses will create 30 subnets and 2,046 valid hosts per subnet.

Example 3-12, Applying GSS for Class B IP address 172.17.0.0 and Subnet mask 255.255.255.0.

172.17.0.0   Network B address
255.255.255.0   Subnet mask

- 255=11111111. This means there are eight-Subnetting bits.
- 2^8-2=254 Subnets
- 2^8-2=254 hosts per each subnet
- 256-255=1. The valid subnets are 1,2,3,4 ....253, and 254.
- State the valid hosts. See the table below, please.
- State the broadcast address for each subnet. See the table below, please.

Table 3-11 The 255.255.255.0 Subnets. (First and last two subnets)

Subnet	1.0	2.0	253.0	254.0
First host	1.1	2.1	253.1	254.1
Last host	1.254	2.254	253.254	254.254
Broadcast	1.255	2.255	253.255	254.255

As a conclusion, using mask 255.255.255.0 for Class B IP addresses will create 254 subnets and 254 valid hosts per subnet.

Example 3-13, Applying GSS for Class B IP address 172.17.0.0 and Subnet mask 255.255.255.128.

172.17.0.0   Network B address
255.255.255.128   Subnet mask

- 255.128=11111111.10000000 this means there are nine-Subnetting bits.
- 2^9-2=510 Subnets
- 2^7-2=126 hosts per each subnet
- 256-255=1. For third octet the subnets are 1,2,3,4 ....253, and 254. In forth octet there is only one-Subnetting bit, two subnets. Therefore, there are TWO subnets for each third octet value, hence the 2*256-2=510 subnets. For example, if the third octet was showing subnet 2, the two subnets would actually be 2.0 and 2.128.
- State the valid hosts. See the table below, please.
- State the broadcast address for each subnet. See the table below, please.

Table 3-12 The 255.255.255.128 Subnets. (First and last three subnets)

Subnet	0.128	1.0	1.128	254.0	254.128	255.0
First Host	0.129	1.1	1.129	254.1	254.129	255.1
Last Host	0.254	1.126	1.254	254.126	254.254	255.126
Broadcast	0.255	1.127	1.255	254.127	254.255	255.127

As a conclusion, using mask 255.255.255.128 for Class B IP addresses will create 510 subnets and 126 valid hosts per subnet.

Example 3-14, Applying GSS for Class B IP address 172.17.0.0 and Subnet mask 255.255.255.192.

172.17.0.0   Network B address
255.255.255.192   Subnet mask

- 255.192=11111111.11000000. This means there are ten-Subnetting bits.
- 2^10-2=1022 Subnets
- 2^6-2=62 hosts per each subnet
- 256-255=1. For third octet the subnets are 1,2,3,4 ....253, and 254. In the forth octet there are two-Subnetting bits, four subnets. Therefore, there are FOUR subnets (0, 64, 128, and 192) for each third octet value (This is true for every subnet in the third octet except 0 and 255), hence the (4*256=1022) subnets. For example, if the third octet was showing subnet 2, the two subnets would actually be 2.0, 2.64, 2.128, and 2.192. As long as not all the subnet bits on the third octet are all OFF, the subnet 0 in the fourth octet is valid. In addition, as long as not all the subnet bits in the third octet are all ON, 192 is valid in the fourth octet as a subnet. For subnet 255 in the third octet, there are only 0, 64, 128 subnets in the fourth octet (Until reaching the mask 255.192).
- State the valid hosts. See the table below, please.
- State the broadcast address for each subnet. See the table below, please.

Table 3-13 The 255.255.255.192 Subnets. (Ranges from the first two subnets)

Subnet	0.64	0.128	0.192	1.0	1.64	1.128
First Host	0.65	0.129	0.193	1.1	1.65	1.129
Last Host	0.126	0.190	0.254	1.62	1.126	1.190
Broadcast	0.127	0.191	0.255	1.63	1.127	1.191

As a conclusion, using mask 255.255.255.192 for Class B IP addresses will create 1022 subnets and 62 valid hosts per subnet.

Example 3-15, Applying GSS for Class B IP address 172.17.0.0 and Subnet mask 255.255.255.224.

172.17.0.0   Network B address
255.255.255.224   Subnet mask

- 255.224=11111111.11100000. This means there are eleven-Subnetting bit.
- 2^11-2=2046 Subnets
- 2^5-2=30 hosts per each subnet
- 256-255=1. For third octet the subnets are 1,2,3,4 ....253, and 254. In the forth octet there are three-Subnetting bits, eight subnets. Therefore, there are EIGHT subnets (0, 32, 64, 96, 128, 160, 192, and 224) for each third octet value. Both 0 and 224 subnets can be used as long as the third octet does not show a value of 0 or 255.
- State the valid hosts. See the table below, please.
- State the broadcast address for each subnet. See the table below, please.

Table 3-14 The 255.255.255.224 Subnets. (The first subnet ranges)

Subnet	0.32	0.64	0.96	0.128	0.160	0.192	0.224
First H	0.33	0.65	0.97	0.129	0.161	0.193	0.225
Last H	0.62	0.94	0.126	0.158	0.190	0.222	0.254
Broad.	0.63	0.95	0.127	0.159	0.191	0.223	0.255

Table 3-15 The 255.255.255.224 Subnets. (The second subnet ranges)

Subnet	1.0	1.32	1.64	1.96	1.128	1.160	1.192	1.224
First	1.1	1.33	1.65	1.97	1.129	1.161	1.193	1.225

Last	1.30	1.62	1.94	1.126	1.158	1.190	1.222	1.254
Broad.	1.31	1.63	1.95	1.127	1.159	1.191	1.223	1.255

Table 3-16 The 255.255.255.224 Subnets. (The Last subnet ranges)

Subnet	255.0	255.32	255.64	255.96	255.128	255.160	255.192
First H	255.1	255.33	255.65	255.97	255.129	255.161	255.193
Last H	255.30	255.62	255.94	255.126	255.158	255.190	255.222
Broad.	255.31	255.63	255.95	255.127	255.159	255.191	255.223

As a conclusion, using mask 255.255.255.224 for Class B IP addresses will create 2046 subnets and 30 valid hosts per subnet.

Simplified GSS for Class B IP Addresses

Below, is the simplified strategy that can be followed easily to implement Subnetting.

- State the number of subnetting bits (S)
- State the base subnet value using the 256-subnet mask = base subnet value
- State the subnet of the IP address by mixing the base value with itself until reaching the subnet that contains the required IP address (Subnet1).
- State the next subnet value (Subnet2).
- If S <= 8 then the host addresses' ranges are (Subnet1.1) – ((Subnet2-1).255). i.e., (3rd and 4th octets) are used or TWO DIMENSIONs.
- If S > 8 then the host addresses' ranges are (Subnet1+1) – (Subnet2-1). i.e., (Only 4th octet) is used or ONE DIMENSION.
- State the broadcast address.
- State the valid hosts

Example 3-16, Applying Simplified GSS for Class B IP address 172.17.85.10 and Subnet mask 255.255.192.0

172.17.85.10   Class B IP address
255.255.192.0   Subnet mask

- S=2
- 256-192=64
- 64+64=128, the IP address 85 falls between the two subnets and must be part of the 172.17.64.0 Subnet. (Subnet 1=64.0)
- Subnet 2 = 128.0
- Ranges are 64.0-127.255.
- 127.255 is the broadcast address.
- 64.1-127.254 the valid hosts range.

As a conclusion, first start by using the 256 mask, which in this case is 256-192=64. The first subnet is 64.0; the second subnet is 128.0. The host (85.10) must be in the 64.0 subnet; the broadcast address is 127.255 and the valid host range is 172.17.64.1-172.17.127.254.

Example 3-17, Applying Simplified GSS for Class B IP address 172.17.85.10 and Subnet mask 255.255.255.0.

172.17.85.10   Class B IP address

255.255.255.0   Subnet mask

- S=8
- 256-255=1
- 1+1=2, 3, 4, 5 ... 85, 86... etc. The IP address 85 falls between the two subnets and must be part of the 172.17.85.0 Subnet. (Subnet 1=85.0)
- Subnet 2 = 86.0
- Ranges are 85.0-85.255.
- 85.255 is the broadcast address.
- 85.1-85.254 the valid hosts range.

As a conclusion, first start by using the 256 mask, which in this case is 256-255=1. The first subnet is 1.0; the second subnet is 2.0... 85.0, 86.0. The host (85.10) must be in the 85.0 subnet; the broadcast address is 85.255 and the valid host range is 172.17.85.1-172.17.85.254.

Example 3-18, Applying Simplified GSS for Class B IP address 172.17.85.185 and Subnet mask 255.255.255.192.

172.17.85.185   Class B IP address
255.255.255.192   Subnet mask

- S=10
- 256-192=64
- 64+64=128, 128+64=192 the IP address 185 falls between the two subnets and must be part of the 172.17.85.128 Subnet. (Subnet 1=128)
- Subnet 2 = 192
- Ranges are 128-191.
- 191 is the broadcast address.
- 129-190 the valid hosts range.

As a conclusion, first start by using the 256 mask, which in this case is 256-192=64. The first subnet is 64; the second subnet is 128; the third subnet is 192. The host (85.185) must be in the 85.128 subnet; the broadcast address is 85.191 and the valid host range is 172.17.85.129-172.17.85.190.

Example 3-19, Applying Simplified GSS for Class B IP address 172.17.85.5 and Subnet mask 255.255.255.252.

172.17.85.5   Class B IP address
255.255.255.252   Subnet mask

- S=14
- 256-252=4
- 4+4=8, the IP address 5 falls between the two subnets and must be part of the 172.17.85.4 Subnet. (Subnet 1=4)
- Subnet 2 = 8
- Ranges are 4-7.
- 7 is the broadcast address.
- 5-6 the valid hosts range.

As a conclusion, first start by using the 256 mask, which in this case is 256-252=4. The first subnet is 4; the second subnet is 8; the third subnet is 12. The host (85.5) must be in the 85.4 subnet; the broadcast address is 85.7 and the valid host range is 172.17.85.5-172.17.85.6.

Subnetting Class A IP Addresses

The valid Subnet masks for Class A are:

- 255.128.0.0.
- 255.192.0.0.
- 255.224.0.0.
- 255.240.0.0.
- 255.248.0.0.
- 255.252.0.0.
- 255.254.0.0.
- 255.255.0.0
- 255.255.128.0
- 255.255.192.0
- 255.255.224.0
- 255.255.240.0
- 255.255.248.0
- 255.255.252.0
- 255.255.254.0
- 255.255.255.0
- 255.255.255.128.
- 255.255.255.192.
- 255.255.255.224.
- 255.255.255.240.
- 255.255.255.248.
- 255.255.255.252.

These are the valid subnet masks for class A IP addresses. Mask 255.255.255.255 is used for broadcast, and mask 255.255.255.254 is invalid, because the using of one bit to define hosts is incorrect.

The Class A network address has 24 bits available for hosts addressing. This means that up to 22 bits can be used for subnetting since at least 2 bits must be left for host addressing. There are 22 different patterns can be used to subnet Class A. address. The process of subnetting a Class A network is the same as for a Class B, except, there are more host bits available for masking.

The same subnet numbers for Class B can be used for Class A, except, a ZERO must be added to the network portion and a 255 to the broadcast section in the fourth octet. For example, 64.**0.0** is a Class A subnet address, and 127.**255.255** its broadcast address. The valid hosts' range will be 64.0.1-127.255.254. This addition is only required, if the number of Subnetting bits less than 8.

Based on the GSS, the following is some practice examples for Subnetting Class A IP addresses. The simplified GSS can also be recreated for Class A in the same way of Class B.

Example 3-20, Applying GSS for Class A IP address 77.17.85.5 and Subnet mask 255.192.0.0.

77.0.0.0   Network A address
255.192.0.0   Subnet mask

- 192=11000000. This means there are two-Subnetting bits.
- $2^2-2=2$ Subnets
- $2^{22}-2=4,194,302$ hosts per each subnet
- 256-192=64. The valid subnets are 64.0.0, and 128.0.0.
- State the valid hosts. See the table below, please.

- State the broadcast address for each subnet. See the table below, please.

Table 3-17 The 255.192.0.0 Subnets

Subnet	77.64.0.0	77.128.0.0
First Host	77.64.0.1	77.128.0.1
Last Host	77.127.255.254	77.191.255.254
Broadcast	77.127.255.255	77.191.255.255

As a conclusion, using mask 255.192.0.0 for Class A IP addresses will create 2 subnets and 4,194,302 valid hosts per Subnet.

Example 3-21, Applying GSS for Class A IP address 77.17.85.5 and Subnet mask 255.240.0.0.

77.0.0.0   Network A address
255.240.0.0   Subnet mask

- 240=11110000. This means there are Four-Subnetting bits.
- 2^4-2=14 Subnets
- 2^20-2=1,040,574 hosts per each subnet
- 256-240=16. The valid subnets are 16.0.0, 32.0.0, 44.0.0.....224.0.0.
- State the valid hosts. See the table below, please.
- State the broadcast address for each subnet. See the table below, please.

Table 3-18 The 255.240.0.0 Subnets. (The First and Last subnets ranges)

	First Subnet	Last Subnet
Subnet	77.16.0.0	77.224.0.0
First Host	77.16.0.1	77.224.0.1
Last Host	77.31.255.254	77.239.255.252
Broadcast	77.31.255.255	77.239.255.255

As a conclusion, using mask 255.240.0.0 for Class A IP addresses will create 14 subnets and 1,048,574 valid hosts per Subnet.

Example 3-22, Applying GSS for Class A IP address 77.17.85.5 and Subnet mask 255.255.0.0.

77.0.0.0   Network A address
255.255.0.0   Subnet mask

- 255=11111111. This means there are eight-Subnetting bits.
- 2^8-2=254 Subnets
- 2^16-2=65,534 hosts per each subnet
- 256-255=1. The valid subnets are 1, 2, 3, 4.... 253, and 254.
- State the valid hosts. See the table below, please.
- State the broadcast address for each subnet. See the table below, please.

Table 3-19 The 255.255.0.0 Subnets. (The First and Last subnets ranges)

	First Subnet	Last Subnet
Subnet	77.1.0.0	77.254.0.0
First host	77.1.0.1	77.254.0.1
Last Host	77.1.255.254	77.254.255.254
Broadcast	77.1.255.255	77.254.255.255

As a conclusion, using mask 255.255.0.0 for Class A IP addresses will create 254 subnets and 65,534 valid hosts per Subnet.

Example 3-23, Applying GSS for Class A IP address 77.17.85.5 and Subnet mask 255.255.240.0.

77.0.0.0   Network A address
255.255.240.0   Subnet mask

- 255.240=11111111.11110000. This means there are twelve-Subnetting bits.
- $2^{12}-2=4094$ Subnets
- $2^{12}-2=4094$ hosts per each subnet
- 256-240=16. However, since the 2nd octet is 255 or all Subnet bits ON, It is possible to start with 0 in the 3rd octet as long as a Subnet bit is turned ON in the 2nd octet. Therefore, the subnets become 77.1.0.0, 77.1.16.0, 77.1.32.0, and 77.1.48.0, all the way to 77.1.240.0. The next set of subnets would be 77.2.0.0, 77.2.16.0, 77.2.32.0, 77.2.48.0, all the way to 77.2.240.0. Notice that 240 can be used in the 3rd octet as long as not all the Subnet bits in the 2nd octet are ON. In other words, 77.255.240.0 is invalid because all Subnet bits are turned ON. The last valid Subnet would be 77.255.224.0.
- State the valid hosts. See the table below, please.
- State the broadcast address for each subnet. See the table below, please.

Table 3-20 The 255.255.240.0 Subnets. (The 1st, 2nd, and last subnets ranges)

	First Subnet	Second Subnet	Last Subnet
Subnet	77.1.0.0	77.1.16.0	77.255.224.0
First Host	77.1.0.1	77.1.16.1	77.255.224.1
Last Host	77.1.15.254	77.1.31.254	77.255.239.254
Broadcast	77.1.15.255	77.1.31.255	77.255.239.255

As a conclusion, using mask 255.255.240.0 for Class A IP addresses will create 4094 subnets and 4094 valid hosts per Subnet.

Example 3-24, Applying GSS for Class A IP address 77.17.85.5 and Subnet mask 255.255.255.192.

77.0.0.0   Network A address
255.255.255.192   Subnet mask

- 255.255.192=11111111.11111111.11000000. This means there are 18th -Subnetting bit.
- $2^{18}-2=262,142$ Subnets
- $2^{6}-2=62$ hosts per each Subnet
- Now, Subnet numbers from the 2nd, 3rd, and 4th octets should be added. In the 2nd and 3rd, they can range from 1 to 255, as long as all Subnet bits in the 2nd, 3rd, and 4th octets are not all ON at the same time. For the 4th octet, it will be 256-192=64. However, 0 will be valid as long as at least one other Subnet bit is turned ON in the 2nd or 3rd octet. In addition, 192 will be valid as long as not all the bits in the 2nd and 3rd octets are turned ON.
- State the valid hosts. See the table below, please.
- State the broadcast address for each Subnet. See the table below, please.

Table 3-21 The 255.255.255.192 Subnets. (The 1st three subnets ranges)

Subnet	77.1.0.0	77.1.0.64	77.1.0.128
First Host	77.1.0.1	77.1.0.65	77.1.0.129
Last Host	77.1.0.62	77.1.0.126	77.1.0.190
Broadcast	77.1.0.63	77.1.0.127	77.1.0.191

Table 3-22 The 255.255.255.192 Subnets. (The last three subnets ranges)

Subnet	77.255.255.0	77.255.255.64	77.255.255.128
First Host	77. 255.255.1	77. 255.255.65	77. 255.255.129
Last Host	77. 255.255.62	77. 255.255.126	77. 255.255.190
Broadcast	77. 255.255.63	77. 255.255.127	77. 255.255.191

As a conclusion, using mask 255.255.255.192 for Class A IP addresses will create 262,142 subnets and 62 valid hosts per Subnet.

Variable Length Subnet Masks (VLSMs)

VLSMs is an abbreviation for "Variable Length Subnet Masks". It refers to a way that takes one network and creates many networks using subnet masks of different lengths on different types of network designs.

Classful routing protocols such as RIPv1 and IGRP do not have a field for subnet information, so the subnet information gets dropped from these routing protocols. This means that if a router running RIPv1 has a subnet mask of a certain value; it assumes that all interfaces within the classful address space have the same subnet mask.

Classless routing protocols such as RIPv2, EGRP and OSPF do have a field for subnet information, so the subnet information gets to advertise within these routing protocols. This means that if a router running RIPv2 has a subnet mask of a certain value; it not assumes that all interfaces within the classless address space have the same subnet mask.

Classless routing protocols do support the advertisement of subnet mask information along with each route updates sent by that protocol. Classful routing protocols do not transmit mask information along with each route updates sent by that protocol. So, only classless routing protocols support VLSM. Therefore, it is possible to use VLSM with routing protocols such as RIPv2, EIGRP, or OSPF.

Example 3-25, Classful Network: Looking at Figure 3-1, there are two routers, each with two LANs, connected together with a WAN point-to-point serial link. In a typical classful network design (RIPv1 or IGRP routing protocols), it is possible to subnet the network as follows:

172.18.10.0 = Network
255.255.255.0 (/24) = Mask

Figure 3-1 Classful Network

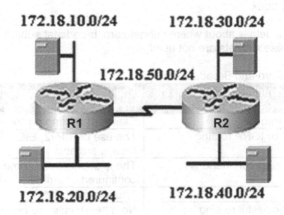

As discussed previously in this chapter, this type of subnetting yields 254 hosts per each subnet. However, the serial link for WAN connectivity requires only two host's numbers. This represents a wasting in the host numbers. All hosts and router interfaces in the Figure 3-1 have the same subnet mask-this is called classful routing. If it requires more efficient network, it definitely needs to add different masks to each router interface. This clears the reasons for transferring to VLSMs and Classless network of course.

Example 3-26, Classless Network: Looking at Figure 3-2, there are two routers, each with two LANs, connected together with a WAN point-to-point serial link. In a classless network design (RIPv2 or EGRP routing protocols), it is possible to subnet the network as follows:

172.18.50.0 = Network
255.255.255.252 (/30) = Mask

Figure 3-2 Classless Network

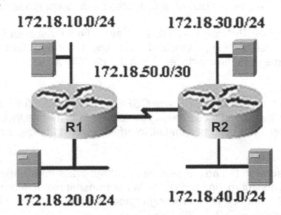

As discussed previously in this chapter, this type of subnetting yields 254 hosts per each subnet with mask /24. Since the serial link for WAN connectivity requires only two host's numbers it is possible to use a different subnet mask, in this example, subnet mask /30 is used to provide 2 hosts per subnet. This represents a gaining in the host numbers as compared with the previous example. Since, not all hosts and router interfaces in the Figure 3-2 have the same subnet mask-this is called classless routing. This represents a more efficient network. Now, remember that it is possible to use different size masks on each router interface.

Detailed information for the routing protocols such as RIP, IGRP, EGRP, OSPF protocols will be obtained in the next chapters and in the ICND2 book.

As a summary, Table 3-22 gives details about where subnet zero, broadcast subnet, and the other special subnets are used and where these subnets are not used.

Table 3-23 The Use of Subnet Zero and Broadcast Subnet

The use of 2^x-2 formula, and avoiding the zero and broadcast subnets	The use of 2^x formula with the zero and broadcast subnets
Classful routing protocol	Classless routing protocol
The use of RIPv1 or IGRP routing protocol	The use of RIPv2, EIGRP, or OSPF routing protocol
The no ip subnet zero command is configured	The ip subnet zero command is configured or omitted (default)
No VLSM	The use of VLSM
Any indication for classful routing	No other details are provided

Not default for answering CISCO examination	The default for answering CISCO examination

*Where X is the amount of unmasked bits, or the 0s.

Summary

In this chapter, a strong foundation for internetworking protocol (IP suite) Subnetting is presented. The information presented in this chapter is essential for designing, configuring IP networks and troubleshooting IP network. To answer CISCO examination questions, the default ip subnet zero command is assumed to be configured, so subnet zero, and broadcast subnet must be used.

Several examples are used to clarify the ideas behind this chapter. The following topics are covered:

- Network Subnetting (Class A, Class B, and Class C)
- Variable Length Subnet Masks (VLSMs)
- IP network troubleshooting

At the end of the chapter, several learning questions are given to evaluate the learning level from this chapter. The correct answers and solutions with complementary discussions are found in appendix A, "Answers to Chapters Learning Questions."

Chapter Three Commands Reference

Table 3-24 lists and briefly describes the new command that is used in this chapter.

Table 3-24 Chapter 3 Command Reference

Command	Description
Router(config)#ip subnet-zero	Makes the router accepts the **subnet-zero** and breaks the rules and uses a 1-bit subnet mask.

Chapter 3 Learning Questions

3-1. What is the Subnetting?

    A.   It refers to the technique, by which networks are removed.
    B.   It refers to the technique, by which one large network is divided into many smaller networks.
    C.   It refers to the technique, by which network optimization is measured.
    D.   It refers to the technique, by which network performance is measured.

3-2.   TRUE/FALSE: Subnetting techniques can be applied on Class A, B, and C networks.

    A.   TRUE
    B.   FALSE

3-3.   Which of the following advantages are obtained by applying the Subnetting? (Select all that apply)

    A.   Reducing network traffic
    B.   Optimizing network performance
    C.   Enhancing network reconfiguration and network fault tolerance
    D.   Simplifying network management
    E.   Providing spanning of large geographical distances
    F.   Creating many sub_networks from one large network
    G.   Reducing the overall network cost

3-4.   TRUE/FALSE: Applying Subnetting creates many small sub_networks. Each small sub_network cannot be assigned to specific administrative function.

    A.   TRUE
    B.   FALSE

3-5.   TRUE/FALSE: Subnetting creates many smaller broadcast domains. Routers (Layer-3 Switches) are used to connect subnets or broadcast domains together. With routers, most traffic will stay on the local network, only packets forwarded to other networks will pass through the router. This will stop broadcast cancer from choking the entire network. The smaller broadcast domains, the less network traffic on that network subnet/segment.

    A.   TRUE
    B.   FALSE

3-6.   TRUE/FALSE: As traffic is increased, network performance is degraded. Since subnetting reduces traffic, network performance is degraded.

    A.   TRUE
    B.   FALSE

3-7.   TRUE/FALSE: Creating smaller connected networks, makes isolating network problems and network troubleshooting difficult.

    A.   TRUE
    B.   FALSE

3-8.   TRUE/FALSE: Subnetting makes network more tolerant of network faults and makes network reconfiguration possible. Subnetting prevents a fault from propagating to all networks. Fault can be isolated within that faulty subnet. Redundant paths for packets can be guaranteed by subnetting. However, this can only be obtained by adopting a suitable subnetting strategy.

A.   TRUE
B.   FALSE

3-9.   TRUE/FALSE: Subnetting makes creating WAN networks more efficient. Since WAN links are considerably slower and more expensive than LAN links, a single large network that spans long distances can create performance problems. Creating smaller connected networks makes WAN network more efficient.

A.   TRUE
B.   FALSE

3-10.   TRUE/FALSE: As nothing can be obtained without paying, Subnetting has a disadvantage, this is relating to the overall network cost. To connect subnets, a layer-3 device or router must be used. The number of routers that required depends on many factors. However, If VLANs is used to create subnets; the required number of routers can be reduced.

A.   TRUE
B.   FALSE

3-11.   How subnetworks are created?

A.   By taking bits from the host portion of the IP address and reserve, those to define the subnet address.
B.   By taking bits from the network and host portions of the IP address and reserve, those to define the subnet address.
C.   By multiplexing IP addresses of multiple networks together.

3-12.   TRUE/FALSE: The more subnets per network, the fewer bits are available for defining hosts.

A.   TRUE
B.   FALSE

3-13. Which of the following is an important factor when designing an IP addressing scheme? (Select all that apply)
A.   The number of hosts
B.   The number of name servers
C.   The number of subnets
D.   The location of internet access points
E.   The location of name servers

3-14. Which of the following is true about subnet mask? (Select all that apply)

A.   This is a 32-bit value that allows the recipient of IP packets to distinguish the network ID portion of the IP address from the host ID portion of the IP address.
B.   This allows every machine on the network to know which part of the host address will be used as the subnet address.
C.   It is assigned on every machine in the network.
D.   It is composed of 1s and 0s. The 1s in the subnet mask represents the portions that refer to the network or subnet addresses.

3-15.   Try to select the correct option to fill the blank.
Networks that do not need subnets, they use the _____.

A.   Default subnet mask
B.   255.255.255.255 subnet mask

3-16.   TRUE/FALSE: If a subnet mask is not assigned to a network, this means that this network does not have subnets.

A.   TRUE
B.   FALSE

3-17.   TRUE/FALSE: 255.255.255.255 can be used as a subnet mask to subnet networks.

A.   TRUE
B.   FALSE

3-18. Which of the following is true about default subnet mask? (Select all that apply)

A.   It cannot be changed.
B.   For a Class A network, the first byte in a subnet mask cannot be changed; it must read 255.0.0.0 at a minimum.
C.   For a Class B network, the first and second bytes in a subnet mask cannot be changed; it must read 255.255.0.0 at a minimum.
D.   For a Class C network, the first, second and third bytes in a subnet mask cannot be changed; it must read 255.255.255.0 at a minimum.

3-19. What is the maximum number of hosts that can be assigned to a class "C," non-subnetted network?

A. 16
B. 48
C. 254
D. 1024

3-20. Which of the following is a valid Subnet mask for class C? (Select all that apply)

A. 255.255.255.128
B. 255.255.255.192
C. 255.255.255.224
D. 255.255.255.240
E. 255.255.255.248
F. 255.255.255.252
G. 255.255.255.254
H. 255.255.255.255

3-21.   What is the state of the 128-bit for IP=194.165.141.2 Subnet Mask = 255.255.255.128?

A. ON
B. OFF

3-22. What is the state of the 128-bit for IP=194.165.141.185 Subnet Mask = 255.255.255.128?

A. ON
B. OFF

3-23. Write the subnet, broadcast address and the valid host range for the following IP address. 196.100.100.10

255.255.255.252

   A. Subnet 16, Broadcast 19, hosts range 17-18.
   B. Subnet 8, Broadcast 11, hosts range 9-10.
   C. Subnet 12, Broadcast 15, hosts range 13-14.
   D. Subnet 20, Broadcast 23, hosts range 21-22.

3-24.   Write the subnet, broadcast address and the valid host range for the following IP address. 196.100.100.13 255.255.255.248

   A. Subnet 8, Broadcast 15, hosts range 9-14.
   B. Subnet 16, Broadcast 23, hosts range 17-22.
   C. Subnet 24, Broadcast 31, hosts range 25-30.
   D. Subnet 32, Broadcast 39, hosts range 33-38.

3-25.   Write the subnet, broadcast address and the valid host range for the following IP address. 196.100.100.20, with 4 bits of Subnetting

   A. Subnet 17, Broadcast 31, hosts range 18-30.
   B. Subnet 18, Broadcast 31, hosts range 19-30.
   C. Subnet 19, Broadcast 31, hosts range 20-30.
   D. Subnet 16, Broadcast 31, hosts range 17-30.

3-26.   Write the subnet, broadcast address and the valid host range for the following IP address. 196.100.100.115, with 3 Subnetting bits

   A. Subnet 96, Broadcast 127, hosts range 97-126.
   B. Subnet 96, Broadcast 111, hosts range 97-110.
   C. Subnet 96, Broadcast 101, hosts range 97-100.
   D. Subnet 96, Broadcast 99, hosts range 97-98.

3-27.   Write the subnet, broadcast address and the valid host range for the following IP address. 196.100.100.190, with 2 Subnetting bits

   A. Subnet 128, Broadcast 143, hosts range 129-142.
   B. Subnet 128, Broadcast 135, hosts range 129-134.
   C. Subnet 128, Broadcast 191, hosts range 129-190.
   D. Subnet 128, Broadcast 131, hosts range 129-130.

3-28.   Write the subnet, broadcast address and the valid host range for the following IP address. 196.100.100.222 255.255.255.128

   A. Subnet 128, Broadcast 255, hosts range 129-254.
   B. Subnet 128, Broadcast 256, hosts range 129-255.
   C. Subnet 128, Broadcast 254, hosts range 129-253.
   D. Subnet 128, Broadcast 253, hosts range 129-252.

3-29.   Which subnet mask provides 12 subnets with a Class C network ID?

   A. 255.255.255.248
   B. 255.255.255.240
   C. 255.255.255.252
   D. 255.255.255.255

3-30.   What broadcast address does the host 194.100.100.5 use? (Assume six bits for Subnetting)

A. 194.100.100.7
B. 194.100.100.255
C. 194.100.100.15
D. 194.100.100.16

3-31.   Which of the following is the valid host range for the IP address 192.100.188.170 /26?

A. 192.100.188.128-192
B. 192.100.188.128-191
C. 192.100.188.129-191
D. 192.100.188.129-190

3-32.   What is the broadcast address of the subnet address 192.100.188.20/30?

A. 192.100.188.127
B. 192.100.188.23
C. 192.100.188.31
D. 192.100.188.63

3-33.   What is the subnet address of the IP address 192.100.188.30/29?

A. 192.100.188.0
B. 192.100.188.16
C. 192.100.188.24
D. 192.100.188.32

3-34.   Given the IP address of 193.250.12.43 and a subnet mask of 255.255.255.128, what is the subnet address?

A.   193.250.12.32
B.   193.250.12.0
C.   193.250.12.43
D.   193.250.12.128
E.   None of the above

3-35.   Which of the following subnet masks can be written as /24 using the dotted notation?

A.   255.0.0.0
B.   224.0.0.0
C.   255.255.0.0
D.   255.255.255.0

3-36.   Given the IP address 192.168.185.129 and the subnet mask 255.255.255.192. What is the network ID and the broadcast address for the subnet where this host is located?

A.   Network ID = 192.168.185.128, broadcast address is 192.168.185.255.
B.   Network ID = 192.168.185.0, broadcast address is 192.168.185.255.
C.   Network ID = 192.168.185.129, broadcast address is 192.168.185.224.
D.   Network ID = 192.168.185.128, broadcast address is 192.168.185.191.

3-37.   Given a Class C Network ID 192.168.1.0 and subnet mask 255.255.255.252, how many subnets and how many hosts per subnet will this allow for?

   A.   62 subnets with each 2 hosts
   B.   126 subnets with each 4 hosts
   C.   30 subnets with each 6 hosts
   D.   2 subnets with each 62 hosts

3-38.   You are designing an IP addressing scheme for a small network with 4 subnets. You expect to add a subnet each year for the next 5 years. The network ID is 194.165.141.80. What subnet mask should you assign to allow for the maximum amount of hosts per subnet?

   A. 255.255.255.128
   B. 255.255.255.192
   C. 255.255.255.224
   D. 255.255.255.240
   E. 255.255.255.252

3-39.   Which of the following is a valid Subnet mask for class B? (Select all that apply)

   A. 255.255.128.0
   B. 255.255.192.0
   C. 255.255.224.0
   D. 255.255.240.0
   E. 255.255.248.0
   F. 255.255.252.0
   G. 255.255.254.0
   H. 255.255.255.0
   I.   255.255.255.128
   J. 255.255.255.192
   K. 255.255.255.224
   L. 255.255.255.240
   M. 255.255.255.248
   N. 255.255.255.252
   O. 255.255.255.254
   P. 255.255.255.255

3-40.   How many bits can be used to subnet Class B address?

   A. 16
   B. 15
   C. 14
   D. 13

3-41.   How many subnetting patterns are available for Class B address?

   A. 13
   B. 14
   C. 15
   D. 16

3-42.   What is the main difference between subnetting Class C address and subnetting Class B address?

   A. There is no difference.

    B. Class C has more host bits.
    C. Class B has more host bits.

3-43.   TRUE/FALSE: The same subnet numbers for Class C can be used for Class B, except a ZERO must be added to the network portion and a 255 to the broadcast section in the fourth octet.

    A. TRUE
    B. FALSE

3-44.   Write the subnet, broadcast address and the valid host range for the following IP address. 172.17.10.25/25.

    A. Subnet 0, Broadcast 127, hosts range 1-126.
    B. Subnet 64, Broadcast 127, hosts range 65-126.
    C. Subnet 32, Broadcast 63, hosts range 33-62.
    D. Subnet 32, Broadcast 47, hosts range 33-46.

3-45.   Write the subnet, broadcast address and the valid host range for the following IP address 172.17.10.126/26.

    A. Subnet 0, Broadcast 127, hosts range 1-126.
    B. Subnet 64, Broadcast 127, hosts range 65-126.
    C. Subnet 32, Broadcast 63, hosts range 33-62.
    D. Subnet 32, Broadcast 47, hosts range 33-46.

3-46.   Write the subnet, broadcast address and the valid host range for the following IP address. 172.17.10.56/27.

    A. Subnet 0, Broadcast 127, hosts range 1-126.
    B. Subnet 64, Broadcast 127, hosts range 65-126.
    C. Subnet 32, Broadcast 63, hosts range 33-62.
    D. Subnet 32, Broadcast 47, hosts range 33-46.

3-47.   Write the subnet, broadcast address and the valid host range for the following IP address. 172.17.10.35/28.

    A. Subnet 0, Broadcast 127, hosts range 1-126.
    B. Subnet 64, Broadcast 127, hosts range 65-126.
    C. Subnet 32, Broadcast 63, hosts range 33-62.
    D. Subnet 32, Broadcast 47, hosts range 33-46.

3-48.   Write the subnet, broadcast address and the valid host range for the following IP address. 172.17.10.9/29.

    A. Subnet 0, Broadcast 127, hosts range 1-126.
    B. Subnet 8, Broadcast 15, hosts range 9-14.
    C. Subnet 32, Broadcast 63, hosts range 33-62.
    D. Subnet 32, Broadcast 47, hosts range 33-46.

3-49.   Write the subnet, broadcast address and the valid host range for the following IP address. 172.17.10.18/30.

    A. Subnet 0, Broadcast 127, hosts range 1-126.

      B. Subnet 64, Broadcast 127, hosts range 65-126.
      C. Subnet 16, Broadcast 19, hosts range 17-18.
      D. Subnet 32, Broadcast 47, hosts range 33-46.

3-50.   Which subnet mask provides 12 subnets with a Class B network ID?

      A. 255.255.248.0
      B. 255.255.240.0
      C. 255.255.252.0
      D. 255.255.255.0

3-51.   What broadcast address does the host 128.100.100.5/30 use?

      A. 128.100.100.7
      B. 128.100.100.255
      C. 128.100.100.15
      D. 128.100.100.16

3-52.   Which of the following is a valid host range for the IP address 172.16.10.22/28?

      A. 172.16.10.17-30/28
      B. 172.16.10.17-31/28
      C. 172.16.10.16-30/28
      D. 172.16.10.16-31/28

3-53.   What is the broadcast address of the subnet address 172.17.17.0/24?

      A. 172.17.17.127/24
      B. 172.17.17.31
      C. 172.17.17.63
      D. 172.17.17.255

3-54.   Which of the following is the broadcast address for a Class B network ID using the default subnet mask?

      A. 172.17.17.255
      B. 172.17.255.255
      C. 172.255.255.255
      D. 255.255.255.255

3-55.   What is the subnet address of the IP address 172.17.17.17/25?

      A. 172.17.17.0/25
      B. 172.17.17.127/25
      C. 172.17.17.128/25
      D. 172.17.17.255/25

3-56.   What is the subnet address of the IP address 172.17.0.17/25?

      A. 172.17.0.0/25
      B. 172.17.0.128/25
      C. 172.17.0.1/25
      D. It is invalid.

3-57. Which of the following subnet masks can be written as /22 using the dotted notation?

    A. 255.220.0.0
    B. 224.222.0.0
    C. 255.255.255.0
    D. 255.255.252.0

3-58. What is the broadcast address of the address 172.17.126.255/18?

    A. 172.17.127.255/18
    B. 172.17.255.255/18
    C. 172.255.255.255/18
    D. 172.17.126.255/18

3-59. Given a Class B Network ID 172.17.0.0 and subnet mask 255.255.255.0, how many subnets and how many hosts per subnet will this allow for?

    A. 128 subnets with each 510 hosts
    B. 254 subnets with each 254 hosts
    C. 510 subnets with each 128 hosts
    D. It is an invalid subnet mask.

3-60. What subnet mask should be used to subnet Class B address into 510 subnets?

    A. 255.255.128.0
    B. 255.255.254.0
    C. 255.255.255.0
    D. 255.255.255.128

3-61. You are designing an IP addressing scheme for a middle-size network with 4 subnets. You expect to add a subnet each year for the next 5 years. The network ID is 172.17.16.0. What subnet mask should you assign to allow for the maximum amount of hosts per subnet?

    A. 255.255.128.0
    B. 255.255.192.0
    C. 255.255.224.0
    D. 255.255.240.0
    E. 255.255.255.240

3-62. Your network is divided into 20 subnets and is used a class B network ID. Each subnet should allow for at least 1500 hosts. Which subnet mask should you assign?

    A. 255.255.248.0
    B. 255.255.252.0
    C. 255.255.255.0
    D. 255.255.255.128
    E. 255.255.255.192

3-63. Which one of the following does not belong to the same subnet as the other three when using 255.255.224.0 as the subnet mask?

    A. 172.17.63.51
    B. 172.17.66.24

C.   172.17.65.33
D.   172.17.64.42

3-64.   Given the IP address 172.18.71.12 and the subnet mask 255.255.248.0, what is the network ID and the broadcast address for the subnet where this host is located.

A. Network ID = 172.18.64.0, broadcast address is 172.18.80.255.
B. Network ID = 172.18.32.0, broadcast address is 172.18.71.255.
C. Network ID = 172.18.32.0, broadcast address is 172.18.80.255.
D. Network ID = 172.18.64.0, broadcast address is 172.18.71.255.

3-65.   Which of the following is a valid subnet number in the network 130.1.0.0 when using a mask 255.255.248.0?

A. 130.1.2.0
B. 130.1.4.0
C. 130.1.8.0
D. 130.1.16.0
E. 130.1.24.0
F. 130.1.32.0
G. 130.1.40.0
H. 130.1.256.0

3-66.   Which of the following is not a valid subnet number in the network 130.1.0.0 when using a mask 255.255.255.0?

A.   130.3.2.0
B.   130.1.4.0
C.   130.1.8.0
D.   130.1.16.0
E.   130.1.24.0
F.   130.1.32.0
G.   130.1.40.0
H.   130.1.256.0

3-67.   Which of the following is a valid Subnet mask for class A? (Select all that apply)

A. 255.128.0.0
B. 255.192.0.0
C. 255.224.0.0
D. 255.240.0.0
E. 255.248.0.0
F. 255.252.0.0
G. 255.254.0.0
H. 255.255.0.0
I. 255.255.128.0
J. 255.255.192.0
K. 255.255.224.0
L. 255.255.240.0
M. 255.255.248.0
N. 255.255.252.0
O. 255.255.254.0
P. 255.255.255.0

Q. 255.255.255.128
R. 255.255.255.192
S. 255.255.255.224
T. 255.255.255.240
U. 255.255.255.248
V. 255.255.255.252
W. 255.255.255.254
X. 255.255.255.255

3-68.   How many bits can be used to subnet Class A address?

A. 22
B. 23
C. 24
D. 25

3-69.   How many subnetting patterns are available for Class A address?

A. 22
B. 23
C. 24
D. 25

3-70.   What is the main difference between subnetting Class B address and subnetting Class A address?

A. There is no difference.
B. Class A has more host bits.
C. Class B has more host bits.

3-71.   TRUE/FALSE: The same subnet numbers for Class B can be used for Class A, except a ZERO must be added to the network portion and a 255 to the broadcast section in the fourth octet.

A. TRUE
B. FALSE

3-72.   Write the Subnet, broadcast address and the valid host range for the following IP address. 77.10.10.5/30.

A. Subnet 0, Broadcast 127, hosts range 1-126.
B. Subnet 4, Broadcast 7, hosts range 5-6.
C. Subnet 32, Broadcast 63, hosts range 33-62.
D. Subnet 32, Broadcast 47, hosts range 33-46.

3-73.   Write the Subnet, broadcast address and the valid host range for the following IP address. 77.77.77.77/28.

A. Subnet 16, Broadcast 31, hosts range 17-30.
B. Subnet 32, Broadcast 47, hosts range 33-46.
C. Subnet 48, Broadcast 63, hosts range 49-62.
D. Subnet 64, Broadcast 79, hosts range 65-78.

3-74.   Which Subnet mask provides 12 subnets with a Class A network ID?

A. 255.248.0.0
B. 255.240.0.0
C. 255.255.252.0
D. 255.255.255.0

3-75.   What broadcast address does the host 77.255.255.17/29 use?

A. 77.255.255.23/29
B. 77.255.255.24/29
C. 77.255.255.255/29
D. 77.255.255.22/29

3-76.   What is the broadcast address of the Subnet address 77.17.16.0/23?

A. 77.17.18.255/23
B. 77.17.16.0/23
C. 77.17.17.255/23
D. 77.17.255.255/23

3-77.   Which of the following is the broadcast address for a Class A network ID using the default Subnet mask?

A. 77.17.17.255
B. 77.17.255.255
C. 77.255.255.255
D. 255.255.255.255

3-78.   You are designing an IP addressing scheme for a large network with 4 subnets. You expect to add a Subnet each year for the next 4 years. The network ID is 77.1.1.0. What Subnet mask should you assign to allow for the maximum amount of hosts per Subnet?

A.   255.0.0.0
B.   255.254.0.0
C.   255.240.0.0
D.   255.255.255.0

3-79.   Assuming a class A network, a subnet mask of 255.248.0.0 will allow for how many subnets.

A.   60
B.   62
C.   30
D.   32

3-80.   Which of the following is true about **VLSMs**? (Select all that apply)

A.   It is an abbreviation for "Variable Length Subnet Masks."
B.   It refers to a way that takes one network and creates many networks using subnet masks of different lengths on different types of network designs.

3-81.   Try to decide which option gets in which blank.

Classful routing protocols such as the RIPv1 and IGRP do _____ a field for subnet mask information, so the subnet information is dropped from these routing protocols. This means that if a router running RIPv1 has a subnet mask of a certain value, it _____ that all interfaces within the classful address space have the same subnet mask.

A.   not have
B.   have
C.   assumes
D.   not assumes

3-82.   Try to decide which option gets in which blank.

Classless routing protocols such as the RIPv2, EGRP, and OSPF do _____ a field for subnet mask information, so the subnet information gets advertises within these routing protocols. This means that if a router running RIPv2 has a subnet mask of a certain value, it _____ that all interfaces within the classless address space have the same subnet mask. The benefit of this type of network is that it is possible to save a bunch of IP address space with it.

A.   not have
B.   have
C.   assumes
D.   not assumes

3-83.   TRUE/FALSE: Classless routing protocols do support the advertisement of subnet mask information along with each route update sent by that protocol. Classful routing protocols do not transmit mask information along with each route update sent by that protocol. Therefore, only classless routing protocols support VLSM.

A. TRUE
B. FALSE

3-84.   Which of the following IP addresses could not be assigned to the router's interface? Assume that the router is configured with the **ip subnet-zero.**

A.   225.1.1.2/24
B.   172.18.0.200/25
C.   99.100.153.191/26
D.   172.18.0.200/24

3-85.   Match each of the following subnetting formula to its suitable using.

1.   The use of 2^X-2 formula, and avoiding the zero and broadcast subnets
2.   The use of 2^X formula with the zero and broadcast subnets

A.   Classful routing protocol
B.   Classless routing protocol
C.   The use of RIPv1 or IGRP routing protocol
D.   The use of RIPv2, EIGRP, or OSPF routing protocol
E.   The **no ip subnet zero** command is configured.
F.   The **ip subnet zero** command is configured or omitted (default).
G.   No VLSM
H.   The use of VLSM
I.   Any indication for classful routing.
J.   No other details are provided.
K.   Not default for answering CISCO examination.
L.   The default for answering CISCO examination.

CHAPTER 4
INTERNETWORKING OS
CISCO DEVICES

This chapter begins with an introduction to the CISCO Internetwork Operating System (IOS), and continues with an in-depth view of the CISCO IOS router configuration options using both the initial setup mode and the CISCO IOS Command-Line Interface (CLI). IOS is the operating system that makes CISCO routers and switches work, which allows configuring and managing these devices as well. Basics of router configurations and examples of well-designed networks are given in this chapter.

The following topics are emphasized in this chapter:
- Logging into a router
- Performing editing and help features
- Establishing hostnames
- Setting enabled (or privileged mode) passwords
- Setting virtual terminal passwords
- Enabling interface configurations
- Gathering router information
- Viewing, saving, and verifying router configurations

A firm understanding of the fundamentals behind this chapter and answering the 239 learning questions at the end of this chapter are important for both Configuring CISCO networks and answering the CCNA/CCENT exam related questions. The questions herein are intended to reflect the type of questions presented on the CCENT Test.

Router User Interface

In this section, IOS definition will be given firstly. Secondly, a CISCO router connection and the procedure to bring the router UP at the first time will be outlined. Finally, a Step-by-Step CISCO router configuration during setup mode will be detailed.

CISCO Router IOS

The CISCO IOS is the kernel of CISCO routers and most CISCO switches. IOS is a software system that manages CISCO routers and Switches, both their hardware and software resources. It is what runs the CISCO routers and some CISCO switches, which allows configuring these devices as well. CISCOFusion is proposed by CISCO to make all CISCO devices run the same OS. Almost all CISCO routers run the same IOS, but only about half of the switches currently run the CISCO IOS.

The IOS was created to deliver network services and applications. The CISCO IOS runs on most CISCO routers and on some CISCO Catalyst switches, like the CAT2.96K switch.

All network OS facilities can be obtained by IOS, and the following are some functions of the IOS:

- Managing network resources.
- Carrying network protocols and functions.
- Connecting high-speed traffic between networking devices.
- Adding security rules to network access.

The CISCO IOS can be accessed using the following ways:

- Through the console port of a router.
- Through the network by using Telnet application.

- Through a modem.

For example, A HyperTerminal Windows application can be used to access IOS through the console port of a Router. LAN Router interfaces can be used to access IOS using Telnet utility. Access to the IOS command line is called an EXEC session. IOS command line is called Command Line Interface (CLI).

Physical Installation

To physically install a router for the first time, it is recommended to follow the following steps:

Step 1.	Connecting the router LAN ports to an Ethernet if it is required using any LAN cables.
Step 2.	Connecting the router's serial interface to the CSU/DSU, and the CSU/DSU to the line from the Telco, if an external CSU/DSU is used.
Step 3.	Connecting the router's serial interface to the line from the Telco, if an internal CSU/DSU is used.
Step 4.	Connecting the router's console port to a PC (using a rollover cable), to configure the router.
Step 5.	Connecting a power cable from a power outlet to the power port on the router.
Step 6.	Turning ON the router.

Most of the CISCO Catalyst switches do not have a power ON/OFF switch—once the switch is connected to the power, the switch is ON. However, CISCO routers do have ON/OFF switches.

Connecting to a Router

Connecting to a CISCO router is required for configuring the router, verifying the router configuration, and checking statistics. Any active interface can be used to connect and configure a router. The following ways can be used for a router connection:

- Console port connection.
- Auxiliary port connection.
- Ethernet port connection.

Console port connection is used to connect and configure the router at the first time setup. It is an RJ-45 connection on the rear panel of the router. No password is set on this port by default. Windows HyperTerminal software is an example of programs that used to access the router through this port. The default Console port parameters are: 9600 baud, 8 data bits, no parity, 2 stop bits. However, this type of connection does not support hardware flow control.

Auxiliary port connection is really the same as a console port and can be used in the same way. It is used to connect and configure the router. It is an RJ-45 connection on the rear panel of the router. No password is set on this port by default. It is also used to configure modem commands. In this way, a modem can be connected to the router. This provides dialing-up and configuring a remote router if it's down. Windows HyperTerminal software is an example of programs that used to access the router through this port. The default Auxiliary port parameters are 9600 baud, 8 data bits, no parity, 2 stop bits. However, this type of connection does support hardware flow control.

Ethernet port connection can be accessed using telnet. Telnet is the most common way for router connection and configuration. It is an emulation program that used to connect and configure the router. It uses any active interface on a router like an Ethernet (RJ-45, DB-15...etc) or serial port (DB-60) for router connection. Password can be set for Telnet access. However, a router can be configured to prohibit telnet access.

Figure 4-1 shows an illustration rear panel of an 1841 CISCO *Integrated Services Router (ISR)*. Notice the different interfaces and connections. Integrated Services Routers (ISR) means that many functions are integrated into a single device.

Figure 4-1 The CISCO 1841 Router Rear Panel

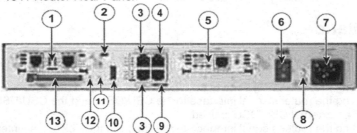

The CISCO 1841 router rear panel has a console port, an auxiliary port, Universal Serial Bus (USB) port, two high-speed WAN Interface Card/WAN Interface Card/Voice Interface Card (HWIC/WIC/VIC) slots, two 10/100 Fast Ethernet RJ45 ports, and a Compact Flash (CF) drive. CISCO 1841 router supports AIM-VPN/BPII-Plus card and two fast Ethernet connections. The front panel contains two LEDs that output status data about the system status (SYS OK) and system activity (SYS ACT). The back panel consists of eight LEDs: two duplex LEDs, two speed LEDs, two link LEDs, CF LED, and AIM LED.

The CISCO 1841 router rear panel contains the following:

(1)	HWIC/WIC/VIC slot 1
(2)	Lock
(3)	FE ports
(4)	Console port
(5)	HWIC/WIC/VIC slot 0
(6)	Power switch
(7)	Power inlet
(8)	Ground connector
(9)	Auxiliary port
(10)	USB port
(11)	AIM LED
(12)	CF LED
(13)	CF drive

Router Memory Specifications

Several types of memories are used in CISCO devices such as; Dynamic random-access memory (DRAM), Nonvolatile random-access memory (NVRAM) and Flash memory.

DRAM is used for main system memory and shared memory. DRAM needs refresh every ms, it is a small chip, simple, cheap, easy to make, and hold = 4 times as much info a SRAM (Static RAM) hold.

NVRAM is used for storing configuration information.

Flash Memory is used for running CISCO IOS software. It is an electronically erasable programmable read-only memory (EEPROM).

Starting a CISCO Router

During bringing UP period, the router at first will run a Power-On Self Test (POST). Loading the CISCO IOS from Flash Memory (by default) is the second step. The third step is loading the Startup-config from NVRAM if it's found. Entering the setup mode if no configuration is found in NVRAM is the fourth step.

After the IOS is loaded, it looks for a valid configuration called Startup-Config that is stored by default in NVRAM. If there is no configuration, then the router will bring up what is called Setup mode. So, setup mode is called automatically if no startup-config in NVRAM.

Configuration 4-1, First time Router Booting: The following Configuration is what will appear on the Console if the router is booting for the first time. When this information is shown, the router has been successfully booted. However, the messages displayed vary, depending on the CISCO IOS release and the selected features. The screen displays in this section are for reference only and may not exactly reflect the screen displays on the actual console. Notice that, it is possible to press the Ctrl-C key combination at any time to leave the setup mode and go back to the previous CLI mode.

System Bootstrap, Version 12.3(8r)YI, RELEASE SOFTWARE
Technical Support: http://www.cisco.com/techsupport
Copyright (c) 2005 by Cisco Systems, Inc.

C850 series (Board ID: 4-149) platform with 65536 Kbytes of main memory

Booting flash:/c850-advsecurityk9-mz.123-8.YI2.bin
Self decompressing the image : ################################## [
OK]

Restricted Rights Legend

Use, duplication, or disclosure by the Government is
subject to restrictions as set forth in subparagraph
(c) of the Commercial Computer Software - Restricted
Rights clause at FAR sec. 52.227-19 and subparagraph
(c) (1) (ii) of the Rights in Technical Data and Computer
Software clause at DFARS sec. 252.227-7013.

Cisco Systems, Inc.
170 West Tasman Drive
San Jose, California 95134-1706

Cisco IOS Software, C850 Software (C850-ADVSECURITYK9-M), Version 12.3(8)YI2, RELEASE SC
FTWARE (fc1)
Synched to technology version 12.3(10.3)T2
Technical Support: http://www.cisco.com/techsupport
Copyright (c) 1986-2005 by Cisco Systems, Inc.
Compiled Tue 14-Jun-05 20:08 by ealyon
Image text-base: 0x8002008C, data-base: 0x80F991F8

Changing crypto engine : Onboard: 0 state change to: INIT
This product contains cryptographic features and is subject to United
States and local country laws governing import, export, transfer and
use. Delivery of Cisco cryptographic products does not imply
third-party authority to import, export, distribute or use encryption.

Importers, exporters, distributors and users are responsible for compliance with U.S. and local country laws. By using this product you agree to comply with applicable laws and regulations. If you unable to comply with U.S. and local laws, return this product immediately.

A summary of U.S. laws governing Cisco cryptographic products may found at: http://www.cisco.com/ww1/export/crypto/stqrg.html

If you require further assistance please contact us by sending email to export@cisco.com

Cisco 851W (MPC8272) processor (revision 0x100) with 59392K/6144K bytes of memory.
Processor board ID FHK0945307S
MPC8272 CPU Rev: Part Number 0xC, Mask Number 0x10
5 FastEthernet interfaces.
1 802.11 radio
128K bytes of non-volatile configuration memory.
20480K bytes of processor board System flash (Intel Strataflash)

First-Time Router Startup

Setup mode is a step-by-step process for configuring a router. It is only covering some very global commands, but it is helpful to configure easily certain protocols, such as, bridging or DECnet. It is simply, an easy step-by-step setup configuration tool.

A Router can enter in setup mode in one of the following ways:

- During first time booting.
- During Router booting and there is no startup-config stored in NVRAM.
- From Privileged EXEC mode, by issuing the **setup** command (Router#**setup**).

Two options are available during setup mode: Basic Management and Extended Setup. A basic Management option only gives enough configurations to allow connectivity to the router. An extended setup option allows configuring some global parameters as well as interface configuration parameters.

Configuration 4-2, Using the extended setup mode: The following Configuration shows in step-by-step how to configure a router at the first time. If the following messages are appeared, the router has booted, and it is ready for initial configuration using the **setup** command facility or the command-line interface (CLI).

--- System Configuration Dialog ---

At any point you may enter a question mark '?' for help.
Use ctrl-c to abort configuration dialog at any prompt.
Default settings are in square brackets '[ ]'.

Step 1 When the following message appears; enter **yes** to begin the initial configuration dialog:

--- System Configuration Dialog ---

Would you like to enter the initial configuration dialog? [yes/no]: y

At any point you may enter a question mark '?' for help.
Use ctrl-c to abort configuration dialog at any prompt.

Default settings are in square brackets '[ ]'.

Step 2 When the following message appears; press **n** to enter Extended setup option:

Basic management setup configures only enough connectivity
for management of the system, Extended Setup will ask you
to configure each interface on the system.

Would you like to enter basic management setup? [yes/no]: n

Step 3 When the following message appears, press **Return** to see the current interface summary:

First, would you like to see the current interface summary? [yes]: return

Any interface listed with OK? value "NO" does not have a valid configuration

Interface	IP-Address	OK?	Method	Status	Protocol
Dot11Radio0	unassigned	NO	unset	initializing	down
FastEthernet0	unassigned	NO	unset	initializing	down
FastEthernet1	unassigned	NO	unset	initializing	down
FastEthernet2	unassigned	NO	unset	initializing	down
FastEthernet3	unassigned	NO	unset	initializing	down
FastEthernet4	unassigned	NO	unset	initializing	down
Vlan1	unassigned	YES	unset	up	down

Step 4 Enter a host name for the router (this example uses THAAR):

Configuring global parameters:

Enter host name [Router]: THAAR

The enable secret is a password used to protect access to privileged EXEC and configuration modes.
This password, after entered, becomes encrypted in the configuration.

Step 5 Enter an enable secret password. This password is encrypted (more secure) and cannot be seen when viewing the configuration:

Enter enable secret: altaiey

The enable password is used when you do not specify an enable secret password, with some older
software versions, and some boot images.

Step 6 Enter an enable password that is different from the enable secret password. This password is not encrypted (less secure) and can be seen when viewing the configuration:

Enter enable password: guess

The setup mode asks to configure two enable passwords. Only the enabled secret password will be used. The enable password is for pre-10.3 IOS routers. However, the password must be configured in the setup mode, and it must be different. It will never be used if the enable secret is configured.

The virtual terminal password is used to protect access to the router over a network interface. If a password for the VTY lines is not set during setup mode, there is no possibility to telnet into a router by default. However, it is possible to configure VTY password later, but it requires the using of a console port.

Step 7 Enter the virtual terminal password, which prevents unauthenticated access to the router through ports other than the console port:

Enter virtual terminal password: altaiey

Step 8 Respond to the following prompts as appropriate for the network. Notice that, the following configuration parts are not part of the C850 router model. It is added to provide a better understanding to the startup configuration mode of the router.

Configure SNMP Network Management? [yes]: enter or no
Community string [public]: enter
Configure LAT? [no]: enter
Configure AppleTalk? [no]: enter
Configure DECnet? [no]: enter
Configure IP? [yes]: enter
Configure IGRP routing? [yes]: n
Configure RIP routing? [no]: enter

Note if you answer **no** to IGRP, you are prompted to configure RIP.

Configure CLNS? [no]: enter
Configure IPX? [no]: enter
Configure Vines? [no]: enter
Configure XNS? [no]: enter
Configure Apollo? [no]: enter
Configure bridging? [no]: enter

Step 9 Configure the ISDN switch-type used by the Basic Rate Interface (BRI) module:

BRI interface needs isdn switch-type to be configured
Valid switch types are :
[0] none..........Only if you don't want to configure BRI.
[1] basic-1tr6....1TR6 switch type for Germany
[2] basic-5ess....AT&T 5ESS switch type for the US/Canada
[3] basic-dms100..Northern DMS-100 switch type for US/Canada
[4] basic-net3....NET3 switch type for UK and Europe
[5] basic-ni......National ISDN switch type
[6] basic-ts013...TS013 switch type for Australia
[7] ntt...........NTT switch type for Japan
[8] vn3...........VN3 and VN4 switch types for France
Choose ISDN BRI Switch Type [2]:

Step 10 Configure the asynchronous serial lines for the integrated modems on the modules installed in the router. (If you want to allow users to dial in through the integrated modems, you must configure the async lines.)

Async lines accept incoming modems calls. If you will have
users dialing in via modems, configure these lines.

Configure Async lines? [yes]: enter
Async line speed [115200]: enter

Note Cisco recommends that you do not change this speed.
Will you be using the modems for inbound dialing? [yes]: enter
Note If your asynchronous interfaces will be using the same basic configuration parameters, Cisco recommends answering yes to the next prompt. That way, you group the modems so that they can be configured as a group. Otherwise, you will need to configure each interface separately.

Would you like to put all async interfaces in a group and configure them all at one time?[yes]: enter

Allow dial-in users to choose a static IP addresses? [no]: enter
Configure for TCP header compression? [yes]: enter
Configure for routing updates on async links? [no]: enter

Enter the starting address of IP local pool? [X.X.X.X]: 172.17.18.1

Note Make sure the starting and ending addresses of the IP pool are in the same subnet.

Enter the ending address of IP local pool? [X.X.X.X]: 172.17.18.254

You can configure a test user to verify that your
dial-up service is working properly
What is the username of the test user? [user]:
What is the password of the test user? [passwd]:
Will you be using the modems for outbound dialing? [no]:

Step 11 Configure the router interfaces including IP addresses. The Configuration shows you how to configure two FastEthernet interfaces on the router.

Do you want to configure FastEthernet 0/0 interface [yes]: enter
Use the 100 Base-TX (RJ-45) connector? [yes]: enter
Operate in full-duplex mode? [no]:y and enter
Configure IP on this interface? [yes]: enter
IP address for this interface: 172.17.17.17
Subnet mask for this interface [255.0.0.0]: 255.255.255.0
Class B network is 172.17.0.0, 8 subnet bits; mask is /24

Do you want to configure FastEthernet 0/1 interface [yes]: enter
Use the 100 Base-TX (RJ-45) connector? [yes]: enter
Operate in full-duplex mode? [no]:y and enter
Configure IP on this interface? [yes]: enter
IP address for this interface: 172.18.18.18
Subnet mask for this interface [255.0.0.0]: 255.255.255.0
Class B network is 172.18.0.0, 8 subnet bits; mask is /24

The mask is displayed as /24, which means 24 out of 32 bits are used.

Completing the Configuration of a CISCO Router

Configuration 4-3, Showing all the configuration parameters: When you have provided all the information prompted for by the **setup** command facility, messages similar to the following appear:

The following configuration command was created:

hostname THAAR

```
enable secret 5 $1$zxxT$YZMzUP1/wQvyLn5cWey/
enable password guess
line vty 0 4
password altaiey
snmp-server community public
!
no appletalk routing
no decnet routing
ip routing
no clns routing
no ipx routing
no vines routing
no xns routing
no apollo routing
no bridge 1
!
line 1 64
speed 115200
flowcontrol hardware
login local
autoselect during-login
autoselect ppp
modem dialin
ip local pool setup_pool 172.17.18.1 172.17.18.254
!
username user password passwd
line 1 64
modem output
transport input all
!
interface FastEthernet0/0
media-type 100BaseX
full-duplex
no shutdown
ip address 172.17.17.17 255.255.255.0
no mop enabled
!
interface FastEthernet0/1
media-type 100BaseX
full-duplex
no shutdown
ip address 172.18.18.18 255.255.255.0
no mop enabled
!
end


[0] Go to the IOS command prompt without saving this config.
[1] Return back to the setup without saving this config.
[2] Save this configuration to nvram and exit.

Enter your selection [2]: 0
```

To complete your router configuration, the following should be implemented:

A **setup** command facility prompt asks if you want to save this configuration. If you select **0**, the configuration information you entered is not saved, and you return to the CLI mode. If you select **1**, the configuration information you entered is not saved, and you return to the CISCO router enable prompt (THAAR#). Type **setup** command to return to the System Configuration dialog. If you select **2**, the configuration is saved in NVRAM, and you are returned to the EXEC prompt (THAAR>).

Command-Line Interface (CLI)

In this section, basic configuration commands from CLI will be described. The CLI is the best way to configure a router. It gives a greatest flexibility when configuring a router. However, it is possible to type several configuration commands into a word processor for later pasting into the router's CLI configuration.

The Switch and Router CLIs

Several features can be configured using the CLI in the same way on both switches and routers. However, some features are configured in different ways.

The following features are using the same configuration commands on both routers and switches:

- Console configuration
- Reaching setup mode either by reloading the router with an empty startup-config or by using the **setup** command
- Telnet, and enable secret password.
- SSH encryption keys and username/password login authentications configurations
- User and Enable (privileged) modes
- Entering and exiting configuration mode, using the **configure terminal**, **end**, and **exit** commands, and the Ctrl-Z key sequence.
- CLI help, command editing, and command recall features
- The host name and interface description configurations
- Ethernet interfaces that can negotiate speed, using the **speed** and **duplex** commands configurations.
- Administratively disabling (**shutdown**) and administratively enabling (**no shutdown**) an interface
- The use of commands like **line console 0** and **interface** to navigate through different configuration mode contexts.
- The meaning and the use of the startup-config (in NVRAM), running-config (in RAM), and external servers (like TFTP)
- The **copy** command to copy the configuration files and IOS images are the same.

The following features are using different configuration commands on routers as compared with switches:

- IP addresses configuration.
- Routers have an auxiliary (Aux) port which can be used to connect the router to an external modem and phone line, so that, remote users can dial into the router, and access the CLI, by making a phone call.
- Questions in setup mode configuration.

Configuration 4-4, Invoking the CLI during the Router startup: The following Configuration shows how CLI is entered during the Router startup by just saying **no** to enter the Initial Configuration Dialog. Then, the router will display the following messages, which indicate the status of all the router interfaces.

> **Would you like to enter the initial configuration dialog? [yes]:n**
> **Would you like to terminate autoinstall? [yes]:return**

Press RETURN to get started!

%LINK-3-UPDOWN: Interface Ethernet0/0, changed state to up
%LINK-3-UPDOWN: Interface Ethernet0/1, changed state to up
%LINK-3-UPDOWN: Interface Serial0/0, changed state to up
%LINK-3-UPDOWN: Interface Serial0/1, changed state to down
%LINK-3-UPDOWN: Interface Serial0/2, changed state to down
%LINK-3-UPDOWN: Interface Serial1/0, changed state to up
%LINK-3-UPDOWN: Interface Serial1/1, changed state to down
%LINK-3-UPDOWN: Interface Serial1/2, changed state to down

<Additional messages are omitted.>

Logging into the router

Configuration 4-5, Logging into the Router: The following Configuration shows the steps that must be followed for logging into a router user mode, then switching to privileged mode, and logging out the router.

Step 1: Press **Return**, after the interface status messages are completed, and enter user mode. Then list all available commands.

```
Return
Router> ?
Exec commands:
  Connect            Open a terminal connection
  Disconnect         Disconnect an existing telnet session
  Enable             Turn on privileged commands
  Exit               Exit from the EXEC
  Help               Description of the interactive help system
  Lock               Lock the terminal
  Login              Log in as a particular user
  logout             Exit from the EXEC
  name-connection    Name an existing telnet connection
  Ping               Send echo messages
  resume             Resume an active telnet connection
  show               Show running system information
  systat             Display information about terminal lines
  telnet             Open a telnet connection
  terminal           Set terminal line parameters
  where              List active telnet connections
Router>
```

The list of commands might vary slightly from this example, depending on the software features set and configurations of your router.

Step 2: log into the privileged mode and then list all available commands.

```
Router>enable
Router#?
Exec commands:
  access-enable      Create a temporary Access-List entry
  access-profile     Apply user-profile to interface
  access-template    Create a temporary Access-List entry
```

bfe	For manual emergency modes setting
clear	Reset functions
clock	Manage the system clock
configure	Enter configuration mode
connect	Open a terminal connection
copy	Copy a config file to or from a tftp server
debug	Debugging functions
disable	Turn off privileged commands
disconnect	Disconnect an existing telnet session
enable	Turn on privileged commands
exit	Exit from the EXEC
help	Description of the interactive help system
llc2	Execute llc2 tests
lock	Lock the terminal
login	Log in as a particular user
logout	Exit from the EXEC
name-connection	Name an existing telnet connection
ping	Send echo messages
reload	Halt and perform a cold restart
resume	Resume an active telnet connection
send	Send a message to other tty lines
setup	Run the SETUP command facility
show	Show running system information
systat	Display information about terminal lines
telnet	Open a telnet connection
terminal	Set terminal line parameters
test	Test subsystems, memory, and interfaces
trace	Trace route to destination
where	List active telnet connections
which-route	Do route table lookup and display results
write	Write running configuration to memory, network, or terminal

The list of commands might vary slightly from this example, depending on the software features set and configurations of your router.

Step 3: log out the privileged mode.

Router#disable
Router>

Step 4: log out the router console.

Router>logout

Router con0 is now available
Press RETURN to get started

Step 5: log out the router from the privileged mode.

Router>en
Router#logout

Router con0 is now available
Press RETURN to get started

It is possible to use the **exit** command instead of using the **logout** command as shown in the following Configuration.

Router>en
Router#exit

Router con0 is now available
Press RETURN to get started

Router Modes of Operation

Configuration 4-6, Operating in different Router modes of operation: The following Configuration shows the steps that must be followed for logging into the router different modes of operation.

Step 1: Enter the Global Configuration Mode from the privileged EXEC mode and list all available commands.

Router#config
Configuration from terminal, memory, or network
[terminal]?return
Enter configuration commands, one per line. End with CNTL/Z
Router(config)# ?

access-list	Add an access list entry
Apollo	Apollo global configuration commands
Appletalk	Appletalk global configuration commands
Arp	Set a static ARP entry
async-bootp	Modify system bootp parameters
autonomous-system	Specify local AS number to which we belong
banner	Define a login banner
boot	Modify system boot parameters
bridge	Transparent bridging
buffers	Adjust system buffer pool parameters
busy-message	Display message when connection to host fails
chat-script	Define a modem chat script
clns	Global CLNS configuration subcommands
clock	Configure time-of-day clock
decent	Global DECnet configuration subcommands
default-value	Default character-bits values
dialer-list	Create a dialer list entry
enable	Modify enable password parameters
end	Exit from configure mode
exit	Exit from configure mode
frame-relay	Global frame relay configuration commands
help	Description of the interactive help system
hostname	Set system's network name
interface	Select an interface to configure
ip	Global IP configuration subcommands
ipx	Novell/IPX global configuration commands
line	Configure a terminal line
lnm	IBM Lan Manager
locaddr-priority-list	Establish queueing priorities based on LU address

logging	Modify message logging facilities
login-string	Define a host-specific login string
mop	The DEC MOP Server
netbios	NETBIOS access control filtering
no	Negate a command or set its defaults
ntp	Configure NTP
priority-list	Build a priority list
queue-list	Build a custom queue list
rif	Source-route RIF cache
route-map	Create route-map or enter route-map command mode
router	Enable a routing process
scheduler-interval	Maximum interval before running lowest priority process
service	Modify use of network based services
smt-queue-threshold	Set the max number of unprocessed SMT frames
snmp-server	Modify SNMP parameters
source-bridge	Source-route bridging ring groups
stun	STUN global configuration commands
tacacs-server	Modify TACACS query parameters
tftp-server	Provide TFTP service for netload requests
tn3270	tn3270 configuration command
username	Establish User Name Authentication
vines	Vines global configuration commands
x25	X.25 Level 3
xns	XNS global configuration commands

Any changes made in the global configuration mode will affect the global configuration, which means it will affect the router as a whole. The **running-config** parameters will be changed in this mode. Notice also that, the list of commands might vary slightly from this example, depending on the software features set and configurations of your router.

Step 2: Enter the global configuration mode from the privileged EXEC mode to change the **running-config** parameters.

Router#config terminal
Router(config)#

The **config t** command can also be used here.

Step 3: Enter the global configuration mode to change the **startup-config** parameters.
Router#config memory
Router(config)#

The **config mem** will change the configuration stored in NVRAM, which is known as a **startup-config**.

Step 4: Enter the global configuration mode to change the router configuration parameters stored on a TFTP host on the network.

Router#config network
Router(config)#

The **config net** command can also be used here.

Actually, for a router to make a change to a configuration, it needs to put the configuration in DRAM. Therefore, when the commands **config mem** or **config net** are issued, the current running-config will be replaced by the config stored in NVRAM or a configuration stored on a TFTP host.

Step 5: Enter the Interface Configuration Mode to configure the fastethernet 0/0 interface.

```
Router(config)#interface ?
    Async              Async interface
    BVI                Bridge-Group Virtual Interface
    Dialer             Dialer interface
    FastEthernet       FastEthernet IEEE 802.3
    Group-Async        Async Group interface
    Lex                Lex interface
    Loopback           Loopback interface
    Multilink          Multilink-group interface
    Null               Null interface
    Port-channel       Ethernet Channel of interfaces
    Tunnel             Tunnel interface
    Virtual-Template   Virtual Template interface
    Virtual-TokenRing  Virtual TokenRing
```

```
Router(config)#interface fastethernet 0/0
Router(config-if)#
```

Step 6: Enter the Subinterface Configuration Mode to configure a virtual (Subinterface) fastethernet 0/0.1 interface.
```
Router(config)#int f0/0.?
   <0-4294967295>    FastEthernet interface number
Router(config)#int f0/0.1
Router(config-subif)#
```

Subinterfaces allow for creating virtual interfaces on a single physical interface within the router. Subinterfaces appear to be distinct physical interfaces to the various networking protocols. For example, Frame Relay networks provide multiple point-to-point links called Permanent Virtual Circuits (PVCs). PVCs can be grouped under separate Subinterfaces that in turn are configured on a single physical interface. In a bridging spanning-tree, each Subinterface is a separate bridge port, and a frame arriving on one Subinterface can be sent out on another Subinterface.

Step 7: Enter the Line Configuration Mode to configure Console 0.

```
Router(config)#line ?
    <0-70>     First Line number
    aux        Auxiliary line
    console    Primary terminal line
    tty        Terminal controller
    vty        Virtual terminal
```

```
Router(config)#line console 0
Router(config-line)#
```

The user mode passwords can be set up in this way. The **line console 0** command is known as a major, or global, command, and any command typed from the (config-line) prompt is known as a subcommand.

Step 8: Enter into the Router Configuration Mode to configure an OSPF protocol.

```
Router(config)#router ?
    bgp          Border Gateway Protocol (BGP)
    egp          Exterior Gateway Protocol (EGP)
    igrp         Interior Gateway Routing Protocol (IGRP)
    isis         ISO IS-IS
    iso-igrp     IGRP for OSI networks
    ospf         Open Shortest Path First (OSPF)
    rip          Routing Information Protocol (RIP)
    static       Static CLNS Routing

Router(config)#router ospf
Router(config-router)#
```

Editing and Help Features

Configuration 4-7, Using the help, and editing facilities: The following Configuration shows the steps that must be followed for helping during Router configuring process. The Configuration will show how CISCO is providing advanced help features.

Feature 1: Use a question mark (**?**) at any EXEC prompt, to see the list of commands available from that prompt.

```
Router(config-line)# ?
Line configuration commands:
```

access-class	Filter connections based on an IP access list
activation-character	Define the activation character
autobaud	Set line to autobaud
autocommand	Automatically execute an EXEC command
autohangup	Automatically hangup when last connection closes
autohost	Automatically connect to a host
cts-required	Require CTS on line
data-character-bits	Size of characters being handled
databits	Set number of data bits per character
disconnect-character	Define the disconnect character
dispatch-character	Define the dispatch character
dispatch-timeout	Set the dispatch timer
editing	Enable command line editing
escape-character	Change the current line's escape character
exec	Start an EXEC process
exec-banner	Enable the display of the EXEC banner
exec-character-bits	Size of characters to the command exec
exec-timeout	Set the EXEC timeout
exit	Exit from line configuration mode
flowcontrol	Set the flow control
help	Description of the interactive help system
history	Enable the command history function
hold-character	Define the hold character
length	Set number of lines on a screen
location	Enter terminal location description
lockable	Allow users to lock a line
login	Enable password checking

modem	Configure the Modem Control Lines
monitor	Copy debug output to the current terminal line
no	Negate a command or restore its defaults
notify	Inform users of output from concurrent sessions
padding	Set padding for a specified output character
parity	Set terminal parity
password	Set a password
private	Configuration options that user can set will remain in effect between terminal sessions
refuse-message	Define a refuse banner
rotary	Add line to a rotary group
rxspeed	Set the receive speed
session-limit	Set maximum number of sessions
session-timeout	Set interval for closing connection when there is no input traffic
special-character-bits	Size of the escape (and other special) characters
speed	Set the transmit and receive speeds
start-character	Define the start character
stop-character	Define the stop character
stopbits	Set async line stop bits
telnet	Telnet protocol-specific configuration
telnet-transparent	Send a CR as a CR followed by a NULL instead of a CR followed by a LF
terminal-type	Set the terminal type
transport	Define transport protocols for line
txspeed	Set the transmit speeds
vacant-message	Define a vacant banner
width	Set width of the display terminal

By default, one page at a time will be displayed. Pressing the **spacebar** will display the next page. Pressing **Return** will display one command at a time. Pressing any other key will quit the list and return to the prompt.

Feature 2: Use a question mark (**?**) at any EXEC prompt to find the commands that start with a certain letter. The letter(s) must be followed by "**?**" with no space between them.

```
Router#c?
clear   clock   configure   connect   copy
Router#c
Router# co?
configure  connect  copy
Router# configure ?
memory    Configure from NV memory
network   Configure from a TFTP network host
terminal  Configure from the terminal
<cr>
```

Feature 3: Use a question mark (**?**) at any EXEC prompt to find the next command in a string. Type the first command and then a question mark "**?**" with a space between them.

```
Router#clock ?
        set    Set the time and date
Router#clock set ?
      hh:mm:ss      current Time
```

Router#clock set 12:50:10 ?
          <1-31>   Day of the month
         MONTH   Month of the year
Router#clock set 12:50:10 15 ?
         MONTH   Month of the year
Router#clock set 12:50:10 15 march ?
     <1993-2035> Year
Router#clock set 12:50:10 15 march 2003 ?
    RETURN
Router#

Here are some of the error messages that can be received from the incorrect typing of the commands:

Router#clock set 12:50:10
% Incomplete command.

Router(config)#access list 190 permit host 194.165.141.82
                       ^

% Invalid input detected at '^' marker.

Router#sh th
% Ambiguous command: "sh th"

It means that not all required commands or values are entered. Use the question mark to find the required command.

Router#sh te?
Word   tech-support   terminal

Table 4-1 shows the list of enhanced editing commands available on a CISCO router.

Table 4-1 Enhanced Editing Commands

Command	Meaning
Ctrl+A	Moves the cursor to the beginning of the line
Ctrl+E	Moves the cursor to the end of the line
Ctrl+R	Redisplays a line
Ctrl+U	Erases a line
Esc+B	Moves back one word
Esc+F	Moves forward one word
Ctrl+W	Erases a word
Ctrl+F	Moves forward one character
Ctrl+B	Moves back one character
Ctrl+D	Deletes a single character to the left of the cursor
Backspace	Deletes a single character to the left of the cursor
Ctrl+Z	Ends configuration mode and returns to EXEC
Tab	Finishes typing a partial command name entry

An additional editing feature: The automatic scrolling of long lines is a feature in the CISCO CLI. When the command typed had reached the right margin, it is automatically moved ten spaces to the left. This is indicated by dollar sign ($), as shown in the following example.

Router(config)#$ 190 permit tcp host 194.165.141.82 0.0.0.0 eq 23

Feature 4: Use the command **show history** to see the **last 10** commands entered on the router.

Router#sh history
     enable
     sh users
     sh history
     sh flash
     sh int e0
     sh int s0
     sh ver
     sh terminal
     sh users
     sh history

Feature 5: Use the command **show terminal** to verify the terminal configuration and its history size.

Router#sh terminal
Line 0, Location: "",Type: ""
....
History is enabled, history size is 10.
Full user help is disable
Allowed transports are lat pad v120 telnet mop rlogin
Nasi. Preferred is lat.
No output characters are padded
No special data dispatching characters
Group codes: 0

Feature 6: Use the **terminal history size** command to change the size of history buffer and verify that the change has been implemented correctly.

Router#terminal history size ?
<0-256>   Size of history buffer

Router# terminal history size 20

Router#sh terminal
Line 0, Location: "",Type: ""
....
History is enabled, history size is 20.
Full user help is disable
Allowed transports are lat pad v120 telnet mop rlogin
Nasi. Preferred is lat.
No output characters are padded
No special data dispatching characters
Group codes: 0

Table 4-2 shows the list of Router history commands that are available on a CISCO router.

Table 4-2 Router History Commands

Command	Meaning
Ctrl+P or UP arrow	It recalls commands in the history buffer in a backward sequence, beginning with the most recent Command. Repeat the key sequence to recall successively older

	commands.
Ctrl+N or down arrow	It returns to more recent commands in the history buffer after recalling commands with Ctrl-P or the Up Arrow. Repeat the key sequence to recall successively more recent commands.
Show history	It shows the last 10 commands entered by default
Show terminal	It shows terminal configurations and history buffer size
Terminal history size	It changes buffer size (max 256)

Gathering Routing Information

Configuration 4-8, Displaying the basic System Configuration Parameters: The following Configuration shows how basic system configuration would be obtained. The command is used to obtain hardware as well as the software version, the names and sources of configuration files, the router uptime, the router configuration register, and the boot images.

Use the **show version** command to list the basic system configuration.

THAAR#sh version
Cisco IOS Software, 2800 Software (C2800NM-ADVIPSERVICESK9-M), Version 12.4(12), RELEASE SOFTWARE (fc1)
Technical Support: http://www.cisco.com/techsupport
Copyright (c) 1986-2009 by Cisco Systems, Inc.
Compiled Fri 17-Nov-06 12:02 by prod_rel_team

ROM: System Bootstrap, Version 12.4(13r)T, RELEASE SOFTWARE (fc1)

THAAR uptime is 13 days, 11 hours, 48 minutes
System returned to ROM by power-on
System image file is "flash:c2800nm-advipservicesk9-mz.124-12.bin"
This product contains cryptographic features and is subject to United States and local country laws governing import, export, transfer and use. Delivery of Cisco cryptographic products does not imply third-party authority to import, export, distribute or use encryption. Importers, exporters, distributors and users are responsible for compliance with U.S. and local country laws. By using this product you agree to comply with applicable laws and regulations. If you are unable to comply with U.S. and local laws, return this product immediately.

A summary of U.S. laws governing Cisco cryptographic products may be found at:
http://www.cisco.com/wwl/export/crypto/tool/stqrg.html

If you require further assistance please contact us by sending email to export@cisco.com.

Cisco 2811 (revision 53.50) with 249856K/12288K bytes of memory.
Processor board ID FTX1107A6BB
2 FastEthernet interfaces
2 Serial(sync/async) interfaces
1 Virtual Private Network (VPN) Module
DRAM configuration is 64 bits wide with parity enabled.
239K bytes of non-volatile configuration memory.
62720K bytes of ATA CompactFlash (Read/Write)
Configuration register is 0x2102

THAAR#

The **show version** command provides the following information: how long the Router has been running, how it was restarted, the IOS filename running, the model hardware and processor versions, the amount of DRAM, and the configuration register value. The following is a list of all valuable information that can be provided by **sh ver** command.

- The IOS version
- The IOS filename running
- The model hardware and processor versions
- The number and types of interfaces
- The uptime
- The time of the last loading of IOS (if the router's clock has been set)
- The amount of RAM memory
- The amount of NVRAM memory
- The amount of Flash memory
- The reason for the last reload of IOS (**reload** command, power OFF/ON, software failure).
- The source from which the router loaded the current IOS
- The configuration register's current and future value (if different)

Setting the System Passwords

Five types of passwords can be used to secure the CISCO Router:

- Enable Password.
- Enable secret password.
- Console password.
- Auxiliary password.
- Telnet password.

Enable and enable secret passwords are used to secure the Router privileged mode. Enable and enable secret passwords are used when the **enable** command is issued. Console, auxiliary and telnet passwords are activated when the user mode is accessed.

Enable Passwords

Configuration 4-9, Setting the enabled passwords: The following Configuration shows how enable, and enable secret passwords are set up on a Router.

Router(config)#enable ?
    last-resort   Define enable action if no TACACS servers respond
    password   Assign the privileged level password
    secret   Assign the privileged level secret
    use-tacacs   Use TACACS to check enable passwords

Router(config)#enable secret altaiey
Router(config)#enable password altaiey
The enable password you have chosen is the same as your enable secret. This is not recommended. Re-enter the enable password.

Router(config)#enable password thaar

The following options are available by the **enable** command:

Last-resort: It is used when an authentication through a tacacs server is set up and the server is not available. By this option, the administrator will still have the opportunity to enter the Router. If the tacacs server is working, this option is not used.

Password: It is used to set the enable password on older, pre 10.3 systems. However, it is not used if an enable secret password is set.

Secret: It is the newer, encrypted enable password. It will override the enable password if set.

Use-tacacs: This option tells the Router to authenticate through a tacacs server. The tacacs server is used to manage the authentication for too many (hundreds) routers. Therefore, you can only change the password once for hundreds of routers.

User-Mode Passwords

Configuration 4-10, Setting up the user-mode passwords: The following Configuration shows how the user-mode passwords are set up on the Router.

Step 1: Use the command **line ?** to list the user-mode available lines. To configure the user-mode passwords, the required line should be configured at first, and then the **login** or **no login** command must be issued to tell the Router whether to prompt for authentication or not.

```
Router(config)#line ?
  <0-4>       First Line number
  aux         Auxiliary line
  console     Primary terminal line
  vty         Virtual terminal
```

The following options are available by the **line** command:

Aux It is used to set the user-mode password for the auxiliary port.

Console It is used to set a console user-mode password.

Vty It is used to set a Telnet password on the Router. By default, Telnet utility cannot be used, if this password is not set.

Step 2: Use the command **line aux** to configure the auxiliary line password.

```
Router(config)#line aux ?
  <0-0>     First Line number
Router(config)#line aux 0
Router(config-line)#login
Router(config-line)#password thaar
```

The **0-0** means that there is only one port. The **login** command must be entered or the auxiliary port will not prompt for authentication.

Step 3: Use the command **line console** to configure the console line password.

```
Router(config)#line console ?
  <0-0>     First Line number
Router(config)#line console 0
Router(config-line)#login
Router(config-line)#password thaarm
```

The following is important commands for the console port.

Exec-timeout 0 0 command sets the timeout for the console EXEC session to zero, or to never time out. It is used to set the interval that the EXEC command interpreter waits until user input is detected. Use the **no** form of this command to remove the timeout definition. The default value is 10 minutes. If no input is detected, the EXEC facility resumes the current connection, or if no connections exist, it returns the terminal to the idle state and disconnects the incoming session. It is the same as entering **exec-timeout 0**.

Logging synchronous command stops console messages from popping up and disrupting your input. This makes reading your input messages much easier. It should be a default command. This command can also be used for the auxiliary port line and virtual terminal line.

The following is an example of how to configure these commands.

```
Router(config)#line console 0
Router(config-line)#exec-timeout ?
  <0-35791>      Timeout in minutes
Router(config-line)# exec-timeout 0 ?
  <0-2147483>  Timeout in seconds
Router(config-line)# exec-timeout 0 0
Router(config-line)#logging synchronous
```

Step 4: Use the command **line vty** to set the user-mode password for Telnet access into the Router. Configure a Telnet password for 0-100 lines.

```
Router(config)#line vty 0 ?
  <0-197>     First Line number
  <cr>
Router(config)#line vty 0 100
Router(config-line)#login
Router(config-line)#password thaarmj
```

Routers that are not using the Enterprise edition of the CISCO IOS have five VTY lines, by default, 0 through 4. However, more vty lines are available with the enterprise edition. After the Router is configured with an IP address, Telnet program can be used to configure and check the Router instead of having to use a console cable. When telnet into a Router that does not have a VTY password set, an error message is received stating that the connection is refused because the password is not set. However, the Router can be configured to allow Telnet connections without a password by using the **no login** command.

```
Router(config-line)#line vty 0 100
Router(config-line)#no login
```

Step 5: Use the command **show running-config** to see the configured passwords. The command will show that only enable secret password is encrypted by default. However, user-mode and enable passwords can manually be encrypted.

```
Router#sh run
```

```
!
enable secret 5 $1$zxxT$YZMzUP1/wQvyLn5cWey/
enable password thaar
!
line vty 0 4
password thaarmj
login
line vty 5 100
password thaarmj
```

```
login
line con 0
password thaarm
login
line aux 0
password thaar
login
!
line con 0
exec-timeout 0 0
!
end
```

Step 6: Use the command **service password-encryption** to encrypt the enable and user-mode configured passwords. To check if these passwords are encrypted or not, again, use the **sh run** command for this purpose.

```
Router(config)#service password-encryption
Router(config)#enable password thaar
Router(config)#line vty 0 100
Router(config-line)#login
Router(config-line)#password thaarmj
Router(config-line)#line con 0
Router(config-line)#login
Router(config-line)#password thaarm
Router(config-line)#line aux 0
Router(config-line)#login
Router(config-line)#password thaar
Router(config-line)#exit
Router(config)#no service password-encryption
Router(config)#^Z
```

```
Router#sh run
```

```
!
enable secret 5 $1$zxxT$YZMzUP1/wQvyLn5cWey/
enable password 7 070220464b0c1d
!
line vty 0 4
password 7 01070e055a190b05
login
line vty 5 100
password 7 01070e055a190b05
login
line con 0
password 7 01070e055a190b
login
line aux 0
password 7 01070e055a19
login
!
line con 0
exec-timeout 0 0
!
```

end

Banner

Configuration 4-11, Configuring Banners on the Router: The following Configuration shows how the **banner** command is used. A banner gives the users and administrators pre-configured messages when they log into the Router. A banner can also be used to add a security notice to users dialing into the internetwork.

Step 1: List all available banner commands.

```
Router(config)#banner ?
    LINE           c  banner-text  c, where 'c' is a delimiting character
    exec           set EXEC process creation banner
    incoming       set incoming terminal line banner
    login          set login banner
    motd           set        Message Of The Day banner
```

Four different banners are available:
Exec banner: A line-activation (exec) banner can be configured to display when an EXEC process (such as incoming connection to a VTY line) is created.
Incoming banner: This banner is configured to be displayed on terminals connected to reverse Telnet lines. Users, who use reverse Telnet, can see the useful instructions created by this banner.
Login banner: A login banner is configured to be displayed on all connected terminals. When this banner is configured with other banners, it will be displayed after the MOTD banner but before the login prompts. The login banner can only be disabled globally using the **no banner login** command, which can be used to delete this banner. Therefore, this banner cannot be disabled on a per-line basis.
Motd banner: This banner is widely used and provides a message to every-person dialing in or connecting to the Router via Telnet, auxiliary port, or console port.

Step 2: Configure a Motd banner on the Router.

```
Router(config)#banner motd ?
        LINE          c  banner-text  c, where 'c' is a delimiting character
Router(config)#banner motd #
        Enter TEXT message. End with the character '#'.
        Building power will be off from 6:00 AM until 8:00 AM this coming Friday.          <cr>
        # <cr>
Router(config)#^Z
Router#
        13:55:54: %SYS-CONFIG_I: Configured from console by console
Router#exit
        Router con0 is now available

        Press RETURN to get started.
        Building power will be off from 6:00 AM until 8:00 AM this coming Friday.

Router>
```

The above MOTD banner tells anyone connecting to the Router that building power will be off from 6:00 AM until 8:00 AM this coming Friday. The delimiting character can be any character of your choice --a pound sign (#) for example. It tells the Router when the message is done. The delimiting character must not be used in the message. Once the message is completed, the **Return** key must be pressed, then the **delimiting character**, then the **Return** key again. MOTD will still work, if the previous sequence is not implemented correctly, but if there is more than one banner, it will combine them as one message and put them on one line.

Router Interfaces

Configuration 4-12, Configuring the Router Interfaces: The following Configuration shows how Router interfaces are configured. Interface configuration is one of the most important issues of the Router configurations. Without interfaces, the Router is useless. Interface configurations must be accurate to communicate with other devices in the internetwork. Configure an interface includes setting parameters such as, Network Layer address (IP address), Subnet mask, Media-type, Bandwidth, Clock rate, and other administrator commands. However, not all routers use the same methods to configure interfaces.

Step 1: lists all available interfaces on the Router and invoke the interface configuration mode.

```
Router(config)#interface ?
  Async            Async interface
  BVI              Bridge-Group Virtual Interface
  CTunnel          CTunnel Interface
  Dialer           Dialer interface
  FastEthernet     FastEthernet IEEE 802.3
  Group-Async      Async Group interface
  Lex              Lex interface
  Loopback         Loopback interface
  MFR              Multilink Frame Relay bundle interface
  Multilink        Multilink-group interface
  Null             Null interface
  Serial           Serial
  Tunnel           Tunnel interface
  Vif              PGM Multicast Host interface
  Virtual-Template Virtual Template interface
  Virtual-TokenRing Virtual TokenRing
  range            interface range command
Router(config)#interface fastethernet 0/0
Router(config-if)#
```

Step 2: lists all available Ethernet ports on 2522 Router, and then invoke an Ethernet port.

```
Router(config)#int ethernet ?
<0-0>   Ethernet interface number
Router(config)#int ethernet 0
Router(config-if)#
```

The 2500 Router is a fixed configuration Router, which means that when the model of the Router is brought, it is restricted with that configuration. To configure an interface, the **interface type interface_number** sequence is always used. However, some Router series use a physical slot in the Router and a port number on the module plugged into that slot.

Step 3: lists all available FastEthernet ports on 2600 Router then invoke a port on that Router.

```
Router(config)#int fastethernet ?
<0-1>      FastEthernet interface number
Router(config)#int fastethernet 0?
/
```

Router(config)#int fastethernet 0/?
<0-1>   FastEthernet interface number
Router(config)# int fastethernet 0/0
Router(config-if)#

To configure an interface on such routers, the interface must be configured using the following syntax: **interface type slot_number/port_number**.

If you try to configure the FastEthernet ports on 2600 Router using **interface type number** syntax an error message is received.

Router(config)#int fastethernet 0
 % Incomplete command.

Step 4: Set the type of connector for the FastEthernet ports on 2600 Router.

Router(config)#int fa 0/0
Router(config-if)#media-type ?
 100BaseX   Use RJ45   for -TX; SC F0 for -FX
 MII   Use MII connector

Router(config-if)#media-type 100BaseX

The above step shows how to configure a media-type 100BaseX for a fastethernet interface. However, this is typically auto-detected.

Step 5: Bring the Ethernet interface UP using **no shutdown** command. Before bring it UP, check its status.

Router#sh int e0
Ethernet0 is administratively down, line protocol is down
<cr>
Router#config t
Enter configuration commands, one per line. End with CNTL/Z.
Router(config)#int e0
Router(config-if)#no shutdown
Router(config-if)#^Z
12:57:09: %LINK-3-UPDOWN: Line protocol Ethernet0, changed state to up
12:57:10: %LINEPROTO-5-UPDOWN: Line protocol on Interface Ethernet0, changed state to up
Router#sh int e0
Ethernet0 is up, line protocol is up

All interfaces are shut down by default. The status of an interface can be displayed using **show interface** and **show running-config** commands. The **no shutdown** command brings the interface UP and the **shutdown** command brings it OFF.

Step 6: Configure an IP address on an Ethernet interface using the **ip address** command from interface configuration mode.

Router(config)#int e0
Router(config-if)#ip address 172.17.17.17 255.255.255.0
Router(config-if)#no shut

IP is typically used on all routers. If another IP address is typed on the same interface and an **Enter** key is pressed, the new IP address and subnet mask will replace the old setting. However, a secondary IP address can be defined on the same interface.

Step 7: Configure the same Ethernet interface on a second subnet using the **ip address ... secondary** command and verify the new setting.

```
Router(config)#int e0
Router(config-if)#ip address 172.17.18.18 255.255.255.0 secondary
Router(config-if)# exit
Router(config)#^Z
Router#sh run
Building configuration...
Current configuration:
   .....
!
   interface Ethernet0
   ip address 172.17.18.18 255.255.255.0 secondary
   ip address 172.17.17.17 255.255.255.0
!
```

Step 8: Configure an Ethernet interface on VIP (Versatile Interface Processor) Card for 7000 series router using the **interface type slot/port adapter/port number** command.

```
Router7000(config)#int ethernet 1/0/0
```

To configure an interface on 7000 or 7500 series router with VIP (Versatile Interface Processor) cards, the **interface type slot/port adapter/port number** command must be used as shown above.

Step 9: lists all available serial ports on 2522 Router using the **int serial ?** command.

```
Router(config)#int serial ?
 <0-9>      serial interface number
Router(config)#int serial 1
Router(config-if)#
```

Step 10: configure a DCE (Data Communication Equipment) serial interface clocking with the **clock rate** command.

```
Router(config)#int s0
Router(config-if)#clock rate ?
Speed (bits per second)
1200
2400
4800
9600
19200
38400
56000
64000
72000
125000
148000
250000
```

500000
800000
1000000
1300000
2000000
4000000
8000000

<300-8000000>   Choose clock rate from list above

Router(config-if)#clock rate 32000
%Error: This command applies only to DCE interfaces
Router(config-if)#int s1
Router(config-if)#clock rate 32000

To configure the clock rate for the hardware connections on serial interfaces such as network interface modules (NIMs) and interface processors to an acceptable bit rate, use the **clock rate** interface configuration command. Notice also that the **clock rate** command is in the bits per second. Use the **no** form of this command to remove the clock rate if you change the interface from a DCE to a DTE device. Using the **no** form of this command on a DCE interface sets the clock rate to the hardware-dependent default value.

Router(config)#int s5/0
Router(config-if)#clock rate 1234567
%Clockrate rounded to nearest value that your hardware can support.
%Use Exec Command 'show running-config' to see the value rounded to.

Router# show running-config
Building configuration...
...
!
interface Serial5/0
no ip address
clockrate 1151526
!
...

Step 11: Configure the bandwidth of a serial interface with the **bandwidth** command.

Router(config-if)#bandwidth ?
  <1-10000000>   Bandwidth in kilobits
Router(config-if)#bandwidth 128

Every CISCO Routers are shipped with a default serial link bandwidth of a T1, or 1.544Mbps. The bandwidth of a serial link is used by routing protocols such as EIGRP, and OSPF to calculate the best cost to a remote network, and it has no effect on the data transfer over the serial link. The bandwidth setting of a serial link that using RIP routing is irrelevant.

Setting the Router Hostnames

Configuration 4-13, Naming the Router: The following Configuration shows how Router hostnames are configured using **the** hostname command.

Router#config t

```
Enter configuration commands, one per line. End with CNTL/Z.
Router(config)#hostname thaar
thaar(config)#hostname world
world(config)#^Z
world#
```

The hostname is only locally significant on the Router, which means it has no effect on how the Router performs name resolution lookups on the internetwork.

Setting the Router interface Descriptions

Configuration 4-14, Defining Router's Descriptions: The following Configuration shows how Router descriptions are configured using the **description** command.

```
Router#config t
Enter configuration commands, one per line. End with CNTL/Z.
Router(config)#int e0
Router(config-if)#description Training LAN
Router(config-if)int s0
Router(config-if)#description WAN to Internet connection
circuit:9999abc11
```

The description is only locally significant on the Router, which means it is not appeared on the internetwork. Setting descriptions on an interface is very helpful to the administrator.

```
Router#sh run
.......
 Interface Ethernet0
 description Training LAN
 ip address 172.17.17.17 255.255.255.0
 no ip directed-broadcast
 !
 Interface serial0
 description WAN to Internet connection circuit:9999abc11
 ip address 212.77.200.77 255.255.255.252
 no ip directed-broadcast
 no ip mroute-cache
 !
Router#sh int e0
Ethernet0 is up, line protocol is up
Hardware is Lance, address is 0001.754b.2555 (bia 00B0.644b.2555)
description Training LAN
......
Router#sh int s0
Serial0 is up, line protocol is up
Hardware is HD64570
description WAN to Internet connection circuit:9999abc11
.......
Router#
```

The previous sections focus on the CISCO router configurations. Commands that used for setting passwords, banner, interfaces and hostnames are identical with CISCO switches as well.

Viewing and Saving Configurations

Configuration 4-15, Displaying, and checking the router configuration: The following Configuration shows how Router configurations are viewed and saved.

Step 1: Manually save the running configuration in DRAM to startup configuration in NVRAM using the **copy run start** command.

```
Router#copy running-config startup-config
Destination filename [startup-config]?return
Warning: Attempting to overwrite an NVRAM configuration previously written by a different version of
the system image.
Overwrite the previous NVRAM configuration?[confirm]return
Building configuration....
......
[OK]
Router#
```

The message stated that there is an attempt to write over the older startup-config. The IOS had been just upgraded to the new version, and the last line indicates that the file was saved and the old version was running. The copying process takes about 2 to 3 minutes and when the process is completed, the OK message will appear.

Step 2: list the system startup configuration using the **show startup-config** command.

```
Router# show start
Using 419 out of 32762 bytes
!
version 12.0
service udp-small-servers
service tcp-small-servers
!
hostname Router
!
!
!
interface Ethernet0
 no ip address
 shutdown
!
interface Serial0
 no ip address
 shutdown
 no fair-queue
!
no ip classless
!
!
line con 0
line 1 8
line aux 0
line vty 0 4
 login
```

```
!
end
```

This command shows the configuration that will be used the next time the Router is reloaded. It presents the amount of NVRAM, which is used to store the startup-config file.

Step 3: list the system running configuration using the **show running-config** command.

```
Router# show run
Building configuration  ...
Current configuration:
!
version 12.0
service udp-small-servers
service tcp-small-servers
!
hostname Router
!
!
!
interface Ethernet0
 no ip address
 shutdown
!
interface Serial0
 no ip address
 shutdown
 no fair-queue
!
no ip classless
!
!
line con 0
line 1 8
line aux 0
line vty 0 4
 login
!
end
```

This command shows the current configuration of the Router.

Step 4: Delete the system startup configuration using the **erase startup-config** command.

```
Router# erase startup-config
Erasing the nvram filesystem will remove all files! Continue?[confirm]Enter
.....
[OK]
Erase of nvram: complete
Router#sh start
%% Non-volatile configuration memory is not present
Router#
```

If the startup configuration is deleted, the **sh start** command will give an error message as shown above.

Verifying the Router Configuration

Configuration 4-16, Checking the Router Configuration: The following Configuration shows how the Router configurations are checked and verified. It is strongly recommended to follow the steps below in the same order.

Step 1: Display the system hardware configuration using the **show version** command.

Router#sh ver
....

Step 2: Verify the Router configuration using **show running-config** and **show startup-config** commands.

Router#sh run
......
Router#sh start

The **sh run** command is the best way to verify the current configuration. The **sh start** command is the best way to verify the configuration that will be used the next time the Router is reloaded.

Step 3: Find the network layer addresses for the neighbor routers using the **show cdp nei detail** command. Other verifying utilities will use the discovered addresses.

Router#sh cdp nei detail
Device ID: device.cisco.com
Entry address(es):
  IP address: 198.92.68.18
  CLNS address: 490001.1111.1111.1111.00
  DECnet address: 10.1
Platform: AGS, Capabilities: Router Trans-Bridge
Interface: Ethernet0, Port ID (outgoing port): Ethernet0
Holdtime : 143 sec
....

The obtained network layer addresses will be used with the **ping** and **Telnet** utilities.

Step 4: Check the basic network connectivity using the **ping** command.

Router#ping ?
WORD   Ping destination address or hostname
appletalk   Appletalk echo
decnet   DECnet echo
ip   IP echo
ipx   Novell/IPX echo
<cr>

Router# ping
Protocol [ip]:
Target IP address: 198.92.68.18
Repeat count [5]:
Datagram size [100]:
Timeout in seconds [2]:

Extended commands [n]:
Sweep range of sizes [n]:
Type escape sequence to abort.
Sending 5, 100-byte ICMP Echos to 198.92.68.18, timeout is 2 seconds:
!!!!!
Success rate is 100 percent, round-trip min/avg/max = 1/2/4 ms

Clearly, different protocols can be used with the ping utility. Ping can be used from user configuration mode (user-level ping) and it can be used from privileged configuration mode (privileged ping). The Configuration above shows the using of an extended ping utility.

Step 5: Discover the path a packet takes as it traverses an internetwork using the **trace** utility.

Router#trace ?
WORD   Trace route to destination address or hostname
appletalk   Appletalk trace
clns   ISO CLNS Trace
ip   IP Trace
<cr>

Step 6: Test the network connectivity using the **Telnet** utility.

Router#telnet ?
WORD   IP address or hostname of a remote system
<cr>
Router#198.92.68.18
Trying 198.92.68.18 … Open

User Access Verification

Password:

Telnet is the best testing utility, since it uses IP at the Network layer and TCP at the Transport layer to create a session with a remote host. If Telnet session is established with another device, the IP connectivity must be good. It is possible to telnet only to IP addresses. However, any TCP/IP hosts' names can be used, instead of IP addresses. It is also possible to telnet from the Router prompts or from any hosts OSs. From the Router prompt, there is no need to type telnet; just type a hostname or IP address, and the Router will assume that the Telnet utility is required.

Step 7: Verify the network configuration using the **show interface** command.

Router#sh int ?
Ethernet   IEEE 802.3
Null   Null interface
Serial   Serial
Accounting   Show interface accounting
<cr>

Router# show interface-e0/0
Ethernet0/0 is up, line protocol is up
    Hardware is QUICC Ethernet, address is 00B0.6401.0249 (bia 0800.3e01.0249)
    Internet address is 172.16.72.1
    MTU 1500 bytes, BW 10000 Kbit, DLY 1000 usec, rely 255/255, load 1/255

Encapsulation ARPA, loopback not set, keepalive set (10 sec)
ARP type: ARPA, ARP Timeout 04:00:00
Last input 00:00:00, output 00:00:00, output hang never
Last clearing of "show interface" counters never
Queueing strategy: fifo
Output queue 0/40, 0 drops; input queue 0/75, 0 drops
5 minute input rate 0 bits/sec, 0 packets/sec
5 minute output rate 0 bits/sec, 0 packets/sec
28816 packets input, 12153458 bytes, 0 no buffer
Received 28783 broadcasts, 0 runts, 0 giants
0 input errors, 0 CRC, 0 frame, 0 overrun, 0 ignored, 0 abort
0 input packets with dribble condition detected
1237 packets output, 146472 bytes, 0 underruns
0 output errors, 101 collisions, 2 interface resets
0 babbles, 0 late collision, 49 deferred
0 lost carrier, 0 no carrier
0 output buffer failures, 0 output buffers swapped out

The last command shows the hardware address, IP address, encapsulation methods, and statistics on collisions for ethernet 0/0 interface. The output of the line and data-link protocol status represents the most important status that can be obtained from the show interface command.

Interface Status Codes

Two *interface status codes* are used to indicate the interface status as shown in Table 4-3. Both status codes on the interface must be in an "up" state for a functioning router interface. The first status code refers essentially to whether Layer 1 is functioning, and the second status code mainly refers to whether the data link layer protocol is working.

Table 4-3 Interface Status Codes

Status Name	Meaning
First status Code (Line status)	It indicates a Layer 1 status. If the cable is correctly cabled, if it is the right type cable, and if the device on the other end is powered ON, this status shows UP.
Second status code (Protocol status)	Generally, it indicates a Layer 2 status. It is always DOWN if the line status is DOWN. A mismatched data link layer configuration causes a protocol status of DOWN even if the line status is UP.

When troubleshooting a network, four interface status combinations can be faced as shown in Table 4-4.

Table 4-4 Interface Status Codes: Typical Combinations

Line and Protocol Status	Reasons
Administratively down, down	A **shutdown** command has been configured on the interface.
down, down	A **no shutdown** command has been configured on the interface, but the physical layer has a problem, such as no cable has been attached to the interface. On Ethernet, the switch interface on the other end of the cable maybe shut down, or the switch is not working.
up, down	Data link layer problems have been presented; it most often means incorrect configuration problems. For example, on a point-to-point serial links, one router is

	configured as PPP and the other is configured as HDLC.
up, up	The interface is functioning well.

Router#sh int e0
Ethernet0 is up, line protocol is up

The first parameter refers to the Physical layer and is UP when it receives a signal. The second parameter refers to the Data Link layer and looks for keepalives from the connecting end. If Ethernet 0 is UP, line protocol is UP, the interface is UP and running.

Router#sh int s0
Serial0 is up, line protocol is down

When the line is UP and the protocol is DOWN, maybe there is a clocking (keeplive) or framing problem. To solve this problem, check the keepalives on both ends and make sure they match; the clock rate is set, if needed; and the encapsulation type is the same on both sides.

Router#sh int s0
Serial0 is down, line protocol is down

When the line interface and protocol are DOWN, maybe there is a cable or interface problem. In addition, if one end is administratively shut down, then the remote end would show down and down. The **no shutdown** command will recover this problem.

Router#sh int s0
Serial0 is administratively down, line protocol is down.

Other useful commands that can be used to verify the interfaces status are as follows, assuming Router 1841 in this case.

Router #show ip interface brief

Interface	IP-Address	OK?	Method	Status	Protocol
FastEthernet0/0	172.17.17.20	YES	unset	up	up
FastEthernet0/1	unassigned	YES	unset	administratively down	down
Serial0/0/0	10.0.0.1	YES	unset	up	up
Serial0/0/1	unassigned	YES	unset	up	up
Serial0/1/0	unassigned	YES	unset	up	up
Serial0/1/1	unassigned	YES	unset	administratively down	down

Router #show protocols fa0/0
FastEthernet0/0 is up, line protocol is up

Step 8: Verify the configuration of the serial interface s0 using the **show interface** command, and then clear its counter using **the clear counters** command.

Router#sh int s0
 Serial0 is up, line protocol is down
 Hardware is MCI Serial
 Internet address is 131.108.174.48, subnet mask is 255.255.255.0
 MTU 1500 bytes, BW 1544 Kbit, DLY 20000 usec, rely 246/255, load 1/255
 Encapsulation FRAME-RELAY, loopback not set, keepalive set (10 sec)
 LMI enq sent 2, LMI stat recvd 0, LMI upd recvd 0, DTE LMI down
 LMI enq recvd 266, LMI stat sent 264, LMI upd sent 0

LMI DLCI 1023 LMI type is CISCO frame relay DTE
Last input 0:00:04, output 0:00:02, output hang never
Last clearing of "show interface" counters 0:44:32
Output queue 0/40, 0 drops; input queue 0/75, 0 drops
Five minute input rate 0 bits/sec, 0 packets/sec
Five minute output rate 0 bits/sec, 0 packets/sec
  307 packets input, 6615 bytes, 0 no buffer
  Received 0 broadcasts, 0 runts, 0 giants
  0 input errors, 0 CRC, 0 frame, 0 overrun, 0 ignored, 0 abort
  0 input packets with dribble condition detected
  266 packets output, 3810 bytes, 0 underruns
  0 output errors, 0 collisions, 2 interface resets, 0 restarts
  178 carrier transitions

The above command demonstrates the serial line s0 and the Maximum Transmission Unit (MTU), which is 1500 bytes by default. The command also shows the default T1 bandwidth (B/W) on all CISCO serial links: 1.544Mbps. Keepalive is also obtained by this command, which is 10 seconds by default. Each Router sends a keepalive message to its neighbor every 10 seconds. Both connected routers must be configured for the same keepalive time, or the internetwork will not work.

Router#clear counter ?
Ethernet   IEEE 802.3
Null   Null interface
Serial   Serial
<cr>

Router#clear counters s0
Clear "show interface" counters on this interface [confirm]return
Router#
01:15:55: %CLEAR-5-COUNTERS: Clear counter on interface Serial0 by console
Router#

Step 9: Verify the interface physical configuration using the **show controllers** command.

Router# show controllers fastethernet 0
DEC21140
Setup Frame
(0) 00e0.1e3e.c125
(1) 0100.0ccc.cccc
dec21140_ds=0x606A0078, registers=0x3C210000, ib=0x4002F75C, ring entries=128
rxring=0x4002F844, rxr shadow=0x606F5168, rx_head=47, rx_tail=47
txring=0x4003006C, txr shadow=0x606F5388, tx_head=63, tx_tail=63, tx_count=0
tx_size=128, rx_size=128
PHY link up
Duplex mode sensed by auto-negotiation is half-duplex and
Fast Ethernet speed is 100 Mbps.

Router#sh controllers s 0
HD unit 0, idb = 0x1229E4, driver structure at 0x127E70
buffer size 1524 HD unit 0, V.35 DTE cable
cpb = 0xE2, eda = 0x4140, cda = 0x4000

Router#sh controllers s 1
HD unit 1, idb = 0x12C174, driver structure at 0x131600
buffer size 1524 HD unit 1, V.35 DCE cable
 cpb = 0xE3, eda = 0x2940, cda = 0x2800

The above command gives the type of cable plugged into a port. For serial interfaces, this will typically only be a DTE cable, which then plugs into a type of DSU. Since Serial 1 has a DCE cable, it would have to provide clocking and must be configured by the clock rate command. Serial 0 has a DTE cable, so it would get its clocking from the DSU.

Router#sh controllers s0
                              ^

% Invalid input detected at '^' marker.

This is the only command that needs to have a space after the interface type.

Summary

In this chapter, a strong foundation for Internetwork Operating System is presented. The information presented in this chapter is essential for all CISCO network engineers. The IOS consists of a number of commands and utilities, such as setup, ping, Telnet, trace, show ...etc. These commands and utilities are designed to serve all network operations. Several configurations are used to clarify the ideas behind this chapter. The following topics are covered:

- Logging into a Router
- Performing editing and help features
- Establishing hostnames
- Setting enabled (or privileged mode) passwords.
- Setting virtual terminal passwords
- Enabling interface configurations
- Gathering Router information
- Viewing, saving and verifying Router configurations

At the end of the chapter, several learning questions are given to evaluate the learning level from this chapter. The correct answers and solutions with complementary discussions are found in appendix A, "Answers to Chapters Learning Questions."

Chapter Four Commands Reference

Table 4-5 lists and briefly describes all the new commands and keys that are used in this chapter.

Table 4-5 Chapter 4 Commands Reference

Command	Description
Router> ?	Lists all the available commands
Router>enable	Logs into the privileged mode
Router#disable	Logs out the privileged mode
Router>logout	Logs out the router console
Router#logout	Logs out the router from privileged mode
Router#exit	Logs out the router from privileged mode
Router#config then return	Enters into the Global Configuration Mode from the privileged EXEC mode
Router#config terminal OR config t	Enters into the Global Configuration Mode from the privileged EXEC mode
Router#config memory OR config mem	Enters into the global configuration mode to change the startup-config parameters
Router#config network OR config net	Enters into the global configuration mode to change the router configuration parameters stored on a TFTP host on the network
Router(config)#interface ?	Lists all the available types of the interfaces
Router(config)#interface fastethernet 0/0	Enters into the Interface Configuration Mode to configure fastethernet 0/0 interface
Router(config)#int f0/0.1	Enters into the Subinterface Configuration Mode to configure a virtual (Subinterface) fastethernet 0/0.1 interface
Router(config)#line console 0	Enters into the Line Configuration Mode to configure Console 0
Router(config)#router ospf	Enters into the Router Configuration Mode to configure an OSPF protocol
Router#c?	Finds commands that start with a certain letter (ex. c here). The letter(s) must be followed by ? with no space between them
Router#clock ?	Finds the next command in a string (ex. clock here). Type the first command and then a question mark?, with space between them
Router#sh history	Sees the last 10 commands entered on the router
Router#sh terminal	Verifies the terminal configuration and its history size
Router# terminal history size 20	Changes the size of history buffer to 20
Ctrl+A	Moves the cursor to the beginning of the line
Ctrl+E	Moves the cursor to the end of the line
Ctrl+R	Redisplays a line
Ctrl+U	Erases a line
Esc+B	Moves back one word
Esc+F	Moves forward one word
Ctrl+W	Erases a word
Ctrl+F	Moves forward one character
Ctrl+B	Moves back one character
Ctrl+D	Deletes a single character
Backspace	Deletes a single character
Ctrl+Z	Ends configuration mode and returns to EXEC

Tab	Finishes typing a command
Ctrl+P or UP arrow	Recalls commands in the history buffer in a backward sequence, beginning with the most recent Command. Repeat the key sequence to recall successively older commands.
Ctrl+N or down arrow	Returns to more recent commands in the history buffer after recalling commands with Ctrl-P or the Up Arrow. Repeat the key sequence to recall successively more recent commands.
Router#sh version	Obtains the hardware as well as the software version, the names and sources of configuration files, and the boot images
Router(config)#enable secret altaiey	Sets up the enable secret password on the Router to altaiey
Router(config)#enable password thaar	Sets up the enable password on the Router to thaar
Router(config)#line aux 0	Configures the auxiliary line 0
Router(config-line)#login Router(config-line)#password thaar	Configures the auxiliary line 0 password to thaar
Router(config)#line console 0	Configures the console line 0
Router(config-line)# exec-timeout 0 0	Sets the timeout for the console EXEC session to zero, or to never time out
Router(config-line)#logging synchronous	Stops the console messages from popping up and disrupting your input
Router(config)#line vty 0 4	Enters into the virtual terminal mode (Telnet access) into the Router
Router#sh run	Sees the router configuration
Router(config)#service password-encryption	Encrypts the enable and user-mode configured passwords
Router(config)#no service password-encryption	Stops encrypting the enable and user-mode configured passwords
Router(config)#banner motd #	Starts typing the motd message
Router(config-if)#media-type 100BaseX	Configures a media-type 100BaseX for a fastethernet interface
Router#sh int e0	Checks the e0 interface status
Router(config-if)#no shutdown	Brings an interface to UP status
Router(config-if)#ip address 172.17.17.17 255.255.255.0	Configures an IP address (172.17.17.17 255.255.255.0) on an interface
Router(config-if)#ip address 172.17.18.18 255.255.255.0 secondary	Configures a secondary IP address (172.17.18.18 255.255.255.0) on an interface
Router(config)#int serial 1	Configures a serial port on the Router
Router(config-if)#clock rate 32000	Sets up the clock rate for the hardware connections on serial interfaces and make this interface as DCE. The clock rate command is in bits per second
Router(config-if)#bandwidth 128	Sets up the bandwidth for the hardware connections on serial interfaces. The bandwidth command is in kilobits per second
Router(config)#hostname thaar	Configures the Router hostname to thaar
Router(config-if)#description Training LAN	Configures the Router description
Router#copy running-config startup-config	Saves the running configuration in DRAM to startup configuration in NVRAM
Router# show start	Lists the system startup configuration
Router# erase startup-config	Deletes the system startup configuration
Router#sh cdp nei detail	Finds the network layer addresses for the neighbor routers

Router# ping	Checks the basic network connectivity using the ping command
Router#trace	Discovers the path a packet takes as it traverses an internetwork
Router#telnet	Tests the network connectivity
Router#clear counters s0	Clears the "show interface" counters on this interface
Router# show controllers fastethernet 0	Verifies the interface physical configuration

Chapter 4 Learning Questions

4-1. What is the IOS? (Select all that apply)

    A. IOS is a software system that manages CISCO routers and Switches, both their hardware and software resources.

    B. IOS is what runs the CISCO routers and some CISCO switches, which allows configuring these devices as well.

    C. IOS is the kernel of CISCO routers and most CISCO switches.

4-2. TRUE/FALSE: All CISCO Devices run the same OS.

    A. TRUE

    B. FALSE

4-3. Why IOS is created?

    A. IOS is created to help CISCO in its operation

    B. IOS is created to deliver network services and applications.

    C. IOS is created to help programmers.

4-4. What are the functions of the IOS? (Select all that apply)

    A. Managing network resources.

    B. Carrying network protocols and functions.

    C. Connecting high-speed traffic between networking devices.

    D. Adding security rules to network access.

4-5. How CISCO IOS can be accessed?

    A. Through the console port of a router.

    B. Through the network by using Telnet application.

    C. Through a modem.

    D. Through the Router's power socket.

4-6. Try to select the correct option to fill the blank.
Access to the IOS command line is called _____.

    A. Enabled session

    B. EXEC session

4-7. TRUE/FALSE: CAT2.96K switches use IOS.

    A. TRUE

    B. FALSE

4-8. TRUE/FALSE: To install a router for the first time physically, it is recommended to follow the following steps:

    Step 1. Connecting the router LAN ports to an Ethernet if it is required using any LAN cables.

    Step 2. Connecting the router's serial interface to the CSU/DSU, and the CSU/DSU to the line from the Telco, if an external CSU/DSU is used.

    Step 3. Connecting the router's serial interface to the line from the Telco, if an internal CSU/DSU is used.

Step 4. Connecting the router's console port to a PC (using a rollover cable), to configure the router.

Step 5. Connecting a power cable from a power outlet to the power port on the router.

Step 6. Turning ON the router.

    A.   TRUE

    B.   FALSE

4-9.   Try to decide which option gets in which blank.

Connecting to a CISCO router is required for _____, _____, and _____.

    A.   configuring the router

    B.   verifying the router configuration

    C.   checking the Router statistics

4-10.   Which of the following ways are used for router connection? (Select all that apply)

    A.   Console port connection

    B.   Auxiliary port connection

    C.   Ethernet port connection

4-11.   Which of the following is true about **Console port connection**? (Select all that apply)

    A.   It is used to connect and configure the router at the first time setup.

    B.   It is an RJ-45 connection on the rear panel of the router.

    C.   No password is set on this port by default.

    D.   Windows HyperTerminal software is an example of programs that used to access the router through this port.

    E.   The default Console port parameters are: 9600 baud, 8 data bits, no parity, 2 stop bits.

    F.   It does not support hardware flow control.

4-12.   Which of the following is true about **Auxiliary port connection**? (Select all that apply)

    A.   It is used to connect and configure the router.

    B.   It is an RJ-45 connection on the rear panel of the router.

    C.   No password is set on this port by default.

    D.   It is also used to configure the modem commands, .so that, the modem can be connected to the router.

    E.   Windows HyperTerminal software is an example of programs that used to access the router through this port.

    F.   The default Auxiliary port parameters are 9600 baud, 8 data bits, no parity, and 2 stop bits.

    G.   It does support hardware flow control.

4-13.   Which of the following is true about **Telnet access** to a CISCO router? (Select all that apply)

    A.   An emulation program used to connect and configure the router.

    B.   It uses any active interface on a router like an Ethernet (RJ-45, DB-15...etc) or serial port (DB-60) for router connection.

    C.   Password can be set for Telnet access.

    D.   A router can be configured to prohibit Telnet access.

4-14.   Which of the following ports can be used to dial up a remote router and configure it?

A. Console port
B. Auxiliary port
C. Ethernet port

4-15. Which of the following memories do CISCO Routers use? (Select all that apply)

A. Dynamic random-access memory (DRAM)
B. Nonvolatile random-access memory (NVRAM)
C. Flash memory

4-16. Which of the following is true about **DRAM**? (Select all that apply)

A. It is used for main system memory and for shared memory.
B. It is used for storing configuration information.
C. It is used for running CISCO IOS software.
D. It is an electronically erasable programmable read-only memory (EEPROM).

4-17. Which of the following is true about **NVRAM**? (Select all that apply)

A. It is used for main system memory and for shared memory.
B. It is used for storing configuration information.
C. It is used for running CISCO IOS software.
D. It is an electronically erasable programmable read-only memory (EEPROM).

4-18. Which of the following is true about **Flash Memory**? (Select all that apply)

A. It is used for main system memory and for shared memory.
B. It is used for storing configuration information.
C. It is used for running CISCO IOS software.
D. It is an electronically erasable programmable read-only memory (EEPROM).

4-19. Which of the following steps is the first step that a CISCO Router is followed during bringing up period? (Select all that apply)

A. The router will run a Power-On Self Test (POST).
B. The router loads the CISCO IOS from Flash Memory.
C. The router will load startup-config from NVRAM if it is found.
D. The router will enter setup mode, if no configuration is found in NVRAM.

4-20. Which of the following steps is the second step that a CISCO Router is followed during bringing up period? (Select all that apply)

A. The router will run a Power-On Self Test (POST).
B. The router loads the CISCO IOS from Flash Memory.
C. The router will load Startup-config from NVRAM if it is found.
D. The router will enter setup mode, if no configuration is found in NVRAM.

4-21. Which of the following steps is the third step that a CISCO Router is followed during bringing up period? (Select all that apply)

A. The router will run a Power-On Self Test (POST).
B. The router loads the CISCO IOS from Flash Memory.
C. The router will load Startup-config from NVRAM if it is found.

    D.   The router will enter setup mode, if no configuration is found in NVRAM.

4-22.   Which of the following steps is the fourth step that a CISCO Router is followed during bringing up period? (Select all that apply)

    A.   The router will run a Power-On Self Test (POST).
    B.   The router loads the CISCO IOS from Flash Memory.
    C.   The router will load Startup-config from NVRAM if it is found.
    D.   The router will enter setup mode, if no configuration is found in NVRAM.

4-23.   Try to decide which option gets in which blank.

After the IOS is loaded, it looks for a valid configuration called startup-Config that is stored by default in _____.
If there is no configuration, then the router will bring up what is called _____.

    A.   setup mode
    B.   NVRAM

4-24.   Which of the following memories is used to load the IOS by default?

    A.   ROM
    B.   Flash memory
    C.   NVRAM
    D.   Boot ROM

4-25.   What is the setup mode? (Select all that apply)

    A.   It is a Step-by-Step process for configuring a router.
    B.   It only covers some very global commands, but it is helpful to configure easily certain protocols, such as, bridging or DECnet.

4-26.   How a Router can enter in setup mode? (Select all that apply)

    A.   During the first time booting.
    B.   From User configuration mode, by issuing the setup command (Router>**setup**).
    C.   During Router booting and there is no startup-config stored in NVRAM.
    D.   From Privileged EXEC mode, by issuing the setup command (Router#**setup**).

4-27.   Which of the following options is available during the setup mode? (Select all that apply)

    A.   Basic Management
    B.   Extended setup

4-28.   Which of the following options is only used for defining the router connectivity?

    A.   Basic Management
    B.   Extended setup

4-29.   Which of the following options is used for configuring some global parameters as well as interface configuration parameters?

    A.   Basic Management
    B.   Extended setup

4-30.   During the setup mode, what are the two different management setup configurations?

   A.   Basic
   B.   Extended
   C.   Advanced
   D.   Enhanced

4-31.   Which of the following capabilities does a Setup Facility provide? (Select all that apply)

   A.   Establish hostnames
   B.   Set enable (or privileged mode) passwords
   C.   Set virtual terminal passwords
   D.   Enable SNMP network management
   E.   Enable routing of protocols
   F.   Enable transparent Ethernet bridging
   G.   Configure IP, including IGRP and RIP dynamic routing
   H.   Configure Novell IPX
   I.   Configure AppleTalk Phase 1 and Phase 2

4-32.   What does the brackets ([ ]) mean in the setup mode?

   A.   A default entry.
   B.   A Control^C combination should be pressed to continue.
   C.   An invalid entry is entered.
   D.   A blank password entry.

4-33.   What does the question mark '?' mean in the setup mode?

   A.   A default entry.
   B.   A help can be obtained.
   C.   More entries are found.
   D.   A blank password entry.

4-34.   What does the ctrl-c mean in the setup mode?

   A.   A default entry.
   B.   A Control^C combination should be pressed to continue.
   C.   An invalid entry is entered.
   D.   The configuration dialog can be aborted at any prompt.

4-35.   What will happen when you decide to terminate the AutoInstall procedure during the setup mode?

   A.   The Router will be shutdown.
   B.   The Router will be rebooted.
   C.   The CISCO IOS software CLI will be invoked.
   D.   Nothing will be done.

4-36.   What will happen when you decide to enter basic management setup procedure during the setup mode?

   A.   Extended setup options are not considered.
   B.   The Router will be rebooted.
   C.   The CISCO IOS software CLI will be invoked.

D.   Nothing will be done.

4-37.   Which of the following passwords is only used for the pre-10.3 IOS versions?

A.   The enabled secret password.
B.   The enable password.
C.   The VTY password.
D.   The enabled secure password.

4-38.   Which of the following passwords is more secure than the others that used in the CISCO Router?

A.   The enabled secret password.
B.   The enable password.
C.   The VTY password.
D.   The enabled secure password.

4-39.   Which of the following passwords is used to secure the Telnet session in the CISCO Router?

A.   The enabled secret password.
B.   The enable password.
C.   The VTY password.
D.   The enabled secure password.

4-40.   Which of the following subnet masks is corresponding to the following output, which is appeared during the setup mode?
"Class B network is 172.17.0.0, 8 subnet bits; mask is /24"

A.   255.0.0.0
B.   255.255.0.0
C.   255.255.255.0
D.   255.255.255.255

4-41.   What does the '0' mean at the end of the setup mode?

A.   Go to the IOS command prompt without saving this config.
B.   Return to the setup without saving this config.
C.   Save this configuration to nvram and exit.
D.   Nothing.

4-42.   What does the '1' mean at the end of the setup mode?

A.   Go to the IOS command prompt without saving this config.
B.   Return to the setup without saving this config.
C.   Save this configuration to nvram and exit.
D.   Nothing.

4-43.   What does the '2' mean at the end of the setup mode?

A.   Go to the IOS command prompt without saving this config.
B.   Return to the setup without saving this config.
C.   Save this configuration to nvram and exit.
D.   Nothing.

4-44.   How you can enter the CLI mode in the Router setup mode? (Select all that apply)

A.   By terminating the autoinstall procedure at the beginning of setup procedure.
B.   By selecting '0' at the end of setup procedure.
C.   None of the above.

4-45.   TRUE/FALSE: The following features are using the same configuration commands on both routers and switches:

- Console configuration
- Reaching setup mode either by reloading the router with an empty startup-config or by using the **setup** command
- Telnet, and enable secret password.
- SSH encryption keys and username/password login authentications configurations
- User and Enable (privileged) modes
- Entering and exiting configuration mode, using the **configure terminal**, **end**, and **exit** commands, and the Ctrl-Z key sequence.
- CLI help, command editing, and command recall features
- The host name and interface description configurations
- Ethernet interfaces that can negotiate speed, using the **speed** and **duplex** commands configurations.
- Administratively disabling (**shutdown**) and administratively enabling (**no shutdown**) an interface
- The use of commands like **line console 0** and **interface** to navigate through different configuration mode contexts.
- The meaning and the use of the startup-config (in NVRAM), running-config (in RAM), and external servers (like TFTP)
- The **copy** command to copy the configuration files and IOS images are the same.

A.   TRUE
B.   FALSE

4-46.   TRUE/FALSE: The following features are using different configuration commands on routers as compared with switches:

- IP addresses configuration.
- Routers have an auxiliary (Aux) port which can be used to connect the router to an external modem and phone line, so that, remote users can dial into the router, and access the CLI, by making a phone call.
- Questions in the setup mode configuration.

A.   TRUE
B.   FALSE

4-47.   Which of the following is typically required during a CISCO router configuration, but not typically required during a CISCO switch configuration? (Select all that apply)

A.   Turning to "ON" the ON/OFF switch
B.   Configuring serial cables
C.   Connecting to the console port
D.   Configuring Fast Ethernet ports
E.   Connecting the power cable
F.   Configuring the AUX port

4-48.   Which of the following is true about router user EXEC mode? (Select all that apply)

    A.   It is mostly used to view statistics.
    B.   It is an initial step to logging into a privileged mode.
    C.   It is used to view and change the configuration of a CISCO router.
    D.   To enter a user-mode, a configured user-mode password is required.
    E.   To enter a user-mode, a configured enable-mode password is required.

4-49.   Which of the following is true about router enabled EXEC mode? (Select all that apply)

    A.   It is mostly used to view statistics.
    B.   It is an initial step to logging into a privileged mode.
    C.   It is used to view and change the configuration of a CISCO router.
    D.   To enter an enabled EXE mode, a configured user-mode password is required.
    E.   To enter an enabled-mode, a configured enable-mode password is required.

4-50.   Which of the following commands is used to log into a privileged EXEC mode? (Select all that apply)

    A.   disable
    B.   en
    C.   logout
    D.   exit
    E.   enable
    F.   quit
    G.   ena

4-51.   Which of the following commands is used to turn OFF the privileged EXEC mode? (Select all that apply)

    A.   disable
    B.   en
    C.   logout
    D.   exit
    E.   enable
    F.   quit
    G.   Contol+Z

4-52.   Which of the following commands is used to logout a router console from the privileged EXEC mode? (Select all that apply)

    A.   disable
    B.   en
    C.   logout
    D.   exit
    E.   enable
    F.   quit
    G.   Contol+Z

4-53.   Which command is used to switch from the Privileged EXEC mode to the User EXEC mode? (Select all that apply)

    A.   disable
    B.   en
    C.   logout
    D.   exit
    E.   enable

  F. quit
  G. Contol+Z

4-54. Which command is used to switch from the User EXEC mode to the Privileged EXEC mode? (Select all that apply)

  A. Login
  B. Setup
  C. Exec
  D. Enable
  E. Privexec
  F. enableexec

4-55. Which command prompt is shown in the User EXEC Mode?

  A. >
  B. Router>
  C. Router#
  D. Router(config)#
  E. Router(config-if)#

4-56. Which command prompt is shown in the Privileged EXEC Mode?
  A. >
  B. Router>
  C. Router#
  D. Router(config)#
  E. Router(config-if)#

4-57. Which command prompt is used to issue the **setup** command?
  A. >
  B. Router>
  C. Router#
  D. Router(config)#
  E. Router(config-if)#

4-58. TRUE/FALSE: Any changes made in the global configuration mode will affect the router as a whole.
  A. TRUE
  B. FALSE

4-59. Which of the following configs is changed by the **config t** command?

  A. startup-config
  B. running-config
  C. router-config
  D. nvram-config

4-60. Which of the following configs is changed by the **config mem** command?

  A. startup-config
  B. running-config
  C. router-config
  D. nvram-config

4-61.   Which of the following commands is used to enter the global configuration mode? (Select all that apply)

    A.   Router>config
    B.   Router#config t
    C.   Router#config interface
    D.   Router#config
    E.   Router#router ospf

4-62.   Which of the following commands is used to change the running-config parameters? (Select all that apply)

    A.   Router>config
    B.   Router#config t
    C.   Router>config interface
    D.   Router#config
    E.   Router>router ospf

4-63.   Which of the following commands is used to the change startup-config? (Select all that apply)

    A.   Router>config
    B.   Router#config t
    C.   Router#config mem
    D.   Router#config
    E.   Router#router ospf
    F.   Router#config memory

4-64.   Which command is used to change the router configuration parameters stored on a TFTP host? (Select all that apply)

    A.   Router>config net
    B.   Router#config network
    C.   Router#config mem
    D.   Router#config
    E.   Router#config net
    F.   Router#config memory

4-65.   Which command is used to configure fastethernet interface on the router? (Select all that apply)

    A.   Router>int f0/0
    B.   Router(config)#int f0/0
    C.   Router(config)#interface f0/0
    D.   Router#interface f0/0
    E.   Router(config)#interface fastethernet 0/0

4-66.   Which command is used to configure fastethernet Subinterface 1 on the router? (Select all that apply)

    A.   Router>int f0/0.1
    B.   Router(config)#int f0/0.1
    C.   Router# interface f0/0/1
    D.   Router(config)#interface f0/0/1
    E.   Router(config)#interface fastethernet 0/0.1

4-67.   Which command is used to configure the console port parameters? (Select all that apply)

A.   Router>line console 0
B.   Router(config)#line console 0
C.   Router#config line
D.   Router(config)#config console 0
E.   Router(config)#config line
F.   Router#line console 0

4-68.   Which command is used to configure the routing protocols on a router? (Select all that apply)

A.   Router>router rip
B.   Router#router ospf
C.   Router(config)#router rip
D.   Router#config rip
E.   Router(config)#router ospf
F.   Router#router rip

4-69.   Which command prompt is shown in the Global Configuration Mode?

A.   >
B.   Router>
C.   Router#
D.   Router(config)#
E.   Router(config-sub)#

4-70.   Which command prompt is shown in the Interface Configuration Mode?

A.   >
B.   Router>
C.   Router(config-line)#
D.   Router(config)#
E.   Router(config-if)#

4-71.   Which command prompt is shown in the Subinterface Configuration Mode?

A.   >
B.   Router>
C.   Router(config-subif)#
D.   Router(config-line)#
E.   Router(config-if)#

4-72.   Which command prompt is shown in the Line Configuration Mode?

A.   >
B.   Router(config-line)#
C.   Router#
D.   Router(config)#
E.   Router(config-if)#

4-73.   Which command prompt is shown in the Router Configuration Mode?

A.   >

B.   Router(config-line)#
C.   Router#
D.   Router(config-router)#
E.   Router(config-if)#

4-74.   Which Exit method is used to end the Global Configuration Mode session? (Select all that apply)

A.   end
B.   exit
C.   CTRL+T
D.   CTRL+Z
E.   CTRL+E
F.   Logout

4-75.   Which Exit method is used to end the Interface Configuration Mode session? (Select all that apply)

A.   end
B.   exit
C.   CTRL+C
D.   CTRL+Z
E.   CTRL+X
F.   Logout

4-76.   Which Exit method is used to end the Subinterface Configuration Mode session? (Select all that apply)

A.   end
B.   exit
C.   CTRL+C
D.   CTRL+Z
E.   CTRL+X
F.   Logout

4-77.   Which Exit method is used to end the Line Configuration Mode session? (Select all that apply)

A.   end
B.   exit
C.   CTRL+C
D.   CTRL+Z
E.   CTRL+X
F.   Logout

4-78.   Which Exit method is used to end the Router Configuration Mode session? (Select all that apply)

A.   end
B.   exit
C.   CTRL+C
D.   CTRL+Z
E.   CTRL+X
F.   Logout

4-79.   Which character is used to list all available commands at any prompt? (Select all that apply)

A. #
B. ?
C. %
D. $

4-80. Which character is used to find commands that start with a certain letter?

A. #
B. ?
C. %
D. $

4-81. Which of the following is used to find the next command in a **clock** command string?

A. clock?
B. clock ^?
C. clock ?
D. clock !

4-82. Which error message is solved by issuing the following command? "Router#**clock set 12:50:10**"

A. % Incomplete command. Press the up arrow key and type a ?.
B. % Invalid input detected at '^' marker. Press the up arrow key and type a ?.
C. % Ambiguous command: "clock set 12:50:10". Press the up arrow key and type a ?.
D. %IP-3-BADIPALIGN: Invalid alignment in packet for IP. [chars]=[hex]. Press the up arrow key and type a ?.
E. %IP-4-DUPADDR: Duplicate address [inet] on [chars], sourced by [enet]. Press the up arrow key and type a ?.

4-83. Which of the following error messages is generated by issuing the command: Router# **access list 190 permit host 194.165.141.82**?

A. % Incomplete command.
B. % Invalid input detected at '^' marker.
C. % Ambiguous command: "**access list**".
D. %IP-3-BADIPALIGN: Invalid alignment in packet for IP. [chars]=[hex].
E. %IP-4-DUPADDR: Duplicate address [inet] on [chars], sourced by [enet].

4-84. Which of the following error messages is generated by issuing the command: Router#**sh te**?

A. % Incomplete command: "sh te".
B. % Invalid input detected at '^' marker.
C. % Ambiguous command: "sh te".
D. %IP-3-BADIPALIGN: Invalid alignment in packet for IP. [chars]=[hex].
E. %IP-4-DUPADDR: Duplicate address [inet] on [chars], sourced by [enet].

4-85. Which of the following keystrokes moves the cursor back one character?

A. CTRL-Z
B. ESC,B
C. CTRL-F
D. CTRL-B
E. CTRL-W

4-86.   Which key sequence moves the cursor to the beginning of a line?

A.   CTRL-A
B.   CTRL-C
C.   CTRL-P
D.   CTRL-E
E.   CTRL-N

4-87.   Which of the following keystrokes moves the cursor to the end of the line?

A.   CTRL-Z
B.   ESC,B
C.   CTRL-F
D.   CTRL-B
E.   CTRL-E

4-88.   Which of the following keystrokes redisplays a line?

A.   CTRL-Z
B.   ESC,B
C.   CTRL-R
D.   CTRL-B
E.   CTRL-W

4-89.   Which of the following keystrokes erases a line?

A.   CTRL-U
B.   ESC,B
C.   CTRL-F
D.   CTRL-B
E.   CTRL-W

4-90.   Which of the following keystrokes moves the cursor back one word?

A.   CTRL-Z
B.   ESC+B
C.   CTRL-F
D.   CTRL-B
E.   CTRL-W

4-91.   Which of the following keystrokes moves the cursor forward one word?

A.   CTRL-Z
B.   ESC+F.
C.   CTRL-F
D.   CTRL-B
E.   CTRL-W

4-92.   Which of the following keystrokes erases a word?

A.   CTRL-Z
B.   ESC,B
C.   CTRL-F

    D.   CTRL-B
    E.   CTRL-W

4-93.   Which of the following keystrokes deletes a single character?

    A.   CTRL-Z
    B.   ESC,B
    C.   CTRL-D
    D.   CTRL-B
    E.   CTRL-W

4-94.   Which of the following keystrokes moves the cursor forward one character?

    A.   CTRL-Z
    B.   ESC,B
    C.   CTRL-F
    D.   CTRL-B
    E.   CTRL-W

4-95.   Which of the following keystrokes deletes a single character?

    A.   CTRL-Z
    B.   Backspace
    C.   CTRL-F
    D.   CTRL-B
    E.   CTRL-W

4-96.   Which of the following keystrokes ends configuration mode and returns to EXEC?

    A.   CTRL-Z
    B.   ESC,B
    C.   CTRL-F
    D.   CTRL-B
    E.   CTRL-W

4-97.   Which of the following keystrokes can finish typing a command for you?

    A.   CTRL-Z
    B.   Backspace
    C.   CTRL-F
    D.   CTRL-B
    E.   Tab

4-98.   Which of the following keystrokes indicates an automatic scrolling of long lines?

    A.   ?
    B.   &
    C. $
    D.   %
    E.   #

4-99.   Which of the following lists the last commands entered on the Router?

    A.   sh history
    B.   sh users
    C.   sh network
    D.   sh old commands
    E.   sh old

4-100. Which of the following verifies the Router terminal configuration?

    A.   sh history
    B.   sh users
    C.   sh network
    D.   sh ver
    E.   sh terminal

4-101. Which of the following verifies the Router terminal history size?

    A.   sh history
    B.   sh users
    C.   sh network
    D.   sh ver
    E.   sh terminal

4-102. Which of the following can change the Router terminal history size?

    A.   terminal history size 300
    B.   terminal history_size 300
    C.   terminal history size 30
    D.   terminal history_size 30
    E.   sh terminal

4-103. Which of the following editing commands shows the last command entered? (Select all that apply)

    A.   CTRL-P
    B.   ESC-B
    C.   CTRL-F
    D.   CTRL-B
    E.   UP arrow

4-104. Which of the following keystrokes shows the next commands that you entered? (Select all that apply)

    A.   CTRL-P
    B.   ESC,B
    C.   CTRL-N
    D.   Down arrow
    E.   UP arrow

4-105. Which of the following commands turns OFF the key sequences such as CTRL-B?

    A.   no edit
    B.   terminal no editing
    C.   no editing
    D.   no short keys
    E.   disable terminal editing

4-106. How the entries in the command history buffer can be displayed?

    A.   Sh history
    B.   Sh commands
    C.   Sh buffer
    D.   Debug history
    E.   debug command

4-107. Which of the following commands is used to obtain the basic system configuration? (Select all that apply)

    A.   sh ver
    B.   sh hardware
    C.   sh software
    D.   sh version

4-108. Which of the following information does the **show version** command provide? (Select all that apply)

    A.   The IOS version currently running on the Router
    B.   The source of configuration files.
    C.   The boot images.
    D.   How long the Router has been running.
    E.   How the Router was restarted.
    F.   The IOS filename running.
    G.   The model hardware and processor versions.
    H.   The amount of DRAM.
    I.   The configuration register value.
    J.   The amount of NVRAM.
    K.   The amount of flash memory.
    L.   The available network ports.

4-109. How many passwords are available to secure the CISCO Router?

    A.   3
    B.   4
    C.   5
    D.   2
    E.   1

4-110. Which of the following passwords are used to secure the CISCO Router? (Select all that apply)

    A.   Enable Password
    B.   Enable secret password
    C.   Console password
    D.   Auxiliary password
    E.   Telnet password

4-111. Which of the following passwords are used to secure the privileged mode? (Select all that apply)

    A.   Enable Password
    B.   Enable secret password
    C.   Console password
    D.   Auxiliary password

E.   Telnet password

4-112.   Which of the following passwords are used when the user mode is accessed? (Select all that apply)

A.   Enable Password
B.   Enable secret password
C.   Console password
D.   Auxiliary password
E.   Telnet password

4-113.   Which of the following passwords are used when the **enable** command is issued? (Select all that apply)

A.   Enable Password
B.   Enable secret password
C.   Console password
D.   Auxiliary password
E.   Telnet password

4-114.   Which of the following is used to assign the privileged level password thaar on the Router?

A.   enable thaar
B.   enable secret thaar
C.   enable password altaiey
D.   enable password thaar

4-115.   Which of the following is used to assign the privileged level secret altaiey on the Router?

A.   enable thaar
B.   enable secret altaiey
C.   enable password altaiey
D.   enable password secret altaiey

4-116.   Which configuration mode is used to set up the enable passwords?

A.   User EXEC mode
B.   Privileged EXEC mode
C.   Global configuration mode
D.   Line configuration mode
E.   Interface configuration mode

4-117.   Which of the following is true about enable secret passwords? (Select all that apply)
A.   The enable secret password is encrypted by default.
B.   The enable password is encrypted by default.
C.   The enable secret password supersedes the enable password.
D.   The enable password supersedes the enable secret password.

4-118.   Which of the following is used to configure the auxiliary line password on the Router?

A.   line aux 0
B.   aux 0
C.   line aux
D.   line 0

4-119.   Which of the following is used to configure the console line password on the Router? (Select all that apply)

    A. line console 0
    B. line con 0
    C. console 0
    D. console line

4-120.   Which of the following is used to configure the Telnet password for only line 1? (Select all that apply)

    A. line vty 0 1
    B. line vty 0 4
    C. line telnet 1
    D. line vty 1

4-121.   Which configuration mode can be used to set the user-mode passwords?

    A. User configuration mode
    B. Global configuration mode
    C. Line configuration mode
    D. Interface configuration mode

4-122.   When trying to establish a Telnet session the following message is appeared "connection refused, password not set,". How this problem is recovered and how could the Telnet session be established without prompting for a password?

    A.   config t, line con 0 4, no login
    B.   config t, line vty 0 4, no password
    C.   config t, line vty 0 4, no login
    D.   config t, line vty 0 4

4-123.   Which of the following sets a user-mode password for the console port?

    A.   config t, line con 0, login, password thaar
    B.   config t, line con 0, password thaar, login
    C.   config t, line con 0, login
    D.   config t, line con port, login, password thaar

4-124.   Which of the following sets a user-mode password for the auxiliary port?

    A.   config t, line aux 0, login, password thaar
    B.   config t, line aux 0, password thaar, login
    C.   config t, line aux 0, login
    D.   config t, line aux port, login, password thaar

4-125.   Which of the following allows the users to Telnet into a Router and without the need for a user-mode password?

    A.   login
    B.   no login
    C.   password thaar
    D.   no password
    E.   No command is needed; Telnet is enabled by default

4-126.   Which of the following stops the console messages from writing over the command you are trying to type in?

    A.   logging synchronous
    B.   logging asynchronous
    C.   logging
    D.   no logging

4-127.   Which of the following sets the time out of the console to only one second?

    A.   time-out 0 1
    B.   exec-timeout 0 1
    C.   time-out 1 0
    D.   exec-timeout 1 0

4-128.   Which of the following encrypts the Telnet password on the Router?

    A.   service password-encryption, line vty 0 4, login, password thaar
    B.   line vty 0 4, password-encryption on, login, password thaar
    C.   password-encryption, line vty 0 4, login, password thaar
    D.   service encryption, line vty 0 4, login, password thaar

4-129.   What does the command **line aux 0** perform?

    A.   restart the Router
    B.   shutdown the Router
    C.   Entering the auxiliary line mode
    D.   disable auxiliary connection

4-130.   Which of the following shows the configured passwords on the Router?

    A.   sh passwords
    B.   sh run
    C.   sh enable-passwords
    D.   sh user-mode passwords

4-131.   Which of the following defines the banner messages on the Router?

    A. banner ?
    B. banner thaar
    C. banner today
    D. banner mtod

4-132.   How many different banners are available?

    A.   3
    B.   4
    C.   5
    D.   6

4-133.   Which of the following is a banner type that can be defined on the Router? (Select all that apply)

    A. motd banner

B. login banner
C. exec banner
D. incoming banner

4-134.   Which of the following is used to configure the motd banner on the Router? (Select all that apply)

A. banner motd ?
B. banner login ?
C. banner exec ?
D. banner incoming ?
E. banner motd hello

4-135.   Which of the following is used to configure the login banner on the Router? (Select all that apply)

A. banner motd ?
B. banner login ?
C. banner exec ?
D. banner incoming ?
E. banner login hello

4-136.   Which of the following is used to configure the exec banner on the Router? (Select all that apply)

A. banner motd ?
B. banner login ?
C. banner exec ?
D. banner incoming ?
E. banner exec hello

4-137.   Which of the following is used to configure the incoming banner on the Router? (Select all that apply)

A. banner motd ?
B. banner login ?
C. banner exec ?
D. banner incoming ?
E. banner incoming hello

4-138.   Which of the following configuration modes can be used to apply the banner on the Router?

A. User configuration mode
B. Global configuration mode
C. Line configuration mode
D. Interface configuration mode

4-139.   Which of the following is used to delete the motd banner from the Router?

A.   no banner motd
B.   delete banner motd
C.   remove banner motd
D.   banner no motd
E.   no motd banner

4-140.   Which of the following is used to delete the exec banner from the Router?

A.   banner no exec
B.   delete banner exec

C.   remove banner exec
D.   no banner exec
E.   no exec banner

4-141.   Which of the following is used to delete the incoming banner from the Router?

A.   remove banner incoming
B.   delete banner incoming
C.   no banner incoming
D.   banner no incoming
E.   no incoming banner

4-142.   Which of the following is used to delete the login banner from the Router?

A.   delete banner login
B.   no banner login
C.   banner no login
D.   remove banner login
E.   no login banner

4-143.   Which of the following is used to disable the EXEC banner on a particular line? (Select all that apply)

A.   no exec-banner
B.   no motd-banner
C.   no banner-exec
D.   no banner exec
E.   No way to disable it. It must be deleted completely from the Router.

4-144.   Which of the following is used to disable the motd banner on a particular line? (Select all that apply)

A.   no exec-banner
B.   no motd-banner
C.   no banner-motd
D.   no banner motd
E.   No way to disable it. It must be deleted completely from the Router.

4-145.   Which of the following is used to disable the incoming banner on a particular line? (Select all that apply)

A.   no exec-banner
B.   no motd-banner
C.   no banner-exec
D.   no banner exec
E.   No way to disable it. It must be deleted completely from the Router.

4-146.   Which of the following is used to disable the login banner on a particular line? (Select all that apply)

A.   no exec-banner
B.   no motd-banner
C.   no banner-exec
D.   no banner exec
E.   No way to disable it. It must be deleted completely from the Router.

4-147.   From which configuration mode can, the banner be disabled on a particular line?

    A. User configuration mode
    B. Global configuration mode
    C. Line configuration mode
    D. Interface configuration mode

4-148.   Which of the following is true about banner? (Select all that apply)

    A.   A banner gives the users and administrators pre-configured messages when they log into the Router.
    B.   A banner adds a security notice to users dialing into the internetwork.
    C.   There are four different banners available.
    D.   The banner message must start by delimiting character and ends with the same character.

4-149.   TRUE/FALSE: A delimiting character can be used within the banner message body.

    A.   TRUE
    B.   FALSE

4-150.   Which of the following defines an Ethernet interface on the Router? (Select all that apply)

    A. int e0
    B. interface ethernet 0
    C. ethernet 0
    D. interface ethernet 1/0/1

4-151.   Which of the following configures a FastEthernet interface on the Router? (Select all that apply)

    A. int fa 0
    B. interface fastethernet 0
    C. interface fastethernet 0/0
    D. interface fastethernet 1/0/1

4-152.   From which configuration mode can, the Router interface be selected?

    A. User configuration mode
    B. Global configuration mode
    C. Line configuration mode
    D. Interface configuration mode

4-153.   Which of the following is used to set a serial interface to provide clocking to another Router at 64kbps?

    A.   clock rate 64k
    B.   clock rate 6400
    C.   clock rate 64000

4-154.   Which of the following is used to set a serial interface to provide a bandwidth of 2Mbps?

    A.   bandwidth 2M
    B.   bandwidth 2000k
    C.   bandwidth 2000000
    D.   bandwidth 2000

4-155.   Which of the following configuration modes can be used to adjust the bandwidth and clock rate for a serial Router interface?

A. User configuration mode
B. Global configuration mode
C. Line configuration mode
D. Interface configuration mode

4-156.   Which of the following is true regarding the command **media-type 100BaseX**? (Select all that apply)

A.   It is used to set the connector type to Fastethernet type.
B.   It is typically auto-detected.
C.   It is used to set the connector type to Ethernet type.
D.   It is typically not auto-detected.
E.   It is configured from Interface configuration mode.

4-157.   TRUE/FALSE: All Router interfaces are shut down by default.

A.   TRUE
B.   FALSE

4-158.   Which of the following is used to bring an interface up?

A.   shutdown
B.   no shutdown
C.   interface up
D.   interface down
E.   interface ON
F.   interface OFF

4-159.   Which of the following is used to bring an interface down?

A.   shutdown
B.   no shutdown
C.   interface up
D.   interface down
E.   interface ON
F.   interface OFF

4-160.   Which of the following is used to set an IP address 172.17.17.17/24 to an interface?

A.   ip address 172.17.17.17 255.255.255.0
B.   ip address 172.17.17.17
C.   ip address 172.17.17.17 255.255.255.0 secondary

4-161.   Which of the following is used to set a secondary IP address 172.17.17.17/24 to an interface?

A.   ip address 172.17.17.17 255.255.255.0
B.   ip address 172.17.17.17
C.   ip address 172.17.17.17 255.255.255.0 secondary

4-162.   What is the problem with an interface if the following Error message is received "Ethernet0 is administratively down, line protocol is down"?

A.   The administrator shutdowns the interface.
B.   The administrator is pinging from the interface.
C.   Network Cable is not attached to the interface.

4-163.   Which of the following is used to recover an interface from the following problem "Ethernet0 is administratively down, line protocol is down"?

A.   config t,int e0, shutdown
B.   config t,int e0, shut
C.   config t,int e0, no shutdown
D.   config t,int e0, no shut

4-164.   TRUE/FALSE: All routers use the same methods to choose interfaces.

A.   TRUE
B.   FALSE

4-165.   Which of the following is part of an interface configuration?

A.   Network Layer addresses
B.   Media-type
C.   Bandwidth
D.   Clock rate

4-166.   Which of the following syntax is used for an interface configuration? (Select all that apply)

A.   interface interface_type interface_number
B.   interface interface_type slot_number/port_number
C.   Interface interface_type slot_number/port adapter/port_number

4-167.   Which of the following shows the configured interfaces on the Router?

A.   sh int e0
B.   sh run
C.   sh int s0
D.   sh router_interfaces

4-168.   Which of the following is used to restore clock rate to its default values? (Select all that apply)

A.   no ip address
B.   no clock rate
C.   Clock rate no
D.   Clock rate off

4-169.   Which of the following is used to restore the bandwidth setting to its default values? (Select all that apply)

A.   no ip address
B.   no bandwidth
C.   bandwidth no
D.   bandwidth off

4-170.   Which of the following is used to remove and disable IP processing on a particular interface? (Select all that apply)

    A. no ip address
    B. no_ip address
    C. ip address no
    D. ip address off

4-171. Which of the following commands should be used to provide the Router with a 64000bps serial link, if the Router is facilitating a CSU/DSU?

    A. clock rate 64000
    B. clockrate 64000
    C. clock rate 64
    D. bandwidth 64
    E. bandwidth 64000

4-172. Which of the following cases require the **no clock rate** command to be issued on the serial interfaces? (Select all that apply)

    A. Transferring that interface from DCE to DTE
    B. Turning the clock rate off
    C. Reconfiguring that interface
    D. Transferring that interface from DTE to DCE

4-173. Which of the following types of interfaces require the clock rate command to be issued? (Select all that apply)

    A. DCE
    B. DTE
    C. CSU
    D. DSU

4-174. Why the bandwidth is set on the Router serial interfaces? (Select all that apply)

    A. To be used for calculating the best route.
    B. It is required by Dynamic routing protocol.
    C. Router interfaces cannot work without setting this command.

4-175. What is the default Bandwidth setting on the CISCO Router serial interfaces?

    A. T1 (1.544Mbps)
    B. T3 (45Mbps)
    C. 100 kbps
    D. 128kbps

4-176. Which of the following Dynamic Routing Protocols uses the Bandwidth? (Select all that apply)

    A. OSPF
    B. RIP
    C. IGRP
    D. EIGRP

4-177. Which CISCO prompt allows you to issue commands to configure multiple virtual interfaces on a single physical interface?

    A.   Router(config-subif)#
    B.   Router(config-if)#
    C.   Router(config)#
    D.   Router#

4-178. Which of the following features is typically associated with the router CLI, but not with the switch CLI? (Select all that apply)

    A.   The interface vlan x command
    B.   The ip address w.x.y.z 255.x.y.z command
    C.   Configuring the AUX port
    D.   The ip address dhcp command
    E.   The clock rate xxxx command

4-179. Which of the following is used to set the name of a Router to BOSS?

    A.   config t,host name BOSS
    B.   config t,hostname BOSS
    C.   config t,name BOSS

4-180. TRUE/FALSE: The hostname setting is only locally significant.

    A. TRUE
    B. FALSE

4-181. Which of the following is used to set the Router identification to the name CISCO, which an administrator would see when connecting with Telnet or through the console?

    A. banner motd @
    B. host name CISCO
    C. set prompt CISCO
    D. hostname CISCO
    E. description CISCO

4-182. Which of the following configuration modes can be used to set the Router name?

    A. User configuration mode
    B. Global configuration mode
    C. Line configuration mode
    D. Interface configuration mode

4-183. What is the default setting for the CISCO routers hostnames?

    A.   router
    B.   CISCO
    C.   CISCO_router
    D.   Router_CISCO

4-184. What is the correct order of displaying the following at the startup? (Select all that apply)

    A.   banner message-of-the-day (MOTD)

B.   login and password prompt
C.   EXEC banner
D.   Hostname

4-185.   Which of the following commands defines the router hostname? (Select all that apply)

A.   Router(config)#hostname router
B.   Router#hostname router
C.   Router(config)#setup
D.   Router#setup

4-186.   Which of the following is used to set the description "My LAN" of an interface?

A.   config t, int e0, description my LAN
B.   config t, description my LAN
C.   config t, int e0, my LAN

4-187.   TRUE/FALSE: The interface description setting is only locally significant.

A.   TRUE
B.   FALSE

4-188.   Which of the following configuration modes can be used to set the interface description?

A.   User configuration mode
B.   Global configuration mode
C.   Line configuration mode
D.   Interface configuration mode

4-189.   Which of the following shows the interface description? (Select all that apply)

A.   sh int e0
B.   sh run.
C.   sh int s0
D.   sh router_interfaces

4-190.   Which of the following is used to copy the running config to startup config? (Select all that apply)

A.   config t, copy run start
B.   enable, copy run start
C.   config t, copy start run
D.   enable, copy start run

4-191.   Which of the following is used to copy the startup config to running config? (Select all that apply)

A.   config t, copy run start
B.   enable, copy run start
C.   config t, copy start run
D.   enable, copy start run

4-192.   From which configuration mode can, the running configuration file be copied to startup configuration file?

A. User EXEC mode
B. Privileged EXEC mode
C. Global Configuration Mode
D. Interface configuration mode

4-193.   Which of the following shows the content of the running configuration file? (Select all that apply)

A.   sh int e0
B.   sh run
C.   sh int s0
D.   sh start

4-194.   Which of the following shows the content of the startup configuration file? (Select all that apply)

A.   sh int e0
B.   sh run
C.   sh int s0
D.   sh start

4-195.   From which configuration mode can, the startup configuration file be copied to running configuration file?

A. User EXEC mode
B. Privileged EXEC mode
C. Line configuration mode
D. Interface configuration mode

4-196.   Which of the following is used to delete the content of the startup configuration file? (Select all that apply)

A. config t, erase startup-config
B. enable, erase startup-config
C. config t, delete startup-config
D. enable, delete startup-config

4-197.   From which configuration mode can, the startup configuration file be deleted?

A. User EXEC mode
B. Privileged EXEC mode
C. Line configuration mode
D. Interface configuration mode

4-198.   Which of the following is used to copy the NVRAM contents to DRAM?

A. config t, copy run start
B. enable, copy run start
C. config t, copy start run
D. enable, copy start run

4-199.   Which of the following is used to copy the DRAM contents to NVRAM?
A. config t, copy run start
B. enable, copy run start
C. config t, copy start run

D. enable, copy start run

4-200.   What are the two ways that can be used to enter in the setup mode of a Router?

A. By typing the **erase start** command and rebooting the Router.
B. By typing the **setup** command from Privileged EXEC mode.
C. By typing the **clear flash** command.
D. By typing the **setup mode** command.

4-201.   Which of the following is used to back up the currently running-configuration and have it reload if the Router is restarted?

A. Router#copy run startup
B. Router#copy start run
C. Router(config)#copy running-config start
D. Router(config)#copy current starting

4-202.   Which of the following deletes the contents of the NVRAM on a Router? (Select all that apply)

A. erase nvram
B. erase start
C. erase startup
D. erase startup-config

4-203.   Which of the following configuration modes is used to configure the router?

A. User EXEC mode
B. Privileged EXEC mode
C. Global configuration mode
D. Specific configuration mode
E. Setup mode.

4-204.   Which of the following is used to verify the hardware configuration of the Router? (Select all that apply)

A. sh interface e0
B. sh ver
C. sh controllers s 0
D. sh interface s0

4-205.   Which of the following finds the network layer addresses for the neighbor routers? (Select all that apply)

A. config t, sh cdp nei detail
B. enable, sh cdp nei detail
C. config t, show cdp neighbor detail
D. enable, show cdp neighbor detail

4-206.   From which configuration mode can, the show cdp neighbor detail command be issued?

A. User EXEC mode
B. Privileged EXEC mode
C. Line configuration mode
D. Interface configuration mode

4-207. Which of the following can check the basic network connectivity? (Select all that apply)

A. ping
B. sh run
C. trace
D. sh start

4-208. Which of the following discovers the path that a packet takes as it traverses an internetwork? (Select all that apply)

A. ping
B. sh run
C. trace
D. sh start

4-209. From which configuration mode can, the ping utility be issued? (Select all that apply)

A User EXEC mode
B. Privileged EXEC mode
C. Line configuration mode
D. Interface configuration mode

4-210. From which configuration mode can, the trace utility be issued? (Select all that apply)

A. User EXEC mode
B. Privileged EXEC mode
C. Line configuration mode
D. Interface configuration mode

4-211. Which of the following can check the network connectivity? (Select the best answer)

A. ping
B. telnet
C. trace
D. sh start

4-212. From which configuration mode can, the Telnet utility be issued?

A. User EXEC mode
B. Privileged EXEC mode
C. Line configuration mode
D. Interface configuration mode

4-213. Which of the following is used to verify the network configuration of an interface? (Select all that apply)

A. sh interface e0
B. sh ver
C. sh controllers s 0
D. sh interface s0

4-214. Which of the following is used to verify the physical configuration of an interface? (Select all that apply)

A. sh interface e0

    B. sh ver
    C. sh controllers s 0
    D. sh interface s0

4-215.   Which of the following clears the "show interface" counters of the interface? (Select all that apply)

    A. delete counters
    B. zero counters
    C. clear controllers s 0
    D. clear counters e0

4-216.   Which of the following shows if s0 interface needed to provide clocking?

    A.   Router#sh controllers s 0
    B.   Router# sh controllers s0
    C.   Router(config)# sh controllers s 0
    D.   Router(config)# sh controllers s0

4-217.   Which of the following shows if either a DTE or DCE cable is plugged into serial 0?

    A.   Router#sh controllers s 0
    B.   Router# sh controllers s0
    C.   Router# sh int s 0
    D.   Router# sh int s0

4-218.   If the following message is obtained from sh int s0 command, what could the problem be? "Serial0 is up, line protocol is up"

    A.   There is no problem. The interface is working.
    B.   The keepalives could be set wrong between the point-to-point links.
    C.   The interface is defective.
    D.   No cable is attached to the interface.
    E.   no shutdown command must issue on the interface.

4-219.   If the following message is obtained from sh int s0 command, what could the problem be? "Serial0 is up, line protocol is down"

    A.   There is no problem. The interface is working.
    B.   The keepalives could be set wrong between the point-to-point links.
    C.   The interface is defective.
    D.   No cable is attached to the interface.
    E.   no shutdown command must issue on the interface.

4-220.   If the following message is obtained from sh int s0 command, what could the problem be? "Serial0 is down, line protocol is down"

    A.   There is no problem. The interface is working.
    B.   The keepalives could be set wrong between the point-to-point links.
    C.   The interface is defective.
    D.   No cable is attached to the interface.
    E.   no shutdown command must issue on the interface.

4-221.   If the following message is obtained from sh int s0 command, what could the problem be? "Serial0 is administratively down, line protocol is down."

    A.   There is no problem. The interface is working.
    B.   The keepalives could be set wrong between the point-to-point links.
    C.   The interface is defective.
    D.   No cable is attached to the interface.
    E.   no shutdown command must issue on the interface.

4-222.   Which of the following can be used with the different types of protocols? (Select all that apply)

    A.   ping
    B.   trace
    C.   telnet

4-223.   Which of the following can only be used with the TCP/IP protocol? (Select all that apply)

    A.   ping
    B.   trace
    C.   telnet

4-224.   TRUE/FALSE: Telnet is the best utility, since it uses IP at the Network layer and TCP at the Transport layer to create a session with a remote host.

    A.   TRUE
    B.   FALSE

4-225.   TRUE/FALSE: At the Router prompt, there is no need to type telnet, just type a hostname or IP address, and the Router will assume that Telnet utility is required.

    A.   TRUE
    B.   FALSE

4-226.   What are the first and second parameters referring to in the following sh int e0 command output? "Ethernet0 is up, line protocol is up"

    A.   The first parameter refers to the physical layer, whereas the second one refers to the data link layer.
    B.   The first parameter refers to the data link layer, whereas the second one refers to the physical layer.
    C.   The first parameter refers to the physical layer, whereas the second one refers to the network layer.
    D.   The first parameter refers to the network layer, whereas the second one refers to the physical layer.

4-227.   Which of the following will show the B/W of the s0 interface?

    A.   Router#sh controllers s 0
    B.   Router# sh controllers s0
    C.   Router# sh int s 0
    D.   Router# sh int s0

4-228.   Which of the following will show the MTU of the s0 interface?

    A.   Router#sh controllers s 0
    B.   Router# sh controllers s0
    C.   Router# sh int s 0
    D.   Router# sh int s0

4-229.   Which of the following will show the keepalive time of the s0 interface?

A.   Router#sh controllers s 0
B.   Router# sh controllers s0
C.   Router# sh int s 0
D.   Router# sh int s0

4-230.   What is the default value for the s0 interface MTU parameter?

A. 1500 bytes
B. 2500 bytes
C. 1500 bits
D. 2500 bits

4-231.   What is the default value for the s0 interface B/W parameter?

A. 1500 kbit
B. 1544 kbit
C. 1500 bits
D. 2500 bits

4-232.   What is the default value for the s0 interface keepalive time?

A. 15 second
B. 20 second
C. 25 second
D. 10 second

4-233.   What is the default value for the e0 interface B/W parameter?

A. 1500 kbit
B. 1544 kbit
C. 1500 bits
D. 10000 kbits

4-234.   What does the command **show controllers s0** provide? (Select all that apply)

A. It verifies the physical configuration of s0 interface.
B. The type of connection (e.g., DTE or DCE).
C. The configurations of the interface including the IP address and clock rate.
D. The type of serial port connection (e.g., Ethernet or Token Ring).
E. The controlling processor of s0 interface.

4-235.   If an interface is administratively down, what is the problem?

A. There is no problem. **no shutdown** command needs to be issued.
B. The interface is defective.
C. The interface is looped.
D. The interface is not connected to another device.

4-236.   Which of the following will show the contents of the EEPROM in the Router?

A. show flash

B. show ver
C. show EEPROM
D. show flash file
E. show ip flash

4-237.   Based on Figure 4-2, which of the following steps is not required to be able to forward IP packets on both routers' interfaces? (Select all that apply)

Figure 4-2 Question 4-237 Network

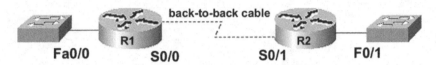

A.   Configuring the interface IP address commands on each router's FastEthernet and serial interfaces
B.   Configuring the bandwidth command on one router's serial interface
C.   The interface vlan x command
D.   Configuring the AUX port on the routers.
E.   The ip address dhcp command
F.   Configuring the clock rate command on one router's serial interface
G.   Setting the interface description on both the FastEthernet and serial interface of each router

4-238.   Which of the following is true regarding Figure 4-2, if the output of the show ip interface brief command on R2 lists interfaces status codes of "down" and "down" for interface Serial 0/1? (Select all that apply)

A.   R2's serial interface has been configured to use HDLC, but the router on the other end of the serial link has been configured to use PPP.
B.   The shutdown command is issued for that interface.
C.   Only one router has been configured with a serial interface IP address command.
D.   A serial cable is not inserted correctly into the R2's serial interface.

4-239.   Which of the following commands does not list the IP address and mask of at least one interface? (Select all that apply)

A.   show version
B.   show interfaces
C.   show ip interface brief
D.   show run
E.   show protocols type number
F.   show start

CHAPTER 5
INTERNETWORKING
ROUTING PROTOCOLS

This chapter begins with an introduction to the IP routing process, and continues with an in-depth view of the routing protocols. Two types of routing protocols will be discussed in this chapter, the Routing Information Protocol (RIP) and Interior Gateway Routing Protocol (IGRP).

Today, with CISCO Routers many routing protocols can be configured at the same time. IP routing is the process of moving packets from one network to another network through the routers and delivering the packets to the hosts. Routing Protocols configuration in the CISCO IOS and their traffic monitoring will be detailed and examples of well-designed networks will be given in this chapter.

The following topics are emphasized in this chapter:

- The Routing Process.
- Static Routing.
- Default Routing.
- Dynamic Routing.
- Routing Information Protocol.
- Interior Gateway Routing Protocol.
- Verifying the routing configurations.

A firm understanding of the fundamentals behind this chapter and answering the 228 learning questions at the end of this chapter are important for Configuring, Managing and troubleshooting a CISCO internetwork and answering the CCNA/CCENT exam related questions. The questions herein are intended to reflect the type of questions presented on the CCENT Test.

The Routing Process

This section defines the routing process in general, and then, presents the minimum Router requirements to be able to routing a packet throughout the internetwork. The section also introduces static routing and dynamic routing processes.

Routing process is a process of moving a packet from one host and sending it through the internetwork to another host on a different network/subnet. So, it takes a packet from one network and sends it to another network. It requires routing software, which is implemented in a Router or in any other automated machines. By adding the routing software and the suitable networks' interfaces, any automated machine can work as a Router.

Routing process is the core of the Router processes. The Router learns about remote networks from a network administrator or from neighbor Routers. From this information the Router builds a routing table that describes how to find the remote networks. If the network is directly connected, their interfaces must be defined on the Router, then the Router knows how to get to this network and there are no needs for any further interventions. If the network is not directly connected, the Router must learn how to obtain the remote network with either the configuring of the static routing or dynamic routing.

The routing process can be either static or dynamic. Static routing process means that the administrator must type all network locations into the routing tables of all routers in the internetwork by hand. The administrator is responsible for updating manually, all changes into all routers. Dynamic routing, on the hand, is implemented and supported by dynamic routing protocols running on the Routers, but it still needs some administrator's interventions. Dynamic routing protocols discover all routes by communicating with neighbor routers in the internetwork. The routers use dynamic routing protocols to update each other about all the networks they know about. When changes occur in the network topology, the dynamic routing protocols automatically inform all routers about those changes.

Example 5-1, The IP Routing Process in a Simple Network: The following example describes the IP routing process. The example uses Figure 5-1 to clarify in step by step the communication between Host A and Host B on a different network. Notice that, the IP routing process is simple and does not change regardless of the size of the network.

Figure 5-1 IP Routing Process in a Simple Network

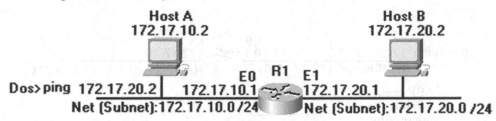

The following steps illustrate what will happen when Host A on the net 10.0 tries to ping Host B on the net 20.0.

Step 1: Issuing the ping command. The user issues **ping 172.17.20.2** command from Host A. Host A used the IP and ICMP Network layer protocols to generate a packet.

Step 2: Determining the destination Host B's Network. IP and the ARP protocols on the host are working together to determine what network this packet is destined for by calculating the binary multiplication of (the destination IP address * the source subnet mask) and (the source IP address * the source subnet mask). If both are equal, this means that the destination address is in the local network (the packet will be sent directly to that destination host), otherwise the destination will be on the remote network. In this example, the destination is in the remote network. The packet then must be sent to the Router (R1) so that it will be routed to the correct remote network.

Step 3: Determining the R1 MAC address. Host A has the IP address of E0 as a default gateway. However, to communicate with R1, the R1's MAC address must be obtained. To obtain the hardware address of E0, Host A looks in a location in memory called the ARP cache. However, if it's not found in ARP cache (i.e., The E0 IP address has not already been resolved to a MAC address), Host A sends an ARP broadcast on the local network looking, for the MAC address of IP address 172.17.10.1. This step is usually times out. Finally, the R1 responds with the MAC address of the E0.

Step 4: Completing the Packet. The network layer takes the packet it generated with the ICMP echo request (ping) to the Data Link layer, along with the MAC address of where Host A wants to send the packet. The packet includes in addition to the source IP address and the destination IP address, the ICMP specific in the Network layer protocol field.

Step 5: Generating the frame by Host A. The Data Link layer generates the frame, by encapsulating the packet with the control information needed to transmit. The frame includes the source and destination MAC addresses, and the type field specifying the Network layer protocol (IP uses an Ethernet_II frame by default). This process is depicted in Figure 5-2.

The frame contains the source and destination MAC addresses, the source and destination IP addresses, and the data and the frame's CRC inside the Frame Check Sequence (FCS) field.

Step 6: Sending the frame. The data Link layer of Host A takes the frame to the Physical layer, encodes the frame into 1s and 0s and transmits this out on the network.

Step 7: Receiving the data by R1. R1's E0 receives the signal and the interface synchronizes on the digital signal preamble and extracts the frame. R1's interface, then builds the frame, runs a CRC and, at the end of the frame, checks the FCS field to be sure that the CRC matches and no fragmentation or collisions are occurred during transmission.

Figure 5-2 Generating the Frame from Host A

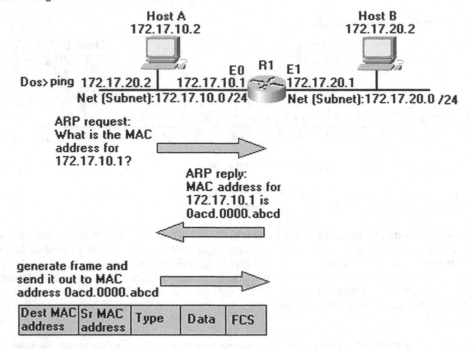

Step 8: Checking the destination MAC address. The frame destination MAC address is checked. Since it is a match, the frame type field will be checked to see what R1 should do with the data packet. IP is in the type field. Therefore, R1 must hand the packet to the IP protocol running on R1. The frame is discarded, and the original-generated packet by Host A is put in R1's buffer.

Step 9: Checking the Destination IP address. IP in R1 determines if the packet is for R1 by looking at the packet's destination IP address. IP 172.17.20.2 is in the packet and from the routing table; R1 determines that 172.17.20.0 net is a directly connected network on the interface E1.

Step 10: Generating the frame by R1. R1 places the packet in the buffer of the interface E1. Now, to send the packet to the destination host B, R1 needs to create a frame at first and the frame must have a MAC address of the destination Host B. The same process described in steps 2 and 3 are applied here. Assuming that the MAC is not in the ARP cache, R1 must then send an ARP broadcast out E1 to find the MAC address of 172.17.20.2.

Step 11: Replying to R1 broadcast. Host B responds to R1's ARP broadcast with the MAC address of its NIC by an ARP reply. R1's E1 interface now creates the packet to Host B. This process is depicted in Figure 5-3.

At this point, notice the following important thing; the IP source and destination addresses are never changed. The packet was never modified at all; only the frame is changed. The frame's source and destination MAC addresses are changed at every interface of R1 during transmission.

Step 12: Checking the IP address by Host B. Host B receives the frame from R1 and runs a CRC checking. According to CRC result, the frame is discarded and the packet is handled to IP of Host B. The destination IP address in the packet is checked by IP. Since the IP destination address matches the IP of Host B, it looks in the protocol field of the packet to determine what the purpose of the packet is.

Figure 5-3 Generating the Frame from R1's E1

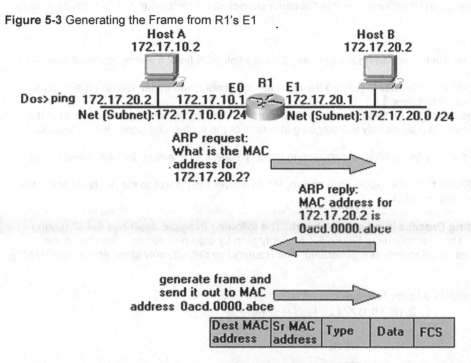

Step 13: Generating the reply by Host B. Since the packet is an ICMP echo request, Host B generates a new ICMP echo-reply packet with a source IP address of Host B and a destination IP address of Host A. Host B sends an ICMP echo-reply to Host A by the same processes above, except that it goes in the opposite direction and each device only needs to look in its ARP cache to determine the MAC address of each interface, since the MAC address of each device along the path is already known in the ARP cache of each device.

The IP routing process illustrated in example 5-1 would be the same if the network were much larger. The only difference is that the packet would simply go through more hops (routers) before it finds the destination host. However, on point-to-point WAN links, ARP is not needed, and the data link addressing is unused.

In IP routing, the frame is replaced at each hop as the packet traverses the internetwork, so the frame changes at each hop. The packet from the source to the destination was never modified at all, regardless the number of hops passing through. Only, the source and destination MAC addresses change at each hop.

In IP routing, the source host would send a packet to the Router, only if the packet is destined to that Router or the packet is destined to the remote network. With the help of the routing table, the Router will decide for which network the packet must be gone. The Router, by default, only knows about their directly connected networks. So, in example 5-1, the routing table of R1 already has both IP networks (10.0 and 20.0) in the routing table because these nets are directly connected to R1.

The following are the general rules that must be implemented by hosts and routers for a successful IP routing process.

- **By Host**

Rule1. If the destination IP address is in the same subnet, send the packet directly to that destination host.

Rule2. If the destination IP address is not in the same subnet, send the packet to the default gateway.

▪ **By Router**

Rule1. Ensure that the frame had no errors using the data-link FCS field. If errors occurred, discard the frame.

Rule2. If errors not found in **Rule1**, discard the old data-link header and trailer, leaving the IP packet and handled it to Layer 3.

Rule3. Check the routing table to find the route that matches the destination IP packet address. If a route is found, it may identify the outgoing interface of the router, and possibly the next-hop router.

Rule4. Forward the new frame after encapsulating the IP packet inside a new data-link header and trailer.

Rule5. Repeat **Rule1** to **Rule4** inside each hop router, to deliver the packet to the destined address host in the internetwork.

Example 5-2, The IP Routing Process in a Large Network: The following example describes the IP routing process in a large network. The example uses Figure 5-4 to clarify step by step how Routers interfaces are configured and routing tables for all routers are generated. The Routers, by default, only know about their directly connected networks.

Figure 5-4 IP Routing Process in a Large Network

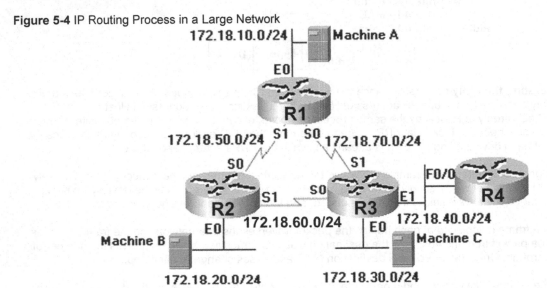

Routes to remote networks can be added to the routing tables of the routers using the following routing types: Static routing, default routing and dynamic routing. However, the best way for one network is not necessarily best for another. The best way should be selected depending on the network requirements.

The rest of this chapter will emphasize configuring the network in Figure 5-4. The first step is to configure the routers interfaces. This will make the routers to know about all directly connected networks. The second step is to add the static routes to these routers. The third step is to add the default routes to these routers. Then, Dynamic routes will be added in the fourth step, by configuring the dynamic routing protocols on the routers. RIP and IGRP dynamic routing protocols will be configured on this network. However, this internetwork is a lab WAN, and the routers are connected using back-to-back connections. Therefore, one Router must be configured to supply clocking on both interfaces. R1 will be used for this purpose.

Step 1, Configuring the routers interfaces: Router configuration is a simple process, since it only requires adding IP addresses to the interfaces and then the **no shutdown** command must be performed. However, configuring the IP addresses for router interfaces can be done dynamically using DHCP servers. The following Configurations are used to clarify how routers interfaces are configured for directly connected networks. The Configurations will use Table 5-1 for an IP addressing scheme. Each network in Figure 5-4 has a 24-bit subnet mask (255.255.255.0).

Table 5-1 IP Addressing Scheme for Internetwork in Figure 5-4

Router	Network Address	Interface	Address
R1	172.18.10.0	E0	172.18.10.1
	172.18.70.0	S0	172.18.70.1
	172.18.50.0	S1	172.18.50.2
R2	172.18.20.0	E0	172.18.20.1
	172.18.50.0	S0	172.18.50.1
	172.18.60.0	S1	172.18.60.2
R3	172.18.30.0	E0	172.18.30.1
	172.18.40.0	E1	172.18.40.1
	172.18.60.0	S0	172.18.60.1
	172.18.70.0	S1	172.18.70.2
R4	172.18.40.0	F0/0	172.18.40.2

Configuration 5-1, R1 Interfaces Configuration: The following Configuration shows how to configure R1 interfaces using the **ip address** and **no shutdown** commands.

```
R1(config)#interface ethernet 0
R1(config-if)#ip address 172.18.10.1 255.255.255.0
R1(config-if)#no shut
R1(config-if)#int s0
R1(config-if)#ip address 172.18.70.1 255.255.255.0
R1(config-if)#clock rate 64000
R1(config-if)#no shut
R1(config-if)#int s1
R1(config-if)#ip address 172.18.50.2 255.255.255.0
R1(config-if)#clock rate 64000
R1(config-if)#no shut
```

The preceding Configuration configured Ethernet 0 into network 172.18.10.0, serial 0 into network 172.18.70.0, and serial 1 into network 172.18.50.0. The serial interfaces need to add the **clock rate** command to the DCE interfaces connected to both serial interfaces. The created IP routing tables on a CISCO Router can be displayed using the privileged mode command **show ip route** as shown below. Notice that only the configured network is shown in the routing table.

```
R1#sh ip route
Codes:  C – connected, S – static, I - IGRP, R - RIP, M – Mobile, B – BGP, D – EIGRP, EX – EIGRP external,
O - OSPF, ......
Gateway of last resort is not set

     172.18.0.0/24 is subnetted, 3 subnets
C    172.18.70.0 is directly connected, Serial0
C    172.18.50.0 is directly connected, Serial1
```

```
C    172.18.10.0 is directly connected, Ethernet0
R1#
```

The preceding routing table shows the directly connected networks to R1 with the "C" character at the beginning of each line; which means that the networks are directly connected.

It is possible to change the format of the display of the subnet mask in **show** commands, for the duration of the login session to the router, using the **terminal ip netmask-format decimal** EXEC command, as shown below.

```
R1#terminal ip netmask-format decimal
R1#show ip route
Codes:  C – connected, S – static, I - IGRP, R - RIP, M – Mobile, B – BGP, D – EIGRP, EX – EIGRP external,
O - OSPF, ......
Gateway of last resort is not set

     172.18.0.0 255.255.255.0 is subnetted, 3 subnets
C    172.18.70.0 is directly connected, Serial0
C    172.18.50.0 is directly connected, Serial1
C    172.18.10.0 is directly connected, Ethernet0
R1#
```

Notice in the output above, the **/24** is displayed in the decimal format equivalent, i.e., **255.255.255.0**.

Configuration 5-2, R2 Interfaces Configuration: The following Configuration shows how to configure R2 interfaces using the **ip address** and **no shutdown** commands.

```
R2(config)#int e0
R2(config-if)#ip address  172.18.20.1 255.255.255.0
R2(config-if)#no shut
R2(config-if)#int s0
R2(config-if)#ip address  172.18.50.1 255.255.255.0
R2(config-if)#no shut
R2(config-if)#int s1
R2(config-if)#ip address  172.18.60.2 255.255.255.0
R2 (config-if)#no shut
```

The preceding Configuration configured Ethernet 0 into network 172.18.20.0, serial 0 into network 172.18.50.0, and serial 1 into network 172.18.60.0. To view the IP routing tables created on a CISCO Router, use the privileged mode command **show ip route**. The command output is shown as follows. Notice that only the configured network is shown in the routing table.

```
R2#sh ip route
........
     172.18.0.0/24 is subnetted, 3 subnets
C    172.18.60.0 is directly connected, Serial1
C    172.18.50.0 is directly connected, Serial0
C    172.18.20.0 is directly connected, Ethernet0
R2#
```

Notice that R1 and R2 can now communicate because they are on the same WAN network.

Configuration 5-3, R3 Interfaces Configuration: The following Configuration shows how to configure R3 interfaces using the **ip address** and **no shutdown** commands.

```
R3(config)#int e0
R3(config-if)#ip address  172.18.30.1 255.255.255.0
R3(config-if)#no shut
R3(config-if)#int e1
R3(config-if)#ip address 172.18.40.1 255.255.255.0
R3(config-if)#no shut
R3(config-if)#int s0
R3(config-if)#ip address 172.18.60.1 255.255.255.0
R3(config-if)#no shut
R3(config-if)#int s1
R3(config-if)#ip address 172.18.70.2 255.255.255.0
R3(config-if)#no shut
```

The preceding Configuration configured Ethernet 0 into network 172.18.30.0, Ethernet 1 into network 172.18.40.0, serial 0 into network 172.18.60.0, and serial 1 into network 172.18.70.0. To view the IP routing tables created on a CISCO Router, use the privileged mode command **show ip route**. The command output is shown as follows. Notice that only the configured network is shown in the routing table.

R3#sh ip route
....
```
      172.18.0.0/24 is subnetted, 4 subnets
C     172.18.70.0 is directly connected, Serial1
C     172.18.60.0 is directly connected, Serial0
C     172.18.40.0 is directly connected, Ethernet1
C     172.18.30.0 is directly connected, Ethernet0
R3#
```

Notice that R1, R2, and R3 can now communicate because all WAN connections are configured. However, these routers cannot communicate with R4 yet.

Configuration 5-4, R4 Interfaces Configuration: The following Configuration shows how to configure R4 interfaces using the **ip address** and **no shutdown** commands.

```
R4(config)#interface fa0/0
R4(config-if)#ip address 172.18.40.2 255.255.255.0
R4(config-if)#no shut
```

The preceding Configuration configured Fastethernet 0/0 into network 172.18.40.0. To view the IP routing tables created on a CISCO Router, use the privileged mode command **show ip route**. The command output is shown as follows. Notice that only the configured network is shown in the routing table.
R4#sh ip route
....
```
      172.18.0.0/24 is subnetted, 1 subnets
C     172.18.40.0 is directly connected, FastEthernet0/0
R4#
```

Notice that R4 and R3 can now communicate because they are on the same LAN network. However, R4, by default, cannot communicate with the R1 and R2 yet because it does not know about networks 172.18.50.0, 172.18.60.0, and 172.18.70.0. However, R3 can ping both the R1 and R2, but R2 and R1 cannot see R4.

Configuring Static Routing on the CISCO Routers

Static Routing is the process of configuring network routes in each router's routing table manually by an administrator. There are several advantages of static routing process:

- Improving security in the internetwork, since the administrator could only allow routing to certain networks.
- No overhead on the Router CPU.
- No bandwidth usage between routers.
- Routes could be not volatile when rebooting the router.

On the hand, there are several disadvantages of static routing process:

- The administrator must add a new route to any new networks on all routers.
- It is unsuitable in large networks because too many routes must be added manually when a new network is added and this would be a full-time job, and errors could happen.
- Troubleshooting and maintenance of the internetwork would be difficult.
- The administrator must fully understand the internetwork and how each Router is connected.

Static Routing Command Explanation

The command used to add a static route to a routing table is:

ip route destination_network mask next_hop_address or exit interface [administrative_distance] [permanent].

The following describes each command in the string:

destination_network: IP route prefix for the destination network.
mask: Prefix subnet mask for the destination network.
next_hop_address: IP address of the next hop Router that can be used to reach the destination network. The next hop Router will receive the packet and forward it to the remote network in the internetwork. This Router interface is on a directly connected network. Try to **ping** the next hop Router interface before adding it to the route.
exit interface: Network interface to use. It can be used in place of the next hop address. It must be on a point-to-point link, such as WAN link. This command does not work on a LAN.
administrative_distance: (Optional) By default, the static routes have an administrative distance of 1. However, adding an administrative weight at the end of the command can change the default value.
permanent: (Optional) Specifies that the route will not be removed, even if the interface shuts down. In case of the interface shuts down or in case of the Router cannot communicate to the next hop Router, the route is automatically removed from the routing table.

Step 2, Configuring the routers static routes: The following Configurations are used to clarify how routers are configured for static routing using the **ip route** command. The Configurations will use Table 5-1 for an IP addressing scheme. Each network in Figure 5-4 has a 24-bit subnet mask (255.255.255.0). Before starting configuring the routers, remember that, each routing table automatically includes directly connected networks. To be able to route to all networks in the internetwork, the routing table must include information that defines where these other networks are located and how to get there.

Configuration 5-5, R1 static routing configuration: The following Configuration shows how to configure static routes on the R1 Router using **ip route** and then, shows the routing table using the **sh ip route** command. Before starting, notice that networks 172.18.10.0, 172.18.50.0, and 172.18.70.0 are directly connected to the R1 Router. For R1 Router to be able to route to all networks, the following networks must be configured in the routing table: 172.18.20.0, 172.18.30.0, 172.18.40.0, and 172.18.60.0. Notice also that, each static route sends the packets either to 172.18.50.1 or to 172.18.70.2. These interfaces are the R1 Router's next hops.

R1(config)#ip route 172.18.20.0 255.255.255.0 172.18.50.1
R1(config)#ip route 172.18.30.0 255.255.255.0 172.18.70.2
R1(config)#ip route 172.18.40.0 255.255.255.0 172.18.70.2
R1(config)#ip route 172.18.60.0 255.255.255.0 172.18.50.1

Any one of the two next hop interfaces for R1 Router can be used; however careful configuration should be taken, since the R2 and R3 routers must be configured with same routing table. If the R2 or R3 routers are not configured with all the same information as R1 Router, the packets will be discarded at R2 or R3. To view the routing table, the **show running-config** or **show ip route** commands can be used.

R1#sh ip route
Codes: C – connected, S – static, I - IGRP, R - RIP, M – Mobile, B – BGP, D – EIGRP, EX – EIGRP external,
O - OSPF, ...
Gateway of last resort is not set

       172.18.0.0/24 is subnetted, 7 subnets
C   172.18.70.0 is directly connected, Serial0
S   172.18.60.0 [1/0] via 172.18.50.1
C   172.18.50.0 is directly connected, Serial1
S   172.18.40.0 [1/0] via 172.18.70.2
S   172.18.30.0 [1/0] via 172.18.70.2
S   172.18.20.0 [1/0] via 172.18.50.1
C   172.18.10.0 is directly connected, Ethernet0
R1#

The preceding routing table shows the directly connected networks to R1 as well as the remote networks that are using static routes. Notice the "S"; this means that the networks are statically defined.

Configuration 5-6, R2 static routing configuration: The following Configuration shows how to configure static routes on the R2 Router using **ip route** and then, shows the routing table using the **sh ip route** command. Before starting, notice that networks 172.18.20.0, 172.18.50.0, and 172.18.60.0 are directly connected to the R2 Router. For R2 Router to be able to route to all networks, the following networks must be configured in the routing table: 172.18.10.0, 172.18.30.0, 172.18.40.0, and 172.18.70.0. Notice also that, each static route sends the packets either to 172.18.50.2 or to 172.18.60.1. These interfaces are the R2 Router's next hops.

R2(config)#ip route 172.18.10.0 255.255.255.0 172.18.50.2
R2(config)#ip route 172.18.30.0 255.255.255.0 172.18.60.1
R2(config)#ip route 172.18.40.0 255.255.255.0 172.18.60.1
R2(config)#ip route 172.18.70.0 255.255.255.0 172.18.50.2

To view the routing table, the **show running-config** or **show ip route** commands can be used.

R2#sh ip route
Codes: C – connected, S – static, I - IGRP, R - RIP, M – Mobile, B – BGP, D – EIGRP, EX – EIGRP external,
O - OSPF, ...
Gateway of last resort is not set

       172.18.0.0/24 is subnetted, 7 subnets
S   172.18.70.0 [1/0] via 172.18.50.2
C   172.18.60.0 is directly connected, Serial1

```
C   172.18.50.0 is directly connected, Serial0
S   172.18.40.0 [1/0] via 172.18.60.1
S   172.18.30.0 [1/0] via 172.18.60.1
C   172.18.20.0 is directly connected, Ethernet0
S   172.18.10.0 [1/0] via 172.18.50.2
R2#
```

The preceding routing table shows the directly connected networks to R2 as well as the remote networks that are using static routes. Notice the [1/0], it is the administrative distance and hops to the remote network, which is 0. Notice also that, R2 Router now has a complete routing table. As long as the other routers in the internetwork have the same routing table, R2 can communicate to all remote networks.

Configuration 5-7, R3 static routing configuration: The following Configuration shows how to configure static routes on the R3 Router using **ip route** and then, shows the routing table using the **sh ip route** command. Before starting, notice that networks 172.18.30.0, 172.18.40.0, 172.18.70.0, and 172.18.60.0 are directly connected to the R3 Router. For R3 Router to be able to route to all networks, the following networks must be configured in the routing table: 172.18.10.0, 172.18.20.0, and 172.18.50.0. Notice also that, each static route sends the packets either to 172.18.70.1 or to 172.18.60.2. These interfaces are the R3 Router's next hops.

```
R3(config)#ip route 172.18.10.0 255.255.255.0 172.18.70.1
R3(config)#ip route 172.18.20.0 255.255.255.0 172.18.60.2
R3(config)#ip route 172.18.50.0 255.255.255.0 172.18.60.2
```

To view the routing table, the **show running-config** or **show ip route** commands can be used.

```
R3#sh ip route
Codes:  C – connected, S – static, I - IGRP, R - RIP, M – Mobile, B – BGP, D – EIGRP, EX – EIGRP external,
O - OSPF, ......
Gateway of last resort is not set

     172.18.0.0/24 is subnetted, 7 subnets
C   172.18.70.0 is directly connected, Serial1
C   172.18.60.0 is directly connected, Serial0
S   172.18.50.0  [1/0] via 172.18.60.2
C   172.18.40.0 is directly connected, Ethernet1
C   172.18.30.0 is directly connected, Ethernet0
S   172.18.20.0  [1/0] via 172.18.60.2
S   172.18.10.0 [1/0] via 172.18.70.1
R3#
```

The preceding routing table shows the directly connected networks to R3 as well as the remote networks that are using static routes. Notice that, R3 Router now has a complete routing table. R3 can now communicate to all remote networks in this internetwork, since all other routers in the internetwork have the same routing table.

Configuration 5-8, R4 static routing configuration: The following Configuration shows how to configure static routes on the R4 Router using **ip route** and then, shows the routing table using the **sh ip route** command. Before starting, notices that only network 172.18.40.0 is directly connected to the R4 Router. For R4 Router to be able to route to all networks, the following networks must be configured in the routing table: 172.18.10.0, 172.18.20.0, 172.18.30.0, 172.18.50.0, 172.18.60.0, and 172.18.70.0. Notice also that, each static route sends the packets to 172.18.40.1. This interface is the only R4 Router's next hops.

```
R4(config)#ip route 172.18.10.0 255.255.255.0 172.18.40.1
R4(config)#ip route 172.18.20.0 255.255.255.0 172.18.40.1
```

R4(config)#ip route 172.18.30.0 255.255.255.0 172.18.40.1
R4(config)#ip route 172.18.50.0 255.255.255.0 172.18.40.1
R4(config)#ip route 172.18.60.0 255.255.255.0 172.18.40.1
R4(config)#ip route 172.18.70.0 255.255.255.0 172.18.40.1

To view the routing table, the **show running-config** or **show ip route** commands can be used.

R4#sh ip route
Codes: C – connected, S – static, I - IGRP, R - RIP, M – Mobile, B – BGP, D – EIGRP, EX – EIGRP external,
O - OSPF, ...
Gateway of last resort is not set

    172.18.0.0/24 is subnetted, 7 subnets
S   172.18.70.0 [1/0] via 172.18.40.1
S   172.18.60.0 [1/0] via 172.18.40.1
S   172.18.50.0 [1/0] via 172.18.40.1
C   172.18.40.0 is directly connected, FastEthernet0/0
S   172.18.30.0 [1/0] via 172.18.40.1
S   172.18.20.0 [1/0] via 172.18.40.1
S   172.18.10.0 [1/0] via 172.18.40.1
R4#

The preceding routing table shows the directly connected networks to R4 as well as the remote networks that are using static routes. Notice that, R4 Router now has a complete routing table. R4 can now communicate to all remote networks in this internetwork, since all other routers in the internetwork have the same routing table.

Since, the correct routing tables are now configured on all routers; the hosts throughout this internetwork should be able to communicate without any problem. However, if one more route or another Router is added to the internetwork, all routers' routing tables must be updated by hand. Of course, this is a complicated and time-consuming task for a large internetwork.

To verify that all routers' routing tables are correctly configured, **ping** utility can be used. The following is the output of a **ping** to network 172.18.10.0 from R4 router:

R4#ping 172.18.10.1
Type escape sequence to abort.
Sending 5, 100-byte ICMP Echos to 172.18.10.1, timeout is 2 seconds:
.!!!!
Success rate is 80 percent (4/5), round-trip min/avg/max = 42/44/46 ms

Notice that, the first response to the **ping** command is a period, since, the first Ping times out waiting for the ARP request and response. When the ARP has found the MAC address of the default gateway, the IP-to-Ethernet mapping will be added in the ARP cache, and the Ping will not be time out for any other IP connectivity to the next hop router, as no ARP broadcasts have to be performed.

The following is the output of a **ping** to network 172.18.40.0 from R1 router. This is to be performed on a WAN not a LAN and therefore, there are no ARP broadcasts.

R1#ping 172.18.40.2
Type escape sequence to abort.
Sending 5, 100-byte ICMP Echos to 172.18.40.2, timeout is 2 seconds:
!!!!!
Success rate Is 100 percent (5/5), round-trip min/avg/max = 44/46/48 ms

An extended IOS Ping utility can be used from privileged EXEC mode, which allows the user to change many options for what the **ping** command does, including the source IP address used for the ICMP echo requests sent by the command. This is helpful, in case there are some difficulties to ask a user to **ping** to another host and test his network. The CISCO **ping** command uses, by default, the output interface's IP address as the packet's source address, unless otherwise specified in an extended **ping**. The following shows how to test the network connectivity between Machine A in network 172.18.10.0 and Machine B in network 172.18.20.0 from R1 CLI.

```
R1#ping
Protocol [ip]:
Target IP address: 172.18.10.2
Repeat count [5]:
Datagram size [100]:
Timeout in seconds [2]:
Extended commands [n]: y
Source address or interface: 172.18.20.2
Type of service [0]:
Set DF bit in IP header? [no]:
Validate reply data? [no]:
Data pattern [0xABCD]:
Loose, Strict, Record, Timestamp, Verbose[none]:
Sweep range of sizes [n]:
Type escape sequence to abort.
Sending 5, 100-byte ICMP Echos to 10.1.2.252, timeout is 2 seconds:
!!!!!
Success rate is 100 percent (5/5), round-trip min/avg/max = 4/4/8 ms.
```

Configuring the Default Routing on a CISCO Router

Default routing is used to send packets with a remote destination network not in the routing table to the next hop router. However, it can only be used on stub networks. Stub networks have only one connection to an internetwork. Therefore, default routes can only be set on a stub network, or network loops may occur. Default route can be created by defining a static route and using all 0s in place of the network and mask.

Step 3, Configuring the routers default routes: The following Configurations are used to clarify how routers are configured for default routing using the **ip route** command. The Configurations will use Table 5-1 for an IP addressing scheme. Each network in Figure 5-4 has a 24-bit subnet mask (255.255.255.0). Before starting configuring the routers, remember that, each routing table automatically includes directly connected networks. To be able to route to all networks in the internetwork, the routing table must include information that defines where these other networks are located and how to get there. However, for stub networks, default routing can be defined instead of defining the static route. The only router that is considered a stub network is R4. It is incorrect idea to define the default routes on the R1, R2, and R3 routers, since packets would not be forwarded to the correct networks because each router will have more than one interface routing to other routers. For this reason, it is assumed that the second network on R4 does not have a router that needs packets sent to it.

Configuration 5-9, R4 default routing configuration: The following Configuration shows how to configure default routes on the R4 Router using **ip route** and then, shows the routing table using the **sh ip route** command. Before starting, notices that, only network 172.18.40.0 is directly connected to the R4 Router. For R4 Router to be able to route to all networks, the following networks must be configured in the routing table: 172.18.10.0, 172.18.20.0, 172.18.30.0, 172.18.50.0, 172.18.60.0, and 172.18.70.0. The default route is used here to forward the packets to R3 router. Then R3 router will send the packets to R1 and R2 routers, since R3 router has already configured to reach R2 and R1 routers using static routing. Notice also that, R4 router will only send the packets to 172.18.40.1, which is the interface of R3 router. This interface is the only R4 Router's next hops. Moreover, before implementing the default routing in R4, you must remove all static routes to remote networks.

R4(config)#no ip route 172.18.10.0 255.255.255.0 172.18.40.1
R4(config)#no ip route 172.18.20.0 255.255.255.0 172.18.40.1
R4(config)#no ip route 172.18.30.0 255.255.255.0 172.18.40.1
R4(config)#no ip route 172.18.50.0 255.255.255.0 172.18.40.1
R4(config)#no ip route 172.18.60.0 255.255.255.0 172.18.40.1
R4(config)#no ip route 172.18.70.0 255.255.255.0 172.18.40.1
R4(config)#ip route 0.0.0.0 0.0.0.0 172.18.40.1

Default routing uses wildcards in the network address and mask locations of a static route. Notice that, by using default route, it is possible to create just one static route entry instead of six entries when static routing is used. To view the routing table, the **show running-config** or **show ip route** commands can be used.

R4#sh ip route
Codes: C – connected, S – static, I - IGRP, R - RIP, M – Mobile, B – BGP, D – EIGRP, EX – EIGRP external,
O - OSPF, ...
L2 – IS-IS level-2, * - candidate default, U – per-user static route, o – ODR

Gateway of last resort is 172.18.40.1 to network 0.0.0.0
172.18.0.0/24 is subnetted, 7 subnets
C   172.18.40.0 is directly connected, FastEthernet0/0
S*   0.0.0.0/0 [1/0] via 172.18.40.1
R4#

The preceding routing table shows the directly connected network to R4 as well as the default route to five remote networks. Notice the "S*", this means that the network is a candidate for a default route. The [1/0] is the administrative distance and hops to the remote network. Notice also that, the gateway of last resort is now set. This message indicates that R3 is a router to which all unroutable packets are sent. R3 now, acts as a repository for all unroutable packets, ensuring that all messages are at least handled in some way.

All CISCO routers are classful routers by default, which means they expect a default subnet mask on each interface of the router. Hence, when a router receives a packet for a destination subnet not in the routing table, it will drop the packet by default. Therefore, when the default routing is used, the **ip classless** command must be issued from global configuration mode because no remote subnets will be in the routing table. However, the **ip classless** command is ON by default on all new IOS versions.

R4(config)#ip classless

Now, instead of dropping the packet, the router will forward the packet on the default route.

Default routes decrease network traffic by eliminating the routing update traffic. It also decreases administration of routing tables since just one route entry can be used to represent many routes. However, no overhead on the Router CPU is added when the default routing is used.

In Figure 5-5, RC is unable to successfully ping RB, even if default routing is defined. The problem is RB and RA are not on the same network. "RB" interface "S0" is on network 172.15.0.0/28 with Range (172.15.0.0 - 172.15.0.15) and "RA" interface "S1" is on network 172.15.0.16/28 Range (172.15.0.16 - 172.15.0.31). This Figure illustrates were two default routes must reside and a problem that even occurred when the administrator incorrectly configures the network.

Figure 5-5 Default Routing in a Problem

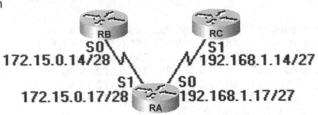

System Config.

RA no static route defined

RB default route
0.0.0.0 0.0.0.0 172.15.0.17

RC default route
0.0.0.0 0.0.0.0 192.168.1.17

Dynamic Routing Protocols

Dynamic routing is the process of using dynamic routing protocols to find and update automatically routing tables on routers. Dynamic routing is easier than static or default routing, since it requires little administration when routes are created, but it is used at the expense of the Router CPU processes and bandwidth on the network links, since it exchanges routes update messages throughout the internetwork.

Dynamic route is created by adopting the dynamic routing protocols in the routers. Routing protocols create dynamic routes automatically. A routing protocol defines the set of rules used by a Router when it communicates between neighbor routers. Two types of routing protocols are used in the internetwork: Interior Gateway Protocol (IGP) and Exterior Gateway Protocol (EGP). Open Shortest Path First (OSPF) is an example of an IGP. Border Gateway Protocol (BGP) is an example of an EGP. IGP routing protocols are used to exchange routing information with routers in the same Autonomous System (AS). EGP routing protocols are used to exchange routing information between Autonomous Systems (ASs). An Autonomous System (AS) is a collection of networks under a common administrative routing domain. To uniquely identifying each AS in the Internet, an AS number (ASN) is assigned to each AS. This number is included by BGP in the routing updates to prevent loops.

Today, BGP is used by ISPs to exchange routing information between different ISPs and between ISPs and customers. BGP advertises only routing information to specifically defined peers using TCP. BGP does not use a metric like IGPs to decide what route to use, instead BGP uses policies. Routing policy can be based on a business relationship between ISPs.

Using of the Administrative Distances in the Routing Protocols

Administrative distance AD is used to measure the trustworthiness of routing information received on a Router from a neighbor Router. AD is an integer from 0 to 255, where 0 is the most trusted and 255 means no traffic (no trust) will be passed via this route.

Table 5-2 shows the default administrative distances that a CISCO Router will use to decide which route to use to a remote network.

Table 5-2 The CISCO Default ADs

Route Source	Default AD
Directly connected interface	0
Static Route	1
Default Route	1
EIGRP	90
IGRP	100
OSPF	110
IS-IS	115
RIP v1 and v2	120
External EIGRP	170
Unknown	255(the route will never be used)

The following strategy (in the same order) is used by the router when it receives two route updates for the same remote network.

1. The router checks the AD's. The lowest AD will be placed in the routing table.
2. If both advertised routes to the same network have the same AD, then the routing protocol metrics (such as hop count or bandwidth of the lines) will be used to find the best path to the remote network. The advertised route with the lowest metric will be placed in the routing table.
3. If both advertised routes have the same AD as well as the same metrics, then the routing protocol will load-balance to the remote network.

Types of Routing Protocols

There are three types or classes of IGP routing protocols: Distance Vector, Link State and Hybrid. RIP and IGRP are examples of the distance vector routing protocols. OSPF and Integrated IS-IS are examples of the link state routing protocols. EIGRP is an example of the Hybrid routing protocols. Hybrid is sometimes called Balanced Hybrid or Advanced Distance Vector. Original IGP protocols use broadcast to send their route updates to the IP all-local-hosts broadcast address of 255.255.255.255, whereas the newest version of IGP protocols use multicast for this purpose. Also note that the Original IGP protocols did not include any authentication features, which make these protocols suffer from an attacker, whereas, the newer IGPs typically support some type of authentication, hoping to mitigate the exposure to types of DoS attacks.

Distance vector: This type uses a distance to a remote network to find the best path, which is the route with the least number of hops to the destination network. Each time a packet goes through a Router, it is called a hop. The vector is the determination of direction to the remote network. RIP and IGRP send the entire routing table to directly connected neighbors and are examples of this type.

Link State: This type of routing protocols is more complex than distance vector routing protocols, and they also consume more Router resources. However, link state protocols are used to exchange routing information in a larger internetwork, and typically called the shortest path first. Link state protocols create three separate tables in each Router, and hence, provide the routers more information about internetwork topology than distance-vector routing protocols. In general, distance Vector periodic updates are sent more frequent than Links state protocol updates.

Link state routing protocols create three separate tables in each Router. As a result, they know more about the internetwork than any distance-vector routing protocol. These tables are:

1. Table for keep tracking of the directly attached neighbors.
2. Table for determining the entire internetwork topology.
3. Table for all internetwork routes (routing table).

An example of an IP routing protocol that is completely Link State is OSPF. It uses only bandwidth as a way to determine the best path to a remote network.

Hybrid: This type of routing protocols uses features of the distance vector and link state. An example of a hybrid routing protocol is EIGRP.

Note: Only the distance vector routing protocol is required for CCENT test.

Too many types of metrics can be adopted by routing algorithms to determine the best route:

1. Path Length
2. Reliability
3. Delay
4. Bandwidth
5. Load
6. Communication Cost

In general, all routing protocols have several general goals:

1. Learning and filling the routing table dynamically with a route to all subnets in the internetwork.
2. Placing the best route in the routing table if more than one route to a subnet is available.
3. Removing no longer valid routes from the routing table.
4. Adding new routes or replacing lost routes with the best currently available route, as quickly as possible. The time between losing the route and finding a working replacement route is called *convergence time*.
5. Preventing routing loops.

Auto-Summarization and Manual Summarization

To short the routing tables in a large internetwork, route summarization is used. This will speed up the routers while retaining all the needed routes in the network. Two general types of route summarization can be implemented: *auto-summarization* and *manual summarization*. Manual summarization means that the network administrator supplies the route summarization manually. This gives the administrator a great control and flexibility and makes the administrator to choose what summary routes to advertise. Therefore, manual summarization is the more useful feature as compared to auto-summarization. The complete details for the summarizations will be given in the ICND2 book.

Convergence

In some cases, there are reconfigurations in the internetwork topology. Internetwork topology reconfigurations are occurred when a router link comes up or fails, or when a router fails or turns ON for the first time or a router is removed from the internetwork. These made routes in the router's routing table change and reconfigure. The term *convergence* refers to the processes used by dynamic routing protocols to recognize the changes, to discover the new best routes to each subnet, and to reconfigure all the routers' routing tables. A more quickly converge routing protocols are required by almost all modern internetworks to make routing tables up-to-date as soon as possible. Users might not be able to connect to the internetwork and send their packets to particular subnets during convergence.

Since, distance-vector routing protocols send a complete routing table during routing updates, their convergence will be slow; this can cause inconsistent routing tables and routing loops. Routing loops can occur because not every Router is updated at the same time.

Classless and Classful Routing Protocols

Routing protocols can be classified as *Classless* and *Classful* Routing Protocols. Protocols that consider the Class A, B, or C network number that a subnet resides in are called classful. Whereas, protocols that ignore Class A, B, and C rules altogether are called classless. Table 5-3 lists the criteria that must be used to identify the type of routing protocols.

Table 5-3 Classless and Classful Routing Protocols

Feature	Classless	Classful
Supporting VLSM	Yes	No
Sending subnet mask in routing updates	Yes	No
Supporting manual route summarization	Yes	No
Supporting auto route summarization	Yes	Yes

As a summary in this section, Table 5-4 compares several IGP's routing protocols.

Table 5-4 Comparing IGP Protocols

Feature	RIP-1	RIP-2	IGRP	EIGRP	OSPF	IS-IS
Classless	NO	YES	NO	YES	YES	YES
Supporting VLSM	NO	YES	NO	YES	YES	YES
Sending subnet mask in routing updates	NO	YES	NO	YES	YES	YES
Distance vector	YES	YES	YES	NO	NO	NO
Link-state	NO	NO	NO	NO	YES	YES
Supporting auto-summarization	YES	YES	YES	YES	NO	NO
Supporting manual summarization	NO	YES	NO	YES	YES	YES
CISCO Proprietary	NO	NO	YES	YES	NO	NO
Sending routing updates to a multicast IP address	NO	YES	NO	YES	YES	N/A
Supporting authentication	NO	YES	NO	YES	YES	YES
Convergence	Slow	Slow	Slow	Very fast	Fast	Fast

Distance-Vector Routing Protocols

This algorithm passes the complete routing tables to neighbor routers in a route update message. All routers that received the routing update combine the received routing table with their own routing tables to complete the internetwork map. Simply, this is called routing by rumor, because a router receiving an update from a neighbor router believes the information about remote networks without it actually finds out the remote networks.

The administrative distance is first checked. In case of there are multiple links to the same remote network and the links have the same administrative distances, the distance vector algorithm uses another metrics to determine the best path to use to that remote network. RIP uses the only hop count as a metric for determining the best route to an internetwork. If RIP finds more than one link to the same remote network with the same hop count, it will automatically perform a round-robin load balance between the two paths. RIP can perform load balancing for up to six equal-cost links (four by default).

Distance vector protocols primarily base their routing decisions on finding the shortest route to a destination, in other words, a route with the lowest hop count. So, Distance Vector routing protocols make path selections based upon the number of hops that must be traversed to the destination. Distance-vector protocols, by definition, use metrics (distance) and next-hop data (vectors) to make forwarding decisions.

Routing Information Protocol (RIP)

This section introduces the RIP dynamic routing protocol, and then, presents the RIP configuration throughout the internetwork. The section also shows how RIP configuration is verified.

RIP is a dynamic, true distance-vector routing protocol. It sends the complete routing table out to all active interfaces every 30 seconds. It works well in small networks, but it is inefficient on the large networks with slow WAN links or on networks with a large number of routers installed. RIP versions can be version 1, version 2 or next generation (ng).

RIP only uses a hop count to determine the best path to a remote network, but it has a maximum allowable hop count of 15, meaning that 16 is considered unreachable. RIP has an administrative distance of 120 by default. It slowly converges, often taking 3 to 5 minutes.

The main differences between RIPv1 and RIPv2 are: RIPv1 uses only classful routing, which means that all devices in the internetwork must use the same subnet mask. RIPv2 uses only classless routing, which means that devices in the internetwork may use the different subnet masks. This is because RIPv1 does not send updates with subnet mask information in the internetwork, whereas RIPv2 does send updates with subnet mask information in the internetwork.

Configuring RIP Routing

RIP configuration is simple, after turning it ON from global Configuration mode, the networks to be advertising must be specified. Here is an example of how RIP routing should be configured.

Step 4, Configuring RIP Routing: The following Configurations are used to clarify how routers are configured for RIP routing using the **router rip** and **network w.x.y.z** commands. To configure RIP routing, just turn ON the protocol with the **router rip** command and tell the RIP routing protocol, which networks to advertise.

The **network** command only uses a classful network number as its one parameter. The router will do the following three things for any of the router's interface in that entire classful network:

- Multicasting routing updates to a reserved multicast IP address, 224.0.0.9.
- Listening for incoming updates on that same interface.
- Advertising about the subnet connected to the interface.

The configurations will use Table 5-1 for an IP addressing scheme. Each network in Figure 5-4 has a 24-bit subnet mask (255.255.255.0). Before starting configuring the routers, remember that, each routing table automatically includes the directly connected networks. To be able to route to all networks in the internetwork, the routing table must include information that defines where these other networks are located and how to get there. The RIP routing is used to obtain information about remote networks automatically.

Configuration 5-10, R1 RIP routing configuration: The following Configuration shows how to configure RIP routing on the R1 Router using **router rip** and **network** commands and then, shows the routing table using the **sh ip route** command. Before starting, notices that the networks 172.18.10.0, 172.18.50.0, and 172.18.70.0 are directly connected to the R1 Router. RIP will be used to provide information about other remote networks. The following networks must be obtained automatically by RIP: 172.18.20.0, 172.18.30.0, 172.18.40.0, and 172.18.60.0. Before implementing RIP routing on R1, you must remove all static routes to remote networks. The routing tables are not propagated with RIP information if R1 is configured with static routing. Notice also that static routing has AD of 1, whereas RIP routing has AD of 120 by default.

R1(config)#no ip route 172.18.20.0 255.255.255.0 172.18.50.1
R1(config)#no ip route 172.18.30.0 255.255.255.0 172.18.70.2

R1(config)#no ip route 172.18.40.0 255.255.255.0 172.18.70.2
R1(config)#no ip route 172.18.60.0 255.255.255.0 172.18.50.1
R1(config)#router rip
R1(config-router)#network 172.18.0.0
R1(config-router)#^Z
R1#

Notice that, in the above RIP configuration, the routing protocol does not tell which networks to advertise. RIP will find the networks and advertise them. The configuration above shows also how it is easy to configure the router for RIP as compared with static routing. However, dynamic routing consumes much of Router's CPU process and bandwidth.

Configuration 5-11, R2 RIP routing configuration: The following Configuration shows how to configure RIP routing on the R2 Router using **router rip** and **network** commands and then, shows the routing table using the **sh ip route** command. Before starting, notice that networks 172.18.20.0, 172.18.50.0, and 172.18.60.0 are directly connected to the R2 Router. Networks 172.18.10.0, 172.18.30.0, 172.18.40.0, and 172.18.70.0 will be discovered automatically by RIP routing.

R2(config)#no ip route 172.18.10.0 255.255.255.0 172.18.50.2
R2(config)#no ip route 172.18.30.0 255.255.255.0 172.18.60.1
R2(config)#no ip route 172.18.40.0 255.255.255.0 172.18.60.1
R2(config)#no ip route 172.18.70.0 255.255.255.0 172.18.50.2
R2(config)#router rip
R2(config-router)#network 172.18.0.0
R2(config-router)#^Z
R2#

Notice that, the completely **no ip route** command must be issued to delete static entry in the routing table. This will make sure that no routes are in the routing table with a better AD than 120 and then RIP can be configured. RIP will never be used on the router if static routes are not removed first. To turn OFF the RIP routing process, use the **no router rip** command. To remove a network entry, use the **no network w.x.y.z** command.

Configuration 5-12, R3 RIP routing configuration: The following Configuration shows how to configure RIP routing on the R3 Router using **router rip** and **network** commands and then, shows the routing table using the **sh ip route** command. Before starting, notice that networks 172.18.30.0, 172.18.40.0, 172.18.70.0, and 172.18.60.0 are directly connected to the R3 Router. Networks 172.18.10.0, 172.18.20.0, and 172.18.50.0 will be discovered automatically by RIP routing.

R3(config)#no ip route 172.18.10.0 255.255.255.0 172.18.70.1
R3(config)#no ip route 172.18.20.0 255.255.255.0 172.18.60.2
R3(config)#no ip route 172.18.50.0 255.255.255.0 172.18.60.2
R3(config)#router rip
R3(config-router)#network 172.18.0.0
R3(config-router)#^Z
R3#

Configuration 5-13, R4 RIP routing configuration: The following Configuration shows how to configure RIP routing on the R4 Router using **router rip** and **network** commands and then, shows the routing table using the **sh ip route** command. Before starting, notices that, only network 172.18.40.0 is directly connected to the R4 Router. Networks 172.18.10.0, 172.18.20.0, 172.18.30.0, 172.18.50.0, 172.18.60.0, and 172.18.70.0 will be discovered automatically by RIP routing. Using RIP routing in R4 is implemented after removing all default routes to remote networks. The routing tables are not propagated with RIP information if R4 is configured with default routing. Notice also that default routing has AD of 1 whereas RIP routing has AD of 120 by default.

R4(config)#no ip route 0.0.0.0 0.0.0.0 172.18.40.1
R4(config)#router rip
R4(config-router)#network 172.18.0.0
R4(config-router)#^Z
R4#

Verifying the Configured RIP Routing Tables

The following Configurations are used to clarify how routers RIP configurations are verified using the **show ip route** command. Each routing table should now have the routers' directly connected routes as well as RIP-learned routes received from neighbor routers. Other commands that can be used to verify RIP configuration are **show ip route [rip], show ip protocols and show ip interface brief**. The **show ip interface brief** command, lists one line per router interface, including the IP addresses and interface status. An interface must have an IP address, and must be in an "UP-UP" status, before RIP begins to work on the interface. The other commands will be explained in more details at the end of this chapter.

Configuration 5-14, R1 RIP routing table verification: The following Configuration shows how the routing table is verified using the **sh ip route** command. To view the routing table, the **show running-config** command can also be used.

R1#sh ip route
Codes: C – connected, S – static, I - IGRP, R - RIP, M – Mobile, B – BGP, D – EIGRP, EX – EIGRP external,
O - OSPF, ...
Gateway of last resort is not set

      172.18.0.0/24 is subnetted, 7 subnets
C   172.18.70.0 is directly connected, Serial0
R   172.18.60.0 [120/1] via 172.18.50.1, 00:00:08, Serial1
C   172.18.50.0 is directly connected, Serial1
R   172.18.40.0 [120/1] via 172.18.70.2, 00:00:08, Serial0
R   172.18.30.0 [120/1] via 172.18.70.2, 00:00:08, Serial0
R   172.18.20.0 [120/1] via 172.18.50.1, 00:00:08, Serial1
C   172.18.10.0 is directly connected, Ethernet0
R1#

The preceding routing table shows the directly connected networks to R1 as well as the remote networks that are discovered automatically by RIP routing. Notice the "R"; this means that the networks were added dynamically using the RIP routing protocol. In the RIP routes, the [120/1] indicates the default AD of the route (120) and the number of hops to the remote network (1).

Configuration 5-15, R2 RIP routing table verification: The following Configuration shows how the routing table is verified using the **sh ip route** command. To view the routing table, the **show running-config** command can also be used.

R2#sh ip route
Codes: C – connected, S – static, I - IGRP, R - RIP, M – Mobile, B – BGP, D – EIGRP, EX – EIGRP external,
O - OSPF, ...
Gateway of last resort is not set

      172.18.0.0/24 is subnetted, 7 subnets
R   172.18.70.0 [120/1] via 172.18.50.2, 00:00:12, Serial0
C   172.18.60.0 is directly connected, Serial1
C   172.18.50.0 is directly connected, Serial0

R   172.18.40.0 [120/1] via 172.18.60.1, 00:00:08, Serial1
R   172.18.30.0 [120/1] via 172.18.60.1, 00:00:08, Serial1
C   172.18.20.0 is directly connected, Ethernet0
R   172.18.10.0 [120/1] via 172.18.50.2, 00:00:12, Serial0
R2#

The preceding routing table shows the directly connected networks to R2 as well as the remote networks that are discovered automatically by RIP routing. Notice that, R2 Router now has a complete routing table. As long as the other routers in the internetwork have the same routing table, R2 can communicate to all remote networks.

Configuration 5-16, R3 RIP routing table verification: The following Configuration shows how the routing table is verified using the **sh ip route** command. To view the routing table, the **show running-config** command can also be used.

R3#sh ip route
Codes: C – connected, S – static, I - IGRP, R - RIP, M – Mobile, B – BGP, D – EIGRP, EX – EIGRP external,
O - OSPF, ...
Gateway of last resort is not set

      172.18.0.0/24 is subnetted, 7 subnets
C   172.18.70.0 is directly connected, Serial1
C   172.18.60.0 is directly connected, Serial0
R   172.18.50.0 [120/1] via 172.18.60.2, 00:00:22, Serial0
C   172.18.40.0 is directly connected, Ethernet1
C   172.18.30.0 is directly connected, Ethernet0
R   172.18.20.0 [120/1] via 172.18.60.2, 00:00:16, Serial0
R   172.18.10.0 [120/1] via 172.18.70.1, 00:00:22, Serial1
R3#

The preceding routing table shows the directly connected networks to R3 as well as the remote networks that are discovered automatically by RIP routing. Notice that, R3 Router now has a complete routing table. As long as the other routers in the internetwork have the same routing table, R3 can communicate to all remote networks.

Configuration 5-17, R4 RIP routing table verification: The following Configuration shows how the routing table is verified using the **sh ip route** command. To view the routing table, the **show running-config** command can also be used.

R4#sh ip route
Codes: C – connected, S – static, I - IGRP, R - RIP, M – Mobile, B – BGP, D – EIGRP, EX – EIGRP external,
O - OSPF, ...
Gateway of last resort is not set

      172.18.0.0/24 is subnetted, 7 subnets
R   172.18.70.0 [120/1] via 172.18.40.1, FastEthernet0/0
R   172.18.60.0 [120/1] via 172.18.40.1, FastEthernet0/0
R   172.18.50.0 [120/2] via 172.18.40.1, FastEthernet0/0
C   172.18.40.0 is directly connected, FastEthernet0/0
R   172.18.30.0 [120/1] via 172.18.40.1, FastEthernet0/0
R   172.18.20.0 [120/2] via 172.18.40.1, FastEthernet0/0
R   172.18.10.0 [120/2] via 172.18.40.1, FastEthernet0/0
R4#

Holding Down RIP Propagation's

Configuration 5-18, Stopping RIP broadcast: The following Configuration shows how the stop unwanted RIP updates from propagating across the LANs and WANs using the **passive-interface** command.

```
Router(config)#router rip
Router(config-router)#network 172.20.0.0
Router(config-router)#passive-interface serial 1
```

The above command will prevent RIP updates from being propagated out serial interface 1, but serial interface 1 can still receive RIP updates. This will be required to prevent RIP network advertised every route on a LAN and WAN. Issuing this command is a requirement when connecting a local RIP network on the Internet, since there is no advantage for route advertising in this case. Other ways to stop unwanted RIP updates from propagating across the LANs and WANs are available but the above method is the easiest way.

RIP uses broadcast UDP data packets to exchange routing updates. Every 30 seconds, the router sends routing updates to all other routers in the internetwork; this process is termed **advertising**. If the router does not receive an update from a router (nonupdating router) for 90 seconds or more, it marks all routes from the nonupdating router as being unusable. The router then will wait 240 seconds to remove all routing table entries for the nonupdating router, if there is no update from the nonupdating router.

RIP maintains only the best route to a destination. When better route information is coming, this information replaces old route information in the routing tables. Network topology changes can make changes to routes, causing, for example, a new route to become the best route to a particular destination. Network topology changes are reflected directly in routing update messages. When a router receives a routing update message that includes an update of the changes; the router updates its tables and advertises the change.

RIP Version 2 (RIPv2)

RIP is an open standard, so it is possible to use RIP with any brand of routers. OSPF is also an open standard with better performance, especially in a large internetwork.

Both RIPv1 and RIPv2 are distance-vector protocols, this means that each router running RIP sends its complete routing tables out all active interfaces periodically. RIPv1 is classful routing protocol, whereas, RIPv2 is considered classless because subnet information is sent with each route update and its support VLSM of course. Both RIP versions have the same administrative distance (120) and the same maximum number of hops (16). In both RIP versions, the timers and loop-avoidance schemes are the same. RIPv2 is defined in RFC 2453. With all enhancements in RIPv2, it still converges relatively slowly. Table 5-5 lists the RIPv2 improvements to RIPv1.

Table 5-5 RIPv2 Improvements

Improvement	Description
authentication	Clear text and MD5 encryption can be used to authenticate the source of a routing update.
subnet mask with route	RIPv2 is considered classless because subnet information is sent with each route update and its support VLSM of course.
next-hop router IP address in the routing update	A RIP router can direct any listeners to a different router on the same subnet.
external route tags	RIPv2 helping other routing protocol pass information. RIP can pass information about routes learnt from an external source and redistributed into RIP.
multicast routing updates	Instead of broadcasting updates to 255.255.255.255 like

	RIPv1, the destination IP address is 224.0.0.9, an IP multicast address. 224.0.0.9 is reserved specifically for using by RIPv2. This makes update to send to only RIP hosts in the internetwork.

Configuration 5-19, R1 RIPv2 routing configuration: The following Configuration shows how to configure RIPv2 routing on the R1 Router using **router rip** and **network** and **version 2** commands. R2, R3, and R4 can be configured in the same manner.

```
R1(config)#router rip
R1(config-router)#network 172.18.0.0
R1(config-router)#version 2
R1(config-router)#^Z
R1#
```

Interior Gateway Routing Protocol (IGRP)

Interior Gateway Routing Protocol (IGRP) is a CISCO proprietary distance-vector routing protocol. This means that all routers in the internetwork must be CISCO routers. It is created to overcome the problems associated with RIP. This section introduces the IGRP dynamic routing protocol, and then, presents the IGRP configuration throughout the internetwork. The section also shows how IGRP configuration is verified. IGRP is not required for CCENT exam, and it is possible to skip this section. It is added here to provide the reader more practical information about dynamic routing protocol.

IGRP is a dynamic, distance-vector routing protocol. The default administrative distance of IGRP is 100. It converges relatively slow. It has a maximum hop count of 255 with a default of 100. IGRP uses a different metric from RIP. By default, RIP uses a composite metric to determine the best path. IGRP uses bandwidth and delay of the line by default as a metric for determining the best route to a network. Load, reliability, and maximum transmission unit (MTU) can also be used, although they are not used by default. The mathematical formula that used by IGRP to calculate the metrics uses bandwidth and delay as input and results in an integer value, the metric, between 1 and 4,294,967,295.

Configuring IGRP Routing

IGRP routing configuration is as simple as RIP routing configuration and the same command that used for configuring the RIP is used to configure the IGRP routing except that IGRP uses an Autonomous System (AS) number. All routers within an AS must use the same AS number, or they will not communicate with other IGRP routing information.

Step 5, Configuring IGRP Routing: The following Configurations are used to clarify how routers are configured for IGRP routing using the **router igrp AS_number** and **network w.x.y.z** commands. To configure IGRP routing, just turn ON the protocol with the **router igrp** command within a specified AS and tell the IGRP routing protocol, which networks to advertise. The Configurations will use Table 5-1 for an IP addressing scheme. Each network in Figure 5-4 has a 24-bit subnet mask (255.255.255.0). Before starting configuring the routers, remember that, each routing table automatically includes directly connected networks. To be able to route to all networks in the internetwork, the routing table must include information that defines where these other networks are located and how to get there. The IGRP routing is used to obtain information about the remote networks automatically.

Configuration 5-20, R1 IGRP routing configuration: The following Configuration shows how to configure IGRP routing on the R1 Router using **router igrp AS_number** and **network w.x.y.z** commands and then, shows the routing table using the **sh ip route** command. Before starting, notices that the networks 172.18.10.0, 172.18.50.0, and 172.18.70.0 are directly connected to the R1 Router. IGRP will be used to provide information about other remote networks. The following networks must be obtained automatically by IGRP: 172.18.20.0,

172.18.30.0, 172.18.40.0, and 172.18.60.0. Configuring IGRP is straightforward and not much different from configuring RIP. AS number must be decided before configuring the routers. All routers in the internetwork must use the same AS number if the routers sharing the routing information. AS 20 will be used to configure the routers in Figure 5-4 internetwork.

```
R1(config)#router igrp ?
  <1-65535>   Autonomous system number
R1(config)#router igrp 20
R1(config-router)#network 172.18.0.0
R1(config-router)#^Z
R1#
```

Notice that in the router configuration for IGRP above, the routing protocol does not tell which subnets to advertise; it tells the classful boundary. IGRP will find the subnets and advertise them. Both RIP and IGRP are classful routing, which means that subnet mask information is not sent with the routing protocol updates. The configuration above shows also how it is easy to configure the router for IGRP as compared with static routing. However, dynamic routing consumes more router CPU processes and bandwidth. Notice also that, the AS number, as shown in the second line of the router configuration above, can be any number from 1 to 65535. A router can be configured to participate in many ASs at the same time depending on the internetwork design.

Configuration 5-21, R2 IGRP routing configuration: The following Configuration shows how to configure IGRP routing on the R2 Router using **router igrp and network** commands and then, shows the routing table using the **sh ip route** command. Before starting, notice that networks 172.18.20.0, 172.18.50.0, and 172.18.60.0 are directly connected to the R2 Router. Networks 172.18.10.0, 172.18.30.0, 172.18.40.0, and 172.18.70.0 will be discovered automatically by IGRP routing.

```
R2(config)#router igrp 20
R2(config-router)#network 172.18.0.0
R2(config-router)#^Z
R2#
```

To turn OFF the IGRP routing process, use the **no router igrp AS_number** command. To remove a network entry, use the **no network w.x.y.z** command.

Configuration 5-22, R3 IGRP routing configuration: The following Configuration shows how to configure IGRP routing on the R3 Router using the **router igrp** and **network** commands and then, shows the routing table using the **sh ip route** command. Before starting, notice that networks 172.18.30.0, 172.18.40.0, 172.18.70.0, and 172.18.60.0 are directly connected to the R3 Router. Networks 172.18.10.0, 172.18.20.0, and 172.18.50.0 will be discovered automatically by IGRP routing.

```
R3(config)#router igrp 20
R3(config-router)#network 172.18.0.0
R3(config-router)#^Z
R3#
```

Configuration 5-23, R4 IGRP routing configuration: The following Configuration shows how to configure IGRP routing on the R4 Router using the **router igrp** and **network** commands and then, shows the routing table using the **sh ip route** command. Before starting, notices that, only network 172.18.40.0 is directly connected to the R4 Router. Networks 172.18.10.0, 172.18.20.0, 172.18.30.0, 172.18.50.0, 172.18.60.0, and 172.18.70.0 will be discovered automatically by IGRP routing.

```
R4(config)#router igrp 20
R4(config-router)#network 172.18.0.0
```

R4(config-router)#^Z
R4#

IGRP can load balance up to six unequal links, and uses bandwidth to determine for this purpose. The **variance** command is used to control the load balancing between different metrics.

To control traffic distribution among IGRP load-sharing routes, two more commands can be used: **traffic-share balanced** and **traffic-share min**.

Router(config-router)#variance ?
<1-128>   Metric variance multiplier
Router(config-router)#traffic-share ?
balanced   share inversely proportional to metric
min   all traffic share among min metric paths

The **traffic-share balanced** command makes the IGRP router to share inversely proportional to the metrics, and the **traffic-share min** command makes the IGRP router to use only minimum cost routes.

Verifying the Configured IGRP Routing Tables

The following Configurations are used to clarify how routers IGRP configurations are verified using the **show ip route** command. Each routing table should now have the routers' directly connected routes as well as IGRP-injected routes received from neighbor routers. Since RIP routing is not turned OFF, it is still running in the background. However, RIP routes will never be used, since the AD of IGRP is 100 and its better than RIP AD of 120.

Configuration 5-24, R1 IGRP routing table verification: The following Configuration shows how the routing table is verified using the **sh ip route** command. To view the routing table, the **show running-config** command can also be used.

R1#sh ip route
Codes: C – connected, S – static, I - IGRP, R - RIP, M – Mobile, B – BGP, D – EIGRP, EX – EIGRP external,
O - OSPF, ...
Gateway of last resort is not set
      172.18.0.0/24 is subnetted, 7 subnets
C   172.18.70.0 is directly connected, Serial0
I   172.18.60.0 [100/160370] via 172.18.50.1, 00:00:30, Serial1
C   172.18.50.0 is directly connected, Serial1
I   172.18.40.0 [100/160270] via 172.18.70.2, 00:00:32, Serial0
I   172.18.30.0 [100/160170] via 172.18.70.2, 00:00:35, Serial0
I   172.18.20.0 [100/160070] via 172.18.50.1, 00:00:40, Serial1
C   172.18.10.0 is directly connected, Ethernet0
R1#

The preceding routing table shows the directly connected networks to R1 as well as the remote networks that are discovered automatically by IGRP routing. Notice the "I"; this means that the networks were added dynamically using the IGRP routing protocol. The [100/160170] is the default AD of the route (100) along with the composite metric. The lower the composite metric is the better route.

Configuration 5-25, R2 IGRP routing table verification: The following Configuration shows how the routing table is verified using the **sh ip route** command. To view the routing table, the **show running-config** command can also be used.

R2#sh ip route
Codes: C – connected, S – static, I - IGRP, R - RIP, M – Mobile, B – BGP, D – EIGRP, EX – EIGRP external,
O - OSPF, ...
Gateway of last resort is not set

     172.18.0.0/24 is subnetted, 7 subnets
I   172.18.70.0 [100/160360] via 172.18.50.2, 00:00:12, Serial0
C   172.18.60.0 is directly connected, Serial1
C   172.18.50.0 is directly connected, Serial0
I   172.18.40.0 [100/160260] via 172.18.60.1, 00:00:15, Serial1
I   172.18.30.0 [100/160160] via 172.18.60.1, 00:00:14, Serial1
C   172.18.20.0 is directly connected, Ethernet0
I   172.18.10.0 [100/160060] via 172.18.50.2, 00:00:12, Serial0
R2#

The preceding routing table shows the directly connected networks to R2 as well as the remote networks that are discovered automatically by IGRP routing. Notice that, R2 now has a complete routing table. As long as the other routers in the internetwork have the same routing table, R2 can communicate to all remote networks. IGRP and RIP are now running concurrently on R2. However, the IGRP information will override the RIP information by default because of IGRP's administrative distance.

Configuration 5-26, R3 IGRP routing table verification: The following Configuration shows how the routing table is verified using the **sh ip route** command. To view the routing table, the **show running-config** command can also be used.

R3#sh ip route
Codes: C – connected, S – static, I - IGRP, R - RIP, M – Mobile, B – BGP, D – EIGRP, EX – EIGRP external,
O - OSPF, ...
Gateway of last resort is not set

     172.18.0.0/24 is subnetted, 7 subnets
C   172.18.70.0 is directly connected, Serial1
C   172.18.60.0 is directly connected, Serial0
I   172.18.50.0 [100/160370] via 172.18.60.2, 00:00:42, Serial0
C   172.18.40.0 is directly connected, Ethernet1
C   172.18.30.0 is directly connected, Ethernet0
I   172.18.20.0 [100/160360] via 172.18.60.2, 00:00:46, Serial0
I   172.18.10.0 [100/160350] via 172.18.70.1, 00:00:44, Serial1
R3#

The preceding routing table shows the directly connected networks to R3 as well as the remote networks that are discovered automatically by IGRP routing. Notice that, R3 Router now has a complete routing table. As long as the other routers in the internetwork have the same routing table, R3 can communicate to all remote networks.

Configuration 5-27, R4 IGRP routing table verification: The following Configuration shows how the routing table is verified using the **sh ip route** command. To view the routing table, the **show running-config** command can also be used.

R4#sh ip route
Codes: C – connected, S – static, I - IGRP, R - RIP, M – Mobile, B – BGP, D – EIGRP, EX – EIGRP external,
O - OSPF, ...
Gateway of last resort is not set

172.18.0.0/24 is subnetted, 7 subnets
I   172.18.70.0   [100/150370] via 172.18.40.1, FastEthernet0/0
I   172.18.60.0   [100/150360] via 172.18.40.1, FastEthernet0/0
I   172.18.50.0   [100/150350] via 172.18.40.1, FastEthernet0/0
C   172.18.40.0 is directly connected, FastEthernet0/0
I   172.18.30.0   [100/150340] via 172.18.40.1, FastEthernet0/0
I   172.18.20.0   [100/160370] via 172.18.40.1, FastEthernet0/0
I   172.18.10.0   [100/160270] via 172.18.40.1, FastEthernet0/0
R4#

Example 5-3: In Figure 5-6 below, the following configuration is applied.

1. RA has RIP and IGRP enabled on the interface E0.
2. RB has IGRP enabled on E0.
3. RC has RIP enabled on F0/0.

RC is not receiving routing updates from RA. The problem is either an access-list may be defined incorrectly or RA's RIP interface is passive.

Figure 5-6 RIP and IGRP Example

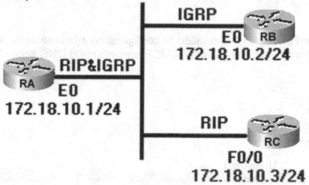

To control the set of interfaces that a router wants to exchange routing updates with, it is possible to disable the sending of routing updates on specified interfaces by configuring the **passive-interface** command. However, if an access-list is wrongly configured, the routes may be filtered from updates. Access lists filter network traffic by controlling whether routed packets are forwarded or blocked at the router's interfaces.

Monitoring IP Routing on the CISCO Routers

In this section, the commands that can be used to verify and track the correctly configured the routed and routing protocols will be given. Several Microsoft Windows 7/XP commands that can be used for verifying and troubleshooting IP routing network are given in brief. However, following the rules and recommendations that are presented in Chapters 2 and 3 (IP addressing and subnetting) of this book will prevent several types of problems and troubles, which could be occurred in the IP routing network.

Ping

The **ping** utility is the easiest way to check the network connectivity as a first troubleshooting utility as shown in several examples throughout this book. However, here are some of the comments regarding the use of this utility in the IP routing.

1. Testing the network connectivity within the same subnet. If this test fails, the problem maybe one of the following:

   - The host's IP configurations are not fallen in the same subnet. Correcting the IP address and subnet masks are the solution in this case.
   - The underlying Ethernet Layer 1 and Layer 2 have a problem, if the hosts on the same subnet have the correct IP configuration. In this case, you need to follow the troubleshooting steps, which will be described in Chapter 6 of this book.

2. Testing the network connectivity between different internetwork subnets. If the test in point 1 is OK so that the host can ping other hosts in the same subnet, try to ping between hosts on different subnets, as follows:

   - Checking the connection and correct the IP configurations between a host and the default gateway/Router using the **ping** utility. If this test is failed, the problem may be in the IP configurations or some Layer 1 or 2 problems on the LAN.
   - Checking the connection and correct the IP configurations between hosts on different subnets (not the same LAN) using the **Ping** utility. If this test is not succeeded, the problem may be the IP configurations between subnets or the router's other interface has failed.

ipconfig /all

This command prompt is used to display the detailed IP configuration information for all interfaces on the PC, including IP address, subnet mask, default gateway, DHCP server(s) and DNS server(s) IP addresses.

C:\>ipconfig /all

Windows IP Configuration

```
    Host Name . . . . . . . . . . . . : thaar
    Primary Dns Suffix  . . . . . . . :
    Node Type . . . . . . . . . . . . : Unknown
    IP Routing Enabled. . . . . . . . : No
    WINS Proxy Enabled. . . . . . . . : No
```

Ethernet adapter Local Area Connection:

```
    Media State . . . . . . . . . . . : Media disconnected
    Description . . . . . . . . . . . : Intel(R) PRO/100 VE Network Connection
    Physical Address. . . . . . . . . : 00-15-F2-F3-C1-D4
     Dhcp Enabled. . . . . . . . . . . : Yes
     Autoconfiguration Enabled . . . . : Yes
     IP Address. . . . . . . . . . . . : 192.168.0.2
     Subnet Mask . . . . . . . . . . . : 255.255.255.0
     Default Gateway . . . . . . . . . : 192.168.0.1
     DHCP Server . . . . . . . . . . . : 192.168.2.1
     DNS Servers . . . . . . . . . . . : 4.2.2.2
                                         4.1.1.1
     Lease Obtained. . . . . . . . . . : Friday, January 8, 2010 8:11:11 AM
     Lease Expires . . . . . . . . . . : Friday, January 22, 2010 8:11:11 AM
```

PPP adapter thaar-evdo:

```
Connection-specific DNS Suffix  . :
Description . . . . . . . . . . . : WAN (PPP/SLIP) Interface
Physical Address. . . . . . . . . : 00-53-45-00-00-00
Dhcp Enabled. . . . . . . . . . : No
IP Address. . . . . . . . . . . . : 213.188.87.63
Subnet Mask . . . . . . . . . . . : 255.255.255.255
Default Gateway . . . . . . . . . : 213.188.87.63
DNS Servers . . . . . . . . . . . : 82.205.200.10
                          82.205.200.11
```

C:\>

ipconfig /release

This command prompt is used to release any DHCP-leased IP addresses for all interfaces on the PC.

C:\>ipconfig /release

Windows IP Configuration

Ethernet adapter Local Area Connection:

```
Connection-specific DNS Suffix  . :
IP Address. . . . . . . . . . . . : 0.0.0.0
Subnet Mask . . . . . . . . . . . : 0.0.0.0
Default Gateway . . . . . . . . . :
```

C:\>

ipconfig /renew

This command prompt is used to acquire an IP address and related information from the DHCP server.

C:\>ipconfig /renew

Ethernet adapter Local Area Connection:

```
Media State . . . . . . . . . . . : Media disconnected
Description . . . . . . . . . . . : Intel(R) PRO/100 VE Network Connection
Physical Address. . . . . . . . . : 00-15-F2-F3-C1-D4
  Dhcp Enabled. . . . . . . . . . : Yes
  Autoconfiguration Enabled . . . . : Yes
  IP Address. . . . . . . . . . . . : 192.168.0.2
  Subnet Mask . . . . . . . . . . . : 255.255.255.0
  Default Gateway . . . . . . . . . : 192.168.0.1
  DHCP Server . . . . . . . . . . . : 192.168.2.1
  DNS Servers . . . . . . . . . . . : 4.2.2.2
                          4.1.1.1
  Lease Obtained. . . . . . . . . . : Friday, January 8, 2010 8:11:11 AM
  Lease Expires . . . . . . . . . . : Friday, January 22, 2010 8:11:11 AM
```

C:\>

Nslookup *name*

This command prompt is used to send a DNS request for the listed name.

```
C:\>nslookup www.cisco.com
DNS request timed out.
    timeout was 2 seconds.
*** Can't find server name for address 4.2.2.2: Timed out
DNS request timed out.
    timeout was 2 seconds.
*** Can't find server name for address 4.1.1.1: Timed out
Server:  DNS1.thaartechnologies.com
Address:  10. 5.2.10

DNS request timed out.
    timeout was 2 seconds.
Non-authoritative answer:
Name:   origin-www.cisco.com
Address:  72.163.4.161
Aliases:  www.cisco.com, www.cisco.com.akadns.net
     geoprod.cisco.com.akadns.net

C:\>
```

arp –a

This command prompt is used to list the host's ARP cache.

```
C:\>arp -a

Interface: 192.168.0.2 --- 0x2
  Internet Address      Physical Address     Type
  192.168.0.3        00-03-0d-29-8d-7f    dynamic

C:\>
```

ipconfig /displaydns

This command prompt is used to list the host's name cache.

```
C:\>ipconfig /displaydns

Windows IP Configuration

     tis17-5-en.url.trendmicro.com
     ----------------------------------------
     Record Name . . . . . . : tis17-5-en.url.trendmicro.com
     Record Type . . . . . . : 5
     Time To Live  . . . . . . : 4
     Data Length . . . . . . . : 4
     Section . . . . . . . . . . . : Answer
     CNAME Record  . . . . : trendmicro.com.edgesuite.net
```

tis17-5-en.url.trendmicro.com

Record Name . . . . . . : tis17-5-en.url.trendmicro.com
Record Type . . . . : 5
Time To Live . . . . . . : 4
Data Length . . . . : 4
Section . . . . : Answer
CNAME Record . . . . : trendmicro.com.edgesuite.net

1.0.0.127.in-addr.arpa

Record Name . . . . : 1.0.0.127.in-addr.arpa.
Record Type . . . .. : 12
Time To Live . . . . : 586057
Data Length . . . . . : 4
Section . . . . : Answer
PTR Record . . . . . : localhost

thaartechnologies.com

Record Name . . . . . : thaartechnologies.com
Record Type . . . . . : 1
Time To Live . . . . . : 6231
Data Length . . . . . . : 4
Section . . . . : Answer
A (Host) Record . . . : 76.163.122.170

biscotti.lsops.net

Record Name . . . . . : biscotti.lsops.net
Record Type . . . . . : 1
Time To Live . . . . . : 2
Data Length . . . . . . : 4
Section . . . . : Answer
A (Host) Record . . . : 78.129.203.9

Record Name . . . . : biscotti.lsops.net
Record Type . . . .. : 1
Time To Live . . . . . : 2
Data Length . . . . . . : 4
Section . . . . : Answer
A (Host) Record . . . : 78.129.203.10

Record Name . . . . . : a.ns.lsops.net
Record Type . . . .. . : 1
Time To Live . . . . . : 2

Data Length . . . . . . : 4
Section . . . . : Additional
A (Host) Record . . . : 78.129.203.2

Record Name . . . . . : b.ns.lsops.net
Record Type . . . . .. : 1
Time To Live . . . . . : 2
Data Length . . . . . . : 4
Section . . . . : Additional
A (Host) Record . . . : 82.211.118.63

public.ibe-ta.com

Record Name . . . . . . : public.ibe-ta.com
Record Type . . . . . . : 5
Time To Live . . . . . . : 507
Data Length . . . . : 4
Section . . . . : Answer
CNAME Record . . . . : cluster.ibe-ta.com

backup30.url.trendmicro.com

Record Name . . .. . . : backup30.url.trendmicro.com
Record Type . . . . : 5
Time To Live . . . . . . : 18
Data Length . . . . : 4
Section . . . . : Answer
CNAME Record . . . . : trendmicro-g.georedirector.akadns.net

cisco.com

Record Name . . . . . . : cisco.com
Record Type . . . . . . : 1
Time To Live . . . . . : 1300
Data Length . . . . . : 4
Section . . . . : Answer
A (Host) Record . . . : 198.133.219.25

Record Name . . . . .. : ns1.cisco.com
Record Type . . . . . . : 1
Time To Live . . . .. : 1300
Data Length . . . . .. : 4
Section . . . . : Additional
A (Host) Record . . . : 128.107.241.185

Record Name . . . . .. : ns2.cisco.com
Record Type . . . . . . : 1

Time To Live . . . . . : 1300
Data Length . . . . . . : 4
Section . . . . : Additional
A (Host) Record . . . : 64.102.255.44

downloads.privatepost.com

Record Name . . . . . . : downloads.privatepost.com
Record Type . . . . : 5
Time To Live . . . . . . : 1716
Data Length . . . . . . : 4
Section . . . . : Answer
CNAME Record . . . . : fw.identum.com

www.amazon.com

Record Name . . . . . : www.amazon.com
Record Type . . . . .. : 1
Time To Live . . . . . : 11
Data Length . . . . . . : 4
Section . . . . : Answer
A (Host) Record . . . : 207.171.166.252

Record Name . . . . . : ns-911.amazon.com
Record Type . . . .. . : 1
Time To Live . . . . . : 11
Data Length . . . . . . : 4
Section . . . . : Additional
A (Host) Record . . . : 207.171.178.13

Record Name . . . . . : ns-912.amazon.com
Record Type . . . .. . : 1
Time To Live . . . . . : 11
Data Length . . . . . . : 4
Section . . . . : Additional
A (Host) Record . . . : 207.171.191.123

Record Name . . . . . : ns-921.amazon.com
Record Type . . . .. . : 1
Time To Live . . . . . : 11
Data Length . . . . . . : 4
Section . . . . : Additional
A (Host) Record . . . : 72.21.192.209

Record Name . . . . . : ns-923.amazon.com
Record Type . . . .. . : 1
Time To Live . . . . . : 11

```
        Data Length . . . . . . : 4
        Section . . . . . . . . . . : Additional
        A (Host) Record . . . : 72.21.204.208


        localhost
        ----------------------------------------
        Record Name . . . . . . : localhost
        Record Type . . . . . . : 1
        Time To Live . . . . . : 586057
        Data Length . . . . . : 4
        Section . . . . . . . . .. : Answer
        A (Host) Record . . . : 127.0.0.1
```

C:\>

ipconfig /flushdns

This command prompt is used to remove all DNS-found name cache entries.

C:\>ipconfig /flushdns

Windows IP Configuration

Successfully flushed the DNS Resolver Cache.

C:\>

arp –d

This command prompt is used to flush (empty) the host's ARP cache.

C:\>arp -d

C:\Documents and Settings\oracle>arp -a
No ARP Entries Found

C:\>

netstat –rn

This command prompt is used to display a host's routing table.

C:\>netstat -rn

```
Route Table
===============================================================
Interface List
0x1 .............................................. MS TCP Loopback interface
0x2 ...00 15 f2 f3 c1 d4 ................ Intel(R) PRO/100 VE Network Connection – Packet Scheduler Miniport
0x20004 ...00 53 45 00 00 00 ...... WAN (PPP/SLIP) Interface
===============================================================
===============================================================
Active Routes:
Network Destination          Netmask          Gateway     Interface  Metric
```

0.0.0.0	0.0.0.0	213.188.87.63	213.188.87.63	1
127.0.0.0	255.0.0.0	127.0.0.1	127.0.0.1	1
192.168.3.91	255.255.255.255	213.188.87.63	213.188.87.63	1
213.188.87.63	255.255.255.255	127.0.0.1	127.0.0.1	50
213.188.87.255	255.255.255.255	213.188.87.63	213.188.87.63	50
224.0.0.0	240.0.0.0	213.188.87.63	213.188.87.63	1
255.255.255.255	255.255.255.255	213.188.87.63	213.188.87.63	1
255.255.255.255	255.255.255.255	213.188.87.63	2	1
Default Gateway:	213.188.87.63			

==

Persistent Routes:
  None

C:\>

In addition to these commands, Figure 5-7 shows, an example of how to configure a host's IP address, subnet mask, default gateway, and DNS server(s) IP addresses statically. However, these IP addresses can be configured with XP commands as well, using the **netsh** utility.

Figure 5-7 Statically Configured IP Addresses on Windows XP

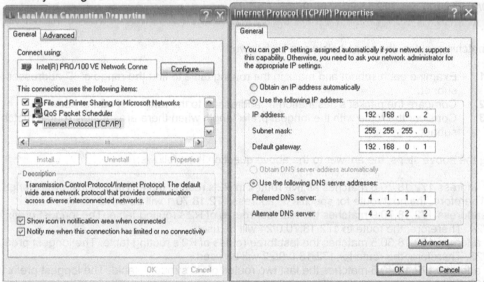

Obtaining the Matching Route

A router uses the steps described in this chapter to obtain a suitable route for a destined IP address. However, there are some cases that more than one route that matches an individual destined IP address can be found in a particular router's routing table. The reasons for overlapping routes in a Router's routing table include the configuration of static routes, auto-summary, and route summarization.

It is easy to find the suitable route for a particular destined IP address. Simply, compare the destination IP address to each subnet in the routing table. The route that matches the packet's destination must be in the suitable subnet's IP addresses range.

Furthermore, the Router will use the most specific route, i.e., the route with the longest prefix length, if a particular destination IP address matches more than one route in the Router's routing table.

The following configuration shows the Router routing table with multiple routes for a particular destination IP address.

Configuration 5-28, Overlapping Routes: For the R2 routing table shown below, which route R2 would match for packets destined to the following IP addresses: 172.18.70.5, 172.18.70.9, 172.18.30.5, and 172.18.40.5? The destination IP address(es) and the Router's routing table are all the requirements to answer this question.

R2#sh ip route
Codes: C – connected, S – static, I - IGRP, R - RIP, M – Mobile, B – BGP, D – EIGRP, EX – EIGRP external,
O - OSPF, ...
Gateway of last resort is not set

```
     172.18.0.0/24 is variably subnetted, 5 subnets
R    172.18.70.1/32 [120/1]  via 172.18.50.2, 00:00:12, Serial0
R    172.18.70.0/24 [120/2]  via 172.18.60.1, 00:00:08, Serial1
R    172.18.0.0/22 [120/1]  via 172.18.50.2, 00:00:12, Serial0
R    172.18.0.0/16 [120/2]  via 172.18.60.1, 00:00:08, Serial1
R    0.0.0.0/0  [120/3]  via 172.18.60.1, 00:00:06, Serial1
R2#
```

To find all matching routes, the steps below can be followed:

Step 1.   Examine each subnet and mask in the routing table to find the range of IP addresses in each subnet.
Step 2.   Compare the packet's destination IP address(es) to the ranges of addresses.
Step 3.   Consider the route with the longest prefix length when there are multiply routes match the same subnet.

By following the above steps, the answer to the above question is as follows:

- IP address 172.18.70.5 matches all five routes in R2's routing table. The longest prefix length is /32. Therefore, the host route for specific IP address 172.18.70.1 will be used.
- IP address 172.18.70.9 matches the last four routes of R2's routing table. The longest prefix length is /24. Therefore, the route to 172.18.70.0/24 will be used.
- IP address 172.18.30.5 matches the last three routes of R2's routing table. The longest prefix length is /22. Therefore, the route for 172.18.0.0/22 will be used.
- IP address 172.18.40.5 matches the last two routes of R2's routing table. The longest prefix length is /16. Therefore, the route for 172.18.0.0/16 will be used.

To show which route the router would match to reach a specific IP address, the **show ip route w.x.y.x** command can be used as shown below.

R2#show ip route 172.18.30.5
Routing entry for 172.18.0.0/22
Known via "rip", distance 120, metric 1
Redistributing via rip
Last update from 172.18.50.2 on Serial0, 00:00:12 ago
Routing Descriptor Blocks:
* 172.18.50.2, from 172.18.50.2, 00:00:12 ago, via Serial0
Route metric is 1, traffic share count is 1

The show ip arp Command

To list the contents of a router's ARP cache, the **show ip arp** command is used.

Configuration 5-29, Display the R3's ARP cache: This command lists the used protocol type (IP or the internet of course here), the used IP address, Age in minutes, MAC address, the interface and its type. The routers use the ARP in the same way that PC's use it and for the same purposes as described in the beginning of this chapter.

```
R3#show ip arp
Protocol    Address      Age (min)    Hardware Addr     Type     Interface
Internet    172.18.30.2      6         0013.197b.5eb1    ARPA     Ethernet0
Internet    172.18.30.1      -         0013.197b.5005    ARPA     Ethernet0
Internet    172.18.40.1      -         0013.197b.5009    ARPA     Ethernet1
```

Notice that, if the Age lists a number, this value represents the number of minutes since the router last received a packet from the host, i.e., Age in minutes of the cache entry. For example, it had been 6 minutes since R3 had received a packet from a host with source IP address 172.10.30.2. The timer of the Age is reset to 0 each time a matching packet is received. If the Age is listed as a hyphen, the ARP entry actually represents an IP address assigned to the router interface, i.e., means the address is local. The Type indicates the encapsulation type the CISCO IOS software is using the network address in this entry. Other values that can be found here are the SNAP and SAP. **ARPA** (default) signifies that the standard Ethernet version 2.0 **encapsulation** is used.

The traceroute Command

To test the route between a router and another host or router and to discover the path that a packet takes as it traverses an internetwork, the CISCO IOS **traceroute** command is used. The **traceroute** command identifies the IP addresses of the routers in the route, i.e. the next-hop device address.

Configuration 5-30, Test the route between Routers: Figure 5-8, shows an internetwork with the **traceroute** command issued from R2 to Machine A. The arrowed lines show the path a packet takes as it traverses from R2 to Machine A with three IP addresses identified by the command output shown below. Table 5-1 is used as a reference for the IP addresses in this internetwork.

```
R2#traceroute 172.18.10.2
Type escape sequence to abort.
Tracing the route to 172.18.10.2
1    172.18.60.1    9 msec     4 msec     4 msec
2    172.18.70.1    20 msec    21 msec    22 msec
3    172.18.10.2    22 msec    22 msec    24 msec
```

Notice that, if a routing problem exists, the command will not complete, and no routers would be listed after the last route that can be discovered, and the user would have to stop the command, typically by pressing the Ctrl-Shift-6 key sequence a few times, as it will be discussed in Chapter 7 of this book.

Two other commands can be used to test the IP routing connectivity in the internetworks; **Telnet** and **ssh** commands. These commands also will be discussed in Chapter 7. As an example, the following configuration shows how to connect to R1 from R2 using username thaar in **ssh** command.

R2#ssh –l thaar R1 172.18.70.1

The **show ssh** command lists the same kind of information that can be obtained from the **show users** command. Both commands list all users logged into the router on which the command is used. These commands list all sessions, including users at the console, and those connecting using both **Telnet** and **SSH**. Whereas, the **show sessions** command lists the suspended Telnet/SSH sessions from a Router to other devices.

Figure 5-8 Traceroute Example

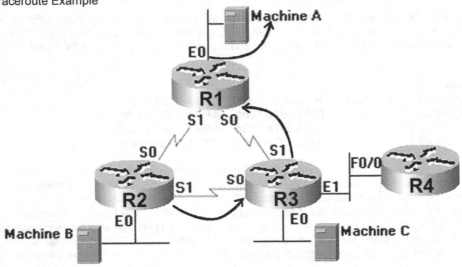

The following CISCO commands can also be used to verify and check the IP networks:

- **show ip route.**
- **show protocols**
- **show ip protocol**
- **debug ip rip**
- **debug ip igrp events**
- **debug ip igrp transactions**

show ip route

Configuration 5-31: The following Configuration shows how to display the IP routing table in a CISCO Router using the command **show ip route.**

R4# show ip route
Codes: C - connected, S - static, I - IGRP derived, R - RIP derived, M – Mobile, B – BGP, D – EIGRP, EX – EIGRP external, O - OSPF, IA – OSPF inter area N1- OSPF NSSA external type 1, N2 – OSPF NSSA external type 2 E1 – OSPF external type 1, E2 – OSPF external type 2, E - EGP i – IS-IS, L1 – IS-IS level-1, L2 – IS-IS level-2, * - candidate default route U – per-user route T – traffic engineered route.
Gateway of last resort is not set

    172.18.0.0/24 is subnetted, 7 subnets
R   172.18.70.0 [120/1] via 172.18.40.1, FastEthernet0/0
R   172.18.60.0 [120/1] via 172.18.40.1, FastEthernet0/0
R   172.18.50.0 [120/2] via 172.18.40.1, FastEthernet0/0
C   172.18.40.0 is directly connected, FastEthernet0/0
R   172.18.30.0 [120/1] via 172.18.40.1, FastEthernet0/0
R   172.18.20.0 [120/2] via 172.18.40.1, FastEthernet0/0

R   172.18.10.0   [120/2] via 172.18.40.1, FastEthernet0/0
R4#

The Router reports the networks to which it is directly connected and the networks that it has learnt dynamically of since the Router had came online. The **clear ip route** command can be used to delete routes from the IP routing table. The command **show ip route 172.18.70.0** will show detailed information about 172.18.70.0 network in the routing table. The **show ip route rip** command will only display RIP related routes. Whereas, the command **show ip route summary** will display the current state of the routing table.

```
Router# show ip route summary
Route Source    Networks    Subnets    Overhead    Memory (bytes)
connected       0           3          126         360
static          1           2          126         360
igrp 109        747         12         31878       91080
internal        3                                  360
Total           751         17         32130       92160
Router#
```

show protocols

Configuration 5-32: The following Configuration shows how to view the IP address of an interface using the command **show protocols**.

```
R1#show protocols
Global values:
  Internet Protocol routing is enabled
Ethernet0 is up, line protocol is up
  Internet address is 172.18.10.1/24
Serial0 is up, line protocol is up
  Internet address is 172.18.70.1/24
Serial1 is up, line protocol is up
  Internet address is 172.18.50.2/24
R1#
```

This command shows the routed protocols configured on the Router and the Network layer addresses configured on each interface. This command will present all configured interfaces even secondaries and subinterfaces. This command also will show other network types such as, IPX if they were configured on the router.

show ip protocol

Configuration 5-33: The following Configuration shows how to display the parameters and the current state of the active routing protocol process on the CISCO Router using the **show ip protocol** command. The following output verifies that both RIP and IGRP are running on the Router, but only IGRP is appeared in the routing table (**Configuration 5-27**) because of its lower AD.

```
R4#sh ip protocol
Routing Protocol is "rip"
  Sending updates every 30 seconds, next due in 2 seconds
  Invalid after 180 seconds, hold down 180, flushed after 240
  Outgoing update filter list for all interfaces is not set
  Incoming update filter list for all interfaces is not set
  Redistributing: rip
  Default version control: send version 1, receive version 1
```

```
Interface          Send Recv  Key-chain
FastEthernet0/0     2    2     trees
Routing for Networks:
 172.18.0.0
Routing Information Sources:
Gateway      Distance    Last Update
172.18.40.1   120         00:00:29
Distance: (default is 120)
```

The information displayed by **show ip protocol** is useful in debugging the routing operations. Information in the Routing Information Sources field of the **show ip protocol** output can help you identify a Router suspected of delivering bad routing information. The command also shows the default values of the timers used in the routing protocol. The output verifies that RIP is sending updates every 30 seconds. The invalid timer is set at 180 seconds. If an update is not received from a Router in 180 seconds, its route became invalid. The holddown timer is 180, which is around six times the update timer. The holddown timer suppressed an invalid route for 180 seconds while waiting for a new update for that route to be received. If a new update is not received before the holddown timer expires, the flush timer will start, and when it expires, the route is deleted from the routing table. The RIP routing for network 172.18.0.0 shows, there is only one neighbor to this network was found that is 172.18.40.1. The last line in the output above is the default AD for RIP (120).

The output below shows the IGRP routing information.

```
Routing Protocol is "igrp 20"
  Sending updates every 90 seconds, next due in 44 seconds
  Invalid after 270 seconds, hold down 280, flushed after 630
  Outgoing update filter list for all interfaces is not set
  Incoming update filter list for all interfaces is not set
  Default networks flagged in outgoing updates
  Default networks accepted from incoming updates
  IGRP metric weight K1=1, K2=0, K3=1, K4=0, K5=0
  IGRP maximum hopcount 100
  IGRP maximum metric variance 1
  Redistributing: igrp 20
  Routing for Networks:
   172.18.0.0
  Routing Information Sources:
   Gateway      Distance    Last Update
   172.18.40.1   100         00:00:41
  Distance: (default is 100)
```

The output above shows the default update timer value = 90 seconds, the AD value = 100 by default, AS = 20, networks being advertised, and gateways. The invalid timer is set at 270 seconds. The holddown timer is 280. If a new update is not received before the holddown timer expires, the flush timer will start. When the flush timer expires, the route is deleted from the Routing table.

Debug ip rip

Configuration 5-34: The following Configurations shows how IP RIP running is checked through the internetwork using the command **debug ip rip**.

```
R4#debug ip rip
RIP protocol debugging is on
R4#
```

08:15:04: RIP: received v1 update from 172.18.40.1 on FastEthernet0/0
08:15:04:   172.18.30.0 in 1 hops
08:12:04: RIP: received v1 update from 172.18.40.1 on FastEthernet0/0
08:12:04:   172.18.60.0 in 1 hops
08:12:04: RIP: received v1 update from 172.18.40.1 on FastEthernet0/0
08:12:04:   172.18.50.0 in 2 hops
08:12:04: RIP: received v1 update from 172.18.40.1 on FastEthernet0/0
08:12:04:   172.18.70.0 in 1 hops
08:12:04: RIP: received v1 update from 172.18.40.1 on FastEthernet0/0
08:12:04:   172.18.20.0 in 2 hops
08:12:04: RIP: received v1 update from 172.18.40.1 on FastEthernet0/0
08:12:04:   172.18.10.0 in 2 hops
08:12:06: RIP: sending v1 update to 255.255.255.255 via FastEthernet0/0 (172.18.40.2)
08:12:06:   subnet 172.18.70.0, metric 1
08:12:06:   subnet 172.18.60.0, metric 1
08:12:06:   subnet 172.18.50.0, metric 2
08:12:06:   subnet 172.18.30.0, metric 1
08:12:06:   subnet 172.18.20.0, metric 2
08:12:06:   subnet 172.18.10.0, metric 2

R4#undebug all
All possible debugging has been turned off
R4#

The **debug ip rip** command shows the routing updates as they are sent and received on the Router. To receive the output of this command through a Telnet session, the command **terminal monitor** should be issued. The output above shows that RIP is both sending and receiving on the FastEthernet0/0 interface of R4 Router. The output shows also that the Router being debugged has received updates from R3 Router at source address 172.18.40.1. That Router sent information about six destinations in the routing table update. The Router being debugged also sent updates, in both cases to broadcast address 255.255.255.255 as the destination. This command can be turned OFF by using **no debug ip rip, undebug all**, **un al** or **no debug all** commands.

Notice that, it is helpful to look at the router's CPU utilization with the **show process** command, before using the **debug** command. This command lists the average percentage of router's CPU utilization over three short time periods. It is not recommended to enable the debug command on routers with a higher CPU utilization, generally above 30 to 40 percent, since this may highly be utilizing the router CPU and slowing packet forwarding.

R4#show process

Another note can be found here. It is useful to configure the time stamps that can be found on the debug output messages, to make the router generate time stamps. For this purpose, the **service timestamps** global configuration command must be configured.

R4(config)# service timestamps

Debug IP IGRP

Configuration 5-35: The following Configurations shows how IP IGRP running is checked through the internetwork using the commands **debug ip igrp.** The following two options are available for this command:

R4#debug ip igrp ?
  events   IGRP protocol events
  transactions IGRP protocol transactions

Debug IP IGRP Events

Configuration 5-36: The following output shows how to view information about IP IGRP events through the internetwork using the command **debug ip igrp events**.

R4#debug ip igrp events
IGRP event debugging is on
08:15:16: IGRP: received request from 172.18.40.1 on FastEthernet0/0
08:15:16: IGRP: sending update to 172.18.40.1 via FastEthernet0/0 (172.18.40.2)
08:15:16: IGRP: Update contains 4 interior, 0 system, and 0 exterior routes.
08:15:16: IGRP: Total routes in update: 3
08:15:16: IGRP: received update from 172.18.40.1 on FastEthernet0/0
08:15:16: IGRP: Update contains 2 interior, 0 system, and 0 exterior routes.
08:15:16: IGRP: Total routes in update: 2
R4#un all
All possible debugging has been turned off
R4#

Use the **debug ip igrp events** EXEC command to display summary information on IGRP routing messages that indicate the source and destination of each update, as well as the number of routes in each update. However, information about individual routes is not gathered by this command. This command is particularly useful when there are many networks in the routing table. In this case, using **debug ip igrp transactions** command could flood the console and make the Router unusable. Therefore, use **debug ip igrp events** command instead to display summary routing information. This command can be turned OFF by using **no debug ip igrp events**, **undebug all**, **un al** or **no debug all** commands.

Debug IP IGRP Transactions

Configuration 5-37: The following output shows message requests from neighbor routers asking for an update and the broadcasts sent from R4 towards that neighbor Router using the **debug ip igrp transactions** command.

R4#debug ip igrp transactions
IGRP protocol debugging is on
08:16:06: IGRP: received request from 172.18.40.1 on FastEthernet0/0
08:16:06: IGRP: sending update to 172.18.40.1 via FastEthernet0/0 (172.18.40.2)
08:16:06:   subnet 172.18.70.0, metric=150370
08:16:06:   subnet 172.18.60.0, metric=150360
08:16:06:   subnet 172.18.50.0, metric=150350
08:16:06:   subnet 172.18.30.0, metric=150350
08:16:06: IGRP: received update from 172.18.40.1 on FastEthernet0/0
08:16:06:   subnet 172.18.20.0, metric=160360
08:16:06:   subnet 172.18.10.0, metric=160350
R4#un all
All possible debugging has been turned off
R4#

The output above shows a request was received from a neighbor Router on network 172.18.40.1 to FastEthernet0/0. The R4 Router responded with an update packet. When there are many networks in the routing table, **debug ip igrp transactions** can flood the console and make the Router unusable. In this case, use **the debug ip igrp events** instead to display summary routing information. This command can be turned OFF by using **no debug ip igrp transactions, undebug all, un al,** or **no debug all** commands.

Summary

In this chapter, a strong foundation for IP (Internet Protocol) routing is presented. The information presented in this chapter is essential for all CISCO network engineers. The IOS consists of several IP routing related commands and utilities, such as ip route, router rip, router igrp, debug ip rip, debug ip igrp, show...etc. These commands and utilities are designed to serve ip network operations. A number of configurations and examples are used to clarify the ideas behind this chapter. The following topics are covered:

- The Routing Process
- Static Routing
- Default Routing
- Dynamic Routing
- Routing Information Protocol
- Interior Gateway Routing Protocol
- Verifying the routing configurations

At the end of the chapter, several learning questions are given to evaluate the learning level from this chapter. The correct answers and solutions with complementary discussions are found in appendix A, "Answers to Chapters Learning Questions."

Chapter Five Commands Reference

Table 5-6 lists and briefly describes all the new commands and keys that are used in this chapter.

Table 5-6 Chapter 5 Commands Reference

Command	Description
R1#sh ip route	Views the IP routing tables created on a CISCO Router
R1#terminal ip netmask-format decimal	Changes the format of the display of the subnet mask in the show commands to decimal
R1(config)#ip route 172.18.20.0 255.255.255.0 172.18.50.1	Adds a static route to a routing table
R1(config)#no ip route 172.18.10.0 255.255.255.0 172.18.40.1	Removes a static route from a routing table
R1(config)#ip route 0.0.0.0 0.0.0.0 172.18.40.1	Adds a default route to a routing table
R1(config)#ip classless	Makes the router classless router so that it can forward the packet on the default route
R1(config)#router rip	Makes the router uses RIP routing protocol.
R1(config-router)#network 172.18.0.0	Configures the network for routing protocol.
R1(config-router)#^Z	Exits the global configuration prompt
Router(config-router)#passive-interface serial 1	Holds Down RIP Propagation's
R1(config-router)#version 2	Makes the router uses RIP v2 routing protocol.
R1(config)#router igrp 20	Makes the router uses IGRP routing protocol with AS 20
Router(config-router)#variance	Controls the load balancing between the best metric and the worst acceptable metric
Router(config-	Helps control traffic distribution among IGRP load-sharing

router)#traffic-share min	routes to minimum costs
Router(config-router)#traffic-share balanced	Tells the IGRP router to share inversely proportional to the metrics
C:\>Ping	Checks the network connectivity from a windows host
C:\>ipconfig /all	Displays a network configuration on a windows host
C:\>ipconfig /release	Releases any DHCP-leased IP addresses for all interfaces on a windows host
C:\>ipconfig /renew	Acquires an IP address and related information using the DHCP server on a windows host
C:\>nslookup www.cisco.com	Sends a DNS request for www.cisco.com
C:\>arp -a	Lists the host's ARP cache
C:\>ipconfig /displaydns	Lists the host's name cache
C:\>ipconfig /flushdns	Removes all DNS-found name cache entries
C:\>arp -d	Empties the host's ARP cache
C:\>netstat -rn	Displays a host's routing table
R1#show ip arp	Lists the contents of a router's ARP cache
R1#traceroute 172.18.10.2	Identifies the IP addresses of the routers in the route to host 172.18.10.2, i.e. the next-hop device address
R1#ssh –l thaar R2 172.18.70.1	Connects to R2 from R1 using username thaar in ssh command
R1#show ssh	Lists all users logged into the router
R1# show users	Lists all users logged into the router
R1# show sessions	Lists suspended Telnet/SSH sessions from a Router to other devices
Router# show ip route summary	Displays the current state of the routing table
R1#show protocols	Shows the routed protocols configured on the Router and the Network layer addresses configured on each interface. This command will present all configured interfaces even secondaries and subinterfaces. If other network types such as, IPX were configured on the router, those network addresses would have appeared as well
R1#sh ip protocol	Displays the parameters and current state of the active routing protocol process on CISCO Router
R1#debug ip rip	Shows how IP RIP running is checked through the internetwork
R1#undebug all OR no debug ip rip OR un al OR no debug all	Turns off debugging
R1#show process	Shows the router's CPU utilization
R1(config)# service timestamps	Makes the router generate time stamps.

Chapter 5 Learning Questions

5-1.   What is the routing process?

    A.   Routing process is a process of moving a packet from one host and sending it through the internetwork to another host on a different network/subnet.

    B.   It is a process of dropping a packet from the router.

5-2.   Which of the following is true about routing process? (Select all that apply)

    A.   It takes a packet from one network and sends it to another network.

    B.   It requires routing software.

    C.   It can be implemented in a Router or in any other automated machines.

    D.   Only CISCO Routers implement this process.

5-3.   Try to clear the basic of routing process in the internetwork by arranging the following statements:

    A. The Router learns about remote networks from a network administrator or from neighbor Routers.

    B. From this information, the Router builds a routing table that describes how to find the remote networks.

    C. If the network is directly connected, their interfaces must be defined on the Router, then the Router knows how to get to this network and there are no needs for any further interventions.

    D. If the network is not directly connected, the Router must learn how to obtain the remote network with either the configuring of the static routing or dynamic routing.

5-4.   Which of the following is a type of the routing process? (Select all that apply)

    A. Static

    B. Dynamic

    C. Extended

    D. Exterior

    E. Interior

    F. Enhanced

5-5.   Which of the following is true about static routing process? (Select all that apply)

    A. Static routing process means that the administrator must type all network locations into the routing tables of all routers in the internetwork by hand.

    B. The administrator is responsible for updating manually, all changes into all routers.

    C. It is implemented and supported by dynamic routing protocols, but it still needs some administrator's interventions.

    D. It discovers all routes by communicating with neighbor routers in the internetwork.

    E. The routers use it to update each other about all the networks they know about.

    F. When changes occur in the network topology, the dynamic routing protocols automatically inform all routers about those changes.

    G. It is implemented by the dynamic routing protocols running on the Routers.

5-6.   Which of the following is true about dynamic routing process? (Select all that apply)

    A. Static routing process means that the administrator must type all network locations into the routing tables of all routers in the internetwork by hand.

    B. The administrator is responsible for updating manually, all changes into all routers.

    C. It is implemented and supported by dynamic routing protocols, but it still needs some administrator's interventions.

D. It discovers all routes by communicating with neighbor routers in the internetwork.

E. The routers use it to update each other about all the networks they know about.

F. When changes occur in the network topology, the dynamic routing protocols automatically inform all routers about those changes.

G. It is implemented by the dynamic routing protocols running on the Routers.

5-7.   Match each of the following steps to its correct description.

1.   **Step 1: Issuing the ping command**
2.   **Step 2: Determining the destination Host B's Network.**
3.   **Step 3: Determining the R1 MAC address.**
4.   **Step 4: Completing the Packet**
5.   **Step 5: Generating the frame by Host A.**
6.   **Step 6: Sending the frame.**
7.   **Step 7: Receiving the data by R1.**
8.   **Step 8: Checking the destination MAC address.**
9.   **Step 9: Checking the Destination IP address.**
10.   **Step 10: Generating the frame by R1.**
11.   **Step 11: Replying to R1 broadcast.**
12.   **Step 12: Checking the IP address by Host B.**
13.   **Step 13: Generating the reply by Host B.**

A.   The user issues' **ping 172.17.20.2** command from Host A. Host A used the IP and ICMP Network layer protocols to generate a packet.

B.   IP and the ARP protocols on a host are working together to determine what network this packet is destined for by calculating the binary multiplication of (the destination IP address * the source subnet mask) and (the source IP address * the source subnet mask). If both are equal, this means that the destination address is in the local network (the packet will be sent directly to that destination host), otherwise the destination will be on the remote network. In this example, the destination is in the remote network. The packet then must be sent to the Router (R1) so that it will be routed to the correct remote network.

C.   Host A has the IP address of E0 as a default gateway. However, to communicate with R1, the R1's MAC address must be obtained. To obtain the hardware address of E0, Host A looks in a location in memory called the ARP cache. However, if it's not found in ARP cache (i.e., The E0 IP address has not already been resolved to a MAC address), Host A sends an ARP broadcast on the local network looking, for the MAC address of IP address 172.17.10.1. This step is usually times out. Finally, the R1 responds with the MAC address of the E0.

D. The network layer takes the packet it generated with the ICMP echo request (ping) to the Data Link layer, along with the MAC address of where Host A wants to send the packet. The packet includes in addition to the source IP address and the destination IP address, the ICMP specific in the Network layer protocol field.

E.   The Data Link layer generates the frame, by encapsulating the packet with the control information needed to transmit. The frame includes the source and destination MAC addresses, and the type field specifying the Network layer protocol (IP uses an Ethernet_II frame by default). This process is depicted in Figure 5-2. The frame contains the source and destination MAC addresses, the source and destination IP addresses, and the data and the frame's CRC inside the Frame Check Sequence (FCS) field.

F.   The data Link layer of Host A takes the frame to the Physical layer, encodes the frame into 1s and 0s and transmits this out on the network.

G.   The R1's E0 receives the signal and the interface synchronizes on the digital signal preamble and extracts the frame. The R1's interface, then builds the frame, runs a CRC and, at the end of the frame, checks the FCS field to be sure that the CRC matches and no fragmentation or collisions are occurred during transmission.

H.   The frame destination MAC address is checked. Since it is a match, the frame type field will be checked to see what the R1 should do with the data packet. IP is in the type field. Therefore, the R1 must hand the packet to the IP protocol running on the R1. The frame is discarded, and the original-generated packet by Host A is put in the R1's buffer.

I.   IP in R1 determines if the packet is for the R1 by looking at the packet's destination IP address. IP 172.17.20.2 is in the packet and from the routing table; R1 determines that 172.17.20.0 net is a directly connected network on the interface E1.

J.   R1 places the packet in the buffer of the interface E1. Now, to send the packet to the destination host B, R1 needs to create a frame at first and the frame must have a MAC address of the destination Host B. The same process described in steps 2 and 3 are applied here. Assuming that the MAC is not in the ARP cache, the R1 must then send an ARP broadcast out E1 to find the MAC address of 172.17.20.2.

K.   Host B responds to the R1's ARP broadcast with the MAC address of its NIC by an ARP reply. The R1's E1 interface now creates the packet to Host B. This process is depicted in Figure 5-3.

L.   Host B receives the frame from R1 and runs a CRC checking. According to CRC result, the frame is discarded and the packet is handled to IP of Host B. The destination IP address in the packet is checked by IP. Since the IP destination address matches the IP of Host B, it looks in the protocol field of the packet to determine what the purpose of the packet is.

M.   Since the packet is an ICMP echo request, Host B generates a new ICMP echo-reply packet with a source IP address of Host B and a destination IP address of Host A. Host B sends an ICMP echo-reply to Host A by the same processes above, except that it goes in the opposite direction. Now, each device only needs to look in its ARP cache to determine the MAC address of each interface, since the MAC address of each device along the path is already known in the ARP cache of each device.

5-8. TRUE/FALSE: The IP routing process illustrated in example 5-1 would be the same if the network were much larger. The only difference is that the packet would simply go through more hops (routers) before it finds the destination host. However, on point-to-point WAN links, ARP is not needed, and the data link addressing is unused.

A.   TRUE
B.   FALSE

5-9.   Which of the following is true about IP routing?

A.   The frame changes at each hop.
B.   The destination IP address changes at each hop.
C.   The source IP address changes at each hop.
D.   The packet from the source to the destination was never modified at all, regardless the number of hops passing through.
E.   The destination MAC address changes at each hop.
F.   The source MAC address changes at each hop.

5-10.   Which of the following cases makes the source host sends a packet to the Router? (Select all that apply)

A.   The packet is destined for the Router.
B.   The packet is destined for the local network.
C.   The packet is destined for the remote network.

5-11.   TRUE/FALSE: The Router would forward the received packet depending on the routing table.

A.   TRUE

B.   FALSE

5-12.   TRUE/FALSE: In example 5-1, the routing table of R1 already has both IP networks (10.0 and 20.0) in the routing table because these nets are directly connected to R1.

A.   TRUE
B.   FALSE

5-13.   Match each of the following with its suitable implemented rule.

1.   By Host
2.   By Router

Rule1.   If the destination IP address is in the same subnet, send the packet directly to that destination host.
Rule2.   If the destination IP address is not in the same subnet, send the packet to the default gateway.
Rule3.   Ensure that the frame had no errors using the data-link FCS field. If errors occurred, discard the frame.
Rule4.   If errors not found in **Rule1**, discard the old data-link header and trailer, leaving the IP packet and handled it to Layer 3.
Rule5.   Check the routing table to find the route that matches the destination IP packet address. If a route is found, it may identify the outgoing interface of the router, and possibly the next-hop router.
Rule6.   Forward the new frame after encapsulating the IP packet inside a new data-link header and trailer.
Rule7.   Repeat **Rule1** to **Rule4** inside each hop router, to deliver the packet to the destined address host in the internetwork.

5-14.   TRUE/FALSE: Routes to remote networks can be added to the routing tables of the routers using the following routing types: Static routing, default routing, and dynamic routing. However, the best way for one network is not necessarily best for another. The best way that should be selected depends on the network requirements.

A.   TRUE
B.   FALSE

5-15.   Which CISCO IOS command will use to see the IP routing table?

A.   sh ip route
B.   display ip route
C.   ip route
D.   sh ip table

5-16.   When looking at the IP routing table, what does the C mean?

A.   Dynamically connected
B.   Directly connected
C.   Statically connected
D.   Sending packets

5-17.   Which of the following is a default method for defining the routes on a Router? (Select all that apply)

A.   Directly connected routing

B.   Static routing
C.   Default routing
D.   Dynamic routing

5-18.   Which of the following methods can be used to define a route on the Router for a directly connected network? (Select all that apply)

A.   Configuring a static route
B.   Configuring a dynamic route
C.   Configuring a default route
D.   Configuring the Router interfaces

5-19.   What does an administrative distance of 0 mean?

A.   0 is the default administrative distance for dynamic routing.
B.   0 is the default administrative distance for default routing.
C.   0 is the default administrative distance for static routing.
D.   0 is the default administrative distance for directly connected routes.
E.   There is no routing allowed on this router.
F.   There are 0 hops to the next destination.

5-20.   Which of the following methods can be used to define routes on the Router to a remote network? (Select all that apply)

A.   Directly connected routing
B.   Static routing
C.   Default routing
D.   Dynamic routing

5-21.   What is the static routing?

A.   It is the process of automatically adding routes in each router's routing table.
B.   It is the process of configuring network routes in each router's routing table manually by an administrator.
C.   It is the process of an administrator manually adding routes for directly connected networks in each router's routing table.

5-22.   Which of the following is an advantage of the static routing process? (Select all that apply)

A.   Improving security in the internetwork, since the administrator could only allow routing to certain networks.
B.   No overhead on the Router CPU.
C.   No bandwidth usage between routers.
D.   Routes could be not volatile when rebooting the router.
E.   The administrator must really understand the internetwork and how each Router is connected to configure the routes correctly.

5-23.   Which of the following is a disadvantage of the static routing process? (Select all that apply)

A.   The administrator must add a new route to any new networks on all routers.
B.   It is unsuitable in large networks because too many routes must be added manually when a new network is added and this would be a full-time job and errors could happen.
C.   Troubleshooting and maintenance of the internetwork would be difficult.

D.   The administrator must fully understand the internetwork and how each Router is connected.
E.   It reduces the internetwork security.

5-24.   What is the default administrative distance for the static routes?

A.   90
B.   100
C.   0
D.   1

5-25.   When looking at a routing table, what does the S mean?

A.   Dynamically connected
B.   Directly connected
C.   Statically connected
D.   Sending packets

5-26.   Which of the following is true when creating the static routes? (Select all that apply)

A.   The mask parameter is optional.
B.   The gateway parameter is required.
C.   The administrative distance is required.
D.   The administrative distance is optional.
E.   The destination network address is required.
F.   None of the above

5-27.   What does a router do with a received packet that is destined for an unknown network?

A.   It drops the packet.
B.   It forwards the packet.
C.   It holds the packet until the next route updates.
D.   It sends a broadcast for the unknown network.

5-28.   Which of the following is not one of the advantages of using the static routes over dynamic routing?

A.   Fast convergence
B.   No CPU usage
C.   No bandwidth usage
D.   Security

5-29.   Which routes are most believable by default?

A.   RIP
B.   OSPF
C.   EIGRP
D.   Static route

5-30.   Which of the following is an advantage of using the static routing tables with the CISCO Routers?

A.   Network bandwidth conservation
B.   Decreased administration of routing tables
C.   Increased security by limiting subnet access
D.   No overhead on the Router CPU

5-31. Which of the following links use the exit interface instead of the next hop address?

    A. Point-to-multipoint link
    B. Multipoint-to-multipoint link
    C. Point-to-point link

5-32. Which command will specify that a route will not be removed from the routing table?

    A. Mask
    B. Destination network address
    C. Next hop
    D. Administrative distance
    E. Permanent

5-33. Which of the following cases tends to remove the route automatically from the routing tables? (Select all that apply)

    A. In case of interface shutdown
    B. In case of the Router cannot communicate to the next hop Router.
    C. In case of the administrator removes the route.

5-34. Which command will add a static route to the routing table?

    A. ip address
    B. static route
    C. ip static route
    D. ip route

5-35. Which command will remove a static route from the routing table?

    A. no ip route
    B. remove static route
    C. no ip static route
    D. no ip address

5-36. Which of the following prompts defines a static route?

    A. Router>
    B. Router#
    C. Router(config)#
    D. Router(config-if)#

5-37. Which of the following prompts removes a static route?

    A. Router>
    B. Router#
    C. Router(config)#
    D. Router(config-if)#

5-38. TRUE/FALSE: Static route is used to define remote networks' routes.

    A. TRUE
    B. FALSE

5-39.   Which command will route the packets for network 131.108.0.0 to a Router at 131.108.6.6?

    A.   ip route 131.108.6.6 255.255.0.0 131.108.0.0.
    B.   ip route 255.255.0.0 131.108.0.0 131.108.6.6.
    C.   ip route 255.255.0.0 131.108.6.6 131.108.0.0.
    D.   ip route 131.108.0.0 255.255.0.0 131.108.6.6.

5-40.   Which command will view the statically defined routes? (Select all that apply)

    A.   show running-config
    B.   show ip route
    C.   show static routes
    D.   display ip route
    E.   view ip route

5-41.   What will happen when an internetwork with five networks is statically routes defined and then one more route or another Router is added to the internetwork? (Select all that apply)

    A.   All routers' routing tables must be updated by hand.
    B.   Only the new router must be updated by hand.
    C.   None of the above

5-42.   If you wanted to change the default administrative distance for a static route to 175, what would you do?

    A.   Add an administrative distance parameter to the end of a static route entry.
    B.   Change the network to a different router interface that runs FastEthernet or Gigabit Ethernet.
    C.   Set the global command static-routing 175
    D.   Add the permanent parameter to the end of a static route entry

5-43.   If you define a static route, but the route does not appear in the routing table. What is the reason for this situation? (Select all that apply)

    A.   The command permanent is not used.
    B.   The router does not accept the route.
    C.   The router does accept the route, but it requires long period to appear in the routing table.
    D.   The router cannot communicate to the next hop address you configured.

5-44.   Try to arrange the following information to complete a static route.

    A.   255.255.255.0
    B.   Administrative distance =175
    C.   172.18.80.1
    D.   172.18.80.0
    E.   S

5-45.   Which of the following ARP table entries would be expected to find if Machine B successfully pings Machine A? Assume that both Machines are configured statically for IP addresses and all the devices in Figure 5-4 just booted, and none of the devices has yet sent any data frames.

    A.   An entry on R2's ARP cache for Machine A IP address
    B.   An entry on R2's ARP cache for Machine B IP address
    C.   An entry on Machine B's ARP cache for Machine A IP address
    D.   An entry on Machine B's ARP cache for IP address 172.18.20.1

5-46. Which of the following ARP requests would be expected to occur if Machine B successfully pings Machine A? Assume that both Machines are configured statically for IP addresses and all the devices in Figure 5-4 just booted, and none of the devices has yet sent any data frames.

    A.   An ARP broadcast would be sent from R2 to look for Machine B's MAC address.
    B.   An ARP broadcast would be sent from Machine B to look for R2's MAC address of the interface with IP address 172.18.20.1.
    C.   An ARP broadcast would be sent from Machine B to look for Machine A's MAC address.
    D.   An ARP broadcast would be sent from R1 to look for Machine A's MAC address.
    E.   An ARP broadcast would be sent from Machine A to look for R1's MAC address of the interface with IP address 172.18.10.1.

5-47. Which of the following is true about packets, if Machine B is successfully pinging Machine A in Figure 5-4? (Select all that apply)

    A.   The Machine A's frame, as it crosses the subnet 172.18.20.0, has a source MAC address of Machine A's MAC address.
    B.   The Machine A's frame, as it crosses the subnet 172.18.10.0, has a source MAC address of Machine A's MAC address.
    C.   The Machine A's frame, as it crosses the serial link, has a source MAC address of R1's MAC address.
    D.   The Machine B's frame, as it crosses the subnet 172.18.20.0, has a destination MAC address of R2's MAC address.
    E.   The Machine B's frame, as it crosses the subnet 172.18.10.0, has a destination MAC address of R1's MAC address.
    F.   The Machine B's frame, as it crosses the serial link, has a destination IP address of Machine A's IP address.

5-48. Which of the following is true about default routing? (Select all that apply)

    A.   It is used to send packets with a remote destination network in the routing table to the next hop router.
    B.   It can only be used on networks with multiple exit ports.
    C.   It is used to send packets with a remote destination network not in the routing table to the next hop router.
    D.   It can only be used on stub networks.

5-49. What is a stub network?

    A.   A network with more than one exit point
    B.   A network with more than one exit and entry point
    C.   A network with only one exit point
    D.   A network that has only one entry.

5-50. What type of network could you consider configuring a default route on?

    A.   Static
    B.   Dynamic
    C.   Stub
    D.   Secondary

5-51. How a default route is created?

    A.   By defining a static route and using all 0s in place of the network and mask
    B.   By using all 1s in place of the network and mask

   C.   By using 255 in place of the network and mask
   D.   By defining a static route and using all 1s in place of the network only.

5-52.   Which of the following is a correct default route?

   A.   ip route 0.0.0.0 0.0.0.0 172.18.20.1
   B.   B ip route 172.0.0.0 255.0.0.0
   C.   ip route 0.0.0.0 255.255.255.255 172.18.20.1
   D.   route ip 0.0.0.0 0.0.0.0 172.18.10.1 150

5-53.   In the following command, what does the 175 mean?
ip route 0.0.0.0 0.0.0.0 100.100.100.150 175

   A.   It defines the next hop.
   B.   It defines the administrative distance.
   C.   It means that the update is broadcasted.
   D.   Nothing, it is an invalid command.

5-54.   What is the administrative distance of the default routes by default?

   A.   0
   B.   100
   C.   10
   D.   1

5-55.   Which of the following commands must be issued with the default routing?

   A.   ip default routing
   B.   ip classful
   C.   ip classless
   D.   ip default classless

5-56.   Which command will view the default routes? (Select all that apply)

   A.   show running-config
   B.   show ip route
   C.   show static routes
   D.   display ip route
   E.   view ip route

5-57.   When looking at a routing table, what does the S* mean?

   A.   Dynamically connected
   B.   Directly connected
   C.   Statically connected
   D.   Sending packets
   E.   Default route

5-58.   Which of the following is true when creating the default routes? (Select all that apply)

   A.   The mask parameter must be 0.0.0.0.
   B.   The gateway parameter is required.
   C.   The administrative distance is required.
   D.   The administrative distance is optional.

E.   The destination network address must be 0.0.0.0.
F.   None of the above

5-59.   What does a router do with a received packet that is destined for an unknown network, assume that the router is implemented a default routing?

A.   It drops the packet.
B.   It forwards the packet on the default route.
C.   It holds the packet until the next route updates.
D.   It sends a broadcast for the unknown network.

5-60.   Which of the following is an advantage of using the default routing tables with the CISCO Routers?

A.   Network bandwidth conservation
B.   Decreased administration of routing tables
C.   Increased security by limiting subnet access
D.   No overhead on the Router CPU

5-61.   Which command will add a default route to the routing table?

A.   ip address
B.   default route
C.   ip default route
D.   ip route

5-62.   Which command will remove a default route to the routing table?

A.   no ip route
B.   remove default route
C.   no ip default route
D.   no ip address

5-63.   Which of the following prompts defines a default route?

A.   Router>
B.   Router#
C.   Router(config)#
D.   Router(config-if)#

5-64.   Which of the following prompts removes a default route?

A.   Router>
B.   Router#
C.   Router(config)#
D.   Router(config-if)#

5-65.   TRUE/FALSE: Default route is used to implement remote networks' routes.

A.   TRUE
B.   FALSE

5-66.   Try to arrange the following information to complete a default route.

    A.   0.0.0.0/0
    B.   Administrative distance =175
    C.   172.18.80.1
    D.   0.0.0.0
    E.   S*

5-67.   Which command will configure a default route on a router to go to 172.17.100.10?

    A.   Router>ip route 0.0.0.0 0.0.0.0 172.17.100.10
    B.   Router# ip route 0.0.0.0 0.0.0.0 172.17.100.10
    C.   Router(config)# ip route 0.0.0.0 0.0.0.0 172.17.100.10
    D.   Router(config-if)# ip route 0.0.0.0 0.0.0.0 172.17.100.10

5-68.   In Figure 5.5, RC is unable to ping successfully RB. What is the problem?

    A.   RA and RB are not on the same subnet.
    B.   RA does not have any static routes defined.
    C.   RIP must be enabled on all routers.
    D.   Both networks must have the same network mask.

5-69.   What is the dynamic routing?

    A.   It is the process of using dynamic routing protocols to find and update automatically routing tables on routers.
    B.   It is the process of using protocols to find and update manually routing tables on routers.
    C.   It is the process used by hubs to find and update automatically routing tables.

5-70.   Which of the following is true about dynamic routing? (Select all that apply)

    A.   It is easier than static or default routing, since it requires little administration when routes are created.
    B.   It consumes Network bandwidth since it exchanges the route update messages throughout the internetwork.
    C.   It increases overhead on the Router CPU.

5-71.   How a dynamic route is created?

    A.   By defining a route manually in the routing table.
    B.   By using all 1s in place of the network and mask.
    C.   By using 255 in places of the network and mask.
    D.   By adopting the dynamic routing protocols in the routers

5-72.   TRUE/FALSE: A routing protocol defines the set of rules used by a Router when it communicates between the neighbor routers.

    A.   TRUE
    B.   FALSE

5-73.   How many types of routing protocols can be used in the internetwork? (Select all that apply)

    A.   One (Interior Gateway Protocol)
    B.   Two (Interior Gateway Protocol and Exterior Gateway Protocol)
    C.   Three (Interior Gateway Protocol, Exterior Gateway Protocol and Border Gateway Protocol)
    D.   Four (Interior Gateway Protocol, Exterior Gateway Protocol, Border Gateway Protocol and Open

Shortest Path First)

5-74. Which of the following is true about IGP? (Select all that apply)

    A.   IGP routing protocols are used to exchange routing information with routers in the same Autonomous System (AS).

    B.   IGP routing protocols are used to exchange routing information between Autonomous Systems (ASs).

5-75. Which of the following is true about EGP? (Select all that apply)

    A.   EGP routing protocols are used to exchange routing information with routers in the same Autonomous System (AS).

    B.   EGP routing protocols are used to exchange routing information between different Autonomous Systems (ASs).

5-76. What is an Autonomous System (AS)? (Select all that apply)

    A.   It Is a collection of networks under a common administrative routing domain.

    B.   It is an IGP routing protocols

    C.   It is an EGP routing protocols.

5-77. TRUE/FALSE: Today, BGP is used by ISPs to exchange routing information between different ISPs and between ISPs and customers. BGP advertises only routing information to specifically defined peers using TCP. BGP does not use a metric like IGPs to decide what route to use, instead BGP uses policies. Routing policy can be based on a business relationship between ISPs.

    A.   TRUE

    B.   FALSE

5-78. What is an administrative distance (AD)? (Select all that apply)

    A.   It is used to rate the trustworthiness of routing information received on a Router from a neighbor Router.

    B.   It is an integer from 0 to 255.

    C.   0 AD is the most trusted.

    D.   255 (no trust) AD means no traffic will be passed via this route.

5-79. Which of the following route sources is the most trusted?

    A.   Directly Connected interfaces

    B.   Static route

    C.   Default route

    D.   Dynamic route

5-80. What does an administrative distance of 1 mean?

    A.   1 is the default administrative distance for dynamic routing.

    B.   1 is the default administrative distance for static routing.

    C.   1 is the default administrative distance for directly connected routes.

    D.   There is no routing allowed on this Router.

    E.   There is one hop to the next destination.

5-81. What does an administrative distance of 1 mean?

A.   1 is the default administrative distance for dynamic routing.
B.   1 is the default administrative distance for default routing.
C.   1 is the default administrative distance for directly connected routes.
D.   There is no routing allowed on this Router.
E.   There is one hop to the next destination.

5-82.   What does an administrative distance of 100 mean?

A.   100 is the default administrative distance for IGRP routing protocol.
B.   100 is the default administrative distance for default routing.
C.   100 is the default administrative distance for directly connected routes.
D.   There is no routing allowed on this Router.
E.   There are 100 hops to the next destination.

5-83.   What does an administrative distance of 120 mean?

A.   There are 120 hops to the next destination.
B.   120 is the default administrative distance for default routing.
C.   120 is the default administrative distance for directly connected routes.
D.   There is no routing allowed on this Router.
E.   120 is the default administrative distance for RIP routing.

5-84.   What does an administrative distance of 255 mean?

A.   255 means that this route will never be used.
B.   There are 255 hops to the next destination.
C.   255 is the default administrative distance for default routing.
D.   255 is the default administrative distance for directly connected routes.
E.   There is no routing allowed on this Router.
F.   255 means unknown route.
G.   255 is the default administrative distance for RIP routing.

5-85.   What is the purpose of the administrative distance in the routing?

A.   Rating the source's trustworthiness, expressed as a numeric value from 0 to 255.
B.   Creating a routing database
C.   Determining the rule for entering that route
D.   Rating the destination's trustworthiness, expressed as a numeric value from 0 to 1023.

5-86.   Which of the following routing types has the highest administrative distance?

A.   Default routing
B.   Static Routing
C.   Directly connected
D.   Dynamic routing

5-87.   What strategy does the router use when it receives two-route updates for the same remote network?

A.   The router checks the AD's. The lowest AD will be placed in the routing table.
B.   If both advertised routes to the same network have the same AD, then the routing protocol metrics (such as hop count or bandwidth of the lines) will be used to find the best path to the remote network. The advertised route with the lowest metric will be placed in the routing table.

C.   If both advertised routes have the same AD as well as the same metrics, then the routing protocol will load-balance to the remote network.

5-88.   How many classes are found for the routing protocols?

A.   One
B.   Two
C.   Three
D.   Four

5-89.   Which of the following is a class of the routing protocols? (Select all that apply)

A.   Distance Vector
B.   Link State
C.   Hybrid
D.   Mixed
E.   Link Vector
F.   Distance State

5-90.   Which of the following is true about dynamic routing protocols? (Select all that apply)

A.   RIP and IGRP are examples of the distance vector routing protocols.
B.   OSPF and Integrated IS-IS are examples of the link state routing protocols.
C.   EIGRP is an example of the Hybrid routing protocols.
D.   Hybrid is sometimes called Balanced Hybrid or Advanced Distance Vector.

5-91.   Which of the following is true about IGP protocols? (Select all that apply)

A.   Original IGP protocols use broadcast to send their route updates to the IP all-local-hosts broadcast address of 255.255.255.255, whereas the newest version of IGP protocols use multicast for this purpose.
B.   Original IGP protocols did not include any authentication features, which make these protocols, suffer from an attacker, whereas the newer IGPs typically support some type of authentication, hoping to mitigate the exposure to types of DoS attacks.

5-92.   Which of the following is true about **Distance Vector** Routing Protocols? (Select all that apply)

A.   These protocols use a distance to a remote network to find the best path.
B.   These protocols select the route with the least number of hops to the destination network as the best route.
C.   These protocols use a link state to a remote network to find the best path.
D.   These protocols select the route with the highest number of hops to the destination network as the best route.

5-93.   What does the word vector refer to in distance vector?

A.   The vector is the determination of direction to the remote network.
B.   The vector is the determination of routes to the remote network.
C.   The vector is the determination of the type of the remote network.

5-94.   TRUE/FALSE: Each time a packet goes through a Router, it is called a hop.

A.   TRUE

B.   FALSE

5-95.   Which of the following protocol is a distance vector routing protocol? (Select all that apply)

A.   OSPF
B.   RIP
C.   IGRP
D.   EIGRP

5-96.   TRUE/FALSE: RIP and IGRP send the entire routing table to the directly connected neighbors and are examples of the distance vector type.

A.   TRUE
B.   FALSE

5-97.   Which of the following is true about **Link State** Routing Protocols? (Select all that apply)

A.   This type of routing protocols is more complex than distance vector routing protocols, and they consume more Router resources.
B.   It is typically called the shortest path first.
C.   It creates three separate tables in each Router.
D.   It provides the routers more information about internetwork topology than distance-vector routing protocol.
E.   These protocols are used to exchange routing information in a larger internetwork.
F.   In general, the distance Vector periodic updates are sent more frequent than the Links state protocol updates.

5-98.   Which of the following tables is created by the Link state routing protocols? (Select all that apply)

A.   Table for keep tracking of the directly attached neighbors
B.   Table for determining the entire internetwork topology
C.   Table for all internetwork routes (routing table)
D.   Table for determining the Router usage

5-99.   Which of the following protocol is an IP link state routing protocol? (Select all that apply)

A.   OSPF
B.   RIP
C.   IGRP
D.   EIGRP

5-100.   TRUE/FALSE: **Hybrid** routing protocols use aspects of the distance vector and link state.

A.   TRUE
B.   FALSE

5-101.   Which of the following protocols is a hybrid routing protocol? (Select all that apply)

A.   OSPF
B.   RIP
C.   IGRP
D.   EIGRP

5-102.   Which routing protocols is only required for the CCENT Test? (Select all that apply)

A.   Distance Vector
B.   Link State
C.   Hybrid
D.   Mixed
E.   Link Vector
F.   Distance State

5-103.   Which of the following statements is correct about routing protocols?

A.   Distance Vector periodic updates are sent more frequent than Links state protocol updates.
B.   Link State periodic updates are sent more frequent than Distance Vector protocol updates.
C.   Link-state routing protocols are also known as Shortest Path First protocols.
D.   Distance Vector routing protocols are also known as Shortest Path First protocols.

5-104.   Which of the following metrics do the routing algorithms use to determine the best route? (Select all that apply)

A.   Path Length
B.   Reliability
C.   Delay
D.   Bandwidth
E.   Load
F.   Communication Cost

5-105.   Which of the following is a general goal for all the routing protocols? (Select all that apply)

A.   Learning and filling the routing table dynamically with a route to all subnets in the internetwork.
B.   Placing the best route in the routing table if more than one route to a subnet is available.
C.   Removing no longer valid routes from the routing table.
D.   Adding new routes or replacing lost routes with the best currently available route, as quickly as possible. The time between losing the route and finding a working replacement route is called convergence time.
E.   Preventing routing loops

5-106.   Which of the following is true about route summarization? (Select all that apply)

A.   To short the routing tables in a large internetwork, route summarization is used.
B.   Route summarization will speed up the routers while retaining all the needed routes in the network.
C.   Two general types of route summarization can be implemented. These are; auto-summarization and manual summarization.

5-107.   TRUE/FALSE: Manual summarization means that the network administrator supplies the route summarization manually. This gives the administrator a great control and flexibility and makes the administrator to choose what summary routes to advertise. Therefore, manual summarization is the more useful feature as compared with auto-summarization.

A.   TRUE
B.   FALSE

5-108.   Which of the following can cause internetwork topology reconfigurations? (Select all that apply)

    A.   When a router link comes up or fails.
    B.   When a router fails.
    C.   When a router turns ON for the first time.
    D.   When a router is removed from the internetwork.

5-109.   TRUE/FALSE: Internetwork topology reconfigurations made routes in the router's routing tables change and reconfigure. The term convergence refers to the processes used by dynamic routing protocols to recognize the changes, to discover the new best routes to each subnet, and to reconfigure all the routers' routing tables.

    A.   TRUE
    B.   FALSE

5-110.   Which of the following is true about router's convergence? (Select all that apply)

    A.   A more quickly converge routing protocols are required by almost all modern internetworks to make routing tables up-to-date as soon as possible.
    B.   Users might not be able to connect to the internetwork and send their packets to particular subnets during convergence.

5-111.   TRUE/FALSE: Since, distance-vector routing protocols send a complete routing table during routing updates, their convergence will be slow; this can cause inconsistent routing tables and routing loops. Routing loops can occur because not every Router is updated at the same time.

    A.   TRUE
    B.   FALSE

5-112.   TRUE/FALSE: Routing protocols can be classified as Classless and Classful Routing Protocols.

    A.   TRUE
    B.   FALSE

5-113.   Which of the following is true about routing protocols? (Select all that apply)

    A.   Protocols that consider the class A, B, or C network number, which a subnet resides in are called classful.
    B.   Protocols that ignore the Class A, B, and C rules altogether are called classless.

5-114.   Which of the following features is supported by the classless routing protocols? (Select all that apply)

    A.   Supporting VLSM
    B.   Sending subnet mask in routing updates
    C.   Supporting manual route summarization
    D.   Supporting auto route summarization

5-115.   Which of the following features is supported by the classful routing protocols? (Select all that apply)

    A.   Supporting VLSM
    B.   Sending subnet mask in routing updates
    C.   Supporting manual route summarization
    D.   Supporting auto route summarization

5-116.   Match each of the following protocols to its feature.

1. RIPv1
2. RIPv2
3. EIGRP
4. OSPF
5. IS-IS

    A. Classless
    B. Supporting VLSM
    C. Sending subnet mask in routing updates
    D. Distance vector
    E. Link-state
    F. Supporting auto-summarization
    G. Supporting manual summarization
    H. CISCO Proprietary
    I. Sending routing updates to a multicast IP address
    J. Supporting authentication
    K. Hybrid

5-117. Which of the following protocols has a very fast convergence?

    A. RIPv1
    B. RIPv2
    C. EIGRP
    D. OSPF
    E. IS-IS

5-118. Try to decide if the following paragraph correctly depicts the distance-vector routing protocols.

"This algorithm passes the complete routing tables to neighbor routers in a route update message. All routers that received the routing update combine the received routing table with their own routing tables to complete the internetwork map. Simply, this is called routing by rumor, because a router receiving an update from a neighbor router believes the information about remote networks without it actually finds out the remote networks."

    A. Correct
    B. Incorrect

5-119. In case of there are multiple links to the same remote network, which of the following is checked firstly by the distance vector algorithm?

    A. Hop count
    B. Reliability
    C. Administrative distance

5-120. In case of there are multiple links to the same remote network and the links have the same administrative distances, which of the following is checked secondly by the distance vector algorithm?

    A. Hop count
    B. Reliability
    C. Administrative distance

5-121. TRUE/FALSE: RIP uses only hop count as a metric for determining the best route to an internetwork.

    A. TRUE

B.   FALSE

5-122.   TRUE/FALSE: If RIP finds more than one link to the same remote network with the same hop count, it will automatically perform a round-robin load balance between these links.

A.   TRUE
B.   FALSE

5-123.   How many equal-cost links can load balancing to be performed on by the RIP?

A.   Three
B.   Four
C.   Five
D.   Six

5-124.   Distance vector protocols primarily base their routing decisions on finding the shortest route to a destination. In other words, a route with:

A.   The lowest bandwidth
B.   The lowest hop count
C.   The highest average bandwidth between all hops.
D.   A pre-configured default route

5-125.   What type of routing protocols makes path selections based upon the number of hops that must be traversed to the destination? (Select the Best Answer)

A.   Distance Vector
B.   Internal
C.   External
D.   Link State
E.   Dynamic
F.   Static

5-126. Which of the following is true about RIP? (Select all that apply)

A.   It is a dynamic, true distance-vector routing protocol.
B.   It sends the complete routing table out to all active interfaces every 30 seconds.
C.   It only uses the hop count to determine the best route to a remote network.
D.   It works well in the small networks, but it is inefficient on the large networks with slow WAN links or on networks with a large number of routers installed.

5-127. What is the maximum allowable hop count for the RIP?

A.   16
B.   15
C.   115
D.   116

5-128. Which of the following is true about RIPv1 and RIPv2? (Select all that apply)

A.   RIPv1 uses only classful routing, which means that all devices in the internetwork must use the same subnet mask.
B.   RIPv2 uses only classful routing, which means that all devices in the internetwork must use the same

subnet mask.

C. RIPv1 uses only classless routing, which means that devices in the internetwork may use the different subnet masks.
D. RIPv2 uses only classless routing, which means that devices in the internetwork may use the different subnet masks.

5-129. Why RIPv1 is considered as a classful routing?

A. This is because, RIPv1 does not send updates with subnet mask information in the internetwork.
B. This is because, RIPv1 does send updates with subnet mask information in the internetwork.
C. This is because, RIPv1 internetwork can be decomposed into classes.
D. This is because, RIPv1 internetwork cannot be decomposed into classes.

5-130. Why RIPv2 is considered as a classless routing?

A. This is because, RIPv2 does not send updates with subnet mask information in the internetwork.
B. This is because, RIPv2 does send updates with subnet mask information in the internetwork.
C. This is because, RIPv2 internetwork can be decomposed into classes.
D. This is because, RIPv2 internetwork cannot be decomposed into classes.

5-131. Which RIP version is the only required for the CCENT Test? (Select all that apply)

A. RIPv1
B. RIPv2
C. RIPv3
D. RIPv6

5-132. What is the routing algorithm of the RIP?

A. Routed information
B. Distance vector
C. Link state
D. Dijkstra algorithm

5-133. What is the routing metric of the RIP?

A. Count to infinity
B. Bandwidth
C. Reliability
D. Hop count
E. TTL
F. Delay
G. Bandwidth
H. Load

5-134. What does a metric of 16 hops represent in a RIP routing network?

A. 16ms
B. Number of routers in the internetwork.
C. Number of hops
D. Last hop available
E. 16 hops—unreachable

5-135.   What is the default administrative distance of the RIP?

    A.   102
    B.   100
    C.   120
    D.   220

5-136.   Distance-vector permits a maximum HOP count so that packets cannot swim around a network indefinitely. For the RIPv1, this value is:

    A.   HOP count metric is Not applicable to RIPv1.
    B.   RIPv1 is not a distance-vector algorithm.
    C.   16
    D.   15

5-137.   TRUE/FALSE: The **network** command only uses a classful network number as its one parameter. The router will do the following three things for any of the router's interface in that entire classful network:

    ▪   Multicasting routing updates to a reserved multicast IP address, 224.0.0.9
    ▪   Listening for incoming updates on that same interface
    ▪   Advertising about the subnet connected to the interface

    A.   TRUE
    B.   FALSE

5-138.   Which command will turn ON the RIP routing?

    A.   RouterA#routing rip
    B.   RouterA#router rip
    C.   Router(config)#router rip
    D.   Router(config)#routing rip
    E.   Router(config-router)#router rip

5-139.   Which command will tell the RIP routing which network to advertise?

    A.   RouterA#network w.x.y.z
    B.   RouterA# network w.x.y.z
    C.   Router(config)# network w.x.y.z
    D.   Router(config-if)# network w.x.y.z
    E.   Router(config-router)# network w.x.y.z

5-140.   What command will show the routing table used by the RIP?

    A.   show ip route
    B.   debug rip routing
    C.   show protocol
    D.   show rip table

5-141.   What does the passive command provide to the dynamic routing protocols?

    A.   Stops the router from receiving any dynamic updates.
    B.   Stops the router from sending any dynamic updates.
    C.   Stops an interface from sending or receiving periodic dynamic updates.

D.   Stops an interface from sending periodic dynamic updates but still receives updates.

5-142.   Which of the following commands can be used to verify the RIP routing? (Select all that apply)

A.   show ip rip
B.   show ip route
C.   show protocol
D.   show rip

5-143.   When looking at a routing table, what does the R mean?

A.   RIP discovered route
B.   Directly connected
C.   Statically connected
D.   Sending packets

5-144.   Which of the following is true when creating the RIPv1 routing? (Select all that apply)

A.   The mask parameter is mandate.
B.   The network is required.
C.   The administrative distance is required.
D.   The administrative distance is optional.
E.   The RIP routing must be enabled.
F.   None of the above.

5-145.   Which of the following is an advantage of using the RIP dynamic routing?

A.   No CPU usage
B.   No bandwidth usage
C.   Security
D.   Easy to create and maintain
E.   Fast convergence

5-146.   Which of the following routing has AD=120 by default?

A.   RIP
B.   OSPF
C.   EIGRP
D.   Static route

5-147.   Which command will stop the RIP routing?

A.   no ip rip
B.   remove router rip
C.   no dynamic rip
D.   no router rip

5-148.   Which command will remove a network entry from the RIP routing?

A.   no network
B.   remove network rip
C.   no rip network
D.   no router network

E.   no network rip

5-149.   Which command will stop a router from propagating RIP information out serial 1?

A.   config t, router rip, passive-interface serial 1
B.   config t, no router rip, passive-interface serial 1
C.   config t, no router rip, no passive-interface serial 1
D.   config t, no router rip

5-150.   Which of the following prompts can be used to turn OFF the RIP routing?

A.   Router>
B.   Router#
C.   Router(config)#
D.   Router(config-if)#

5-151.   Which of the following prompts removes a network entry from the RIP routing?

A.   Router>
B.   Router#
C.   Router(config)#
D.   Router(config-if)#
E.   Router(config-router)#

5-152.   What will happen when one more route or another Router is added to a RIP enabled internetwork with five networks? (Select all that apply)

A.   All routers' routing tables must be updated by hand.
B.   Only the new router must be updated by hand.
C.   None of the above

5-153.   Try to arrange the following information to complete a RIP route.

A.   Administrative distance =175
B.   172.18.80.1
C.   172.18.80.0
D.   R
E.   Hop count=15
F.   FastEthernet0/0

5-154.   What is the main difference between OSPF and RIP? (Select all that apply)

A.   Both are IGP's, but the RIP convergence time is much shorter than that of OSPF.
B.   RIP is a distance vector protocol, whereas OSPF is a link state protocol.
C.   There is no difference between the two protocols; other than RIP is used for IP and OSPF is used for OSI.
D.   OSPF allows for a lower hop count than RIP.
E.   RIP works better in large internetworks than OSPF.

5-155.   Which command will enable networks 10.2.2.0 and 172.16.18.0 to run the RIP protocol?

A.   config t, router rip, network 10.0.0.0, network 172.16.0.0
B.   config t, rip router, network 10.0.0.0, network 172.16.0.0

    C.   config t, routing rip, network 10.0.0.0, network 172.16.0.0
    D.   config t, rip routing, network 10.0.0.0, network 172.16.0.0

5-156. Try to decide if the following paragraph correctly depicts the RIP routing.

    A.   Correct
    B.   Incorrect

"RIP uses broadcast UDP data packets to exchange routing updates. Every 30 seconds, the router sends routing updates to all other routers in the internetwork; this process is termed **advertising**. If the router does not receive an update from a router (nonupdating router) for 90 seconds or more, it marks all routes from the nonupdating router as being unusable. The router then will wait 240 seconds to remove all routing table entries for the nonupdating router, if there is no update from the nonupdating router."

5-157. Try to decide if the following paragraph is correctly depicted The RIP routing.

    A.   Correct
    B.   Incorrect

"RIP maintains only the best route to a destination. When better route information is coming, this information replaces old route information in the routing tables. Network topology changes can make changes to routes, causing, for example, a new route to become the best route to a particular destination. Network topology changes are reflected directly in routing update messages. When a router receives a routing update message that includes an update of the changes; the router updates its tables and advertises the change."

5-158. TRUE/FALSE: RIP is an open standard, so it is possible to use RIP with any brand of routers. OSPF is also an open standard with better performance, especially in a large internetwork.

    A.   TRUE
    B.   FALSE

5-159. Which of the following is true about RIP? (Select all that apply)

    A.   Both RIPv1 and RIPv2 are distance-vector protocols, which mean that each router running RIP sends its complete routing tables out all active interfaces periodically.
    B.   The timers and loop-avoidance schemes are the same in both RIP versions.
    C.   Both RIPv1 and RIPv2 are configured as classful addressing (but RIPv2 is considered classless because subnet information is sent with each route update and its support VLSM of course.
    D.   Both RIP versions have the same administrative distance (120).
    E.   Since RIP is an open standard, it is possible to use RIP with any brand of routers.
    F.   RIPv2 is defined in RFC 2453.
    G.   With all enhancements in RIPv2, it still converges relatively slowly.

5-160. Which of the following is true about IGRP? (Select all that apply)

    A.   It is a dynamic, distance-vector routing protocol.
    B.   It is CISCO propriety protocol.
    C.   It has a maximum hop count of 255 with a default of 100.
    D.   By default, it uses a composite metric to determine the best path.

5-161. What is the maximum allowable hop count for the IGRP?

    A.   25

B.   225
C.   255
D.   555

5-162. What is the default hop count for the IGRP?

A.   10
B.   100
C.   110
D.   101

5-163.   What is the routing algorithm that is used by the IGRP?

A.   Routed information
B.   Distance vector
C.   Link state
D.   Dijkstra algorithm

5-164.   What is the routing metric that is used by the IGRP?

A.   Count to infinity
B.   Bandwidth
C.   delay of the line
D.   Reliability
E.   Hop count
F.   TTL
G.   Load
H.   Maximum Transmission Unit (MTU)

5-165.   Which of the following is a CISCO propriety routing protocol?

A.   RIP
B.   IGRP
C.   OSPF
D.   HELLO

5-166.   What is the default administrative distance of the IGRP?

A.   102
B.   100
C.   120
D.   220

5-167.   Which command will turn ON the IGRP routing?
A.   RouterA#routing igrp
B.   RouterA#router igrp
C.   Router(config)#router igrp
D.   Router(config)#routing igrp
E.   Router(config-router)#router igrp

5-168.   Which command will tell the IGRP routing which network to advertise?

A.   RouterA#network w.x.y.z

B.   RouterA#network w.x.y.z
C.   Router(config)#network w.x.y.z
D.   Router(config)#network w.x.y.z
E.   Router(config-router)# network w.x.y.z

5-169.   What command will show the routing table used by the IGRP?

A.   show ip route
B.   debug igrp routing
C.   show protocol
D.   show igrp table

5-170.   Which of the following commands can be used to verify the IGRP routing? (Select all that apply)

A.   show ip igrp
B.   show ip route
C.   show protocol
D.   show igrp

5-171.   When looking at a routing table, what does the I mean?

A.   IGRP discovered route
B.   Directly connected
C.   Statically connected
D.   Sending packets

5-172.   Which of the following is true when creating the IGRP routing? (Select all that apply)

A.   The mask parameter is mandate.
B.   The network is required.
C.   The administrative distance is required.
D.   The administrative distance is optional.
E.   The IGRP routing must be enabled.
F.   The AS number must be applied.
G.   None of the above.

5-173.   Which of the following is an advantage of using the IGRP dynamic routing?

A.   No CPU usage
B.   No bandwidth usage
C.   Security
D.   Easy to create and maintain
E.   Fast convergence

5-174.   Which of the following routing has AD=100 by default?

A.   RIP
B.   OSPF
C.   IGRP
D.   Static route

5-175.   Which command will stop the IGRP routing?

A.   no ip igrp
B.   remove router igrp
C.   no dynamic igrp
D.   no router igrp

5-176. Which command will remove a network entry from the IGRP routing?

A.   no network
B.   remove network igrp
C.   no igrp network
D.   no router network
E.   no network igrp

5-177. Which of the following prompts can be used to turn OFF the IGRP routing?

A.   Router>
B.   Router#
C.   Router(config)#
D.   Router(config-if)#

5-178. Which of the following prompts removes a network entry from the IGRP routing?

A.   Router>
B.   Router#
C.   Router(config)#
D.   Router(config-if)#
E.   Router(config-router)#

5-179. What will happen when one more route or another Router is added to an IGRP enabled internetwork with five networks? (Select all that apply)

A.   All routers' routing tables must be updated by hand.
B.   Only the new router must be updated by hand.
C.   None of the above.

5-180. Try to arrange the following information to complete an IGRP route.

A.   Administrative distance =100
B.   172.18.80.1
C.   172.18.80.0
D.   I
E.   Composite metric = 160876
F.   FastEthernet0/0

5-181. TRUE/FALSE: IGRP routes do not include subnet information.

A.   TRUE
B.   FALSE

5-182. What command is used to stop the routing updates from exiting out an interface?

A.   Router(config-if)#no routing
B.   Router(config-if)#passive-interface

C.   Router(config-router)#passive-interface s0
D.   Router(config-router)#no routing updates

5-183.   Which of the following routing protocols uses bandwidth and delay of the line when making routing decisions?

A.   IGRP
B.   Static
C.   RIP
D.   OSPF

5-184.   What does the passive command provide to the IGRP routing protocols?

A.   Stops an interface from sending or receiving periodic dynamic updates
B.   Stops an interface from sending periodic dynamic updates but still receives updates.
C.   Stops the router from receiving any dynamic updates
D.   Stops the router from sending any dynamic updates

5-185.   Which command will control the load balancing between the best and the worst acceptable metrics in the IGRP routing?

A.   Router(config-if)#variance multiplier
B.   Router(config-if)# variance multiplier
C.   Router(config-router)#passive-interface s0
D.   Router(config-router)# variance multiplier

5-186.   Which command will use to help control traffic distribution among the IGRP load-sharing routes? (Select all that apply)

A.   Router(config)#traffic-share balanced
B.   Router(config)#traffic-share min
C.   Router(config-router)# traffic-share balanced
D.   Router(config-router)# traffic-share min

5-187.   What does an AS do in an internetwork? (Select all that apply)

A.   It creates routing areas.
B.   AS's are used with IGRP, EIGRP and OSPF.
C.   It creates network subnets.
D.   AS's are used with static and default routes.

5-188.   In Figure 5-6, the following configuration is applied.

- RA has RIP and IGRP enabled on the interface E0.
- RB has IGRP enabled on E0.
- RC has RIP enabled on F0/0.

RC is not receiving routing updates from RA, what is possibly the problem? (Select Two)

A.   RC's RIP interface is passive.
B.   An access-list may be defined incorrectly.
C.   A neighbor command needs to be defined on RA.
D.   The ip address on RC is on a different subnet than RA.

E.   RA's RIP interface is passive.

5-189.   TRUE/FALSE: The following steps should be followed to check IP connectivity using the **Ping** command:

1.   Testing the network connectivity within the same subnet. If this test fails, the problem maybe one of the following:

- The host's IP configurations are not fallen in the same subnet. Correcting the IP address and subnet masks are the solution in this case.
- The underlying Ethernet Layer 1 and Layer 2 have a problem, if the hosts on the same subnet have the correct IP configuration. In this case, you need to follow the troubleshooting steps, which will be described in Chapter 6 of this book.

2.   Testing the network connectivity between different internetwork subnets. If the test in point 1 is OK so that the host can ping other hosts in the same subnet, try to ping between hosts on different subnets, as follows:

- Checking the connection and correct the IP configurations between a host and the default gateway/Router using the **ping** utility. If this test is failed, the problem may be in the IP configurations or some Layer 1 or 2 problems on the LAN.
- Checking the connection and correct the IP configurations between hosts on different subnets (not the same LAN) using the **Ping** utility. If this test is not succeeded, the problem may be the IP configurations between subnets or the router's other interface has failed.

A.   TRUE
B.   FALSE

5-190.   Which of the following commands is useful for troubleshooting an IP routing for MS Windows XP OS?

A.   ipconfig /all
B.   tracert
C.   ipconfig /displaydns
D.   arp –a

5-191.   Which of the following commands is useful for obtaining a host's current IP address and mask for MS Windows XP OS?

A.   ipconfig /all
B.   tracert
C.   ipconfig /displaydns
D.   arp –a

5-192.   TRUE/FALSE: A router uses the steps described in chapter 5 to obtain a suitable route for a destined IP address. However, there are some cases that more than one route that matches an individual destined IP address can be found in a particular router's routing table.

A.   TRUE
B.   FALSE

5-193.   Which of the following can be considered as a reason for overlapping routes in a Router's routing table? (Select all that apply)

A.   the configuration of static routes
B.   auto-summary
C.   route summarization

5-194.   TRUE/FALSE: The Router uses the ANDing process to find the matched route. However, it is easy to find the suitable route for a particular destined IP address. Simply, compare the destination IP address to each subnet in the routing table-the route that matches the packet's destination must be in the suitable subnet's IP addresses range.

A.   TRUE
B.   FALSE

5-195.   TRUE/FALSE: The Router will use the most specific route, i.e., the route with the longest prefix length, if a particular destination IP address matches more than one route in the Router's routing table.

A.   TRUE
B.   FALSE

5-196.   If Machine D is added to the subnet 172.18.20.0/26 in Figure 5-4 with IP address 172.18.20.5, which of the following is/are true? Assume that Machine B's IP address is 172.18.20.2/24.

A.   A ping 172.18.50.1 command from Machine B would use ARP to learn the MAC address of 172.18.50.1.
B.   A ping 172.18.20.5 command from R2 would use ARP to learn the MAC address of 172.18.20.5.
C.   A ping 172.18.20.5 command from Machine B would use ARP to learn Machine D's MAC address.
D.   A ping 172.18.20.2 command from Machine D would use ARP to learn Machine B's MAC address.

5-197.   Which of the following troubleshooting tasks and results would most likely point to a Layer 1 or 2 Ethernet problem(s) on the subnet 172.18.20.0 in Figure 5-4?

A.   A ping 172.18.20.1 command from Machine B succeeded, but a ping 172.18.50.1 was not succeeded.
B.   A ping 172.18.50.2 command from Machine B succeeded, but a ping 172.18.10.1 was not succeeded.
C.   A ping 172.18.20.2 command from Machine B succeeded.
D.   A ping 172.18.20.1 command on Machine B was not succeeded.

5-198.   Which of the following IP addresses could be found in the **tracert 172.18.20.2** Microsoft operating system's command if it is issued from Machine A?

A.   172.18.10.1
B.   172.18.50.2
C.   172.18.50.1
D.   172.18.20.1
E.   172.18.20.2

5-199.   Which command will verify and check the IP networks? (Select all that apply)

A.   show ip route
B.   show protocols
C.   show ip protocol
D.   debug ip rip
E.   debug ip igrp events
F.   debug ip igrp transactions

5-200.   Which of the following information is provided by the **show ip route**? (Select all that apply)

    A.   A symbol to indicate the protocol that derived the route (I--IGRP derived, R--RIP derived, O--OSPF derived, C--connected, S--static, S*--default route, E--EGP derived, B--BGP derived, i--IS-IS derived)

    B.   A symbol to indicate the type of route (*--Indicates the last path used when a packet was forwarded, IA--OSPF interarea route, E1--OSPF external type 1 route, E2--OSPF external type 2 route, L1--IS-IS Level 1 route, L2--IS-IS Level 2 route).

    C.   IP address indicates the address of the remote network.

    D.   The administrative distance of the information source.

    E.   The metric for the route.

    F.   IP address specifies the address of the next router to the remote network.

    G.   Time that specifies the last time the route was updated in hours:minutes:seconds.

    H.   An interface symbol to specify the interface through which the specified remote network can be reached.

    I.   IP address to indicate the Gateway of last resort.

5-201.   Which command will present the subnet mask of the IP route?

    A.   sh ip route
    B.   sh ip route network_number
    C.   sh ip route subnet_mask
    D.   sh ip route summary

5-202.   Which command will show the routed protocols running on your CISCO Router?

    A.   show ip traffic
    B.   show ip route
    C.   show protocols
    D.   show ip routed protocols

5-203.   Which commands will display the IP address of all configured router's interfaces? (Select all that apply)

    A.   sh ip route
    B.   sh prot
    C.   sh ip route summary
    D.   sh ip route detail

5-204.   Which commands will display all configured interfaces even secondaries and subinterfaces?

    A.   sh prot
    B.   sh users
    C.   sh all int
    D.   sh all protocol

5-205.   Which command will show the IGRP timer values?

    A.   show ip route
    B.   show igrp routing
    C.   show ip igrp timer
    D.   show protocol
    E.   show ip protocol

5-206.   Which command will verify the broadcast frequency for IGRP?

A. sh ip route
B. sh ip protocol
C. sh ip igrp broadcast
D. debug ip igrp

5-207. Which command will display the parameters and the current state of the active routing protocol process on CISCO Router?

A. sh ip route
B. debug ip igrp
C. sh ip igrp broadcast
D. sh ip protocol

5-208. Which command will show the autonomous system value for IGRP?

A. sh ip route
B. debug ip igrp
C. sh lp lgrp broadcast
D. sh ip protocol

5-209. Which command will show both RIP and IGRP parameters if both are configured on the same router at the same time?

A. sh ip route
B. debug ip igrp
C. sh ip igrp broadcast
D. sh ip protocol
E. sh run

5-210. Which command will verify that RIP is running on the router? (Select all that apply)

A. sh ip route
B. sh run
C. sh ip rip
D. sh ip protocol

5-211. Which command will display the AD value for RIP and IGRP? (Select all that apply)

A. sh ip route
B. sh ip igrp
C. sh ip rip
D. sh ip protocol

5-212. What commands are available for supporting the RIP networks? (Select all that apply)

A. sh ip route
B. sh ip rip
C. debug ip rip
D. sh rip protocol

5-213. Which of the following commands can be used to verify the RIP routing? (Select all that apply)

A. sh ip route

B.   sh ip rip
C.   debug ip rip
D.   sh rip protocol

5-214.   Which command will show the IP RIP routing updates as they are sent and received on the Router?

A.   sh ip route
B.   sh ip rip
C.   debug ip rip
D.   sh rip protocol

5-215.   Which command can be used to stop the **debug ip rip** command?

A.   un all
B.   undebug all
C.   no debug ip rip
D.   undebug
E.   no debug all

5-216.   TRUE/FALSE: It is a not good idea to issue the **debug ip rip** command wisely.

A.   TRUE
B.   FALSE

5-217.   Which command will verify RIP routing updates through Telnet session?

A.   terminal monitor, debug ip rip
B.   debug ip rip
C.   show ip rip
D.   terminal monitor, show ip rip

5-218.   Which command will check IP IGRP running through the internetwork?

A.   debug ip igrp
B.   debug igrp
C.   show ip igrp
D.   debug igrp protocol

5-219.   Which command will view information about IP IGRP events through the internetwork?

A.   debug ip igrp
B.   debug ip igrp events
C.   show ip igrp events
D.   debug igrp protocol

5-220.   Which command will view message requests from neighbor routers through the internetwork?

A.   debug ip igrp
B.   debug ip igrp transactions
C.   show ip igrp transactions
D.   debug igrp protocol

5-221.   Which command will stop the **debug ip igrp events** command?

A.   un all
B.   undebug all
C.   no debug ip igrp events
D.   undebug
E.   no debug all

5-222.   Which command will stop the **debug ip igrp transactions** command?

A.   un all
B.   undebug all
C.   no debug ip igrp transactions
D.   undebug
E.   no debug all

5-223.   TRUE/FALSE: It is not good to use the **debug ip igrp events** command wisely.

A.   TRUE
B.   FALSE

5-224.   TRUE/FALSE: It is good to use the **debug ip igrp transactions** command wisely.

A.   TRUE
B.   FALSE

5-225.   Which command will show the source and destination of each IGRP update?

A.   debug ip igrp
B.   debug ip igrp events
C.   show ip igrp events
D.   debug ip igrp transactions

5-226.   Which command will show the number of routes in each IGRP update?

A.   debug ip igrp
B.   debug ip igrp events
C.   show ip igrp events
D.   debug ip igrp transactions

5-227.   Which command will better be used to debug the IGRP if there are many networks in your routing table?

A.   debug ip igrp
B.   debug ip igrp events
C.   show ip igrp events
D.   debug ip igrp transactions

5-228.   Which command will show the metric of routes in each IGRP update?

A.   debug ip igrp
B.   debug ip igrp events
C.   show ip igrp events
D.   debug ip igrp transactions

CHAPTER 6
INTERNETWORKING
SWITCHING

In this chapter, switching technology will be described. Switches provide a connection point for the Ethernet devices so that the devices on the LAN can communicate with each other and with the rest of network. The necessary switching background for the CISCO Catalyst 2960 (CAT2.96K) switch configuration will be given in chapter six. Chapter four outlined the user interface for the CISCO routers, which is the same for the CISCO switches, so this chapter will be dedicated only for commands that used by the switches, which are not found in the CISCO routers. The necessary switching background for the CISCO Catalyst 2960 switch configuration will be given and how to configure the CISCO LAN Switches will be described in this chapter.

The following topics are emphasized in this chapter:
- Layer-2 Switching
- Address learning.
- Forward/filtering decisions.
- Loop avoidance.
- Spanning-tree Protocol.
- LAN switches types.
- CISCO Catalyst LAN Switches
- CISCO Catalyst 2960 Switch CLI
- Configuring CISCO switch 2960
- Ethernet Switch Troubleshooting

By understanding perfectly the information presented in this chapter and answering the 219 learning questions at the end of this chapter, configuring and troubleshooting the switches, and answering the CCNA/CCENT exam related questions will be guaranteed. The questions herein are intended to reflect the type of questions presented on the CCENT Test.

Layer-2 Switching

In this section, LAN switching concepts, switching features and the switching problems will be given. Switch functions at OSI layer 2 will be described. Broadcast storm problem will be discussed as well.

Layer-2 Switching is hardware based, which means it uses the MAC address (Layer-2 address) to filter the network. Switches use to build and maintain their filter table an Application-Specific Integrated Circuits (ASICs). ASICs can run up to Gigabit speeds with very low latency. Layer-2 switch is fast, because it looks at the frame's hardware address before deciding to either forward the frame or drop it, whereas routers look at L3 IP address which require more time for processing. Therefore, routing is slower than switching. Layer-2 switching provides: Hardware-based bridging (MAC), wire speeds, Low latency and Low cost features.

Layer-2 switching (and bridging) performs no modification to the data packet, only to the frame encapsulating the packet. This fact makes the switching process faster and so efficient (less error-prone than routing). Moreover, there is no need to enable CSMA/CD algorithm in switching based network, which gives an enhancement in the overall network performance. This will be discussed in more details in the following sections.

Layer-2 switching breaks up collision domains and increases the bandwidth for each user because each connection (interface) into the switch is its own collision domain, so there is a possibility to connect multiple devices to each interface. Layer-2 switching provides network segmentation. If VLANs are defined on the switch, Layer-2 switching can break up broadcast domains.

If twelve stations are connected to separate 100 Mbps ports on a 16-port Layer-2 switch. The switch will give each station a bandwidth equal to 100 Mbps (200 mbps for full duplex connections). This is one of the main factors for using the switch. The switch will give each station 100 Mbps not like a shared bandwidth hub where all 12 stations share the 100 Mbps of a hub bandwidth.

Layer-2 switching network has the same problems as a bridged network. The right way to create Layer-2 switching is by correctly breaks up collision domains, so users should spend 80 percent of their time on the local segment as in bridging network. The rule is 80/20. Layer-2 switching networks break up collision domains but the network is still one large broadcast domain.

Layer-2 switching problems are: Broadcast messages, Multicast messages, and slow convergence of spanning tree. These problems can cause performance issues and limit the size of the network. To reduce the number of collisions on an Ethernet network while maintaining a single broadcast domain, either a switch or a bridge must be used. Switches and bridges actually create separated collision domains on each interface to which a network is connected. This allows several collision domains to exist while retaining a single broadcast domain.

Now let us investigate how Ethernet network works. Ethernet networks allow only one device to place frames on the network media, but all stations receive the frames. Each station must determine whether the frames it receives are intended for it or not. Frequently, more than one device attempts to place frames onto the network at the same time, which causes errors known as collisions. Collisions are normal on Ethernet networks, and mechanisms exist to detect and correct them. However, more collisions can cause slow network throughput. In a situation where more collisions are occurring because of the high number of devices on the network, the network should be broken into segments so that fewer devices are placing frames on the same network segment. By using switches or bridges, it is possible to break the network into multiple collision domains so that the frequency of collisions is greatly reduced. This type of segmentation is sometimes called *micro-segmentation*.

Because switches and bridges forward all broadcasts, they maintain the existing broadcast domains. Broadcasts are messages sent simultaneously to every device on the network, and are part of the normal network traffic. They are usually not a concern on small networks, but on larger networks, broadcasts can consume a significant portion of network bandwidth. To reduce the broadcast traffic, routers (or L3 Switches) must be used to segment the network; hence, broadcasts are contained within the network segments. For example, suppose a network is broken into two segments with a Router. Broadcasts from devices on each segment would not pass through the Router to the other segment, which would reduce the bandwidth broadcasts consumed on each segment.

Routers create separate collision and broadcast domains. If an Ethernet network is segmented with routers, it would create multiple broadcast and collision domains.

Hubs simply forward all traffic. Therefore, you cannot reduce the number of collisions on a network using hubs. Adding a hub to a network with a single collision domain and a single broadcast domain would have no effect on either domain.

As a summary in this section, the following are the features of switching:

- Providing dedicated bandwidth per single device.
- Providing a double bandwidth for each port/device when using full duplex.
- Providing multiple simultaneous conversations between devices on different ports.
- Providing the rate adaptation features, this means that different Ethernet speed devices can communicate through a single switch.

Switch Functions at Layer-2

The primary function of a LAN switch is to receive Ethernet frames and then decide: either forward the frame out some other port(s), or ignore the frame. The following functions are performed by the layer-2 switching:

- Source Address Learning.

- Frame Forward/Filter Decisions.
- Frame Loop avoidance.

These functions will be discussed now in more details.

Source Address Learning

To learn a source address, the switch will follow the following steps:

Step1. Power ON the switch. In this state, the MAC filtering table is empty

Step2. When a switch interface receives a frame from one device, the switch places the device source MAC address (SA) and the switch interface that the device located on in the MAC forward/filter table (MAC address table).

Step3. The switch then, floods the network (except the port that the source frame received from) with this frame because it has no idea on which interface the destination device is located.

Step4. If a destination device is found on the network, it will answer and send a frame back; then the switch will take the source MAC address from that frame and place this address with the interface that received the frame in the MAC forward/filter table.

Step5. The switch makes a point-to-point connection between the two devices, and the frames will only be forwarded between these two devices.

Step6. To keep the MAC address table as up-to-dated as possible, and if these two devices do not communicate through the switch after a certain period, the switch will flush the MAC table from the entries of these two devices.

Example 6-1, The Switch Basic Operations: In Figure 6-1, there are four hosts attached to the switch. When the switch is powered ON, it has nothing in the MAC address table. Station 1 sends a frame to Station 4. Station 1's MAC address is 0000.9E01.1111; Station 4's MAC address is 0000.9E01.4444.

Figure 6-1 Switch Working

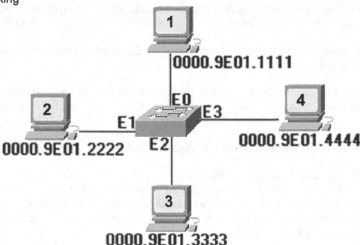

The switch receives the frame from the sending station on the E0 interface and places the source address (Station 1 address) and E0 interface in the MAC address table. The switch now searches in its MAC filter table for destination address. Since the destination address is not in the MAC address table, the frame is forwarded out all interfaces except E0. All stations receive the frame and check the destination address. Only station that its MAC address is identical with the destination address in the frame will respond to the sender. Station 4 responds to station 1. The switch receives this frame on the interface E3 and places the source hardware address (Station

4 address) and E3 interface in the MAC address table. Station 1 and Station 4 can now make a point-to-point connection, and only the two devices will receive the frames. Station 2 and Station 3 will not see the transmitted frames between Station 1 and Station4.

If Station 1 and Station 4 in Figure 6-1 are not communicating again through the switch within a certain amount of time, the switch will flush the entries from the MAC address table to keep it as up-to-dated as possible.

In Figure 6-1, after a point-to-point communication is established between Stations 1 and 4, Station 2 and Station 3 will completely not see all frames traversing between Station 1 and Station 4.

The MAC address table contains a combination of INTERFACE NUMBER and STATION MAC ADDRESS that connected to the same switch port. The complete content of the switch's MAC address table shown in Figure 6-1 is as follows:

    E0: 0000.9E01.1111
    E1: 0000.9E01.2222
    E2: 0000.9E01.3333
    E3: 0000.9E01.4444

Frame Forward/Filter Decisions

When a frame is received at a switch interface, the destination MAC address is compared to the forward/filter MAC address table. After the arrived frame is checked against the MAC address table and the destination MAC address is found in the MAC address table, the switch does not transmit the frame out any interface except for the destination interface. This is called **frame filtering,** and it preserves bandwidth usage on the other network segments.

If the destination MAC address for the incoming frame is not listed in the MAC address table, then the frame is broadcasted out all active interfaces except the interface the frame was received on. When a device answers the broadcast, the switch updates the MAC address table with the device interface and starts a point-to-point communication between the two devices. The MAC address table contains a combination of the filtered devices MAC addresses and their interface. The switch does neglect the frame, if no device answers the broadcast.

Frame Loop Avoidance

Redundant links are extremely helpful in the network design and are used in the switching network to help stop complete network failures if one link fails and to provide some kind of fault tolerance. On the other hand, redundant links may cause problems in the network. Loops can be occurred since the frames can be broadcasted down all the redundant links simultaneously.

The most serious problems that have been caused by the redundant links if no loop avoidance schemes are used are as follows:

- The switches will flood broadcasts without limits throughout the internetwork. This sometimes referred to as a **broadcast storm**.
- Multiple copies of the same frame can be received by a device since the frame can arrive from different segments at the same time.
- Since the switch can receive the frame from more than one link, the MAC address forward/filter table will be confused about where a device is located. Sometimes the switch cannot forward a frame because it is constantly updating the MAC address table with source MAC address locations. This is called **thrashing** the MAC table.

- Multiple loops generating throughout a network is one of the biggest problems. This means that loops can occur within other loops. If the broadcast storm is occurred, the network would not be able to perform frame switching.

All these points are problems of the links if a mechanism is not added to stop loops.

In switched network with redundant links, **Broadcast Storms** occur when a frame is continually broadcasted through the internetwork physical network (no loop avoidance schemes are provided). This occasion is illustrated in Figure 6-2.

Figure 6-2 Broadcast Storms

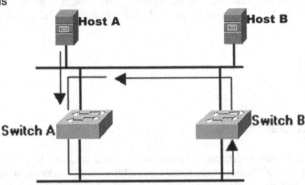

Figure 6-3 shows a switched network with redundant links. If there are no loops avoidance schemes are provided, multiple copies of the same frame can be received by Router A.

Figure 6-3 Router A in a Problem

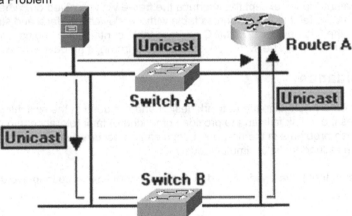

In a switched network with redundant links and there are no loop avoidance schemes are provided, if the switch received the frame from more than one link, the switch cannot forward a frame because it is constantly updating the MAC address table with source hardware address locations. This occasion is called "thrashing the MAC table". If multiple loops are generated throughout an internetwork, and the broadcast storm is occurred, the network would not be able to perform frame switching.

Spanning-Tree Protocol (STP)

In this section, Spanning-Tree Protocol will be given. Root bridge selection and designated port assignment will be described. Blocking, Listening, Learning and Forwarding STP states will be discussed in this section.

STP's main task is to stop network loops from occurring on a meshed Layer-2 switching network (bridges or switches). DEC (Digital Equipment Cooperation) was the original creator of STP. The IEEE 802.1d is the IEEE version of STP. All CISCO switches run the IEEE 802.1d version of STP, which is not compatible with the DEC version and there is no CISCO version for STP. STP is used to prevent loops and ensures data flows through a single network path in a Catalyst switched network environment.

The Spanning Tree Algorithm is a requirement in the meshed switching network. It is used to stop network loops from occurring on a Layer-2 network, by monitoring the network and finding all links and making sure that loops do not occur by shutting down redundant links. So, STP is mainly used to discover a "loop free" topology and provide, as possible, a path between every pair of LAN's.

Spanning-Tree Protocol Operations

STP finds all links in the network, shuts down redundant links and stops any network loops from occurring in the switching network. STP does this by electing a root bridge. There is only one Root Bridge in any given switched network. Root Bridge's ports are called designated ports. The designated ports operate in Forwarding State. Forwarding state ports can send and receive traffic. In STP network, there is only one Root Bridge and all other switches are called nonroot bridges. Nonroot bridges' ports can be categorized into root port (designated port) and nondesignated port.

In Figure 6-4, Root port is selected using the lowest cost rule (as determined by a link's bandwidth).

Figure 6-4 Root Port Selection in STP

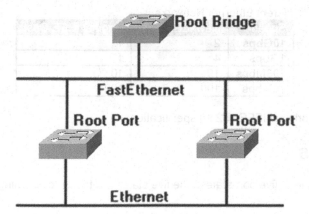

Root port in Nonroot bridges can send and receive traffic. The nondesignated ports operate in Blocking State. Blocking state ports cannot send or receive traffic.

Selecting the Root Bridge

Switches and bridges exchange information between them using a special type of multicast frames called Bridge Protocol Data Units (BPDUs). BPDUs are used to send configuration messages to neighboring switches, including the bridge IDs. Bridge ID is used to determine the root bridge and to determine the root port. The

Bridge ID is 8 bytes long and includes the Priority and the MAC address of the device. The default priority on all devices running the IEEE STP is 32,768. To determine the root bridge in a Layer-2 network, STP combines the priority and MAC address. Root Bridge is selected using the lowest Bridge ID, which is a combination of switch Priority and MAC address.

In Figure 6-5, switch A will be selected as a Root Bridge in the STP network since it has the lowest MAC address. Remember that both switches have the same Priority.

Figure 6-5 Selecting Root Bridge in STP Network

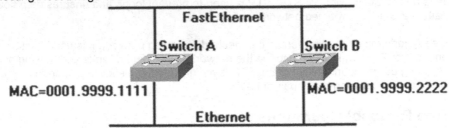

BPDUs are sent out from all active bridge ports every two seconds by default. In a Nonroot bridge, the port with the lowest cost to the root bridge is the root port of the bridge.

Selecting the designated Port

Designated Port is determined on the path cost communication to the root bridge. The port cost is an accumulated total path cost based on the bandwidth of the links.

The following Table 6-1 shows the typical costs associated with the different Ethernet networks.

TABLE 6-1 Typical Costs of Different Ethernet Networks

Speed	New IEEE Cost	Original IEEE Cost
10Gbps	2	1
1Gbps	4	1
100Mbps	19	10
10Mbps	100	100

The 2960 switches use the original IEEE 802.1d specifications.

The Port States

STP switch port can be in one of five port states. The five states are blocking, learning, listening, forwarding and disabled.

- The switches in **blocking state** do not forward frames; they listen to and receive BPDUs. By default, all ports are in this state when the switch is powered UP.
- The switches in **Listening State** listen to BPDU to make sure no loops are occurred on the network before passing data frames.
- The switches in **Learning State** learn MAC addresses and build a filter table but do not forward frames.
- The switches in **Forwarding State** send and receive all data on the bridged port.
- The switches in **Disabled State** (administratively) do not participate in the frame forwarding or STP. A port in the disabled state is virtually nonoperational.

Typical port states of a STP switch are blocking and Forwarding states. A forwarding port has been determined to have the lowest cost to the root bridge. If the network has a topology change, the ports on a switch will be switched into learning and listening states. Once a switch determines the best path to the Root Bridge, then all other ports will be in blocking state. Blocked ports are still receiving BPDUs and are used to prevent network loops. If a switch determines that a blocked port should now be the designated port, the port will go to listening state. It will check all BPDUs heard to make sure that it would not create a loop once the port goes to forwarding state.

The Convergence

Convergence is the time it takes a bridge in the STP network to transition to either the forwarding or blocking states. It is important in the STP network to make sure that all devices have the same MAC address table. No data is forwarded during the convergence period. The main problem with convergence is the time it takes for devices to update, since all devices must be updated before data can be forwarded. The update time takes 50 seconds to go from blocking to forwarding state. This allows an enough time for all switches to update their STP MAC address table. However, it is not recommended to change the default STP timers. Moreover, another term is found here, **Forward delay,** which is the time it takes to transition a port from listening to learning state or from learning to forwarding state.

Example 6-2, The STP operation: Referring to Figure 6-6, the following is the steps that STP will follow to manage and configure the network. Assume that all Switches have the same Priority (32,768), the MAC addresses as shown on the figure and all devices are CISCO Catalyst 2960 (CAT2.96K) switches.

Step 1, Root Bridge selection based on (Priority + MAC address): Since switch A has the lowest MAC address and all three switches use the same default priority, then Switch A will be the root bridge.

Step 2, Root port selection based on the lowest cost path: Because the connection from Switch B and Switch C to the root bridge is from port 0 using FastEthernet link and has the best cost, both switches' root ports will be port 0.

Step 3, Designated ports selection based on bridge ID: the root bridge always has all ports as designated. However, since both switch B and switch C have the same cost to the Root Bridge, the designated port will be on switch B since it has the lowest bridge ID. Because switch B has been determined to have the designated port, switch C will put port 1 in the Blocking state to stop any network loop from occurring.

Figure 6-6 STP Network

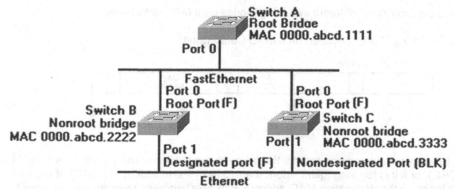

As a summary to the switch functions, the switches take decisions to forward and filter frames, learn MAC addresses, and use STP to avoid loops, as follows:

Step 1.   Forwarding frames based on the destination address:
1.   Flooding the frame, if the destination address is a broadcast, multicast, or unknown destination Unicat.
2.   Forwarding the frame; if the destination address is a known Unicast address:
    A.   Forwarding the frame out the outgoing interface, if the listed outgoing interface in the MAC address table is different from the interface in which the frame was received.
    B.   Filtering/ignoring the frame, if the outgoing interface is the same as the interface in which the frame was received.

Step 2.   Learning MAC address table entries:
1.   Examining the source MAC address for each received frame and noting the interface from which the frame was received.
2.   Adding the address and interface, setting the inactivity timer to 0, if they are not already in the table.
3.   Resetting the inactivity timer for the entry to 0, if it is already in the table.

Step 3.   Using STP to prevent loops by causing some interfaces to block (does not send or receive frames). STP functions are:
1.   Selecting Root Bridge based on the lowest (Priority + MAC address).
2.   Selecting Root port based on the lowest cost path.
3.   Selecting Designated ports based on the lowest bridge ID.

The Types of LAN Switches

In this section, Store and forward, Cut-through, and FragmentFree Switch types will be described, and their differences will be given.

Packet switching Latency depends on the chosen of the switching mode. The primary switching modes are:

Store and forward: The complete data frame is received on the switch's buffer, CRC error detection is implemented, and then the destination address is looked up in the MAC address table.

Cut-through (Real time): The switch looks up the destination address in the MAC address table once it receives the destination MAC address in the frame.

FragmentFree: The switch forwards the frame after checking the first 64bytes of a frame for fragmentation (because of possible collisions). FragmentFree is the default type for the CAT2.96K switch. It is sometimes referred to as *modified cut-through*.

Figure 6-7 shows the location of different switching modes on a MAC data frame.

Figure 6-7 The Switching Modes Location on a MAC Data Frame

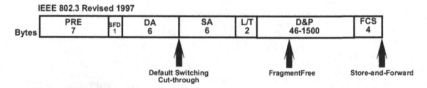

The store-and-forward switching mode checks the frame to see if it is too short (runt -less than 64 bytes, including the CRC), or if it is too long (giant -more than 1518 bytes, including the CRC). If the frame is error free, the LAN switch looks up the destination MAC address in its MAC address table and determines the outgoing interface. It then forwards the frame toward its destination. The main characteristics of the store-and-forward switching mode are:

- Frames with errors are discarded.
- It has the highest latency than the FragmentFree and Cut-through modes.
- The CRC is computed after the frame is copied to the switch's buffer.
- The frame is discarded if it is a runt or a giant.

FragmentFree LAN switching mode waits for the collision window (the first 64 bytes of a frame) to make sure a collision has not occurred before looking up the destination hardware address in the MAC filter table and forwarding the frame. FragmentFree LAN switching mode keeps CRC errors to a minimum but still has a fixed latency rate. It checks into the data portion of the frame to make sure no fragmentation has occurred.

Store-and-forward has a variable latency time depending on the frame length. FragmentFree and cut through modes always read only a fixed amount of a frame, so they have fixed latency times. In store-and-forward mode, latency is measured by the last-bit-received to the first-bit-transmitted or LIFO. This does not include the time it makes to receive the entire packet which can vary, according to packet size, from 65 microseconds to 1.3 milliseconds.

Some switches can be configured to perform cut-through switching on a per-port basis until a user-defined error threshold is reached. When errors reach the threshold point, the mode automatically change over to store-and-forward mode. This will stop forwarding the errors. When the error rate on the port falls below the threshold, the port automatically changes back to cut-through mode. The CAT2.96K switch uses the store-and-forward switching mode and Fragment Free mode.

Virtual LANs (VLANs)

VALN is a virtual configuration tool in the LAN switch to segment the LAN based on broadcast domains or generally, to segment one broadcast domain into multiply domains. By default, a LAN switch put all switch's interfaces into one broadcast domain-the default VLAN 1. Without VLAN configuration, LAN consists of all devices in that broadcast domain. With VLANs, a switch can put some interfaces into one broadcast domain and some into another based on some simple configuration, so a LAN switch can create multiply broadcast domains. These individual broadcast domains created by the switch are called VLANs.

Figure 6-8 illustrates how to segment one broadcast domain using two switches into two broadcast domains. Whereas, Figure 6-9 illustrates how to segment one broadcast domain using one switch and VLANs into two broadcast domains.

Figure 6-8 A LAN with Two Broadcast Domains and No VLANs

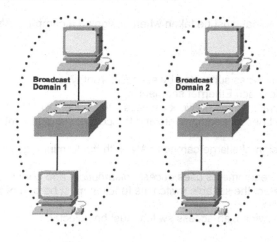

Figure 6-9 A LAN with Two Broadcast Domains Using One Switch and VLANs

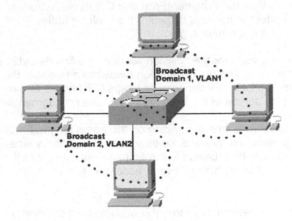

The use of VLANs in a network provides the following features:

- Virtually grouping network users instead of physical location grouping.
- Segmenting large broadcast domains into multiply smaller ones to reduce overhead caused by broadcasts in the network.
- Securing sensitive data on servers by putting the servers on a separate VLAN.
- Separating IP phone traffic (and other important traffics) from traffics sent by PCs connected to the phones to enhance the performance of Voice Over IP
- Reducing the workload for STP by limiting a VLAN to a single access switch.

No more information about VLAN is required for CCENT exam, except some of the design configurations, which will be given in this chapter.

Campus LAN Design

When LAN is extended to support large number of clients in one larger building, or in multiple buildings (close proximity to one another), this LAN is called *campus LAN*. A campus LAN is created by connecting several switches in each building together, and then connecting the switches (usually the *Core* switches) in the buildings by Ethernet links.

There are several considerations that must be taken when designing a campus LAN:

- The number of clients.
- The types of Ethernet available.
- The cabling lengths and types supported by each Ethernet type.
- The speeds required for each Ethernet segment.
- The function of each switch in the network (Access, Distribution, or Core).
- The type of the present network equipments and the cost of development this network.

Figure 6-10 shows a typical design of a large campus LAN, with the terminology included in the figure.

A campus design based CISCO equipments uses *access*, *distribution*, and *core* terms to describe the function of each switch in a campus. To select the suitable switch, its function must be one of the following:

- Connecting end-user devices, an access switch must be selected.

- Connecting multiple different switches in a campus, a distribution or core switch must be selected.

Figure 6-10 CISCO Campus Design

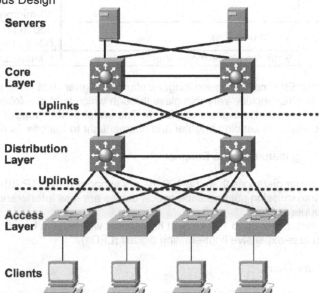

The roles/functions of the campus switches can be one of the following:

- **Access:** Connects end-user devices and should not be used to connect other access switches as shown in Figure 6-10.
- **Distribution:** Connects access switches together, and should not be used to connect directly end-user devices. For redundancy at least two uplinks to two different distribution switches are used to connect each access switch, as shown in Figure 6-10. Usually, distribution switches have faster forwarding rates capability than access switches.
- **Core:** Connects distribution switches together in very large campus LANs to provide very high forwarding rates and should not be used to connect directly end-user devices or access switches. Usually, core switches have the fastest forwarding rates capability than access switches and distribution switches.

Ethernet LAN Cabling and Media

Ethernet LAN media and cable lengths need to be addressed when designing a campus LAN. UTP cabling and categories are discussed in Chapter one of this book. List 6-2 emphasizes the cable lengths and categories that can be used.

Table 6-2 IEEE Ethernet Types and Media Specifications

Type	Media	Maximum Segment Length
10BASE-T	TIA/EIA CAT3 or better, two pairs	100 m (328 feet)
100BASE-TX	TIA/EIA CAT5 UTP or better, two pairs	100 m (328 feet)
100BASE-FX	62.5/125-micron multimode fiber	400 m (1312.3 feet)
1000BASE-CX	STP	25 m (82 feet)
1000BASE-T	TIA/EIA CAT5e UTP or better, four pairs	100 m (328 feet)

1000BASE-SX	Multimode fiber	275 m (853 feet) for 62.5-micron fiber 550 m (1804.5 feet) for 50-micron fiber
1000BASE-LX	Multimode fiber	550 m (1804.5 feet) for 50- and 62.5-micron fiber
1000BASE-LX	9-micron single-mode fiber	5 km (6.2 miles)

Fiber-optic cables are used for Ethernet to support longer distances, higher data rates transmission and better transmission quality. Optical cables include very-thin glass through which light can follow, whereas UTP cables include copper wires over which electrical signals can follow. The switches that support the optical transmission can send bits, by alternating between sending brighter and dimmer light to encode 0s and 1s on the cable.

Optical cables add the following features to the Ethernet:

- Supporting much longer distances than the 100 meters supported by UTP Ethernet.
- Supporting better transmission quality, since optical cables are less interference from outside sources as compared to copper cables.
- Supporting longer distances, up to 100 kms, at higher cost when using Laser, and up to hundred of meters when using less-expensive light-emitting diodes (LEDs).

Two types of optical cables are found:

1. Multimode fiber supports shorter distances, cheaper cabling, and working fine with less-expensive LEDs.
2. Singlemode fiber supports the longest distances, more expensive and working fine with Laser. Furthermore, the switches that support this type are much-expensive than those which use the first type.

CISCO Catalyst LAN Switches

The default settings for CISCO Catalyst switches make it possible to work by only power ON the switch by connecting the power cable to the switch and a power outlet, and connect hosts to the switch using the correct UTP cables. However, connecting to a switch's user interface is essential for doing some crucial jobs such as; checking on the switch's status, looking at information about what the switch is doing, configuring specific features of the switch and enabling security features.

As stated in the beginning of this chapter, the chapter is intended to describe how to access a CISCO switch's user interface, use commands to find out how a switch is currently working, configure a switch, and verity a switch configuration. The chapter focuses only on commands that are not discussed in chapter four of this book.

CISCO Catalyst 2960 Switch CLI

The **command-line interface (CLI)** is used by CISCO in their catalyst switches in the same concepts that used by CISCO routers. Users look to the CLI as a text-based interface in which they can enter a text command and then presses **Enter** key, which sends the command to the switch for telling the switch what to do. What the command requires, the switch will do, and the switch will reply with some messages stating the results of the command.

To access the CLI interface of the switch, either use a rollover cable to connect to the console port or use a straight through cable to connect to any interface in the switch after configuring that interface with an IP address and other required parameters, just like in CISCO routers.

To connect to the console port, a Hyper-terminal emulator software can be used to access the CLI of the switch in Windows based machines. The emulator must be configured to use the PC's serial port, matching the switch's console port settings.

The following are the default console port settings on a switch:

- 9600 bits/second
- No hardware flow control
- 8-bit ASCII
- No stop bits
- 1 parity bit

As the CCNA/CCENT exam references the CISCO Catalyst 2960 model, the focus will be on this model in the coming sections.

CISCO Catalyst 2960 Switch

CISCO introduces the 2900 series of switches as full-featured, low-cost wiring closet switches for the large networks. Usually the 2960 switch is used as an access switch for the large networks, and it is capable of connect to the rest of the network (distribution layer) using the uplinks. Furthermore, this family uses IOS as an operating system not Cat OS as some CISCO switches use. Figure 6-11 shows the 2960 family.

As an example, model WS-2960-24TT-L has 24 auto-negotiate, RJ-45 UTP, 10/100 ports. These ports can be used for connecting 10BASE-T or 100BASE-TX Ethernets. This model has two additional RJ-45 ports on the right those are 10/100/1000 interfaces, intended to connect to the distribution/core layer switches of a campus network. These ports can be used for connecting 10BASE-T or 100BASE-TX or 1000BASE–T Ethernets. The datasheet for this switch can be found on CISCO web site.

Figure 6-11 CISCO Catalyst 2960 Switch Family

In CISCO switches the physical connectors are called either **interfaces** or **ports**. Each port has a number in the style *x/y*, where *x* refers to the slot number and *y* refers to the port number within the slot, just like in CISCO routers. On a 2960, the x is always 0 since this switch is considered as only one slot or without slots. The first

10/100 interface on a 2960 is numbered starting at 0/1; the second is 0/2, and so on. The interfaces also have names; for example, "interface FastEthernet 0/2" is the second of the 10/100 interfaces. Any Gigabit interfaces would be called "GigabitEthernet" interfaces. For example, the second 10/100/1000 interface on a 2960 would be "interface gigabitethernet 0/2."

Recently, in 2010 CISCO adds a new switch to Cat2.96K family. The Catalyst 2960-S switches introduce the following features with LAN Base software:

- 10 and 1 Gigabit Ethernet uplink flexibility with Small Form-Factor Pluggable Plus (SFP+)
- 24 or 48 ports of Gigabit Ethernet desktop connectivity
- CISCO FlexStack stacking module with 40 Gbps of throughput
- PoE+ with up to 30W per port, which supports the latest PoE+ capable devices
- Power supply options, with 740W or 370W fixed power supplies for PoE+ switches are available
- USB storage for file backup, distribution, and simplified operations
- Several additional software features

Switch LEDs Status

In addition to the using of commands from the CISCO IOS CLI to check how a switch is working, verify its current status, and troubleshoot any problems, which may be taking a long period of time, several LEDs on the switch can be used for these purposes. The front of CISCO Cat2.96K switch has one LED over each physical Ethernet interface and five LEDs on the left, and a mode button. Table 6-3 summarizes the LEDs of this switch.

Table 6-3 LEDs on the Front Panel of CISCO Cat2.96K PoE Switch

LED Name	LED Description
(1) SYST (system)	It indicates the overall system status.
(2) RPS (Redundant Power Supply)	It indicates the status of the redundant power supply.
(3) STAT (Status)	If it is ON (green), it indicates that each port LED implies that port's status.
(4) DUPLX (duplex)	If its ON (green), it indicates each port LED implies that port's duplex (ON/green=Full-Duplex; OFF=Half-Duplex)
(5) SPEED	If its ON (green), it indicates each port LED implies the speed of that port, as follows: OFF means 10 Mbps, solid green means 100 Mbps, and flashing green means 1 Gbps.
(6) PoE	It indicates the using of Power Over Ethernet

Figure 6-12 shows the front panel LEDs for CISCO catalyst 2.96K switch. The numbers are described in Table 6-3.

The SYST LED provides a quick overall status of the switch, with the following three different states:

- **OFF:** The switch is powered OFF
- **ON (green):** The switch is powered ON and in a normal operational state (Cisco IOS has been loaded)
- **ON (amber):** The switch's Power-On Self Test (POST) process failed, and the Cisco IOS is not loaded.

Figure 6-12 The Front Panel LEDs for CISCO Cat2.96K PoE Switch

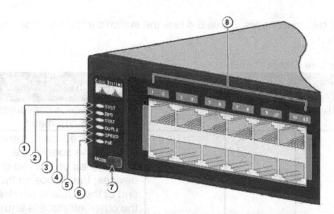

Tho immediato rocponse to the last state is to power the switch OFF and back ON again. If the problem is not solved, a call to the local CISCO partners or CISCO Technical Assistance Center (TAC) is typically the next step.

A mode button when pressed, cycles the port LEDs through three modes: STAT, DUPLX, and SPEED. The current port LED mode is signified by a solid green STAT, DUPLX, or SPEED LEDs in the left of the front panel of the switch.

The meaning of the interface LED, which is sitting above or below each Ethernet port, is different depending on which of the three ports LED modes is currently used on the switch.

For example, in STAT (status) mode, each port LED provides status information about that port. For example:

- **OFF:** The link is OFF (not working).
- **Solid green:** The link is ON (working, with no current traffic).
- **Flashing green:** The link is ON (working, with traffic is currently passing over the interface).
- **Flashing amber:** The interface is OFF (administratively disabled or has been dynamically disabled for a variety of reasons).

In SPEED port LED mode, the port LEDs provide the operating speed of the interface, as follows:

- **Dark:** 10 Mbps
- **Solid green:** 100 Mbps
- **Flashing green:** 1000 Mbps (1 Gbps).

In DUPLX port LED mode, the port LEDs provide the mode of operating of the interface, either Full-duplex or Half-duplex.

When the IEEE autonegotiation process is enabled on a switch port and on a host, both devices agree to the fastest speed supported by both devices, and the mode will be selected as either full duplex if it is supported by both devices, or half duplex if it is not. When autonegotiation is disabled on one device and the other device uses autonegotiation, the device using autonegotiation chooses the default duplex mode setting based on the current speed. The defaults are as follows:

- 10 Mbps, half duplex, if the speed is not known.
- half duplex, if the speed is known to be 10 or 100 Mbps.
- full duplex, if the speed is known to be 1000 Mbps.
- full duplex, if the speed is known to be faster than 1 Gbps.

Switch Port Status

A switch interface has several status codes. Table 6-4 lists the switch's interface code combinations and the corresponding interface status.

Table 6-4 LAN Switch Interface Status Codes

Line Status	Protocol Status	Interface Status	The reason
Administratively Down	Down	disabled	The interface is configured with the **shutdown** command.
Down	Down	notconnect	No cable; bad cable; wrong cable pinouts; the speeds are mismatched on the two connected devices; the device on the other end of the cable is powered OFF or the other interface is **shutdown**.
Up	Down	notconnect	An interface up/down state is not expected on LAN switch interfaces.
Down	Down(err-disabled)	err-disabled	Port security has disabled the interface.
Up	Up	connect	The interface is working.

Configuring CISCO switch 2960

In this section, several commands that can be used to configure the switch are described. The Section begins with Table 6-5, which lists all the commands that can be used for configuring the switch with a brief description. Detailed descriptions are given to those commands, which are not discussed in chapter 4. The descriptions are based on CAT2.96K switch and IOS 12.2 version.

Table 6-5 Configuring CISCO Switch EXEC Commands

Command	Description
line console 0	Issued from Global CLI prompt. Changes the prompt to console configuration mode.
line vty vty-no1 vty-no2	Issued from Global CLI prompt. Changes the prompt to vty (telnet/SSH) configuration mode for the range of vty lines listed in the command. Vty can be any number from 0 to 15.
Login	Issued from Console and vty configuration mode. Tells switch or router to prompt for a password. Usually this is not used for Console since the console user can easily break the password by doing password recovery procedure.
password pass-text	Issued from Console and vty configuration mode. Lists the password required if the login command is configured.
login local	Issued from Console and vty configuration mode. Prompts for an authentication, to be checked against locally configured **username** global configuration commands
username name password passvalue	Issued from Global CLI prompt. Creates usernames and passwords for user authentication. Used when the login local line configuration command has been used.
ip address ip-address subnet-mask	Issued from any switch interface prompt and from VLAN interface prompt. Statically configures an IP address and subnet mask on an interface or set the switch's IP address and subnet mask.
ip address dhcp	Issued from VLAN interface mode. Configures the switch as a DHCP client to discover its IP address, mask, and default gateway.
ip default-gateway address	Issued from global command. Configures the switch's default gateway IP address, if the switch not uses DHCP.

interface type port-number	Issued from global configuration mode. Configure an interface. The type is typically Ethernet, FastEthernet, or gigabit Ethernet. The possible port numbers vary depending on the model of switch—for example, F0/1, F0/2, and so on.
shutdown no shutdown	Issued from Interface mode. Turns OFF or on the interface, respectively. The shutdown command puts the interface in administratively down mode.
description text	Issued from Interface mode. Sets a description text on an interface.
speed {10 | 100 | 1000 | auto}	Issued from interface mode. Sets the speed manually to the listed speed or, with the **auto** setting, automatically negotiates the speed.
duplex {auto | full | half}	Issued from interface mode. Sets the duplex manually to half or full, or to autonegotiate the duplex setting.
hostname name	Issued from Global command prompt. Sets the switch's or router's name.
enable secret pass-value	Issued from Global command prompt. Sets the encrypted enable secret password. Supersedes the enable password if set.
enable password pass-value	Issued from Global command prompt. Sets the clear-text enable password, used only when the enable secret password is not set.
Exit	Takes back to the next higher CLI mode.
End	Issued from any of the configuration sub-modes Exits configuration mode and goes back to enable mode.
Ctrl-Z	Does the same thing as the end command. It is a two-key combination rather than a command
no debug all undebug all	Issued from the enable CLI mode to disable all currently enabled debugs.
show process	Lists statistics about CPU utilization.
terminal monitor	Makes the IOS sends a copy of all syslog messages, including debug messages, to the Telnet or SSH user who issues this command.
reload	Issued from enable CLI mode that reboots the switch or router.
copy from-location to-location	Issued from enable CLI mode that copies files from one file location to another. Location can be any of start-up-config, running-config, TFTP and RPC servers, and flash memory.
copy running-config startup-config	Issued from enable CLI mode that saves the active config into the startup-config file and replacing the last one.
copy startup-config running-config	Issued from enable CLI mode that merges the startup config file with the currently active config file in RAM.
show running-config	Lists the active configuration that found in the running-config file.
write erase erase startup-config erase nvram:	Issued from enable CLI mode to erase the start-up-config file.
Setup	Issued from enable CLI mode that places the user in setup mode to configure the router or the switch.
Quit	Issued from EXEC mode that disconnects the user from the CLI session.
show system:running-config	Does the same job as show running-config command.
show startup-config	Lists the initial configuration that found in the startup-config file.
show nvram:startup-config show nvram:	Does the same job as show startup-config command.
enable	Issued from user mode that takes to enable (privileged) mode and prompts for an enable password if configured.
disable	The opposite to the **enable** command.
history size length	Issued from Line config mode. Defines the number of commands held in the history buffer.
Config t	Puts the switch into global configuration mode and changes the running configuration.
show dhcp lease	Lists IP address, subnet mask, and default gateway information, the switch acquires as a DHCP client
Show version	Shows the IOS information of the switch.
?	Lists all commands available in this mode. There is no need to press ENTER key after ?.

Help	Presents how to get help description.
command ?	Lists all the first parameter options for the command.
com?	Lists commands that start with com.
command parm?	Lists all parameters beginning with parm for the command.
command parm<Tab Key>	Spells the rest of this parameter at the command line or does nothing. The last result means that there is more than one possible next parameter for this string of parm characters.
command parameter1 ?	Lists all the next parameters and gives a brief explanation of each.

When the ENTER key is pressed after the commands, the switch enters the command in a history buffer, storing ten commands by default. Several key sequences can be used to move backward and forward in the historical list of commands and then edit the command before re-issuing it. Table 6-6 lists the key sequences used to manipulate previously entered commands.

Table 6-6 Key Sequences for Command Edit and Recall

Keyboard Command	Functions
Up arrow or Ctrl-p	Displays the most recently used command one after another until the history buffer is exhausted. (The p stands for previous.)
Down arrow or Ctrl-n	Goes forward to the more recently entered commands. (The n stands for next.)
Left arrow or Ctrl-b	Takes the cursor backward in the present command without deleting any character. (The b stands for back.)
Right arrow or Ctrl-f	Takes the cursor forward in the present command without deleting any character. (The f stands for forward.)
Backspace	Takes the cursor backward in the present command, deleting any passed character.
Ctrl-a	Takes the cursor directly to the first character of the present command.
Ctrl-e	Takes the cursor directly to the end of the present command.
Ctrl-r	Redisplays the command line with all characters. It is useful when there are too many messages on the screen.
Ctrl-d	Deletes a single character from the present command line.
Esc-b	Takes the cursor back one word in the present command line.
Esc-f	Takes the cursor forward one word in the present command line..

Configuring SSH

SSH is the preferred method for remote login to switches and routers today, since SSH encrypts all the data sent between the SSH client and the SSH server (Telnet sends all data, including all passwords entered by the user, as clear text). SSH requires that the user supply both a username and password instead of just a password. The Switch can be configured to use authentication on an external server called an Authentication, Authorization, and Accounting (AAA) server or the authentication configured on a switch itself.

Configuration 6-1: The following configuration steps show how to configure SSH on the switch:

1. Changing the vty lines to use usernames, with either locally configured usernames or an AAA server. In this configuration, the **login local** subcommand defines the use of local usernames, replacing the **login** subcommand in vty configuration mode.
2. Telling the switch to accept both Telnet and SSH with the **transport input telnet ssh** vty subcommand. (The default is the **transport input telnet**, omitting the **ssh** parameter.) For more secure environment the Telnet can be removed leaving only SSH (**transport input ssh**).
3. Adding **username** & **password** command to configure the username & password pair(s).
4. Configuring the switch to generate a matched public and private key pair, as well as a shared encryption key, using the **crypto key generate rsa** command.
5. Each SSH client needs a copy of the switch's public key (as shown by **show crypto key mypubkey**

rsa command) before the client can connect. No switch commands are required for this step.

6. The **show running-config | begin line vty** command, as used in this configuration, lists the running configuration, beginning with the first line, which contains the text **line vty**.

```
Switch#config t
Switch(config)#line vty 0 15
Switch(config-line)#login local
Switch(config-line)#transport input telnet ssh
Switch(config-line)#exit
Switch(config)#username thaar password cisco
Switch(config)#crypto key generate rsa
Switch(config)#^Z
Switch#show crypto key mypubkey rsa
Switch#show running-config | begin line vty
```

Configuring Switch Interfaces

CISCO switch contains several Interfaces (ports). These interfaces are used to forward data to and from other devices. Each interface may be configured with several different settings. IOS uses interface subcommands to configure these settings.

Configuration 6-2: The following configuration shows how to statically configure the switch interfaces to use the **duplex** and **speed** interface subcommands, or an interface can use autonegotiation (the default).The configuration shows how to use the **description** command as well.

```
Switch#config t
Switch(config)#interface FastEthernet 0/1
Switch(config-if)#duplex full
Switch(config-if)#speed 100
Switch(config-if)#description MANAGER HOST
Switch(config-if)#exit
Switch(config)#interface range FastEthernet 0/6 - 24
Switch(config-if-range)#description END-USER INTERFACE
Switch(config-if-range)#^Z
Switch#
Switch#show interfaces status
```

Port	Name	Status	Vlan	Duplex	Speed	Type
Fa0/1	MANAGER HOST	connected	1	full	100	10/100BaseTX
Fa0/2		notconnect	1	auto	auto	10/100BaseTX
Fa0/3		connected	1	a-full	a-100	10/100BaseTX
Fa0/4		notconnect	1	auto	auto	10/100BaseTX
Fa0/5		notconnect	1	auto	auto	10/100BaseTX
Fa0/6	END-USER INTERFACE	notconnect	1	auto	auto	10/100BaseTX
Fa0/7	END-USER INTERFACE	notconnect	1	auto	auto	10/100BaseTX
Fa0/8	END-USER INTERFACE	notconnect	1	auto	auto	10/100BaseTX
Fa0/9	END-USER INTERFACE	notconnect	1	auto	auto	10/100BaseTX
Fa0/10	END-USER INTERFACE	notconnect	1	auto	auto	10/100BaseTX
Fa0/11	END-USER INTERFACE	notconnect	1	auto	auto	10/100BaseTX

Fa0/12	END-USER INTERFACE	notconnect	1	auto	auto	10/100BaseTX
Fa0/13	END-USER INTERFACE	notconnect	1	auto	auto	10/100BaseTX
Fa0/14	END-USER INTERFACE	notconnect	1	auto	auto	10/100BaseTX
Fa0/15	END-USER INTERFACE	notconnect	1	auto	auto	10/100BaseTX
Fa0/16	END-USER INTERFACE	notconnect	1	auto	auto	10/100BaseTX
Fa0/17	END-USER INTERFACE	notconnect	1	auto	auto	10/100BaseTX
Fa0/18	END-USER INTERFACE	notconnect	1	auto	auto	10/100BaseTX
Fa0/19	END-USER INTERFACE	notconnect	1	auto	auto	10/100BaseTX
Fa0/20	END-USER INTERFACE	notconnect	1	auto	auto	10/100BaseTX
Fa0/21	END-USER INTERFACE	notconnect	1	auto	auto	10/100BaseTX
Fa0/22	END-USER INTERFACE	notconnect	1	auto	auto	10/100BaseTX
Fa0/23	END-USER INTERFACE	notconnect	1	auto	auto	10/100BaseTX
Fa0/24	END-USER INTERFACE	notconnect	1	auto	auto	10/100BaseTX
Gi0/1		notconnect	1	auto	auto	10/100/1000BaseTX
Gi0/2		notconnect	1	auto	auto	10/100/1000BaseTX

Switch#

In the previous configuration, the **a-** in **a-full** and **a-100** refers to the fact that these values were autonegotiated. To configure an interface IP address dynamically using DHCP server, the following configuration should be used. Checking the dhcp leased IP addresses are also outlined here.

```
Switch#config t
Switch(config)#interface vlan 1
Switch(config-if)#ip address dhcp
Switch(config-if)#no shutdown
Switch(config-if)#^Z
Switch#
Switch#show dhcp lease
Temp IP addr: 172.17.1.10 for peer on Interface: Vlan1
Temp sub net mask: 255.255.255.0
DHCP Lease server: 172.17.1.1, state: 3 Bound
DHCP transaction id: 2105
Lease: 172800 secs, Renewal: 86400 secs, Rebind: 162000 secs
Temp default-gateway addr: 172.17.1.1
.........
Switch#show interface vlan 1
Vlan1 is up, line protocol is up
.........
Internet address is 172.17.1.10/24
..........
```

Configuring Port Security

Port security can be used to restrict an interface so that only the expected devices can use it. This reduces exposure to some types of attacks.

Configuration 6-3: The following configuration shows the steps of how to configure the switch interfaces security. Port security configuration involves several steps. The port should be an access port at first, which means that the port is not doing any VLAN trunking. Secondly, the port security feature should be enabled and the actual MAC addresses of the devices allowed to use that port should be configured.

Example 6-3: Assume the following example: The first fastethernet interface is connected to device1 with MAC address (1111.1111.1111), and the second fastethernet interface is connected to device2 with MAC address (2222.2222.2222). These are the only devices that should be connected to interfaces 1 & 2 so port security should be configured on those interfaces. The switch examines the source MAC address of all frames received on those interfaces, allowing only frames sourced from the configured MAC addresses.

1. Using the **switchport mode access** command to put the switch interface in an access interface state.
2. Using the **switchport port-security** command to enable port security.
3. (Optional) using the **switchport port-security maximum** number command to specify the maximum number of allowed MAC addresses associated with the interface. (The Default is to one MAC address.).
4. (Optional) using the **switchport port-security violation {protect | restrict | shutdown}** command to define the action that should be taken when a frame is received from a MAC address other than the defined addresses. (The default duty is to shut down the interface.).
5. Using the **switchport port-security mac-address** mac-address command to specify the allowed MAC address(es) to send frames into the interface. The same command can be used multiple times to define more than one MAC address.
6. Alternatively, instead of Step 5, using the **switchport port-security mac-address sticky** command to use the "sticky learning" process to learn, and configure the MAC addresses of currently connected hosts, dynamically.
7. (Optional) using the following commands to check the current configuration, **show running-config**, **show port-security interface fastethernet 0/1** and **show port-security interface fastethernet 0/2**.
8. (Optional) saving the current configuration so that only 2222.2222.2222 is used on fa0/2 interface in the future by issuing the **copy running-config startup-config** command to save the configuration.

```
Switch#config t
Switch(config)#interface fastEthernet 0/1
Switch(config-if)#switchport mode access
Switch(config-if)#switchport port-security
Switch(config-if)#switchport port-security mac-address 1111.1111.1111
Switch(config-if)#exit
Switch(config)#interface fastEthernet 0/2
Switch(config-if)#switchport mode access
Switch(config-if)#switchport port-security
Switch(config-if)#switchport port-security mac-address sticky
Switch(config-if)#^Z
Switch#show running-config
Switch#show port-security interface fastEthernet 0/1
Switch#show port-security interface fastEthernet 0/2
Switch#copy running-config startup-config
Switch#
```

Table 6-7 lists the actions of the switch when port security violation occurs.

Table 6-7 Port Security Violations

switchport port-security violation options	Protect	Restrict	Shutdown
Discards offending traffic	Yes	Yes	Yes
Sends log and SNMP messages	No	Yes	Yes
Disables the interface, discarding all traffic	No	No	Yes

VLAN Configuration

This book is dealing only with configuring the access interfaces of the switch. The second type of switch interfaces-Trunk interfaces will be covered in ICND2 book. Access interfaces send and receive frames only in a single VLAN, called the *access VLAN*, whereas Trunking interfaces send and receive traffic in multiple VLANs. By default, CISCO switches already have VLAN 1 configured, and all interfaces are members to VLAN 1.

Configuration 6-4: The following steps should be followed to add another VLAN, and assign the access interfaces to be in that VLAN:

Step 1.   Configuring a new VLAN:
   A.   Using the **vlan** vlan-id global configuration command to create the VLAN and move the user into the VLAN configuration mode.
   B.   (Optional) Using the **name** VLAN subcommand to list a name for the VLAN. If it not configured, the VLAN name is VLANZZZZ, where ZZZZ is the four-digit decimal VLAN ID.
Step 2.   Configuring an access interface to a VLAN:
   A.   Using the **interface** command to move into the interface configuration mode.
   B.   Using the **switchport access vlan** id-number interface subcommand to specify the VLAN number associated with that interface.
   C.   (Optional) using the **switchport mode access** interface subcommand to disable trunking so that the switch will not dynamically decide to use trunking on the interface, and it will remain an access interface.

Example 6-4: Assume the following example shown in Figure 6-13. The figure shows a network with one LAN switch (ACCESS1) and three PCs in each of the two VLANs (7 and 77).

Figure 6-13 Two VLANs on One Switch

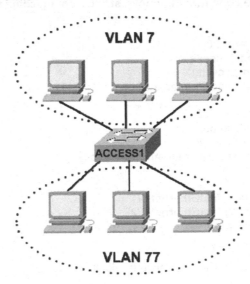

```
ACCESS1#show vlan brief
        VLAN  Name          Status     Ports
        1     default       active     Fa0/1, Fa0/2, Fa0/3, Fa0/4
                                       Fa0/5, Fa0/6, Fa0/7, Fa0/8
                                       Fa0/9, Fa0/10, Fa0/11, Fa0/12
                                       Fa0/13, Fa0/14, Fa0/15, Fa0/16
                                       Fa0/17, Fa0/18, Fa0/19, Fa0/20
                                       Fa0/21, Fa0/22, Fa0/23, Fa0/24
                                       Gi0/1, Gi0/2
        1002  fddi-default  act/unsup
        1003  token-ring-   act/unsup
              default
        1004  fddinet-default act/unsup
        1005  trnet-default  act/unsup

ACCESS1#config t
Enter configuration commands, one per line. End with CNTL/Z.
ACCESS1(config)#vlan 7
ACCESS1(config-vlan)#name Dept7 vlan
ACCESS1(config-vlan)#exit
ACCESS1(config)#interface range fastethernet 0/1 - 3
ACCESS1(config-if)#switchport access vlan 7
ACCESS1(config-if)#exit

ACCESS1#sh run
............................
interface FastEthernet0/1
switchport access vlan 7
switchport mode access
!
interface FastEthernet0/2

switchport access vlan 7
switchport mode access
!
interface FastEthernet0/3
switchport access vlan 7
switchport mode access
!

ACCESS1#show vlan brief
        VLAN  Name          Status     Ports
        1     default       active     Fa0/4
                                       Fa0/5, Fa0/6, Fa0/7, Fa0/8
                                       Fa0/9, Fa0/10, Fa0/11, Fa0/12

                                       Fa0/13, Fa0/14, Fa0/15, Fa0/16
                                       Fa0/17, Fa0/18, Fa0/19, Fa0/20
                                       Fa0/21, Fa0/22, Fa0/23, Fa0/24
                                       Gi0/1, Gi0/2
        7     Dept7-vlan    active     Fa0/1, Fa0/2, Fa0/3
        1002  fddi-default  act/unsup
        1003  token-ring-   act/unsup
              default
        1004  fddinet-default act/unsup
        1005  trnet-default  act/unsup
ACCESS1#show interfaces vlan 7
```

Securing Unused Switch Interfaces

The default interface configurations of a CISCO switch as follows:

- Auto-negotiate speed
- Auto-negotiate duplex
- Each interface begins in an enabled (**no shutdown**) state.
- All interfaces assigned to VLAN 1.
- Auto-negotiate VLAN features, VLAN trunking and VLAN Trunking Protocol (VTP)

These default configurations make the switch working directly after switching ON and without any interventions.

Security threats are the side effects of the default configuration. To overcome this issue, CISCO recommends configuring unused interfaces by the following interface subcommands:

- **shutdown**-to administratively disable it.
- **switchport access vlan** *number*-to assign it to an unused VLAN.
- **switchport mode access**-to force it as an access interface (nontrunking interface) and prevent VLAN trunking and VTP.

Ethernet Switch Troubleshooting

This section explains how to verify and troubleshoot the CISCO switching network. The section suggests some verification and troubleshooting methods and practices that helping to solve the problems with the CISCO networks. However, at first what is the meaning of verification and troubleshooting? The process of examining a network to confirm that it is working as designed this is called Verification, whereas Troubleshooting means examining the network to determine what is causing a particular problem so that it can be fixed.

Verifying and troubleshooting CISCO switching network can be down by using the CISCO Discovery Protocol (**cdp**) and several **show** commands. Many of these commands are described in the previous chapters, and the commands are the same for CISCO routers. CDP commands will be explained in the next chapter of this book. Table 6-8 lists these commands and their description.

Table 6-8 Verifying and Troubleshooting EXEC Commands

Command	Description
switch(config)#cdp run	Enables CDP for the entire switch.
switch(config)#no cdp run	Disables CDP for the entire switch
switch(config-if)#cdp enable	Enables CDP for a particular interface.
switch(config-if)#no cdp enable	Disables CDP for a particular interface.
switch#show cdp neighbors [type number]	Shows the neighbor found on a specific interface if an interface was listed in the command or displaying one summary line of information about each neighbor connected to the switch.
switch#show cdp neighbors detail	Shows one large set of information for every neighbor. Lists the IP address and IOS version and type ....etc.
switch#show cdp entry name	Shows the same information as the **show cdp neighbors detail** command, but only for the named neighbor.
switch#show cdp	Shows whether CDP is enabled globally, and lists the cdp timer and holdtime frequencies.
switch#show cdp interface [type number]	States whether CDP is enabled on each interface, or a single interface if the interface is listed in the command, and states update and holdtime timers on those interfaces.
switch#show cdp traffic	Displays global statistics for the number of CDP

	advertisements sent and received on a switch and any errors.
switch#show mac address-table [dynamic | static] [address hw-addr] [interface interface-id] [vlan vlan-id]	Displays the content of switch's MAC address table.
switch#show interfaces [type number]	Displays detailed information about the listed interface.
switch#show interfaces status [type number]	Displays summary information about the listed interface such as interface status and settings.

Layer 1 Common Problems

Working interfaces with the connect state (up/up) may suffer from several problems. These problems can be identified by monitoring various interface counters. However, there are several reasons for such problems:

- The UTP cable could be damaged. Therefore, an Ethernet frame that passes over such cable may encounter problems and the electrical signal can degrade.
- Several sources of electromagnetic interference (FMI) such as, a nearby electrical power cable to the UTP cable. EMI may change the electrical signal on the UTP cable.

As a result for such problems, the electrical signal degrades and the receiving host may receive incorrect frame bits value. These incorrect frames will be discarded in the receiving host by using the error detection logic as implemented in the FCS field in the Ethernet trailer and the receiving host interface's counters list these errors as CRC errors.

Configuration 6-5: The following configuration shows the using of the CISCO interface counters. From the output, two types of collisions are displayed, the Ethernet collision and the late collision. The first one is the normal Ethernet collisions. The second one is occurred when a switch sense a collision after sending the 64 bytes of a frame. The collision in this case is considered as a late collision. The interface increments the late collision counter in addition to the usual CSMA/CD actions to send a jam signal, wait a random time, and try again.

Switch#show interfaces fa0/1
....
Received 165 broadcasts (0 multicast)
0 runts, 0 giants, 0 throttles
0 input errors, 0 CRC, 0 frame, 0 overrun, 0 ignored
0 watchdog, 121 multicast, 0 pause input
0 input packets with dribble condition detected
65764 packets output, 7492890 bytes, 0 underruns
0 output errors, 0 collisions, 1 interface resets
0 babbles, 0 late collision, 0 deferred
0 lost carrier, 0 no carrier, 0 PAUSE output
0 output buffer failures, 0 output buffers swapped out
....

By using the Ethernet collision and the late collision counters, three common LAN problems can be identified:

- Excessive interference on the cable. This can cause the various input error counters to keep growing larger. By monitoring the CRC errors counter and the collision counters. It is possible to identify if the problem may simply be interference on the cable or not. When the CRC errors counter grows and the collisions' counters do not, this means that excessive interference is occurred.

- A duplex mismatch. The use of **show interface** command can identify if this problem is occurred or not.
- Jabber which refers to cases in which the NIC ignores Ethernet rules and sends a frame after frame without a break between the frames.

With both last two problems, the collisions and late collision counters could keep growing. If the collision counters show that more than 0.1% of all the output frames has collided, a significant problem exists. The percentage of collisions versus output frames can be found by dividing the collisions counter by the "packets' output" counter. Table 6-9 summarizes these three general types of interface problems.

Table 6-9 Layer 1 Interface Problems with (**up/up**) State

The Problem	The Problem as Indicated by Counter Values	The Problem Causes
Excessive noise	Many input errors; few collisions	EMI, Damaged cables or Wrong cable category (Cat 5, 5E, 6)
Collisions	More than roughly 0.1% of all frames are collisions	Duplex mismatch (seen on the half-duplex side) or Jabber or DoS attack
Late collisions	Increasing late collisions	Collision domain or single cable too long or Duplex mismatch

Configuration 6-6: The following configuration shows the using of **show mac address-table [dynamic | static]** [**address** hw-addr] [**interface** interface-id] [**vlan** vlan-id] command. The command is used to display the content of switch's MAC address table. The first command lists all MAC addresses currently known by the switch. The output includes, in addition to dynamically learned MAC addresses, some static MAC addresses that used by the switch and any statically configured MAC addresses, such as those configured with the **switchport port-security** command. The output lists entries that list a port of "CPU" and refer to MAC addresses used by the switch for overhead traffic such as CDP and STP. According to these entries, the switch will send frames destined for these MACs addresses to the switch's CPU. The second command lists only the dynamic learning MAC address, whereas the last command displays only the static MAC addresses.

```
switch#show mac address-table
            Mac Address Table
-------------------------------------------------------------
Vlan    Mac Address         Type        Ports
----    -------------------  ---------   -------
All     0120.bbbb.0000      STATIC      CPU
All     0120.bbbb.0001      STATIC      CPU
All     0120.bbbb.0002      STATIC      CPU
All     0120.bbbb.0003      STATIC      CPU
All     0120.bbbb.0004      STATIC      CPU
All     0120.bbbb.0005      STATIC      CPU
All     0120.bbbb.0006      STATIC      CPU
All     0120.bbbb.0007      STATIC      CPU
All     0120.bbbb.0008      STATIC      CPU
All     0120.bbbb.0009      STATIC      CPU
1       0019.e801.925b      DYNAMIC     Gi0/1
Total Mac Addresses for this criterion: 11
!
switch#show mac address-table dynamic
switch#show mac address-table static
```

Summary

In this chapter, a strong foundation for Layer-2 Switching is presented. Configuring and troubleshooting Layer-2 Switching are presented. The background presented here is essential for understanding the rest of the book and undertaking the examination. The following topics are covered:

- Layer-2 switching and bridging differences
- MAC address filter table manipulation
- Layer-2 switches decisions and how they make them.
- Problems within Layer-2 switches and their remedy
- Spanning-Tree Protocol and how it prevents loops.
- Store-and-forward LAN switching mode
- Cut-through LAN switching mode
- FragmentFree LAN switching mode
- CISCO Catalyst LAN Switches
- CISCO Catalyst 2960 Switch CLI
- Configuring CISCO switch 2960
- Ethernet Switch Troubleshooting

At the end of the chapter, several learning questions are given to evaluate the learning level from this chapter. The correct answers and solutions with complementary discussions are found in appendix A, "Answers to Chapters Learning Questions."

Chapter Six Commands Reference

Table 6-10 lists and briefly describes all the new commands and keys that are used in this chapter.

Table 6-10 Chapter 6 Commands Reference

Command	Description
line console 0	Issued from Global CLI prompt. Changes the prompt to console configuration mode.
line vty *vty-no1 vty-no2*	Issued from Global CLI prompt. Changes the prompt to vty (telnet/SSH) configuration mode for the range of vty lines listed in the command. Vty can be any number from 0 to 15.
Login	Issued from Console and vty configuration mode. Tells switch or router to prompt for a password. Usually this is not used for Console since the console user can easily break the password by doing password recovery procedure.
password *pass-text*	Issued from Console and vty configuration mode. Lists the password required if the login command is configured.
login local	Issued from Console and vty configuration mode. Prompts for an authentication, to be checked against locally configured **username** global configuration commands
username *name* password *passvalue*	Issued from Global CLI prompt. Creates usernames and passwords for user authentication. Used when the login local line configuration command has been used.

ip address *ip-address subnet-mask*	Issued from any switch interface prompt and from VLAN interface prompt. Statically configures an IP address and subnet mask on an interface or set the switch's IP address and subnet mask.
ip address dhcp	Issued from VLAN interface mode. Configures the switch as a DHCP client to discover its IP address, mask, and default gateway.
ip default-gateway *address*	Issued from global command. Configures the switch's default gateway IP address, if the switch not uses DHCP.
interface *type port-number*	Issued from global configuration mode. Configure an interface. The type is typically Ethernet or FastEthernet or gigabit Ethernet. The possible port numbers vary depending on the model of switch—for example, F0/1, F0/2, and so on.
shutdown no shutdown	Issued from Interface mode. Turns off or on the interface, respectively. The shutdown command puts the interface in administratively down mode.
description *text*	Issued from Interface mode. Sets a description text on an interface.
speed {10 | 100 | 1000 | auto}	Issued from interface mode. Sets the speed manually to the listed speed or, with the **auto** setting, automatically negotiates the speed.
duplex {auto | full | half}	Issued from interface mode. Sets the duplex manually to half or full, or to autonegotiate the duplex setting.
hostname *name*	Issued from Global command prompt. Sets the switch's or router's name.
enable secret *pass-value*	Issued from Global command prompt. Sets the encrypted enable secret password. Supersedes the enable password if set.
enable password *pass-value*	Issued from Global command prompt. Sets the clear-text enable password, used only when the enable secret password is not set.
Exit	Takes back to the next higher CLI mode.
End	Issued from any of the configuration sub-modes Exits configuration mode and goes back to enable mode.
Ctrl-Z	Does the same thing as the end command. It is a two-key combination rather than a command
no debug all undebug all	Issued from the enable CLI mode to disable all currently enabled debugs.
show process	Lists statistics about CPU utilization.
terminal monitor	Makes the IOS sends a copy of all syslog messages, including debug messages, to the Telnet or SSH user who issues this command.
reload	Issued from enable CLI mode that reboots the switch or router.
copy *from-location to-location*	Issued from enable CLI mode that copies files from one file location to another. Location can be any of start-up-config, running-config, TFTP and RPC servers, and flash memory.
copy running-config startup-config	Issued from enable CLI mode that saves the active config into the startup-config file and replacing the last one.
copy startup-config running-config	Issued from enable CLI mode that merges the startup config file with the currently active config file in RAM.

show running-config	Lists the active configuration that found in the running-config file.
write erase erase startup-config erase nvram:	Issued from enable CLI mode that erases the start-up-config file.
Setup	Issued from enable CLI mode that places the user in setup mode to configure the router or the switch.
Quit	Issued from EXEC mode that disconnects the user from the CLI session.
show system:running-config	Does the same job as show running-config command.
show startup-config	Lists the initial configuration that found in the startup-config file.
show nvram:startup-config show nvram:	Does the same job as show startup-config command.
enable	Issued from user mode that takes to enable (privileged) mode and prompts for an enable password if configured.
disable	The opposite to the **enable** command.
history size *length*	Issued from Line config mode. Defines the number of commands held in the history buffer.
Config t	Puts the switch into global configuration mode and changes the running configuration.
show dhcp lease	Lists IP address, subnet mask, and default gateway information, the switch acquires as a DHCP client
Show version	Shows the IOS information of the switch.
?	Lists all commands available in this mode. There is no need to press ENTER key after ?.
Help	Presents how to get help description.
command *?*	Lists all the first parameter options for the command.
com*?*	Lists commands that start with com.
command *parm*?	Lists all parameters beginning with parm for the *command*.
command *parm*<Tab Key>	Spells the rest of this parameter at the command line or does nothing. The last result means that there is more than one possible next parameter for this string of *parm* characters.
command *parameter1* ?	Lists all the next parameters and gives a brief explanation of each.
Up arrow or Ctrl-p	Displays the most recently used command one after another until the history buffer is exhausted. (The p stands for previous.)
Down arrow or Ctrl-n	Goes forward to the more recently entered commands. (The n stands for next.)
Left arrow or Ctrl-b	Takes the cursor backward in the present command without deleting any character. (The b stands for back.)
Right arrow or Ctrl-f	Takes the cursor forward in the present command without deleting any character. (The f stands for forward.)
Backspace	Takes the cursor backward in the present command, deleting any passed character.
Ctrl-a	Takes the cursor directly to the first character of the present command.
Ctrl-e	Takes the cursor directly to the end of the present command.
Ctrl-r	Redisplays the command line with all characters. It's useful

	when there are too many messages on the screen.
Ctrl-d	Deletes a single character from the present command line.
Esc-b	Takes the cursor back one word in the present command line.
Esc-f	Takes the cursor forward one word in the present command line.
Switch(config-line)#transport input telnet ssh	Tells the switch to accept both Telnet and SSH
Switch(config)#username thaar password cisco	Configures username & password pair(s)
Switch(config)#crypto key generate rsa	Configures the switch to generate a matched public and private key pair, as well as a shared encryption key
Switch#show crypto key mypubkey rsa	Shows the copy of the switch's public key
Switch#show running-config | begin line vty	Lists the running configuration, beginning with the first line, which contains the text line vty
Switch(config)#interface range FastEthernet 0/6 - 24	Enters into multiple interface configuration lines at the same time, here FastEthernet 0/6 – 24 are used
Switch#show interfaces status	Lists the status of all switch interfaces
Switch(config)#interface vlan 1	Enters into vlan 1 interface configuration mode
Switch(config-if)#ip address dhcp	Configures an interface IP address dynamically using DHCP server
Switch#show dhcp lease	Lists the dhcp configured interfaces with all configured parameters
Switch#show interface vlan 1	Lists the details for interface vlan 1
Switch(config-if)#switchport mode access	Puts the switch interface in an access interface state
Switch(config-if)#switchport port-security	Enables port security
Switch(config-if)#switchport port-security mac-address 1111.1111.1111	Specifies the allowed MAC address associated with the interface. If Max is used instead of the MAC address, it means the maximum number of allowed MAC addresses associated with the interface
Switch(config-if)#switchport port-security mac-address sticky	Makes the "sticky learning" process to dynamically learn and configure the MAC addresses of currently connected hosts
Switch#show port-security interface fastEthernet 0/1	Checks the current interface configuration
switchport port-security violation {protect | restrict | shutdown}	Defines the action that should be taken when a frame is received from a MAC address other than the defined addresses. (The default duty is to shut down the interface.)
ACCESS1#show vlan brief	Lists vlan's configurations in a brief
ACCESS1(config)#vlan 1	Enters vlan 1 configuration mode
ACCESS1(config-vlan)#name Dept7-vlan	Defines a name for vlan, ex. Dept7-vlan
switch(config)#cdp run	Enables CDP for the entire switch.
switch(config)#no cdp run	Disables CDP for the entire switch
switch(config-if)#cdp enable	Enables CDP for a particular interface.
switch(config-if)#no cdp enable	Disables CDP for a particular interface.

switch#show cdp neighbors [*type number*]	Shows the neighbor found on a specific interface if an interface was listed in the command or displaying one summary line of information about each neighbor connected to the switch.
switch#show cdp neighbors detail	Shows one large set of information for every neighbor. Lists the IP address and IOS version and type ....etc.
switch#show cdp entry *name*	Shows the same information as the show cdp neighbors detail command, but only for the named neighbor.
switch#show cdp	Shows whether CDP is enabled globally, and lists the cdp timer and holdtime frequencies.
switch#show cdp interface [*type number*]	States whether CDP is enabled on each interface, or a single interface if the interface is listed in the command, and states update and holdtime timers on those interfaces.
switch#show cdp traffic	Displays global statistics for the number of CDP advertisements sent and received on a switch and any errors.
switch#show mac address-table	Displays the content of switch's MAC address table
switch#show mac address-table dynamic	Displays the dynamically added MAC addresses to switch's MAC table
switch#show mac address-table static	Displays the statically added MAC addresses to switch's MAC table

Chapter 6 Learning Questions

6-1. Try to decide which option gets in which blank.

Layer-2 Switching is _____, which means it uses the _____ address (Layer-2 address) to filter the network.

    A.   MAC
    B.   hardware based.

6-2. Which circuit of the following is used to build and maintain switch's filter table?

    A.   Application-specific Integrated circuits (ASICs)
    B.   Switched circuit
    C.   Analog circuits
    D.   Virtual circuits

6-3. Why Layer-2 switching (multiport bridge) is fast?

    A.   It is fast, because it looks at the Network Layer header information before deciding to either forward the frame or drop it.
    B.   It is fast, because it looks at the frame's hardware address before deciding to either forward the frame or drop it.
    C.   It is fast, because it looks at the Transport Layer header information before deciding to either forward the frame or drop it.
    D.   It is fast, because it looks at the Session Layer header information before deciding to either forward the frame or drop it.

6-4. Which of the following does Layer-2 switching provide? (Select all that apply)

    A.   Hardware-based bridging (MAC)
    B.   Wire speeds
    C.   Low latency
    D.   Low cost
    E.   Network address filtering

6-5. Layer-2 switching performs no modification to the data packet, only to the frame encapsulating the packet. This fact makes:

    A.   The switching process is slower and so efficient (less error-prone than routing).
    B.   The switching process is faster and so efficient (less error-prone than routing).
    C.   The switching process is slower and so efficient (more error-prone than routing).
    D.   The switching process is faster and so efficient (more error-prone than routing).

6-6. Which of the following is a feature of the Layer-2 switching? (Select all that apply)

    A.   Layer-2 switching provides network segmentation.
    B.   Layer-2 switching breaks up collision domains.
    C.   Layer-2 switching increases the bandwidth for each user because each connection (Interface) into the switch is its own collision domain, so there is a possibility to connect multiple devices to each interface.
    D.   Layer-2 switching breaks up broadcast domains.

6-7. Twelve stations connected to separate 10Mbps ports on a 16-port Layer-2 switch. How many Mbps of bandwidth the switch will give each station? (Select the best answer)

    A.   16Mbps
    B.   12Mbps
    C.   10/12Mbps
    D.   10/16Mbps
    E.   10Mbps

6-8.   TRUE/FALSE: Layer-2 switching network has the same problems as a bridged network.

    A.   TRUE
    B.   FALSE

6-9.   Which is the right way to create Layer-2 switching (bridged networks)?

    A.   The right way to create Layer-2 switching is by correctly breaks up collision domains, so users should spend 20 percent of their time on the local segment.
    B.   The right way to create Layer-2 switching is by correctly breaks up collision domains, so users should spend 10 percent of their time on the local segment.
    C.   The right way to create Layer-2 switching is by correctly breaks up collision domains, so users should spend 80 percent of their time on the local segment.
    D.   The right way to create Layer-2 switching is by correctly breaks up collision domains, so users should spend 100 percent of their time on the local segment.

6-10.   TRUE/FALSE: layer-2 switching networks break up collision domains but the network is still one large broadcast domain.

    A.   TRUE
    B.   FALSE

6-11.   Which device should be used to separate the collision domains?

    A.   Access server
    B.   Repeaters
    C.   Hubs
    D.   Switches

6-12.   How many broadcast domains are created when a network is segmented with a 24-port switch?

    A.   1
    B.   3
    C.   4
    D.   24

6-13.   How many collision domains are created when a network is segmented with a 24-port switch?

    A.   1
    B.   3
    C.   4
    D.   24

6-14.   Which of the following is the Layer-2 switching problem that cause performance issues and limit the size of the network? (Select all that apply)

A.   Broadcast messages
B.   Multicast messages
C.   Collisions
D.   Slow convergence of spanning tree

6-15.   TRUE/FALSE: Layer-2 switches can completely replace routers (layer-3 devices).

A.   TRUE
B.   FALSE

6-16.   Which of the following devices is used to reduce the number of collisions while maintaining a single broadcast domain throughout an Ethernet network? (Select all that apply)

A.   Router
B.   Switch
C.   Bridge
D.   Hub

6-17.   Try to decide if the following paragraph correctly depicts the Ethernet Network operation.

A.   Correct
B.   Incorrect

"Ethernet networks allow only one device to place frames on the network media, but all stations receive the frames. Each station must determine whether the frames it receives are intended for it or not. Frequently, more than one device attempts to place frames onto the network at the same time, which causes errors known as collisions. Collisions are normal on Ethernet networks, and mechanisms exist to detect and correct them. However, more collisions can cause slow network throughput. In a situation where more collisions are occurring because of the high number of devices on the network, the network should be broken into segments so that fewer devices are placing frames on the same network segment. By using switches or bridges, it is possible to break the network into multiple collision domains so that the frequency of collisions is greatly reduced. This type of segmentation is sometimes called micro-segmentation."

6-18.   Try to decide if the following paragraph correctly depicts the broadcast.

A.   Correct
B.   Incorrect

"Because switches and bridges forward all broadcasts, they maintain the existing broadcast domains. Broadcasts are messages sent simultaneously to every device on the network, and are part of the normal network traffic. They are usually not a concern on small networks, but on larger networks, broadcasts can consume a significant portion of network bandwidth. To reduce the broadcast traffic, routers (or L3 Switches) must be used to segment the network; hence, broadcasts are contained within the network segments. For example, suppose a network is broken into two segments with a Router. Broadcasts from devices on each segment would not pass through the Router to the other segment, which would reduce the bandwidth broadcasts consumed on each segment."

6-19.   Try to decide if the following paragraph correctly depicts the Routers.

A.   Correct
B.   Incorrect

"Routers create separate collision and broadcast domains. If an Ethernet network is segmented with routers, it would create multiple broadcast and collision domains."

6-20.   Try to decide if the following paragraph correctly depicts the Hubs.

   A.   Correct
   B.   Incorrect

"Hubs simply forward all traffic. Therefore, you cannot reduce the number of collisions on a network using hubs. Adding a hub to a network with a single collision domain and a single broadcast domain would have no effect on either domain."

6-21.   Which of the following is a feature of the switching? (Select all that apply)
   A.   Providing dedicated bandwidth per single device
   B.   Providing a double bandwidth for each port/device when using full duplex
   C.   Providing multiple simultaneous conversations between devices on different ports
   D.   Providing a rate adaptation feature, this means that different Ethernet speed devices can communicate through a single switch.

6-22.   What are the functions of the layer-2 switching? (Select all that apply)

   A.   Address Decomposition
   B.   Source Address Learning
   C.   Frame Forward/Filter Decisions
   D.   Routing decisions
   E.   Frame Loop avoidance

6-23.   TRUE/FALSE: When a switch is powered ON, the MAC filtering table is empty.

   A.   TRUE
   B.   FALSE

6-24.   Try to decide if the following steps are correctly depicting the basic operation of a switch.

   A.   Correct
   B.   Incorrect

   Step1.   Power ON the switch. In this state, the MAC filtering table is empty
   Step2.   When a switch interface receives a frame from one device, the switch places the device source MAC address (SA) and the switch interface that the device located on in the MAC forward/filter table (MAC address table).
   Step3.   The switch then, floods the network (except the port that the source frame received from) with this frame because it has no idea on which interface the destination device is located.
   Step4.   If a destination device is found on the network, it will answer and send a frame back; then the switch will take the source MAC address from that frame and place this address with the interface that received the frame in the MAC forward/filter table.
   Step5.   The switch makes a point-to-point connection between the two devices, and the frames will only be forwarded between these two devices.
   Step6.   To keep the MAC address table as up-to-dated as possible, and if these two devices do not communicate through the switch after a certain period, the switch will flush the MAC table from the entries of these two devices.

6-25.   What is the difference between Layer-2 switches and hubs? (Select all that apply)

A. Switches forward all frames out all ports every time
B. Hubs forward all frames out all ports every time
C. Switches make a point-to-point connection, and the frames will only be forwarded between the source and destination devices.
D. Hubs make a point-to-point connection, and the frames will only be forwarded between the source and destination devices.

6-26. What does a switch do when a frame is received on an interface and the destination MAC address is unknown or not in switch MAC address table?

A. Drops the received frame
B. Floods the network with the frame looking for destination device
C. Forwards the switch to the first available link
D. Sends back a message to the originating station asking for a name resolution

6-27. What does a switch do with a multicast frame received on an interface?

A. Drops the received frame
B. Floods the network with the frame looking for destination device
C. Forwards the switch to the first available link
D. Sends back a message to the originating station asking for a name resolution

6-28. What does a switch do with a broadcast frame received on an interface?

A. Drops the received frame
B. Floods the network with the frame looking for destination device
C. Forwards the switch to the first available link
D. Sends back a message to the originating station asking for a name resolution

6-29. What will happen if Station 1 and Station 4 in Figure 6-1 are not communicating again through the switch within a certain amount of time?

A. The switch will update the entries frequently in the MAC address table to keep it as current as possible.
B. The switch will flush the entries from the MAC address table to keep it as up-to-dated as possible.
C. The switch will keep the entries in the MAC address table without changing.

6-30. After a point-to-point communication is established between Stations 1 and 4 in Figure 6-1, what will Stations 2 and 3 do to Stations 1 and 4's frames?

A. Station 2 and Station 3 will see all these frames.
B. Station 2 and Station 3 will not see these frames.
C. Station 2 and Station 3 will read all these frames.
D. Station 2 and Station 3 will manipulate all these frames.

6-31. In Figure 6-1, what is the complete content of the switch 's MAC address table?

A. E2: 0000.9E01.1111
   E1: 0000.9E01.2222
   E0: 0000.9E01.3333
   E3: 0000.9E01.4444
B. E1: 0000.9E01.1111

        E3: 0000.9E01.2222
        E0: 0000.9E01.3333
        E2: 0000.9E01.4444
    C. E0: 0000.9E01.1111
        E1: 0000.9E01.2222
        E2: 0000.9E01.3333
        E3: 0000.9E01.4444
    D. E3: 0000.9E01.1111
        E2: 0000.9E01.2222
        E1: 0000.9E01.3333
        E0: 0000.9E01.4444

6-32.   What does a switch do when a frame is received at a switch interface?

   A.   When a frame is received at a switch interface, the Source MAC address is compared with the forward/filter MAC address table.
   B.   When a frame is received at a switch interface, the interface MAC address is compared with the forward/filter MAC address table.
   C.   When a frame is received at a switch interface, nothing will be done.
   D.   When a frame is received at a switch interface, the destination MAC address is compared with the forward/filter MAC address table.

6-33.   If the destination MAC address for the incoming frame is known and listed in the MAC address table, where does the switch send this frame?

   A.   The switch does not transmit the frame out any interface except for the source interface.
   B.   The switch does not transmit the frame out any interface except for the destination interface.
   C.   The switch does not transmit the frame out any interface.
   D.   The switch does not transmit the frame out any interface except for the source and destination interface.

6-34.   The switch does not transmit incoming frames with known destination MAC addresses out any interfaces except for the destination addresses. What is the advantage from this feature?

   A.   This preserves bandwidth on the other network segments, and it is called Frame filtering.
   B.   This preserves the port numbers on the other network segments, and it is called frame filtering.
   C.   This preserves Station numbers on the other network segments, and it is called frame filtering.
   D.   This preserves the interface numbers on the other network segments, and it is called frame filtering.

6-35.   How the frame-filtering feature is implemented by the switch?

   A.   The switch does not transmit incoming frames with known destination MAC addresses out any interfaces except for the source interface. This preserves bandwidth on the other network segments, and it is called frame filtering.
   B.   The switch does not transmit incoming frames with known destination MAC addresses out any interfaces except for the source and destination interface. This preserves bandwidth on the other network segments, and it is called frame filtering.
   C.   The switch does not transmit incoming frames with known destination MAC addresses out any interfaces except for the destination addresses. This preserves bandwidth on the other network segments, and it is called frame filtering.
   D.   The switch does not transmit incoming frames with known destination MAC addresses out any interfaces. This preserves bandwidth on the other network segments, and it is called frame filtering.

6-36.   If the destination MAC address for the incoming frame is unknown and not listed in the MAC address table, where does the switch send this frame?

A.   The switch does broadcast the frame out all active interfaces.
B.   The switch does broadcast the frame out all active interfaces except the interface the frame was received on.
C.   The switch does not broadcast the frame out any interface.
D.   The switch does not broadcast the frame out all interfaces except the interface the frame was received on.

6-37.   If the destination MAC address for the incoming frame is unknown and not listed in the MAC address table, the switch broadcasts the frame out all active interfaces except the interface the frame was received on. What will the switch do when a device answers the broadcast?

A.   The switch updates the MAC address table with the device interface and starts a point-to-point communication between the two devices.
B.   The switch updates the MAC address table with the device IP address and starts a point-to-point communication between the two devices.
C.   The switch updates the MAC address table with the device logical name and starts a point-to-point communication between the two devices.
D.   The switch updates the MAC address table with the device Virtual address and starts a point-to-point communication between the two devices.

6-38.   If the destination MAC address for the incoming frame is unknown and not listed in the MAC address table, the switch broadcasts the frame out all active interfaces except the interface the frame was received on. What will the switch do when no device answers the broadcast?

A.   The switch broadcasts the frame again out of all active interfaces.
B.   The switch broadcasts the frame again out of all active interfaces except the interface the frame was received on.
C.   The switch neglects the frame.
D.   The switch broadcasts the frame again out of all interfaces except the interface the frame was received on.

6-39.   Which device looks up the frame's destination in an address table and sends the frame to the destination host?

A.   Router
B.   Switch
C.   Repeater
D.   Hub

6-40.   Which of the following is an advantage for using the redundant links between the switches? (Select all that apply)

A.   Redundant links are used in the switching network to help stop complete network failures if one link fails.
B.   Redundant links are used in the switching network to help stop complete network maintenance.
C.   Redundant links are used in the switching network to help stop complete network support.
D.   Redundant links are used in the switching network to provide some kind of fault tolerance.

6-41.   TRUE/FALSE: Although redundant links are useful in the switching network, they cause problems in the network.

A.   TRUE
B.   FALSE

6-42.   Try to decide which option gets in which blank.
Because frames can be _____ down all the redundant links simultaneously, network _____ problem can occur.

A.   loops
B.   broadcast

6-43.   What are the most serious problems that have been caused by the redundant links if no loop avoidance schemes are used? (Select all that apply)

A.   The switches will flood broadcasts without limits throughout the internetwork. This sometimes referred to as a **broadcast storm**.
B.   Multiple copies of the same frame can be received by a device since the frame can arrive from different segments at the same time.
C.   Since the switch can receive the frame from more than one link, the MAC address forward/filter table will be confused about where a device is located. Sometimes the switch cannot forward a frame because it is constantly updating the MAC MAC address table with source MAC address locations. This is called **thrashing** the MAC table.
D.   Multiple loops generating throughout a network is one of the biggest problems. This means that loops can occur within other loops. If the broadcast storm is occurred, the network would not be able to perform frame switching.

6-44.   In Figure 6-2, if a frame is continually broadcasted through the internetwork, what this occasion is called? (Assume that no loops avoidance schemes are provided.)

A.   This occasion is called "network competition."
B.   This occasion is called "network cognition."
C.   This occasion is called "network flooding."
D.   This occasion is called "broadcast storms."

6-45.   Figure 6-3 shows a switched network with redundant links. What will happen to Router A? (Assume that no loops avoidance schemes are provided.)

A.   Router A will receive multiple copies of the same frame.
B.   Router A will receive multicast messages.
C.   Router A will receive Unicat message from the server only.
D.   Router A will receive broadcast messages.

6-46.   In a switched network with redundant links and no loops avoidance schemes are provided, what will happen if the switch received the frame from more than one link?

A.   The switch can forward the frame.
B.   The switch cannot forward the frame.
C.   The switch can refuse the frame.
D.   The switch cannot refuse the frame.

6-47.   In a switched network with redundant links and no loop avoidance schemes are provided. If the switch cannot forward a frame because it is constantly updating the MAC filter table with source hardware address locations, what this occasion is called?

A. This occasion is called "thrashing the MAC table."
B. This occasion is called "removing the MAC table."
C. This occasion is called "zeroing the MAC table."
D. This occasion is called "addressing the MAC table"

6-48.   Try to decide which option gets in which blank.
If a _____ are generating throughout an internetwork, and the broadcast storm is occurred, the network would not be able to perform _____.

A. multiple loops
B. frame switching

6-49.   Which are the two reasons that can make the switch unable to perform frame switching? (Select all that apply)

A. Filtering the MAC table
B. Multiple loops generated throughout an internetwork.
C. Broadcast storms
D. Refreshing the MAC table

6-50.   What is the main task of the STP in a meshed network?

A. The main task of STP is to provide routing management in multiple links Layer-2 switching network.
B. The main task of STP is to prevent loops in multiple links Layer-2 switching network.
C. The main task of STP is to prevent routing in multiple links Layer-2 switching network.
D. The main task of STP is to provide path management in multiple links Layer-2 switching network.

6-51.   Which IEEE specification will describe the Spanning Tree Algorithm?

A. 802.1q
B. 802.1u
C. 802.1d
D. 803.2u

6-52.   Which STP specifications are adopted by CISCO switches?

A. All CISCO switches run the DEC version of STP.
B. All CISCO switches run the IEEE 802.1d version of STP.
C. All CISCO switches run the CISCO version of STP.

6-53.   Which of the following is used to prevent loops and ensure data flows through a single network path in a Catalyst switched network environment?

A. Dijkstra Algorithm
B. Spanning Tree Protocol
C. Split Horizon
D. Forward Fragment Latency

6-54.   What is the purpose of the **Spanning Tree Algorithm**? (Select all that apply)

A. To keep routing updates from being transmitted onto the same port on which they were received.
B. To stop network loops from occurring on Layer-2 network.
C. To monitor the network, find all links, and make sure that loops do not occur by shutting down redundant links.

    D.   To discover a "loop free" topology and provide, as possible, a path between every pair of LAN's

6-55.   What protocol is used at layer 2 to help stopping the switched network loops?

    A.   VLANs
    B.   BPDUs
    C.   STP
    D.   RIP

6-56.   How STP ensures that loops do not occur in the mashed network? (Select all that apply)

    A.   STP monitors the network and finds all links.
    B.   STP shuts down the redundant links.
    C.   STP provides the redundant links.
    D.   STP supports the redundant links.

6-57.   How the following duty is implemented by STP? "STP finds all links in the network, shuts down redundant links, and stops any network loops from occurring in the network."

    A.   Electing a root bridge that will decide on the network topology.
    B.   Arranging the network topology
    C.   Distributing the network topology
    D.   Managing the network topology

6-58.   How many root bridges can be found on STP network?

    A.   2
    B.   3
    C.   1
    D.   0

6-59.   In a network with 10 of switches, how many root bridges are found?

    A.   1
    B.   3
    C.   5
    D.   10

6-60.   What are the names of the Root Bridge ports?

    A.   Root Bridge's ports are called Nonroot ports.
    B.   Root Bridge's ports are called Nondesignated ports.
    C.   Root Bridge's ports are called root ports.
    D.   Root Bridge's ports are called designated ports.

6-61.   What is the operational state of the designated ports?

    A.   The designated ports operate in Blocking State.
    B.   The designated ports operate in Forwarding State.
    C.   The designated ports operate in Pending State.
    D.   The designated ports operate in Stopping State.

6-62.   Try to select the correct option to fill the blank.

Forwarding state ports can _____.

A.   Send traffic only
B.   Receive traffic only
C.   Send and Receive traffic
D.   Do nothing

6-63.   In STP network, there is only one Root Bridge. What is the name of other switches in the network?

A.   Other switches are called network bridges.
B.   Other switches are called network switches.
C.   Other switches are called nonroot bridges.
D.   Other switches are called root bridges.

6-64.   Try to decide which option gets in which blank.
Nonroot bridge ports can be categorized into _____ and _____.

A.   Root port (designated port)
B.   Nondesignated port

6-65.   Which rule is used to select the root port in Figure 6-4?

A.   Root port is selected using the Highest cost path to root bridge rule (as determined by a link's bandwidth).
B.   Root port is selected using the Lowest cost path to root bridge rule (as determined by a link's bandwidth).
C.   Root port is selected using the Highest cost path to root bridge rule (as determined by a link's length).
D.   Root port is selected using the Lowest cost path to root bridge rule (as determined by a link's length).

6-66.   Try to select the correct option to fill the blank.
Root port in Nonroot bridges can _____.

A.   Send and Receive traffic
B.   Send traffic only
C.   Receive traffic only
D.   Do nothing

6-67.   What is the operational state for the nondesignated ports?

A.   The nondesignated ports operate in Blocking State.
B.   The nondesignated ports operate in Forwarding State.
C.   The nondesignated ports operate in Pending State.
D.   The nondesignated ports operate in Stopping State.

6-68.   Try to select the correct option to fill the blank.
Blocking state ports can _____.

A.   Send traffic only
B.   Receive traffic only
C.   Send and Receive traffic
D.   Not Send or Receive traffic

6-69.   Try to select the correct option to fill the blank.

Nondesignated ports can _____.

A.   Not Send or Receive traffic
B.   Receive traffic only
C.   Send and Receive traffic
D.   Send traffic only

6-70.   How many types of switches are in the STP network?

A.   One
B.   Two
C.   Three
D.   Four

6-71.   Which of the following is a type of a switch in the STP networks? (Select all that apply)

A.   Nonroot bridges
B.   Root bridge
C.   Designated bridges
D.   Nondesignated bridges

6-72.   How many types of switch's ports are in the STP network?

A.   One
B.   Two
C.   Three
D.   Four

6-73.   Which of the following is a type of a switch's port in the STP network? (Select all that apply)

A.   Nonroot port
B.   Root port
C.   Designated port
D.   Nondesignated port

6-74.   TRUE/FALSE: Switches/bridges can exchange information between them.

A.   TRUE
B.   FALSE

6-75.   How Switches/bridges can exchange information between them?

A.   Switches/bridges exchange information between them using Packet Data Units (PDUs).
B.   Switches/bridges exchange information between them using Bridge Protocol Data Units (BPDUs).
C.   Switches/bridges exchange information between them using Bridge Data Units (BDUs).
D.   Switches/bridges exchange information between them using Data Units (DUs).
E.   Switches/bridges exchange information between them using Bridge Packet Data Units (BPDUs).

6-76.   What is true about BPDUs?

A.   They are used to send configuration messages using IPX messages.
B.   They are used to send configuration messages using DECnet messages.
C.   They are only used to set the bridge ID of a switch.

D.   They are used to send configuration messages using multicast frames.

6-77.   How bridge ID of a switch is sent to neighboring switches?

A.   Broadcasts during convergence times
B.   Bridge Packet Data Units
C.   STP
D.   BPDU

6-78.   What is the using of the bridge ID? (Select all that apply)

A.   Bridge ID is used to determine the Root Bridge.
B.   Bridge ID is used to determine the root port.
C.   Bridge ID is used to determine the nonroot bridge.
D.   Bridge ID is used to determine the nonroot port.

6-79.   Try to select the correct option to fill the blanks.
The bridge ID is _____ long and includes the _____ and the _____ of the device.

A.   MAC address
B.   Priority
C.   8 bytes
D.   IP address

6-80.   What is the default priority on all devices running the IEEE STP?

A.   32,768
B.   1
C.   0
D.   32,767

6-81.   Which of the following is used to determine the Root Bridge in a network? (Select all that apply)

A.   MAC address
B.   IP address
C.   Bandwidth of the links
D.   Priority

6-82.   Which rule is used to select the Root Bridge in the STP network?

A.   Root Bridge is selected using the highest Bridge ID (Priority + MAC address).
B.   Root Bridge is selected using the lowest Bridge ID (Priority + MAC address).
C.   Root Bridge is selected using the highest cost path.
D.   Root Bridge is selected using the lowest cost path.

6-83.   In Figure 6-5, which switch should be selected as a root bridge in STP network (Assume that both switches have the same priority = 32,768)?

A.   Switch A
B.   Switch B

6-84.   What is the time that a switch will need to send BPDUs through STP network?

A.   Every 4 seconds by default
B.   Every 3 seconds by default
C.   Every 2 seconds by default
D.   Every 1 second by default

6-85.   Which port is select as the root port in a Nonroot bridge?

A.   Any active port
B.   Any FastEthernet port
C.   The port with the lowest cost to the root bridge
D.   The port with the highest cost to the root bridge

6-86.   How often BPDUs are sent from a layer-2 device?

A.   Every 3 seconds
B.   Every 2 seconds
C.   Every 1 second
D.   Never

6-87.   TRUE/FALSE: A Designated Port is determined on the path cost communication to the root bridge.

A.   TRUE
B.   FALSE

6-88.   Try to decide which option gets in which blank.
The Port cost is _____ total path cost based on the _____ of the links.

A.   bandwidth
B.   an accumulated

6-89.   What are the new and the Original IEEE typical cost path for 10Gbps Ethernet network?

A.   0,0
B.   1,1
C.   2,1
D.   1,2

6-90.   What are the new and the Original IEEE typical cost path for 1Gbps Ethernet network?

A.   4,1
B.   1,1
C.   2,2
D.   4,2

6-91.   What are the new and the Original IEEE typical cost path for 100Mbps Ethernet network?

A.   19,19
B.   19,10
C.   19,11
D.   10,19

6-92.   What are the new and the Original IEEE typical cost path for 10Mbps Ethernet network?

A. 100,200
B. 200,100
C. 10,10
D. 100,100

6-93. What IEEE path cost specification does 2960-switch use?

A. New IEEE path cost
B. Original IEEE path cost 802.1d

6-94. What are the five port states of a STP switch? (Select all that apply)

A. Learning
B. Gathering
C. Listened
D. Listening
E. Forwarding
F. Blocking
G. Disabled

6-95.
1. Which of the following is true about the **blocking state** of the STP switch?
2. Which of the following is true about the **Listening State** of the STP switch?
3. Which of the following is true about the **Learning State** of the STP switch?
4. Which of the following is true about the **Forwarding State** of the STP switch?
5. Which of the following is true about the **Disabled State** of the STP switch?

A. The switches in this state do not forward frames; they listen to and receive BPDUs. By default, all ports are in this state when the switch is powered UP.
B. The switches in this state listen to BPDU to make sure that there are no loops have been occurred on the network before passing data frames.
C. The switches in this state learn MAC addresses and build a filter table but do not forward frames.
D. The switches in this state send and receive all data on the bridged port.
E. The switches in this state (administratively) do not participate in the frame forwarding or STP. A port in the disabled state is virtually nonoperational.

6-96. What are the typical port states of a STP switch?

A. Learning
B. Gathering
C. Listened
D. Listening
E. Forwarding
F. Blocking

6-97. Which rule is used to select the forwarding port?

A. Forwarding port has determined to have the lowest cost path to Root Bridge.
B. Forwarding port has determined to have the highest cost path to Root Bridge.
C. Forwarding port has determined to have the lowest length to Root Bridge.
D. Forwarding port has determined to have the highest length to Root Bridge.

6-98. When the switch ports will be in listening or learning states? (Select all that apply)

    A.   During network topology changes
    B.   During adding a new switch to the network
    C.   During failed links
    D.   During the network shutdown state

6-99.   What will happen after a switch determines the best path to the Root Bridge and selects the forwarding port?

    A.   All other ports are put in the listening state.
    B.   All other ports are put in the learning state.
    C.   All other ports are put in the forwarding state.
    D.   All other ports are put in the blocking state.

6-100.   TRUE/FALSE: Blocked ports cannot receive BPDUs.

    A.   TRUE
    B.   FALSE

6-101.   What will happen after a switch determines that a blocked port should now be the designated port?

    A.   The port will go to listening state.
    B.   The port will go to learning state.
    C.   The port will go to forwarding state.
    D.   The port will go to blocking state.

6-102.   What is true about blocking state of a STP switch port? (Select all that apply)

    A.   Blocking ports do not forward or receive any frames.
    B.   Blocking ports forward all types of the frames
    C.   Blocking ports receive and listen for BPDUs.
    D.   Blocking ports do not listen for BPDUs.

6-103.   When the switch is powered ON, what is the port state?

    A.   Learning
    B.   Gathering
    C.   Listened
    D.   Listening
    E.   Forwarding
    F.   Blocking

6-104.   Which states indicate that a port will be unable to send and receive data frames? (Select all that apply)

    A.   Learning
    B.   Gathering
    C.   Listened
    D.   Listening
    E.   Forwarding
    F.   Blocking

6-105.   Which states indicate that a port will be able to listen to and receive BPDUs? (Select all that apply)

    A.   Learning

B.   Gathering
C.   Listened
D.   Listening
E.   Forwarding
F.   Blocking

6-106.   Which states indicate that a port will be able to listen to BPDU and to make sure no loops occur on the network before passing data frames? (Select all that apply)

A.   Learning
B.   Gathering
C.   Listened
D.   Listening
E.   Forwarding
F.   Blocking

6-107.   Which states indicate that a port will be able to learn MAC addresses and build a filter table? (Select all that apply)

A.   Learning
B.   Gathering
C.   Listened
D.   Listening
E.   Forwarding
F.   Blocking

6-108.   Which states indicate that a port will be able to send and receive all data on the bridged port? (Select all that apply)

A.   Learning
B.   Gathering
C.   Listened
D.   Listening
E.   Forwarding
F.   Blocking

6-109.   What is the convergence?

A.   Convergence is the time it takes a bridge in the STP network to transition to either the forwarding or blocking states.
B.   Convergence is the time it takes a bridge in the STP network to transition to either the listening or blocking states.
C.   Convergence is the time it takes a bridge in the STP network to transition to either the forwarding or listening states.
D.   Convergence is the time it takes a bridge in the STP network to transition to either the learning or blocking states.

6-110.   In STP networks, when convergence period is occurred?

A.   During transitioned to either the listening or blocking states.
B.   During transitioned to either the forwarding or blocking states.
C.   During transitioned to either the forwarding or listening states.
D.   During transitioned to either the learning or blocking states.

6-111.   TRUE/FALSE: No data is forwarded during the convergence time.

A.   TRUE
B.   FALSE

6-112.   Why convergence is important in the STP network?

A.   To make sure that all devices are operated
B.   To make sure that all devices are not operated
C.   To make sure that all devices have the same MAC address table.
D.   To make sure that not all devices have the same MAC address table.

6-113.   What is the main problem with the convergence?

A.   The time it takes devices to update
B.   The time it takes devices to run
C.   The time it takes devices to stop

6-114.   How much update time the convergence takes?

A.   It takes 5 seconds to go from blocking to forwarding state.
B.   It takes 50 seconds to go from blocking to forwarding state.
C.   It takes 150 seconds to go from blocking to forwarding state.
D.   It takes 55 seconds to go from blocking to forwarding state.

6-115.   What is a Forward delay?

A.   A time it takes to transition a port from blocking to learning state or from learning to forwarding state.
B.   It is the time it takes to transition a port from listening to blocking state or from learning to forwarding state.
C.   A time it takes to transition a port from listening to learning state or from forwarding to learning state.
D.   A time it takes to transition a port from listening to learning state or from learning to forwarding state.

6-116.   What is the typical time a switch port will go from blocking to forwarding state?

A.   5 seconds
B.   10 seconds
C.   50 seconds
D.   55 seconds

6-117.   Try to decide which option gets in which blank.
The _____ for packet switching through the switch depends on the chosen of the _____.

A.   Latency
B.   Switching mode

6-118.   What are the primary switching modes? (Select all that apply)

A.   Store and receive
B.   Cut-through
C.   FragmentFree
D.   Store and forward.

6-119.
1. What is correct about the **Store and forward** switching modes?
2. What is correct about the **cut-through** (Real Time) switching modes?
3. What is correct about the **FragmentFree** switching modes?

    A. After receiving the complete data frame on the switch's buffer, a CRC is run, and then the destination address is looked up in the MAC address table.
    B. The switch only waits for the destination MAC address to be received and then looks up the destination address in the MAC address table.
    C. It is the default for the CAT2.96K switch. It checks the first 64 bytes of a frame for fragmentation (because of possible collisions) before forwarding the frame. It is sometimes referred to as "modified cut-through."

6-120. Which LAN switching mode waits for the destination addresses and checks the filter table?

    A. Cut-and-forward
    B. Cut-Through
    C. Store-and Forward
    D. Store-Through
    E. FragmentFree

6-121. Which LAN switching mode runs a CRC on every frame?

    A. Cut-and-forward
    B. Cut-Through
    C. Store-and-Forward
    D. Store-Through
    E. FragmentFree

6-122. Which LAN switching mode has the highest latency of any LAN switch type?

    A. Cut-and-forward
    B. Cut-Through
    C. Store-and-Forward
    D. Store-Through
    E. FragmentFree

6-123. Which LAN switching mode only checks the destination hardware address before forwarding a frame?

    A. Cut-and-forward
    B. Cut-Through
    C. Store-and-Forward
    D. Store-Through
    E. FragmentFree

6-124. Which LAN switching mode has the lowest latency of any LAN switch type?

    A. Cut-and-forward
    B. Cut-Through
    C. Store-and-Forward
    D. Store-Through
    E. FragmentFree

6-125.   Which LAN switching mode has no error checking?

    A.   Cut-and-forward
    B.   Cut-Through
    C.   Store-and-Forward
    D.   Store-Through
    E.   FragmentFree

6-126.   Which of the following LAN switching modes can filter all errors?

    A.   Cut-and-forward
    B.   Cut-Through
    C.   Store-and-Forward
    D.   Store-Through
    E.   FragmentFree

6-127.   Which of the following LAN switching modes can check only for collisions?

    A.   Cut-and-forward
    B.   Cut-Through
    C.   Store-and-Forward
    D.   Store-Through
    E.   FragmentFree

6-128.   What is the default LAN switching mode on a CAT2.96K switch?

    A.   Cut-and-forward
    B.   Cut-Through
    C.   Store-and-Forward
    D.   Store-Through
    E.   FragmentFree

6-129.   TRUE/FALSE: The CAT2.96K switch can use the store-and-forward switching mode in addition to the Fragment Free mode.

    A.   TRUE
    B.   FALSE

6-130.   Where the different switching modes are taken place on the frame shown in Figure 6-7-1?

Figure 6-7-1 The Switching Modes Location on a MAC Data Frame

IEEE 802.3 Revised 1997

	PRE 7	SFD 1	DA 6	SA 6	L/T 2	D&P 46-1500	FCS 4
Bytes							

6-131.   Which LAN switching modes are included in a CAT2.96K switch?

    A.   FragmentFree
    B.   Cut-Through
    C.   Store and Forward

6-132.   Which LAN switching mode checks the frame to see if it is too short (runt - less than 64 bytes including the CRC), or if it is too long (giant - more than 1518 bytes including the CRC)?

    A.   Cut-and-forward
    B.   Cut-Through
    C.   Store-and-Forward
    D.   Store-Through
    E.   FragmentFree

6-133.   What are the characteristics of the store-and-forward switching mode? (Select all that apply)

    A.   Frames with errors are discarded.
    B.   It has the highest latency than the FragmentFree and Cut-through modes.
    C.   The CRC is computed after the frame is copied to the switch's buffer.
    D.   The frame is discarded if it is a runt or a giant.
    E.   Only the destination address is copied into the switch's buffer before the frame is forwarded to its destination.
    F.   It waits for the collision window to overtake before looking up the destination hardware address in the MAC filter table and forwarding the frame.

6-134.   TRUE/FALSE: Some switches can be configured to perform cut-through switching on a per-port basis until a user-defined error threshold is reached.

    A.   TRUE
    B.   FALSE

6-135.   Which LAN switching mode waits for the collision window to overtake before looking up the destination hardware address in the MAC filter table and forwarding the frame?

    A.   Cut-and-forward
    B.   Cut-Through
    C.   Store-and-Forward
    D.   Store-Through
    E.   FragmentFree

6-136.   Which LAN switching mode has a variable latency time?

    A.   Cut-and-forward
    B.   Cut-Through
    C.   Store-and-Forward
    D.   Store-Through
    E.   FragmentFree

6-137.   Which LAN switching mode keeps CRC errors to a minimum but still has a fixed latency rate?

    A.   Cut-and-forward
    B.   Cut-Through
    C.   Store-and-Forward
    D.   Store-Through
    E.   FragmentFree

6-138.   Which LAN switching mode has a fixed latency time? (Select all that apply)

    A.   Cut-and-forward

B.   Cut-Through
C.   Store-and-Forward
D.   Store-Through
E.   FragmentFree

6-139.   Which of the following is true about VLANs? (Select all that apply)

A.   VLAN is a virtual configuration tool in the LAN switch to segment the LAN, based on broadcast domains or generally, to segment one broadcast domain into multiply domains.
B.   By default, a LAN switch put all switch's interfaces into one broadcast domain-the default VLAN 1.
C.   Without VLAN configuration, LAN consists of all devices in that broadcast domain.
D.   With VLANs, a switch can put some interfaces into one broadcast domain and some into another based on some simple configuration, so a LAN switch can create multiply broadcast domains. These individual broadcast domains created by the switch are called VLANs.

6-140.   Which of the following is a feature that can be added to the network by defining the VLANs? (Select all that apply)

A.   Virtually grouping network users instead of physical location grouping
B.   Segmenting large broadcast domains into multiply smaller ones to reduce overhead caused by broadcasts in the network.
C.   Securing sensitive data on servers by putting the servers on a separate VLAN
D.   Separating IP phone traffic (and other important traffics) from traffics sent by PCs connected to the phones to enhance the performance of Voice over IP.
E.   Reducing the workload for STP by limiting a VLAN to a single access switch

6-141.   TRUE/FALSE: When LAN is extended to support large number of clients in one larger building, or in multiple buildings (close proximity to one another), this LAN is called campus LAN. A campus LAN is created by connecting several switches in each building together, and then connecting the switches (usually the Core switches) in the buildings by Ethernet links.

A.   TRUE
B.   FALSE

6-142.   Which of the following considerations must be taken when designing a campus LAN? (Select all that apply)

A.   The number of clients
B.   The types of Ethernet available
C.   The cabling lengths and types supported by each Ethernet type.
D.   The speeds required for each Ethernet segment.
E.   The function of each switch in the network (Access, Distribution, or Core)
F.   The type of the present network equipments and the cost of development this network

6-143.   TRUE/FALSE: A campus design based CISCO equipments uses access, distribution, and core terms to describe the function of each switch in a campus. To select the suitable switch, its function must be one of the following:

▪   Connecting end-user devices, an access switch must be selected.
▪   Connecting multiple different switches in a campus, a distribution or core switch must be selected.

A.   TRUE
B.   FALSE

6-144.   Match each role of the campus switches to its suitable description.

1.   Distribution
2.   Access
3.   Core

A.   It connects end-user devices and it should not be used to connect other access switches, as shown in Figure 6-10.
B.   It connects access switches together, and it should not be used to connect directly end-user devices. For redundancy, at least two uplinks to two different distribution switches are used to connect each access switch, as shown in Figure 6-10. Usually, distribution switches have faster forwarding rate capability than access switches.
C.   It connects distribution switches together in very large campus LANs to provide very high forwarding rates and should not be used to connect directly end-user devices or access switches. Usually, core switches have the fastest forwarding rates' capability than access switches and distribution switches.

6-145.   Which of the following supports a maximum cable length of longer than 100 meters? (Select all that apply)

A.   100BASE-FX
B.   100BASE-TX
C.   1000BASE-SX
D.   1000BASE-CX
E.   1000BASE-T
F.   1000BASE-LX

6-146.   TRUE/FALSE: Fiber-optic cables are used for Ethernet to support longer distances, higher data rates transmission, and better transmission quality. Optical cables include very-thin glass through which light can flow, whereas UTP cables include copper wires over which electrical signals can flow. The switches that support the optical transmission can send bits, by alternating between sending brighter and dimmer light to encode 0s and 1s on the cable.

A.   TRUE
B.   FALSE

6-147.   Which of the following features is provided by using Optical cables in the Ethernet? (Select all that apply)

A.   Supporting much longer distances than the 100 meters supported by UTP Ethernet.
B.   Supporting better transmission quality, since optical cables are less interference from outside sources as compared to copper cables.
C.   Supporting longer distances, up to 100 kms, at higher cost when using Laser, and up to hundred of meters when using less-expensive light-emitting diodes (LEDs)

6-148.   Which of the following is a type of optical cable that can be used in the Ethernet? (Select all that apply)

A.   Multimode fiber supports shorter distances, cheaper cabling, and working fine with less-expensive LEDs.
B.   Singlemode fiber supports the longest distances, more expensive and working fine with Laser. In addition, the switches that support this type is much expensive than those which use the first type.

6-149.   Try to decide if the following paragraph is true or false.

    A.   TRUE
    B.   FALSE

"The default settings for CISCO Catalyst switches make it possible to work by only power ON the switch by connecting the power cable to the switch and a power outlet, and connect hosts to the switch using the correct UTP cables."

6-150.   Try to decide which option gets in which blank.

However, connecting to switch's user interface is essential for doing crucial jobs such as; checking on the _____, looking at information about what the switch is _____, configuring specific features of the switch and enabling _____.

    A.   switch's status
    B.   doing
    C.   security features

6-151.   Try to decide if the following paragraph is true or false.

"Users look to the CLI as a text-based interface in which they can enter a text command and then presses **Enter** key, which sends the command to the switch for telling the switch what to do. What the command requires, the switch will do, and the switch will reply with some messages stating the results of the command."

    A.   TRUE
    B.   FALSE

6-152.   TRUE/FALSE: To access the CLI interface of the switch, either use a rollover cable to connect to console port or use a straight through cable to connect to any interface in the switch after configuring that interface with an IP address and other required parameters, just like in CISCO routers.

    A.   TRUE
    B.   FALSE

6-153.   TRUE/FALSE: To connect to the console port, Hyper-terminal emulator software can be used to access the CLI of the switch in Windows based machines. The emulator must be configured to use the PC's serial port, matching the switch's console port settings.

    A.   TRUE
    B.   FALSE

6-154.   Which of the following is a default console port setting on a switch? (Select all that apply)

    A.   9600 bits/second
    B.   No hardware flow control
    C.   8-bit ASCII
    D.   No stop bits
    E.   1 parity bit

6-155.   Which of the following is true about CISCO CAT2.96K switch?

    A.   CISCO introduces the 2960 series of switches as full-featured, low-cost wiring closet switches for the large networks.
    B.   Usually the 2960 switch is used as an access switch for the large networks, and it is capable of

connect to the rest of the network (distribution layer) using the uplinks.

C.   In addition, this family uses IOS as an operating system not Cat OS as some CISCO switches use.

6-156.   Which of the following is true about CAT2.96K switch ports?

A.   In CISCO switches, the physical connectors are called either **interfaces** or **ports**. Each port has a number in the style x/y, where x refers to slot number and y refers to the port number within the slot, just like in CISCO routers.

B.   On a 2960, the x is always 0 since this switch is considered as only one slot or without slots. The first 10/100 interface on a 2960 is numbered starting at 0/1; the second is 0/2, and so on.

C.   The interfaces also have names; for example, "interface FastEthernet 0/2" is the second of the 10/100 interfaces. Any Gigabit interfaces would be called "GigabitEthernet" interfaces. For example, the second 10/100/1000 interface on a 2960 would be "interface gigabitethernet 0/2."

6-157.   TRUE/FALSE: In addition to the using of commands from the CISCO IOS CLI to check how a switch is working, verify its current status, and troubleshoot any problems, which may be taking a long period of time, several LEDs on the switch can be used for these purposes..

A.   TRUE
B.   FALSE

6-158.   Try to decide which option gets in which blank.
The front of CISCO Cat2.96K switch has _____ over each physical Ethernet interface and _____ on the left, and a mode button.

A.   five LEDs
B.   one LED

6-159.   Match each of the following LED name to its suitable description.

1.   SYST (system)
2.   RPS (Redundant Power Supply)
3.   STAT (Status)
4.   DUPLX (duplex)
5.   SPEED

A.   It indicates the overall system status.
B.   It indicates the status of the redundant power supply.
C.   If it is ON (green), indicates that each port LED implies that port's status.
D.   If it is ON (green), indicates each port LED implies that port's duplex (ON/green=Full-Duplex; OFF=Half-Duplex)
E.   If it is ON (green), indicates each port LED implies the speed of that port, as follows: OFF means 10 Mbps, solid green means 100 Mbps, and flashing green means 1 Gbps.

6-160.   The SYST LED provides a quick overall status of the switch, Which of the following different states is provided? (Select all that apply)

A.   **OFF:** The switch is powered OFF.
B.   **ON (green):** The switch is powered ON and in the normal operational state (CISCO IOS has been loaded)
C.   **ON (amber):** The switch's Power-On Self Test (POST) process failed, and the CISCO IOS is not loaded.

6-161. TRUE/FALSE: The immediate response to the **ON (amber)** state is to power the switch OFF and back on again. If the problem is not solved, a call to the local CISCO partners or CISCO Technical Assistance Center (TAC) is typically the next step.

    A.   TRUE
    B.   FALSE

6-162. TRUE/FALSE: A mode button when pressed, cycles the port LEDs through three modes: STAT, DUPLX, and SPEED. The current port LED mode is signified by a solid green STAT, DUPLX, or SPEED LEDs in the left of the front panel of the switch.

    A.   TRUE
    B.   FALSE

6-163. TRUE/FALSE: The meaning of the interface LED that is sitting above or below each Ethernet port is different depending on which of three ports LED modes is currently used on the switch.

    A.   TRUE
    B.   FALSE

6-164. For example, in STAT (status) mode, each port LED provides status information about that port. Which of the following status it provides? (Select all that apply)

    A.   **OFF:** The link is OFF (not working).
    B.   **Solid green:** The link is ON (working, with no current traffic).
    C.   **Flashing green:** The link is ON (working, with traffic is currently passing over the interface).
    D.   **Flashing amber:** The interface is OFF (administratively disabled or has been dynamically disabled for a variety of reasons.)

6-165. TRUE/FALSE: In SPEED port LED mode, the port LEDs provide the operating speed of the interface, as follows:

- **Dark:** 10 Mbps
- **Solid green:** 100 Mbps
- **Flashing green:** 1000 Mbps (1 Gbps)

    A.   TRUE
    B.   FALSE

6-166. TRUE/FALSE: In DUPLX port LED mode, the port LEDs provide the mode of operating of the interface, either Full-duplex or Half-duplex.

    A.   TRUE
    B.   FALSE

6-167. TRUE/FALSE: When the IEEE autonegotiation process is enabled on a switch port and on a host, both devices agree to the fastest speed supported by both devices and the mode will be selected as either full duplex if it is supported by both devices, or half duplex if it is not.

    A.   TRUE
    B.   FALSE

6-168. TRUE/FALSE: When autonegotiation is disabled on one device and the other device uses autonegotiation, the device using autonegotiation chooses the default duplex mode setting based on the current speed. The defaults are as follows:

- 10 Mbps, half duplex, if the speed is not known
- half duplex, if the speed is known to be 10 or 100 Mbps
- full duplex, if the speed is known to be 1000 Mbps
- full duplex, if the speed is known to be faster than 1 Gbps

    A.   TRUE
    B.   FALSE

6-169.   Which of the following is true regarding the way that can be used to disable IEEE standard autonegotiation on a 10/100/1000 port on a CISCO CAT2.69K switch?

    A.   Use the disable auto-negotiate interface subcommand.
    B.   Configure the speed 1000 and full-duplex interface subcommands.
    C.   Use the not negotiate interface subcommand.

6-170.   Match each of the following Interface status to its suitable Line and Protocol status combinations.
    1.   Disabled
    2.   Notconnect
    3.   err-disabled
    4.   connect

    A.   Administratively Down/Down
    B.   Down/Down
    C.   Up/Down
    D.   Down/Down(err-disabled)
    E.   UP/UP

6-171.   Match each of the following interface status to its suitable reasons.

    1.   disabled
    2.   notconnect
    3.   err-disabled
    4.   connect

    A.   The interface is configured with the **shutdown** command.
    B.   No cable; bad cable; wrong cable pinouts; the speeds are mismatched on the two connected devices; the device on the other end of the cable is powered OFF or the other interface is **shutdown**.
    C.   An interface up/down state is not expected on LAN switch interfaces.
    D.   Port security has disabled the interface.
    E.   The interface is working.

6-172.   Which of the following is true about interface Fa0/2 if the output of the show interfaces status command indicates that interface Fa0/2 in a "disabled" state? (Select all that apply)

    A.   Interface Fa0/2 is configured with the shutdown command.
    B.   The show interfaces Fa0/2 command will list the interface with two status codes of administratively down and down.
    C.   The show interfaces Fa0/2 command will list the interface with two status codes of up and up.
    D.   Currently interface Fa0/2 cannot be connected by network.

E.   Currently interface Fa0/2 can be connected by network.
F.   Currently interface Fa0/2 cannot be used to forward frames.
G.   Currently interface Fa0/2 can be used to forward frames.

6-173.   TRUE/FALSE: When the ENTER key is pressed after the commands, the switch enters the command in a history buffer, storing ten commands by default. Several key sequences can be used to move backward and forward in the historical list of commands and then edit the command before re-issuing it.

A.   TRUE
B.   FALSE

6-174.   What command statement is used to backup the configuration from RAM into NVRAM?

A.   copy run-config start-config
B.   copy tftp run-config
C.   copy run-config tftp

6-175.   Try to decide if the following paragraph is true or false.

"SSH is the preferred method for remote login to switches and routers today, since SSH encrypts all the data sent between the SSH client and the SSH server (Telnet sends all data, including all passwords entered by the user, as clear text)."

A.   TRUE
B.   FALSE

6-176.   Try to decide which option gets in which blank.

SSH requires that the user supply both a _____ and _____ instead of just a password.

A.   username
B.   password

6-177.   Try to decide which option gets in which blank.

The switch can be configured to use authentication on an _____ called an Authentication, Authorization, and Accounting (AAA) server or the authentication configured on a _____.

A.   external server
B.   switch itself

6-178.   Which of the following commands is used to tell the switch to use the local authentication?

A.   login locally
B.   login local
C.   login localized

6-179.   Which of the following commands is used to tell the switch to accept only ssh connections?

A.   transport input telnet ssh
B.   transport input telnet
C.   transport input ssh

6-180.   Which of the following commands is used to tell the switch to generate a matched public and private key pair, as well as a shared encryption key?

A.   crypto key generate rsa
B.   crypto generate rsa
C.   crypto key rsa

6-181.   Which of the following commands is used to display a copy of the switch's key which is generated using the crypto key generate rsa command?

A.   show crypto key mypubkey rsa
B.   show key mypubkey rsa
C.   show mypubkey rsa

6-182.   Which of the following commands is used to configure an interface to use the duplex full?

A.   Switch(config-if)#duplex full
B.   Switch(config)#duplex full
C.   Switch#duplex full

6-183.   Which of the following commands is used to configure an interface to use the speed of 100Mbps?

A.   Switch(config-if)#100 speed
B.   Switch(config-if)#speed 100
C.   Switch(config-if)#speed 100Mbps

6-184.   On a CAT2.96K switch, which of the following is true about interface Fa0/2 if the output of the **show interfaces status** command shows the interface Fa0/2 in a "disabled" state? (Select all that apply)

A.   The interface is configured with the **shutdown** command.
B.   The **show interfaces fa0/2** command will list the interface with two status codes of administratively down and down (line status and protocol status).
C.   The interface cannot currently be used to forward frames.

6-185.   On a CAT2.96K switch, which of the following is true about interface Fa0/2 if the output of the **show interfaces status** command shows the interface Fa0/2 in a "notconnect" state? (Select all that apply)

A.   The interface is connected to No cable or bad cable or wrong cable pinouts.
B.   The speeds are mismatched on the two connected sides.
C.   The device on the other end of the cable is powered OFF or the other interface is **shutdown**.
D.   The **show interfaces fa0/2** command will list the interface with two status codes of administratively down and down (line status and protocol status).
E.   The interface cannot currently be used to forward frames.

6-186.   On a CAT2.96K switch, which of the following is true about interface Fa0/2 if the output of the **show interfaces status** command shows the interface Fa0/2 in a "notconnect" state? (Select all that apply)

A.   The **show interfaces fa0/2** command will list the interface with two status codes of administratively up and down (line status and protocol status).
B.   The interface cannot currently be used to forward frames.

6-187.   On a CAT2.96K switch, which of the following is true about interface Fa0/2 if the output of the **show interfaces status** command shows the interface Fa0/2 in a "err-disabled" state? (Select all that apply)

A.   Port security has disabled the interface.
B.   The **show interfaces fa0/2** command will list the interface with two status codes of administratively down and down (err-disabled).
C.   The interface cannot currently be used to forward frames.

6-188.   On a CAT2.96K switch, which of the following is true about interface Fa0/2 if the output of the **show interfaces status** command shows the interface Fa0/2 in a "connect" state? (Select all that apply)

A.   The interface is working well.
B.   The **show interfaces fa0/2** command will list the interface with two status codes of administratively up and up (line status and protocol status).
C.   The interface can currently be used to forward frames.

6-189.   Which of the following is true about the link between the following two switches after it comes up? Switch SW1 uses its fa0/1 interface to connect to switch SW2's fa0/2 interface. SW2's fa0/2 interface is configured with the **speed 100** and **duplex full** commands. SW1 uses all defaults for interface configuration commands on its fa0/1 interface.

A.   The link works at 100 Mbps.
B.   Both switches use full duplex.

6-190.   Which of the following is true about interface? (Select all that apply)

A.   The following line of output was taken from a **show interfaces fa0/1** command:
     Full-duplex, 100Mbps, media type is 10/100BaseTX
B.   The speed was configured with the **speed 100** interface subcommand.
C.   The duplex was configured with the **duplex full** interface subcommand.

6-191.   Try to decide if the following statement is true or false.
"Many interfaces that use copper wiring are capable of multiple speeds, and duplex settings using the IEEE standard (IEEE 802.3X) autonegotiation process."

A.   TRUE
B.   FALSE

6-192.   Which of the following is true regarding the following output from a show interfaces fa0/2 command:
Full-duplex, 100Mbps, media type is 10/100BaseTX? (Select all that apply)

A.   The interface duplex must be configured with the duplex full interface subcommand.
B.   The interface duplex may be configured with the duplex full interface subcommand.
C.   The interface speed must be configured with the speed 100 interface subcommand.
D.   The interface speed may be configured with the speed 100 interface subcommand.

6-193.   Try to decide if the following paragraph is true or false.

"Port security can be used to restrict an interface so that only the expected devices can use it. This reduces exposure to some types of security attacks."

A.   TRUE
B.   FALSE

6-194.   What is the first step that should be followed to configure port security?

    A.   Switch(config-if)#switchport mode access
    B.   Switch(config-if)#switchport port-security
    C.   Switch(config-if)#switchport port-security mac-address 2222.2222.2222

6-195.   What is the second step that should be followed to configure port security?

    A.   Switch(config-if)#switchport mode access
    B.   Switch(config-if)#switchport port-security
    C.   Switch(config-if)#switchport port-security mac-address 2222.2222.2222

6-196.   What is the third step that should be followed to configure port security?

    A.   Switch(config-if)#switchport mode access
    B.   Switch(config-if)#switchport port-security
    C.   Switch(config-if)#switchport port-security mac-address 2222.2222.2222

6-197.   Which of the following commands is used to configure the "sticky learning" process on an interface?

    A.   Switch(config-if)#switchport mode access sticky
    B.   Switch(config-if)#switchport port-security mac-address 2222.2222.2222
    C.   Switch(config-if)#switchport port-security mac-address sticky

6-198.   Which of the following commands is used to display the port security details on an interface?

    A.   Switch#show port-security interface fastEthernet 0/1
    B.   Switch#port-security interface fastEthernet 0/1
    C.   Switch#show switchport port-security

6-199.   The interface shows it's in err-disable, how it is possible to recover this interface from this state? (Arrange the following steps)

    A.   Issue the shutdown subcommand.
    B.   Recover the interface to working state by no shutdown command.

6-200.   Which of the following steps are required when configuring port security without sticky learning? (Select all that apply)

    A.   Setting the maximum number of allowed MAC addresses on the interface with the **switchport port-security maximum** interface subcommand.
    B.   Enabling port security with the **switchport port-security** interface subcommand.
    C.   Defining the allowed MAC addresses using the **switchport port-security mac-address** interface subcommand.

6-201.   Which of the following describes a way to disable IEEE standard autonegotiation (802.3X) on a 10/100 interface on a switch?

    A.   Configure the **negotiate disable** interface subcommand.
    B.   Configure the **no negotiate** interface subcommand.
    C.   Configure the **speed 100** and **duplex full** interface subcommands.

6-202.   Which of the following modes is used to configure the duplex setting for the interface fastethernet 0/1?

    A.   User mode

    B.   Enable mode
    C.   Global configuration mode
    D.   Interface configuration mode

6-203.   Which of the following is a default interface configuration of a CISCO switch? (Select all that apply)

    A.   Auto-negotiate speed
    B.   Auto-negotiate duplex
    C.   Each interface begins in an enabled (**no shutdown**) state.
    D.   All interfaces assigned to VLAN 1.
    E.   Auto-negotiate VLAN features, VLAN trunking and VLAN Trunking Protocol (VTP)

6-204.   TRUE/FALSE: The default configurations in the previous question make the switch working directly after switching ON and without any interventions.

    A.   TRUE
    B.   FALSE

6-205.   Security threats are the side effects of the default configuration. To overcome this issue, CISCO recommends configuring unused interfaces by the interface subcommands. Which of the following subcommands can be used for this issue? (Select all that apply)

    A.   **shutdown-**to administratively disable it.
    B.   **switchport access vlan** number-to assign it to an unused VLAN.
    C.   **switchport mode access-**to force it as an access interface (nontrunking interface) and prevent VLAN trunking and VTP.

6-206.   What is the meaning of verification and troubleshooting? (Select all that apply)

    A.   The process of examining a network to confirm that it is working as designed, this is called Verification.
    B.   Troubleshooting means examining the network to determine what is causing a particular problem so that it can be fixed.

6-207.   TRUE/FALSE: Working interfaces with the connect state (up/up) may suffer from several problems. These problems can be identified by monitoring various interface counters.

    A.   TRUE
    B.   FALSE

6-208.   There are several reasons for the problems in the previous question. Which of the following can be considered as a reason for these problems? (Select all that apply)

    A.   The UTP cable could be damaged. Therefore, an Ethernet frame that passes over such cable may encounter problems and the electrical signal can degrade.
    B.   Several sources of electromagnetic interference (EMI) such as, a nearby electrical power cable to the UTP cable, may change the electrical signal on the UTP cable.

6-209.   TRUE/FALSE: As a result, for such problems, the electrical signal degrades and the receiving host may receive incorrect frame bits value. These incorrect frames will be discarded in the receiving host by using the error detection logic as implemented in the FCS field in the Ethernet trailer and the receiving host interface's counters list these errors as CRC errors.

A. TRUE
B. FALSE

6-210. By using the Ethernet collision and the late collision counters, Some common LAN problems can be identified. Which of the following problems can be identified in this issue? (Select all that apply)

A. Excessive interference on the cable. This can cause the various input error counters to keep growing larger. By monitoring the CRC errors counter and the collisions counters, it is possible to identify if the problem may simply be interference on the cable or not. When the CRC errors counter grows and the collision's counters do not, this means that excessive interference is occurred.

B. A duplex mismatch. The use of **show interface** command can identify if this problem is occurred or not

C. Jabber, which refers to cases in which the NIC ignores Ethernet rules and sends a frame after frame without a break between the frames.

6-211. TRUE/FALSE: With both last two problems, the collisions and late collision counters could keep growing. If the collision counters show that more than 0.1% of all the output frames has collided, a significant problem exists. The percentage of collisions versus output frames can be found by dividing the collisions counter by the "packet's output" counter.

A. TRUE
B. FALSE

6-212. Match each of the following problems with its suitable indication by a switch counter.

1. Excessive noise
2. Collisions
3. Late collisions

A. Many input errors; few collisions
B. More than roughly .1% of all frames are collisions.
C. Increasing late collisions

6-213. Match each of the following switch problems with its problem reason.

1. Excessive noise
2. Collisions
3. Late collisions

A. EMI or Damaged cables Wrong cable category (Cat 5, 5E, 6)
B. Duplex mismatch (seen on the half-duplex side) or Jabber or DoS attack
C. Collision domain or single cable too long or Duplex mismatch

6-214. What is the first step in the switch troubleshooting process?

A. Examining the switch LEDs
B. Doing CDP process
C. Using the show command

6-215. Which of the following commands is used to verify the CISCO networks?

A. Switchport command
B. Help command

    C.   CDP commands

6-216.   Which of the following commands is used to display the whole contents of the mac address table?

    A.   switch#show mac address-table
    B.   switch#show mac address-table dynamic
    C.   switch#show mac address-table static

6-217.   Which of the following commands is used to display only the dynamically learned mac addresses in the mac address table?

    A.   switch#show mac address-table
    B.   switch#show mac address-table dynamic
    C.   switch#show mac address-table static

6-218.   Which of the following commands is used to display only the statically configured mac addresses in the mac address table?

    A.   switch#show mac address-table
    B.   switch#show mac address-table dynamic
    C.   switch#show mac address-table static

6-219.   Which of the following commands is used to display the MAC address table entries for MAC addresses configured by port security?

    A.   show mac address-table
    B.   show mac address-table dynamic
    C.   show mac address-table static
    D.   show mac address-table port-security

CHAPTER 7
INTERNETWORKING OS
MANAGEMENT
FACILITIES

This chapter begins with an introduction to the CISCO Router main internal components, and continues with an in-depth view of the CISCO IOS, configuration files and their locations in the CISCO devices. IOS is the operating system that manages all device resources, so that, makes a CISCO device work, which allows configuring these devices as well as devices management. Router boot sequence, and configuration register, including how to use the configuration register for password recovery and examples of well-designed networks will be given in this chapter.

The following topics are emphasized in this chapter:

- Backing up and restoring the CISCO IOS.
- Backing up and restoring the CISCO configuration.
- Gathering information about neighbor devices using CDP and Telnet utility.
- Resolving hostnames using host table and DNS.
- Testing the network connectivity using the ping and trace utilities.

A firm understanding of the fundamentals behind this chapter and answering the 216 learning questions at the end of this chapter are important for Configuring, Managing and Troubleshooting a CISCO internetwork and answering CCNA/CCENT exam related questions. The questions herein are intended to reflect the type of questions presented on the CCENT Test.

The CISCO Router Booting Components

In this section, major internal booting components of the CISCO Router will be given. Understanding these components is essential for both configuring and troubleshooting a CISCO Internetwork. Table 7-1 summarizes these components. Definition of the several types of memories will be given at first, where those used by the CISCO devices, are underlined.

- **RAM/DRAM:** Dynamic Random-Access Memory, DRAM is used by the router or switch just as it is used by any other automated machine to store working data. It stores information in capacitors that must be periodically refreshed. Delays can occur because they are inaccessible to the processor when refreshing their contents. However, they are less complex and have a greater capacity than SRAMs. It is used by CISCO Routers to store packet buffers and routing tables, along with the hardware addresses cache. Running configuration is stored in DRAM. It is a volatile memory that can be read and written by a microprocessor. The RAM loses its contents when a unit is powered OFF.
- **SRAM:** Static Random Access Memory retains its contents for as long as power is supplied. It does not require constant refreshing, like DRAM. It is a volatile memory that can be read and written by a microprocessor.
- **NVRAM:** Nonvolatile RAM holds the initial or startup-config file that is used when the router or switch is first switched ON and when the device is reloaded. The NVRAM retains its contents intact when a unit is powered OFF.
- **ROM:** Read-Only Memory Chip boots and maintains the Router. CISCO Routers use it to store the bootstrap, which runs a POST, and then finds and loads the IOS in flash memory by default. It is used to hold ROM monitor and the Mini-IOS or bootloader. Read-Only Memory stores a bootstrap (or boothelper) program that is loaded when the router or switch first powers ON. This bootstrap program then finds the full CISCO IOS image and manages the process of loading CISCO IOS into RAM, at which point CISCO IOS takes over the operation of the router/switch.
- **EEPROM:** Electrically Erasable Programmable Read-Only Memory that can be erased using electrical signals applied to specific pins on the chip.
- **Flash memory:** It is either a chip inside the router/switch or a removable memory card. Flash memory stores the CISCO IOS images by default. Flash memory can also be used to store any other files,

including backup copies of configuration files. It is an EEPROM chip used on the Router to hold the CISCO IOS by default. Nonvolatile storage can be electrically erased and reprogrammed so that software images can be stored, booted, and rewritten as necessary. It is not erased when the Router is reloaded.

Table 7-1 CISCO Router Booting Components

Component	Description
Bootstrap	It is used during initialization to bring a Router up. It will boot the Router and load the IOS and is stored in the ROM.
POST (Power-On-Self-Test)	It is used to check the basic functionality of the Router hardware and determines which interfaces are present. It is like Bootstrap, stored in the ROM.
ROM monitor	It is used for manufacturing testing and troubleshooting. It is like Bootstrap, stored in the ROM.
Mini-IOS	A small IOS in ROM, which can be used to bring up an interface and to load a CISCO IOS into flash memory. The mini-IOS can also perform some maintenance operations. CISCO calls the Mini-IOS, RXBOOT or bootloader
RAM (Random Access Memory)	A device buffer, which stores packet buffers, routing tables, and the software and data structures that allow the CISCO device to function. Running-config is stored in RAM. CISCO IOS can also be run from RAM.
ROM (Read-Only-Memory)	It is used to start and maintain the Router. CISCO routers use a ROM chip to load the bootstrap, which runs a power-on-self-test, and then finds and loads the IOS in the flash memory by default.
Flash Memory	It is used on the CISCO devices to store the CISCO IOS, by default. Flash memory is not erased when the device is reloaded. It is an EEPROM created by Intel and licensed to other semiconductor manufacturers.
NVRAM (NonVolatile RAM)	It is used to store the device configuration. It is not erased when the Router or Switch is reloaded. Startup-config is stored in NVRAM.
Configuration Register	It is used to control how the Router boots up. The typical value of this register is 0x2102, which tells the device to load the IOS from flash memory and to look for and load startup-config from NVRAM.

Booting the Router

Internally, the Router will follow the following sequence during booting up process. During the boot sequence, the Router will test the hardware and load the necessary software.

POST step (1): When the Router powered ON, it performs a POST. The POST verifies that all hardware components of the device are operational and present. The POST is stored in and run from ROM.

Bootstrap step (2): The bootstrap is a program in ROM that is used to invoke programs. It is responsible for finding where each IOS program is located and then loading the file. By default, the IOS software is loaded from flash memory in all Cisco Routers. The bootstrap main objective is looking for and loading the Cisco IOS software. In this step, the router copy the bootstrap in router's RAM for executing. Then, the bootstrap program selects which OS image (IOS) to load into RAM, and loads that OS. The newly loaded IOS image takes the control of the router hardware from bootstrap program.

IOS step (3): The IOS software looks for a valid configuration file stored in NVRAM and loads it into RAM as the running-config. The configuration file in NVRAM is called startup-config and is only there if the command copy run start is issued. This command copies the running-config of the Router to startup-config in NVRAM.

Setup step (4): The Router will start the setup mode configuration upon bootup, if this is the first time booting or there is no startup-config file in NVRAM. The Router will be operational, after completing the setup steps or after executing the configuration file in NVRAM.

Several configuration options can be applied for Steps 2 and 3, which tell the router what to do next.

Notice that, the CISCO router has the following three OS:

1. CISCO IOS image: It allows the router to perform its normal function of routing packets.
2. ROMMON in ROM: Its operating environment is the ROM Monitor and it operates on the old and new routers.
3. RxBoot, boot helper in ROM: Its operating environment is the Boot ROM and it operates only in the older routers.

The last two types are used to perform some troubleshooting, recover router passwords, and to copy the new IOS files into Flash when Flash has been erased or corrupted for any reason. This book will mainly refer to the OS that continues to be available for these special functions, the ROMMON OS, since the RxBoot OS is only available in the older routers and is no longer needed in the newer routers.

The resent CISCO router product lines (for example, 1800 and 2800 series routers) use only one additional OS to perform the special functions, whereas the older CISCO routers (for example, 2500 series routers) actually had two different operating systems to perform these special functions.

The Configuration Registers

In this section, configuration register values will be given firstly. Secondly, the procedure to recover the Router lost password and the using of the configuration register in this procedure will be outlined. Finally, the procedure to change the configuration register values will be detailed.

The configuration register is a 16-bit configurable value stored in the hardware or software that determines how CISCO routers function during initialization. In the hardware, the bit position is set using a jumper. While, in the software, it is set by specifying specific bit patterns used to set startup options, and is configured using a hexadecimal value with the configuration commands. The 16-bit software register is found on all CISCO routers, which is written into NVRAM. By default, the configuration register is set to load the CISCO IOS from flash memory and to look for and load the startup-config file from NVRAM.

The Configuration Register Bits Meanings

As stated in the previous section, the default configuration setting on the CISCO Routers is 0x2102 (hexadecimal). This will make the Router to load the CISCO IOS from flash memory. It is important to know how this value is mapped, which is as shown in table 7-2.

TABLE 7-2 The Default Configuration Register Bit Numbers

Configuration Register	2	1	0	2
Bit number	15 14 13 12	11 10 9 8	7 6 5 4	3 2 1 0
Binary	0 0 1 0	0 0 0 1	0 0 0 0	0 0 1 0

Several configuration operations can be obtained by setting the configuration register to different values. The values of the configuration register are used to determine how CISCO routers function during initialization. Table 7-3 shows how the setting of the bits in configuration register will affect the router initialization and Table 7-4 shows boot field setting in details.

TABLE 7-3 Software Configuration Bit Meanings

Bit	Hex	Description
0-3	0x0000-0x000F	Boot Field (see Table 7-4)
6	0x0040	Ignore NVRAM contents (password recovery).
7	0x0080	OEM bit enable.
8	0x0100	Break disable
10	0x0400	IP broadcast with all zeros.
5,11-12	0x0800-0x1000	Console line speed.
13	0x2000	Boot default ROM software if network boot fails.
14	0x4000	IP broadcasts do not have net numbers.
16	0x8000	Enable diagnostic messages and ignore NVM contents

TABLE 7-4 The Boot Field Meanings (Configuration Register Bits 0-3)

Boot Field	Meaning	The Using
00	ROM Monitor Mode	To invoke ROM monitor mode, set the configuration register to 2100. Then the Router must manually boot using the **b** command. The Router will show the rommon> prompt.
01	Boot image From ROM	To boot an IOS image stored in ROM, set the configuration register to 2101. The router(boot)> prompt will be displayed
02-0F	Specifies a default boot filename	To make a router to use the boot commands specified in NVRAM, set the register to any value from 2102 through 210F.

Configuration Register: The Current Value

Configuration 7-1, Verifying the configuration register value: Display the current configuration register using the **show version** command.

```
THAAR#sh version
Cisco IOS Software, 2800 Software (C2800NM-ADVIPSERVICESK9-M), Version 12.4(12), RELEASE SOFTWARE (fc1)
Technical Support: http://www.cisco.com/techsupport
Copyright (c) 1986-2009 by Cisco Systems, Inc.
Compiled Fri 17-Nov-06 12:02 by prod_rel_team

ROM: System Bootstrap, Version 12.4(13r)T, RELEASE SOFTWARE (fc1)

THAAR uptime is 13 days, 11 hours, 48 minutes
System returned to ROM by power-on
System image file is "flash:c2800nm-advipservicesk9-mz.124-12.bin"

This product contains cryptographic features and is subject to United States and local country laws governing import,
export, transfer and use. Delivery of Cisco cryptographic products does not imply third-party authority to import,
export, distribute or use encryption. Importers, exporters, distributors and users are responsible for compliance with
U.S. and local country laws. By using this product you agree to comply with applicable laws and regulations. If you
are unable to comply with U.S. and local laws, return this product immediately.

A summary of U.S. laws governing Cisco cryptographic products may be found at:
http://www.cisco.com/wwl/export/crypto/tool/stqrg.html

If you require further assistance please contact us by sending email to
export@cisco.com.

Cisco 2811 (revision 53.50) with 249856K/12288K bytes of memory.
Processor board ID FTX1107A6BB
2 FastEthernet interfaces
2 Serial(sync/async) interfaces
1 Virtual Private Network (VPN) Module
DRAM configuration is 64 bits wide with parity enabled.
239K bytes of non-volatile configuration memory.
62720K bytes of ATA CompactFlash (Read/Write)
Configuration register is 0x2102
THAAR#
```

The **show version** (**sh version**, **show ver** or **sh ver**) command gives the value of the configuration register in the last information. The default value is 0x2102. This command also presents the IOS version.

The show version command is very useful. It provides the following information about the router.

- The IOS version
- The uptime (the length of time that has passed since the last reload)
- The reason for the last reload of IOS (**reload** command, power off/on, software failure)
- The time of the last loading of IOS (if the router's clock has been set)
- The source from which the router loaded the current IOS
- The amount of RAM memory
- The number and types of interfaces
- The amount of NVRAM memory
- The amount of Flash memory
- The configuration register's current and future setting (if different)

Chosen the OS by the Configuration Register

On more modern CISCO routers that do not have an RxBoot OS, the process to choose which OS to load as follows:

Step1. If the boot field = 0, use the ROMMON OS.
Step2. If the boot field = 1, load the first IOS file found in Flash memory.
Step3. If the boot field = 2-F:
  1. Try each **boot system** command in the startup-config file, in order, until one works.
  2. If none of the **boot system** commands work, load the first IOS file found in Flash memory.

Table 7-5 shows several examples of the boot system command.

Table 7-5 Boot System Command Options

Command	Result
boot system flash	Loading the first file from Flash memory.
boot system flash *filename*	Loading IOS with the name *filename* from Flash memory.
boot system tftp *filename* **107.100.100.100**	Loading IOS with the name *filename* from the TFTP server 107.100.100.100.

Changing the Configuration Register Value

Changing the configuration register value provides the possibility to modify how the Router boots and runs. By modifying the configuration register value, the following operations can be implemented on the Router:

- Force the system into the ROM monitor.
- Select a boot source and default boot filename.
- Enable or disable the Break function.
- Recover a lost password.
- Control broadcast addresses.
- Set the console terminal baud rate.
- Load operating software from ROM.
- Enable booting from TFTP server.

Configuration 7-2, Loading to ROM monitor: Change the configuration register value using the **config-register** command so that the Router will boot to ROM monitor mode next time reloaded.

Router(config)#config-register 0x2100

Router(config)#^Z
Router#

To invoke the ROM monitor mode, set the configuration register to 2100. Then the Router must manually boot using the **b** command. The Router will show the rommon> prompt.

Configuration 7-3, Loading ROM Software: Change the configuration register value using the **config-register** command so that the Router will load IOS from ROM next time reloaded.

Router(config)#config-register 0x0101
Router(config)#^Z

To boot an IOS image stored in ROM, set the configuration register to 2101. The router will show the router(boot)> prompt.

Router#sh ver
......
Configuration register is 0x2102 (will be 0x0101 at next reload)

The show version command shows the current configuration register value, as well as what it will be when the router reboots. After, any changes to the configuration register, the router needs to be reloaded to make these changes take effect.

Configuration 7-4, Loading Flash Memory Contents: Set the software configuration register so that the Router will boot from onboard Flash memory, and it will ignore **Break** at the next reboot of the Router.

Router#conf term
Enter configuration commands, one per line. End with CNTL/Z.
Router(config)#config-register 0x102
Router(config)#boot system flash [filename]
Router(config)#Crtl-z
Router#

Note: Several default boot filenames can be found from www.cisco.com.

Password Recovery Procedure

Password recovery is required if the password is lost when the administrator in User-configuration mode or the password is lost when the administrator out of the Router. If the administrator in Privileged EXEC mode, he simply can set a new password or he can erase the configuration. Password recovery can only be done from the console port on the Router. This section provides important information on how to recover a lost password.

The value of bit 6 in the default virtual configuration register (0x2102) is 0 or OFF. This will tell the Router to look for and to load a Router configuration stored in NVRAM (startup-config). To recover a password, bit 6 must be turned ON, this will tell the router to ignore the NVRAM contents. The configuration register value 0x2142 is used to recover a lost password since the bit 6 is turned ON.

The following is an overview of the overall Password recovery procedure:

1.   Boot the Router and interrupt the boot sequence by performing a **Break** to the rommon prompt.
2.   Change the configuration register to ignore NVRAM by turning ON bit 6 (with the value 0x2142).

To recover a lost password, set the configuration register to (0x0040) so that the contents of NVRAM are ignored.

3.   Reload the Router.
4.   Enter the privileged level in the system EXEC.
5.   Copy the startup-configuration file to running-config.
6.   Change the password.
7.   Change the configuration register value back to its original setting.
8.   Copy the running-config file to startup-configuration.
9.   Reload the Router.

Configuration 7-5, Recovering lost password: To recover a lost password, the following Configuration should be followed.

Step 1: Attach an ASCII terminal to the Router console port, which is located on the rear panel.

Step 2: Configure the terminal to operate at 9600 bps, 8 data bits, no parity, and 2 stop bits.

Step 3. Interrupting the Router Boot Sequence. Boot the Router and perform a **Break** (System Interrupt). If **Break** function is disabled, powers cycle the Router. (To power cycle, turn OFF the Router, wait five seconds, and then turn it ON again.) If **Break** function is enabled on the Router, press the **Break** key or send a break (**^[**). When using HyperTerminal, just press **Ctrl+Break**. Within five seconds of turning ON the Router, press the **Break** key. This action causes the terminal to display the ROM monitor prompt:

SYSTEM BOOTSTRAP, VERSION 12.3(8R)YI, RELEASE SOFTWARE
TECHNICAL SUPPORT: HTTP://WWW.CISCO.COM/TECHSUPPORT
....
monitor: command "boot" aborted due to user interrupt
rommon >

Notice the line **"boot" aborted due to user interrupt**. This is because of pressing the system interrupt.

Step 4: Changing the Configuration Register. Set the configuration register to ignore the configuration file information as follows:

rommon>confreg
Configuration Summary
      enabled are:
      console baud: 9600
      boot: image specified by the boot system command
      or default to: Adv-cisco-image
      do you wish to change the configuration? y/n [n]: y
      enable "diagnostic mode"? y/n [n]:
      enable "use net in IP bcast address"? y/n [n]:
      enable "load rom after netbootfails"? y/n [n]:
      enable "use all zero broadcast"? y/n [n]:
      enable "break/abort has effect?" y/n [n]:
      enable "ignore system config info?" [n]: y
      change console baud rate? y/n [n]:
      change boot characteristics? y/n [n]
      Configuration Summary
      enabled are:
      console baud: 9600

boot: image specified by the boot system command
or default to: Adv-cisco-image
do you wish to change the configuration? y/n [n]:y
You must reset or power cycle for the new config to take effect

To change the bit value on 2600 CISCO Routers, simply, enter the following commands:

rommon>confreg 0x2142

The command that should be entered here will depend on the used platform. On 2500 platforms the >o/r 0x2142 command should be entered.

Step 5: Reloading the Router. Initialize the Router by entering the i command as follows:

rommon>i

On some platforms, the reset command should be used to reload the Router from rommon prompt. However, the Router will power cycle, the configuration register will be set to ignore the configuration file, and the Router will boot the boot system image and then prompt the system configuration dialogue as follows:

    --- System Configuration Dialog ---
Would you like to enter the initial configuration dialog? [yes/no]:no

Step 6: Entering the User EXEC mode. Enter no in response to the system configuration dialogue prompts until the following system message is displayed:

Press RETURN to get started! Enter
Router>

Step 7: Entering the Privileged EXEC mode Enter the enable command to enter enabled mode. The prompt changes to the following:

Router>enable
Router#

Step 8: Copying the Configuration. Copy the startup configuration to running configuration. This will make the configuration in RAM and ready for changing.

Router#copy start run

At this point, forgotten the enable password can be viewed if it is not encrypted. This is by using the show start command.

Step 9: Changing the enable secret password. Although the enable secret password cannot be viewed at this point, it can be changed as follows:

Router# configure terminal
Enter configuration commands, one per line. End with CNTL/Z.
Router(config)# enable secret thaarm
Router(config)#^Z

Step 10: Changing the configuration register. Change the configuration register value back to its original value 0x2102 using the config-register 0xvalue command.

Router# config t
Enter configuration commands, one per line. End with CNTL/Z.
Router(config)# config-register 0x2102

Step 11: Exit configuration mode by entering **Ctrl-Z**.

Step 12: **Copying the Configuration.** Copy the currently running configuration to startup configuration. This will store the configuration in DRAM into NVRAM.

Router#copy run start

Step 13: Reloading the Router and enable it using the recovered password.

Router#reload

The **reload** command halts the system. If the system is set to restart on error, it reboots itself. Use the reload command after configuration information is entered into a file and saved to the startup configuration. It is impossible to reload from a virtual terminal if the system is not set up for automatic booting. This prevents the system from dropping to the ROM monitor and thereby taking the system out of the remote user's control. If the configuration file is modified, the system prompts to save the configuration. Therefore, step 12 is listed here for confirmation and there is no problem to skip this step.

This completes the procedure for recovering a lost password.

Backing Up and Restoring the CISCO IOS System

In this section, checking the amount of flash memory will be described firstly. Secondly, backing up the CISCO IOS from flash memory to a TFTP host will be outlined. Finally, restoring the CISCO IOS from a TFTP server to flash memory will be detailed.

As a **rule** in this field, before upgrading or restoring a CISCO IOS, a copy of the existing file to a TFTP server should be taken. This copy is considered as a backup in case the new image does not work.

Verifying Flash Memory

The flash memory should be verified before attempting to upgrade the CISCO IOS, to find if the Router flash memory has enough space to hold the new image or not.

Configuration 7-6: Verify the amount of flash memory on the Router using the **show flash** command.

Router#sh flash
System flash directory:
File   Length   Name/status
 1   8121000   c2500-js-l.112-18.bin
 [8121064 bytes used, 8656152 available, 16777216 total]
16384K bytes of processor board System flash (Read ONLY)
Router#

This command provides the amount of flash memory and the file or files being stored in flash memory. The last line in the **show flash** command output shows that the flash is 16384K bytes (16MB). The filename here is c2500-js-1.112-18.bin. The name of the file platform-specific and is derived as follows:

- **c2500** is the platform (CISCO 2500).
- **j** indicates that the file is an enterprise image.
- **s** indicates the file contains extended capabilities.
- **l** indicates that the file can be moved from flash memory if needed and is not compressed.
- **11.2-18** indicates the revision number.
- **bin** indicates that the CISCO IOS is a binary executable file.

Backing Up the CISCO IOS

Configuration 7-7: Backup the CISCO IOS to a TFTP host using the **copy flash tftp** command.

```
Router#copy flash tftp
System flash directory:
File    Length      Name/status
 1     8121000     c2500-js-l.112-18.bin
 [8121064 bytes used, 8656152 available, 16777216 total]
16384K bytes of processor board System flash (Read ONLY)
Address or name of remote host [255.255.255.255]? 172.17.17.17
Source file name? c2500-js-l.112-18.bin
Destination file name [default = source name]? Enter
Verifying checksum for 'c2500-js-l.112-18.bin'(file #1)… OK
Copy '/c2500-js-l.112-18.bin' from Flash to server as '/c2500-js-l.112-18.bin'? [yes/no]y
!!!!!!!!!! ……..
Upload to server done
Flash copy took 0:01:01 [hh:mm:ss]
Router#
```

In the above example, the content of flash memory was copied successfully to the TFTP host. All you need is to enter the address of the remote host, which is the IP address of the TFTP host and the source filename, which is the file in flash memory. It is a straightforward command that requires only the source filename and the IP address of the TFTP host. However, keep in your mind, to implement this command successfully, the connectivity to the TFTP host must be verified first. The **ping 172.17.17.17** utility can be used to check this connectivity before implementing this command. Notice also that, the TFTP host must have a default directory specified, or it will not work, since, the **copy flash tftp** command does not prompt for the location of any file.

Restoring or Upgrading the CISCO IOS

Configuration 7-8: Replace the damaged or old CISCO IOS copy by a new copy from a TFTP host using the **copy tftp flash** command. The command contains the following main parts:

```
Router#copy tftp flash
               **** NOTICE ****
Flash load helper v1.0
This process will accept the copy options and then terminate
the current system image to use the ROM based image for the copy.
Routing functionality will not be available during that time.
If you are logged in via telnet, this connection will terminate.
Users with console access can see the results of the copy operation.
               ---- ******** ----
```

This command downloads the file from a TFTP host to flash memory. It requires the IP address of the TFTP host and the name of the file to be downloaded to flash memory. After issuing this command, the above messages will be displayed stating that the Router will be rebooted, and a ROM-based IOS image will be ran to perform this operation. Therefore, before issuing this command, the following considerations should be taken:

- The network connectivity to the TFTP host must be available. The **ping** command can be used for this purpose.
- The required file to be placed in flash memory should be placed in the default TFTP directory on the TFTP host. When this command is issued, TFTP will not ask where the file is. If the file to be restored is not in the default directory of the TFTP host, this procedure will not work.
- The time of implementing this command should be in the low load time. This command requires rebooting the Router, and all connections will be cut within this period.

Proceed? [confirm] Enter
System flash directory:
File   Length   Name/status
 1   8121000   /c2500-js-I.112-18.bin
[8121064 bytes used, 8656152 available, 16777216 total]
16384K bytes of processor board System flash (Read ONLY)
Address or name of remote host [172.17.17.17]? Enter
Source file name? c2500-js56i-I.120-9.bin
Destination file name [c2500-js56i-I.120-9.bin]? Enter
Accessing file 'c2500-js56i-I.120-9.bin' on 172.17.17.17 …
Loading c2500-js56i-I.120-9.bin from 172.17.17.17 (via Ethernet0): ! [OK]

After pressing **Enter** to confirm the rebooting message, the above Router output is displayed. Once the Router has used the TFTP host, it will remember the address and just prompt to press **Enter**. The source file name that must be in the TFTP host default directory is entered next.

Erase flash device before writing? [confirm] Enter
Flash contains files. Are you sure you want to erase? [confirm] Enter
System configuration has been modified. Save? [yes/no]: y
Building configuration...
[OK]
Copy ' c2500-js56i-I.120-9.bin' from TFTP server
as ' c2500-js56i-I.120-9.bin' into Flash WITH erase? [yes/no] yes

If the flash memory is full or do not have enough space to store both copies, or if the flash memory is new and no file has been written to flash memory before, the Router will ask to delete the contents of the flash memory before writing the new file into the flash memory. The above messages prompt three times, before erasing flash memory. If the **copy run start** command is not issued yet, the Router will prompt for this to be done, since the router needs to reboot, as shown above.

%SYS-5-RELOAD: Reload requested
%FLH: c2500-js56i-I.120-9.bin from 172.17.17.17 to flash …..
System flash directory:
File   Length   Name/status
 1   8121000   /c2500-js-I.112-18.bin
 [8121064 bytes used, 8656152 available, 16777216 total]
16384K bytes of processor board System flash (Read ONLY)
Accessing file 'c2500-js56i-I.120-9.bin' on 172.17.17.17 …
Loading c2500-js56i-I.120-9.bin from 172.17.17.17 (via Ethernet0): ! [OK]

Erasing device...
eeeeeeeeeeeeeeeeeeeeeeeeeeeeeeeeeeeeeeeeeeeeeeeeeeeeeeeeeeeeeeee ...erased

Loading c2500-js56i-l.120-9.bin from 172.17.17.17 (via Ethernet0):
!!!!!!!!!!!!!!!!!!! ....

After confirming to erase the flash memory contents, the router must be rebooted to load a small IOS from ROM, the contents of flash are erased, and finally, the file from the TFTP host is accessed and copied to flash memory. However, the flash file cannot be deleted if it is in use. Once the copy is completed, the following message should be received:

[OK – 10935532/16777216 bytes]
Verifying checksum... OK (0x62EA)
Flash device copy took 00:10:30 [hh:mm:ss]
%FLH: Re-booting system after download

After the file is loaded into flash memory and a checksum is performed, the router is rebooted to load and run the new IOS file. Notice also that, CISCO routers can function as a TFTP-server for a router system image that is run in flash. For this purpose, the global configuration command **tftp-server** can be used.

Backing Up and Restoring the System Configuration

In this section, verifying the system configuration will be described firstly. Secondly, backing up the system configuration from DRAM to a TFTP host or to NVRAM will be outlined. Finally, restoring the system configuration from a TFTP server to the Router's DRAM will be detailed.
As a **rule** in this field, before restoring the system configuration, a copy of the existing configuration to a NVRAM should be taken. This copy is considered as a backup in case the new configuration does not work. Furthermore, a copy of any configuration changes to NVRAM should be taken before rebooting the Router. All changes to running configuration will be lost if the **copy run start** command is not issued before rebooting the Router. The tftp backup is required as an extra precaution in case of dying the Router.

Figure 7-1 shows how the files can be copied between any two storage locations.

Figure 7-1 Copy Command to Different Locations

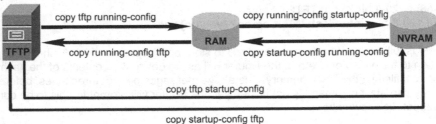

Backing Up the System Configuration

The following commands can be used to backup the Router's configuration:

- copy running-config tftp.
- copy run tftp.
- copy startup-config tftp
- copy start tftp.
- copy running-config startup-config.
- copy run start.

Verifying the Current System Configuration

Configuration 7-9: Verify the system running configuration in DRAM using the **show running-config** command.

Router# show run
Building configuration ...
Current configuration:
!
version 12.0
......

The current configuration information indicates that the Router is now running version 12.0 of the IOS.

Verifying the Stored System Configuration

Configuration 7-10: Verify the stored system configuration in NVRAM using the **show startup-config** command.

Router# show start

Using 419 out of 32762 bytes
!
version 12.0
....

The output indicates that NVRAM is 32KB and only 419 bytes of it are used. It also indicates that the version of the IOS in NVRAM is 12.0, which is up-to-date.

Storing the Current System Configuration to NVRAM

Configuration 7-11: Store the running configuration in DRAM to startup configuration in NVRAM using the **copy run start** command.

Router#copy running-config startup-config
Destination filename [startup-config]?return
Warning: Attempting to overwrite an NVRAM configuration previously written by a different version of the system image.
Overwrite the previous NVRAM configuration?[confirm]return
Building configuration....
......
[OK]
Router#

By performing this command, it is guaranteed that running-config will always be reloaded if the Router is rebooted. The startup-config in NVRAM is considered as a backup to running-config in DRAM. This command replaces the **write memory** command.

Storing the Current System Configuration to a TFTP Host

Configuration 7-12: Store the running configuration in DRAM to a TFTP host using the **copy running-config**

tftp command.

THAAR#copy run tftp
Address or name of remote host? 172.17.17.17

Destination filename [thaar-config]? Enter
!!
419 bytes copied in 10.55 sec (40 bytes/sec)
THAAR#

This command performs a second backup to the running configuration in a tftp host. It required only two !!, which are two UDP acknowledgments. The default destination file name is the hostname plus the extension **–config**. This command replaces the **write network** command.

Restoring the System Configuration from NVRAM

Configuration 7-13: Restore the system configuration stored in NVRAM to DRAM using the **copy startup-config running-config** command.

Router#copy start run
......

This is the easiest way to restore the system configuration. Older CISCO command **config men** can also be used to do this job.

Restoring the System Configuration from a TFTP Host

Configuration 7-14: Restore the system configuration stored in a tftp host to DRAM using the **copy tftp running-config** command.

Router#copy tftp run
Address or name of remote host []? 172.17.17.17
Source filename []? thaar-config
Destination filename [running-config]? Enter
Accessing tftp://172.17.17.17/thaar-config …
Loading thaar-config from 172.17.17.17 (via Ethernet0):
!!
[OK – 419/4096 bytes]
419 bytes copied in 4:410 secs (97 bytes/sec)
Router#

00:35:28: %SYS-5-CONFIG: Configured from tftp://172.17.17.17/thaar-config
Router#

The **copy tftp startup-config** (**copy tftp start**) command can be used to perform the same job. An older CISCO command **config net** can also be used to do this job. Notice also that, the configuration file is an ASCII text file. This means that changes can be made on this file using any text editor before copying the configuration stored in a tftp host to DRAM or NVRAM.

Erasing the System Configuration

Configuration 7-15: Delete the system startup configuration using the **erase startup-config** command.

Router#erase start
Erasing the nvram filesystem will remove all files! Continue?[confirm]Enter
.....
[OK]
Erase of nvram: complete
Router#

The preceding command deletes the contents of NVRAM on the Router. The next time the Router boots, it will run in setup mode, unless the configuration is backed up again.

As a final comment in the backup and restore section, Table 7-6 shows pre–CISCO IOS Release 12.0 and the newer CISCO IOS Release 12.x commands used for configuration file movement and management. Notice that the CISCO IOS Release 12.x commands identify the location of the configuration files following the colon as [[[//location]/directory]/filename], as applicable.

Table 7-6 Copy Command Uses IFS

Pre–CISCO IOS Release 12.0 Commands	CISCO IOS Release 12.x Commands
configure network (before CISCO IOS Release 10.3) copy rcp running-config copy tftp running-config	copy ftp: system:running-config copy rcp: system:running-config copy tftp: system:running-config
configure overwrite-network (before CISCO IOS Release 10.3) copy rcp startup-config copy tftp startup-config	copy ftp: nvram:startup-config copy rcp: nvram:startup-config copy tftp: nvram:startup-config
show configuration (before CISCO IOS Release 10.3) show startup-config	nvram:startup-config
write erase (before CISCO IOS Release 10.3) erase startup-config	erase nvram:
write memory (before CISCO IOS Release 10.3) copy running-config startup-config copy system:running-config	nvram:startup-config
write network (before CISCO IOS Release 10.3) copy running-config rcp copy running-config tftp	copy system:running-config ftp: copy system:running-config rcp: copy system:running-config tftp:
write terminal (before CISCO IOS Release 10.3) show running-config	more system:running-config

The CISCO Discovery Protocol (CDP)

CDP is a CISCO proprietary protocol that runs on CISCO devices (including routers, bridges, access servers, and switches). It allows CISCO network management applications to learn the device type and SNMP agent address of neighboring devices. It is designed to help administrators collect information about locally attached and remote devices. Hardware and protocol information is gathered by CDP. CDP runs at Layer 2 and is media- and network-layer independent, allowing network management to be performed from a system that supports a different network-layer protocol from that being managed. The information that gathered by CDP is useful for troubleshooting and documenting the internetwork.

Obtaining CDP Timers and Holdtime Information

CDP timer information provides how often CDP packets are transmitted to all active interfaces. It is a global parameter that can be configured on CISCO switches as well as CISCO Routers. The **show cdp** command can be used to show this information.

CDP Holdtime information provides the amount of time that the device will hold packets received from neighbor devices.

Configuration 7-16: Display the cdp protocol information using the **show cdp** command.

```
Router# show cdp
Global CDP information:
    Sending CDP packets every 60 seconds
    Sending a holdtime value of 180 seconds
```

Global CDP timer and hold-time parameters are set to the defaults of 60 and 180 seconds, respectively. Notice that, both the CISCO Routers and switches use the same parameters.

Configuration 7-17: Configure the cdp protocol information using the **cdp timer** and **cdp holdtime** commands.

```
Router#config t
Enter configuration commands, one per line. End with CNTL/Z.
Router(config)#cdp ?
  holdtime   Specify the holdtime (in sec) to be sent in packets
  timer      Specify the rate at which CDP packets are sent( in sec)
  run

Router(config)#cdp timer 120
Router(config)#cdp holdtime 240
Router(config)#^Z
Router#
```

The cdp can be turned OFF completely using the command Router(config)#**no cdp run**.

Obtaining Neighbor Information

The **show cdp neighbors** command shows information about directly connected devices.

Configuration 7-18: Display information about directly connected devices using the **show cdp neighbors** command. Table 7-7 shows the description to **sh cdp nei** command.

```
THAAR#sh cdp nei
    Capability Codes: R - Router, T - Trans Bridge, B - Source Route Bridge
    S - Switch, H - Host, I - IGMP, r - Repeater
```

Device ID	Local Interface	Holdtme	Capability	Platform	Port ID
Switch1	fa0/1	122	S I	WS-C2960	-fa0/3
Router2	s0/0/1	177	R S I	2811	s0/0/0

Table 7-7 The **show cdp neighbors** Command Output

Field	Description
Device ID	The hostname of the device directly connected.
Local Interface	The port or interface on which the CDP packets are received.
Holdtime	The amount of time the CISCO device will hold the information before discarding it if no more CDP packets are received.
Capability	The neighbor's capability, such as router or switch.
Platform	The type of CISCO device.
Port ID	The neighbor device's interface on which the CDP packets are broadcast.

It is important to remember that CDP packets are not passed through a CISCO switch, and only what is directly attached will be seen. On a Router connected to a switch, other devices connected to the switch will not be seen on the Router console.

Configuration 7-19: Display the detailed information about directly connected devices using the **show cdp neighbors detail** command.

THAAR#sh cdp nei de

Device ID: Router2
Entry address(es):
IP address: 171.17.17.17
Platform: Cisco 2811, Capabilities: Router Switch IGMP
Interface: Serial0/0/1, Port ID (outgoing port): Serial0/0/0
Holdtime : 156 sec
Version :
Cisco IOS Software, 2800 Software (C2800NM-ADVIPSERVICESK9-M), Version 12.4(12), RELEASE
SOFTWARE (fc1)
Technical Support: http://www.cisco.com/techsupport
Copyright (c) 1986-2006 by Cisco Systems, Inc.
Compiled Fri 17-Nov-06 12:02 by prod_rel_team
THAAR#

In addition to the same information displayed by the **show cdp neighbor** command, the **show cdp neighbor detail** command shows the IOS version of the neighbor device.

Configuration 7-20: Display the detailed information about directly connected devices using the **show cdp entry *** command.

THAAR#sh cdp entry *

Device ID: Router2
Entry address(es):
IP address: 171.17.17.17
Platform: Cisco 2811, Capabilities: Router Switch IGMP
Interface: Serial0/0/1, Port ID (outgoing port): Serial0/0/0
Holdtime : 156 sec

Version :
Cisco IOS Software, 2800 Software (C2800NM-ADVIPSERVICESK9-M), Version 12.4(12), RELEASE
SOFTWARE (fc1)
Technical Support: http://www.cisco.com/techsupport

Copyright (c) 1986-2006 by Cisco Systems, Inc.
Compiled Fri 17-Nov-06 12:02 by prod_rel_team
THAAR#
....
To show all the CDP neighbors information, the (*) should be used. However, the hostname can be used instead of (*). The above output can be obtained using the **sh cdp entry Router2** command. The **sh cdp entry Rou***
command can also be used to display detailed information regarding all devices start with Rou characters.

Obtaining Interface Traffic Information

Configuration 7-21: Display information about interface traffic, including the number of CDP packets sent and received and the errors with CDP using the **show cdp traffic** command.

Router#sh cdp traffic
CDP counters :
Total packets output: 4260, Input: 4348
Hdr syntax: 0, Chksum error: 0, Encaps failed: 2
No memory: 0, Invalid packet: 0, Fragmented: 0
CDP version 1 advertisements output: 0, Input: 0
CDP version 2 advertisements output: 4260, Input: 4348
Router#

In this example, traffic information from CDP table is displayed including the numbers of packets sent; the number of packets received, header syntax, checksum errors, failed encapsulations, memory problems, and invalid and fragmented packets are displayed. Header syntax indicates the number of packets CDP receives with that have an invalid header format.

Obtaining port and Interface Information

Configuration 7-22: Display information about CDP status on Router interfaces or switch ports using the **show cdp interface** command.

Router#sh cdp interface
Serial0/0/0 is up, line protocol is up, encapsulation is SMDS
  Sending CDP packets every 60 seconds
  Holdtime is 180 seconds
FastEthernet0/1 is up, line protocol is up, encapsulation is ARPA
  Sending CDP packets every 60 seconds
  Holdtime is 180 seconds

Router#sh cdp interface FastEthernet 0/1
Ethernet0/1 is up, line protocol is up, encapsulation is ARPA
  Sending CDP packets every 60 seconds
  Holdtime is 180 seconds
Router#

The **show cdp interface** command shows information about each interface using CDP, including the encapsulation on the line, the timer, and the holdtime for each interface. CDP can be turned OFF completely on a Router by **no cdp run** command. However, CDP can also be turned OFF per interface with the **no cdp enable** command. The port can be enabled with CDP by the **cdp enable** command. All ports and interfaces are default to cdp enable.

Configuration 7-23: Turn OFF CDP on a serial interface on the Router using the **no cdp enable** command.

Then verify the changes.

```
Router(config)#int s0/0/0
Router(config-if)#no cdp enable
Router(config-if)#^Z
Router#sh cdp int
Ethernet0/1 is up, line protocol is up, encapsulation is ARPA
  Sending CDP packets every 60 seconds
  Holdtime is 180 seconds
Router#
```

The output above shows that serial 0 does not up in the Router output.

Managing Telnet

Telnet is a virtual terminal protocol that is part of the TCP/IP protocol suite. Telnet allows dedicated connections to remote devices, gathering information, and running programs remotely.

Telnet Overview

Telnet is the best utility for checking network connectivity, since it uses IP at the Network layer and TCP at the Transport layer to create a session with a remote host. Telnet is a virtual terminal protocol that is part of the TCP/IP protocol. Telnet allows dedicated connections to remote devices, gathering information, and running programs. Telnet can only be used after the Routers or switches are configured for IP networking, i.e. VTY lines are configured correctly. Telnet can be used to configure the Routers or switches without using a console port. Telnet can be issued by typing **telnet** from any command prompt (DOS, Linux, or CISCO).

Now, let us investigate the differences between CDP and Telnet. It can be summarized as follows:

- Both are used to gather information about routers and switches.
- CDP can only be used to gather information about directly connected neighbor routers and switches.
- Telnet can be used to gather information about directly and indirectly connected routers and switches.
- It is possible to Telnet into remote routers and switches and then run CDP to gather CDP information about indirectly connected routers and switches that cannot be obtained by normally running CDP.
- The CDP cannot be used for running programs as Telnet does.

Configuration 7-24: Access the **Telnet** utility from any Router prompt, as in the following:

```
Router#telnet 172.17.17.17
Trying 172.17.17.17 … Open
Password required, but none set

[Connection to 172.17.17.17 closed by foreign host]
  Router#
```

The connection is refused, since no VTY port is configured. To configure the user-mode passwords, the required line should be configured at first, and then the commands **login** or **no login** must be issued to tell the Router whether to prompt for authentication or not.

THAAR(config)#line vty 0 4
THAAR(config-line)#login
THAAR(config-line)#password thaamj
THAAR(config-line)#^Z
THAAR#
%SYS-5-CONFIG_I: Configured from console by console

Router#172.17.17.17
Trying 172.17.17.17 ... Open

User Access Verification

Password: "thaamj"
THAAR>

At the Router prompt, there is no need to type **telnet**; just type a hostname or IP address, and the Router will assume that **Telnet** utility is required. Notice that, the VTY password is the User-mode password, not the enable mode password. The double quotation is used to indicate that when the password is entered it will not appear on the Router console.
Router# "Console"
THAAR>en
% No password set
THAAR>

Anyone telnetting into the remote device must use the enable mode password or the enable secret password to be able to configure remote devices.

Telnetting into Multiple Devices at the Same Time

To terminate an active Telnet connection, the following commands can be used:

- close
- disconnect
- exit
- logout
- quit

To keep open multiple Telnet sessions use the **CTRL+SHIFT+6**, then **X** keystroke combination.

Configuration 7-25: From Router prompt, **telnet** into router THAAR, then **suspend** the session.

Router#172.17.17.17
Trying 172.17.17.17 ... Open

User Access Verification

Password: "thaamj"
THAAR> "CTRL+SHIFT+6 X"
Router#

To end the connection from THAAR> prompt, enter the **exit** command. To suspend the connection from THAAR> prompt, press **Ctrl+Shift+6** combination, release it, and then press **X**. The double quotation is used to indicate that when the password and the keystrokes are entered, they will not appear on the Router console.

Configuration 7-26: From Router prompt, **telnet** into a Switch while the session with Router THAAR still suspended.

Router#172.18.18.18
Trying 172.18.18.18... Open
....
Router#

To **telnet** into Switch1, the enable mode password level 15 must be configured on the switch. If the keystrokes **Ctrl+Shift+6** and **X** are pressed at the end of the switch's Menu Console Logon Screen, the access will return to Router prompt.

Checking Telnet Sessions

Configuration 7-27: Display the connections made from your Router to remote devices using the **show sessions** command.

```
Router#sh sessions
  Conn     Host              Address         Byte   Idle   Conn Name
    1      172.17.17.17      172.17.17.17      0      0     172.17.17.17
  * 2      172.18.18.18      172.18.18.18      0      0     172.18.18.18
```

Router#

The asterisk (*) next to connection 2 means that session 2 was the last session. However, pressing **Enter** key twice can access the last session again. Typing the number of the connection and pressing **Enter** key twice can access any opened session.

Checking Telnet Users

Configuration 7-28: List all active consoles and VTY ports in use on the Routers using the **show users** command.

```
Router#sh users
       Line       User      Host(s)        Idle Location
   *   0 con 0              172.17.17.17    01:15:05
                           172.18.18.18    01:05:25


THAAR>sh users
       Line       User      Host(s)        Idle Location
       0 con 0              idle            7
   *   2 vty 0
```

In the command output, the **con** represents the local console. In the first example, the console is connected to two remote IP addresses, or devices. In the second example, the command is issued on THAAR Router, which Router had telnetted into. The output shows that the console is active and that VTY port 2 is being used. The asterisk (*) represents the current terminal session user. The **show users all** command can be used to present all available lines regardless of whether anyone is using them.

Terminating Telnet Sessions

Configuration 7-29: Terminate a switch session using the **exit** command.

Router# "Enter+Enter"
[Resuming connection 2 to 172.18.18.18 …]

Switch>exit

[Connection to 172.18.18.18 closed by foreign host]
Router#

The **exit** command is used to end session from a remote device prompt.

Configuration 7-30: Terminate the THAAR router session using the **disconnect** command.

Router#disconnect ?
  <1-2>   The number of an active network connection

  WORD   The name of an active network connection

  <cr>

Router#disconnect 1
Closing connection to 172.17.17.17 [confirm]
Router#

The **disconnect** command is used to end a session from a local device prompt.

Configuration 7-31: Terminate a device session that attached to the Router through **Telnet**, using **clear line #** command. Then verify that the user has been disconnected.

Router#sh users

	Line	User	Host(s)	Idle	Location
*	0 con 0		idle	0	
	1 aux 0		idle	0	
	2 vty 0		Idle	0	172.17.17.16

Router#clear line 2
[confirm]
[OK]
Router#sh users

	Line	User	Host(s)	Idle Location
*	0 con 0		idle	0
	1 aux 0		idle	1

At the beginning, the Configuration checks if any devices are attached to the Router using the **show users** command. Then the **clear line #** command is used to disconnect VTY 2 from the Router. The **show users** command is used again to verify that VTY 2 is disconnected.

Resolving Hostnames

In CISCO devices, there are two techniques to resolve hostnames to IP addresses; building a host table on each Router or building a Domain Name System (DNS) server, which is like a Dynamic Host table. CISCO devices use these techniques to translate the hostname to an IP address. Using hostnames rather than IP addresses to connect to remote machines provides an easiest way to configure, manage, and troubleshoot the system. This section describes these two techniques and gives some examples.

Building a Host Table

Configuration 7-32: Build a host table on the Router using **ip host name tcp_port_number ip_address.**

```
Router(config)#ip host ?
  WORD    Name of host
Router(config)#ip host THAAR ?
  <0-65535>    Default telnet port number
  A.B.C.D      Host IP address (maximum of 8)
Router(config)#ip host THAAR 172.17.17.17
Router(config)#ip host Switch1 172.18.18.18
Router(config)#^Z
```

To define a static host name-to-address mapping in the host cache, use the **ip host** global configuration command. To remove the name-to-address mapping, use the **no** form of this command. The created host table provides name resolution only on the Router on which it was built. The default is TCP port number 23. It is possible to create a session using **Telnet** with a different TCP port number, if needed, and up to eight IP addresses to a hostname can be assigned.

Configuration 7-33: Display the entries in the created host table using the **show hosts** command.

```
Router# show hosts
Default domain is not set
Name/address lookup uses domain service
Name servers are 255.255.255.255
```

Host	Flags	Age	Type	Address(es)
THAAR	(perm, OK)	0	IP	172.17.17.17
Switch1	(perm, OK)	0	IP	172.18.18.18

In this Router output, two hostnames and their associated IP addresses are shown. The **perm** in the Flags column means that the entry is manually configured. Entries resolved by DNS will mark as **temp**. Entries marked **OK** are believed to be valid. Entries marked **??** are considered suspect and subject to revalidation. Entries marked **EX** are expired.

Configuration 7-34: Verify that the host table resolves names using the **telnet** command.

```
Router# telnet Thaar
Trying 172.17.17.17 … Open
```

User Access Verification

Password: "thaarmj"

THAAR> "CTRL+SHIFT+6 X"
Router#Switch1
Trying 172.18.18.18... Open

....

Router#

The configuration above shows that the host table is working correctly. The hostnames are used instead of IP addresses to telnet into two devices. The hostnames must now appear in the output of **show sessions** command.

Router#sh sessions

Conn	Host	Address	Byte	Idle	Conn Name
1	thaar	172.17.17.17	0	0	thaar
* 2	Switch1	172.18.18.18	0	0	Switch1

Router#

To remove a hostname from the host table the **no ip host** command should be used, as in the following example:

Router(config)#no ip host Switch1

Resolving Names with DNS

Configuration 7-35, **DNS names resolution configuration**: If the internetwork has a DNS server, the following configurations should be applied to the CISCO devices to make the DNS name resolution works:

1.   **ip domain-lookup**, which is turned ON by default. It only needs to be issued if it is previously turned OFF (with the **no ip domain-lookup** command).
2.   **ip name-server**. This sets the IP address of the DNS server. It is possible to enter the IP addresses of up to six servers.
3.   (optional) **ip domain-name**. This command appends the domain name to the typed host-name.

The following Configuration shows how these commands are configured on CISCO Routers:

Router(config)#ip domain-lookup
Router(config)#ip name-server ?
 A.B.C.D   Domain server IP address (maximum of 6)
Router(config)#ip name-server 172.17.17.254
Router(config)#ip domain-name edu.com
Router(config)#^Z
Router#

DNS is used to resolve hostnames in a network with many devices where creating a host table for each device is not recommended. Anytime, a CISCO device receives a command it does not understand. Therefore, it tries to resolve this command through DNS resolution by default. As an example, if the **majeed** command is executed before configuring the DNS, the following error messages will be received:

Router#majeed
Translating "majeed"...domain server (255.255.255.255)

% Unknown command or computer name, or unable to find computer address
Router#

Configuration 7-36: Verify the DNS name resolution using the **ping** and **trace** commands. Then check what happened with the **sh hosts** command.

Router#ping thaar
Translating "thaar"... domain server (172.17.17.254) [OK]
Type escape sequence to abort.
Sending 5, 100-byte ICMP Echos to 172.17.17.17, timeout is 2 seconds:
!!!!!
Success rate is 100 percent (5/5), round-trip min/avg/max = 1/2/4 ms

Notice that the DNS server is used by the Router to resolve the host name. The **ping** output displays the minimum, average, and maximum times it takes for a Ping packet to find a system and return. Each exclamation point (!) indicates a receipt of a reply. A period (.) indicates that the network server is timed out while waiting for a reply. Other characters may appear in the output of the ping command, depending on the protocol type. The success rate is the percentage of packets successfully echoed back to the Router. Anything less than 80 percent is usually considered problematic.

Router#sh hosts
Default domain is edu.com
Name/address lookup uses domain service
Name servers are 172.17.17.254

Host	Flag	Age	Type	Address(es)
Thaar.edu.com	(temp, OK)	0	IP	172.17.17.17
Switch1	(perm, OK)	0	IP	172.18.18.18

Router#

The above table shows the DNS resolved entries with **temp**, but the **Switch1** device is still **perm**, which means that it is a manual entry. Keep in your mind, that the hostname is a full domain name. Therefore, if the command **ip domain-name edu.com** is not used, the FQDN must be used to access the network devices. As an example, the last **ping** command must be issued like this: **ping thaar.edu.com**.

Router#trace thaar
Type escape sequence to abort.
Tracing the route to thaar.edu.com (172.17.17.17)
    1 thaar.edu.com (172.17.17.17)10 msec 10 msec
Router#

The **trace** command shows the hops (routers) that a packet traverses on its way to a remote host. In the above example, the packet went through only one hop to find the destination host.

Summary

After an introduction to the CISCO Router main internal components, this chapter gave an in-depth view of the CISCO IOS configuration files and their locations in the CISCO devices. Basics of the Router Managements, Router boot sequence, and configuration register, including how to use the configuration register for password recovery and examples of well-designed networks are given in this chapter. Several configurations are used to clarify the ideas behind this chapter.

The following topics are covered:

- Backing up and restoring the CISCO IOS
- Backing up and restoring the CISCO configuration
- Gathering information about neighbor devices through CDP and Telnet utility
- Resolving hostnames using host table and DNS
- Testing the network connectivity using the ping and trace utilities.

At the end of the chapter, several learning questions are given to evaluate the learning level from this chapter. The correct answers and solutions with complementary discussions are found in appendix A, "Answers to Chapters Learning Questions."

Chapter Seven Commands Reference

Table 7-8 lists and briefly describes all the new commands and keys that are used in this chapter.

Table 7-8 Chapter 7 Commands Reference

Command	Description
boot system flash	Loading the first file from Flash memory
boot system flash filename	Loading IOS with the name filename from Flash memory
boot system tftp filename 107.100.100.100	Loading IOS with the name filename from the TFTP server 107.100.100.100
Router(config)#config-register 0x2100	Changes the configuration register value using config-register command so that the Router will boot to ROM monitor mode next time reloaded
rommon>confreg	Invokes the configuration register configuration
rommon>confreg 0x2142	Changes the configuration register bit value on 2600 CISCO Routers directly from ROM monitor
rommon>i	Initializes the Router directly from ROM monitor
Router#reload	Reloads the router from enabled mode
Router#sh flash	Lists the content of router's flash
Router#copy flash tftp	Copies the content of flash memory to predefined tftp server
Router#copy tftp flash	Copies the configuration file from tftp server to flash memory
Router# show start	Shows the startup configurations
Router#copy running-config startup-config	Backups the running configuration to flash
Router #copy run tftp	Backups the running configuration to predefined tftp server
Router#copy start run	Restores the running configuration from flash to DRAM
Router#copy tftp run	Restores the running configuration from tftp server to DRAM
Router#erase start	Deletes the configuration from flash
copy rcp running-config	Restores the running configuration from network server to DRAM
copy rcp startup-config	Restores the configuration file from network server to flash memory
copy system:running-config	Restores the running configuration from flash to DRAM
copy running-config rcp	Backups the running configuration to predefined network server
copy ftp: system:running-config copy rcp: system:running-config copy tftp: system:running-config	Restores the running configuration from network server to DRAM
copy ftp: nvram:startup-config copy rcp: nvram:startup-config copy tftp: nvram:startup-config	Restores the configuration file from network server to flash memory
nvram:startup-config	Lists the content of the flash
erase nvram:	Deletes the content of the flash
nvram:startup-config	Backs up the content of DRAM to flash
copy system:running-config ftp: copy system:running-config rcp: copy system:running-config tftp:	Backs up the content of DRAM to network server
more system:running-config	Lists the content of DRAM

Router(config)#ip host THAAR 172.17.17.17	Defines a name resolution on the router (host name, THAAR, and IP address, 172.17.17.17, pairs)
Router# show hosts	Displays the entries in the created host table
Router(config)#ip domain-lookup	Turns ON the name resolution on CISCO devices
Router(config)#ip name-server 172.17.17.254	Sets the IP address of the DNS server
Router(config)#ip domain-name edu.com	Appends the domain name to the typed host-name

Chapter 7 Learning Questions

7-1   Which of the following is true about **RAM**? (Select all that apply)

A.   RAM retains its contents for as long as power is supplied. It does not require constant refreshing, like DRAM.

B.   RAM stores information in capacitors that must be periodically refreshed. Delays can occur because they are inaccessible to the processor when refreshing their contents. However, they are less complex and have a greater capacity than SRAMs.

C.   Volatile memory can be read and written by a microprocessor.

D.   RAM retains its contents intact when a unit is powered OFF.

E.   Used by all computers to store information. CISCO Routers use RAM to store packet buffers and routing tables, along with the hardware addresses cache.

7-2   Which of the following is true about **SRAM**? (Select all that apply)

A.   A type of RAM that retains its contents for as long as power is supplied. It does not require constant refreshing, like DRAM.

B.   A type of RAM that stores information in capacitors that must be periodically refreshed. Delays can occur because they are inaccessible to the processor when refreshing their contents. However, they are less complex and have a greater capacity than SRAMs.

C.   Volatile memory can be read and written by a microprocessor.

D.   RAM that retains its contents intact when a unit is powered OFF.

E.   Used by all computers to store information. CISCO Routers use RAM to store packet buffers and routing tables, along with the hardware addresses cache.

7-3   Which of the following is true about **DRAM**? (Select all that apply)

A.   A type of RAM that retains its contents for as long as power is supplied. It does not require constant refreshing, like DRAM.

B.   A type of RAM stores information in capacitors that must be periodically refreshed. Delays can occur because they are inaccessible to the processor when refreshing their contents. However, they are less complex and have a greater capacity than SRAMs.

C.   Volatile memory that can be read and written by a microprocessor.

D.   RAM that retains its contents intact when a unit is powered OFF.

E.   Used by all computers to store information. CISCO Routers use RAM to store packet buffers and routing tables, along with the hardware addresses cache. Running configuration is stored in DRAM.

7-4   Which of the following is true about **NVRAM**? (Select all that apply)

A.   A type of RAM retains its contents for as long as power is supplied. It does not require constant refreshing, like DRAM.

B.   A type of RAM that stores information in capacitors that must be periodically refreshed. Delays can occur because they are inaccessible to the processor when refreshing their contents. However, they are less complex and have a greater capacity than SRAMs.

C.   Volatile memory that can be read and written by a microprocessor.

D.   RAM that retains its contents intact when a unit is powered OFF.

E.   It is used to hold the Router and Switch startup configuration.

7-5   Which of the following is true about **ROM**? (Select all that apply)

A.   Chip used to boot and maintain the Router.

B.   CISCO Routers use it to load the bootstrap, which runs a POST, and then find and load the IOS in

flash memory by default.
C.   Chip used to hold the bootstrap, POST, ROM monitor and the Mini-IOS or bootloader.
D.   Chip used on the Router to hold the CISCO IOS by default.

7-6   Which of the following is true about **EEPROM**? (Select all that apply)

A.   Chip used to boot and maintain the Router.
B.   CISCO Routers use it to load the bootstrap, which runs a POST, and then find and load the IOS in flash memory by default.
C.   Chip used to hold the bootstrap, POST, ROM monitor and the Mini-IOS or bootloader.
D.   Chip used on the Router to hold the CISCO IOS by default.

7-7   Which of the following is true about **Flash Memory**? (Select all that apply)

A.   Nonvolatile storage that can be electrically erased and reprogrammed so that software images can be stored, booted, and rewritten as necessary.
B.   CISCO Routers use it to load the bootstrap, which runs a POST, and then find and load the IOS in flash memory by default.
C.   Chip used to hold the bootstrap, POST, ROM monitor and the Mini-IOS or bootloader.
D.   EEPROM Chip used on the Router to hold the CISCO IOS by default.
E.   It is not erased when the Router is reloaded.

7-8   Try to decide which option gets in which blank.
Bootstrap is stored in the _____of the ROM. It is used to bring a Router up during _____. It will boot the Router and then load the IOS.

A.   Initialization
B.   microcode

7-9   Try to decide which option gets in which blank.
POST is stored in the microcode of the _____. It is used to check the basic functionality of the _____ and determines which interfaces are present.

A.   ROM
B.   Router hardware

7-10   Try to decide which option gets in which blank.
ROM monitor is stored in the _____of the ROM. It is used for manufacturing testing and _____.

A.   Troubleshooting
B.   microcode

7-11   Try to decide which option gets in which blank.
Mini-IOS is called the RXBOOT or _____by CISCO. The mini-IOS is a _____ stored in ROM that can be used to bring up an interface and load a _____ into flash memory.

A.   bootloader
B.   CISCO IOS
C.   Small IOS

7-12   Try to decide which option gets in which blank.
Configuration Register is used to control how the Router _____. The typical value of this register is 0x2102, which tells the Router to load the IOS from _____.

A.   Boots up
B.   Flash memory

7-13   Which of the following is used to load the CISCO IOS? (Select all that apply)

A.   Configuration register
B.   Flash memory
C.   RAM

7-14   Which of the following commands displays the value of the configuration register?

A.   show configuration
B.   show register
C.   show version
D.   show all

7-15   TRUE/FALSE: The Router and Switch startup configuration is erased when the device is reloaded.

A.   TRUE
B.   FALSE

7-16   Which of the following is hold by the RAM? (Select all that apply)

A.   Running configuration
B.   Packet buffers
C.   Routing tables
D.   The software that allows the device function
E.   The data structures that make the device function

7-17   TRUE/FALSE: The flash memory contents are erased when the Router is reloaded.

A.   TRUE
B.   FALSE

7-18   Which of the following memories is used by the CISCO Router to store packet buffers and routing tables?

A.   Flash
B.   RAM
C.   NVRAM
D.   EEPROM

7-19   Which of the following is part of the Router boot sequence? (Select all that apply)

A.   POST step
B.   Bootstrap step
C.   Power OFF step
D.   IOS step
E.   Setup step
F.   Operational step

7-20   Which of the following is true about POST booting step? (Select all that apply)

A.   This step is repressible for testing the hardware to verify that all components of the device are operational and present.
B.   This step is repressible for looking for and loading the CISCO IOS software.
C.   This step is repressible for looking for a valid configuration file stored in NVRAM.
D.   This step is repressible for operating the device either from setup mode or from the startup-config file.

7-21   Which of the following is true about Bootstrap booting step? (Select all that apply)

A.   This step is repressible for testing the hardware to verify that all components of the device are operational and present.
B.   This step is repressible for looking for and loading the CISCO IOS software.
C.   This step is repressible for looking for a valid configuration file stored in NVRAM.
D.   This step is repressible for operating the device either from setup mode or from the startup-config file.

7-22   Which of the following is true about IOS booting step? (Select all that apply)

A.   This step is repressible for testing the hardware to verify that all components of the device are operational and present.
B.   This step is repressible for looking for and loading the CISCO IOS software.
C.   This step is repressible for looking for a valid configuration file stored in NVRAM.
D.   This step is repressible for operating the device either from setup mode or from the startup-config file.

7-23   Which of the following is true about setup booting step? (Select all that apply)

A.   This step is repressible for testing the hardware to verify that all components of the device are operational and present.
B.   This step is repressible for looking for and loading the CISCO IOS software.
C.   This step is repressible for looking for a valid configuration file stored in NVRAM.
D.   This step is repressible for operating the device either from setup mode or from the startup-config file.

7-24   Which of the following is a CISCO router OS? (Select all that apply)

A.   CISCO IOS image: It allows the router to perform its normal function of routing packets.
B.   ROMMON in ROM: Its operating environment is the ROM Monitor and it operates on the old and new routers.
C.   RxBoot, boot helper in ROM: Its operating environment is the Boot ROM and it operates only in the older routers.

7-25   TRUE/FALSE: The last two types are used to perform some troubleshooting, recover router passwords, and to copy the new IOS files into Flash when Flash has been erased or corrupted for any reason.

A.   TRUE
B.   FALSE

7-26   TRUE/FALSE: The resent CISCO router product lines (for example, 1800 and 2800 series routers) use only one additional OS to perform the special functions, whereas the older CISCO routers (for example, 2500 series routers) actually had two different operating systems to perform these special functions.

A.   TRUE
B.   FALSE

7-27   Try to decide if the following paragraph is correctly defining the configuration register.

A.   Correct
B.   Incorrect

"The configuration register is a 16-bit configurable value stored in the hardware or software that determines how CISCO routers function during initialization. In the hardware, the bit position is set using a jumper. While, in the software, it is set by specifying specific bit patterns used to set startup options, and is configured using a hexadecimal value with the configuration commands."

7-28   Which of the following is set by default using the configuration register?

A.   Loading the CISCO IOS from flash memory
B.   Loading the CISCO IOS from RAM
C.   Loading the startup-config file from NVRAM
D.   Loading the startup-config file from ROM

7-29   Which of the following is used to hold the software configuration register?

A.   ROM
B.   RAM
C.   SRAM
D.   NVRAM

7-30   Which is true about configuration register? (Select all that apply)

A.   The default value of the configuration register is 0x2102(hexadecimal).
B.   The 16 bits of the configuration register are read 15-0, from left to right.
C.   It is a hardware and software register.
D.   It can be set by software as well as by jumpers.

7-31   TRUE/FALSE: Several configuration operations can be obtained by setting the configuration register to different values.

A.   TRUE
B.   FALSE

7-32   Which of the following bits are used for the boot field? (Select all that apply)

A.   6
B.   7
C.   0-3
D.   0-4

7-33   Which of the following provides the current value of the configuration register?
A.   sh config
B.   sh register
C.   sh ver
D.   sh all

7-34   What is the default value of the configuration register?

A.   0x2100
B.   0x2101
C.   0x2102

D.   0x2112

7-35   From which configuration mode can, the **show version** command be issued?

A.   User-Configuration mode
B.   Privileged EXEC mode
C.   Interface configuration mode
D.   Global Configuration mode

7-36   Which of the following is true regarding the default configuration register value of 0x2102? (Select all that apply)

A.   The first 2 from left makes the Router to boot the default ROM software, which then will load the IOS from flash memory.
B.   The 1 tells the Router to disable the break at the startup.
C.   The 0 tells the Router to use the NVRAM contents during the startup.
D.   The last 2 in the right tells the Router to use the boot commands specified in NVRAM.

7-37   On more modern CISCO routers that do not have a RxBoot OS, the process to choose, which OS to load, depend on the value of boot field using the following steps. Try to rearrange the steps below in the correct order.

A.   **Step1**: If the boot field = 1, load the first IOS file found in Flash memory.
B.   **Step2**: If the boot field = 0, use the ROMMON OS.
C.   **Step3**: If the boot field = 2-F:
    1.   Try each **boot system** command in the startup-config file, in order, until one works.
    2.   If none of the **boot system** commands work, load the first IOS file, found in Flash memory.

7-38   Match each of the following boot system commands to its suitable result.

1.   boot system flash
2.   boot system flash filename
3.   boot system tftp filename 107.100.100.100

A.   Loading IOS with the name filename from the TFTP server 107.100.100.100
B.   Loading IOS with the name filename from Flash memory
C.   Loading the first file from Flash memory

7-39   Try to decide which option gets in which blank.
Changing the configuration register value provides the possibility to _____ how the Router _____ and
_____.

A.   Modify
B.   Boots
C.   Runs

7-40   Which of the following can be implemented by modifying the configuration register value? (Select all that apply)

A.   Force the system into the ROM monitor.
B.   Select a boot source and default boot filename.
C.   Enable or disable the Break function.
D.   Control broadcast addresses.

E.   Set the console terminal baud rate.
F.   Load operating software from ROM.
G.   Enable booting from TFTP server.
H.   Recover a lost password.

7-41   Which of the following sets the configuration register to a new value?

A.   config-register 0x2142
B.   config register 0x2142
C.   config 0x2142
D.   register 0x2142

7-42   From which configuration mode can, the **config-register** command be issued?

A.   User-Configuration mode
B.   Global Configuration mode
C.   Interface configuration mode
D.   Line interface mode

7-43   Which of the following tells the router to boot the system image from the Flash memory? (Select all that apply)

A.   config-register 0x210F
B.   config-register 0x2102
C.   config-register 0x2101
D.   config-register 0x2100

7-44   Where would a router boot from, if a configuration register was set to 0x0101?

A.   Boot ROM
B.   ROM
C.   Flash memory
D.   NVRAM

7-45   TRUE/FALSE: Configuration register changes take effect only when the system reloads.

A.   TRUE
B.   FALSE

7-46   Which of the following invokes the ROM monitor mode? (Select all that apply)

A.   config-register 0x210F
B.   config-register 0x2102
C.   config-register 0x2101
D.   config-register 0x2100

7-47   When the password recovery is required? (Select all that apply)

A.   The password is lost when the administrator in User-configuration mode.
B.   The password is lost when the administrator out of the Router.
C.   The password is lost when the administrator in privileged EXEC mode.

7-48   TRUE/FALSE: Password recovery can only be done from the console port on the Router.

A.   TRUE
B.   FALSE

7-49   TRUE/FALSE: The value of bit 6 in the default virtual configuration register (0x2102) is 0 or OFF. This will tell the Router to look for and to load a Router configuration stored in NVRAM (startup-config).

A.   TRUE
B.   FALSE

7-50   TRUE/FALSE: To recover a password, bit 6 in the virtual configuration register must be turned ON, which will tell the router to ignore the NVRAM contents.

A.   TRUE
B.   FALSE

7-51   Which of the following virtual configuration register values can be used in the password recovery procedure?

A.   0x2101
B.   0x2142
C.   0x2401
D.   0x2402

7-52   Which of the following can be considered as part of the overall Password recovery procedure? (Select all that apply)

A.   Boot the Router and interrupt the boot sequence by performing a **Break** to the rommon prompt.
B.   Change the configuration register to ignore NVRAM by turning ON bit 6 (with the value 0x2142).
C.   Reload the Router
D.   Enter the privileged level in the system EXEC.
E.   Copy the startup-configuration file to running-config.
F.   Change the password.
G.   Change the configuration register value back to its original setting.
H.   Copy the running-config file to startup-configuration.
I.   Reload the Router

7-53   TRUE/FALSE: To recover a lost password, set the configuration register to (0x0040) so that the contents of NVRAM are ignored.

A.   TRUE
B.   FALSE

7-54   Which of the following keywords interrupts the system booting?

A.   Ctrl+A
B.   Ctrl+Break
C.   Ctrl+delete
D.   Ctrl+Insert

7-55   Why system interrupt is required during the password recovery procedure? (Select all that apply)

A.   To prevent normal system booting.
B.   To make the Router boots from ROM monitor prompt.

C.   To provide a normal system booting and starting setup mode.
D.   To make the Router boots from flash memory.

7-56   Which of the following commands changes the configuration register from ROM monitor on 2600 platforms?

A.   config-register 0x2142
B.   config register 0x2142
C.   confreg 0x2142
D.   register 0x2142

7-57   Which of the following initializes the Router from ROM monitor? (Select all that apply)

A.   reload
B.   reinitialize
C.   reset
D.   i

7-58   Which of the following initializes the Router immediately from the privileged EXEC mode? (Select all that apply)

A.   reload
B.   reinitialize
C.   reset
D.   i

7-59   Which of the following initializes the Router after 10 minutes from the privileged EXEC mode? (Select all that apply)

A.   reload 10
B.   Reload at 10
C.   reset in 10
D.   reload in 10

7-60   Which of the following initializes the software on the Router at 1:00 p.m. today from the privileged EXEC mode? (Select all that apply)

A.   reload at 1:00
B.   reload at 13:00
C.   reset at 13:00
D.   reload in 13:00

7-61   Which of the following initializes the software on the Router on April 10 at 2:00 a.m. from the privileged EXEC mode? (Select all that apply)

A.   reload at 14:00 apr 10
B.   reload at 02:00
C.   reset at 14:00 apr 10
D.   reload at 02:00 apr 10

7-62   Which of the following cancels a pending reload from the privileged EXEC mode? (Select all that apply)

A.   clear reload all

B.   reload cancel
C.   reset all
D.   no reload

7-63   Which of the following modes of operations is used to issue the **confreg 0x2142** command?

A.   User-Configuration mode
B.   Privileged EXEC mode
C.   ROM monitor mode
D.   Line interface mode

7-64   Which of the following modes of operations is used to issue the **i** command?

A.   User-Configuration mode
B.   Privileged EXEC mode
C.   ROM monitor mode
D.   Line interface mode

7-65   Which of the following modes of operations is used to issue the **reset** command?

A.   User-Configuration mode
B.   Privileged EXEC mode
C.   ROM monitor mode
D.   Line interface mode

7-66   From which configuration mode can, the **reload** command be issued?

A.   User-Configuration mode
B.   Privileged EXEC mode
C.   Interface configuration mode
D.   Line interface mode

7-67   What should you do to make a Router boot from the ROM and skip NVRAM?

A.   Set the config-reg to 0x2140
B.   Set the config-reg to 0x2101
C.   router#boot system rom
D.   Run the reload command and press Ctrl-Break within 5 sec.

7-68   Which privileged mode command can be used to halt Router operations and restart or reboot the Router?

A.   cycle
B.   reset
C.   reload
D.   Setup

7-69   What does the 0x0101 config-register setting do?

A.   The Router will boot the IOS.
B.   The Router will load configuration in NVRAM.
C.   The Router will load startup configuration.
D.   The Router will boot normally.

7-70   What would the virtual configuration register set to be, if you changed the baud to 1200? Given a configuration register setting of 0x2102

A.   0x3102
B.   0x2902
C.   0x3902
D.   0x2901
E.   0x3101
F.   0x3922
G.   0x2942

7-71   Which of the following commands makes a router to change the IOS that is loaded when the router boots? (Select all that apply)

A.   boot system
B.   Load
C.   reload
D.   reboot system
E.   reload system
F.   boot
G.   reboot
H.   configuration register

7-72   Which of the following is the last stage that occurs during a CISCO router bootup?

A.   POST
B.   Finding and loading the configuration
C.   loading the CISCO IOS image
D.   Finding and loading the bootstrap

7-73   Which of the following stages verifies that all router components are operational during a CISCO router bootup process?

A.   Finding and loading the configuration
B.   loading the CISCO IOS image
C.   POST
D.   Finding and loading the bootstrap

7-74   What does a router do if the boot field value of 0x2 is found during the CISCO router bootup process?

A.   checking the startup-config file for boot system commands
B.   running the ROM monitor
C.   loading the CISCO IOS image from flash
D.   finding and loading the bootstrap.

7-75   TRUE/FALSE: As a **rule** in this field, before upgrading or restoring a CISCO IOS, a copy of the existing file to a TFTP server should be taken. This copy is considered as a backup in case the new image does not work.

A.   TRUE
B.   FALSE

7-76   Try to decide which option gets in which blank.

Verifying the Router _____, before attempting _____ the CISCO IOS on the Router with a new IOS file, is important, since it will show if the Router flash memory has _____ to hold the new image or not.

    A.   enough space
    B.   to upgrade
    C.   flash memory

7-77   Which of the following verifies the amount of the flash memory?

    A.   flash
    B.   show flash
    C.   display flash
    D.   view flash
    E.   verify flash

7-78   Which of the following information is provided by the **show flash** command? (Select all that apply)

    A.   The CISCO IOS image name in the Router
    B.   The file size of the CISCO IOS image in the Router
    C.   The total amount of the flash memory in the Router
    D.   The available amount of the flash memory in the Router
    E.   The used amount of the flash memory in the Router

7-79   What does c3600 indicate in the CISCO image name c3600-js-l.112-18.bin?

    A.   To image name itself.
    B.   To platform type
    C.   To flash memory type
    D.   To CISCO version

7-80   What does the 112-18 indicate in the CISCO image name c3600-js-l.112-18.bin?

    A.   To image name itself.
    B.   To platform type
    C.   To flash memory type
    D.   To the CISCO revision number

7-81   Which of the following commands displays the current system image version? (Select all that apply)

    A.   sh run
    B.   sh start
    C.   sh flash
    D.   sh version

7-82   From which configuration mode can, the **show flash** command be issued?

    A.   User-Configuration mode
    B.   Privileged EXEC mode
    C.   Interface configuration mode
    D.   Line interface mode

7-83   Which of the following commands copies the IOS image from flash memory to tftp server?

A.   flash copy to tftp server
B.   copy flash to tftp server
C.   Back up flash to tftp server
D.   backup flash tftp
E.   copy flash tftp

7-84   Which of the following information must be supplied by the administrator to the **copy flash tftp** command? (Select all that apply)

A.   The CISCO IOS image name to be copied.
B.   The file size of the CISCO IOS image in the Router
C.   The address or name of remote tftp server
D.   The destination file name
E.   The hostname of the Router

7-85   What does the "!" character indicate in the output of the **copy flash tftp** command?

A.   To image name itself.
B.   Ten packets have been successfully transferred.
C.   To flash memory type
D.   To CISCO version

7-86   What is the default destination file name that can be supplied to the **copy flash tftp** command?

A.   No default name, the administrator must supply a new name.
B.   The platform type name
C.   The hostname of the Router
D.   The source CISCO IOS image name

7-87   From which configuration mode can, the **copy flash tftp** command be issued?

A.   User-Configuration mode
B.   Privileged EXEC mode
C.   Interface configuration mode
D.   Line interface mode

7-88   TRUE/FALSE: It is recommended to check the network connectivity before **copy flash tftp** is issued.

A.   TRUE
B.   FALSE

7-89   TRUE/FALSE: Before **copy flash tftp** command is issued, the TFTP host must have a default directory specified, or it will not work.

A.   TRUE
B.   FALSE

7-90   Which of the following restores the IOS image in flash memory from tftp server?

A.   tftp server copy to flash
B.   copy tftp flash
C.   copy tftp to flash
D.   restore tftp to flash

     E.   upgrade tftp flash

7-91   Which of the following commands upgrades the IOS image in flash memory from a tftp server?

     A.   tftp server copy to flash
     B.   copy tftp flash
     C.   copy tftp to flash
     D.   restore tftp to flash
     E.   upgrade tftp flash

7-92   Which of the following information must be supplied by the administrator to the **copy tftp flash** command? (Select all that apply)

     A.   The CISCO IOS image name to be copied.
     B.   The file size of the CISCO IOS image in the Router
     C.   The address or name of remote tftp server
     D.   The destination file name
     E.   The source file name

7-93   What does the "!" character indicate in the output of the **copy tftp flash** command?

     A.   To image name itself.
     B.   One UDP segment has been successfully transferred.
     C.   To flash memory type
     D.   To CISCO version

7-94   What does the "e" character indicate in the output of the **copy tftp flash** command?

     A.   The contents of flash memory being erased.
     B.   One UDP segment has been successfully transferred.
     C.   To flash memory type
     D.   To CISCO version

7-95   What is the default destination file name that can be supplied to the **copy tftp flash** command?

     A.   No default name, the administrator must supply a new name.
     B.   The platform type name
     C.   The hostname of the Router
     D.   The source CISCO IOS image name

7-96   From which configuration mode can, the **copy tftp flash** command be issued?

     A.   User-Configuration mode
     B.   Privileged EXEC mode
     C.   Interface configuration mode
     D.   Line interface mode

7-97   TRUE/FALSE: It is recommended to check the network connectivity before **copy tftp flash** is issued.

     A.   TRUE
     B.   FALSE

7-98   TRUE/FALSE: Before the **copy tftp flash command** is issued, the required file to be placed in flash memory should be placed in the default TFTP directory on the TFTP host.

    A.   TRUE
    B.   FALSE

7-99   Which of the following is true about **copy tftp flash** command? (Select all that apply)

    A.   It is used to upgrade the CISCO IOS in flash.
    B.   It is used to replace the damaged CISCO IOS in tftp.
    C.   It is used to upgrade the CISCO IOS in tftp.
    D.   It is used to replace the damaged CISCO IOS in flash.

7-100   How many reboots the **copy tftp flash** command requires?

    A.   No reboots
    B.   One reboot
    C.   Two reboots
    D.   Three reboots

7-101   Which of the following is true about **copy tftp flash** command? (Select all that apply)

    A.   It erases the contents of the flash memory in case it has no enough room.
    B.   It erases the contents of the flash memory in case it is new.
    C.   It erases the contents of the flash memory in all cases.

7-102   Which of the following confirmations is required by the **copy tftp flash** command? (Select all that apply)

    A.   Erasing the flash memory contents
    B.   Saving the system configuration
    C.   Accepting the rebooting process
    D.   Accepting the address of the tftp host if the Router has used it before.
    E.   Erasing the system configuration

7-103   How many confirmations the **copy tftp flash** command prompts you for erasing the flash memory content?

    A.   One
    B.   Two
    C.   Three
    D.   No one

7-104   What command is used to configure a Router to become a TFTP server for a Router-system image that is run in flash?

    A.   boot system tftp
    B.   copy tftp flash
    C.   tftp-server system image-name
    D.   copy flash tftp

7-105   What command will tell a Router to run a CISCO IOS from a tftp host?

    A.   boot system tftp [ios file name] [ip address of tftp host]
    B.   boot tftp flash

    C.   boot flash tftp
    D.   boot tftp [ip address of tftp host]

7-106   TRUE/FALSE: As a **rule** in this field, before restoring the system configuration, a copy of the existing configuration to a NVRAM should be taken. This copy is considered as a backup in case the new configuration does not work. In addition, a copy of any configuration changes to NVRAM should be taken before rebooting the Router. All changes to running configuration will be lost if the **copy run start** command is not issued before rebooting the Router. The tftp backup is required as an extra precaution in case of dying the Router.

    A.   TRUE
    B.   FALSE

7-107   Which command will backup the Router's configuration? (Select all that apply)

    A.   copy running-config tftp
    B.   copy run tftp
    C.   copy startup-config tftp
    D.   copy start tftp
    E.   copy running-config startup-config
    F.   copy run start

7-108   Which of the following verifies the stored system configuration in NVRAM?

    A.   sh run
    B.   sh start
    C.   sh ver
    D.   sh users

7-109   Which of the following verifies the system running configuration in DRAM?

    A.   sh run
    B.   sh start
    C.   sh ver
    D.   sh users

7-110   Which of the following backs up the running configuration in DRAM to startup configuration in NVRAM?

    A.   copy start run
    B.   copy run start
    C.   copy run tftp
    D.   copy start tftp
    E.   copy tftp start
    F.   copy tftp run

7-111   Which of the following commands backs up the running configuration in DRAM to a TFTP host?

    A.   copy start run
    B.   copy run start
    C.   copy run tftp
    D.   copy start tftp
    E.   copy tftp start
    F.   copy tftp run

7-112   Which of the following backs up the Router configuration stored in NVRAM to Router's RAM?

    A.   copy start run
    B.   copy run start
    C.   copy run tftp
    D.   copy start tftp
    E.   copy tftp start
    F.   copy tftp run

7-113   Which of the following is a pre-10.3 IOS command and restores the system configuration stored in NVRAM to DRAM?

    A.   config net
    B.   config mem
    C.   write net
    D.   write mem

7-114   Which of the following restores the system configuration stored in a tftp host? (Select all that apply)

    A.   copy start run
    B.   copy run start
    C.   copy run tftp
    D.   copy start tftp
    E.   copy tftp start
    F.   copy tftp run

7-115   Which of the following is a pre-10.3 IOS command and restores the system configuration stored in a tftp host?

    A.   config netw
    B.   config mem
    C.   write net
    D.   write mem

7-116   Which of the following is true regarding the configuration file stored in a tftp host?

    A.   It is a binary file.
    B.   It is an EXE file.
    C.   It is an mp3 file.
    D.   It is an ASCII text file.

7-117   Which of the following deletes the Router configuration?

    A.   erase start
    B.   erase run
    C.   delete start
    D.   delete run

7-118   Which of the following is a pre-10.3 IOS command and backs up the system configuration stored in DRAM to NVRAM?

    A.   config net
    B.   config mem

C.   write net
D.   write mem

7-119   Which of the following is a pre-10.3 IOS command and backs up the system configuration stored in DRAM to tftp?

A.   config net
B.   config mem
C.   write net
D.   write mem

7-120   Which of the following is true about CDP timers' information? (Select all that apply)

A.   It is how often CDP packets are transmitted to all active interfaces.
B.   An amount of time that the device is needed to hold packets received from neighbor devices.
C.   A CDP global parameter that can be configured on CISCO devices.
D.   The **show cdp** command can be used to show this information.

7-121   Which of the following is true about CDP Holdtime information? (Select all that apply)

A.   It is how often CDP packets are transmitted to all active interfaces.
B.   An amount of time that the device is needed to hold packets received from neighbor devices.
C.   A CDP global parameter that can be configured on CISCO devices.
D.   The **show cdp** command can be used to show this information.

7-122   Which of the following displays the cdp protocol timer information?

A.   sh cdp timer
B.   sh cdp holdtime
C.   sh cdp
D.   display cdp timer
E.   display cdp holdtime

7-123   Which of the following displays the cdp protocol holdtime information?

A.   sh cdp timer
B.   sh cdp holdtime
C.   sh cdp
D.   display cdp timer
E.   display cdp holdtime

7-124   What is the default value for cdp protocol timer information?

A.   60 seconds
B.   120 seconds
C.   180 seconds
D.   240 seconds

7-125   What is the default value for cdp protocol holdtime information?

A.   60 seconds
B.   120 seconds
C.   180 seconds

D.   240 seconds

7-126   Which of the following configures the cdp protocol timer information to be equal to 120 seconds?

A.   Router#cdp timer 120
B.   Router#cdp holdtime 240
C.   Router(config)#cdp timer 120
D.   Router(config)#cdp holdtime 240

7-127   Which of the following configures the cdp protocol holdtime information to be equal to 240 seconds?

A.   Router#cdp timer 120
B.   Router#cdp holdtime 240
C.   Router(config)#cdp timer 120
D.   Router(config)#cdp holdtime 240

7-128   From which configuration mode can, the **show cdp** command be issued?

A.   User-Configuration mode
B.   Privileged EXEC mode
C.   Global configuration mode
D.   Line interface mode

7-129   From which configuration mode can, the **cdp timer 120** command be issued?

A.   User-Configuration mode
B.   Privileged EXEC mode
C.   Global configuration mode
D.   Line interface mode

7-130   From which configuration mode can, the **cdp holdtime 240** command be issued?

A.   User-Configuration mode
B.   Privileged EXEC mode
C.   Global configuration mode
D.   Line interface mode

7-131   From which configuration mode can, the **no cdp run** command be issued?

A.   User-Configuration mode
B.   Privileged EXEC mode
C.   Global configuration mode
D.   Line interface mode

7-132   Which of the following turns OFF completely the cdp protocol operations?

A.   Router#cdp off
B.   Router#no cdp
C.   Router(config)#off cdp
D.   Router(config)#no cdp run

7-133   What does the command **cdp timer 120** do?

A.   It adjusts the CDP neighbor command to 120 lines.
B.   It changes the holdtime of CDP packets.
C.   It changes the update frequency of CDP packets.
D.   It shows the update frequency of CDP packets.

7-134   Which of the following is true about **show cdp neighbor** command? (Select all that apply)

A.   It shows information about directly and indirectly connected devices.
B.   It shows information about indirectly connected devices.
C.   It shows detailed information about directly connected devices.

7-135   Which command will show information about neighbor devices?

A.   sh cdp timer
B.   sh cdp nei
C.   sh cdp
D.   display cdp timer
E.   display cdp holdtime

7-136   Which command will show detailed information about neighbor devices?

A.   sh cdp timer
B.   sh cdp nei
C.   sh cdp
D.   sh cdp nei detail
E.   display cdp nei detail

7-137   Which command will give the same output as the **show cdp neighbor detail** command?

A.   sh cdp entry *
B.   sh cdp nei
C.   sh cdp
D.   sh cdp detail
E.   display cdp nei detail

7-138   From which configuration mode can, the **show cdp nei** command be issued?

A.   User-Configuration mode
B.   Privileged EXEC mode
C.   Global configuration mode
D.   Line interface mode

7-139   Which of the following configuration modes is used to issue the **sh cdp nei de** command?

A.   User-Configuration mode
B.   Privileged EXEC mode
C.   Global configuration mode
D.   Line interface mode

7-140   Which of the following configuration modes is used to issue the **sh cdp entry *** command?

A.   User-Configuration mode
B.   Privileged EXEC mode

C.   Global configuration mode
D.   Line interface mode

7-141   TRUE/FALSE: The CDP packets are not passed through a CISCO switch, and only what is directly attached will be seen.

A.   TRUE
B.   FALSE

7-142   Which command will show the IOS version of the neighbor device? (Select all that apply)

A.   sh cdp entry *
B.   sh cdp nei
C.   sh cdp
D.   sh cdp nei detail
E.   display cdp nei detail

7-143   In the output of sh cdp nei command, what does R character refer to?

A.   It refers to the remote device.
B.   It refers to the Router device.
C.   It refers to the repeater device.
D.   It refers to nothing.

7-144   In the output of sh cdp nei command, what does the r character refer to?

A.   It refers to the remote device.
B.   It refers to the Router device.
C.   It refers to the repeater device.
D.   It refers to nothing.

7-145   In the output of sh cdp nei command, what does the S character refer to?

A.   It refers to the switch device.
B.   It refers to the Router device.
C.   It refers to the sensor device.
D.   It refers to nothing.

7-146   In the output of sh cdp nei command, what does the B character refer to?

A.   It refers to the system Bus device.
B.   It refers to the Router device.
C.   It refers to the Source Route Bridge device.
D.   It refers to nothing.

7-147   In the output of sh cdp nei command, what does the T character refer to?

A.   It refers to the Trans Bridge device.
B.   It refers to the Router device.
C.   It refers to the Source Route Bridge device.
D.   It refers to nothing.

7-148   In the output of sh cdp nei command, what does the H character refer to?

A.   It refers to the switch device.
B.   It refers to the Router device.
C.   It refers to the Host device.
D.   It refers to the Hub device.

7-149   In the output of sh cdp nei command, what does the I character refer to?

A.   It refers to the IGMP device.
B.   It refers to the Internal device.
C.   It refers to the IGRP device.
D.   It refers to nothing.

7-150   Which of the following is provided by the **sh cdp nei** command? (Select all that apply)

A.   Speed of the link
B.   Throughput of the link
C.   Local port/interface
D.   MAC address of neighbor
E.   IP address of neighbor
F.   Capability
G.   Remote port ID
H.   Neighbor device ID
I.   Holdtime
J.   Hardware platform
K.   The same information as **the show version** command provides.
L.   The same information as the **show cdp entry *** command provides.

7-151   Which command will show the neighbor router's IP address from the Router prompt? (Select all that apply)

A.   sh cdp nei
B.   sh cdp nei de
C.   sh cdp nei entry *
D.   sh cdp interface
E.   sh cdp traffic

7-152   Which command will show the hostname, local interface, platform, and remote port of a neighbor Router? (Select all that apply)

A.   sh cdp
B.   sh cdp nei
C.   sh cdp nei de
D.   sh cdp entry *
E.   sh cdp traffic
F.   sh cdp interface

7-153   Which of the following is provided by the **sh cdp nei de** command? (Select all that apply)

A.   Speed of the link
B.   Throughput of the link
C.   Local port/interface
D.   MAC address of neighbor switch
E.   IP address of neighbor Router

F.   Capability
G.   Remote port ID
H.   Neighbor device ID
I.   Holdtime
J.   Hardware platform
K.   The same information as **the show version** command provides.
L.   The same information as the **show cdp entry** * command provides.
M.   Protocol information
N.   Time

7-154   Which command will show information about interface traffic?

A.   sh cdp traffic
B.   sh cdp nei
C.   sh cdp
D.   sh cdp nei detail
E.   display cdp nei detail

7-155   From which configuration mode can, the **sh cdp traffic** command be issued?

A.   User-Configuration mode
B.   Privileged EXEC mode
C.   Global configuration mode
D.   Line interface mode

7-156   Which of the following is provided by the **sh cdp traffic** command? (Select all that apply)

A.   The numbers of packets sent.
B.   The number of packets received.
C.   Header syntax
D.   Checksum errors
E.   Failed encapsulations
F.   Memory problems
G.   Invalid packets
H.   Fragmented packets

7-157   Which command will show information about CDP status on Router interfaces or switch ports?

A.   sh cdp traffic
B.   sh cdp nei
C.   sh cdp int
D.   sh cdp nei detail
E.   display cdp nei detail

7-158   Which of the following configuration modes is used to issue the **sh cdp int** command?

A.   User-Configuration mode
B.   Privileged EXEC mode
C.   Global configuration mode
D.   Line interface mode

7-159   Which of the following is provided by the **sh cdp int** command? (Select all that apply)

A.   It gives information regarding all interfaces.
B.   The encapsulation on the line for each interface
C.   The timer for each interface
D.   The holdtime for each interface

7-160   Which command will enable the CDP operations on the Router interfaces or the switch ports?

A.   enable cdp
B.   cdp enable
C.   int enable cdp
D.   int cdp enable

7-161   Which command will disable the CDP operations on the Router interfaces or the switch ports?

A.   disable cdp
B.   no cdp enable
C.   int disable cdp
D.   int cdp disable

7-162   From which configuration mode can, the **cdp enable** command be issued?

A.   User-Configuration mode
B.   Privileged EXEC mode
C.   Global configuration mode
D.   Line interface mode

7-163   From which configuration mode can, the **no cdp enable** command be issued?

A.   User-Configuration mode
B.   Privileged EXEC mode
C.   Global configuration mode
D.   Line interface mode

7-164   Which command will see the CDP-enabled interfaces on a Router?

A.   sh interface
B.   sh cdp interface
C.   sh cdp
D.   sh cdp traffic

7-165   How do you clear the CDP table where CISCO Router keeps information about neighboring devices?

A.   Reset cdp
B.   reset cdp table
C.   clear cdp table
D.   delete cdp

7-166   TRUE/FALSE: To use CDP you have to configure IP or IPX.

A.   TRUE
B.   FALSE

7-167   Which of the following commands displays the frequency at which packets are sent by a switch?

A.   show cdp interface
B.   show cdp neighbors
C.   show cdp entry
D.   show cdp traffic

7-168   Which of the commands displays the CDP packet checksum errors?

A.   show cdp traffic
B.   show cdp entry
C.   show cdp neighbors
D.   show cdp interface

7-169   Which of the following is true about Telnet utility? (Select all that apply)

A.   Telnet is a virtual terminal protocol that is part of the TCP/IP protocol suite.
B.   Telnet allows dedicated for making connections to remote devices, gathering information, and running programs.
C.   Telnet can only be used after the Routers or switches are configured for IP networking.
D.   Telnet can be used to configure the Routers or switches without using a console port.
E.   Telnet can be issued by typing **telnet** from any command prompt (DOS, Linux, or CISCO).
F.   Telnet can only be worked after the Router's or switch's VTY lines are configured correctly.
G.   Telnet can be used to check the network connectivity.

7-170   Which of the following is true regarding the relationship between CDP and Telnet? (Select all that apply)

A.   Both are used to gather information about routers and switches.
B.   CDP can only be used to gather information about directly connected neighbor routers and switches.
C.   Telnet can be used to gather information about directly and indirectly connected routers and switches.
D.   It is possible to Telnet into remote routers and switches and then run CDP to gather CDP information about indirectly connected routers and switches that cannot be obtained by normally running CDP.
E.   Both are identical.

7-171   Which error message will appear on your router console, if you try to telnet into another Router with no VTY lines configured?

A.   % No password set
B.   %SYS-5-CONFIG_I: Configured from console by console
C.   Password required, but none set
D.   VTY Lines are not configured

7-172   TRUE/FALSE: It is possible to configure the remote router using Telnet even enable and enable secret passwords are not set.

A.   TRUE
B.   FALSE

7-173   Which error message will appear on your router console, if you try to access the enable mode on the remote router and no enable password is set?

A.   % No password set
B.   %SYS-5-CONFIG_I: Configured from console by console
C.   Password required, but none set
D.   Lines required, but none set

7-174   TRUE/FALSE: By using Telnet, there is a possibility to access, check, and configure remote, directly and indirectly connected devices.

A.   TRUE
B.   FALSE

7-175   Which command will terminate the Telnet connection? (Select all that apply)

A.   **close**
B.   **disconnect**
C.   **exit**
D.   **logout**
E.   **quit**

7-176   Which of the following keystrokes will suspend a Telnet session?

A.   **CTRL+SHIFT+6 X**
B.   **CTRL+SHIFT+6 Z**
C.   **ALT+SHIFT+x**
D.   **ALT+SHIFT+6 s**
E.   **ALT+SHIFT+6 X**

7-177   TRUE/FALSE: It is possible to telnet into multiple devices simultaneously.

A.   TRUE
B.   FALSE

7-178   TRUE/FALSE: To telnet into a Switch1, the enable mode password level 15 must be configured on the switch.

A.   TRUE
B.   FALSE

7-179   Which command will show the active Telnet connections made to neighbor and remote devices? (Select all that apply)

A.   show people
B.   sh sess
C.   sh sessions
D.   sh connections
E.   sh conn

7-180   What does the asterisk (*) indicate in the output of the **sh sessions** command?

A.   The last session
B.   The first session
C.   Any session
D.   The current terminal session

7-181   Which of the following returns the Router prompts back to the last session?

A.   Pressing End Twice
B.   Pressing Home Twice

C.   Pressing Enter Twice
D.   Pressing Shift twice

7-182   Which of the following returns the Router prompts back to the session number five?

A.   5+Pressing Enter Twice
B.   5+Pressing Home Twice
C.   5+Pressing End Twice
D.   5+Pressing Shift twice

7-183   Which of the following is provided by the **sh session** command? (Select all that apply)

A.   Name or address of the remote host to which the connection is made.
B.   Remote host to which the Router is connected through a Telnet session.
C.   IP address of the remote host
D.   Number of unread bytes displayed for the user to receive.
E.   Interval (in minutes) since data was last sent on the line.
F.   Assigned name of the connection.

7-184   Which command will show you the active consoles in use on your Routers? (Select all that apply)

A.   show users
B.   sh sess
C.   sh sessions
D.   sh connections
E.   sh conn

7-185   Which command will show you the active VTY ports in use on your Routers? (Select all that apply)

A.   show users
B.   sh sess
C.   sh sessions
D.   sh connections
E.   sh conn

7-186   What does the asterisk (*) indicate in the output of **sh users** command?

A.   The last session
B.   The first session
C.   Any session
D.   The current terminal session user

7-187   The output of show users command states that the line 3 vty 0 is active, what do the numbers (3) and (0) refer to in this output?

A.   3 refers to the absolute line number and 0 refer to the relative line number within the type.
B.   0 refers to the absolute line number and 3 refer to the relative line number within the type.
C.   3 refers to the maximum number of lines and 0 refer to the minimum number of lines.

7-188   Which of the following is provided by the **sh users** command? (Select all that apply)

A.   Line type and number
B.   User using the line

    C.   Host to which the user is connected (outgoing connection)
    D.   Interval (in minutes) since the user has typed something.
    E.   Hard-wired location for the line

7-189   Which of the following is a type of the line that appears in the **show users** command? (Select all that apply)

    A.   con--Console
    B.   aux--Auxiliary port
    C.   tty--Asynchronous terminal port
    D.   vty--Virtual terminal

7-190   Which command will terminate a switch session from the switch prompt? (Select all that apply)

    A.   terminate
    B.   no connect
    C.   exit
    D.   no login

7-191   Which command will clear a connection to a remote Router? (Select all that apply)

    A.   terminate
    B.   clear connection
    C.   clear line
    D.   disconnect

7-192   Which command will cut a VTY connection into your Router? (Select all that apply)

    A.   terminate line #
    B.   clear connection
    C.   clear line #
    D.   disconnect line

7-193   Which command will check if any devices are attached to your Router? (Select all that apply)

    A.   show users
    B.   sh sess
    C.   sh sessions
    D.   sh connections
    E.   sh conn

7-194   Which command will build a host table on your Router?

    A.   ip host
    B.   no ip host
    C.   ip hostname
    D.   ip domain-lookup
    E.   ip name-server
    F.   ip domain-name

7-195   Which command will create a host table entry for zoo, using ip addresses 172.17.17.10 and 172.17.17.20?

A.   ip hostname zoo 172.17.17.10 172.17.17.20
B.   ip hostname zoo 172.17.17.10 172.17.17.20
C.   ip host-table zoo 172.17.17.10 172.17.17.20
D.   ip host zoo 172.17.17.10 172.17.17.20

7-196   Which command will show the hostname resolved to the IP address on a Router?

A.   sh Router.
B.   sh name resolving.
C.   sh hosts.
D.   sh ip hosts.
E.   sh hostname.

7-197   From which configuration mode can, the **ip host** command be issued?

A.   User-Configuration mode.
B.   Privileged EXEC mode.
C.   Global configuration mode.
D.   Line interface mode.

7-198   TRUE/FALSE: The created host table by **ip host** command provides name resolution only on the Router on which it was built.

A.   TRUE
B.   FALSE

7-199   Which command will remove the name-to-address mapping?

A.   ip host
B.   no ip host
C.   ip hostname
D.   ip domain-lookup
E.   ip name-server
F.   ip domain-name

7-200   TRUE/FALSE: The default port_number in the **ip host** command is TCP port number 23. However, it is possible to create a session using Telnet with a different TCP port number.

A.   TRUE
B.   FALSE

7-201   How many IP addresses can be assigned to a hostname in the ip host command?

A.   6
B.   7
C.   8
D.   Only one

7-202   What does perm mean in the output of the show hosts command?

A.   The entry is automatically configured by the ip host command.
B.   The entry is automatically configured by the DNS resolution process.
C.   The entry is manually configured by the ip host command.

   D.   The entry is manually configured by the DHCP resolution process.

7-203   What does temp mean in the output of the show hosts command?

   A.   The entry is automatically configured by the ip host command.
   B.   The entry is automatically configured by the DNS resolution process.
   C.   The entry is manually configured by the ip host command.
   D.   The entry is manually configured by the DHCP resolution process.

7-204   TRUE/FALSE: When the network has many devices and you do not want to create a host table in each device, you can use a DNS server to resolve hostnames.

   A.   TRUE
   B.   FALSE

7-205   Which command will test the correct implementation of a host table on your Router?

   A.   telnet
   B.   ping
   C.   trace
   D.   sh sessions

7-206   Which command shows the IP-address-to-hostname-resolution table?

   A.   show address table
   B.   show mac address table
   C.   show host
   D.   sho ip hosts

7-207   Which command will resolve the name thaar to IP address 172.17.17.17?

   A.   DNS lookup thaar 172.17.17.17
   B.   ip host 172.17.17.17 thaar
   C.   thaar ip host 172.17.17.17
   D.   ip host thaar 172.17.17.17

7-208   Which of the following commands should be configured on the Router to make DNS resolution works?

   A.   ip domain-lookup
   B.   ip name-server
   C.   ip domain-name
   D.   ip host
   E.   ip address

7-209   TRUE/FALSE: Anytime a CISCO device receives a command it does not understand, it tries to resolve this through DNS by default.

   A.   TRUE
   B.   FALSE

7-210   Which command will test or verify the correct implementation of the DNS resolution on your Router?

   A.   telnet

B.   ping
C.   trace
D.   sh hosts
E.   sh sessions

7-211   From which configuration mode can, the **ip domain-lookup** command be issued?

A.   User-Configuration mode
B.   Privileged EXEC mode
C.   Global configuration mode
D.   Line interface mode

7-212   From which configuration mode can, the **ip name-server** command be issued?

A.   User-Configuration mode
B.   Privileged EXEC mode
C.   Global configuration mode
D.   Line interface mode

7-213   From which configuration mode can, the **ip domain-name** command be issued?

A.   User-Configuration mode
B.   Privileged EXEC mode
C.   Global configuration mode
D.   Line interface mode

7-214   TRUE/FALSE: If the command **ip domain-name** is not configured with DNS name resolution, The FQDN must be used to access the network devices.

A.   TRUE
B.   FALSE

7-215   How many name-server IP addresses could be configured with **ip name-server** command?

A.   6
B.   7
C.   8
D.   Only one

7-216   Which command will set up a DNS server to resolve names on a CISCO Router?

A.   ip name-lookup
B.   ip name-server
C.   ip domain-name
D.   ip host

CHAPTER 8
INTERNETWORKING
WAN TECHNOLOGIES

In this chapter, CISCO IOS Wide-Area Network (WAN) technologies, which help in extending the LAN to WAN network, will be described. How WAN standards and protocols are implemented in the OSI L1 and L2 will be discussed. Point-to-point leased lines, circuit-switched networks, and packet-switched networks are types of WAN's that will be covered here. Many physical network devices, which are used in the WAN, as well as many access and encapsulation technologies such as digital subscriber line (DSL), Frame Relay, Asynchronous Transfer Mode (ATM), Point-to-Point Protocol (PPP), High-Level Data Link Control (HDLC), and Integrated Services Digital Network (ISDN) will be outlined in this chapter. Popular Internet access technologies such as DSL and cable, along with a variety of configuration topics will be discussed as well.

The configuration and verification part of this chapter, describes how to implement, configure and verify several features related to WAN connections, including leased-line configuration using both HDLC and PPP. Then, the chapter shows how to configure the L3 features required for an Internet access router, specifically Dynamic Host Configuration Protocol (DHCP) and Network Address Translation/Port Address Translation (NAT/PAT). NAT and PAT are two protocols that can be used to solve common addressing issues, which are occurred when a network using a private addressing is connected to the Internet. The web-based router Security Device Manager (SDM) interface is used to clarify these configurations.

The following topics are emphasized in this chapter:

- Point-to-Point WANs implementation at OSI L1
- Standard WAN Cables
- Serial Connections
- DTE, DCE, Clock Rate, Bandwidth, Link Speed and Synchronization
- Back-to-back serial connection
- Types of WAN Connections
- Point-to-Point WANs Implementation at OSI L2
- High-Level Data Link Control (HDLC) Protocol
- Point-to-Point Protocol (PPP)
- Frame Relay
- Integrated Services Digital Network (ISDN)
- Public Switched Telephone Network (PSTN)
- Analog Modems
- Internet Connection
- Digital Subscriber Line (DSL)
- DSL Types, Speeds, Distances, and Standards
- IP over Ethernet Internet Cable Network
- Cell Switching: The ATM
- IP Services for Internet Access Routers
- Network Address Translation (NAT) and Port Address Translation (PAT)
- WAN Configuration and Configuration including, HDLC, PPP, Internet Access Router NAT/PAT and DHCP.

By understanding perfectly the information presented in this chapter and answering the 188 learning questions at the end of this chapter, configuring WAN, and answering the CCNA/CCENT exam related questions will be guaranteed. The questions herein are intended to reflect the type of questions presented on the CCENT Test.

WAN Technology

WAN standards and protocols define how to network between devices that are relatively far apart. WAN is required when an enterprise grows beyond a single location or even a country, and interconnecting these enterprise parts (LANs) to each other becomes necessary. This interconnection will form a WAN.

In this section, WAN concepts, WAN functions in relation to the OSI model, WAN terms and the WAN connection types will be given. CISCO IOS WAN technologies will be discussed as well.

There are several differences between LAN and WAN:

- WAN covers a wide area (connect devices that are relatively far apart) while LAN covers a local area (single building or other small geographical area).
- WAN protocols are different than LAN protocols.
- Usually WAN bandwidth is less than LAN bandwidth.
- LANs are owned by the company while WANs connections usually are leased from services of carriers (service providers), such as public telephone companies, cable companies, satellite systems, and network providers.
- Both WANs and LANs carry a variety of traffic types, such as voice, data, and video.
- WANs use serial connections of various types.
- Except for wireless WAN, WAN cabling is usually installed underground to prevent accidental damage by people or cars.

WANs function focuses primarily on L1 and L2 of the OSI model. A number of recognized authorities, including the ISO, the Telecommunications Industry Association (TIA), and the Electronics Industry Alliance (EIA) defined and managed WAN access standards. These standards typically describe both L1 delivery methods and L2 requirements.

Point-to-Point WANs Implementation at the OSI L1

L1 defines the standards and protocols used to create the physical network and to send and receive the data (bits) from one device to another across that network. To implement a point-to-point WAN link in L1, it is simple; it acts like an Ethernet trunk between two CISCO switches. The trunk link between two CISCO switches is implemented using crossover cable. But this link is unsuitable for WAN link, since the WAN link is typically used for connecting far apart locations. Therefore, a *leased line* should be used to implement a point-to-point WAN link instead of a crossover cable. It is called a leased line since an organization that needs to send data over the WAN circuit does not actually own the cable or line or link, and the connection is always available as long as the leased is paid and the exclusive right to use that line is valid. The actual physical cabling of such long links are owned, installed, and managed by Telco (the local telephone company) that has the right of way to run cables under streets through cities. Telco is sometimes called Public Telephone and Telegraph (PTT) company. With the internet exploration in 1990's, the generic term *service provider* is used to refer to a company that provides any form of WAN connectivity, including Internet services. Usually, Telco has a large network runs around the country, and to connect the customer to Telco network, Telco runs extra cables from the local central office (CO) to the customer (subscriber) building. Figure 8-1 demonstrates the typical WAN networks.

Figure 8-1 shows that at both sites, the router is connected to a device called an external Channel Service Unit/Data Service Unit (CSU/DSU) or modem using a short cable, typically less than 50 feet long (the CSU/DSUs get placed in a rack near the router). To connect the CSU/DSU to Telco network, another type of cable is used (copper or fiber), which is much longer than the first one. It plugs into the CSU/DSU of the subscriber. Usually, it is a *four-wire cable* from the Telco, composed of two twisted-pair wires. Each pair is used to send in one direction, so a four-wire circuit allows full-duplex communication. This cabling is often called the *local loop*. The other end of this cable ends up in the nearest exchange or the CO WAN switch of the Telco. Now, the routers at both sites can send and receive data simultaneously across this point-to-point WAN link.

Figure 8-1 Point-to-Point Leased Line WAN

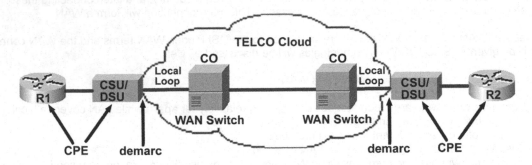

A device such as a DSU/CSU or modem is required to make the local loop carrying data in a suitable form (digital or analog) and to prepare the data for transmission. Other terms can be found here, the Data Communications Equipment (DCE) and Data Terminal Equipment (DTE). DCE's are devices that put data on the local loop, whereas, DTE's are the customer devices that pass the data to the DCE. Clearly, the DCE primarily function is providing an interface for the DTE into the WAN circuit (cloud).

The connectivity between the DTE and the DCE is described by the WAN access physical layer. Figure 8-2 shows the DTE and DCE equipments.

Figure 8-2 DTE and DCE Connectivity

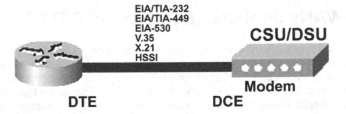

Telco uses the term *demarc* (demarcation point), to refer to the point at which the Telco's responsibility is on one side ends, and the subscriber's responsibility is on the other side starts. For instance, in Figure 8-1, the router cable and the CSU/DSU at the subscriber side are owned by the subscriber, and the wiring (copper or fiber) to the CO and all devices inside the CO are owned by the Telco. Another term is used by Telco to refer to both the CSU/DSU and the router at the subscriber side. Telco called these devices "*customer premises equipment*" (CPE). The subscriber owns the CPE or leases the CPE from the Telco. When, Telco owns and manages the CSU/DSU and maybe the router at the subscriber site, the demarc would be moved to the nearest point that owned by Telco's subscriber.

The following are some important definitions in WAN:

Customer premises equipment (CPE): It is the equipment that's owned by the subscriber site and located on the subscriber's sites. Equipments such as telephones, modems, and terminals which are located at the customer sites and connected to the service provider network are examples of the CPEs.

Demarcation point: It is the point where the service provider's (carrier) responsibility ends and the CPE begins (the separation point between carrier equipment and the CPE). It's generally a communication device in a telecommunications closet owned and installed by the carrier. The customer is responsible to cable (extended demarc) from this box to the CPE, which is usually a connection to a CSU/DSU or ISDN interface.

Local loop: It connects the demarcation point to the closest switching office, called a *central office*. It's sometimes referred to a line from the premises of a telephone subscriber to the telephone company CO.

Central office (CO): The local telephone company office where all loops in a certain area are connected and where circuit switching of subscriber lines occurs. It connects the customers to the provider's switching network. A central office (CO) is sometimes referred to as a *point of presence* (POP).

Toll network: It is a trunk line inside a WAN provider's network. This network is a collection of switches and facilities owned by the ISP. It uses the public switched telephone network (PSTN).

To summarize, the following devices can be used for WAN access at the physical layer (L1):

- **Routers:** To provide WAN access interface ports.
- **Communication servers:** To concentrate the dialing (in and out) for user communications.
- **(DSU/CSU) or Modem:** To provide data transmission, DSU and CSU are required for digital lines. Modem is required for analog lines to convert the digital signal into analog format and vice versa. Both can be combined into a single piece of equipment, called the DSU/CSU, which can also be built into the interface card of the router.
- **WAN networking devices:** To support the network connectivity within the cloud, other devices, such as core routers, ATM switches, Frame Relay switches, and public switched telephone network (PSTN) switches, are also used. All of these devices are part of Telco network.

Note: Wireless can also be used for WAN. It requires several unique requirements. Wireless WANs are not covered in CCENT exam.

Standard WAN Cables

In the following sections, various types of WAN connections will be described. The focus will be on those protocols, which are required by CCNA/CCENT exam.

Several types of WAN interface cards (WIC's) are introduced by CISCO for its routers. In general, these serial interfaces are either synchronous or asynchronous. CISCO routers support the EIA/TIA-232, EIA/TIA-449, EIA-530, V.35, and X.21 standards for serial connections (For more information on these standards bodies, see, the websites http://www.tiaonline.org and http://www.ansi.org). In this chapter and for any of the point-to-point serial links or Frame Relay links, the router uses an interface that supports synchronous communication.

CISCO serial connections support almost any type of WAN service. The typical WAN connections are HDLC, PPP, ISDN, and Frame Relay. Typical speeds are from 2.4kbps to 45Mbps (T3). HDLC, PPP, and Frame Relay can use the same Physical layer specifications. ISDN has different specifications at the Physical layer.

The 60-pin D-shell connector (DB-60 connector) is one of a variety of proprietary physical connector types that CISCO routers use it in synchronous serial interfaces. This connector connects to the DB-60 port on a serial WIC of the router. Because five different cable types are supported with this router port, the port is called a five-in-one serial port. This port is shown at the top of the cable drawings in Figure 8-3. This cable connects the router to the CSU/DSU. Figure 8-3 shows some of the serial cabling WAN connectors' options that can be used on a CISCO router with the typical DTE-DCE connection.

Depending on the attached cable, the synchronous serial port on the router is configured as either DTE or DCE (except EIA-530, which is DTE only). The attached cable can be ordered as either DTE or DCE to match the router configuration. If the port is configured as DTE (the default setting), an external clocking from the DCE device is required.

Figure 8-3 WAN Serial Cabling

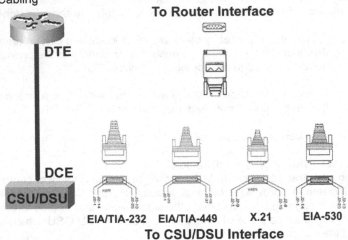

The CSU/DSU is connected to the Telco CO by a cable using a typical RJ-48 connector. The RJ-48 connector is similar in shape and size to the RJ-45 connector used for TP Ethernet cables.

As stated previously in this chapter, both (the modem and the DSU/CSU) can be combined into a single piece of equipment, called the DSU/CSU, which can also be built internally into the interface card of the router. In such cases, the serial cables shown in Figure 8-3 are not required, and Telco is connected to a port on the router serial interface card directly using a cable with an RJ-48 port.

Finally, in addition to a proprietary 60-pin serial connector, CISCO routers also have a new, smaller proprietary serial connection that is about one-tenth the size of the 60-pin basic serial cable. This is called the "*smart serial cable*". The connector of this cable is just a 26-pin connector, which is much smaller than the DB-60 connector. This small cable also supports the same five serial standards in either DTE or DCE configuration.

Serial Connections

Serial WAN transmission requires serial WAN connectors. CISCO routers use a proprietary 60-pin serial connector. CISCO also has a new, smaller proprietary serial connection that is about one-tenth the size of the 60-pin basic serial cable. This is called the "smart-serial. Serial transmission is working by taking place one bit at a time over a single channel. Serial transmissions are measured in frequency or cycles per second (hertz). The amount of data that can be carried within these frequencies is called bandwidth. Bandwidth is the amount of data in bits per second that the serial channel can carry.

There are several types of connectors that the service provider may use to connect a network with the service provider network. These include the following:

- EIA/TIA-232
- EIA/TIA-449
- EIA-530
- V.35 (used to connect to a CSU/DSU)

- X.21 (used in X.25)

DTE, DCE, Clock Rate, Bandwidth, Link Speed and Synchronization

Usually, the following steps will be followed when a subscriber wants to buy a point-to-point leased link from Telco:

Step 1: The subscriber determines how fast the circuit should run, in kilobits per second (kbps), according to the subscriber expected using.

Step 2: The subscriber contacts a service provider and orders the circuit.

Step 3: Usually, Telco recommends the circuit specifications and the required devices that the must purchase.

Step 4: The subscriber purchases two routers, two CSU/DSUs, one at each site.

Step 5: The subscriber installs and configures each router and CSU/DSU and connects the serial cables from each router to the respective CSU/DSU.

Step 6: Telco installs the new line into the customer premises, and connects the line to the CSU/DSUo.

Notice that, in some cases, Telco sells the routers, the CSU/DSUs and the cables, and in many cases, Telco does the installation and configuration of the whole circuit.

Step 1, is the most important step. It means, that the line speed must be specified at first. There are many possible predefined speeds that can be ordered from the service provider. Clock rate, bandwidth, or link speed, are terms that can be used to refer to the line speed. The devices on both sides must be configured to match the defined line speed. This is done by synchronizing the clocks on all devices of the link so that they run at exactly the same speed. This process is called *synchronization*. Synchronization means that both sides agree to send and receive bits at predefined time intervals. Practically, synchronization is done by one side makes small adjustments in its clock rate to match the other side.

In a leased line, synchronization occurs between the two CSU/DSUs. One CSU/DSU (the slave) adjusts its clock to match the clock rate of the other CSU/DSU (the master). The synchronization process will be repeated several times per second between both devices. The two CSU/DSUs, then, take their synchronization from the service provider and adjust their speeds to match the clocking signals from the service provider. Then each CSU/DSUs supply clocking signals to the routers so that the routers can send and receive data at the correct clock rate. Today, the service provider can provide the subscriber by several leased lines speed channels. Table 8-1 lists some of the standards for WAN channel speeds that may be ordered. Two of these speeds are important for the CCNA/CCENT exam, the T1 and E1.

Table 8-1 WAN Speed Standards

Name of Line	Speed of Line
DS0	64 kbps
DS1 (T1-US)	1.544 Mbps (24 DS0s, plus 8 kbps overhead)
DS3 (T3)-US	44.736 Mbps (28 DS1s, plus management overhead)
E1- Europe	2.048 Mbps (32 DS0s)
E3- Europe	34.064 Mbps (16 E1s, plus management overhead)
J1 (Y1)-Japan	2.048 Mbps (32 DS0s)

In the United States, the DS1 standard defines a single line that supports 24 DS0s, plus an 8-kbps overhead channel, for a speed of 1.544 Mbps. (The standard of a single 64-kbps line is referred by the term digital signal level 0 (DS0).) A DS1 is also called a T1 line in US. In Europe and Japan another standards are used, an E1 line standard holding 32 DS0s, and an E3 line holding 16 E1s.

When talking about clocking and speed, both DTE and DCE have another meaning. The DCE is the device that provides clocking, typically the CSU/DSU and the DTE is the device that receives clocking, typically the router. DTE is any device located at the user end of a user-network interface. DTE includes devices such as multiplexers, routers, computers …etc. The connection to a data network is made through DCE such as a modem using the clocking signals generated by that device. Router interfaces are, by default, DTE, and they connect into DCE —for example, a CSU/DSU. The CSU/DSU plugs into a demarcation location (demarc) and is the service provider's last responsibility. The demarc is a jack that has an RJ-45 female connector located in a telecommunications closet.

Note: When a problem occurs, usually the service provider says that it tests fine up to the demarc and that the problem must be the CPE. i.e., it's a customer problem, not the service provider problem.

Figure 8-4 shows DTE-DCE-DTE connection and some devices that may be used in the network. The idea behind a WAN is to be able to connect two DTE networks together. The DCE network includes the links from the CSU/DSU, through the provider's network, all the way to the CSU/DSU at the other end. The network's DCE device (CSU/DSU) provides clocking to the DTE-connected interface (the router's serial interface). For non-production networks which use a WAN crossover type of cable and do not have a CSU/DSU, clocking should be provided on the DCE end of the cable by using the router **clock rate** command. In non-production environments, a DCE network does not always present.

Figure 8-4 WAN Connections

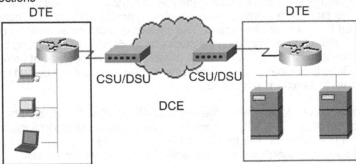

Back-to-Back Serial Connection

To purchase a serial cable from CISCO, it is possible to order either a DTE or a DCE cable, depending on whether the router is acting as a DTE or a DCE. For a real WAN link, a DTE cable must be ordered, since the router acts as DTE by default. However, two CISCO routers can be connected directly in a lab using a Back-to-back serial connection as shown in Figure 8-5. This circuit is usually used for training, so that anyone can have it in home without the need for any CSU/DSUs or real WAN link. To do so, one router must supply clocking. Of course, the router with the DCE cable in it. This router can be configured to supply clocking to the other router that acts as DTE. To connect the two cables together, the male connector of the DTE cable must be inserted into the female connector of the DCE cable. To supply clocking from a router (with DCE cable installed), the **clock rate** command must be issued from that router. Notice that, the combined DCE/DTE cables reverse the transmit and receive pins, much like a crossover TP Ethernet cable allows two directly connected devices to communicate. The DCE cable swaps transmit (Tx) and Receive (Rx) pins, whereas the DTE cable does not swap the Tx and Rx pins. Therefore, one router can transmit on one pin, and the other router will receive it on the same pin and vice versa as shown in Figure 8-5.

Figure 8-5 Back-to-Back Serial Connection

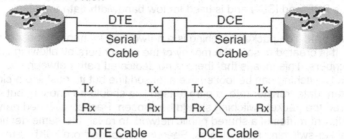

Types of WAN Connections

Depending on the data transmission requirements for the WANs, a number of ways can be used to access a WAN. Figure 8-6 shows several types of the WAN Connectivity options.

Figure 8-6 Types of WAN Connectivity

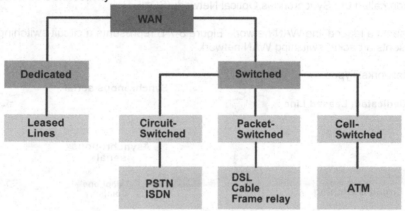

As shown in Figure 8-6, dedicated and switched communications are the two major categories of communication links for WANs. Within each category, individual types of link options exist. These types of links can be summarized as follows:

- **Dedicated link:** The point-to-point line is used, when a permanent, pre-established, dedicated connection is required. This link provides a WAN communications path from the subscriber CPE's through the provider network to a remote location, which allows the subscriber DTE networks to communicate at any time with no setup procedures (only during initial setup) before transmitting data. It uses synchronous serial lines up to 45Mbps. HDLC and PPP encapsulations are frequently used on this type of link. Point-to-point lines are usually leased from a carrier (service provider), and therefore, it is called leased line. The terms leased line, leased circuit, link, serial link, serial line, point-to-point link, dedicated link/line, and circuit are used to refer to a point-to-point leased line.

- **Circuit-switched link:** The circuit switching is working like a phone call, to pass data it needs, the connection must be set up at first. This means, before communication can start, the connection between the sender and the receiver through the networks of the service provider must be established. This also means that circuit switching dynamically establishes a dedicated virtual connection for voice or data between the sender and the receiver. Unlike the leased line where the cost is paid for the whole leasing period, the cost, here is paid only for the time of the actual using. Circuit switching uses dial-up networks such as PPP and ISDN and is used for low bandwidth data transfers.

- **Packet-switched link:** The packet switching is a networking technology based on the transmission of data in packets. It is created to save the money of the subscribers by allowing sharing the bandwidth with other subscribers. This means that there is no dedicated path between the source and destination endpoints. Packet switching can be looked like a leased line but its cost like a circuit switching. If it requires a constant data transfer rate, a pure leased line should be chosen, but when bursty data transfer is required the packet switching should be chosen. Packet-switched networks send data packets over different routes of a shared public network to reach the same destination. Frame Relay and X.25 are packet-switching technologies. Speeds can range from 56Kbps to T3 (45Mbps). This technology transmits data in labeled cells, frames, or packets.

- **Cell-switched link:** It is based on using ATM switches inside the service provider's network (cloud). Unlike the switching technology where the packets/frames are used throughout the network, the cells are used. A cell, just like a packet or frame, is a string of bits sent over ATM networks. The difference is that while packets and frames can vary in size, ATM cells are always fixed 53 bytes in length. Furthermore, ATM typically supports much higher-speed physical links, especially those using a specification called the Synchronous Optical Network (SONET).

Figure 8-7-A represents a leased line WAN network. Figure 8-7-B represents a circuit switching WAN network. Figure 8-7-C represents a packet switching WAN network.

Figure 8-7 WAN Networks Types

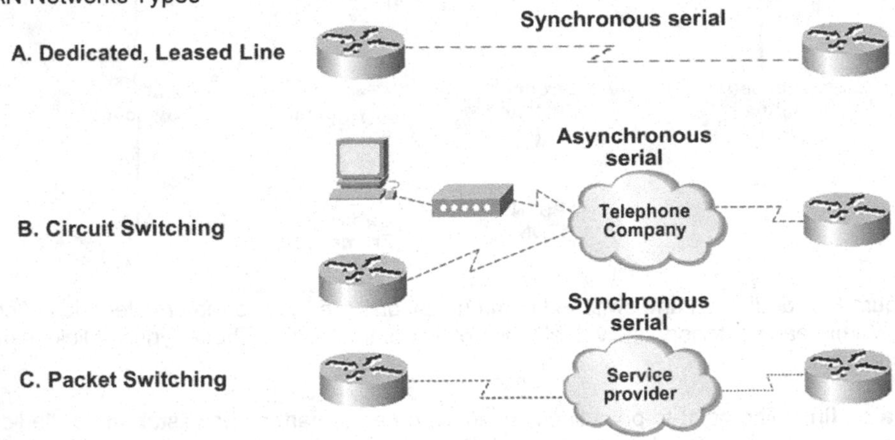

There are several differences between circuit switching and packet switching services. The main differences are:

- Circuit switching creates a physical ability (electrical circuit) to send data between two endpoints without interpreting the data that flow through the circuits. Packet switching means that the devices in the WAN do more than pass electrical signal or the bits from one device to another, the service provider devices interpret the data that flow through their networking devices and then the data can be sent to one direction or to multi-directions.
- Circuit switching is implemented at layer 1 of the OSI layers; whereas packet switching is implemented at layer 2.
- Circuit switching are point-to-point services; whereas, packet switching is multipoint services (more than two).

Point-to-Point WANs Implementation at the OSI L2

L2 protocols define how data is encapsulated for transmission toward a remote location and the mechanisms for transferring the resulting frames. WAN uses a variety of different encapsulation technologies. Frame Relay. ISDN. ATM, PPP and HDLC are WAN techniques that use different encapsulation methods. HDLC and Point-to-Point Protocol (PPP) encapsulation technologies are the most popular data link layer protocols used on Point-to-Point serial links.

Configuration 8-1, CISCO WAN Technologies. CISCO WAN technologies can be accessed from any serial interfaces by invoking the **encapsulation ?** command. It is impossible to configure Ethernet or Token Ring encapsulation on a serial interface. Sample of these technologies are given below:

Thaar#config t
Enter configuration commands, one per line. End with CNTL/Z.
Thaar(config)#int s0/0
Thaar(config-if)#encapsulation ?

atm-dxi	ATM-DXI encapsulation
bstun	Block Serial tunneling (BSTUN)
frame-relay	Frame Relay networks
hdlc	Serial HDLC synchronous
lapb	LAPB (X.25 Level 2)
ppp	Point-to-Point protocol
sdlc	SDLC
sdlc-primary	SDLC (primary)
sdlc-secondary	SDLC (secondary)
smds	Switched Megabit Data Service (SMDS)
stun	Serial tunneling (STUN)
x25	X.25

Thaar (config-if)#

High-Level Data Link Control (HDLC) Protocol

Like Ethernet framing, there is HDLC framing as shown in Figure 8-8. Figure 8-8 shows the standard ISO HDLC framing, CISCO HDLC framing, and PPP framing.

HDLC High-Level Data Link Control. A bit-oriented synchronous data link layer protocol created by ISO and derived from Synchronous Data Link Control (SDLC). HDLC specifies a data encapsulation method on synchronous serial links using frame characters and checksums. No authentication can be used with HDLC. However, most HDLC vendors' implementations (including CISCO) are proprietary. HDLC cannot be configured on an asynchronous serial connection.

The address field is not really needed for Point-to-Point links, since there are only two known address and only one intended recipient at the other end. It used in the past years when Telco sold multidrop circuits.

An FCS field in the HDLC trailer is used to perform error detection; just like in the Ethernet. If a received frame has errors, the device receiving the frame discards the frame, with no error recovery performed by HDLC.

The standard ISO HDLC does not support multiprotocol. When a router receives an HDLC frame, it wants to know what type of packet is held inside the frame. To identify the network protocol being encapsulated, CISCO added a Type field. This produces CISCO's HDLC. CISCO's HDLC is proprietary—it won't communicate with any other vendor's HDLC implementation. Each vendor has a different HDLC implementation for the proprietary field. To connect routers from different vendors, the default HDLC serial encapsulation on CISCO routers should not be used, because it wouldn't work. Instead, something like PPP can be used. PPP is an ISO-standard way of identifying the upper-layer protocols. Figure 8-8 shows the CISCO HDLC format.

Figure 8-8 PPP and HDLC framing

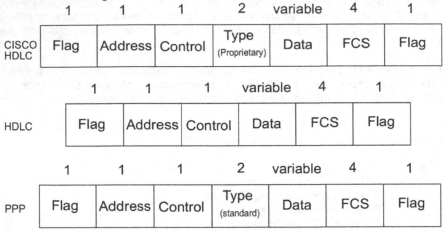

Bit oriented and byte oriented protocols are two different protocols. In byte-oriented protocols, control information is encoded using entire bytes. Bit-oriented protocols may use single bits to represent control information. Bit-oriented protocols include HDLC, TCP, IP …etc.

Connecting Routers from different vendor's: To Connect routers from different vendors, the default HDLC serial encapsulation on CISCO routers should not be used, because it wouldn't work. Instead, something like PPP can be used. PPP is an ISO-standard way of identifying the upper-layer protocols.

Point-to-Point Protocol (PPP)
IETF created PPP in 1994 to connect routers over a point-to-point link from different vendors. It is similar to CISCO HDLC with many additional features. PPP protocol stack is specified at the Physical and Data Link layers only.
PPP Point-to-Point Protocol (PPP) is an industry-standard protocol. It is a data-link protocol that provides router-to-router and host-to-network connections over synchronous and asynchronous circuits. The protocol most commonly used for dial-up Internet access, replacing the earlier SLIP. Because all multi-protocol versions of HDLC are proprietary, PPP can be used to create point-to-point links between different vendors' equipment. It can be run over asynchronous and synchronous links. Its features include address notification, authentication via CHAP or PAP, support for multiple protocols, and link monitoring. PPP has two layers: the Link Control Protocol (LCP) establishes, configures, and tests a link, and then any of various Network Control Protocols (NCPs) transport traffic for a specific protocol suite, such as IPX.

LCP (Link Control Protocol) is used by PPP to build and support data link connections. Network Control Protocol (NCP) is used by PPP to allow the multiple network layer protocols (routed protocols) to be used on a point-to-point connection. PPP is a Data Link layer protocol that can be used over either asynchronous serial or synchronous serial links. The basic purpose of PPP is to transport layer 3 packets across a Data Link layer point-to-point link. It is nonproprietary, which means that if the routers in the network are from different venders, PPP would be needed on the serial interfaces—HDLC encapsulation would not work because it is CISCO proprietary on CISCO routers.

PPP provides the following techniques:

- Authentication
- dynamic addressing
- callback

Figure 8-9 shows the PPP protocol stack as compared to the OSI model.

Figure 8-9 PPP Protocol Stack

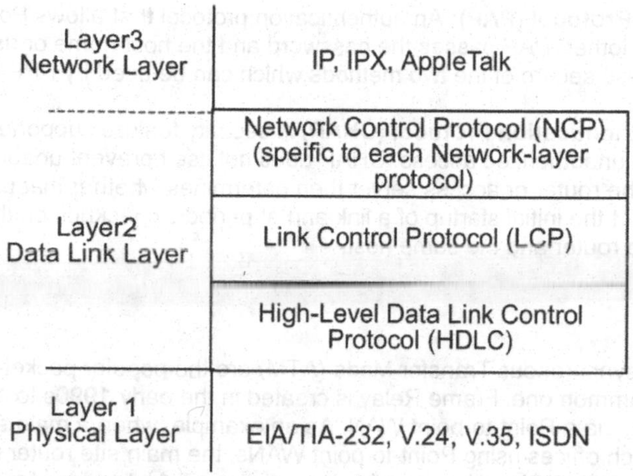

Layer3 Network Layer	IP, IPX, AppleTalk
	Network Control Protocol (NCP) (speific to each Network-layer protocol)
Layer2 Data Link Layer	Link Control Protocol (LCP)
	High-Level Data Link Control Protocol (HDLC)
Layer 1 Physical Layer	EIA/TIA-232, V.24, V.35, ISDN

PPP includes the following main components:

- EIA/TIA-232-C, V.24, V.35, and ISDN
- HDLC
- LCP
- NCP

EIA/TIA-232-C, V.24, V.35, and ISDN are serial communication physical layer international standards. HDLC is a method for encapsulating frames over serial links. LCP is a method of establishing, configuring and supporting the point-to-point connection. NCP purposes include establishing and configuring different Network layer protocols. It makes multiple Network layer protocols to be used simultaneously. Example of protocols here is IPCP (Internet Protocol Control Protocol).

PPP Session Phases

When PPP connection is started, the link goes through three phases of session establishment.
PPP session establishment pass into the following phases:

- Link establishment phase
- Authentication phase
- Network layer protocol phase

Link establishment phase: To configure and test the link, LCP packets are sent by each PPP device. These packets contain a field called the Configuration Option. This field allows each device to see the size of the data, compression, and authentication. Default configurations are used if no Configuration Option field is present.

Authentication phase: Authentication takes place before Network layer protocol information is read. Either CHAP or PAP can be used to authenticate a link. This is an optional phase.

Network layer protocol phase: It is used by the PPP to make the multiple network layer protocols to be encapsulated and sent over a PPP link.

PPP Authentication Protocols

PPP links can use one of the following authentications methods:

Password Authentication Protocol (PAP): An authentication protocol that allows Point-to-Point Protocol (PPP) peers to authenticate one another. PAP passes the password and the host name or username in the clear text (unencrypted). PAP is the less secure of the two methods which can be used by PPP links.

Challenge Handshake Authentication Protocol (CHAP) A security feature supported on lines using PPP encapsulation that prevents unauthorized access. CHAP does not itself prevent unauthorized access; it merely identifies the remote end. The router or access server then determines whether that user is allowed to access the network. CHAP is used at the initial startup of a link and at periodic checkups on the link to validate the communication between the router and the same host.

Frame Relay

Today, Frame Relay and Asynchronous Transfer Mode (ATM) are the popular packet-switching services, but Frame Relay is the more common one. Frame Relay is created in the early 1990s to overcome the problems when connecting many sites via a Point-to-point WAN. As an example, when a main site company wants to connect to two remote branch offices using Point-to-point WANs, the main site router requires two serial interfaces and two separate CSU/DSUs. Now imagine how many serial interfaces for the main site router and how many CSU/DSUs are required, if the company wants to connect to 5 branch offices using any-to-any Point-to-point WANs connectivity. Of course, for each point-to-point line, the main site router needs a separate physical serial interface and a separate CSU/DSU. Ten of routers, with many interfaces, and ten of CSU/DSUs are needed for the overall network with four routers/interfaces and four CSU/DSUs per site. For this reason, Frame Relay is an ideal solution for connecting enterprise LANs, because a router on each LAN needs only a single WAN interface, even when multiple virtual circuits (VC) are used.

Frame Relay is a Data Link and Physical layer specification that provides high performance. Frame Relay is the more efficient replacement of the X.25 protocol and leased lines. Frame Relay can be more cost-effective than point-to-point links and can typically run at speeds of 64Kbps up to 45Mbps (T3). Frame Relay provides features for dynamic bandwidth allocation and congestion control. Frame Relay is an industry-standard, data link layer protocol that handles multiple virtual circuits. Frame Relay implements no error or flow control. This reduces the latency and enhances the performance of the Frame Relay network. Frame Relay cannot be configured on an asynchronous serial connection. Frame Relay protocol works between the subscriber main router and the service provider Frame Relay switch (in the cloud), as shown in Figure 8-10.

Frame Relay Essentials

Frame Relay network is a multi-access network, which means that more than two devices can be attached to the network, similar to LANs. This is done by little changes in the Data link protocol. In Figure 8-11, a leased line is installed between each router and a nearby Frame Relay switch; these links are called *access links,* which are the same Layer 1 features as a point-to-point leased lines. Both access links and leased lines use the same signaling standards and run at the same speed. Figure 8-11 illustrates a VC through the Frame Relay cloud.

Figure 8-10 Frame Relay Typical Network

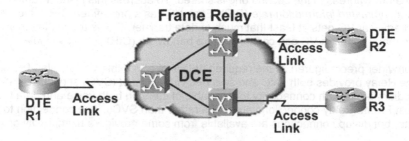

Figure 8-11 Virtual Circuit Created by Frame Relay

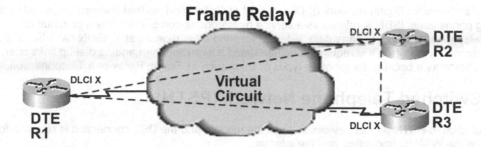

Frame Relay defines its own framing technology, which is defined by a protocol called Link Access Procedure–Frame (LAPF). Each Frame Relay header holds an address field called a Data Link Connection Identifier (DLCI). The WAN switch forwards the frame based on the DLCI, sending the frame through the service provider's network (Frame Relay cloud) until it gets to the destination router.

Frame Relay is also called a *frame-switching service*, because the switches in the service provider cloud can forward one frame to one remote site and another frame to another remote site, just like the packet switching service do.

The Frame Relay switches are also called DCEs, and in this case, the subscriber routers are called DTEs. Clearly, DCE here refers to the device providing the frame-switching service to the subscriber device, and the term DTE refers to the subscriber device needing this service.

The logical path that a frame travels between each pair of routers is called a Virtual Circuit (VC). The VC in Figure 8-11 is represented by the dashed line between the routers. When R1 needs to forward a packet to R2 or R3, it encapsulates the packet into a Frame Relay header (adds DLCI address) and trailer and then, sends the frame to R2 or R3 depending on the established VC which is identified by a unique DLCI to the service provider. The process seems similar to a point-to-point serial link, but here the frames are forwarded over a logical (virtual) VC between routers, not physical link. VCs provide a bidirectional communications path from one DTE device to another. A data-link connection identifier (DLCI) within the Frame Relay address header uniquely identifies a virtual circuit. The DLCI is specific only to the router where it is configured. A VC can pass through any number of intermediate DCE devices located within the network. Numerous VCs can be multiplexed into a single physical circuit for access to and transmission across the network.

One of the main advantages of Frame Relay is that a router usually, uses a single access link to support multiple VCs, with each VC allowing the router to send data to a different remote router. To identify each VC, the router must use a different DLCI, because the DLCI identifies the VC.

One of the differences between Leased Line based networks and Frame Relay based networks is that in the first one the link is dedicated, whereas in the second one is shared. To address this issue, Frame Relay is designed with the concept of a *committed information rate* (CIR). Each VC has a predefined CIR, which is a guarantee by the provider that a particular VC gets at least that much of data transfer. CIR is the minimum value for a particular VC and in many cases; a VC can consume more bandwidth (CIR) if it is available.

When the service provider preconfigured all the required details of a VC; this VC is called *Permanent Virtual Circuit* (PVC).Frame Relay provides both PVC and *switched virtual circuit* (SVC) services using the service provider shared medium-bandwidth connectivity that capable of carrying both voice and data traffic simultaneously. Most Frame Relay connections are PVCs rather than SVCs. The connection to the network edge is often a leased line, but dialup connections are available from some providers using ISDN or xDSL lines.

Integrated Services Digital Network (ISDN)

ISDN Integrated Services Digital Network (ISDN) is a set of digital services that transmit voice, video and data over existing phone lines. ISDN is offered as a service by telephone companies. It is a communication protocol that allows telephone networks to carry data, video, voice, and other digital traffic. ISDN can offer a cost-effective solution for remote users when it is required a higher-speed connection than analog dial-up links offer. ISDN is also a good choice as a backup link for other types of links, such as Frame Relay or a T1 connection.

Public Switched Telephone Network (PSTN)

A brief introduction to PSTN and its devices such as the modem and the DSL connection is required for better understanding the WAN technologies, and the internet.

The term PSTN refers to the equipment and devices that Telcos use to create basic telephone service between any two phones in the world. This term refers to the combined networks of all telephone companies. In addition to original voice support, PSTN supports data transmission as well. Several Internet access technologies use PSTN to transmit data.

To make a home phone work, Telco has to install a cable with a pair of wires, called the *local loop*, between that home and some nearby Telco central office (CO). One end of the cable enters that house and connects to the phone outlets in the house. The other end connects to a computer in the CO, called a *voice switch*. Telco cloud makes a *circuit* between the two endpoints, which provides the physical ability to send voice or data. Figure 8-12 shows the concept of PSTN.

Figure 8-12 Digital PSTN

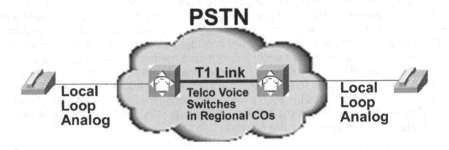

The local loop supports analog electrical signals to create a voice call. Analog signals must be converted to digital to pass the PSTN digital network, and must be converted back to analog for transmission over the destination local loop. To convert analog voice to a digital signal (A/D) a *pulse-code modulation (PCM)* technique is used. PCM defines that an incoming analog voice signal should be sampled 8000 times per second by the A/D converter, using an 8-bit code for each sample. As a result, a single voice call requires (8*8000) 64,000 bits per second—which fits into one of the DS0 channels in a T1. (T1 supports 24 separate DS0 channels, 64 kbps each, plus 8 kbps of management, for a total of 1.544 Mbps.)

Analog Modems

Modems are relatively the lowest cost, remote-access technologies, and usable most anywhere that a PSTN phone line is available. Modems are widely using for internet access and especially, by home users. However, modems suffer from the low bit rate capabilities, a little faster than 100 kbps, even when new compression technologies are adopted. However, there are wireless modems, which support a higher bandwidth (more than 1 Mbps) and does not require a PSTN phone line, are used today by the modern wireless ISP's, especially in the past two years. The costs of wireless modems are relatively higher than the usual modems.

To connect two computers over the PSTN cloud, a modem is required. Analog modem coverts bits (digital signals) generated by one computer to analog signal that can be sent over the local loop. No physical changes are required on the normal local loop cabling, and no changes are required on the voice switch at the Telco's CO.

The term *modem* is a shortened version of the combination of the two words *modulation* and *demodulation*. The modem modulates (changes) digital signals to analog signals and demodulates analog signals back to digital signals that can be understood by the computers and digital devices.

PSTN refers to a communications path between the two modems as a *circuit*. Because the modems can switch to a different destination just by hanging up and dialing another phone number, this type of WAN service is called a *switched circuit*. Figure 8-13 shows an example of such a switched circuit.

Figure 8-13 Modems and PSTN

A Layer 1 service is established between the connected modems, meaning that they can pass bits between each other. PPP protocol is also used as a data link layer protocol on this circuit.

A modem can be either internal modem-built into the computer or external modem located outside the computer. To be used as an Internet access WAN technology, the home-based user connects via a modem to a router owned by an ISP. The home-based user dials into the ISP's router which typically has a large bank of modems, and thus into a phone number into the ISP's router.

The link circuit between two modems differs in regard to clocking and synchronization when compared with a leased link circuit. Modems link create an *asynchronous* circuit, which means that the two modems try to use the same speed, without adjusting their clock rates to match the other modem. Leased link, on the other hand, creates what is called a *synchronous* circuit, because the CSU/DSUs on both sides of the link try to run at the same speed (clocking) and adjust their speeds (synchronization) to match with the other CSU/DSU.

Internet Connection

The largest WAN network is the internet. Today, several ISPs can provide the internet services to an enterprise network or even to home users. The physical connection is usually provided using DSL, cable network, wireless network or VSAT using packet switching networking.

Several documents about the internet development can be found from www.google.com. However, the internet developed through the following main events:

1. In 1957, The USSR launches Sputnik, the first artificial earth satellite.
2. In the 1960s, the U.S. Department of Defense (DoD) started to build a command-and-control network for their computing facilities around the USA.
3. In 1964, the DoD system was made public by the military.
4. Several researchers from the Massachusetts Institute of Technology (MIT), the University of California, Los Angeles (UCLA), and the National Physical Laboratory in the UK were started developing their scientific networks.
5. In the 1969, UCLA installed the first computer on this network and then four computers added to this network. This network was named the Advanced Research Projects Agency Network (ARPANET); the network was wired together via 50 Kbps circuits as a backbone.
6. In 1972, the first e-mail messaging software was developed by Ray Tomlinson of BBN so that ARPANET developers could more easily communicate.
7. Later in 1972, a program that allowed users to read, file, forward, and respond to messages was developed and the network expanded. ARPANET was currently using the Network Control Protocol or NCP to transfer data. This allowed communications between hosts running on the same network. The Backbone was 50Kbps ARPANET, and the number of hosts on the network equal to 23.
8. In 1973, development began on the protocol later to be called TCP/IP; it was developed by a group headed by Vinton Cerf from Stanford and Bob Kahn from DARPA. This new protocol was to allow diverse computer networks to interconnect and communicate with each other.
9. In 1974, first use of the term INTERNET by Vint Cerf and Bob Kahn in paper on Transmission Control Protocol
10. In 1976, Dr. Robert M. Metcalfe develops Ethernet, which allowed coaxial cable to move data extremely fast. This was a crucial component to the development of LANs.
11. In 1979, USENET (the decentralized news group network) was created by Steve Bellovin, a graduate student at University of North Carolina, and programmers Tom Truscott and Jim Ellis. It was based on UUCP.
12. In 1981, National Science Foundation created a backbone called CSNET 56 Kbps network for institutions without access to ARPANET. Vinton Cerf proposed a plan for an inter-network connection between CSNET and the ARPANET.
13. In 1983, Internet Activities Board (IAB) was created. On January 1, every machine connected to ARPANET had to use TCP/IP. TCP/IP became the core Internet protocol and replaced NCP entirely.
14. In 1984, the Domain Name System (DNS) was introduced. The University of Wisconsin created Domain Name System (DNS). This allowed packets to be directed to a domain name, which would be translated by the server database into the corresponding IP number. This made it much easier for people to access other servers, because they no longer had to remember numbers.
15. In 1989, Timothy Berners-Lee began work on a means to better facilitate communication among CERN physicists around the world, based on the concept of hypertext.
16. In 1992, World Wide Web is created and released by CERN.
17. The web was popularized by the 1993 release of a graphical, easy-to-use browser called Mosaic for x and then Netscape.
18. In the 1990s, personal computers (PC) became more powerful, less expensive, and easy to use especially after developing the Windows OS by Microsoft, allowing millions of people to buy them for their homes and offices.

19. In 1995, The National Science Foundation announced that as of April 30, 1995 it would no longer allow direct access to the NSF backbone. The National Science Foundation contracted with four companies that would be providers of access to the NSF backbone (Merit). These companies would then sell connections to groups, organizations, and companies. $50 annual fee is imposed on domains, excluding .edu and .gov domains, which are still funded by the National Science Foundation.
20. In 1996, ISPs, such as America Online (AOL), AT&T, CompuServe, and many other local service providers throughout the word, began offering affordable dialup connections to the Internet.
21. The cable service providers began to offer higher-speed internet access through cable network techniques.
22. In 1999, a wireless technology called 802.11b, more commonly referred to as Wi-Fi, is standardized. Over the years that follow, this technology begins appearing as a built-in feature of portable computers and many handheld devices.
23. Throughout the 1990s and 2000s, several easily users' access applications created and became available for the internet.
24. In 2003, social networking is started over the internet.
25. In 2005, several ISP's began to offer wireless internet access to home users and offices.
26. In December 2009, the first multi-touch website is reported

Today, the Internet becomes the largest source of information and communication for education, business and home users on the earth. The Internet is really a network of networks, combines a worldwide mesh of millions of networks connected by complicated sets of routers, switches and servers, owned and operated by millions of organizations and individuals all over the world, all connected through thousands of ISPs. Figure 8-14 shows how different businesses and organizations are connected by the Internet.

Figure 8-14 WAN and the Internet

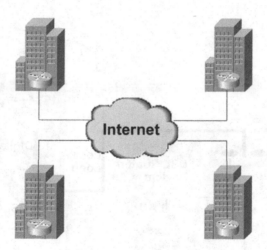

Today, the Internet is using as a utility, that provides IP connectivity to the rest of the world, so if a connection to the Internet is available; communication with anyone else in the world is possible.

Client address for the interface that is connected to the Internet can be obtained from the ISP either as a static address as a dynamic address using DHCP servers.

To solve IPv4 address space limitations, CISCO IOS Network Address Translation (NAT) and Port Address Translation (PAT) are mechanisms that can be used to conserve registered IP addresses in large networks. NAT and PAT translate IP addresses within private internal networks to legal IP addresses for transport over public external networks such as the Internet without requiring a registered subnet address. Incoming traffic is translated for delivery within the inside private networks. This translation of IP addresses eliminates the need for host renumbering and allows the same IP address range to be used in multiple intranets, networks that exist within a companies' boundaries. The following sections describe the DSL and cable internet connections and the features of NAT and PAT.

Digital Subscriber Line (DSL)

For better accessing to the internet utility, DSL was defined. It is created to provide high-speed internet access between a home or business and the local CO.

The following are the key features of the DSL as compared with modem:

- DSL's data circuit is always ON; so there is no need to signal or dial a phone number to set up a data circuit like in modem.
- DSL allows for a concurrent voice call to be up at the same time as the data connection. Both analog voice signal and digital data signal can be sent over the same PSTN-local loop wiring at the same time and of course, the same phone number.
- A *DSL access multiplexer (DSLAM)* device must be added besides a traditional PSTN-voice switch at the local CO.

DSL technology uses existing twisted-pair telephone lines to transport high-bandwidth data and provides IP services to subscribers. The cable from the phone or DSL modem to the telephone wall jack in a home uses RJ-11 telephone connectors. Figure 8-15 shows an example of the DSL connectivity.

Figure 8-15 DSL Network

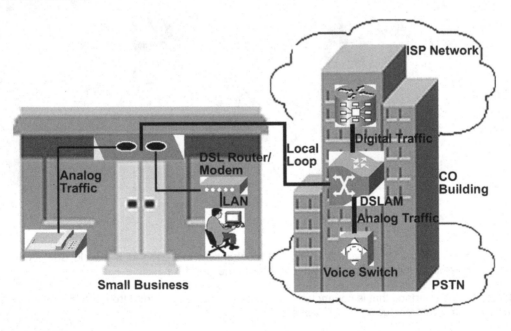

The DSL Router/Modem in Figure 8-15 is connected via a standard telephone cable to the same phone jack on the wall. DSL hardware could be a separate router and DSL modem or a combination of both. A LAN switch and a wireless AP can be added to the router and the DSL modem.

To support voice and DSL at the same line, the PSTN phone company has to disconnect the local loop cable from the old voice switch and move it to a *DSLAM*, as shown in Figure 8-15. The DSLAM directs (multiplexes) the analog voice signal to a PSTN-voice switch and the voice switch treats that signal just like any other analog voice line. The frequency ranges between 0 Hz and 4000 Hz. The DSLAM multiplexes the data traffic to the ISP's router. DSLAMs adopt time-division multiplexing (TDM) technology to multiplex many DSL lines into a single medium, generally a T3 (DS3). Current DSL technologies use sophisticated coding and modulation techniques to achieve data rates up to 8.192 Mbps.

DSL Types, Speeds, Distances, and Standards

Generally, there are two types of DSL either symmetric or asymmetric. *Symmetric* DSL means that the link speed in each direction (upload and download) is the same, whereas *asymmetric* means that the speeds are different. Almost home users need high speed download, to receive much more data than they need to send. Asymmetric DSL allows for much faster downstream speeds, but with lower upstream speeds, as compared with symmetric DSL. For example, an ADSL connection might use a 1.5-Mbps speed downstream, and a 384-Kbps speed upstream.

The following are the two basic types of DSL:

- **Asymmetric DSL (ADSL):** Provides higher download bandwidth than the upload bandwidth
- **Symmetric DSL (SDSL):** Provides the same capacity of bandwidth in both directions

Several varieties of asymmetric and symmetric exist, as follows:

ADSL

- ADSL.
- Consumer DSL (CDSL), also called G.Lite or G.992.2
- Very-high-data-rate DSL (VDSL)

SDSL

- SDSL
- High-data-rate DSL (HDSL)
- ISDN DSL (IDSL)
- Symmetric high-bit-rate DSL (G.shdsl)

The actual received DSL speeds vary widely than the maximum speeds set by standard. There are many factors that affect the actual received DSL speed by the users, as follows:

- The distance between the CO and the users. As distance is longer, the speed will be slower.
- The quality of the local loop cabling, worse wiring-slower speed.
- The type of DSLAM used in the CO.

For ADSL, the CISCO ICND1 course currently is using a maximum of 8.192 Mbps (theoretically, it is close to 10 Mbps). However, the actual speeds received by the users' maybe reach to 1.5 Mbps downstream, and 384 kbps upstream. In contrast, ADSL requires that the customer to be within 18,000 feet (a little over 3 miles/5 kilometers) of the CO location of the provider.

DSL is now a popular choice for enterprise IT organizations to support home workers. The connection between the subscriber and the enterprise must be through the ISP, and it cannot be directly.

IP over Ethernet Internet Cable Network

Today, the internet service delivered by cable networks is another WAN communications access technology that can be used by home users. Cable modem technology does not use a phone line from the PSTN for physical connectivity. It uses a cable TV service supplied by a coaxial cable/over the cable TV (CATV). Cable internet provides an always-on Internet access service in addition to the ability to watch favorites TV channels at the same time. Now, digital voice services can also be supported by cable network. The voice traffic passes over the same CATV cable. Cable modem/Cable router is similar in concept to DSL modem/router; it uses some of the capacity in the CATV cable for transferring data with the same frequency bands that may be allocated for TV channels.

Originally, cable was a one-directional medium designed to carry broadcast analog video channels to the subscribers. It sends electrical signals down the cable for all the channels. Figure 8-16 shows a typical cable network.

Figure 8-16 Cable TV Network

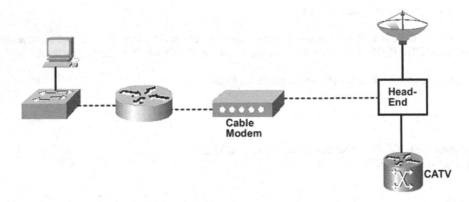

One end of the cable is connected into the house equipments and the other end of the cable is connected to equipment in the cable company's facilities, which is called the head-end (router). The head-end can split the channels used for the Internet over to an ISP router. Other details in the figure are cleared.

Like DSL internet service, Cable Internet service is an always-on and available service. It is also asymmetric, with much faster downstream speeds than DSL (from two to five times faster). Cable speeds also do not degrade due to the length of the cable. The problem with cable internet is that it is shared among users in certain parts of the CATV cable plant. Therefore, the effective speed of cable Internet does degrade as more and more traffic is sent over the cable. DSL does not suffer from this problem.

Remote-Access Technologies, In Brief

To choose which remote internet access technology is suitable, Table 8-2 lists some of the key comparison points for these technologies.

Table 8-2 Comparison of Remote-Access Technologies

	Analog Modems	Cable Modems	DSL
Transport media	Telco local loop	CATV cable	Telco local loop
Supports symmetric speeds	Yes	No	Yes

Supports asymmetric speeds	Yes	Yes	Yes
Practical speeds	Up to 100 kbps	3 to 6 Mbps downstream	1.5 Mbps downstream
Transmits voice and data simultaneously	No	Yes	Yes
Always-on Internet service	No	Yes	Yes
Local loop distance issues	No	No	Yes
Shared service (throughput degrades under higher loads)	No	Yes	No
Overall Cost	Lowest	Lower	Low

Cell Switching: The ATM

Asynchronous Transfer Mode (ATM) is one of the WAN technologies available today. It is used either as a cell-switching service, similar in purpose to the Frame Relay, or as a switching technology used inside the Telcos' core network. It can be used for remote Internet access from the home or a small office.

ATM is based on cell-switching technology that is capable of transferring voice, video, and data simultaneously, through several types of networks. In enterprise, ATM is primarily used as the backbones or WAN links. Figure 8-17 shows a sample of an ATM connection.

Figure 8-17 ATM Network

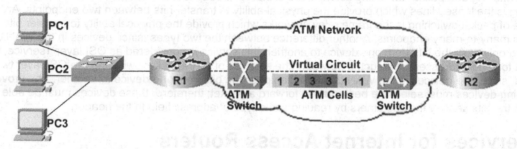

ATM has data rates beyond 155 Mbps. ATM WANs look similar to other switching technologies, such as X.25 and Frame Relay. The enterprise router connects to an ATM service via an access link to an ATM switch inside the service provider's cloud. ATM is implemented using VCs that can be either PVC or SVC; just like Frame Relay. However, there are some differences between ATM and Frame Relay.ATM can support much higher-speed physical links using a Synchronous Optical Network (SONET). Another difference is that, ATM use cells instead of frames (frame relay) or packet (packet switching). A cell is a string of bits sent over ATM network with fixed 53 bytes in length (not variable length like frame or packet).

The 53-byte ATM cell contains a 5-byte ATM header followed by 48 bytes of ATM payload (data). The header contains two fields named *Virtual Path Identifier (VPI)* and *Virtual Channel Identifier (VCI)* that together indicate to which VC an ATM cell belongs and acts, like the data-link connection identifier (DLCI) for Frame Relay by identifying each VC. Just like Frame Relay switches forward frames based on the DLCI, ATM switches forward cells based on the VPI/VCI pair. However, numerous VCs can be multiplexed into a single physical circuit for transmission across the cloud.

A router is used to connect the enterprise LAN (based Ethernet) and the ATM WAN cloud via an access link. Figure 8-18 shows the *segmentation* process that will be done by R1 to a received frame from the Ethernet. The remote router R2 will reassemble the received cells into frames by a reverse process called *reassembly*. The processes done by R1 and R2 are called *segmentation and reassembly (SAR)*.

ATM can run over a variety of physical media, including fiber optics using Synchronous Optical Network (SONET)/Synchronous Digital Hierarchy (SDH) and coaxial cable using DS3.

Figure 8-18 ATM SAR Processes

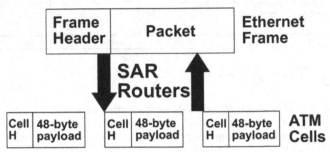

Circuit Switching Vs Packet Switching

Circuit-switching and packet-switching services are explained throughout this chapter. An example of circuit-switching is the leased lines which provide the physical ability to transfer bits between two endpoints. An example of packet switching is the frame relay networks which provide the physical ability to transfer bits between many-to-many endpoints. Another difference between the two types, since devices in the WAN circuit-switching only pass the bits from one device to another, this service is considered as OSI layer 1service, there is no need to send addresses over such a network. The services of WAN packet switching are OSI layer two services, since; the devices in the WAN do more than pass the bits from one device to another. The provider's networking devices must select the best route to forward a packet; therefore, these devices must be able to interpret the bits sent by the customers by reading some type of address field in the header.

IP Services for Internet Access Routers

For DSL and cable Internet access to be implemented in the home users (SOHO), several IP-related services must be performed on the DSL/cable router, including assigning IP addresses, using DHCP service, as well as adopting a Network Address Translation (NAT) feature. A DSL/cable router can be single integrated device that combines (switch, wireless access point, router and modem), or multiplies separated devices. Figure 8-19 shows how SOHO is connected to the ISP using separated DSL Internet Access Router devices (R1).

Figure 8-19 Connecting SOHO to ISP

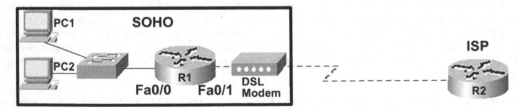

The following steps are followed when PC1 tries to send data to the internet through the ISP:

1. PC1 sends data to its default gateway, which is the local access router interface.
2. The LAN switch forwards frames to the access router.
3. The router makes a routing decision to forward the packet to the ISP router as the next-hop router.
4. The DSL modem converts the Ethernet frame received from the router to meet local loop specifications.
5. The ISP router forwards the packet to the internet based on its routing table.

Assigning IP Address to the Internet Access Router

The following rules should be followed when configuring the IP addresses for the two interfaces of the DSL access router in Figure 8-19:

- One public (globally routable) IP address for the Internet interface of the DSL access router. Usually, assigned by the ISP statically or dynamically using DHCP server, in this case the interface will be a DHCP client
- One static IP address on the local subnet interface of the DSL access router acts as a default gateway to the local subnet, using a private network number.
- Typically, the access router will act as a DHCP server for the local subnet hosts; the local subnet hosts will dynamically learn their IP addresses (including the network details, such as ISP DNS server) from it using a private network number.

Figure 8-20 shows a sample of such network configurations.

Figure 8-20 Internet Access Router Configurations and Functions

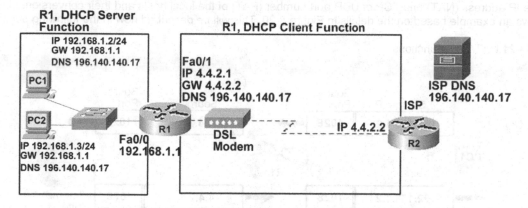

The routing function of the DSL Internet Access Router is deeply described in Chapter 5 of this book; simply, the function is to route all traffic from local private network (PC1 & PC2) to the internet ISP's routers which will route this traffic to the destination internet sites. It should also be able to route all traffic came from the internet sites to the local private network (PC1 & PC2) through the internet ISP's routers. This function will be implemented by the DSL Internet Access Router after configuring its two interfaces (the public one and the local private network one). However, R1 can use a default route. Instead of requiring a static route configuration, the DSL Internet Access Router can add a default route based on the default gateway learnt by the DHCP client function, in this case the IP address of ISP's R2, which will be used as the next-hop router.

To make the whole network works, the process of routing should be done in combination with NAT/PAT functions of the DSL Internet Access Router. The second function is important for the network since the Internet routers should never have any routes for local private IP addresses (PC1 & PC2). NAT/PAT makes PC1 & PC2 as if they are using R1's publicly registered IP address. Internet sites will send the packets to the DSL Internet Access Router's public IP address, and R1 will translate the address to match the correct IP address on the hosts on the local private LAN. The function of NAT/PAT will be described in more details in the next section.

Network Address Translation (NAT) and Port Address Translation (PAT)

The Internet Corporation for Assigned Names and Numbers (ICANN) assigns and manages the global, public IP addresses. IPv4 address space. This space supports a limited number of unique IP addresses, unsuitable for huge growth in the global, as shown in chapter 3 of this book. The ISP must assign at least one unique, global, and routable IP address to any DSL or cable customer and usually the ISP uses DHCP server for this assignment. In particular, the ISP does not want to assign multiple public IP addresses to each PC in the local network such as PC1 and PC2 in Figure 8-20, to conserve the global and public IPv4 address space.

The private local LAN, then, is implemented using private IP addressing and not public IP addresses. When connecting this type of network to public networks such as the Internet, a method to convert the private IP addressing to the public addressing is needed. NAT (as defined in RFC 1631) operates on CISCO routers and is designed for such IP address conversion. NAT enables private IP LANs that use non registered IP addresses to connect to the public and global internet. NAT operates on any device that sits between an internal network and the public network, such as a firewall, a router, or a computer. NAT can be configured to advertise only one address for the entire network to the outside world. Advertising only one address to the public hides the internal network from the world, thus providing additional security to the local LAN.

So, to support lots of local hosts at the local LAN, using a single publicly routable IP address on the router, PAT translates the local hosts' private IP addresses to the one registered public IP address. The router keeps track of both the IP address (NAT) and TCP or UDP port number (PAT) of the local hosts and their conversion. Figure 8-21 shows an example based on the details in Figure 8-20. This will be described now in the following points:

Figure 8-21 NAT/PAT Functions

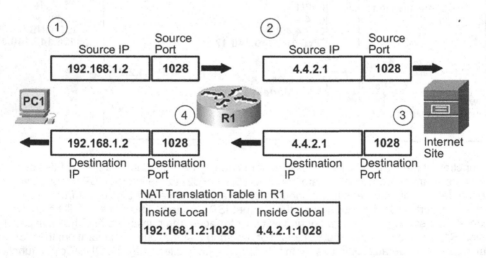

1.   PC1 (IP 192.168.1.2) sends a packet to an internet site through ISP gateway 4.4.2.2 through PC1's default gateway setting (R1).
2.   PC1 sends the packet to R1.

3. R1 performs PAT, based on the details in the R1's NAT translation table, changing the PC1's IP from the private IP address used on the local LAN to the one globally routable public IP address available to R1, namely 4.4.2.1.
4. R1 forwards the packet based on its default route.
5. When the site replies to the packet sent from PC1, the site sends the packet, based on the values in the source fields of the packet at step 3, to same sender, destination IP address 4.4.2.1, and destination port 1028.
6. When R1 receives the packet sent from an internet site, it changes the destination IP address and port per its NAT table, switching from destination address/port 4.4.2.1/1028 to 192.168.1.2/1028.
7. R1 sends the packet (the reply from the internet site) to PC1, IP 192.168.1.2.

NAT uses the following important terms:

Inside host: It refers to a host in the enterprise LAN network (PC1 and PC2 in the previous figures.)
Inside local (Inside local address): The IP address assigned to a host on the inside network (enterprise LAN). The inside local address is not an IANA address. It is used in the IP headers of the packets overtake over the local enterprise network. In this case, 192.168.1.2 and 192.168.1.3 are inside local IP addresses, and the packets at steps 1, 2, and 7 in Figure 8-21 show inside local IP addresses.
Inside global (Inside global address): An IANA IP address assigned by the ISP that represents inside local enterprise LAN IP addresses to the outside world. It is used in the IP headers of the packets overtake over the global Internet (not the enterprise). In this case, 4.4.2.1 is the one inside global IP address, and the packets at steps 3-5 in Figure 8-21 show the inside global IP address.
Inside interface: The router interface connected to the same LAN as the inside hosts. In this case, the default gateway, IP 192.168.1.1 is the inside.
Outside interface: The router interface connected to the Internet. In this case, the IP 4.4.2.1 is the outside interface.

NAT refers to the translation of network layer (IP) addresses, with no translation of ports, whereas PAT refers to the translation of IP addresses as well as transport layer (TCP and UDP) port numbers. PAT is used by the DSL internet access router (R1 in the previous examples) to differentiate packets send from several local hosts on local LAN enterprise based on transport layer port number (described in chapter 2 of this book). Generally, the NAT is used to refer to both NAT and PAT functions.

WAN Configuration

The following subsections clarify the configuration steps that must be followed to configure WAN interfaces on CISCO devices.

Configuring HDLC WANs

Configuration 8-2: To configure the HDLC encapsulation on the leased lines between two CISCO routers, do nothing since it is configured by default. However, several optional configuration steps can be useful so this section explains those optional steps and their impact on the links.

R1(config)#int S0/1/1
R1(config-if)#ip address 172.17.18.18 255.255.255.0
R1(config-if)#encapsulation hdlc
R1(config-if)#no shutdown
R1(config-if)#clock rate 32000
R1(config-if)#bandwidth 128

If the serial link is a back-to-back serial link in a lab, the clock rate should be configured using the **clock rate** *speed* interface subcommand, but only on the router with the DCE cable (the **show controllers serial** *number* command can be used to check this). The **clock rate** command would not be needed on R2, as R1 has the DCE cable, so R2 must be connected to a DTE cable.

Verifying HDLC WANS

Configuration 8-3: To verify the previous hdlc encapsulating, the following steps can be followed:

1. To confirm that R1 indeed has a DCE cable installed.

R1#show controllers S0/1/1
Interface Serial0/1/1
Hardware is GT96K
DCE V.35, clock rate 32000
....

2. To list the various configuration settings, including the default encapsulation value (HDLC) and the bandwidth setting on the serial interface.

R1#show interfaces S0/1/1
Serial0/1/1 is up, line protocol is up
Hardware is GT96K Serial
Internet address is 172.17.18.18/24
MTU 1500 bytes, BW 128 Kbit, DLY 20000 usec,
reliability 255/255, txload 1/255, rxload 1/255
Encapsulation HDLC, loopback not set
Keepalive set (10 sec)
....

3. To display a short status of the interfaces, with both list the line status and protocol status codes.

R1#show ip interface brief
R1#show interfaces description

4. To list the interface configuration for interface S0/1/1.

R1#show running-config interface S0/1/1
Building configuration...
Current configuration: 100 bytes
!
interface Serial0/1/1
ip address 172.17.18.18 255.255.255.0
encapsulation hdlc
clockrate 32000
end

Configuring PPP WANs

Configuration 8-4: To configure the PPP encapsulation on the leased lines between two routers, only add one interface subcommand on each router's serial interface (**encapsulation ppp**). However, several optional configuration steps can be useful as explained in HDLC configuration.

Router#config t
Enter configuration commands, one per line. End with CNTL/Z.
Router(config)#int S0/1/1
Router(config-if)#encapsulation ppp
Router(config-if)#^Z
Router#

PPP encapsulation must be enabled on both interfaces connected to a serial line to work.

Configuring PPP Authentication Protocols

Configuration 8-5: To configure authentication-using PPP between two routers. First, set the hostname of the router if it is not already set. Then set the username and password for the remote router connecting to the local router.

Router#config t
Enter configuration commands, one per line. End with CNTL/Z.
Router(config)#hostname campusA
campusA(config)#username campusB password cisco
campusA(config))#^Z
campusA #

Telnet 172.16.10.2
....
Router>
Router>enable
Router#config t
Enter configuration commands, one per line. End with CNTL/Z.
Router(config)#hostname campusB
campusB(config)#username campusA password cisco
campusB(config)#^Z
campusB #

The username is the hostname of the remote router connecting to the local router, and it is case sensitive. The password is a plain-text password, and it must be the same on both routers. The **show run** command can be used to display this password. However, the password can be encrypted using the **service password-encryption** command. The remote routers must also be configured with usernames and passwords as shown above.

After setting the hostname, usernames, and passwords, the authentication type, either CHAP or PAP can be configured as follows:

campusA #config t
Enter configuration commands, one per line. End with CNTL/Z.
campusA(config)#int S0/1/1
campusA(config-if)#ppp authentication chap pap
campusA(config-if)#^Z
campusA #

Only the first authentication method will be used during link negotiation, the second will be used in case of the first method fails.

Verifying PPP WANs

Configuration 8-6: To verify the previous PPP encapsulating, the following steps should be followed:

campusA#sh int S0/1/1
Serial0/1/1 is up, line protocol is up
Hardware is GT96K Serial
Internet address is 172.16.10.1/24
MTU 1500 bytes, BW 128 Kbit, DLY 20000 usec,
reliability 255/255, txload 1/255, rxload 1/255
Encapsulation PPP, loopback not set Keepalive set (10 sec)
LCP Open
Open: IPCP, CDPCP
....

The sixth line in the command output above lists encapsulation as PPP and the next line shows that the LCP is open, which means that it has negotiated the session establishment and is good! The eight lines tell that the NCP is listening for the protocols IP and CDP.

Configuring Internet Access Routers

Configuration 8-7: To configure the Internet Access Router, only connect its interfaces to the suitable cables (if it's not a wireless router), also, it is requiring to configure the internet-facing interface/port, which is usually done by the ISP. This type of Routers is usually shipping from the factory with DHCP client services enabled on the Internet-facing interface, DHCP server functions enabled on the local LAN-facing interface, and NAT/PAT functions enabled. To clarify the configuration of such routers, this section shows how to configure these functions on a CISCO enterprise-class router (CISCO 1841 Router (Modular) -data sheet can be found on http://cisco.com/en/US/prod/collateral/routers/ps5853/product_data_sheet0900aecd8016a59b.html) where these functions are not configured by default. This router contains an Integrated Channel Service Unit (CSU)/Data Service Unit (DSU). In addition, several optional configuration steps are added to make this section more useful.

CISCO Router and Security Device Manager (SDM) tools are used in this section for the configuration instead of the CLI. Web based access can be used instead of SSH and Telnet tools. The use of SDM is one of the requirements in the CISCO ICND1 CCENT exam. However, the router must first be configured from the CLI with at least one IP address, usually on local LAN interface. Notice that, CISCO switches also allow web access for configuration, using a tool called *CISCO Device Manager (CDM)*, which is identical to the SDM in the routers.

To configure the router, the following steps can be followed, using the network and IP addresses in Figure 8-19:

1. **Configure IP addresses on local LAN:** From the CLI of the router, configure the IP address of one of the router interfaces, which faces the local network. This will make accessing the router using CLI is possible. Make sure that the local hosts (PC1 or PC2) can connect to the router using the **ping** utility.
2. **Install and access SDM.** Install SDM on the router and configure SDM using the configuration steps founded on, http://www.cisco.com/en/US/products/sw/secursw/ps5318/prod_installation_guide09186a00803e4727.html. Access the router's SDM interface using PC1 web browser as shown in Figure 8-22 after the SDM launch page is displayed.

Figure 8-22 SDM Home Page

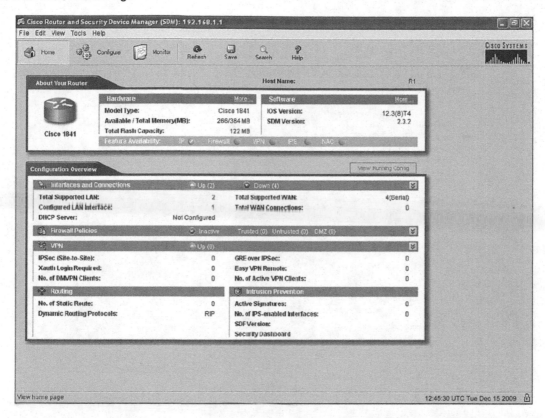

3. **Configure DHCP and PAT:** Use SDM to configure both the DHCP client services and the PAT service on the router as follows:

- Click **Configure** at the top of the window.
- Click **Interfaces and Connections** at the top of the Tasks pane on the left side of the window.

Figure 8-23 shows the Interfaces and Connections window after creation, with the Create Connection tab displayed.

Figure 8-23 SDM Configure Interfaces and Connections Window

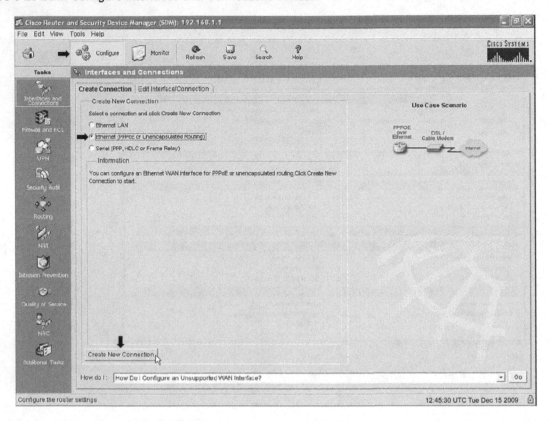

On the Create Connection tab, do the following:

- Choose the **Ethernet (PPPoE or Unencapsulated Routing)** radio group button.
- Click the **Create New Connection** button near the bottom of the tab.

SDM Ethernet Wizard, shown in Figure 8-24 will be opened.

Figure 8-24 SDM Ethernet Wizard Welcome Page

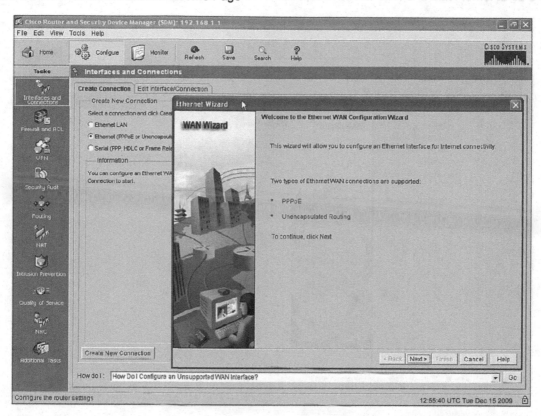

- **Click Next.**

The Wizard shown in Figure 8-25 will be opened. It needs to select a check box that, if checked, enables the protocol PPP over Ethernet (PPPoE). This depends on the ISP. Usually, the ISP wants to leave this box unchecked. This tends to use unencapsulated routing. Unencapsulated routing means that the router forwards Ethernet frames onto the interface, with an IP packet inside the Ethernet frame.

Figure 8-25 Ethernet Wizard: Choice to Use Encapsulation with PPPoE

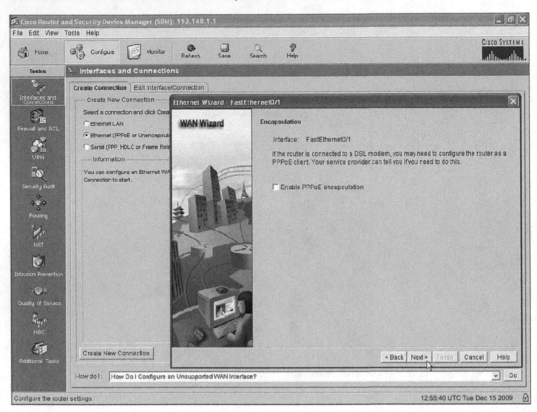

In Figure 8-25, the wizard picked a Fast Ethernet interface (Fa0/1) automatically, as the interface to configure (the only other interface Fa0/0 of the router is already configured in step 1). On this interface DHCP client and NAT/PAT functions need to configure. This is the outside interface.

- Click **Next**.

The wizard shown in Figure 8-26 will be displayed.

- Select the default radio button option of **Dynamic (DHCP Client)**.

Figure 8-26 Ethernet Wizard: Static or DHCP Address Assignment

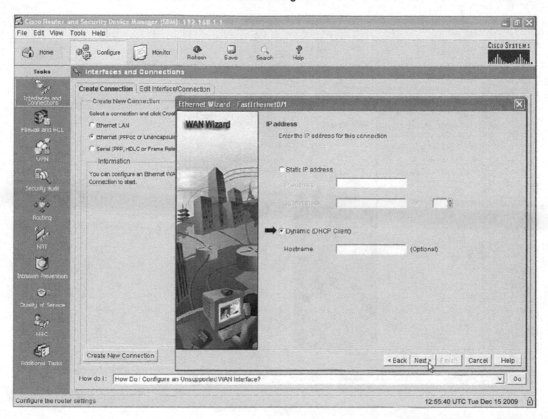

- Click **Next**.

The Advanced Options page shown in Figure 8-27 will be displayed. The page shows the options to enable PAT or not.

- Click the **Port Address Translation** check box.

Figure 8-27 Ethernet Wizard: Enable PAT on the Inside Interface

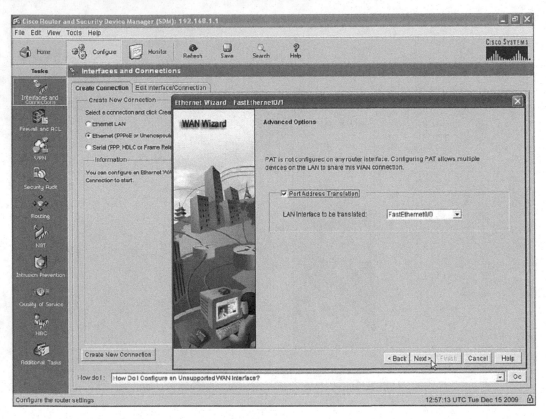

- Check the LAN Interface to Be Translated from the list box, it must be the inside interface, FastEthernet0/0.
- Click **Next** to move to the Summary page shown in Figure 8-28.

Figure 8-28 Ethernet Wizard: Summary Page

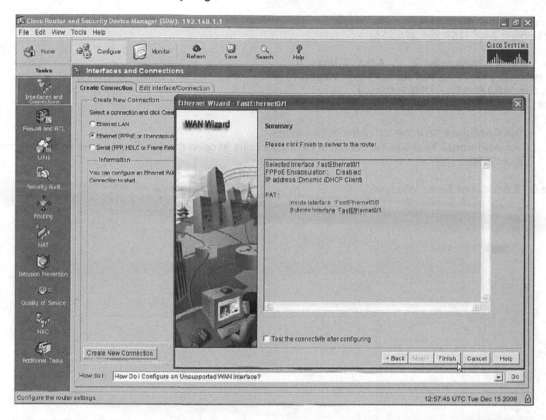

- Click **Finish**. SDM builds the configuration and loads it into the router's running-config file.
- Select save button near the top of the SDM to save the configuration to flash (copy **running-config startup-config**).

4. **Configure DHCP services:** Before using the SDM to configure the DHCP server features on the router, the IP addresses to be assigned by the router to the hosts on the local LAN, along with the DNS IP addresses, domain name, and default gateway settings that the router will advertise, need to be identified. Use the following steps:

- From step 1, the local subnet will use, IP network 192.168.1.0 with mask /24.
- Find the DNS server IP addresses and the domain name learnt by the router using DHCP client services, using the **show dhcp server** command. This will be used by the router to inform the DHCP clients on the local LAN about the DNS server IP address(es) and the domain name.

Configuration 9-7-1: The output of the **show dhcp server** command.

DSLRouter#show dhcp server
DHCP server: ANY (255.255.255.255)
Leases: 2
Offers: 2   Requests: 2   Acks: 2 Naks: 0
Declines: 0   Releases: 11   Bad: 0
DNS0: 196.140.140.17,   DNS1: 0.0.0.0
Subnet: 255.255.255.240 DNS Domain: thaartechnologies.com

- Click **Configure** near the top of the SDM window.
- Click **Additional Tasks** at the bottom of the Tasks pane to open the Additional Tasks window shown in Figure 8-29.

Figure 8-29 Additional Tasks Window

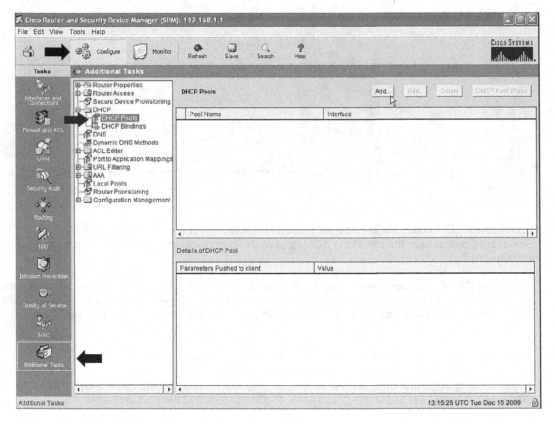

- Select the **DHCP Pools** option on the left (CISCO uses the term *DHCP pool* for the IP addresses that can be assigned using the DHCP service by the router).

- Click the **Add** button to open the Add DHCP Pool dialog box shown in Figure 8-30.
- Add all the information gathered in the previous steps, along with other settings. This includes the following: Range of addresses to be assigned with DHCP server, DNS server IP addresses, Domain name and Default router settings.

Figure 8-30 DHCP Pool Dialog Box

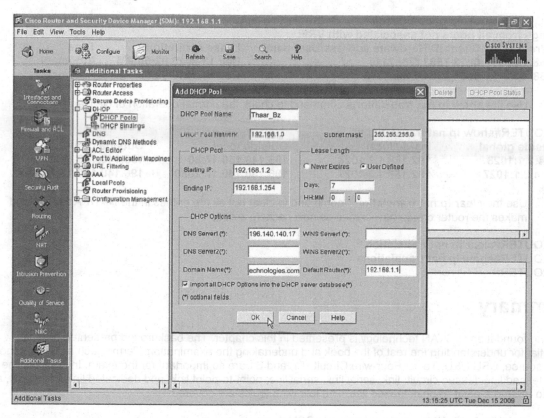

Verifying Internet Access Routers

Configuration 8-8: To verify the previous internet access router configurations, the following steps should be followed:

1. From PC1 try to access the internet (for example, www.thaartechnologies.com.) If a web page opens, that is the network configuration is OK, go to 2.
2. From the DOS prompt of PC1, type: **ipconfig /all** command to find out if the PC learnt an IP address, mask, default gateway, Domain name and DNS IP addresses as configured in the DHCP server configuration on the router. DHCP client function can be checked using the SDM.
3. Cable checking is important to ensure that all interfaces of the router are connected as required by the configuration. The cable should be checked between the router and the local LAN, and between the router and the DSL modem.
4. Using the SDM, ensure that the outside interface per the PAT configuration is connected to the DSL modem (if it is separated from the router) and ensure that the inside interface per the PAT configuration is the interface connected to the local LAN.

5. Generate traffic from PC1 to www.thaartechnologies.com web site to test the PAT function and by using the following CLI commands:

- Use the **show ip dhcp binding** command to list information about the IP addresses assigned to local LAN hosts by the DHCP server function in the access router. The output must be part of the DHCP pool.

```
DSLROUTER#show ip dhcp binding
Bindings from all pools not associated with VRF:
IP address      Client-ID/Hardware address/User name     Lease expiration       Type
192.168.1.2     0c13.7583.f26f.211c                      Dec 13 2010 02:55 PM   Automatic
192.168.1.3     0c01.2354.213a.122b                      Dec 13 2010 02:55 PM   Automatic
```

- Use the **show ip nat translations** command to check the normal operation of NAT and PAT.

```
DSLROUTER#show ip nat translations
Pro Inside global      Inside local         Outside local         Outside global
tcp 4.4.2.1:1028       192.168.1.2:1028     196.140.140.17:80     196.140.140.17:80
udp 4.4.2.1:1027       192.168.1.3:1027     196.140.140.17:2080   196.140.140.17:2080
```

- Use the **clear ip nat translation *** command to clear out all the entries in the NAT/PAT table, and makes the router create new entries as new packets arrive.

```
DSLROUTER#clear ip nat translation *
DSLROUTER#show ip nat translations
DSLROUTER#
```

Summary

A strong foundation for WAN technology is presented in this chapter. The background presented here is essential for understanding the rest of the book and undertaking the examination. Terms such as Synchronous, Clock source, CSU/DSU, Telco, Four-wire Circuit, T1, and E1 are so important for the exam. In addition, the terms leased line, leased circuit, link, serial link, serial line, point-to-point link, and dedicated link/line circuit, are used to refer to a point-to-point leased line. The following topics are covered:

- Point-to-Point WANs implementation at OSI L1
- Standard WAN Cables
- Serial Connections
- DTE, DCE, Clock Rate, Bandwidth, Link Speed and Synchronization
- Back-to-back serial connection
- Types of WAN Connections
- Point-to-Point WANs Implementation at OSI L2
- High-Level Data Link Control (HDLC) Protocol
- Point-to-Point Protocol (PPP)
- Frame Relay
- Integrated Services Digital Network (ISDN)
- Public Switched Telephone Network (PSTN)
- Analog Modems
- Internet Connection
- Digital Subscriber Line (DSL)
- DSL Types, Speeds, Distances, and Standards
- IP over Ethernet Internet Cable Network

- Cell Switching: The ATM
- IP Services for Internet Access Routers
- Network Address Translation (NAT) and Port Address Translation (PAT)
- WAN configuration including, HDLC, PPP, Internet Access Router, NAT/PAT, and DHCP

At the end of the chapter, several learning questions are given to evaluate the learning level from this chapter. The correct answers and solutions with complementary discussions are found in appendix A, "Answers to Chapters Learning Questions."

Chapter Eight Commands Reference

Table 8-3 lists and briefly describes all the new commands and keys that are used in this chapter.

Table 8-3 Chapter 8 Commands Reference

Command	Description
Router(config-if)#encapsulation ?	Lists the available encapsulation types on the router
Router (config-if)#encapsulation hdlc	Defines hdlc encapsulation on the serial router interface
Router(config-if)#encapsulation ppp	Defines PPP encapsulation on the serial router interface
Router (config-if)#ppp authentication chap pap	Configures the authentication type, either CHAP or PAP on a serial interface
Router#show dhcp server	Finds the DNS server IP addresses and the domain name learned by the router
Router #show ip dhcp binding	Lists information about the IP addresses assigned to local LAN hosts by the DHCP server
Router #show ip nat translations	Checks the normal operation of NAT and PAT on the router
Router #clear ip nat translation	Clears out all the entries in the NAT/PAT table, and makes the router creates new entries as new packets arrive

Chapter 8 Learning Questions

8-1 TRUE/FALSE: WAN standards and protocols define how to network between devices that are relatively far apart. WAN is required when an enterprise grows beyond a single location or even a country, and interconnecting these enterprise parts (LANs) to each other becomes necessary. This interconnection will form a WAN.

    A. TRUE
    B. FALSE

8-2 What are the differences between the LAN and WAN? (Select all that apply)

    A. WAN covers a wide area (connect devices that are relatively far apart) while LAN covers a local area (single building or other small geographical area).
    B. WAN protocols are different from LAN protocols.
    C. Usually WAN bandwidth is less than LAN bandwidth.
    D. LANs are owned by the organization (an enterprise) while WANs connections usually are leased from services of carriers (service providers), such as public telephone companies, cable companies, satellite systems, and network providers. The service provider must have permission from the appropriate government agencies to install and maintain the WAN cabling.
    E. Both WANs and LANs carry a variety of traffic types, such as voice, data, and video.
    F. WANs use serial connections of various types.
    G. Except for wireless WAN; WAN cabling is usually installed underground to prevent accidental damage by people or cars.

8-3 TRUE/FALSE: WANs function focuses primarily on L1 and L2 of the OSI model. A number of recognized authorities, including the ISO, the Telecommunications Industry Association (TIA), and the Electronics Industry Alliance (EIA) defined and managed WAN access standards. These standards typically describe both L1 delivery methods and L2 requirements.

    A. TRUE
    B. FALSE

8-4 Which of the following communications types needs a WAN communication? (Select all that apply)

    A. SOHO users need to be able to communicate and share data with each other.
    B. A school needs to share large data files quickly.
    C. Administrative staff within an organization needs to share timetable information with the employees.
    D. A building wants to exchange information with other buildings within a campus.
    E. Customer wants to access the internet.
    F. Branches of a company want to share information with other branches across large distances.

8-5 TRUE/FALSE: L1 defines the standards and protocols used to create the physical network and to send and receive the data (bits) from one device to another across that network.

    A. TRUE
    B. FALSE

8-6 WAN protocols and standards describe how to provide electrical, mechanical, operational, and functional connections to the services of a communications service provider. At which OSI layer this occurs.

    A. Layer 7
    B. Layer 6

    C.   Layer 5
    D.   Layer 4
    E.   Layer 3
    F.   Layer 2
    G.   Layer 1

8-7 Which of the following is true? (Select all that apply)

    A.   To implement a point-to-point WAN link in L1, it is simple; it acts like an Ethernet trunk between two CISCO switches.

    B.   The trunk link between two CISCO switches is implemented using crossover cable. However, this link is unsuitable for WAN link, since the WAN link is typically used for connecting far apart locations. Therefore, a *leased line* should be used to implement a point-to-point WAN link instead of a crossover cable.

    C.   It is called a leased line since an organization that needs to send data over the WAN circuit does not actually own the cable, line, or link and the connection is always available as long as the leased is paid and the exclusive right to use that line is valid.

    D.   The actual physical cabling of such long links are owned, installed, and managed by Telco (the local telephone company) that has the right of way to run cables under streets through cities. Telco is sometimes called the Public Telephone and Telegraph (PTT) company. With the internet exploration in 1990's, the generic term *service provider* is used to refer to a company that provides any form of WAN connectivity, including Internet services.

    E.   Usually, Telco has large network runs around the country, and to connect the customer to Telco's network, Telco runs extra cables from the local central office (CO) to the customer (subscriber) building.

8-8 Which of the following is true? (Select all that apply)

    A.   Figure 8-1 shows that at both sites, the router is connected to a device called an external Channel Service Unit/Data Service Unit (CSU/DSU) or modem using a short cable, typically less than 50 feet long (the CSU/DSUs get placed in a rack near the router).

    B.   To connect the CSU/DSU to Telco's network, another type of cable is used (copper or fiber), which is much longer than the first one. It plugs into the CSU/DSU of the subscriber. Usually, it is a four-wire cable from the Telco, composed of two twisted-pair wires. Each pair is used to send in one direction, so a four-wire circuit allows full-duplex communication. This cabling is often called the local loop. The other end of this cable ends up in the nearest exchange or the CO WAN switch of the Telco.

    C.   Now (after implementing A & B), the routers at both sites can send and receive data simultaneously across this point-to-point WAN link.

8-9 TRUE/FALSE: A device such as a DSU/CSU or modem is required to make the local loop carrying data in a suitable form (digital or analog) and to prepare the data for transmission.

    A.   TRUE
    B.   FALSE

8-10   TRUE/FALSE: Other terms can be found here, the Data Communications Equipment (DCE) and Data Terminal Equipment (DTE). DCE's are devices that put data on the local loop, whereas DTE's are the customer devices that overtake the data to the DCE. Clearly, the DCE primarily function is providing an interface for the DTE into the WAN circuit (cloud).

    A.   TRUE
    B.   FALSE

8-11 TRUE/FALSE: Telco uses the term *demarc* (demarcation point), to refer to the point at which the Telco's responsibility is on one side ends and the subscriber's responsibility is on the other side starts. For instance, in Figure 8-1, the router cable and the CSU/DSU at the subscriber side are owned by the subscriber, and the wiring (copper or fiber) to the CO and all devices inside the CO are owned by the Telco.

A. TRUE
B. FALSE

8-12 TRUE/FALSE: Another term is used by Telco to refer to both the CSU/DSU and the router at the subscriber side. Telco called these devices "customer premises equipment" (CPE). The subscriber owns the CPE or leases the CPE from the Telco. When, the Telco owns and manages the CSU/DSU and maybe the router at the subscriber site, demarc would be moved to the nearest point that owned by Telco's subscriber.

A. TRUE
B. FALSE

8-13 Which of the following typically connects to a four-wire line provided by a Telco? (Select all that apply)

A. CSU/DSU
B. Router serial interface
C. Transceiver
D. Ethernet port on CISCO switches
E. Telco WAN switch interface

8-14
A. Which of the following is true about **Customer premises equipment (CPE)**?
B. Which of the following is true about **Demarcation point**?
C. Which of the following is true about **Local loop**?
D. Which of the following is true about **Central office (CO)**?
E. Which of the following is true about **Toll network**?

1. It is the equipment, which, owned by the subscriber site, located on the subscriber's sites, and connected to the service provider network. Equipments such as telephones, modems, and terminals are examples of the CPEs.
2. It is the point where the service provider's (carrier) responsibility ends and the CPE begins (the separation point between carrier equipment and the CPE). It is generally a communication device in a telecommunications closet owned and installed by the carrier. The customer is responsible to cable (extended demarc) from this box to the CPE, which is usually a connection to a CSU/DSU or ISDN interface.
3. It a cable that connects the demarcation point to the closest switching office (CO). It is sometimes referred to a line from the CPE's of a telephone subscriber to the telephone company CO.
4. The local telephone company office where all loops in a certain area are connected and where circuit switching of subscriber lines occurs. It connects the customers to the provider's switching network. A central office (CO) is sometimes referred to as a point of presence (POP).
5. It is a trunk line inside a WAN provider's network. This network is a collection of switches and facilities owned by the ISP. It uses the public switched telephone network (PSTN).

8-15 Which of the following devices can be used for WAN access at the physical layer (L1)? (Select all that apply)

A. **Routers:** To provide WAN access interface ports.
B. **Communication servers:** To concentrate the dialing (in and out) for user communications.

C. **(DSU/CSU) or Modem:** To provide data transmission. DSU and CSU are required for digital lines. Modem is required for analog lines to convert the digital signal into analog format and vice versa. Both can be combined into a single piece of equipment, called the DSU/CSU, which can also be built into the interface card of the router.

D. **WAN networking devices:** To support the network connectivity within the cloud, other devices, such as core routers, ATM switches, Frame Relay switches, and, public switched telephone network (PSTN) switches, are also used. All of these devices are part of Telco's network.

8-16   TRUE/FALSE: Several types of WAN interface cards (WIC's) are introduced by CISCO for its routers. In general, these serial interfaces are either synchronous or asynchronous. CISCO routers support the EIA/TIA-232, EIA/TIA-449, EIA-530, V.35, and X.21 standards for serial connections.

A. TRUE
B. FALSE

8-17   TRUE/FALSE: CISCO serial connections support almost any type of WAN service. The typical WAN connections are HDLC, PPP, ISDN, and Frame Relay. Typical speeds are from 2.4kbps to 45Mbps (T3). HDLC, PPP, and Frame Relay can use the same Physical layer specifications. ISDN has different specifications at the Physical layer.

A. TRUE
B. FALSE

8-18   TRUE/FALSE: The 60-pin D-shell connector (DB-60 connector) is one of a variety of proprietary physical connector types that CISCO routers use it in synchronous serial interfaces. This connector connects to the DB-60 port on a serial WIC of the router. Because five different cable types are supported with this router port, the port is called a five-in-one serial port. This port is shown at the top of the cable drawings in Figure 8-3. This cable connects the router to the CSU/DSU. Figure 8-3 shows some of the serial cabling WAN connectors' options that can be used on a CISCO router with the typical DTE-DCE connection.

A. TRUE
B. FALSE

8-19   TRUE/FALSE: Depending on the attached cable, the synchronous serial port on the router is configured as either DTE or DCE (except EIA-530, which is DTE only.) The attached cable can be ordered as either DTE or DCE to match the router configuration. If the port is configured as DTE (the default setting), an external clocking from the DCE device is required. The CSU/DSU is connected to the Telco CO by a cable using a typical RJ-48 connector. The RJ-48 connector is similar in shape and size to the RJ-45 connector used for TP Ethernet cables.

A. TRUE
B. FALSE

8-20   TRUE/FALSE: As stated previously in chapter 8, both (the modem and the DSU/CSU) can be combined into a single piece of equipment, called the DSU/CSU, which can also be built internally into the interface card of the router. In such cases, the serial cables shown in Figure 8-3 are not required, and Telco is connected to a port on the router serial interface card directly using a cable with an RJ-48 port.

A. TRUE
B. FALSE

8-21   Try to decide which option gets in which blank.

Finally, in addition to a proprietary _____, CISCO routers also have a new, smaller proprietary serial connection that is about one-tenth the size of the 60-pin basic serial cable. This is called the "_____". The connector of this cable is just a_____, which is much smaller than the DB-60 connector. This small cable also supports the same five serial standards in either DTE or DCE configuration.

    A.   26-pin connector
    B.   smart serial cable
    C.   60-pin serial connector

8-22   What type of connector does the WAN serial transmission require?

    A.   Parallel connectors
    B.   Serial connectors

8-23   Try to decide if the following paragraph correctly depicts CISCO router serial connectors.

"CISCO routers use a proprietary 60-pin serial connector. CISCO also has a new, smaller proprietary serial connection that is about one-tenth the size of the 60-pin basic serial cable. This is called the "smart-serial."

    A.   Correct
    B.   Incorrect

8-24   How serial transmission is working?

    A.   It takes place one bit at a time over a single channel.
    B.   It takes place 60 bits at a time over a single channel.

8-25   Which of the following is a type of connector that the service provider may use to connect a network with the service provider network?

    A.   EIA/TIA-232
    B.   EIA/TIA-449
    C.   EIA-530
    D.   V.35 (used to connect to a CSU/DSU)
    E.   X.21 (used in X.25)

8-26   TRUE/FALSE: Serial transmissions are measured in frequency or cycles per second (hertz).

    A.   TRUE
    B.   FALSE

8-27   The following steps will be followed when a subscriber wants to buy a point-to-point leased link from Telco (service provider). Which of the following steps must be followed for this purpose? (Select all that apply)

    A.   **Step 1:** The subscriber determines how fast the circuit should run, in kilobits per second (kbps), according to the subscriber expected using.
    B.   **Step 2:** The subscriber contacts a service provider and orders the circuit.
    C.   **Step 3:** Usually, Telco recommends the circuit specifications and the required devices that the subscriber must purchase.
    D.   **Step 4:** The subscriber purchase two routers, two CSU/DSUs, one at each site.
    E.   **Step 5:** The subscriber installs and configures each router and CSU/DSU and connects serial cables from each router to the respective CSU/DSU.

F.   **Step 6:** Telco installs the new line into the customer premises, and connects the line to the CSU/DSUs.

8-28   TRUE/FALSE: Notice that, in some cases, Telco sells the routers, the CSU/DSUs, and the cables, and in many cases, Telco does the installation and configuration of the whole circuit.

A.   TRUE
B.   FALSE

8-29   TRUE/FALSE: Step 1 in question 8-27, is the most important step. It means, that the line speed must be specified at first. Many possible predefined speeds can be ordered from the service provider.

A.   TRUE
B.   FALSE

8-30   TRUE/FALSE: Clock rate, bandwidth, or link speed, are terms that can be used to refer to the line speed. The devices on both sides must be configured to match the defined line speed. This is done by synchronizing the clocks on all devices of the link so that they run at exactly the same speed. This process is called *synchronization*. Synchronization means that both sides agree to send and receive bits at predefined time intervals. Practically, synchronization is done by one-side makes small adjustments in its clock rate to match the other side.

A.   TRUE
B.   FALSE

8-31   TRUE/FALSE: In a leased line, synchronization occurs between the two CSU/DSUs. One CSU/DSU (the slave) adjusts its clock to match the clock rate of the other CSU/DSU (the master). The synchronization process will be repeated several times per second between both devices.

A.   TRUE
B.   FALSE

8-32   TRUE/FALSE: The two CSU/DSUs take their synchronization from the service provider and adjust their speeds to match the clocking signals from the service provider. Then each CSU/DSUs supply clocking signals to the routers so that the routers can send and receive data at the correct clock rate.

A.   TRUE
B.   FALSE

8-33   Match each speed to the appropriate name.

1.   1.544Mbps
2.   64 kbps
3.   2.048 Mbps

A.   DS0
B.   E1
C.   T1

8-34   Try to decide which option gets in which blank.

In the United States, the DS1 standard defines a single line that supports _____, plus an 8-kbps overhead channel, for a speed of _____. (The standard of a single 64-kbps line is referred by the term digital signal level

0 (DS0).) A DS1 is also called a _____ in US. In Europe and Japan another standard are used, an E1 line standard holding 32 DS0s, and an E3 line holding 16 E1s.

    A. 24 DS0s
    B. 1.544 Mbps
    C. T1 line

8-35   Which of the following statements is true regarding the available bandwidth for a WAN connection? (Select all that apply)

    A. Bandwidth refers to the rate at which data is transferred over the communication link.
    B. The bandwidth on a serial connection can be incrementally increased to accommodate the need for faster transmission.
    C. In North America, bandwidth is usually expressed as a "DS" number (DS0, DS1, and so forth) that technically refers to the rate and format of the signal.
    D. DS1 line (also called a T1 line) can be obtained by bundling 22 DS0s channels to achieve a total speed of 1.544 Mbps.
    E. DS1 with line speed is 1.544 Mbps represent the most fundamental link speed.

8-36   TRUE/FALSE: When talking about clocking and speed, both DTE and DCE have another meaning. The DCE is the device that provides clocking, typically the CSU/DSU and the DTE is the device that receives clocking, typically the router.

    A. TRUE
    B. FALSE

8-37   Which of the following statements is true? (Select all that apply)

    A. DTE is any device located at the user end of a user-network interface. DTE includes devices such as multiplexers, routers, computers ...etc. The connection to a data network is made through DCE such as a modem using the clocking signals generated by that device.
    B. Router interfaces are, by default, DTE, and they connect into DCE —for example, a CSU/DSU.
    C. The CSU/DSU plugs into a demarcation location (demarc) and is the service provider's last responsibility. Demarc is a jack that has an RJ-48 female connector located in a telecommunications closet.

8-38   Try to decide if the following paragraph correctly depicts Figure 8-4.

"Figure 8-4 shows DTE-DCE-DTE connection and some devices that may be used in the network. The idea behind a WAN is to be able to connect two DTE networks together. The DCE network includes the links from the CSU/DSU, through the provider's network, all the way to the CSU/DSU at the other end. The network's DCE device (CSU/DSU) provides clocking to the DTE-connected interface (the router's serial interface). For non-production networks which are using a WAN crossover type of cable and do not have a CSU/DSU, clocking should be provided on the DCE end of the cable by using the router **clock rate** command. In non-production environments, a DCE network does not always present."

    A. Correct
    B. Incorrect

8-39   Which of the following typically connects to a V.35 or RS-232 end of a cable in a leased line WAN?

    A. Router serial interface
    B. Transceiver

C. Receiver
D. CSU/DSU

8-40   Which of the following devices can be considered as a DTE device that can be used for a point-to-point WAN link using a leased line between two routers located hundreds of miles apart? (Select all that apply)

A. Routers
B. The Telco
C. The CO equipment
D. CSU/DSU

8-41   TRUE/FALSE: To purchase a serial cable from CISCO, it is possible to order either a DTE or a DCE cable, depending on whether the router is acting as a DTE or a DCE. For a real WAN link, a DTE cable must be ordered, since the router acts as DTE by default.

A. TRUE
B. FALSE

8-42   Which of the following is true? (Select all that apply)

A. Two CISCO routers can be connected directly in a lab using a Back-to-back serial connection as shown in Figure 8-5. This circuit is usually used for training, so that anyone can have it in home without the need for any CSU/DSUs or real WAN link.
B. To do so, one router must supply clocking. Of course; the router with the DCE cable in it. This router can be configured to supply clocking to the other router that acts as DTE.
C. To connect the two cables together, the male connector of the DTE cable must be inserted into the female connector of the DCE cable.
D. To supply clocking from a router (with DCE cable installed), the **clock rate** command must be issued from that router.
E. Notice that, the combined DCE/DTE cables reverse the transmit and receive pins, much like a crossover TP Ethernet cable allows two directly connected devices to communicate. The DCE cable swaps transmit (Tx) and Receive (Rx) pins, whereas the DTE cable does not swap the Tx and Rx pins. Therefore, one router can transmit on one pin and the other router will receive it on the same pin and vice versa as shown in Figure 8-5.

8-43   Which of the following is true regarding how to install and configure two back-to-back connected routers (R1 & R2) using interface serial 0/0 on each router?

A. The clock rate command must be configured on R1's serial interface if the DTE cable is installed in R2.
B. The clock rate command must be configured on R1's serial interface if the DCE cable is installed in R2.
C. The clock rate command must be configured on both routers.
D. None of the above answers is correct.

8-44   Match each WAN communication with its description.

1. **Dedicated link**
2. **Circuit-switched link**
3. **Packet-switched link**
4. **Cell-switched link**

A. The point-to-point line is used, when a permanent, pre-established, dedicated connection is required. This link provides a WAN communications path from the subscriber CPE's through the provider network to a remote location, which allows the subscriber DTE networks to communicate at any time with no setup procedures (only during initial setup) before transmitting data. It uses synchronous serial lines up to 45Mbps. HDLC and PPP encapsulations are frequently used on this type of link. Point-to-point lines are usually leased from a carrier (service provider) and therefore, it is called leased line. The terms; leased line, leased circuit, link, serial link, serial line, point-to-point link, dedicated link/line circuit, are used to refer to a point-to-point leased line.

B. The circuit switching is working like a phone call, to overtake data it needs, the connection must be setup at first. This means, before communication can start, the connection between the sender and the receiver through the networks of the service provider must be established. This also means that circuit switching dynamically establishes a dedicated virtual connection for voice or data between the sender and the receiver. Unlike the leased line where the cost is paid for the whole leasing period, the cost, here is paid only for the time of the actual using. Circuit switching uses dial-up networks such as PPP and ISDN and is used for low bandwidth data transfers.

C. The packet switching is a networking technology based on the transmission of data in packets. It is created to save the money of the subscribers by allowing sharing the bandwidth with other subscribers. This means that there is no dedicated path between the source and destination endpoints. Packet switching can be looked like a leased line but its cost like a circuit switching. If it requires a constant data transfer rate, a pure leased line should be chosen, but when bursty data transfer is required, the packet switching should be chosen. Packet-switched networks send data packets over different routes of a shared public network to reach the same destination. Frame Relay and X.25 are packet-switching technologies. Speeds can range from 56Kbps to T3 (45Mbps). This technology transmits data in labeled cells, frames, or packets.

D. It is based on using ATM switches inside the service provider's network (cloud). Unlike the switching technology where the packets/frames are used throughout the network, the cells are used. A cell, just like a packet or frame, is a string of bits sent over ATM networks. The difference is that while packets and frames can vary in size, ATM cells are always fixed 53 bytes in length. Furthermore, ATM typically supports much higher-speed physical links, especially those using a specification called the Synchronous Optical Network (SONET).

8-45   Which of the following is a type of WAN connection? (Select all that apply)

A. Dedicated or leased line
B. Circuit switching
C. Packet switching
D. Bit switching

8-46   Try to decide which option gets in which blank.

Leased lines: Leased line is a point-to-point connection or _____ connection. It is leased from the telephone companies. A leased line is a pre-established WAN communications path from the CPE through the _____ device to the CPE of the remote site, allowing DTE networks to communicate at any time with no setup procedures (only during initial setup) before transmitting data. It uses _____ serial lines up to 45Mbps. HDLC and PPP encapsulations are frequently used on leased lines.

A. dedicated
B. synchronous
C. DCE
D. asynchronous

8-47   Try to decide which option gets in which blank.

Circuit switching: The circuit switching is working like a phone call, to pass data it needs to set up the connection first. Unlike the leased line where the cost is paid for the _____ leasing period, the cost, here is paid only for the time of actually using. No data can be transferred before an _____ connection is established. Circuit switching uses dial-up networks such as PPP and ISDN, and it is used for _____ data transfers.

A. whole
B. end-to-end
C. low-bandwidth

8-48   Try to decide which option gets in which blank.

Packet switching: A networking technology based on the transmission of data in packets. It allows _____ the bandwidth with other users to_____. Packet switching can be looked like a _____ but its cost like_____. If its require a constant data transfer rate, pure leased line should be chosen, but when bursty data transfer is required packet switching should be chosen. Frame Relay and X.25 are packet-switching technologies. Speeds can range from 56Kbps to T3 (45Mbps).

A. sharing
B. save money
C. circuit switching
D. leased line

8-49   Try to decide if Figure 8-7 correctly depicts the connection types of the WAN networks.

A. Correct
B. Incorrect

8-50   Which of the following best describes the main function of the OSI Layer 1 protocols?

A. Delivery of bits from one device to another over some type of media
B. Addressing the bits before sending through a network
C. Framing the received packet from layer 2
D. Segmenting the received packet from layer 2

8-51   Match each type of communication link to its function in a WAN.

1.   Dedicated communication links
2.   Circuit-switched communication links
3.   Packet-switched communication links
4.   Cell-switched communication links

A. It transmits data in labeled cells. Typically, it supports much higher-speed physical links, especially those using a specification called Synchronous Optical Network (SONET).
B. It transmits data in labeled frames, or packets.
C. It dynamically establishes a dedicated virtual connection for voice or data between a sender and a receiver.
D. It provides a pre-established WAN communications path from the CPEs through the provider network to a remote destination.

8-52   Which of the following statements accurately describe the functions of a packet-switching WAN communication link? (Select all that apply)

A. Packet-switched networks send data packets over different routes of a shared public network owned by a carrier to reach the same destination.
B. Customers have a dedicated path between source and destination endpoints.

C. The route that the packets take to reach the destination site varies.
D. Customers use the full bandwidth on its virtual circuit.
E. It is used by the PSTN.
F. The cost of a packet-switched network to the customer is generally lower than with the point-to-point leased lines.
G. Frame relay is a type of packet switching.

8-53   Which of the following statements accurately describe the characteristics and functions of the circuit switched networks? (Select all that apply)

A. By this type, a dedicated physical circuit is established, maintained, and terminated through a carrier network for each communication session.
B. It is used by the PSTN.
C. It allows multiple sites to connect to the switched network of a carrier and communicate with each other.
D. Only two sites per a single connection can be connected by this type of communications.
E. ISDN is an example of a circuit-switched network.
F. This type uses dedicated leased line.

8-54   Which of the following statements accurately describe a point-to-point communication link? (Select all that apply)

A. Carriers usually lease point-to-point lines for a fixed charge, which is why point-to-point lines are often called leased lines.
B. It is usually connecting two relatively close sites.
C. The carrier dedicates fixed transport capacity and facility hardware to the line of a customer. Therefore, it is called dedicated link.
D. No multiplexing technologies are used by this type.
E. A DSU/CSU is used by this type of communications at both endpoints, to ensure reliable delivery of data packets over the connection.
F. A router is used by this type of communications at both endpoints, to ensure reliable delivery of data packets over the connection.
G. A serial link provides a single, pre-established WAN communications path from the CPEs through a carrier network, such as a telephone company, to a remote network.

8-55   TRUE/FALSE: L2 protocols define how data is encapsulated for transmission toward a remote location and the mechanisms for transferring the resulting frames. WAN uses a variety of different encapsulation technologies. Frame Relay, ISDN, ATM, PPP and HDLC are WAN techniques that use different encapsulation methods. HDLC and Point-to-Point Protocol (PPP) encapsulation technologies are the most popular data link layer protocols used on Point-to-Point serial links.

A. TRUE
B. FALSE

8-56   WAN protocols and standards define the encapsulation of data for transmission toward a remote location and the mechanisms for transferring the resulting frames. At which OSI layer this occurs.

A. Layer 7
B. Layer 6
C. Layer 5
D. Layer 4
E. Layer 3
F. Layer 2
G. Layer 1

8-57   TRUE/FALSE: The HDLC header includes an Address field and a Protocol Type field, with the trailer containing a frame check sequence (FCS) field.

    A.   TRUE
    B.   FALSE

8-58   Try to decide if the following paragraph correctly depicts a HDLC.

        A.   Correct
        B.   Incorrect

"**HDLC** High-Level Data Link Control. A bit-oriented synchronous data link layer protocol created by ISO and derived from Synchronous Data Link Control (SDLC). HDLC specifies a data encapsulation method on synchronous serial links using frame characters and checksums. No authentication can be used with HDLC. However, most HDLC vendors' implementations (including CISCO) are proprietary. HDLC cannot be configured on an asynchronous serial connection. "

8-59   TRUE/FALSE: The address field is not really needed for Point-to-Point links, since there are only two known address and only one intended recipient at the other end. It used in the past years when Telco sold multidrop circuits.

    A.   TRUE
    B.   FALSE

8-60   TRUE/FALSE: An FCS field in the HDLC trailer is used to perform error detection just like Ethernet. If a received frame has errors, the device receiving the frame discards the frame, with no error recovery performed by HDLC.

    A.   TRUE
    B.   FALSE

8-61   TRUE/FALSE: The standard ISO HDLC does not support multiprotocol. When a router receives an HDLC frame, it wants to know what type of packet is held inside the frame. To identify the network protocol being encapsulated, CISCO added a Type field. This produces CISCO's HDLC. CISCO's HDLC is proprietary—it will not communicate with any other vendor's HDLC implementation. Each vender has a different HDLC implementation for the proprietary field.

    A.   TRUE
    B.   FALSE

8-62   TRUE/FALSE: To connect routers from different vendors, the default HDLC serial encapsulation on CISCO routers should not be used, because it would not work. Instead, something like PPP can be used. PPP is an ISO-standard way of identifying the upper-layer protocols.

    A.   TRUE
    B.   FALSE

8-63   Which of the following statements is true about HDLC? (Select all that apply)

    A.   HDLC protocol is a popular ISO-standard, bit-oriented Data Link layer protocol.
    B.   It specifies an encapsulation method for data on synchronous serial data links using frame characters and checksums.
    C.   It is a point-to-point protocol used on leased lines.

D.   No authentication can be used with HDLC.
E.   HDLC is the default encapsulation used by CISCO routers over synchronous serial links.

8-64   What is the difference between a bit oriented protocol and a byte-oriented protocol? (Select all that apply)

A.   In byte-oriented protocols, control information is encoded using entire bytes.
B.   Bit-oriented protocols may use single bits to represent control information. Bit-oriented protocols include HDLC, TCP, IP ...etc.

8-65   Which of the following functions of OSI Layer 2 is implemented with a CISCO proprietary header field for HDLC, but is specified by the protocol standard for PPP?

A.   Identifying the type of protocol that is inside the frame.
B.   Framing the packet
C.   Addressing the packet
D.   Error detection during transmission

8-66   RouterA has four point-to-point serial links, one link to each separated remote router. Which of the following is true about HDLC addressing requirements at RouterA?

A.   RouterA must use HDLC addresses 1, 2, 3, and 4.
B.   RouterA must use any four unique addresses between 4 and 16523.
C.   There is no need for addressing.

8-67   Which of the statements accurately describe data-link protocols in a WAN? (Select all that apply)

A.   Many data link layer protocols use a framing mechanism similar to HDLC.
B.   Data link layer protocols define how data is encapsulated for transmission to remote sites.
C.   Data link layer protocols define the mechanisms for transferring the frames to establish the connection across the communication line from the sending to the receiving device.
D.   Data link layer protocols determine the physical and mechanical characteristics of WAN.
E.   PPP is an example of a data-link protocol.

8-68   TRUE/FALSE: IETF created PPP in 1994 to connect routers over a point-to-point link from different vendors. It is similar to CISCO HDLC with many additional features.

A.   TRUE
B.   FALSE

8-69   Try to decide if the following paragraph correctly depicts a PPP.

A.   Correct
B.   Incorrect

"**PPP** Point-to-Point Protocol (PPP) is an industry-standard protocol. A data-link protocol provides router-to-router and host-to-network connections over synchronous and asynchronous circuits. The protocol most commonly used for dial-up Internet access, replacing the earlier SLIP. Because all multi-protocol versions of HDLC are proprietary, PPP can be used to create point-to-point links between different vendors' equipment. It can be run over asynchronous and synchronous links. Its features include address notification, authentication via CHAP or PAP, support for multiple protocols, and link monitoring. PPP has two layers: the Link Control Protocol (LCP) establishes, configures, and tests a link, and then any of various Network Control Protocols (NCPs) transport traffic for a specific protocol suite, such as IPX."

8-70   Which of the following statements is true about PPP? (Select all that apply)

A.   LCP (Link Control Protocol) is used by PPP to build and support data link connections.
B.   Network Control Protocol (NCP) is used by PPP to allow multiple Network layer protocols (routed protocols) to be used on a point-to-point connection.
C.   PPP is a Data Link layer protocol that can be used over either asynchronous serial or synchronous serial links.
D.   The basic purpose of PPP is to transport layer 3 packets across a Data Link layer point-to-point link.
E.   It is nonproprietary, which means that if the routers in the network are from different venders, PPP would be needed on the serial interfaces—the HDLC encapsulation would not work because it is CISCO proprietary on CISCO routers.
F.   PPP provides router-to-router and host-to-network connections over synchronous and asynchronous circuits.

8-71   What does PPP provide? (Select all that apply)

A.   Authentication
B.   dynamic addressing
C.   callback

8-72   What are the main components of PPP? (Select all that apply)

A.   EIA/TIA-232-C, V.24, V.35, and ISDN
B.   HDLC
C.   LCP
D.   NCP

8-73   Which of the following is true about EIA/TIA-232-C, V.24, V.35, and ISDN standards? (Select all that apply)

A.   A serial communication physical layer international standard
B.   A method for encapsulating frames over serial links
C.   A method of establishing, configuring, and supporting the point-to-point connection
D.   NCP purposes include establishing and configuring different Network layer protocols. It makes multiple Network layer protocols to be used simultaneously. Example of protocols; here is IPCP (Internet Protocol Control Protocol).

8-74   Which of the following is true about HDLC? (Select all that apply)

A.   A serial communication physical layer international standard
B.   A method for encapsulating frames over serial links
C.   A method of establishing, configuring, and supporting the point-to-point connection
D.   NCP purposes include establishing and configuring different Network layer protocols. It makes multiple Network layer protocols to be used simultaneously. Example of protocols; here is IPCP (Internet Protocol Control Protocol).

8-75   Which of the following is true about LCP? (Select all that apply)

A.   A serial communication physical layer international standard
B.   A method for encapsulating frames over serial links
C.   A method of establishing, configuring, and supporting the point-to-point connection
D.   NCP purposes include establishing and configuring different Network layer protocols. It makes multiple Network layer protocols to be used simultaneously. Example of protocols; here is IPCP (Internet

Protocol Control Protocol).

8-76   Which of the following is true about NCP? (Select all that apply)

A.   A serial communication physical layer international standard
B.   A method for encapsulating frames over serial links
C.   A method of establishing, configuring, and supporting the point-to-point connection
D.   NCP purposes include establishing and configuring different Network layer protocols. It makes multiple Network layer protocols to be used simultaneously. Example of protocols; here is IPCP (Internet Protocol Control Protocol).

8-77   Try to decide if the following statement is true or false.

"The PPP protocol stack is specified at the Physical and Data Link layers only."

A.   TRUE
B.   FALSE

8-78   Try to decide if the following statement is true or false.

"When PPP connection is started, the link goes through three phases of session establishment."

A.   TRUE
B.   FALSE

8-79   Which of the following is a phase of PPP session establishment phases? (Select all that apply)

A.   Link establishment phase
B.   Authentication phase
C.   Network layer protocol phase

8-80   Try to decide which option gets in which blank.

Link establishment phase: To _____ and _____ the link, LCP packets are sent by each PPP device. These packets contain a field called the _____. This field allows each device to see the size of the data, compression, and authentication. Default configurations are used if no Configuration Option field is present.

A.   test
B.   configure
C.   Configuration Option

8-81   Try to decide which option gets in which blank.

Authentication phase: Either Authentication takes place before Network layer protocol information is_____. CHAP or PAP can be used to _____ a link. This is an optional phase.

A.   read
B.   authenticate

8-82   Try to decide which option gets in which blank.

Network layer protocol phase It is used by the PPP to make _____Network layer protocols to be _____ and _____ over a PPP WAN link.

    A.   single
    B.   multiple
    C.   encapsulated
    D.   sent

8-83   Which of the following can be used by PPP links as a method of authentication? (Select all that apply)

    A.   Password Authentication Protocol (PAP)
    B.   Challenge Handshake Authentication Protocol (CHAP)
    C.   Kerberos

8-84   Try to decide which option gets in which blank.

Password Authentication Protocol (PAP): An authentication protocol that allows Point-to-Point Protocol (PPP) peers to authenticate one another. PAP passes the password and the host name or username in the _____ (unencrypted). PAP is the _____ methods that can be used by PPP links.

    A.   clear text
    B.   higher secure
    C.   less secure
    D.   encrypted text

8-85   Try to decide which option gets in which blank.

Challenge Handshake Authentication Protocol (CHAP) A security feature supported on lines using PPP encapsulation that prevents_____. CHAP does not itself prevent unauthorized access, it merely _____the remote end. The router or access server then determines whether that user is allowed to access the network. CHAP is used at the _____ of a link and at _____ on the link to validate the communication between the router and the same host.

    A.   unauthorized access
    B.   identifies
    C.   initial startup
    D.   periodic checkups

8-86   Try to decide if the following paragraph correctly depicts a Frame Relay.

"Today, Frame Relay, and Asynchronous Transfer Mode (ATM) are the popular packet-switching services, but Frame Relay is the more common one. Frame Relay is created in the early 1990s to overcome the problems when connecting many sites via a Point-to-point WAN. As an example, when a main site company wants to connect to two remote branch offices using Point-to-point WANs, the main site router requires two serial interfaces and two separate CSU/DSUs. Now imagine how many serial interfaces for the main site router and how many CSU/DSUs are required, if the company wants to connect to five branch offices using any-to-any Point-to-point WANs connectivity. Of course, for each point-to-point line, the main site router needs a separate physical serial interface and a separate CSU/DSU. Ten of routers, with many interfaces, and ten of CSU/DSUs are needed for the overall network with four routers/interfaces and four CSU/DSUs per site."

    A.   Correct
    B.   Incorrect

8-87   TRUE/FALSE: Frame Relay is an ideal solution for connecting enterprise LANs, because a router on each LAN needs only a single WAN interface, even when multiple virtual circuits (VC) are used.

A.   TRUE
B.   FALSE

8-88   Which of the following is true about Frame Relay? (Select all that apply)

A.   Frame Relay is a Data Link and Physical layer specification that provides high performance.
B.   Frame Relay is a more efficient replacement of the X.25 protocol and leased lines. Frame Relay can be more cost-effective than point-to-point links and can typically run at speeds of 64Kbps up to 45Mbps (T3).
C.   Frame Relay provides features for dynamic bandwidth allocation and congestion control. Frame Relay is an industry-standard, data link layer protocol that handles multiple virtual circuits.
D.   Frame Relay implements no error or flow control. This reduces the latency and enhances the performance of the Frame Relay network.
E.   Frame Relay cannot be configured on an asynchronous serial connection.

8-89   TRUE/FALSE: Frame Relay network is a multi-access network, which means that more than two devices can be attached to the network, similar to LANs. This is done by little changes in the Data link protocol.

A.   TRUE
B.   FALSE

8-90   TRUE/FALSE: In Figure 8-11, a leased line is installed between each router and a nearby Frame Relay switch; these links are called *access links,* which are the same Layer 1 features as a point-to-point leased lines. Both access links and leased lines use the same signaling standards and run at the same speed. Figure 8-11 illustrates a VC through the Frame Relay cloud.

A.   TRUE
B.   FALSE

8-91   Which of the following is true about Frame Relay? (Select all that apply)

A.   Frame Relay defines its own framing technology, which is defined by a protocol called Link Access Procedure–Frame (LAPF).
B.   Each Frame Relay header holds an address field called a Data Link Connection Identifier (DLCI).
C.   The WAN switch forwards the frame based on the DLCI, sending the frame through the service provider's network (Frame Relay cloud) until it gets to the destination router.

8-92   TRUE/FALSE: Frame Relay is also called a *frame-switching service*, because the switches in the service provider cloud can forward one frame to one remote site and another frame to another remote site, just like the packet switching service do.

A.   TRUE
B.   FALSE

8-93   TRUE/FALSE: The Frame Relay switches are also called DCEs, and in this case, the subscriber routers are called DTEs. Clearly, DCE here refers to the device providing the frame-switching service to the subscriber device, and the term DTE refers to the subscriber device needing this service.

A.   TRUE
B.   FALSE

8-94   Which of the following is true about Frame Relay? (Select all that apply)

A.   The logical path that a frame travels between each pair of routers is called a Virtual Circuit (VC).
B.   The VC in Figure 8-11 is represented by the dashed line between the routers. When R1 needs to forward a packet to R2 or R3, it encapsulates the packet into a Frame Relay header (adds DLCI address) and trailer and then sends the frame to R2 or R3 depending on the established VC which is identified by a unique DLCI to the service provider.
C.   The process seems similar to a point-to-point serial link, but the frames, here are forwarded over a logical (virtual) VC between routers, and not over a physical link.
D.   VCs provide a bidirectional communications path from one DTE device to another.
E.   A data-link connection identifier (DLCI) within the Frame Relay address header uniquely identifies a virtual circuit.
F.   The DLCI is specific only to the router where it is configured.
G.   A VC can overtake through any number of intermediate DCE devices located within the network.
H.   Numerous VCs can be multiplexed into a single physical circuit for access to and transmission across the network.

8-95   Which of the following Frame Relay fields is used to identify the Frame Relay virtual circuits? (Select all that apply)

A.   Data-link current identifier (DLCI)
B.   Data-link connection identifier (DLCI)
C.   Data-link connect identifier (DLCI)
D.   Data-link circuit indicator (DLCI)
E.   Data-link connection identifier and indicator (DLCI)

8-96   TRUE/FALSE: One of the differences between Leased Line based networks and Frame Relay based networks is that in the first one the link is dedicated, whereas in the second one is shared. To address this issue, Frame Relay is designed with the concept of a committed information rate (CIR). Each VC has a predefined CIR, which is a guarantee by the provider that a particular VC gets at least that much of data transfer. CIR is the minimum value for a particular VC and in many cases, a VC can consume more bandwidth (CIR) if it is available.

A.   TRUE
B.   FALSE

8-97   TRUE/FALSE: When the service provider preconfigured all the required details of a VC, this VC is called Permanent Virtual Circuit (PVC).

A.   TRUE
B.   FALSE

8-98   TRUE/FALSE: Frame Relay provides both permanent virtual circuit (PVC), switched virtual circuit (SVC) services using the service provider shared medium-bandwidth connectivity that capable of carry both voice, and data traffic simultaneously. Most Frame Relay connections are PVCs rather than SVCs. The connection to the network edge is often a leased line, but dialup connections are available from some providers using ISDN or xDSL lines.

A.   TRUE
B.   FALSE

8-99   Which of the following is true about Frame Relay virtual circuits (VCs)? (Select all that apply)

A.   A separate access link is required for each VC.
B.   All VCs sharing the same access link must connect to the same router on the other side of the VC.
C.   The same access link can be shared by multiple VCs.
D.   All VCs on the same access link must use the same DLCI.

8-100   TRUE/FALSE: One of the main advantages of Frame Relay is that a router usually, uses a single access link to support multiple VCs, with each VC allowing the router to send data to a different remote router. To identify each VC, the router must use a different DLCI, because the DLCI identifies the VC.

A.   TRUE
B.   FALSE

8-101   Try to decide if the following paragraph correctly depicts an ISDN.

"**ISDN** Integrated Services Digital Network (ISDN) is a set of digital services that transmit voice, video, and data over existing phone lines. ISDN is offered as a service by telephone companies. Therefore, it can be defined as a communication protocol allows telephone networks to carry data, video, voice, and other digital traffic. ISDN can offer a cost-effective solution for remote users when it is required a higher-speed connection than analog dial-up links offer. ISDN is also a good choice as a backup link for other types of links, such as Frame Relay or a T1 connection."

A.   Correct
B.   Incorrect

8-102   TRUE/FALSE: The term PSTN refers to the equipment and devices that Telco's use to create basic telephone service between any two phones in the world. This term refers to the combined networks of all telephone companies.

A.   TRUE
B.   FALSE

8-103   TRUE/FALSE: In addition to original voice support, PSTN supports data transmission as well. Several Internet access technologies use PSTN to transmit data.

A.   TRUE
B.   FALSE

8-104   TRUE/FALSE: To make a home phone work, Telco has to install a cable with a pair of wires, called the *local loop*, between that home and some nearby Telco central office (CO). One end of the cable enters that house and connects to the phone outlets in the house. The other end connects to a computer in the CO, called a *voice switch*. Telco cloud makes a *circuit* between the two endpoints, which provides the physical ability to send voice or data.

A.   TRUE
B.   FALSE

8-105   Which of the following is true about PSTN? (Select all that apply)

A.   The local loop supports analog electrical signals to create a voice call. Analog signals must be converted to digital to overtake the PSTN digital network, and must be converted back to analog for transmission over a destination local loop.
B.   To convert analog voice to a digital signal (A/D) a *pulse-code modulation (PCM)* technique is used.

C. PCM defines that an incoming analog voice signal should be sampled 8000 times per second by the A/D converter, using an 8-bit code for each sample. As a result, a single voice call requires (8*8000) 64,000 bits per second—which fits into one of the DS0 channels in a T1. (T1 supports 24 separate DS0 channels, 64 kbps each, plus 8 kbps of management, for 1.544 Mbps.)

8-106   Which of the following considerations is used to select a PSTN as a communication link? (Select all that apply)

A. The implementation of a PSTN customer connection link for a WAN can be implemented with relatively low cost.
B. The transmission rate for large data files is fast.
C. The time required to connect through the WAN is fast.
D. Only a modem is required for communication.
E. Connecting the modem through the local loop to PSTN is relatively well known.
F. In case of lines are not available, the maintenance of a public telephone network is very high quality and simple.

8-107   Which of the following is true about modems? (Select all that apply)

A. Modems are relatively the lowest cost, remote-access technologies, and usable most anywhere that a PSTN phone line is available.
B. Modems are widely using for internet access and especially, by home users.
C. However, modems suffer from the low bit rate capabilities, a little faster than 100 kbps, even when new compression technologies are adopted.
D. However, there are wireless modems, which support a higher bandwidth (more than 1 Mbps) and does not require a PSTN phone line, are used today by the modern wireless ISP's, especially in the past two years. The costs of wireless modems are relatively higher than the usual modems.

8-108   Which of the following is true about modems? (Select all that apply)

A. To connect two computers over the PSTN cloud, a modem is required.
B. Analog modem coverts bits (digital signals) generated by one computer to analog signal that can be sent over the local loop.
C. No physical changes are required on the normal local loop cabling and no changes are required on the voice switch at the Telco's CO.
D. The term *modem* is a shortened version of the combination of the two words *modulation* and *demodulation*. The modem modulates (encode or change) digital signals to analog signals and demodulate (decode) analog signals back to digital signals that can be understood by the computers and digital devices.

8-109   TRUE/FALSE: PSTN refers to a communications path between the two modems as a circuit. Because the modems can switch to a different destination just by hanging up and dialing another phone number, this type of WAN service is called a *switched circuit*. Figure 8-13 shows an example of such a switched circuit.

A. TRUE
B. FALSE

8-110   TRUE/FALSE: A Layer 1 service is established between the connected modems, meaning that they can overtake bits between each other. PPP protocol is also used as a data link layer protocol on this circuit.

A. TRUE
B. FALSE

8-111   TRUE/FALSE: A modem can be either internal modem-built into the computer or external modem located outside the computer. To be used as an Internet access WAN technology, the home-based user connects via a modem to a router owned by an ISP. The home-based user dials into the ISP's router which typically has a large bank of modems, and thus into a phone number into the ISP's router.

    A.   TRUE
    B.   FALSE

8-112   TRUE/FALSE: The link circuit between two modems differs about clocking and synchronization when compared with a leased link circuit. Modems links create an *asynchronous* circuit, which means that the two modems try to use the same speed, without adjusting their clock rates to match the other modem. Leased link, on the other hand, creates what is called a *synchronous* circuit, because the CSU/DSUs on both sides of the link try to run at the same speed (clocking) and adjust their speeds (synchronization) to match with the other CSU/DSU.

    A.   TRUE
    B.   FALSE

8-113   Which of the following is true regarding the function of demodulation by a modem?

    A.   Decoding an incoming analog electrical signal from the PSTN into a digital signal.
    B.   Encoding an incoming analog signal from the PC into a digital signal for transmission over the PSTN.
    C.   Encoding an analog signal to digital form.
    D.   Encoding a digital signal sent from PC to analog signal to be sent over PSTN.
    E.   Decoding an incoming digital signal from the PSTN into an analog signal.

8-114   TRUE/FALSE: The largest WAN network is the internet. Today, several ISPs can provide the internet services to an enterprise network or even to home users. The physical connection is usually provided using DSL, cable network, wireless network, or VSAT using packet switching networking.

    A.   TRUE
    B.   FALSE

8-115   TRUE/FALSE: Today, the Internet becomes the largest source of information and communication for education, business, and home users on the earth. The Internet is really a network of networks, combines a worldwide mesh of millions of networks connected by complicated sets of routers, switches and servers, owned and operated by millions of organizations and individuals all over the world, all connected through thousands of ISPs.

    A.   TRUE
    B.   FALSE

8-116   TRUE/FALSE: Today, the Internet is using as a utility, that provides IP connectivity to the rest of the world, so if a connection to the Internet is available; communication with anyone else in the world is possible.

    A.   TRUE
    B.   FALSE

8-117   TRUE/FALSE: Client address for the interface that is connected to the Internet can be obtained from the ISP either as a static address as a dynamic address using DHCP servers.

    A.   TRUE

   B.   FALSE

8-118   Which of the following is true? (Select all that apply)

   A.   To solve IPv4 address space limitations, CISCO IOS Network Address Translation (NAT) and Port
        Address Translation (PAT) are mechanisms that can be used to conserve registered IP addresses in
        large networks.
   B.   NAT and PAT translate IP addresses within private internal networks to legal IP addresses for transport
        over public external networks such as the Internet without requiring a registered subnet address.
   C.   Incoming traffic is translated for delivery within the inside private networks.
   D.   This translation of IP addresses eliminates the need for host renumbering and allows the same IP
        address range to be used in multiple intranets, networks that exist within a companies' boundaries.

8-119   TRUE/FALSE: For better accessing to the internet utility, DSL was defined. It is created to provide high-
        speed internet access between a home or business and the local CO.

   A.   TRUE
   B.   FALSE

8-120   Which of the following can be considered as the key feature of the DSL as compared with modem?
        (Select all that apply)

   A.   DSL's data circuit is always ON; so there is no need to signal or dial a phone number to set up a data
        circuit like in modem.
   B.   DSL allows a concurrent voice call to be up at the same time as the data connection. Both analog voice
        signal and digital data signal can be sent over the same PSTN-local loop wiring at the same time and of
        course, the same phone number.
   C.   A *DSL access multiplexer (DSLAM)* device must be added besides a traditional PSTN-voice switch at
        the local CO.

8-121   TRUE/FALSE: DSL technology uses existing twisted-pair telephone lines to transport high-bandwidth
        data and provides IP services to subscribers. The cable from the phone or DSL modem to the telephone
        wall jack in a home uses RJ-11 telephone connectors.

   A.   TRUE
   B.   FALSE

8-122   TRUE/FALSE: The DSL Router/Modem in Figure 8-15 is connected via a standard telephone cable to
        the same phone jack on the wall. DSL hardware could be a separate router and DSL modem or a
        combination of both. A LAN switch and a wireless AP can be added to the router and the DSL modem.

   A.   TRUE
   B.   FALSE

8-123   TRUE/FALSE: To support voice and DSL at the same line, the PSTN phone company has to disconnect
        the local loop cable from the old voice switch and move it to a DSLAM, as shown in Figure 8-15. The
        DSLAM directs (multiplexes) the analog voice signal to a PSTN-voice switch and the voice switch treats that
        signal just like any other analog voice line. The frequency ranges between 0 Hz and 4000 Hz. The DSLAM
        multiplexes the data traffic to the ISP's router.

   A.   TRUE
   B.   FALSE

8-124   TRUE/FALSE: DSLAMs adopt time-division multiplexing (TDM) technology to multiplex many DSL lines into a single medium, generally a T3 (DS3). Current DSL technologies use sophisticated coding and modulation techniques to achieve data rates up to 8.192 Mbps.

A.   TRUE
B.   FALSE

8-125   Which of the following is true about DSLAM? (Select all that apply)

A.   Typically used at a SOHO to connect the PC to a DSL router.
B.   Typically used at a SOHO instead of a DSL router.
C.   Typically used inside the Telco's CO to separate, or multiplexes, the voice traffic from the data traffic, splitting the voice traffic off to a voice switch, and the data traffic to a router.
D.   Typically used at a SOHO instead of a modem.

8-126   Which of the following is true about DSL? (Select all that apply)

A.   Generally, there are two types of DSL either symmetric or asymmetric.
B.   *Symmetric* DSL means that the link speed in each direction (upload and download) is the same, whereas *asymmetric* means that the speeds are different.
C.   Almost home users need high speed download, to receive much more data than they need to send. Asymmetric DSL allows for much faster downstream speeds, but with lower upstream speeds, as compared with symmetric DSL.
D.   An ADSL connection might use a 1.5-Mbps speed downstream, and a 384-Kbps speed upstream.

8-127   TRUE/FALSE: The following is the two basic types of DSL:

▪   **Asymmetric DSL (ADSL):** It Provides higher download bandwidth than the upload bandwidth
▪   **Symmetric DSL (SDSL):** It Provides the same capacity of bandwidth in both directions

A.   TRUE
B.   FALSE

8-128   Which of the following is a variety of asymmetric ADSL? (Select all that apply)

A.   ADSL
B.   Consumer DSL (CDSL) also called G.Lite or G.992.2
C.   Very-high-data-rate DSL (VDSL)

8-129   Which of the following is a variety of symmetric SDSL? (Select all that apply)

A.   SDSL
B.   High-data-rate DSL (HDSL)
C.   ISDN DSL (IDSL)
D.   Symmetric high-bit-rate DSL (G.shdsl)

8-130   TRUE/FALSE: The actual received DSL speeds vary widely than the maximum speeds set by standard. There are many factors that affect the actual received DSL speed by the users, as follows:

▪   The distance between the CO and the users. As distance is longer, the speed will be slower
▪   The quality of the local loop cabling, worse wiring-slower speed.
▪   The type of DSLAM used in the CO

A. TRUE
B. FALSE

8-131   TRUE/FALSE: DSL is now a popular choice for enterprise IT organizations to support home workers. The connection between the subscriber and the enterprise must be through the ISP, and it cannot be directly.

A. TRUE
B. FALSE

8-132   Which of the following statements is true about DSL? (Select all that apply)

A. A customer can connect to a DSL enterprise network directly and without ISP connection.
B. DSL technology is an always-on connection.
C. Up-to-date DSL technologies can support data rates of up to 20 Mbps.
D. DSL technology is a circuit-switched connection technology that uses existing twisted-pair telephone lines (local-loop line for normal telephone voice connection).
E. An ISP is required for DSL customers to connect their local LAN PCs.
F. DSL technology transports high-bandwidth data, such as multimedia and video, to service subscribers.
G. DSL technology supports upstream and downstream data transmissions at frequencies above a 4-kHz window, allowing both voice and data transmissions to occur simultaneously on a DSL service.

8-133   Which of the following is a type of DSL? (Select all that apply)

A. ADSL
B. GDSL
C. IDSL
D. A-lite
E. MDSL

8-134   Which of the following is true about DSL? (Select all that apply)

A. DSL coverage has distance limitations.
B. DSL is not universally available in all geographic locations.
C. DSL service can be incrementally added in any area.
D. DSL technology cannot use the present analog voice connections.
E. The customer must be within 20,000 feet of the CO location of the provider.
F. Downstream speed is usually faster than the upstream speed.

8-135   Which of the following services has a limit of 18,000 feet for the length of the local loop?

A. ADSL
B. ISDN
C. PSTN with analog modems
D. Cable Internet service

8-136   Which of the following is true about Cable Networks? (Select all that apply)

A. Today, the internet service delivered by cable networks is another WAN communications access technology that can be used by home users.
B. Cable modem technology does not use a phone line from the PSTN for physical connectivity.
C. It uses a cable TV service supplied by a coaxial cable/over the cable TV (CATV).

D. Cable internet provides an always-on Internet access service in addition to the ability to watch favorites TV channels at the same time.
E. Now, digital voice services can also be supported by cable network. The voice traffic passes over the same CATV cable.
F. Cable modem/Cable router is similar in concept to DSL modem/router; it uses some of the capacity in the CATV cable for transferring data with the same frequency bands that may be allocated for TV channels.

8-137   TRUE/FALSE: Originally, cable was a one-directional medium designed to carry broadcast analog video channels to the subscribers. It sends electrical signals down the cable for all the channels. Figure 8-16 shows a typical cable network.

A. TRUE
B. FALSE

8-138   TRUE/FALSE: One end of the cable is connected into the house equipments and the other end of the cable is connected to equipment in the cable company's facilities, which is called the head end (router). The head-end can split the channels used for Internet over to an ISP router.

A. TRUE
B. FALSE

8-139   Which of the following is true regarding the comparison between DSL and Cable internet services? (Select all that apply)

A. Like DSL internet service, Cable Internet service is an always-on and available service.
B. Cable Internet service is also asymmetric, with much faster downstream speeds than DSL (from two to five times faster).
C. Cable speeds also do not degrade due to the length of the cable.
D. The problem with cable internet is that it is shared among users in certain parts of the CATV cable plant. Therefore, the effective speed of cable Internet does degrade as more and more traffic is sent over the cable. DSL does not suffer from this problem.

8-140   Which of the following remote-access technologies supports both symmetric speeds and asymmetric speeds? (Select all that apply)

A. DSL
B. Analog modems
C. Cable modems
D. ISDN

8-141   Which of the following remote-access technologies are considered an "always on" Internet service? (Select all that apply)

A. DSL
B. Analog modems
C. Cable modems
D. ISDN

8-142   Which of the following remote-access technologies support Telco's local loop as transport media? (Select all that apply)

A. DSL

B.   Analog modems
C.   Cable modems
D.   ISDN

8-143   Which of the following remote-access technologies support CATV cable as transport media? (Select all that apply)

A.   DSL
B.   Analog modems
C.   Cable modems
D.   ISDN

8-144   Which of the following remote-access technologies supports only asymmetric speeds? (Select all that apply)

A.   DSL
B.   Analog modems
C.   Cable modems

8-145   Which of the following remote-access technologies supports the highest downstream capabilities? (Select all that apply)

A.   DSL
B.   Analog modems
C.   Cable modems

8-146   Which of the following remote-access technologies does not capable of transmit voice and data simultaneously? (Select all that apply)

A.   DSL
B.   Analog modems
C.   Cable modems

8-147   Which of the following remote-access technologies is considered as the lowest overall Cost? (Select all that apply)

A.   DSL
B.   Analog modems
C.   Cable modems

8-148   TRUE/FALSE: Asynchronous Transfer Mode (ATM) is one of the WAN technologies available today. It is used either as a cell-switching service, similar in purpose to the Frame Relay, or as a switching technology used inside the Telco's' core network. It can be used for remote Internet access from the home or a small office.

A.   TRUE
B.   FALSE

8-149   TRUE/FALSE: ATM is based on cell-switching technology that is capable of transferring voice, video, and data simultaneously, through several types of networks. In enterprise, ATM is primarily used as the backbones or WAN links. Figure 8-17 shows a sample of an ATM connection.

A.   TRUE

B.   FALSE

8-150   Which of the following is true about ATM? (Select all that apply)

A.   ATM has data rates beyond 155 Mbps.
B.   ATM WANs look similar to other switching technologies, such as X.25 and Frame Relay.
C.   The enterprise router connects to an ATM service via an access link-to an ATM switch inside the service provider's cloud.
D.   ATM is implemented using VCs that can be either PVC or SVC just like Frame Relay.

8-151   Which of the following is considered as a difference between the ATM and the Frame Relay technologies? (Select all that apply)

A.   ATM can support much higher-speed physical links using a Synchronous Optical Network (SONET).
B.   ATM use cells instead of frames (frame relay) or packet (packet switching). A cell is a string of bits sent over ATM network with fixed 53 bytes in length. It is a not variable length like frame or packet.

8-152   Which of the following is true? (Select all that apply)

A.   The 53-byte ATM cell contains a 5-byte ATM header followed by 48 bytes of ATM payload (data).
B.   The header for ATM cells contains two fields named *Virtual Path Identifier (VPI)* and *Virtual Channel Identifier (VCI)* that together indicate to which VC an ATM cell belongs and acts like the data-link connection identifier (DLCI) for Frame Relay by identifying each VC.
C.   Just as Frame Relay switches forward frames based on the DLCI, ATM switches forward cells based on the VPI/VCI pair.
D.   However, numerous VCs can be multiplexed into a single physical circuit for transmission across the ATM cloud.

8-153   TRUE/FALSE: A router is used to connect the enterprise LAN (based Ethernet) and the ATM WAN cloud via an access link. Figure 8-18 shows the *segmentation* process that will be done by R1 to a received frame from the Ethernet. The remote router R2 will reassemble the received cells into frames by a reverse process called *reassembly*. The processes done by R1 and R2 are called *segmentation and reassembly (SAR)*.

A.   TRUE
B.   FALSE

8-154   TRUE/FALSE: ATM can run over a variety of physical media, including fiber optics using Synchronous Optical Network (SONET)/Synchronous Digital Hierarchy (SDH) and coaxial cable using DS3.

A.   TRUE
B.   FALSE

8-155   Which of the following is true about ATM? (Select all that apply)

A.   ATM is a type of cell-switched connection technology that is capable of transferring voice, video, and data through private and public networks.
B.   ATM is a type of circuit switching.
C.   ATM is implemented by using virtual circuits.
D.   ATM can run only over optical cable using T3.
E.   Virtual circuits provide a bidirectional communications path between ATM endpoints.
F.   An ATM cloud contains only ATM routers, which are responsible for forwarding cells and packets.
G.   To create ATM VC between two endpoints, a physical connection is necessary.

8-156   Which of the following is true regarding the differences between the circuit and packet switching technologies? (Select all that apply)

A.   An example of circuit switching is the leased lines, which provide the physical ability to transfer bits between two endpoints.
B.   An example of packet switching is the frame relay networks, which provide the physical ability to transfer bits between many-to-many endpoints.
C.   Since devices in the WAN circuit-switching only overtake the bits from one device to another, this service is considered as the OSI layer 1 service; there is no need to send addresses over such a network.
D.   The services of WAN packet switching are OSI layer 2 services, since, the devices in the WAN do more than overtake the bits from one device to another. The provider's networking devices must select the best route to forward a packet; therefore, these devices must be able to interpret the bits sent by the customers by reading some type of address field in the header.

8-157   What are the differences between the circuit switching and packet switching? (Select all that apply)

A.   Circuit switching creates a physical ability (electrical circuit) to send data between two endpoints without interpreting the data that flow through the circuits. Packet switching means that the devices in the WAN do more than overtake electrical signal or the bits from one device to another, the service provider devices interpret the data that flow through their networking devices and then the data can be sent to one direction or to multi-directions.
B.   Circuit switching is implemented at layer 1 of the OSI layers, whereas packet switching is implemented at layer 2.
C.   Circuit switching are point-to-point services, whereas packet switching is multipoint services (more than two).

8-158   TRUE/FALSE: For DSL and cable Internet access to be implemented in the home users (SOHO), several IP-related services must be performed on the DSL/cable router, including assigning IP addresses, using DHCP service, as well as adopting a Network Address Translation (NAT) feature. A DSL/cable router can be single integrated device that combines (switch, wireless access point, router and modem), or multiply separated devices. Figure 8-19 shows how SOHO is connected to the ISP using separated DSL Internet Access Router devices (R1).

A.   TRUE
B.   FALSE

8-159   TRUE/FALSE: The following steps are followed when PC1 tries to send data to the internet through the ISP:

1.   PC1 sends data to its default gateway, which is the local access router interface.
2.   The LAN switch forwards frames to the access router
3.   The router makes a routing decision to forward the packet to the ISP router as the next-hop router.
4.   The DSL modem converts the Ethernet frame received from the router to meet local loop specifications.
5.   The ISP router forwards the packet to the internet based on its routing table.

A.   TRUE
B.   FALSE

8-160   TRUE/FALSE: The following rules should be followed when configuring the IP addresses for the two interfaces of the DSL access router in Figure 8-19:

- One public (globally routable) IP address for the Internet interface of the DSL access router. Usually, assigned by the ISP statically or dynamically using DHCP server, in this case the interface will be a DHCP client.
- One static IP address on the local subnet interface of the DSL access router acts as a default gateway to the local subnet, using a private network number.
- Typically, the access router will act as a DHCP server for the local subnet hosts; the local subnet hosts will dynamically learn their IP addresses (including the network details, such as ISP DNS server) from it using a private network number.

   A.   TRUE
   B.   FALSE

8-161   Which of the following is true? (Select all that apply)

   A.   The routing function of the DSL Internet Access Router is simply to route all traffic from local private network (PC1 & PC2) to the internet ISP's routers, which will route this traffic to the destination internet sites.
   B.   It should also be able to route all traffic came from the internet sites to the local private network (PC1 & PC2) through the internet ISP's routers.
   C.   This function will be implemented by the DSL Internet Access Router after configuring its two interfaces (the public one and the local private network one).
   D.   However, R1 can use a default route. Instead of requiring a static route configuration, the DSL Internet Access Router can add a default route based on the default gateway learnt by the DHCP client function, in this case the IP address of ISP's R2, which will be used as the next-hop router.

8-162   TRUE/FALSE: To make the whole network works, the process of routing should be done in combination with NAT/PAT functions of the DSL Internet Access Router. The second function is important for the network since the Internet routers should never have any routes for local private IP addresses (PC1 & PC2). NAT/PAT makes PC1 & PC2 as if they are using R1's publicly registered IP address. Internet sites will send the packets to the DSL Internet Access Router's public IP address, and R1 will translate the address to match the correct IP address on the hosts on the local private LAN.

   A.   TRUE
   B.   FALSE

8-163   TRUE/FALSE: The ISP must assign at least one unique, global, and routable IP address to any DSL or cable customer and usually the ISP uses DHCP server for this assignment. In particular, the ISP does not want to assign multiple public IP addresses to each PC in the local network such as PC1 and PC2 in Figure 8-20, to conserve the global and public IPv4 address space.

   A.   TRUE
   B.   FALSE

8-164   TRUE/FALSE: The private local LAN, then, is implemented using private IP addressing and not public IP addresses. When connecting this type of network to public networks such as the Internet, a method to convert the private IP addressing to a public addressing is needed. NAT (as defined in RFC 1631) operates on CISCO routers and is designed for such IP address conversion.

   A.   TRUE
   B.   FALSE

8-165   Which of the following is true about NAT/PAT? (Select all that apply)

    A.   NAT enables private IP LANs that use non-registered IP addresses to connect to the public and global internet.

    B.   NAT operates on any device that sits between an internal network and the public network, such as a firewall, a router, or a computer.

    C.   NAT can be configured to advertise only one address for the entire network to the outside world. Advertising only one address to the public hides the internal network from the world, thus providing additional security to the local LAN.

8-166   Referring to Figure 8-21, try to rearrange the following points in the correct order.

1.   PC1 (IP 192.168.1.2) sends a packet to an internet site through ISP gateway 4.4.2.2 through PC1's default gateway setting (R1).

2.   PC1 sends the packet to R1.

3.   R1 performs PAT, based on the details in the R1's NAT translation table, changing the PC1's IP from the private IP address used on the local LAN to the one globally routable public IP address available to R1, namely 4.4.2.1.

4.   R1 forwards the packet based on its default route.

5.   When the site replies to the packet sent from PC1, the site sends the packet, based on the values in the source fields of the packet at step 3, to same sender, destination IP address 4.4.2.1, and destination port 1028.

6.   When R1 receives the packet sent from the internet site, it changes the destination IP address and port per its NAT table, switching from destination address/port 4.4.2.1/1028 to 192.168.1.2/1028.

7.   R1 sends the packet (the reply from the internet site) to PC1, IP 192.168.1.2.

8-167   TRUE/FALSE: NAT uses the following important terms:

Inside host: It refers to a host in the enterprise LAN network (PC1 and PC2 in the previous figures.)
Inside local (Inside local address): The IP address assigned to a host on the inside network (enterprise LAN). The inside local address is not an IANA address. It is used in the IP headers of the packets overtake over the local enterprise network. In this case, 192.168.1.2 and 192.168.1.3 are inside local IP addresses, and the packets at steps 1, 2, and 7 in Figure 8-21 show inside local IP addresses.
Inside global (Inside global address): An IANA IP address assigned by the ISP that represents inside local enterprise LAN IP addresses to the outside world. It is used in the IP headers of the packets overtake over the global Internet (not the enterprise). In this case, 4.4.2.1 is the one inside global IP address, and the packets at steps 3-5 in Figure 8-21 show the inside global IP address.
Inside interface: The router interface connected to the same LAN as the inside hosts. In this case, the default gateway, IP 192.168.1.1 is the inside.
Outside interface: The router interface connected to the Internet. In this case, the IP 4.4.2.1 is the outside interface.

    A.   TRUE
    B.   FALSE

8-168   TRUE/FALSE: NAT refers to the translation of network layer (IP) addresses, with no translation of ports, whereas PAT refers to the translation of IP addresses as well as transport layer (TCP and UDP) port numbers. PAT is used by the DSL internet access router (R1 in the previous examples) to differentiate packets send from several local hosts on local LAN enterprise based on transport layer port number (described in chapter 2 of this book). Generally, the NAT is used to refer to both NAT and PAT functions.

    A.   TRUE
    B.   FALSE

8-169   What is the typical function of the cable/DSL Internet access router-LAN facing interface to the SOHO PCs?

A.   DNS server
B.   DHCP server
C.   DHCP client
D.   It performs NAT/PAT for the source address of packets that exit the interface.

8-170   What is the typical function of the cable/DSL Internet access router-Internet facing interface to the SOHO PCs?

A.   DNS server
B.   DHCP server
C.   DHCP client
D.   It performs NAT/PAT for the source address of packets that exit the interface.

8-171   Assuming a PC in SOHO with a DSL router, and a DSL line. The DSL router uses typical default settings and functions. The obtained PC IP address is 192.168.1.5. This PC tries to access the www.thaattechnologies.com web server. Which of the following is true in this case?

A.   PC cannot access this web server.
B.   The 192.168.1.5 address is an inside global IP address.
C.   The 192.168.1.5 address is an inside local IP address.
D.   The PC learns the IP address of the www.thaattechnologies.com web server as a public IP address.
E.   The 192.168.1.5 address is an outside IP address.

8-172   Match each WAN device to its function.

1.   Router
2.   Communication server
3.   Modem
4.   Another networking device
5.   DSLAM

A.   To provide internetworking and WAN access interface ports.
B.   To concentrate dial-in and dial-out user communications.
C.   To work as A/D converter in analog lines.
D.   To provide access services.
E.   To spilt ISP traffic and voice traffic.

8-173   Match each NAT term with its definition.

1.   Inside interface
2.   Outside interface
3.   Static NAT
4.   Dynamic NAT
5.   Inside network
6.   Outside global IP address

A.   The router interface connected to the Internet.
B.   An inside host IP address as it appears to the outside network (the NAT translated IP address.)
C.   The router interface connected to the same LAN as the inside hosts.
D.   NAT maps an unregistered IP address to a registered IP address on a one-to-one basis.

E.   A set of networks subject to IP address and port translation using NAT.
F.   NAT maps an unregistered IP address to a registered IP address from a group of registered IP addresses.

8-174   Which of the following factors affects the number of simultaneous NAT translations that can be active at the same time?

A.   The number of unused port numbers
B.   The number of unused IP addresses
C.   The number of addresses in the NAT pool
D.   The size of the NAT memory queue

8-175   Which of the following is true about Internet facing interface of the DSL router when configuring NAT?

A.   It is the global interface.
B.   It is the local interface.
C.   It is the outside interface.
D.   It is the inside interface.

8-176   Which of the following commands would be required to migrate from the pre-configured HDLC router to use PPP?

A.   encapsulated ppp
B.   no encapsulated hdlc
C.   encapsulation ppp
D.   no encapsulation hdlc

8-177   Which of the following commands is required on at least one of the two routers in order to forward packets over the 128 kbps leased line, using PPP as the data link protocol? (Select all that apply)

A.   no encapsulation hdlc
B.   clock rate 128000
C.   bandwidth 128
D.   encapsulation ppp

8-178   Which of the following is true about point-to-point communication links? (Select all that apply)

A.   Bandwidth of the line is usually the factor to select this type of communication.
B.   Usually offer a high quality of service.
C.   It can be defined on shared links.
D.   Provide permanent, dedicated capacity that is always available.
E.   Endpoints of this link, share the interfaces on the router.
F.   Minimal expertise to install and maintain is required.
G.   Frame-relay uses this type of link

8-179   Which command enables HDLC?

A.   Router (config)# **hdlc encapsulation**
B.   Router (config)# **encapsulation hdlc**
C.   Router (config-if)# **encapsulation hdlc**
D.   Router (config-if)# **hdlc encapsulation**

8-180   How does the CISCO-proprietary HDLC make it possible for multiple network layer protocols to share the same serial link?

A.   It adds network protocol information within the control field.
B.   It adds network protocol information within the FCS field.
C.   It adds network protocol information within the data field.
D.   It adds a new type field.

8-181   Which of the following CISCO CLI prompts is used to enter the commands to specify PPP authentication?

A.   User mode
B.   ROM monitor mode
C.   Global configuration mode
D.   Interface configuration mode

8-182   Which output from the **show interface** command indicates that PPP is configured properly?

A.   PPP encapsulated
B.   PPP encapsulation
C.   Encapsulated PPP
D.   Encapsulation PPP

8-183   Which of the following settings is typically configured on the DHCP server Internet access router using SDM?

A.   The range of IP addresses to be leased to PCs on the local LAN
B.   The MAC addresses of the PCs on the local LAN
C.   The web server IP address(es) learnt via DHCP from the ISP.
D.   The IP address of the ISP's router on the common cable or DSL link
E.   The DNS server IP address(es) learnt via DHCP from the ISP.

8-184   Which of the following is true regarding the use of SDM wizards to configure DHCP Client and PAT services on an internet access router?

A.   The SDM configuration wizard considers any interfaces that already have IP addresses configured as candidates to become inside interfaces for PAT.
B.   The SDM configuration wizard requires PAT to be configured before the DHCP client service is configured.
C.   The SDM configuration wizard assumes the interface on which DHCP server services have been enabled should be an outside interface.
D.   The SDM configuration wizard assumes the interface on which DHCP client services have been enabled should be an inside interface.

8-185   Which of the following is true about configuration process using SDM?

A.   SDM uses an SSH connection to configure a router.
B.   SDM uses a web interface from the IP network or from the console.
C.   SDM loads configuration commands into a router at the end of each wizard (after the user clicks the Finish button), saving the configuration in the running-config and startup-config files.
D.   SDM uses a web browser on a PC and a web server function on the router, requiring the user to connect through an IP network rather than from the console.
E.   SDM does not use SSH at all.

    F.   SDM loads the configuration into the router only after the user clicks the Finish button on any of the configuration wizards, but the configuration is added only to the running-config file.

    G.   The running-config is saved by pressing the save button near the top of the SDM.

8-186   Which of the following is a common problem when configuring a new Internet access router's Layer 3 features? (Select all that apply)

    A.   Omitting the IP address(es) of the DNS server(s) learnt by DHCP server function.

    B.   Setting the wrong interfaces as the NAT inside and outside interfaces

    C.   Not using default configurations and typing wrong IP addresses to router interfaces.

    D.   Configuring wrong routing protocol that the ISP is not used it.

    E.   Not enabling auto-configuration features on the Internet-facing interface

8-187   Which of the following commands displays the active translations for a NAT translation table? (Select all that apply)

    A.   show ip nat translations

    B.   show ip nat records

    C.   show ip nat information

    D.   show ip nat data

    E.   show ip nat translators

8-188   Which of the following remedies must be taken to troubleshoot a NAT connectivity problem on a CISCO router when the appropriate translation is not found in the translation table using the **show ip nat translations** command?

    A.   Verify that the ACL referenced by the NAT command is permitting all necessary inside local IP addresses.

    B.   Run **debug ip nat detailed** command.

    C.   Check if there are enough addresses in the NAT pool.

    D.   Try to use the **show nat translations** command.

    E.   Verify that the router interfaces are appropriately defined as NAT inside or NAT outside.

CHAPTER 9
INTERNETWORKING
WIRELESS
TECHNOLOGY:
AN INTRODUCTION

In this chapter, Wireless LAN (WLAN) will be described. WLAN play an important role in providing network access to end users. In particular, WLANs allow the user to communicate over the network without requiring any cables, enabling mobile devices. In business, WLAN becomes important for travelling employees, to access the company information and resources from anywhere and anytime. WLAN reduces the cost of building networks and especially when the business wants continuously, rearranging the network. For SOHO users, WLAN provides simple, easy to install and low cost internet access. The necessary WLAN background for CISCO Access points (AP) configuration will be given in chapter nine.

The following topics are emphasized in this chapter:

- WLAN standards organizations and their roles
- Comparison of 802.11a, 802.11b, and 802.11g
- WLAN modes, their formal names, and descriptions
- Unlicensed bands, their general names, and the list of standards to use each band
- DSSS frequencies, showing the three nonoverlapping channels
- Installing a BSS WLAN

By understanding perfectly the information presented in this chapter and answering the 139 learning questions at the end of this chapter, configuring CISCO Access points, and answering the CCNA/CCENT exam related questions will be guaranteed. The questions herein are intended to reflect the type of questions presented on the CCENT Test.

WLAN Basics

Today, WLANs are used by many people regularly. Usually, they use it in conjunction with a laptop in home, in office, in a hotel or at a bookstore. The flexibility of the WLAN makes it widely propagated. To connect a PC to wireless LAN, a PCI adaptor must be added to the PC, if a built-in adaptor does not present. A sample of the 802.11b PCI adaptor is shown in Figure 9-1.

Figure 9-1 802.11b PCI Adaptor

A company can provide an Internet access and a LAN access via WLANs to mobile users while also supporting the normal LAN access via a wired LAN (ELAN). Figure 9-2 shows a typical design for such a company LAN.

Figure 9-2 Typical WLAN Connection

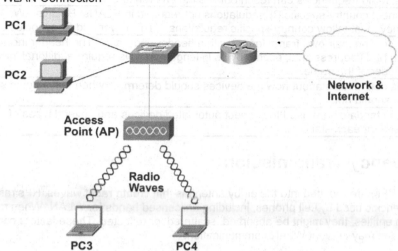

In Figure 9-2, the wireless laptops (PC3 & PC4) connect to the LAN via a WLAN device called an access point (AP). The AP is used to make wireless laptops communicate between each other and to ELAN devices by connecting the laptops to the ELAN through the wired Ethernet switch. The AP makes these laptops send and receive frames with the whole LAN clients.

WLAN Vs ELAN

In many ways, WLANs are similar to ELANs, since both are allowing communications to occur between automated devices. Table 9-1 summarizes the differences and the similarities between WLAN and ELAN.

Table 9-1 WLAN vs. ELAN

WLAN	ELAN
Allowing communications to occur between wireless automated devices.	Allowing communications to occur between wired automated devices.
Defined by IEEE 802.11 family	Defined by IEEE 802.3 family
Use radio waves, to transmit data. Radio waves pass through space, so there is no need for any physical transmission medium.	Use electrical signals or light signals flowing over a cable (TP, Coaxial or optical cabling) to transmit data. It is requiring a physical transmission medium.
If more than one device at the time sends radio waves in the same space at the same frequency, neither signal is used, so a half-duplex (HDX) mechanism must be used. WLANs use the carrier sense multiple access with collision avoidance (CSMA/CA) algorithm to enforce HDX logic and avoid as many collisions as possible.	Ethernet can support full-duplex (FDX) communication if a switch port connects to a single device rather than a hub. This removes the need to control access to the link using carrier sense multiple access collision detect (CSMA/CD).
Transmit data over short distance area using lower data rates (Bandwidth) up to 600 Mbps.	Generally, transmit data over longer distance area using higher data rates (Bandwidth) up to 100 Gbps.
Radio waves cause the following problems not found in ELANs: Connectivity issues: Many factors can affect the WLAN connectivity, such as, the coverage area, RF transmission, multipath distortion, and interference from other wireless services or other WLANs.	

Privacy issues: radio frequencies can reach outside the enterprise/SOHO.
WLANs must meet country-specific RF regulations not required in ELANs. Because WLANs use radio frequencies, they must follow country-specific regulations of RF power and frequencies.
Both standards define their own frame format with a header and trailer. The header includes a source and destination MAC address field, each 6 bytes in length. WLANs require additional information in the Layer 2 header of the frame.
Both standards define rules about how the devices should determine when they should send frames and when they should not.
Of course, both standards are used to connect automated devices and several types of Ethernet devices are used for each standard.

Radio Frequency Transmission

Radio frequencies (RFs) are radiated into the air by antennas that create radio waves. RFs range from the AM radio band to frequencies used by cell phones, including unlicensed bands for WLAN. When radio waves are propagated through entities, they might be absorbed, scattered, or reflected. These factors can cause areas of low signal strength and may prevent WLAN communication.

Generally, the transmission of radio waves is affected by the following factors:

- Reflection: Occurs when RF waves oscillated off entities, such as, metal or glass surfaces.
- Scattering: Occurs when RF waves hit an unlevel surface, such as, a rough surface. Such surfaces cause RF to reflect in many directions
- Absorption: Occurs when RF waves are absorbed by objects, such as, walls.

The following rules must be known for data transmission over radio waves:

- Higher data rates can be obtained by stronger signal with a better signal-to-noise ratio (SNR). This tends to shorter coverage area.
- Higher data rates can be obtained by increasing the bandwidth which is obtained by using higher frequencies or more complex modulation.
- Higher frequencies tend to higher degradation and absorption, which tend to a shorter transmission range. Using more efficient antennas can solve this problem.
- Higher transmit power makes transmission to wider converge areas. To double the range, the power has to be increased by a factor of four.

WLAN Standards & Protocols

At the time this book was written, the IEEE had ratified five major WLAN standards: 802.11, 802.11a, 802.11b, 802.11g, and 802.11n. All these standards will be discussed in brief in this section.

Four organizations have set or influence the standards used for WLANs today. Table 9-2 lists these organizations and describes their roles in brief.

Table 9-2 Organizations that Affect WLAN Standards

Organization	Standardization Role
ITU-R	Worldwide standardization of communications that particularly manage the assignment of frequencies.
IEEE	Standardization of wireless LANs (802.11, 802.11a, 802.11b, 802.11g, 802.11n)
Wi-Fi Alliance	An industry consortium that sets the rules (Wi-Fi certified

	program) for interoperability of WLAN products.
Federal Communications Commission (FCC)	The U.S. government agency that regulates the usage of various communications frequencies in the U.S

The standards for several types of WLANs are created and developed by IEEE. Since, those standards are using radio waves for communications, they must take into account the frequency choices made by the different worldwide regulatory agencies, such as the FCC in the U.S. and the ITU-R, which is controlled by the United Nations (UN).

In 1997, the IEEE created WLAN standards with the creation of the 802.11 standard. This original standard did not have a suffix letter, whereas later WLAN standards have suffix letters, just like in Ethernet IEEE 802.3. Then, the IEEE created several more-advanced WLAN standards: 802.11a, 802.11b, 802.11g, and 802.11n. Table 9-3 lists the WLAN standards, assuming a WLAN in the U.S.

Table 9-3 The WLAN Standards Key Points

Feature	802.11	802.11a	802.11b	802.11g	802.11n
Year ratified	Jun. 1997	Oct. 1999	Oct. 1999	Jun. 2003	Sept 2009
Max net bit rate (FHSS) Mbps	1 or 2	—	—	—	—
Max net bit rate (DSSS) Mbps	1 or 2	—	11	11	20 or 40
Max. net. bit rate (OFDM) Mbps	—	54	—	54	600
Max. cross bit rate Mbps	—	72	—	128	—
Operation frequency band (GHz)	2.4	5	2.4	2.4	2.4 and/or 5
Typical throughput (Mbps)	0.9	20	5	22	50-144
Bandwidth MHz	20	20	20	20	20 or 40
Channels (non overlapped)*	11 (3)	23 (12)	11 (3)	11 (3)	
Speeds required by standard (Mbps)	1, 2	6, 9, 12, 18, 24, 36, 48	1, 2, 5.5, 11	6, 12, 24	7.2, 14.4, 28.9, 45, 60, 90, 120
Max Indoor range	20 meters	50 ft/15 meters	150 ft/45 meters	150 ft/45 meters	70 meters
Max Outdoor range	100 meters	100 ft/30 meters	300 ft/90 meters	300 ft/90 meters	250 meters
Allowable MIMO streams	1	1	1	1	4

The 802.11 Modes of Operations

Two modes of operation are found for WLANs—*ad hoc mode* (peer-to-peer) and *infrastructure* modes.

Ad hoc mode: Independent Basic Service Set (IBSS) is the ad hoc topology mode. This mode is used to connect multiply wireless automated devices directly. It is used for the small workgroups, normally a few numbers of PCs or laptops. Ad hoc coverage is limited, and it's difficult to secure. In this mode, automated devices use their WLAN NIC's (internal, external, or built-in) or modules to send WLAN frames directly to each other and without the use of AP, as shown in Figure 9-3.

Infrastructure mode: This mode is used to connect multiply wireless automated devices through AP devices. It is used to connect wireless devices to the network infrastructure, by connecting the AP to infrastructure switch via wired Ethernet. In this mode, automated devices use their WLAN NIC's or modules to send WLAN frames to the rest of network infrastructure devices through the APs. Wireless devices cannot send frames directly to each other in this mode. Figure 9-3 shows an example of such a network.

Figure 9-3 Peer-to-Peer (Ad Hoc) WLAN

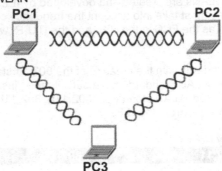

Two sets of services are supported by Infrastructure mode, called *service sets*:

Basic Service Set (BSS): It uses a single AP device to create the WLAN, as shown in Figure 9-2. The Basic Service Set Identifier (BSSID) is used as a Layer 2 MAC address to uniquely identify the BSS AP's within the WLAN. SSID, on the other hand, is used to advertise the availability of the WLAN to mobile clients. The SSID is a wireless network name that is user configurable and can be made up of as many as 32 case-sensitive characters.

Extended Service Set (ESS): It uses multiply AP devices to extend the WLAN to two or more BBSs. It allows roaming in a larger area without changing PC's IP addresses by the use of overlapping wireless cells, as shown in Figure 9-4. BSSs in ESS are connected by a distribution system (DS) or a wired infrastructure. An ESS generally includes a common SSID to allow roaming from one access point to another without requiring client reconfiguration.

Figure 9-4 ESS WLANs

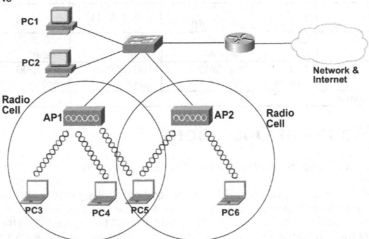

In the enterprise, all APs in the same WLAN must be configured with the same VLAN by the Ethernet switches.

Table 9-4 summarizes the WLAN modes.

Table 9-4 WLAN Modes and Names

Mode	Name of Service Set	Description of Service Set
Ad hoc (Peer-To-Peer)	Independent Basic Service Set (IBSS)	It allows two or more devices to communicate directly, without using AP.
Infrastructure (one AP)	Basic Service Set (BSS)	All devices are connected to a single AP to create a single WLAN.
Infrastructure (more than one AP)	Extended Service Set (ESS)	A single WLAN is created by Multiple APs, allowing roaming and a larger converge area.

WLAN Implementation at Layer 1

Similar to ELAN, WLANs at Layer 1 of the OSI model transmit data by sending and receiving radio waves, using WLAN network interface cards (NIC) or Wireless modules, APs, and other WLAN devices. The WLAN devices make small changes to the radio waves that flow over a medium to encode data. However, there are some differences between Ethernet and WLAN encoding techniques.

WLAN radio waves have a repeating signal that can be oscillated over time, as shown in Figure 9-5. When oscillated, the curve shows a repeating periodic waveform, with a frequency, amplitude, and phase. The frequency which is measured by hertz (Hz) is the most important in discussions the WLANs.

Figure 9-5 8khz Signal

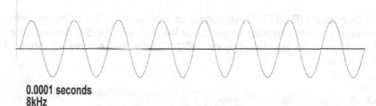

0.0001 seconds
8kHz

FCC defines three unlicensed frequency bands. The frequency band is a range of frequencies. One of the frequencies in the band is used to reference to the whole band. Table 9-5 lists the frequency bands that used for WLAN communications.

Table 9-5 FCC Unlicensed Frequency Bands for Wireless Transmission

Frequency band	Name	Devices
900 MHz	Industrial, Scientific, Mechanical (ISM)	Older cordless phones
2.4 GHz	ISM	Newer cordless phones, Bluetooth, monitors, video, and home gaming consoles, microwave ovens, and 802.11, 802.11b, 802.11g, 802.11n WLANs
5 GHz	Unlicensed National Information Infrastructure (U-NII)	Newer cordless phones and 802.11a, 802.11n WLANs

To operate wireless equipment on unlicensed frequency bands, a license is not required. However, no user has exclusive use of any frequency in the unlicensed bands. The using of unlicensed bands are subject to the local country's code regulations. For example, the 2.4-GHz unlicensed band is used for WLANs, video transmitters, Bluetooth, microwave ovens, and portable phones. Unlicensed frequency bands suffer from interference and degradation.

IEEE 802.11 divided the 2.4-GHz ISM band into 14 channels, but local regulatory agencies (FCC in USA) regulate which channels are allowed, such as channels 1 through 11 in the USA. Each channel in the 2.4 GHz ISM band is 22 MHz wide with 5 MHz separation, resulting in overlap with channels before or after a defined channel. Therefore, a separation of 5 channels is needed to ensure unique nonoverlapping channels. For the FCC example of 11 channels, the maximum of nonoverlapping frequencies are channels 1, 6, and 11. However, the basic throughput is only about half of the data rate, since WLAN uses half-duplex communication.

Wireless Encoding Data and Nonoverlapping DSSS Channels

Encoding means that a device modulates a signal in binary code (0 & 1). For this function, a device can use one or more of signal attributes, such as, frequency, amplitude, and phase. WLAN devices use the same concept when sending data over layer 1 of OSI model. WLAN devices modulate the radio signal's frequency, amplitude, and phase to encode a binary 0 or 1. It is important to know the names of three general classes of encoding that used for WLANs.

Frequency Hopping Spread Spectrum (FHSS): uses all frequencies in the band, hopping to different ones. A device can hopefully avoid interference from other devices that use the same unlicensed frequency band. This is obtained by using slightly different frequencies for consecutive transmissions. The 802.11 WLAN standards used FHSS, but the newest standards (802.11a, 802.11b, 802.11g, and 802.11n) do not.

Direct Sequence Spread Spectrum (DSSS): Designed for use in the 2.4 GHz unlicensed frequency band, DSSS uses just one channel of several separate channels or frequencies. DSSS spreads the data across all frequencies defined by that channel. As regulated by the FCC, this band can have 11 different overlapping DSSS channels, as shown in Figure 9-6.

Figure 9-6 DSSS Channels

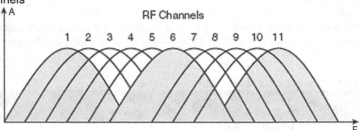

As shown in Figure 9-6, only three of the channels, 1, 6, and 11 can be used in the same space for WLAN communications, since these channels are not overlapped, and they won't interfere with each other. Therefore, when designing an ESS WLAN, APs with overlapping coverage areas should be set to use different nonoverlapping DSSS channels. Figure 9-7 shows this network.

In this network, the devices in the three BSS's can send a frame at the same time and without interfere between each other, because each device uses the different frequencies of the nonoverlapping channels. Although, PC1 and PC2 in Figure 9-7 are located within BSS1, they can communicate between each other and with two different BSS's (APs) using two different channels at the same time.

Figure 9-7 ESS WLAN Using Nonoverlapping DSSS 2.4 GHz Channels

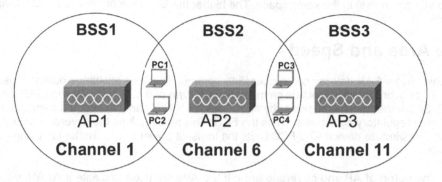

Orthogonal Frequency Division Multiplexing (OFDM): WLANs that use OFDM can use multiple nonoverlapping channels. Figure 9-8 shows the amplitude Vs frequency for OFDM waves

Figure 9-8 OFDM Waves

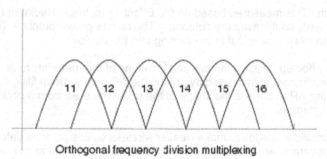

Orthogonal frequency division multiplexing

Table 9-6 summarizes the main three options for encoding and the standards that support each type of encoding.

Table 9-6 Encoding Classes and IEEE Standard WLANs

Encoding Name	Standards
FHSS	802.11
DSSS	802.11b, 802.11g, 802.11n
OFDM	802.11a, 802.11g, 802.11n

Wireless Interferences

There are many sources that can make WLANs suffering from interferences:

- Matters such as, walls, floors, and ceilings. These matters face the WLAN signal through the air. It causes the signal to be partially absorbed, which reduces signal strength and the size of the coverage area. Dead spots areas in which the WLAN simply does not work can also be occurred when the WLAN signals pass through metal, which reflects and scatters the waves.
- Another wireless radio waves in the same frequency range. This causes interference between radio waves and may cause to lose the data which requires lots of retransmissions, and resulting in poor efficiency.

Signal-to-Noise Ratio (SNR) factor is used to measure the interference. SNR compares the WLAN signal and the other undesired signals (noise) in the same space. The higher the SNR, the better the WLAN devices can send data successfully.

Coverage Area and Speed

The space in which two WLAN devices can successfully communicate and exchange data is called a WLAN coverage area. The coverage area depends on many factors. One of these factors is the EIRP which is the power of an AP. Since, the transmitted power by an AP or WLAN NIC cannot exceed a particular level based on the regulations from regulatory agencies such as the FCC. This tends to limit the coverage area that can be covered by an AP or wireless device. The FCC limits the transmit power to ensure the fair using of the unlicensed bands.

Example 10.1, The using of AP and coverage area: If two APs are used to create a WLAN; the products would conform to FCC regulations. However, to obtain wider coverage area, one AP may have high-gain antennas. This will cause to exceed the FCC regulations. In contrast, it might prevent the other AP from working at all because of the interference from the overpowered AP.

Notice that, the power of an AP is measured based on the Effective Isotropic Radiated Power (EIRP) calculation. EIRP = The power of the signal as it leaves the antenna = The radio's power output + The increase in power caused by the antenna gain - Any power lost in the cabling and the device.

The coverage area is also affected by the materials and locations of the materials near the AP. For example, wave reflections and scattering can be increased by putting the AP near a metal filing cabinet, this decreases the coverage area. However, the AP to change the shape of the coverage area from a circle to some other shapes can use different types of antennas

WLAN standards support multiple speeds to make weaker wireless waves passing data at lower speeds. A device at the edge of the coverage area, where the waves are weak, can send and receive data at a slower speed. A device near the AP may have a strong signal, so it can transmit and receive data with the AP at higher rates. The idea of a coverage area, with varying speeds, for an IEEE 802.11b BSS, is illustrated in Figure 9-9.

Figure 9-9 Speeds vs Converge Area

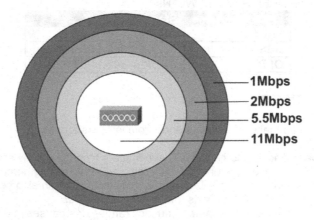

The size of the coverage area of one AP can be increased by using specialized antennas with higher gain, which increase the power of the transmitted signal. For example, to double the coverage area, the antenna gain must be increased to quadruple the original gain but the power output (the EIRP) must still be within FCC rules (in the

U.S.). However, the actual size of the coverage area depends on many factors such as the frequency band used by the WLAN standard, the obstructions between and near WLAN devices, the interference from other sources of RF energy, the antennas used on both the clients and APs, and the options used by DSSS and OFDM when encoding data over the air. In general, WLAN standards that use higher frequencies (U-II band standards 802.11a and 802.11n) can send data faster, but for smaller coverage areas. To cover all the required space, an ESS that uses higher frequencies would then require more APs.

ESS is created by adding additional AP's which tends to add any number of cells to extend the range. It is recommended that ESS cells (also called Extended Service Area (ESA)) have 10 to 15 percent overlap to allow remote users to roam without losing WLAN connections. Bordering cells should be set to different nonoverlapping channels for best performance. However, the combined available bandwidth of the WLAN is affected by the number of nonoverlapping channels supported by a standard.

Example 10.2, WLAN bandwidth capacity: In a WLAN that uses 802.11b, the maximum speed is 11Mbps. However, when three APs sit beside each other to form an ESS and send at the same time, using three nonoverlapping channels, each half-duplex BSS, theoretically, that WLAN could support a throughput of 3 * 11 Mbps, or 33 Mbps, for these devices in that part of the WLAN. An 802.11g WLAN can transmit data at 54 Mbps but with 3 nonoverlapping channels, for a theoretical maximum of 3 * 54 Mbps = 162 Mbps of bandwidth capacity. An 802.11a WLAN can transmit data at 54 Mbps, but with 12 nonoverlapping channels, for a theoretical maximum of 12 * 54 Mbps = 648 Mbps of bandwidth capacity.

WLAN Implementation at Layer 2

Today, ELANs uses switches to connect one device to each port using FDX media. This configuration disabled the use of CSMA/CD algorithm, which is required by shared ELAN that used HDX media.

Unlike ELAN, WLAN devices cannot be separated onto different cable segments to prevent collisions, so collisions can always occur. Now, consider the following question: what will happen when two WLAN devices try to send data at the same time using overlapping frequency bands? Of course, collision will occur within the WLAN, and none of the two transmitted signals can be understood by the receiving WLAN devices. Moreover, the device that is transmitting data cannot concurrently listen for received data, and it has no mechanism to understand that collision occurred.

To solve the above problems, an algorithm called **Carrier Sense Multiple Access with Collision Avoidance** (CSMA/CA) and an **Acknowledgement** mechanism are used. The acknowledgement is required to make the sending device know if its transmitted frame collided with another frame or not. The CSMA/CA does not prevent collusions but it minimizes the statistical chance that collisions could occur. Since, a sending station cannot receive while it transmits; collision detection is impossible in WLANs. Therefore, WLANs use the **Ready To Send** (**RTS**) and **Clear To Send** (**CTS**) protocols to avoid collisions. Figure 9-10 summarizes the working of WLAN network using the CSMA/CA algorithm and acknowledgement.

Figure 9-10 WLAN Working with CSMA/CA

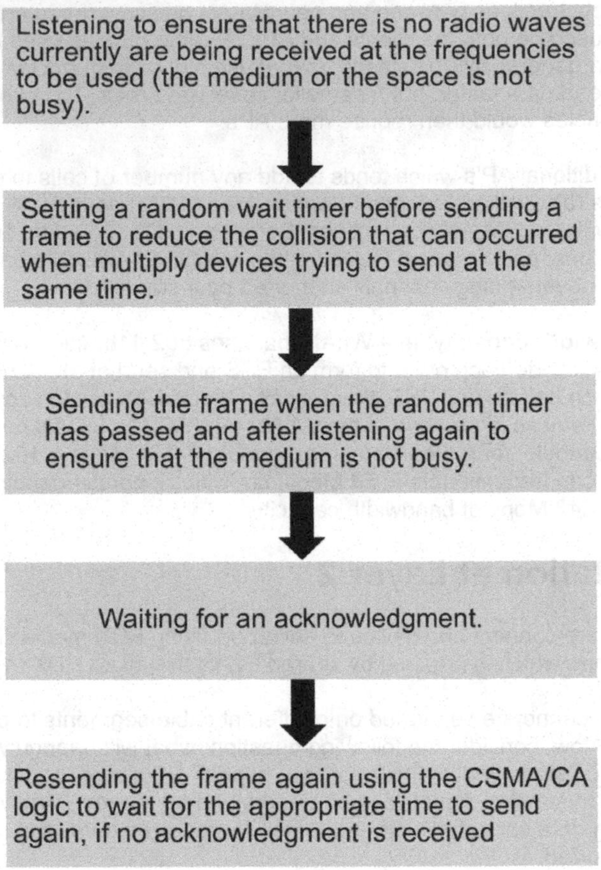

Listening to ensure that there is no radio waves currently are being received at the frequencies to be used (the medium or the space is not busy).

Setting a random wait timer before sending a frame to reduce the collision that can occurred when multiply devices trying to send at the same time.

Sending the frame when the random timer has passed and after listening again to ensure that the medium is not busy.

Waiting for an acknowledgment.

Resending the frame again using the CSMA/CA logic to wait for the appropriate time to send again, if no acknowledgment is received

Installing a BSS WLAN

Figure 9-11 summarizes the steps that required when installing a new BSS WLAN. This procedure can be applied for any WLAN using any type of AP's. Figure 9-12 shows a sample of CISCO Linksys router/AP. Furthermore, the security options will be discussed in chapter ten.

Figure 9-11 Installing New AP.

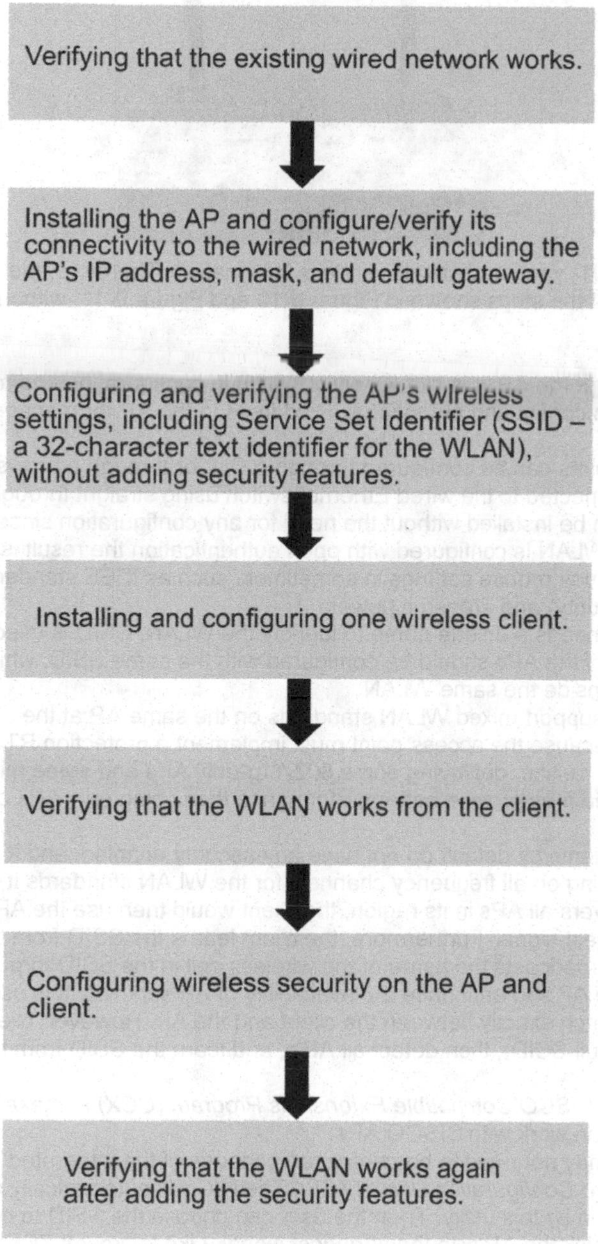

```
┌─────────────────────────────────────────┐
│ Verifying that the existing wired        │
│ network works.                           │
└─────────────────────────────────────────┘
                    ▼
┌─────────────────────────────────────────┐
│ Installing the AP and configure/verify   │
│ its connectivity to the wired network,   │
│ including the AP's IP address, mask,     │
│ and default gateway.                     │
└─────────────────────────────────────────┘
                    ▼
┌─────────────────────────────────────────┐
│ Configuring and verifying the AP's       │
│ wireless settings, including Service Set │
│ Identifier (SSID – a 32-character text   │
│ identifier for the WLAN), without adding │
│ security features.                       │
└─────────────────────────────────────────┘
                    ▼
┌─────────────────────────────────────────┐
│ Installing and configuring one wireless  │
│ client.                                  │
└─────────────────────────────────────────┘
                    ▼
┌─────────────────────────────────────────┐
│ Verifying that the WLAN works from the   │
│ client.                                  │
└─────────────────────────────────────────┘
                    ▼
┌─────────────────────────────────────────┐
│ Configuring wireless security on the AP  │
│ and client.                              │
└─────────────────────────────────────────┘
                    ▼
┌─────────────────────────────────────────┐
│ Verifying that the WLAN works again      │
│ after adding the security features.      │
└─────────────────────────────────────────┘
```

Figure 9-12 CISCO Linksys Router/AP

When you prepare for CCENT, you need simple wireless information. Therefore, the following points summarize the important concepts about the steps shown in Figure 9-10 and Figure 9-11, without confusing you by extra, not required information.

1. It is easy to configure the AP, it is like Ethernet switch in configuration and management. As an example, it requires configuring an optional IP address to the AP for management purposes, just like in Ethernet switch.
2. Wireless access points can be configured through a CLI, or through a browser GUI.
3. The AP can be connected to the wired Ethernet switch using straight through cables.
4. Usually, the AP can be installed without the need for any configuration since it's configured by default settings and if the WLAN is configured with open authentication the result is plug-and-play.
5. Some parameters may require settings in sometimes, such as IEEE standard, Wireless channel, SSID, authentication (security) and Transmit power.
6. Since each WLAN needs a unique name to identify the WLAN, SSID is used. Therefore, to configure an ESS WLAN, each of the APs should be configured with the same SSID, which allows for roaming between APs, but inside the same WLAN.
7. Today, many APs support mixed WLAN standards on the same AP at the same time. This tends to slow down the WLAN because the access point must implement a protection RTS/CTS protocol, particularly with 802.11b/g. In practice, deploying some 802.11g-only APs and some mixed-mode b/g APs in the same coverage area may provide better performance than using only APs configured in b/g mixed mode.
8. Typically, WLAN clients by default do not have any security enabled, and it tries to discover all APs in the region by listening on all frequency channels for the WLAN standards it supports by default. When a WLAN client discovers all APs in its region, the client would then use the AP from which the client receives the strongest signal. Furthermore, the client learns the SSID from the AP.
9. The access point broadcasts the name of the wireless cell in the SSID through beacons. Beacons are broadcasted by the AP's to announce the availability of AP services. It is used to logically separate WLANs. It must match exactly between the client and the AP. However, clients can be configured without an SSID (null-SSID), then detect all AP's, and learn the SSID from the beacons of the access points.
10. CISCO started the *CISCO Compatible Extensions Program (CCX)* to make sure that the clients from different vendors can work with CISCO APs.
11. The wireless NIC may not need to be configured because of the integrated Windows Zero Configuration (WZC) utility or *Zero Configuration Utility (ZCF)*. The NIC will automatically discover the SSIDs of all WLANs in the region by this utility. Then the user can choose the SSID to connect to, or the ZCF utility can automatically pick the AP with the strongest signal. Like Microsoft ZCF, most NIC manufacturers also provide software that can control and configure the NIC automatically. These software can also show the signal strength and quality.
12. To verify proper operation of the first WLAN client, check whether the client can access some neighbor hosts at first after disconnected the WLAN clients from ELAN.

13. In the enterprise with a large number of APs a *site survey* is required during the planning stage of the network. The site survey is required to look for good AP locations, by transmitting and testing signal strength throughout the site.

14. If the new client cannot communicate, the following must be checked:
    - The AP must be located at the center of the area in which the clients reside.
    - The AP's coverage area should be wide enough to reach the client.
    - The AP or client must be not located near a lot of metal.
    - The AP or client must be not located near a source of interference, such as a microwave oven or mobile network or gaming system.

15. The following must also be checked if problems with a new installation is not solved by point 14:

    - Make sure that the NIC and AP's radios are enabled, and its switch/bottom is not turned OFF.
    - Make sure that both the client and AP adopt the correct RF (2.4 GHz ISM or 5 GHz UNII.)
    - Make sure that the external antenna connected and facing the correct direction (straight upward for dipole.)
    - Make sure that the location of the antenna is not too high or not too low relative to wireless clients (within 20 vertical feet.)
    - Update the AP by the latest firmware (OS.)
    - Make sure that the channel configuration of the AP does not use a channel that overlaps with other APs in the same location.
    - Make sure if there is security software (such as antivirus software or firewalls) on the clients that prevent wireless network connection.
    - Make sure that the client laptop is clean, and it is virus and malicious software free.
    - Make sure if security is configured with PSKs for older WEP or current WPA, the key must be an exact match to allow connectivity. Both the wireless client and access point must match for authentication method, EAP or PSK, and encryption method (TKIP or AES.)

Summary

In this chapter, a strong foundation for WLAN is presented. The background presented here is essential for undertaking the examination.

The following topics are covered:

- WLAN standards organizations and their roles
- Comparison of 802.11a, 802.11b, and 802.11g
- WLAN modes, their formal names, and descriptions
- Unlicensed bands, their general names, and the list of standards to use each band
- DSSS frequencies, showing the three nonoverlapping channels
- Installing a BSS WLAN

At the end of the chapter, several learning questions are given to evaluate the learning level from this chapter. The correct answers and solutions with complementary discussions are found in appendix A, "Answers to Chapters Learning Questions."

Chapter 9 Learning Questions

9-1 TRUE/FALSE: The flexibility of the WLAN makes it widely propagated.

    A.   TRUE
    B.   FALSE

9-2 TRUE/FALSE: A company can provide an Internet access and a LAN access via WLANs to mobile users while also supporting the normal LAN access via a wired LAN (ELAN). Figure 9-2 shows a typical design for such a company LAN.

    A. TRUE
    B. FALSE

9-3 Try to decide if the following paragraph correctly depicts Figure 9-2.

"The wireless laptops (PC3 & PC4) in Figure 9-2 connect to the LAN via a WLAN device called an access point (AP). The AP is used to make wireless laptops communicate between each other and to ELAN devices by connecting the laptops to the ELAN through the wired Ethernet switch. The AP makes these laptops send and receive frames with the whole LAN clients."

    A. Correct
    B. Incorrect

9.4 Try to decide which option gets in which blank.

WLAN allowing communications to occur between _____ automated devices.

    A. Wireless
    B. Wired

9-5 Try to decide which option gets in which blank.

ELAN allowing communications to occur between _____ automated devices.

    A. Wireless
    B. Wired

9-6 Which of the following IEEE standards families defines the WLAN?

    A. 802.3
    B. 802.6
    C. 802.11

9-7 Which of the following signals is used to transmit data for the WLAN? (Select all that apply)

    A. Radio waves
    B. Electrical signals
    C. Light signals

9-8 TRUE/FALSE: WLAN requires a physical medium to overtake through space.

    A. TRUE

B. FALSE

9-9 Try to decide which option gets in which blank.

WLANs use the _____ algorithm to enforce _____ logic and avoid as many collisions as possible.

 A. CSMA/CD
 B. CSMA/CA
 C. FDX
 D. HDX

9-10 Match each type of LAN to its suitable characteristics.

 1. WLAN
 2. ELAN

 A. Allowing communications to occur between wireless automated devices.
 B. Allowing communications to occur between wired automated devices.
 C. Defined by IEEE 802.11 family
 D. Defined by IEEE 802.3 family
 E. Uses radio waves, to transmit data. Radio waves pass through space, so there is no need for any physical transmission medium.
 F. Uses electrical signals or light signals flowing over a cable (TP, Coaxial or optical cabling) to transmit data. It is requiring a physical transmission medium.
 G. If more than one device at the time sends radio waves in the same space at the same frequency, neither signal is used, so a half-duplex (HDX) mechanism must be used. WLANs use the carrier sense multiple access with collision avoidance (CSMA/CA) algorithm to enforce HDX logic and avoid as many collisions as possible.
 H. Ethernet can support full-duplex (FDX) communication if a switch port connects to a single device rather than a hub. This removes the need to control access to the link using carrier sense multiple access collision detect (CSMA/CD).
 I. Transmit data over short distance area using lower data rates (Bandwidth) up to 600 Mbps.
 J. Generally, transmit data over longer distance area using higher data rates (Bandwidth) up to 100 Gbps.

9-11 TRUE/FALSE: Radio waves cause the following problems not found in ELANs:

- Connectivity issues: Many factors can affect the WLAN connectivity, such as, the coverage area, RF transmission, multipath distortion, and interference from other wireless services or other WLANs.
- Privacy issues: radio frequencies can reach outside the enterprise/SOHO.

 A. TRUE
 B. FALSE

9-12 TRUE/FALSE: WLANs must meet country-specific RF regulations not required in ELANs. Because WLANs use radio frequencies, they must follow country-specific regulations of RF power and frequencies.

 A. TRUE
 B. FALSE

9-13 TRUE/FALSE: Both WLAN and ELAN standards define their own frame format with a header and trailer. The header includes a source and destination MAC address field, each 6 bytes in length. WLANs require additional information in the Layer 2 header of the frame.

A. TRUE
B. FALSE

9-14 TRUE/FALSE: Both WLAN and ELAN standards define rules about how the devices should determine when they should send frames and when they should not.

A. TRUE
B. FALSE

9-15 TRUE/FALSE: Radio frequencies (RFs) are radiated into the air by antennas that create radio waves. RFs range from the AM radio band to frequencies used by cell phones including unlicensed bands for WLAN. When radio waves are propagated through entities, they might be absorbed, scattered, or reflected. These factors can cause areas of low signal strength and may prevent WLAN communication.

A. TRUE
B. FALSE

9-16 Generally, the transmission of radio waves is affected by many factors. Which of the following factors may affect the transmission of such waves? (Select all that apply)

A.   Reflection: It occurs when RF waves oscillated off entities, such as, metal or glass surfaces.
B.   Scattering: It occurs when RF waves hit an unlevel surface, such as, a rough surface. Such surfaces cause RF to reflect in many directions.
C.   Absorption: It occurs when RF waves are absorbed by objects, such as, walls.

9-17 Which of the following rules must be known for the data transmission over radio waves? (Select all that apply)

A. Higher data rates can be obtained by stronger signal with a better signal-to-noise ratio (SNR). This tends to shorter coverage area.
B. Higher data rates can be obtained by increasing the bandwidth, which is obtained by using higher frequencies or more complex modulation.
C. Higher frequencies tend to higher degradation and absorption, which tends to a shorter transmission range. Using antennas that are more efficient can solve this problem.
D. Higher transmitted power makes transmission to wider converge areas. To double the range, the power has to be increased by a factor of four.

9-18 Which of the following is a WLAN standard?

A. IEEE 802.11a
B. IEEE 802.11
C. IEEE 802.11g
D. IEEE 802.11b
E. IEEE 802.11n

9-19 Which of the following organizations has affected the WLAN standards today? (Select all that apply)

A. ITU-R
B. IEEE
C. FCC
D. Wi-Fi

9-20 TRUE/FALSE: The standards for several types of WLANs are created and developed by the IEEE. Since, those standards are using radio waves for communications, they must take into account the frequency choices made by the different worldwide regulatory agencies, such as the FCC in the U.S. and the ITU-R, which is controlled by the United Nations (UN).

    A. TRUE
    B. FALSE

9-21 Which of the following controls the 801.11 standard that governs the WLANs?

    A. FCC
    B. Wi-Fi Alliance
    C. IEEE

9-22 Which of the following offers certification for interoperability among vendors of 802.11 products?

    A. FCC
    B. Wi-Fi Alliance
    C. IEEE

9-23 Which of the following is unlicensed band, which can be used by WLANs?

    A. 2.4-GHz band
    B. 2.4-MHz band
    C. 5-GHz band
    D. 5-MHz band
    E. 900-GHz band
    F. 900-MHz band

9-24 Which three of the 802.11 standards has the highest possible data rates?

    A. 802.11n
    B. 802.11
    C. 802.11b
    D. 802.11a
    E. 802.11g

9-25 Which 802.11 standard transmits using the 5-GHz band?

    A. 802.11
    B. 802.11a
    C. 802.11b
    D. 802.11g
    E. 802.11n

9-26 IEEE 802.11 is ratified in _____.

        A. 1997
        B. 1999
        C. 2003

9-27 IEEE 802.11a is ratified in _____.

        A. 1997

B. 1999
C. 2003

9-28 IEEE 802.11b is ratified in _____.

A. 1997
B. 1999
C. 2003

9-29 IEEE 802.11g is ratified in _____.

A. 1997
C. 1999
D. 2003

9-30 IEEE 802.11n is ratified in _____.

A. 1997
B. 1999
C. 2009

9-31 The Max net bit rate (FHSS) in Mbps for IEEE 802.11 is _____.

A.   1
B.   2
C.   5
D.   54
E.   None

9-32 The Max net bit rate (FHSS) in Mbps for IEEE 802.11a is _____.

A. 1
B. 2
C. 5
D. 54
E. None

9-33 The Max net bit rate (FHSS) in Mbps for IEEE 802.11b is _____.

A. 1
B. 2
C. 5
D. 54
E. None

9-34 The Max net bit rate (FHSS) in Mbps for IEEE 802.11g is _____.

A. 1
B. 2
C. 5
D. 54
E. None

9-35 The Max net bit rate (FHSS) in Mbps for IEEE 802.11n is _____.

    A. 1
    B. 2
    C. 5
    D. 54
    E. None

9-36 The Max net bit rate (DSSS) in Mbps for IEEE 802.11 is _____.

    A. 1
    B. 2
    C. 11
    D. 20
    E. 40
    F. None

9-37 The Max net bit rate (DSSS) in Mbps for IEEE 802.11a is _____.

    A. 1
    B. 2
    C. 11
    D. 20
    E. 40
    F. None

9-38 The Max net bit rate (DSSS) in Mbps for IEEE 802.11b is _____.

    A. 1
    B. 2
    C. 11
    D. 20
    E. 40
    F. None

9-39 The Max net bit rate (DSSS) in Mbps for IEEE 802.11g is _____.

    A. 1
    B. 2
    C. 11
    D. 20
    E. 40
    F. None

9-40 The Max net bit rate (DSSS) in Mbps for IEEE 802.11n is _____.

    A. 1
    B. 2
    C. 11
    D. 20
    E. 40
    F. None

9-41 The Max net bit rate (OFDM) in Mbps for IEEE 802.11 is _____.

    A. 800
    B. 54
    C. 554
    D. 600
    E. None

9-42 The Max net bit rate (OFDM) in Mbps for IEEE 802.11a is _____.

    A. 800
    B. 54
    C. 554
    D. 600
    E. None

9-43 The Max net bit rate (OFDM) in Mbps for IEEE 802.11b is _____.

    A. 800
    B. 54
    C. 554
    D. 600
    E. None

9-44 The Max net bit rate (OFDM) in Mbps for IEEE 802.11g is _____.

    A. 800
    B. 54
    C. 554
    D. 600
    E. None

9-45 The Max net bit rate (OFDM) in Mbps for IEEE 802.11n is _____.

    A. 800
    B. 54
    C. 554
    D. 600
    E. None

9-46 The Max cross bit rate in Mbps for IEEE 802.11 is _____.

    A. 7.2
    B. 72
    C. 128
    D. 600
    E. Not specified

9-47 The Max cross bit rate in Mbps for IEEE 802.11a is _____.

    A. 7.2
    B. 72
    C. 128

D. 600
E. Not specified

9-48 The Max cross bit rate in Mbps for IEEE 802.11b is _____.

    A. 7.2
    B. 72
    C. 128
    D. 600
    E. Not specified

9-49 The Max cross bit rate in Mbps for IEEE 802.11g is _____.

    A. 7.2
    B. 72
    C. 128
    D. 600
    E. Not specified

9-50 The Max cross bit rate in Mbps for IEEE 802.11n is _____.

    A. 7.2
    B. 72
    C. 128
    D. 600
    E. Not specified

9-51 The Operation frequency band in GHz for IEEE 802.11 is _____.

    A. 2.1
    B. 2.4
    C. 5.1
    D. 5
    E. Not specified

9-52 The Operation frequency band in GHz for IEEE 802.11a is _____.

    A. 2.1
    B. 2.4
    C. 5.1
    D. 5
    E. Not specified

9-53 The Operation frequency band in GHz for IEEE 802.11b is _____.

    A. 2.1
    B. 2.4
    C. 5.1
    D. 5
    E. Not specified

9-54 The Operation frequency band in GHz for IEEE 802.11g is _____.

A. 2.1
B. 2.4
C. 5.1
D. 5
E. Not specified

9-55 The Operation frequency band in GHz for IEEE 802.11n is _____.

A. 2.1
B. 2.4
C. 5.1
D. 5
E. Not specified

9-56 The Typical throughput in Mbps for IFEE 802.11 is _____.

A. 0.9
B. 20
C. 22
D. 5
E. 50-144
F. Not specified

9-57 The Typical throughput in Mbps for IEEE 802.11a is _____.

A. 0.9
B. 20
C. 22
D. 5
E. 50-144
F. Not specified

9-58 The Typical throughput in Mbps for IEEE 802.11b is _____.

A. 0.9
B. 20
C. 22
D. 5
E. 50-144
F. Not specified

9-59 The Typical throughput in Mbps for IEEE 802.11g is _____.

A. 0.9
B. 20
C. 22
D. 5
E. 50-144
F. Not specified

9-60 The Typical throughput in Mbps for IEEE 802.11n is _____.

A. 0.9

B. 20
C. 22
D. 5
E. 50-144
F. Not specified

9-61 The Bandwidth in MHz for IEEE 802.11 is _____.

A. 0.9
B. 20
C. 22
D. 40
E. Not specified

9-62 The Bandwidth in MHz for IEEE 802.11a is _____.

A. 0.9
B. 20
C. 22
D. 40
E. Not specified

9-63 The Bandwidth in MHz for IEEE 802.11b is _____.

A. 0.9
B. 20
C. 22
D. 40
E. Not specified

9-64 The Bandwidth in MHz for IEEE 802.11g is _____.

A. 0.9
B. 20
C. 22
D. 40
E. Not specified

9-65 The Bandwidth in MHz for IEEE 802.11n is _____.

A. 0.9
B. 20
C. 22
D. 40
E. Not specified

9-66 The Max Indoor range for IEEE 802.11 is _____.

A. 20 m
B. 15 m
C. 45 m
D. 70 m
E. Not specified

9-67 The Max Indoor range for IEEE 802.11a is _____.

      A. 20 m
      B. 15 m
      C. 45 m
      D. 70 m
      E. Not specified

9-68 The Max Indoor range for IEEE 802.11b is _____.

      A. 20 m
      B. 15 m
      C. 45 m
      D. 70 m
      E. Not specified

9-69 The Max Indoor range for IEEE 802.11g is _____.

      A. 20 m
      B. 15 m
      C. 45 m
      D. 70 m
      E. Not specified

9-70 The Max Indoor range for IEEE 802.11n is _____.

      A. 20 m
      B. 15 m
      C. 45 m
      D. 70 m
      E. Not specified

9-71 The Max outdoor range for IEEE 802.11 is _____.

      A. 30 m
      B. 100 m
      C. 90 m
      D. 250 m
      E. Not specified

9-72 The Max outdoor range for IEEE 802.11a is _____.

      A. 30 m
      B. 100 m
      C. 90 m
      D. 250 m
      E. Not specified

9-73 The Max outdoor range for IEEE 802.11b is _____.

      A. 30 m
      B. 100 m
      C. 90 m

D. 250 m
E. Not specified

9-74 The Max outdoor range for IEEE 802.11g is _____.

A. 30 m
B. 100 m
C. 90 m
D. 250 m
E. Not specified

9-75 The Max outdoor range for IEEE 802.11n is _____.

A. 30 m
B. 100 m
C. 90 m
D. 250 m
E. Not specified

9-76 Assume three IEEE WLAN devices want to send data with a particular standard. Which of the following is the correct maximum speed they can use?

A. 802.11b, using OFDM, at 54 Mbps
B. 802.11, using OFDM, at 54 Mbps
C. 802.11n, using OFDM, at 600 Mbps
D. 802.11a, using DSSS, at 54 Mbps
E. 802.11g, using DSSS, at 11 Mbps

9-77 TRUE/FALSE: Two modes of operation are found for WLANs—ad hoc mode (peer-to-peer) and infrastructure modes.

A. TRUE
B. FALSE

9-78 Try to decide which option gets in which blank.

Ad hoc mode: Independent Basic Service Set (IBSS) is the ad hoc topology mode. This mode is used to connect _____ wireless automated devices directly. It is used for _____, normally a few numbers of PCs or laptops. Ad hoc coverage is _____ and it is difficult to _____. In this mode, automated devices use their WLAN NIC's (internal, external, or built-in) or modules to send WLAN frames _____ to each other and without the use of _____, as shown in Figure 9-3.

A. small workgroup
B. multiply
C. limited
D. AP
E. secure
F. directly

9-79 Try to decide which option gets in which blank.

Infrastructure mode: This mode is used to connect multiply wireless automated devices through AP devices. It is used to connect wireless devices to the _____, by connecting the AP to infrastructure switch via wired

Ethernet. In this mode, automated devices use their WLAN NIC's or modules to send WLAN frames to the rest of network infrastructure devices through the APs. Wireless devices _____ send frames directly to each other in this mode. Figure 9-2 shows an example of such a network.

> A. network infrastructure
> B. can
> C. cannot

9-80 TRUE/FALSE: Two sets of services are supported by Infrastructure mode, called service sets. These are; Basic Service Set (BSS) and Extended Service Set (ESS).

> A. TRUE
> B. FALSE

9-81 Try to decide if the following paragraph correctly depicts BSS.

Basic Service Set (BSS): "It uses a single AP device to create the WLAN, as shown in Figure 9-2. The Basic Service Set Identifier (BSSID) is used as a Layer 2 MAC address to uniquely identify the BSS AP's within the WLAN. SSID, on the other hand, is used to advertise the availability of the WLAN to mobile clients. The SSID is a wireless network name that is user configurable and can be made up of as many as 32 case-sensitive characters."

> A. Correct
> B. Incorrect

9-82 Try to decide if the following paragraph correctly depicts ESS.

Extended Service Set (ESS): "It uses multiply AP devices to extend the WLAN to two or more BBSs. It allows roaming in a larger area without changing PC's IP addresses by the use of overlapping wireless cells, as shown in Figure 9-4. BSSs in ESS are connected by a distribution system (DS) or a wired infrastructure. An ESS generally includes a common SSID to allow roaming from one access point to another without requiring client reconfiguration."

> A. Correct
> B. Incorrect

9-83 Which of the following is the correct WLAN mode that allows a laptop to roam between different access points?

> A. SSID
> B. ESS
> C. BSS
> D. IBSS

9-84. Which of the following is true about ESS's connections to the wired enterprise?

> A. All APs in the same WLAN must be configured with the same VLAN by the Ethernet switches.
> B. An IP address must be configured on the AP.
> C. All clients connected to the same WLAN should be in the same subnet/VLAN.
> D. A Fast Ethernet or Gigabit Ethernet connection must be used when connecting the APs which using mixed 802.11g mode to an Ethernet switch.
> E. A crossover cable must be used to connect the AP to the Ethernet switch.

9-85 TRUE/FALSE: WLANs at Layer 1 of the OSI model transmit data by sending and receiving radio waves, using WLAN network interface cards (NIC) or Wireless modules, APs, and other WLAN devices. The WLAN devices make small changes to the radio waves that flow over a medium to encode data. However, there are some differences between Ethernet and WLAN encoding techniques.

    A. TRUE
    B. FALSE

9-86 TRUE/FALSE: WLAN radio waves have a repeating signal that can be oscillated over time, as shown in Figure 9-5. When oscillated, the curve shows a repeating periodic waveform, with a frequency, amplitude, and phase. The frequency, which is measured by hertz (Hz), is the most important in discussions the WLANs.

    A. TRUE
    B. FALSE

9-87 Try to decide which option gets in the blank.

WLANs transmit data at Layer 1 of the OSI model by sending and receiving _____.

    A. Electrical signals
    B. Radio waves

9-88 Which of the following FCC frequency bands can be used for the WLANs transmission?

    A. 2.4GHz
    B. 5GHz
    C. 10GHz

9-89 Which of the following IEEE standards uses 2.4GHz frequency bands for transmission?

    A. 802.11
    B. 802.11a
    C. 802.11b
    D. 802.11g
    E. 802.11n

9-90 Which of the following IEEE standards uses 5GHz frequency bands for transmission?

    A. 802.11
    B. 802.11a
    C. 802.11b
    D. 802.11g
    E. 802.11n

9-91 TRUE/FALSE: To operate wireless equipment on unlicensed frequency bands, a license is not required. However, no user has exclusive use of any frequency in the unlicensed bands. The using of unlicensed bands are subject to the local country's code regulations. For example, the 2.4-GHz unlicensed band is used for WLANs, video transmitters, Bluetooth, microwave ovens, and portable phones. Unlicensed frequency bands suffer from interference and degradation.

    A. TRUE
    B. FALSE

9-92 TRUE/FALSE: IEEE 802.11 divided the 2.4-GHz ISM band into 14 channels, but local regulatory agencies (FCC in USA) regulates which channels are allowed, such as channels 1 through 11 in the USA. Each channel in the 2.4 GHz ISM band is 22 MHz wide with 5 MHz separation, resulting in overlap with channels before or after a defined channel. Therefore, a separation of 5 channels is needed to ensure unique nonoverlapping channels. For the FCC example of 11 channels, the maximum of nonoverlapping frequencies are channels 1, 6, and 11. However, the basic throughput is only about half of the data rate, since WLAN uses half-duplex communication.

    A. TRUE
    B. FALSE

9-93 TRUE/FALSE: Encoding means that a device modulates a signal in binary code (0 & 1). For this function, a device can use one or more of signal attributes, such as, frequency, amplitude, and phase. WLAN devices use the same concept when sending data over layer 1 of OSI model. WLAN devices modulate the radio signal's frequency, amplitude, and phase to encode a binary 0 or 1. It is important to know the names of three general classes of encoding that used for WLANs.

    A. TRUE
    B. FALSE

9-94 Which of the following is a WLAN modulation method?

    A. Frequency Hopping Spread Spectrum (FHSS)
    B. Direct Sequence Spread Spectrum (DSSS)
    C. Orthogonal Frequency Division Multiplexing (OFDM)

9-95 Try to decide if the following paragraph correctly depicts a FHSS.

"Frequency Hopping Spread Spectrum (FHSS): uses all frequencies in the band, hopping to different ones. A device can hopefully avoid interference from other devices that use the same unlicensed frequency band. This is obtained by using slightly different frequencies for consecutive transmissions. The 802.11 WLAN standards used FHSS, but the newest standards (802.11a, 802.11b, 802.11g, and 802.11n) do not."

    A. Correct
    B. Incorrect

9-96 Try to decide if the following paragraph correctly depicts a DSSS.

"Direct Sequence Spread Spectrum (DSSS): Designed for use in the 2.4 GHz unlicensed frequency band, DSSS uses just one channel of several separate channels or frequencies. DSSS spreads the data across all frequencies defined by that channel. As regulated by the FCC, this band can have 11 different overlapping DSSS channels, as shown in Figure 9-6."

    A. Correct
    B. Incorrect

9-97 TRUE/FALSE: As shown in Figure 9-6, only three of the channels, 1, 6, and 11 can be used in the same space for WLAN communications, since these channels are not overlapped, and they will not interfere with each other. Therefore, when designing an ESS WLAN, APs with overlapping coverage areas should be set to use different nonoverlapping DSSS channels. Figure 9-7 shows this network.

    A. TRUE
    B. FALSE

9-98 TRUE/FALSE: In Figure 9-7, the devices in the three BSS's can send a frame at the same time and without interfere between each other, because each device uses the different frequencies of the nonoverlapping channels. Although, PC1 and PC2 in Figure 9-7 are located within BSS1, they can communicate between each other and with two different BSS's (APs) using two different channels at the same time.

> A. TRUE
> B. FALSE

9-99 Try to decide if the following paragraph correctly depicts an OFDM.

"Orthogonal Frequency Division Multiplexing (OFDM) WLANs that use OFDM can use multiple nonoverlapping channels. Figure 9-8 shows the amplitude Vs frequency for OFDM waves."

> A. Correct
> B. Incorrect

9-100 Which of the following IEEE standards uses the FHSS encoding method?

> A. 802.11
> B. 802.11a
> C. 802.11b
> D. 802.11g

9-101 Which of the following IEEE standards uses the DSSS encoding method?

> A. 802.11
> B. 802.11a
> C. 802.11b
> D. 802.11g
> E. 802.11n

9-102 Which of the following IEEE standards uses the OFDM encoding method?

> A. 802.11
> B. 802.11a
> C. 802.11b
> D. 802.11g
> E. 802.11n

9-103 Which of the following represents a source that can make WLANs suffering from interferences? (Select all that apply)

> A. Matters such as, walls, floors, and ceilings. These matters face the WLAN signal through the air. It causes the signal to be partially absorbed, which reduces signal strength and the size of the coverage area. Dead spots areas in which the WLAN simply does not work can also be occurred when the WLAN signals pass through metal, which reflects and scatters the waves.
> B. Other wireless radio waves in the same frequency range. This causes interference between radio waves and may cause to lose the data, which requires lots of retransmissions, and resulting in poor efficiency.

9-104 TRUE/FALSE: Signal-to-Noise Ratio (SNR) factor is used to measure the interference. SNR compares the WLAN signal and the other undesired signals (noise) in the same space. The higher the SNR, the better the WLAN devices can send data successfully.

A. TRUE
B. FALSE

9-105 TRUE/FALSE: The space in which two WLAN devices can successfully communicate and exchange data is called a WLAN coverage area. The coverage area depends on many factors.

A. TRUE
B. FALSE

9-106 TRUE/FALSE: One of these factors is the EIRP, which is the power of an AP. Since, the transmitted power by an AP or WLAN NIC cannot exceed a particular level based on the regulations from regulatory agencies such as the FCC. This will limit the coverage area, which can be covered by an AP or wireless device. The FCC limits the transmit power to ensure the fair using of the unlicensed bands.

A. TRUE
B. FALSE

9-107 Try to decide which option gets in the blank.

Notice that, the power of an AP is measured based on the Effective Isotropic Radiated Power (EIRP) calculation. EIRP = _____ = The radio's power output + _____ - Any power lost in the cabling and the device.

A. The power of the signal as it leaves the antenna.
B. The increase in power caused by the antenna gain.

9-108 TRUE/FALSE: The materials and locations of the materials near the AP. also affect the coverage area. For example, wave reflections and scattering can be increased by putting the AP near a metal filing cabinet; however, this decreases the coverage area. However, the AP to change the shape of the coverage area from a circle to some other shapes can use different types of antennas.

A. TRUE
B. FALSE

9-109 TRUE/FALSE: WLAN standards support multiple speeds to make weaker wireless waves passing data at lower speeds. A device at the edge of the coverage area, where the waves are weak, can send and receive data at a slower speed. A device near the AP may have a strong signal, so it can transmit and receive data with the AP at higher rates. The idea of a coverage area, with varying speeds, for an IEEE 802.11b BSS, is illustrated in Figure 9-9.

A. TRUE
B. FALSE

9-110 TRUE/FALSE: The size of the coverage area of one AP can be increased by using specialized antennas with higher gain, which increase the power of the transmitted signal. For example, to double the coverage area, the antenna gain must be increased to quadruple the original gain but the power output (the EIRP) must still be within FCC rules (in the U.S.). However, the actual size of the coverage area depends on many factors such as the frequency band used by the WLAN standard, the obstructions between and near WLAN devices, the interference from other sources of RF energy, the antennas used on both the clients and APs, and the options used by DSSS and OFDM when encoding data over the air. In general, WLAN standards that use higher frequencies (U-II band standards 802.11a and 802.11n) can send data faster, but for smaller coverage areas. To cover all the required space, an ESS that uses higher frequencies would then require more APs.

A. TRUE
B. FALSE

9-111 TRUE/FALSE: ESS is created by adding additional APs, which tends to add any number of cells to extend the range. It is recommended that ESS cells (also called Extended Service Area (ESA)) have 10 to 15 percent overlap to allow remote users to roam without losing WLAN connections. Bordering cells should be set to different nonoverlapping channels for best performance. The combined available bandwidth of the WLAN is affected by the number of nonoverlapping channels supported by a standard.

A. TRUE
B. FALSE

9-112 How many nonoverlapping channels in the IEEE 802.11b standard?

A. 12
B. 3
C. 6

9-113 How many nonoverlapping channels in the IEEE 802.11a standard?

A. 12
B. 3
C. 6

9-114 How many nonoverlapping channels in the IEEE 802.11g standard?

A. 12
B. 3
C. 6

9-115 Which of the following is the term, which is used to define the physical area of radio frequency coverage provided by an AP?

A. The basic service area
B. The RF service area
C. The LAN service area
D. The service area

9-116 How much overlap is suggested by the Extended Service Areas?

A. 20 to 30 percent
B. 16 to 20 percent
C. 10 to 15 percent
D. 5 to 10 percent

9-117 TRUE/FALSE: Unlike ELAN, WLAN devices cannot be separated onto different cable segments to prevent collisions, so collisions can always occur. Now consider the following question: what will be happened when two WLAN devices try to send data at the same time using overlapping frequency bands? Of course, collision will occur within the WLAN, and none of the two transmitted signals can be understood by the receiving WLAN devices. Moreover, the device that is transmitting data cannot concurrently listen for received data, and it has no mechanism to understand that collision occurred.

A. TRUE

B. FALSE

9-118 Try to decide which option gets in which blank.

To solve the above problems, an algorithm called _____ and _____ mechanisms are used.

      A. carrier sense multiple access with collision avoidance (CSMA/CA)
      B. an acknowledgement

9-119 TRUE/FALSE: It is easy to configure the AP, it is like Ethernet switch in configuration and management. As an example, it is requiring configuring an optional IP address to the AP for management purposes, just like in Ethernet switch.

      A. TRUE
      B. FALSE

9-120 TRUE/FALSE: Wireless access points can be configured through a CLI, or through a browser GUI.

      A. TRUE
      B. FALSE

9-121 TRUE/FALSE: The AP can only be connected to the wired Ethernet switch using cross over cables.

      A. TRUE
      B. FALSE

9-122 TRUE/FALSE: Usually, the AP can be installed without the need for any configuration since it is configured by default settings and if the WLAN is configured with open authentication, the result is plug-and-play.

      A. TRUE
      B. FALSE

9-123 Which of the following parameters may require settings in sometimes for a WLAN? (Select all that apply)

      A. IEEE standard
      B. Wireless channel
      C. SSID
      D. authentication (security)
      E. Transmit power

9-124 TRUE/FALSE: Since each WLAN needs a unique name to identify the WLAN, SSID is used. Therefore, to configure an ESS WLAN, each of the APs should be configured with the same SSID, which allows for roaming between APs, but inside the same WLAN.

      A. TRUE
      B. FALSE

9-125 TRUE/FALSE: Today, Many APs support mixed WLAN standards on the same AP at the same time. This tends to slow down the WLAN because the access point must implement a protection RTS/CTS protocol, particularly with 802.11b/g. In practice, deploying some 802.11g only APs and some mixed-mode b/g APs in the same coverage area may provide better performance than using only APs configured in b/g mixed mode.

      A. TRUE

B. FALSE

9-126 TRUE/FALSE: Typically, WLAN clients by default do not have any security enabled, and it tries to discover all APs in the region by listening on all frequency channels for the WLAN standards it supports by default. When a WLAN client discovers all APs in its region, the client would then use the AP from which the client receives the strongest signal. In addition, the client learns the SSID from the AP.

A. TRUE
B. FALSE

9-127 TRUE/FALSE: The access point broadcasts the name of the wireless cell in the SSID through beacons. Beacons are broadcasted by the AP's to announce the availability of AP services. It is used to separate WLANs logically. It must match exactly between the client and the AP. However, clients can be configured without an SSID (null-SSID), then detect all AP's, and learn the SSID from the beacons of the access points.

A. TRUE
B. FALSE

9-128 TRUE/FALSE: CISCO started the CISCO Compatible Extensions Program (CCX) to make sure that the clients from different vendors can work with CISCO APs.

A. TRUE
B. FALSE

9-129 TRUE/FALSE: The wireless NIC may not need to be configured because of the integrated Windows Zero Configuration (WZC) utility or Zero Configuration Utility (ZCF). The NIC will automatically discover the SSIDs of all WLANs in the region by this utility. Then the user can choose the SSID to connect to, or the ZCF utility can automatically pick the AP with the strongest signal. Like Microsoft ZCF, most NIC manufacturers also provide software that can control and configure the NIC automatically. These software can also show the signal strength and quality.

A. TRUE
B. FALSE

9-130 TRUE/FALSE: To verify proper operation of the first WLAN client, check whether the client can access some neighbor hosts at first after disconnected the WLAN clients from ELAN.

A. TRUE
B. FALSE

9-131 TRUE/FALSE: In the enterprise with a large number of APs, a site survey is required during the planning stage of the network. The site survey is required to look for good AP locations, by transmitting and testing signal strength throughout the site.

A. TRUE
B. FALSE

9-132 Which of the following must be checked if the new client cannot communicate with a WLAN? (Select all that apply)

A. The AP must be located at the center of the area in which the clients reside.
B. The AP's coverage area should be wide enough to reach the client.
C. The AP or client must be not located near a lot of metal.

D. The AP or client must be not located near a source of interference, such as a microwave cooker or mobile network or gaming system.

9-133 Which of the following must also be checked if problems with a new installation in a WLAN are not solved by previous question? (Select all that apply)

A. Makes sure that the NIC and AP's radios are enabled and its switch/bottom is not turned OFF.
B. Makes sure that both the client and AP adopt the correct RF (2.4 GHz ISM or 5 GHz UNII.)
C. Makes sure that the external antenna connected and facing the correct direction (straight upward for dipole.)
D. Makes sure that the location of the antenna is not too high or not too low relative to wireless clients (within 20 vertical feet.)
E. Update the AP by the latest firmware (OS).
F. Makes sure that the channel configuration of the AP does not use a channel that overlaps with other APs in the same location.
G. Makes sure, if there is security software (such as antivirus software or firewalls) on the clients that prevent wireless network connection.
H. Makes sure that the client laptop is clean, and it is virus and malicious software free.
I. Makes sure, if security is configured with PSKs for older WEP or current WPA, the key must be an exact match to allow connectivity. Both the wireless client and access point must match for authentication method, EAP or PSK, and encryption method (TKIP or AES.)

9-134 Which of the following are typical configuration choices for AP's?

A. The SSID to use
B. The BSSID to use
C. The wireless standard to use
D. The speed to use
E. The size of the desired coverage area

9-135 Which of the following are common reasons why a client cannot connect through the WLAN into the wired infrastructure?

A. DSSS channel 1 is used instead of the default channel 6, and the client is not configured to use channel 1.
B. A metal filing cabinet is near the AP.
C. Currently used UTP Ethernet cables are near the client PC.
D. A microwave cooker is near the client PC.

9-136 Which of the following factors determines which AP a client is associated with? (Select all that apply)

A. The received weakest signal AP
B. The received strongest signal AP
C. The lowest SSID AP
D. The highest SSID AP
E. The first received SSID AP

9-137 What technique enables a client to communicate while moving?

A. The ability to shift the frequency
B. The ability to vary the frequency
C. The ability to shift the data rates

9-138 Which three are basic wireless access point parameters?

    A. SSID
    B. Authentication
    C. RF channel with optional power
    D. Data transmission rates
    E. Frequency band selection

9-139 Match each wireless client term to its description.

    1. CISCO Compatible Extensions
    2. CISCO Secure Services Client
    3. WZC/ZCF

        A. Advanced features for wireless client
        B. Window operating systems basic wireless supplicant client
        C. Wired and wireless client full-featured supplicant

CHAPTER 10
INTERNETWORKING
SECURITY:
AN INTRODUCTION

In this chapter, an introduction to the networks' security will be described. Networks Security is a big issue, and it requires a serious attention. In particular, studying the networks security gives the engineers some tools to prevent network attackers from attacking the organizations and companies public web sites and networks.

The following topics are emphasized in this chapter:

- Network security
- Sources and Types of Threats
- Firewalls and the Cisco Adaptive Security Appliance (ASA)
- Intrusion Detection and Prevention
- Virtual Private Networks (VPN)
- WLAN security

By understanding perfectly the information presented in this chapter and answering the 94 learning questions at the end of this chapter, understanding network security and answering the CCNA/CCENT exam related questions will be guaranteed. The questions herein are intended to reflect the type of questions presented on the CCENT Test.

Network Security

Today, threatening organizations and companies by network attackers have increased exponentially and become very dangerous. Attackers become very sophisticated and clever. Not only might they attack military, commerce and government networks, but they might try to disrupt infrastructure services. Attackers can extort organizations by threatening a denial of service (DoS) attack on the organizations' servers on the internet. As an example, by one sophisticated attack, attackers can steal identity and credit card information for sometimes millions of people.

Network security is an important issue of every modern network design, and one that requires serious attention and clever working. The bigger problem now is that almost anyone can become a hacker by downloading simple tools from the Internet. A strong security policy then, is required for every up-to-date network. It is easy to protect the network by closing the network completely from the internet and other public networks. However, internal threats still exist, and they may cause 60-80 percent of network security problems. Closing a network is unsuitable for almost all modern networks, simply because these networks require access to the internet and other public networks. The Computer Security Institute (CSI) and some respectable organizations give periodically reports for security threats. The reports confirm that threats from computer crime and other information security breaches continue to affect the networks and that the organizations will lose more and more money by computer crimes.

In this CCENT book, the goal is to know some of the security basics and general terms that can be faced when securing the network. Types of security issues and some of the common tools used to mitigate security risks also need to be understood here. In addition to classes of security tools, the chapter introduces WLAN security.

Sources and Types of Threats

Network topology can adopt a firewall for protection against internet attacks as shown in Figure 10-1. Firewalls represent the best-known security tool that can sit between the organization network and the unsecured Internet and any other public network. By looking at the transport layer port numbers and the application layer headers, the firewall's can stop unsafe packets and prevent certain ports and applications from getting packets into the organization network. However, firewall cannot prevent the inside organization network attacks. Moreover, firewall cannot provide protection from all dangers of connecting to the internet.

Figure 10-1 Organization Network with Firewall

The following is a list to the kinds of attacks that can be occurred from inside the organization network.

- **Denial of service (DoS) attacks:** An attack whose purpose is to break or destroy any entity in the organization network. DoS attacks called *destroyers or crashers or flooders*. Destroyers since it can destroy the hosts within the organization network, such as erasing data and software and destroying applications. Crashers since it can crash a host which means that it can fail hosts or breaking the host's connection to the network. Flooders since it can flood the network with packets to make the network unusable, breaking the connection with organization's servers.
- **Reconnaissance attacks:** The goal of this kind of attack is gathering information to perform an access attack to the network hosts. An example is learning IP addresses and then trying to discover important machines in the network such as servers and then gather more information about services, and vulnerabilities. In most cases, it precedes an actual access or DoS attack and usually, it uses ping utility to do its work.
- **Access attacks:** This kind of attack is an attempt to steal data, typically important data such as financial information or customers list. These types of attacks, exploit known vulnerabilities in authentication services, FTP services, and web services.
- **Password Attacks:** A password attack usually refers to repeated attempts to identify user authentication information. These attacks are implemented using Trojan horse programs, IP spoofing, and packet sniffers.

One tool that can be used to carry out any of these attacks is computer viruses. A virus is a piece of program that is transferred onto an undefending machine by an e-mail attachment or website download or by accessing some suspecting sites. Most computers use some type of anti-virus software, such as, TrendMicro to protect against known viruses and prevent them from harming the computer. To provide best protecting, the machine must be connecting to the internet or local antivirus server to update the software with up-to-date virus *signatures,* which is a list of known characteristics of all current viruses' types. These updates may be several times per hour. All packets entering the machine will be watched be the antivirus so that to protect the machine.

Besides external sources of attacks, there are several types of problems that could commonly occur inside the organization network, such as, Wirelessly accessing the organization network from home or unsafe location with infected laptops through WLAN that bypassing the organization firewall, Mobile Infection accessing the LAN by infected an employee laptop after taking it to home based Cable/DSL internet and Disgruntled employees that steal important information from the network servers before leaving the organization to another one. The last type maybe represents the most dangerous one. Furthermore, the physical security is an important thing that must be addressed well to prevent inside attack and misusing of the organization network.

To prevent several types of inside attacks that can harm the organization network, several CISCO models exist that can work automatically and dynamically to defend the networks. *Self-defending network* is a CISCO term that refers to automation in which the network devices automatically react to network problems. CISCO also uses the term "*security in depth*" to refer to security features included in routers and switches and other networking devices.

Network Admission Control (NAC) is one security tool in the CISCO security in-depth model that can help in preventing some types of attacks from inside the organization network. In summary, NAC functions include the following:

- Monitoring the time of connections to an organization network.
- Monitoring the type of connections if it's wireless device or wired device.
- Preventing a computer from connecting to the organization network until its virus definitions were updated and a machine is scanned recently with the full virus scan.
- Authenticating network clients, NAC includes a requirement that the user supply a username and password before being able to send other data into the organization network.

However, NAC does not prevent an employee from inside the organization network from causing harm, because the employee typically has a legal network authentication.

To form an attack many other tools can be used instead of viruses. The following list summarizes some terms for the tools that can be used by attackers:

- **Scanner:** This tool is used to discover the IP services and the operating systems that run on hosts by sending connection requests to different TCP and UDP ports, for different applications.
- **Spyware:** This virus is used to obtain important and sensitive information or private information, such as, credit card information from victim machines. It is also, used to track what the user does with the machine, and passing the information back to the attacker in the Internet to use it illegally.
- **Malware:** Refers to several types of malicious viruses, such as, spyware.
- **Worm:** Refers to self-propagating program that can quickly iterate itself around the organization networks and the Internet. It can perform DoS attacks on the organization sensitive devices, such as, servers.
- **Keystroke logger:** This virus is used to log all keystrokes and report this information to the attacker. By Loggers authentication information to secure sites can actually be captured before this information leaves the client machine. The captured information can give the attacker access to the sensitive websites.
- **Phishing:** By this type of attack, a website sets up by an attacker that looks like a legitimate website of a well-known organization or a bank. The phisher often sends e-mails listing the illegitimate website's URL like the real organization. When people will apply and connect to the illegitimate website, and enter information such as their name, address, credit card number or social security number (in the U.S.), the attacker will take this information and use it illegally.

By adopting the CISCO "Security in-Depth" model throughout the organization network, several security problems can be solved. This will be introduced in the following sections.

CISCO Adaptive Security Appliance (ASA) and the Firewalls

At the beginning, CISCO sold firewalls with the trade name PIX firewall. Now, CISCO introduced a whole new generation of network security hardware using the trade name Adaptive Security Appliance (ASA). In addition to firewall function, ASA can do more additional functions such as Anti-x.

To filter unwanted traffic, firewalls are used to examine all packets entering and exiting the network core edge. Firewalls sit in the packet-forwarding path between two networks, the local organization network and the unsecured network such as the internet. Based on many characteristics of the packets, such as, source and destination IP addresses, the transport layer (TCP and UDP) port numbers, and application layer headers, firewalls can determine the allowed traffic versus the disallowed traffic.

A network firewall must itself be rigid against security attacks. Unless a firewall rule that allows a specific traffic is configured, the firewall *must disallow all packets*.

The firewalls sit in the packet-forwarding path between two networks. In addition to local LAN interface which connects the firewall to the secure organization network and another interface to the other network usually, the unsecured internet, the firewall has an interface to the demilitarized zone (DMZ) LAN, where the organization's public servers sit. The DMZ LAN is a place to put the organization's devices that need to be accessible from the internet. Figure 10-2 shows a typical design of such a network.

Figure 10-2 Firewall or ASA Design

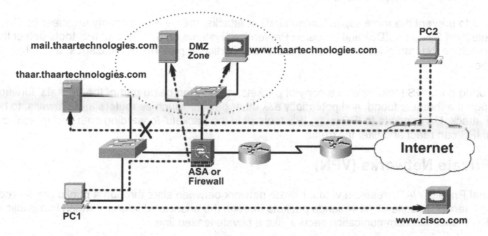

The firewall must be configured to know which interfaces are connected to the organization secure network (inside), unsecured network (outside), and DMZ parts of the network. To tell the firewall which traffic is allowed and, which is not allowed, a series of rules must then be configured. Figure 10-2 depicts the basic firewall functions. It shows four typical flows with dashed lines; three allowed flows and one disallowed flow:

- Allow web clients on the organization network (such as PC1) to access the web servers (www.cisco.com.)
- Allow web clients in the internet (such as PC2) to connect to DMZ servers (www.thaartechnologies.com and mail.thaartechnologies.com.)
- Allow web clients on the organization network (such as PC1) to connect to DMZ servers (www.thaartechnologies.com and mail.thaartechnologies.com.)
- Prevent web clients in the internet (such as PC2) from sending packets to web servers in the organization network (such as the internal web server thaar.thaartechnologies.com.)

Anti-x

Cisco ASA appliances can provide in the overall in-depth security design with a variety of tools that prevent problems such as viruses, spyware, spam and phishing. CISCO uses the term *anti-x* to refer to the whole class of security tools that prevent these various problems-starting with "anti-". Several problems can be prevented using the Cisco ASA:

- **Anti-virus:** Based on virus signatures, the Cisco ASA scans network traffic to prevent the virus's transmission.
- **Anti-spyware:** Preventing the spyware's transmission.
- **Anti-spam:** Cleaning the end user's e-mails from junk e-mail.
- **Anti-phishing:** Preventing the phishing attack from reaching the end users. The Cisco ASA monitors URLs sent in messages through the network, looking for the illegitimate website's URL inside the messages, and then blocking these URL's.
- **URL filtering:** Prevent users from connecting to unsafe sites or unuseful sites.

- **E-mail filtering:** Protecting the organization network from e-mails with unsafe materials in addition to anti-spam filtering.

Intrusion Detection and Prevention Systems (IDS & IPS)

Some types of attacks can be more sophisticated and cannot be easily recovered by anti-x tools. Such attacks may use of new bugs in the operating system.

To detect and to prevent the more sophisticated kinds of attacks, the network security engineer can use the Intrusion Detection Systems (IDS) and Intrusion Prevention Systems (IPS). IDS and IPS tools detect these threats by watching the traffic, looking for attacks that use particular patterns of messages, and other characteristic.

Via a monitoring port, IDS tools receive a copy of packets, rather than being part of the packets' forwarding path, rate and report if a threat is found, and potentially ask other devices, such as routers and firewalls, to help prevent the attack. On opposite to IDS tools, IPS tools sit in the packets' forwarding path and in addition to IDS capabilities, IPS can react and filter the traffic.

Virtual Private Networks (VPN)

VPN or Virtual Private WAN creates a virtual-private network between sites through a public unsecured network, such as, the internet. In spite of, VPN sends packets through the unsecured internet, which is a public WAN network, VPN makes the communication secure, like a private leased line.

VPNs allow the use of the Internet without the risk of others reading the data in transit and without the risks of accepting data from attacking hosts. VPNs use authentication in both VPN's endpoints, meaning that both endpoints can be sure that the other endpoint of the VPN connection is legitimate. In addition to that, VPNs encrypt the transit packets between endpoints so that, even if an attacker managed to obtain a copy of the packets as they pass through the Internet, the attackers cannot understand the data.

VPNs use end-to-end encryption, in which the data remains encrypted while being forwarded through one or more routers. In addition to that, to encrypt data at the data link layer, link encryption can be used so the data is encrypted only as it passes over one data link.

Two types of VPNs are found: an **access VPN** and a **site-to-site intranet VPN**. With an access VPN, the remote office's PC in SOHO typically encrypting the packets. A site-to-site intranet VPN typically connects virtually two sites of the same organization network. The encryption could be done for all devices using different kinds of hardware, including purpose-built VPN concentrator hardware, routers, firewalls, or ASAs.

WLAN Security

WLAN security is one of the important features of WLANs. WLAN suffers from more vulnerabilities than wired Ethernet LANs. For example, someone could sit outside an organization network, pick up the WLAN signals from inside the organization network, reading the data, and enter to the network.

Today, all networks need good security, but WLANs have some unique security requirements. The WLAN security issues are discussed in this section.

WLAN Security Issues

As stated above, WLANs introduce a number of vulnerabilities that do not exist for ELANs. Hackers can use WLAN vulnerabilities to access hosts in the ELAN of the organization network, or prevent services through a DoS attack and much more.

The following categories of threats are discussed here:

- **War drivers:** To gain Internet access for free, the attacker drives around, trying to find breakable security APs with internet accesses.
- **Hackers:** To find information or deny services in the organization network, the hackers try to obtain an access to the organization network through the WLAN bypassing the firewalls.
- **Rogue AP:** After the attacker captures packets from the existing WLAN, finding the SSID and cracking security keys, the attacker can set up a private AP, with the same settings, making the clients of the organization network to access the network through rogue AP capturing their information, such as, authentication details.
- **Employees:** Employees can easily install their own AP within the WLAN organization network. If this AP is without security this will give the attackers the way to enter the organization network from within that AP.

To protect the network against these attacks, three main types of tools can be used on a WLAN:

Mutual Authentication

To prevent a connection to a rogue AP, mutual authentication must be used between the client and AP so that the client can confirm that the AP knows the right key. A key or a secret password is used during the authentication process, on both the client and the AP. The AP and the client can confirm that each of them does indeed know the right key value by using some mathematical algorithms. The key value is never sent through the air during the mutual authentication process, so the attacker will not be able to see or copy or learn the key value, even if the attacker is using any type of network analysis tool to copy every frame inside the WLAN.

Encryption

Encryption uses a secret key and a mathematical formula to encrypt and decrypt the contents of the WLAN frame on both the client and the AP. An attacker cannot read the contents of the frames without the secret encryption key even an attacker may be able to intercept the frames.

Intrusion Tools

These tools include Intrusion Detection Systems (IDS) and Intrusion Prevention Systems (IPS). Cisco also defines the Structured Wireless-Aware Network (SWAN) architecture. SWAN includes many tools. Some of these tools can detect and identify rogue APs.

Table 10-1 lists, the WLAN vulnerabilities and their solutions.

Table 10-1 WLAN Vulnerabilities Solutions

Vulnerability	Solution
War drivers	Powerful authentication
Hackers accessing a WLAN	Powerful encryption
Hackers accessing the organization network	Powerful authentication

| Rogue AP | Powerful authentication, IDS/SWAN |
| Employee AP installation | IDS/SWAN |

WLAN Security Standards

In this section, four significant sets of WLAN security standards for implementing the authentication and encryption will be discussed. These standards are listed in Table 10-2.

Table 10-2 WLAN Security Standards and De-Facto Standards

Name	Year	Standards body
Wired Equivalent Privacy (WEP)	1997	IEEE
The interim CISCO solution	2001	CISCO, IEEE 802.1x Extensible Authentication Protocol (EAP)
Wi-Fi Protected Access (WPA)	2003	Wi-Fi Alliance
802.11i (WPA2)	2005+	IEEE

Wired Equivalent Privacy (WEP)

WEP was the original 802.11 security standard, and it provided only weak authentication and encryption. Its authentication and encryption can be cracked by a hacker today, using easily downloaded tools. Two main problems are found with WEP:

- **Static Preshared Keys (PSK):** Each client and each AP should be configured by the key value and there is no dynamic way to exchange the keys without administrator intervention. This made the configuration so difficult and especially in a large organization network and its security so weak since the employees could not change the keys on a regular basis.
- **Easily cracked keys:** It is 64 bits key with only 40 bits were the actual unique key. This made it easier to predict the key's by a hacker today.

Today, WEP is not used because of the problems shown above.

SSID Cloaking

The *SSID cloaking*, is not part of WEP standard. It is created to address some problems, and to change the process by which clients are associated with an AP. The AP's SSID must be known before a client can communicate with the AP. The client association process can be summarized as following:

1. A periodic Beacon frame is sent by the AP, every 100 ms by default. The Beacon lists the AP's SSID and other configuration information.
2. The client learns about all APs in the range by listening for Beacons on all available channels.
3. Then the client association process is made with the AP with the strongest signal (the default), or with the AP with the strongest signal for the currently preferred SSID.
4. The authentication process occurs as soon as the client has associated with the AP.

The Beacons allow an attacker to easily and quickly find out information about the APs and then gain access to the organization network. To solve this problem, SSID cloaking is used. SSID cloaking tells the AP to stop sending periodic Beacon frames. However, clients still need to be able to find the APs. A null SSID client sends a Probe message, which causes each neighbor AP to respond with its SSID. Therefore, attackers can still find all the APs.

MAC Filtering

The MAC address filtering is a second extra feature often implemented along with WEP. A list of allowed WLAN MAC addresses is configured within the AP, makes it filter the frames sent by WLAN clients whose MAC address is not in the list. It is not secure enough, and it can be broken by attackers.

The Cisco Interim Solution Between WEP and 802.11i

To solve the problems with WEP, vendors such as CISCO, and the Wi-Fi Alliance industry association, introduced de-facto security standards. CISCO improves the encryption, along with the IEEE 802.1x standard for end-user authentication. The main features of Cisco's security enhancements included the following:

- Dynamic key exchange using a Cisco proprietary version of TKIP. (as opposite to WEP static preshared keys)
- User authentication using 802.1x
- A new encryption key per packet

The use of a dynamic key exchange process provides several advantages. It improves the WLAN security, and the clients and AP can dynamically change the keys without administrator interventions, which are slower processes. The security is improved since if the key is discovered, the effect can be short-lived since it's changing dynamically. Furthermore, a new key can be delivered for each packet, allowing encryption to use a different key each time which removes the possibility of discovering the encryption by hackers.

To add another level of security, Cisco added a user authentication to its suite of security features. User authentication means that, the user must supply a username and password.

Wi-Fi Protected Access (WPA)

To solve the problems with WEP, Wi-Fi alliance introduced a multivendor WLAN security standard, i.e. the Wi-Fi Protected Access (WPA) security solution.

WPA essentially performed the same functions as the Cisco proprietary interim solution, but with different details. However, both de-facto standards are incompatible. As an example, dynamic key exchange is used in WPA using the Temporal Key Integrity Protocol (TKIP). IEEE 802.1x user authentication or simple device authentication using preshared keys can be used in WPA. The encryption algorithm of WPA uses the Message Integrity Check (MIC) algorithm, which is similar to the process used in the Cisco-proprietary solution.

IEEE 802.11i and WPA2

To provide better security than Cisco interim and WPA, the IEEE ratified the 802.11i security standard in 2005. It includes dynamic key exchange, much stronger encryption, and user authentication. However, IEEE 802.11i is not backward-compatible with either WPA or the Cisco interim standards.

New encryption standard is used in IEEE 802.11i that is the *Advanced Encryption Standard (AES)*. Longer encryption keys and much more secure encryption algorithms are used in AES making its encryption better than the interim Cisco and WEP standards. The Wi-Fi Alliance calls 802.11i *WPA2*.

Table 10-3 summarizes the key features of the various WLAN security standards.

Table 10-3 Comparisons of WLAN Security Standards

Standard	Security Key	Device Authentication	User Authentication	Encryption
WEP	Static	Weak	None	Weak
CISCO	Dynamic	Strong	802.1x	TKIP
WPA	Both	Strong	802.1x	TKIP
802.11i (WPA2)	Both	Strong	802.1x	AES

Summary

In this chapter, a strong foundation for network security is presented. The background presented here is essential for understanding the network security and undertaking the examination. The following topics are covered:

- Network security
- Sources and Types of Threats
- Firewalls and the Cisco Adaptive Security Appliance (ASA)
- Intrusion Detection and Prevention
- Virtual Private Networks (VPN)
- WLAN security

At the end of the chapter, several learning questions are given to evaluate the learning level from this chapter. The correct answers and solutions with complementary discussions are found in appendix A, "Answers to Chapters Learning Questions."

Chapter 10 Learning Questions

10-1 Which of the following is true about network security? (Select all that apply)

A. Today, threatening organizations, and companies by network attackers have increased exponentially and become very dangerous.

B. Attackers become very sophisticated and clever. Not only might they attack military, commerce and government networks, but also they might try to disrupt infrastructure services.

C. Attackers can extort organizations by threatening a denial of service (DoS) attack on the organizations' servers on the internet.

D. As an example, by one sophisticated attack, attackers can steal identity and credit card information for sometimes millions of people.

10-2 Which of the following is true about network security? (Select all that apply)

A. Network security is an important issue of every modern network design, and one that requires serious attention and clever working.

B. The bigger problem now is that almost anyone can become a hacker by downloading simple tools from the Internet.

C. A strong security policy then, is required for every up-to-date network.

D. It is easy to protect the network by closing the network completely from the internet and other public networks. However, internal threats still exist, and they may cause 60-80 percent of network security problems.

E. Closing a network is unsuitable for almost all modern networks, simply because these networks require access to the internet and other public networks.

F. The Computer Security Institute (CSI) and some respectable organizations give periodically reports for security threats. The reports confirm that threats from computer crime and other information security breaches continue to affect the networks and that the organizations will lose more and more money by computer crimes.

10-3 Try to decide if the following statement correctly depicts the firewalls.

"Firewalls represent the best-known security tool that can sit between the organization network and the unsecured Internet and any other public network."

A. Correct
B. Incorrect

10-4 Try to decide which option gets in which blank.

By looking at the _____ numbers and the _____, the firewall's can stop _____ and prevent certain ports and applications from getting packets into the organization network.

A. unsafe packets
B. application layer headers
C. transport layer port numbers

10-5 Try to decide if the following statement correctly depicts the firewalls.

"However, firewall cannot prevent the inside organization network attacks. Moreover, firewall cannot provide protection from all dangers of connecting to the internet."

    A. Correct
    B. Incorrect

10-6 Which of the following represents a kind of attack that can be occurred from inside the organization network?

    A. **Denial of service (DoS) attacks**
    B. **Reconnaissance attacks**
    C. **Access attacks**
    D. **Password Attacks**

10-7 Try to decide if the following paragraph correctly depicts the **Denial of service (DoS) attacks**.

"An attack whose purpose is to break or destroy any entity in the organization network. DoS attacks called destroyers, crashers, or flooders. Destroyers since it can destroy the hosts within the organization network, such as erasing data and software and destroying applications. Crashers since it can crash a host, which means that it can fail hosts or breaking the host's connection to the network. Flooders since it can flood the network with packets to make the network unusable, breaking the connection with organization's servers."

    A. Correct
    B. Incorrect

10-8 Try to decide if the following paragraph correctly depicts the **Reconnaissance attacks**.
"The goal of this kind of attack is gathering information to perform an access attack to the network hosts. An example is learning IP addresses and then trying to discover important machines in the network such as servers and then gather more information about services, and vulnerabilities. In most cases, it precedes an actual access or DoS attack and usually, it uses ping utility to do its work."

    A. Correct
    B. Incorrect

10-9 Try to decide if the following paragraph correctly depicts the **Access attacks**.

"This kind of attack is an attempt to steal data, typically important data such as financial information or customers list. These types of attacks, exploit known vulnerabilities in authentication services, FTP services, and web services."

    A. Correct
    B. Incorrect

10-10 Try to decide if the following paragraph correctly depicts the **Password Attacks**.

"A password attack usually refers to repeated attempts to identify user authentication information. These attacks are implemented using Trojan horse programs, IP spoofing, and packet sniffers."

    A. Correct
    B. Incorrect

10-11 Try to decide which option gets in which blank.

One tool that can be used to carry out any of these attacks is computer _____. A virus is a piece of a program that is transferred onto an undefending machine by an _____ or website download or by accessing some suspecting sites. Most computers use some type of _____ software, such as, TrendMicro to protect against known viruses and prevent them from harming the computer.

    A. viruses
    B. anti-virus
    C. e-mail attachment

10-12 TRUE/FALSE: To provide best protecting, the machine must be connecting to the internet or local antivirus server to update the software with up-to-date virus signatures, which is a list of known characteristics of all current viruses' types. These updates may be several times per hour. All packets entering the machine will be watched be the antivirus so that to protect the machine.

    A. TRUE
    B. FALSE

10-13 TRUE/FALSE: Besides external sources of attacks, there are several types of problems that could commonly occur inside the organization network, such as, Wirelessly accessing the organization network from home or unsafe location with infected laptops through WLAN that bypassing the organization firewall, Mobile Infection accessing the LAN by infected an employee laptop after taking it to home based Cable/DSL internet and Disgruntled employees that steal important information from the network servers before leaving the organization to another one. The last type maybe represents the most dangerous one. In addition, the physical security is an important thing that must be addressed well to prevent inside attack and misusing of the organization network.

    A. TRUE
    B. FALSE

10-14 Try to decide which option gets in which blank.

To prevent several types of inside attacks that can harm the organization network, a number of CISCO models exist that can work automatically and dynamically to defend the networks. _____ is a CISCO term that refers to automation in which the network devices automatically react to network problems. CISCO also uses the term "_____" to refer to security features included in routers and switches and other networking devices.

    A. *Self-defending network*
    B. *security in depth*

10-15 TRUE/FALSE: Network Admission Control (NAC) is one security tool in the CISCO security in-depth model that can help in preventing some types of attacks from inside the organization network.

    A. TRUE
    B. FALSE

10-16 Which of the following represents a NAC function? (Select all that apply)

    A. Monitoring the time of connections to an organization network.
    B. Monitoring the type of connections if it is a wireless device or wired device.
    C. Preventing a computer from connecting to the organization network until its virus definitions were updated and a machine is scanned recently with the full virus scan.
    D. Authenticating network clients, NAC includes a requirement that the user supply a username and password before being able to send other data into the organization network.

10-17 TRUE/FALSE: However, NAC does not prevent an employee from inside the organization network from causing harm, because the employee typically has a legal network authentication.

A. TRUE
B. FALSE

10-18 Which of the following is a tool that can be used for attack instead of viruses? (Select all that apply)

A. **Scanner**
B. **Spyware**
C. **Malware**
D. **Worm**
E. **Keystroke logger**
F. **Phishing**

10-19 Try to decide if the following statement correctly depicts the **Scanner** tool.

"This tool is used to discover the IP services and the operating systems that run on hosts by sending connection requests to different TCP and UDP ports, for different applications."

A. Correct
B. Incorrect

10-20 Try to decide if the following paragraph correctly depicts the **Spyware** tool.

"This virus is used to obtain important and sensitive information or private information, such as, credit card information from victim machines. It is also, used to track what the user does with the machine, and passing the information back to the attacker in the Internet to use it illegally."

A. Correct
B. Incorrect

10-21 Try to decide if the following statement correctly depicts the **Malware** tool.

"Refers to several types of malicious viruses, such as, spyware."

A. Correct
B. Incorrect

10-22 Try to decide if the following paragraph correctly depicts the **Worm** tool.

"Refers to self-propagating program that can quickly iterate itself around the organization networks and the Internet. It can perform DoS attacks on the organization sensitive devices, such as, servers."

A. Correct
B. Incorrect

10-23 Try to decide if the following paragraph correctly depicts the **Keystroke logger** tool.

"This virus is used to log all keystrokes and report this information to the attacker. By Loggers, authentication information to secure sites can actually be captured before this information leaves the client machine. The captured information can give the attacker access to the sensitive websites."

A. Correct
B. Incorrect

10-24 Try to decide if the following paragraph correctly depicts the **Phishing** tool.

"By this type of attack, a website sets up by an attacker that looks like a legitimate website of a well-known organization or a bank. The phisher often sends e-mails listing the illegitimate website's URL like the real organization. When people will apply and connect to the illegitimate website, and enter information such as their name, address, credit card number or social security number (in the U.S.), the attacker will take this information and use it illegally."

    A. Correct
    B. Incorrect

10-25 Try to decide if the following paragraph correctly depicts the firewalls.

"To filter unwanted traffic, firewalls are used to examine all packets entering and exiting the network core edge. Firewalls sit in the packet-forwarding path between two networks, the local organization network, and the unsecured network such as the internet. Based on many characteristics of the packets, such as, source and destination IP addresses, the transport layer (TCP and UDP) port numbers, and application layer headers, firewalls can determine the allowed traffic versus the disallowed traffic."

    A. Correct
    B. Incorrect

10-26 Try to decide if the following statement correctly depicts the firewalls.

"A network firewall must itself be rigid against security attacks. Unless a firewall rule that allows the traffic is configured, the firewall must disallow all packets."

    A. Correct
    B. Incorrect

10-27 Try to decide which option gets in which blank.
In the _____ between two networks the firewalls are sitting. In addition to local LAN interface, which connects the firewall to the _____ and another interface to the other network usually, the_____, the firewall has an interface to the _____ LAN, where the organization's public servers sit. The DMZ LAN is a place to put the organization's devices that need to be _____ from the internet. Figure 10-2 shows a typical design of such a network.
    A. packet-forwarding path
    B. secure organization network
    C. unsecured Internet
    D. demilitarized zone (DMZ)
    E. accessible

10-28 TRUE/FALSE: The firewall must be configured to know which interfaces are connected to the organization secure network (inside), unsecured network (outside), and DMZ parts of the network. To tell the firewalls which traffics are allowed and, which are not allowed, a series of rules must then be configured.

    A. TRUE
    F. FALSE

10-29 Which of the following is a typical flow that shown in Figure 10-2 with the dashed line? (Select all that apply)

    A. Allows web clients on the organization network (such as PC1) to access the web servers

(www.cisco.com.)
B. Allows web clients in the internet (such as PC2) to connect to DMZ servers (www.thaartechnologies.com and mail.thaartechnologies.com.)
C. Allows web clients on the organization network (such as PC1) to connect to DMZ servers (www.thaartechnologies.com and mail.thaartechnologies.com.)
D. Prevents web clients in the internet (such as PC2) from sending packets to web servers in the organization network (such as the internal web server thaar.thaartechnologies.com.)

10-30 Try to decide which option gets in which blank.

CISCO ASA appliances can provide in the overall _____ with a variety of tools that prevent problems such as _____, spyware, spam, and phishing. CISCO uses the term _____ to refer to the whole class of security tools that prevent these various problems-starting with "anti-." Several problems can be prevented using the CISCO ASA.

    A. in-depth security design
    B. viruses
    C. anti-x

10-31 Several problems can be prevented using the CISCO ASA. Which of the following problems can be solved by CISCO ASA? (Select all that apply)

    A. **Anti-virus**
    B. **Anti-spyware**
    C. **Anti-spam**
    D. **Anti-phishing**
    E. **URL filtering**
    F. **E-mail filtering**

10-32 Match each of the following ASA tools to its suitable definition.

    1. Anti-virus
    2. Anti-spyware
    3. Anti-spam
    4. Anti-phishing
    5. URL filtering
    6. E-mail filtering

        A. Based on virus signatures, the CISCO ASA scans network traffic to prevent the virus's transmission
        B. Preventing the spyware's transmission
        C. Cleaning the end user's e-mails from junk e-mail.
        D. Preventing the phishing attack from reaching the end users. The CISCO ASA monitors URLs sent in messages through the network, looking for the illegitimate website's URL inside the messages, and then blocking these URL's.
        E. Prevent users from connecting to unsafe sites or not useful sites.
        F. Protecting the organization network from e-mails with unsafe materials in addition to anti-spam filtering

10-33 TRUE/FALSE: Some types of attacks can be more sophisticated and cannot be easily recovered by anti-x tools. Such attacks may use of new bugs in the operating system.

    A. TRUE

B. FALSE

10-34 Try to decide which option gets in which blank.

To detect and to prevent the more sophisticated kinds of attacks, the network security engineer can use the _____ and _____. IDS and IPS tools detect these threats by watching the traffic, looking for attacks that use particular patterns of messages, and other characteristic.

      A. Intrusion Detection Systems (IDS)
      B. Intrusion Prevention Systems (IPS)

10-35 Try to decide which option gets in which blank.
Via_____, IDS tools receive a copy of packets, rather than being part of the packets'_____, rate and report if a threat is found, and potentially ask other devices, such as routers and firewalls, to help prevent the attack. On opposite to IDS tools, IPS tools sit in the packets' forwarding path and in addition to IDS capabilities, IPS can _____the traffic.

      A. a monitoring port
      B. forwarding path
      C. react and filter

10-36 TRUE/FALSE: IDS tools sit in the packets' forwarding path.

      A. TRUE
      B. FALSE

10-37 TRUE/FALSE: VPN or virtual private WAN creates a virtual-private network between sites through a public insecure network, such as, the internet. In spite of, VPN sends packets through the insecure internet, which is a public WAN network, VPN makes the communication secure, like a private leased line.

      A. TRUE
      B. FALSE
10-38 Try to decide which option gets in which blank.

VPNs allow the use of the _____ without the risk of others reading the data in transit and without the risks of accepting data from attacking hosts. VPNs use _____ in both VPN's endpoints, meaning that both endpoints can be sure that the other endpoint of the VPN connection is legitimate. In addition to that, VPNs _____ the transit packets between endpoints so that even if an attacker managed to obtain a copy of the packets as they overtake through the Internet, the attackers cannot understand the data.

      A. Internet
      B. Authentication
      C. Encrypt
10-39 TRUE/FALSE: VPNs use end-to-end encryption, in which the data remains encrypted while being forwarded through one or more routers. In addition to that, to encrypt data at the data link layer, link encryption can be used so the data is encrypted only as it passes over one data link.

      A. TRUE
      B. FALSE
10-40 Try to decide which option gets in which blank.
Two types of VPNs are found: an _____ and a _____. With an access VPN, the remote office's PC in _____typically encrypting the packets. A site-to-site intranet VPN typically connects virtually _____ of the same organization network. The encryption could be done for all devices using different kinds of hardware,

including purpose-built VPN concentrator hardware, routers, firewalls, or ASAs.

    A. **access VPN**
    B. **site-to-site intranet VPN**
    C. SOHO
    D. two sites

10-41 TRUE/FALSE: As stated above, WLANs introduce a number of vulnerabilities that do not exist for ELANs. Hackers can use WLAN vulnerabilities to access hosts in the ELAN of the organization network, or prevent services through a DoS attack and much more.

    A. TRUE
    B. FALSE

10-42 Match each of the following threat categories to its suitable definition.

    1. **War drivers**
    2. **Hackers**
    3. **Rogue AP**
    4. **Employees**

    A. To gain free Internet access, the attacker drives around, trying to find breakable security APs with internet accesses.
    B. To find information or deny services in the organization network, the hackers try to obtain an access to the organization network through the WLAN bypassing the firewalls.
    C. After the attacker captures packets from the existing WLAN, finding the SSID and cracking security keys, the attacker can set up a private AP, with the same settings, making the clients of the organization network to access the network through rogue AP capturing their information, such as, authentication details.
    D. Employees can easily install their own AP within the WLAN organization network. If this AP is without security this will give the attackers the way to enter the organization network from within that AP.

10-43 TRUE/FALSE: To protect the network against these attacks, three main types of tools can be used on a WLAN. These are:

- Mutual authentication
- Encryption
- Intrusion tools

    A. TRUE
    B. FALSE

10-44 Try to decide which option gets in which blank.

To prevent a connection to a _____, mutual authentication must be used between the client and AP so that the client can confirm that the AP knows the right key. A _____ or a _____ is used during the authentication process, on both the client and the AP. The AP and the client can confirm that each of them does indeed know the right key value by using some mathematical algorithms. The key value is never sent through _____ during the mutual authentication process, so the attacker will not be able to _____the key value, even if the attacker is using any type of network analysis tool to copy every frame inside the WLAN.

    A. rogue AP
    B. key

C. secret password

D. the air

E. see, copy, or learn

10-45 Try to decide which option gets in which blank.

Encryption uses a _____ and a _____ to _____ the contents of the WLAN frame on both the client and the AP. An attacker cannot read the contents of the frames without the secret encryption key even an attacker may be able to intercept the frames.

A. secret key

B. mathematical formula

C. encrypt and decrypt

10-46 Try to decide which option gets in which blank.

These tools include Intrusion Detection Systems (IDS) and Intrusion Prevention Systems (IPS). CISCO also defines the _____ architecture. SWAN includes many tools; some of these tools can detect and identify _____.

A. Structured Wireless-Aware Network (SWAN)

C. rogue APs

10-47 What is the solution to the "war drivers" Vulnerability?

A. The use of encryption

B. The use of authentication

C. The use of IDS/SWAN

10-48 What is the solution to the "Hackers accessing a WLAN" Vulnerability?

A. The use of encryption

B. The use of authentication

C. The use of IDS/SWAN

10-49 What is the solution to the "Hackers accessing the organization network" Vulnerability?

A. The use of encryption

B. The use of authentication

C. The use of IDS/SWAN

10-50 What is the solution to the "Rogue AP" Vulnerability?

A. The use of encryption

B. The use of authentication

C. The use of IDS/SWAN

10-51 What is the solution to the "Employee AP installation" Vulnerability?

A. The use of encryption

B. The use of authentication

C. The use of IDS/SWAN

10-52 Which of the following is a WLAN security standard or de-facto standard?

A. WEP
B. 802.11a
C. 802.11g

10-53 Which of the following is a WLAN security standard or de-facto standard?

A. 802.11n
B. The interim CISCO solution
C. 802.11g

10-54 Which of the following is a WLAN security standard or de-facto standard?

A. 802.11
B. 802.11a
C. WPA

10-55 Which of the following is a WLAN security standard or de-facto standard?

A. WPA2
B. 802.11a
C. 802.11b

10-56 When WEP is ratified?

A. 1995
B. 1997
C. 2000

10-57 When interim CISCO solution is ratified?
A. 1995
B. 1997
C. 2001

10-58 When WPA is ratified?

A. 2003
B. 1997
C. 2000

10-59 When WPA2 is ratified?

A. 1995
B. 2005
C. 2000

10-60 Which of the following organizations is ratified WEP?

A. IEEE
B. Wi-Fi
C. CISCO

10-61 Which of the following organizations is ratified the interim CISCO solution?

    A. Oracle
    B. Wi-Fi
    C. CISCO

10-62 Which of the following organizations is ratified WPA?

    A. IEEE
    B. Wi-Fi
    C. CISCO

10-63 Which of the following organizations is ratified WPA2?

    A. IEEE
    B. Wi-Fi
    C. CISCO

10-64 TRUE/FALSE: WEP was the original 802.11 security standard, and it provided only weak authentication and encryption.

    A. TRUE
    B. FALSE

10-65 TRUE/FALSE: WEP's authentication and encryption can be cracked by a hacker today, using easily downloaded tools.

    A. TRUE
    B. FALSE

10-66 TRUE/FALSE: Two main problems are found with WEP:

- **Static Preshared Keys (PSK)**
- **Easily cracked keys**

    A. TRUE
    B. FALSE

10-67 Try to decide if the following paragraph correctly depicts the **Static Preshared Keys (PSK)** problem.

"Each client and each AP should be configured by the key value and there is no dynamic way to exchange the keys without administrator intervention. This made the configuration so difficult and especially in a large organization network and its security very weak since the employees could not change the keys on a regular basis."

    A. Correct
    B. Incorrect

10-68 Try to decide if the following paragraph correctly depicts the **Easily cracked key's** problems.
"It is 64 bits key with only 40 bits were the actual unique key. This made it easier to predict the key's by a hacker today."

    A. Correct

B. Incorrect

10-69 TRUE/FALSE: The SSID cloaking, is not part of WEP standard. It is created to address some problems, and to change the process by which clients associate with an AP. The AP's SSID must be known before a client can communicate with the AP.

   A. TRUE
   B. FALSE

10-70 Which of the following is part of the client association process? (Select all that apply)

   A. A periodic Beacon frame is sent by the AP, every 100 ms by default. The Beacon lists the AP's SSID and other configuration information.
   B. The client learns about all APs in the range by listening for Beacons on all available channels.
   C. Then the client association process is made with the AP with the strongest signal (the default), or with the AP with the strongest signal for the currently preferred SSID.
   D. The authentication process occurs as soon as the client has associated with the AP.

10-71 TRUE/FALSE: The Beacons allow an attacker to easily and quickly find out information about the APs and then gain access to the organization network. To solve this problem, SSID cloaking is used. SSID cloaking tells the AP to stop sending periodic Beacon frames. However, clients still need to be able to find the APs. A null SSID client sends a Probe message, which causes each neighbor AP to respond with its SSID. Therefore, attackers can still find all the APs.

   A. TRUE
   B. FALSE

10-72 TRUE/FALSE: The MAC address filtering is a second extra feature often implemented along with WEP. A list of allowed WLAN MAC addresses is configured within the AP, makes it filter the frames sent by WLAN clients whose MAC address is not in the list. It is not secure enough, and it can be broken by attackers.

   A. TRUE
   B. FALSE

10-73 Which of the following are the main features of CISCO security enhancements to WEP? (Select all that apply)

   A. Dynamic key exchange using a CISCO proprietary version of TKIP. (as opposite to WEP static preshared keys)
   B. User authentication using 802.1x
   C. A new encryption key for each packet

10-74 TRUE/FALSE: The use of a dynamic key exchange process provides several advantages. It improves the WLAN security, the clients and AP can dynamically change the keys, and without administrator interventions, which are slower processes. The security is improved since if the key is discovered, the effect can be short-lived since it is changing dynamically. In addition, a new key can be delivered for each packet, allowing encryption to use a different key each time, which removes the possibility of discovering the encryption by hackers.

   A. TRUE
   B. FALSE

10-75 TRUE/FALSE: WPA essentially performed the same functions as the CISCO proprietary interim solution, but with different details and both de-facto standards are incompatible.

A. TRUE
B. FALSE

10-76 Try to decide which option gets in which blank.

As an example, dynamic key exchange is used in WPA using the _____. IEEE 802.1x user authentication or simple device authentication using _____ can be used in WPA. The encryption algorithm of WPA uses the _____, which is similar to the process used in the CISCO-proprietary solution.

    A. Temporal Key Integrity Protocol (TKIP)
    B. preshared keys
    C. Message Integrity Check (MIC) algorithm

10-77 TRUE/FALSE: To provide better security than CISCO interim and WPA, the IEEE ratified the 802.11i security standard in 2005. It includes dynamic key exchange, much stronger encryption, and user authentication. However, the IEEE 802.11i is not backward-compatible with either WPA or the CISCO interim standards.

    A. TRUE
    B. FALSE

10-78 Try to decide which option gets in which blank.

New encryption standard is used in IEEE 802.11i that is the _____. _____ and much more secure _____ are used in AES making its encryption better than the interim CISCO and WEP standards. The Wi-Fi Alliance calls 802.11i _____.

    A. Advanced Encryption Standard (AES)
    B. Longer encryption keys
    C. encryption algorithms
    D. WPA2

10-79 Which of the following security keys is used in the WEP standard?

    A. Static
    B. Dynamic
    C. Static and Dynamic

10-80 Which of the following security keys is used in the CISCO WLAN Security standard?

    A. Static
    B. Dynamic
    C. Static and Dynamic

10-81 Which of the following security keys is used in the WPA standard?

    A. Static
    B. Dynamic
    C. Static and Dynamic

10-82 Which of the following security keys is used in the IEEE 802.11i standard?

    A. Static
    B. Dynamic

C. Static and Dynamic

10-83 TRUE/FALSE: Device authentication in WEP standard is weak.

A. TRUE
B. FALSE

10-84 TRUE/FALSE: Device authentication in CISCO WLAN Security standard is weak.

A. TRUE
B. FALSE

10-85 TRUE/FALSE: Device authentication in WPA standard is weak.

A. TRUE
B. FALSE

10-86 TRUE/FALSE: Device authentication in WPA2 standard is weak.

A. TRUE
B. FALSE

10-87 Which of the following user authentication is used in WEP standard?

A. None
B. 802.1x

10-88 Which of the following user authentication is used in CISCO WLAN Security standard?

A. None
B. 802.1x

10-89 Which of the following user authentication is used in WPA standard?

A. None
B. 802.1x

10-90 Which of the following user authentication is used in WPA2 standard?

A. None
B. 802.1x

10-91 Which of the following encryption is used in WEP standard?

A. Weak
B. TKIP
C. AES

10-92 Which of the following encryptions is used in the CISCO WLAN Security standard?

A. Weak
B. TKIP
C. AES

10-93 Which of the following encryptions is used in the WPA standard?

    A. Weak
    B. TKIP
    C. AES

10-94 Which of the following encryptions is used in the IEEE 802.11i standard?

    A. Weak
    B. TKIP
    C. AES

Conclusion

Congratulations! You have completed the book and ready for the CCENT certification. I wish you could overtake the CCENT/CCNA certification with full marks. CCENT is the essential certification for CISCO internetworking routing and switching track. Understanding CCENT topics and passing this exam successfully, are crucial for those who want to be an Internetworking professional, and is an easy mission, just follow this book. The current track of CCNA routing and switching contains two exams and two certifications, the CCENT/ICND1 exam 640-822 and the ICND2 exam 640-816. However, it is possible to obtain the CCNA exam 640-802 by one exam and one certification. Now, CCENT and CCNA are the most popular entry-level networking and internetworking certification programs. CCENT certification proves that you have a firm foundation in the networking and internetworking field, and it also proves that you have a solid understanding of IP protocol, IP routing, switching, routing and many of CISCO device's configurations.

This book was developed and written not just to tell you the topics of the internetworking, but to make you professional in this field and to help you learn how to apply the topics. No matter what your experience level in this field, the book will help you overtake the exams successfully with full scores. The book is designed to make you pass the CCENT/CCNA certification with extreme confidence and total marks from the first time, in one week.

You must gain the following goals after reading this book:

- Understanding perfectly all CISCO CCNA/CCENT topics for 640-822 (ICND1) exam as well as the ICND1 material of the 640-802 (CCNA) exam
- Obtaining the certification in one week and with one book
- Reading all expected Q&As that can be faced by 640-822 (CCENT) exam as well as the ICND1 part of the 640-802 (CCNA) exam
- Reading the information easily, which makes you prepare the exam directly
- Becoming familiar with CISCO switches, CISCO routers, CISCO internetworking and the associated protocols and technologies
- Taking a solid step to become a professional Internetworking engineer

GOOD LUCK
Thaar AL_Taiey
JAN 2011

Appendix A
Answers to the Chapters
Learning Questions

Answers to the Chapter 1 Learning Questions

1-2.   B, A.
1-3.   A, B.
1-4.   A, B.
1-5.   A-F.
1-6.   B.
1-7.   A.
1-8.   A.
1-9.   A-E.
1-10.   A-J.
1-11.   A-C.
1-12.   A-H.
1-13.   A.
1-14.   C, Γ-II.
1-15.   A-F, H-J, M. Today, applications such as word processing and spreadsheets are not common network-based applications, but these applications will be common in the future with MS Office Live.
1-16.

1-	Speed	H
2-	Security	A
3-	Manageability	B
4-	Availability	E
5-	Scalability	C
6-	Reliability	D
7-	Cost	F
8-	Topology	G

1-16.   A, B, C.
1-17.   B, A.
1-18.

1.	physical topology	A
2.	logical topology	B

1-19.   A. Bus star and ring topologies represent the primary categories of physical topologies.
1-20.   A.
1-21.

A	2
B	1

1-22.   A, B, D.
1-23.   A.
1-24.   A.
1-25.

A	1
B	2

1-26.   A, B, C, D.
1-27.   A.
1-28.   A.
1-29.

A	1
B	1
C	2

1-30.   A.
1-31.   A.
1-32.   A, B.
1-33.   A, B C.
1-34.   D.

1-35.   A-D.
1-36.   A, B.
1-37.   A-C.
1-38.   D-G.
1-39.   A.
1-40.

1	A
2	F
3	D
4	G
5	E
6	B
7	F
8	C

1-41.   A-E.
1-42.   A.
1-43.   A.
1-44.   A.
1-45.   A, B, E.
1-46.

1	A
2	B

1-47.   A, B.
1-48.   A.
1-49.   A.
1-50.   A.
1-51.   A.
1-52.   A.
1-53.   A, C. This is a LAN.
1-54.   A, B. This is a WAN.
1-55.   A.
1-56.   A, B, C, D. Hub is a simple networking device that used to connect devices and from a LAN.
1-57.   A, B, C. Network can be segmented using Bridges, Switches or routers.
1-58.   A, B, C, D. Routers are used to create an internetwork and break up broadcast domains as well as collision domains.
1-59.   A. It is correct for the routers.
1-60.   B, C, F, G.
1-61.   A, C, D.
1-62.   C.
1-63.   A, B, C, D. These are the main functions of the routers.
1-64.   A, B, C, E, D. These are the router operations.
1-65.   A, B, C. Switches main function is optimizing network performance.
1-66.   A, B, C. Every single port on a switch represents its own collision domain.
1-67.

1.	Hub	A
2.	Switch	B
3.	Router	C

1-68.   A. Basically, switch is just a multiple-port bridge with more intelligent functions.
1-69.   A.
1-70.   A.
1-71.   A, B.
1-72.   A.
1-73.   A.

1-74. A-G.
1-75. A.
1-76. A, B.
1-77. B, A, C. This is a reference model.
1-78. A, B, C.
1-79. A.
1-80. A. It is correct.
1-81. A, B, C, D, E, F. This is the layered approach.
1-82. A-C. These are the benefits of using the layered approach.
1-83. B, C. Computerized devices from multiple vendors can work the same network; this is by creating products to meet the same networking standards.
1-84. A, B. modular approach divides the network communication process into smaller and simpler components, thus helping component development, design, and troubleshooting.
1-05. A, B. Several venders can participate in developing the same Software.
1-86. B, A, C.
1-87. A-C.
1-88. A.
1-89. A-C.
1-90.

1.	Application	A
2.	Presentation	B
3.	Session	C
4.	Transport	D
5.	Network	E
6.	data link	F
7.	Physical	G

1-91. A, B.
1-92. A.
1-93. A-H.
1-94. A-J.
1-95. A-G.
1-96. A-C.
1-97. A-E.
1-98. A-G.
1-99. A-G.
1-100. A-C.
1-101. A, B.
1-102. A-E.
1-103. A.
1-104. B-F.
1-105. A, B.
1-106. A, B, C.
1-107. A, B, C, D.
1-108. A, B, C.
1-109. A, B, C, D, E.
1-110. A, B, C.
1-111. A-D.
1-112. A, B.
1-113. A.
1-114. A, B, C. Framing is the main function of this layer.
1-115. D, E.
1-116. A, B. The main duties of this layer are sending bits and receiving bits.

1-117.   A. Yes, Some of the networking devices operate at all seven layers of the OSI model. The following is a list of some of these devices:
- Network hosts
- Gateways
- Web and application servers
- Network management stations

1-118.   C.

1-119.   A.

1-120.   F.

1-121.

1.	Application	G
2.	Presentation	D
3.	Session	E
4.	Transport	F
5.	Network	B
6.	data link	C
7.	Physical	A

1-122.   F.

1-123.   A-B.

1-124.   A-D.

1-125.   A.

1-126.   A.

1-127.   A-C.

1-128.   A-E.

1-129.   A.

1-130.   B. "Encapsulation is defined as the process of adding a header in front of data (and possibly adding a trailer at L2 as well)."

1-131.   A.

1-132.   D.

1-133.   E.

1-134.   C.

1-135.

1.	Step 1	A
2.	Step 2	B
3.	Step 3	C
4.	Step 4	D
5.	Step 5	E
6.	Step 6	F
7.	Step 7	G
8.	Step 8	H

1-136.   A.

1-137.

1.	Transport	C
2.	Network	D
3.	data link	B
4.	Physical	A

1-138.   A.

1-139.   A-E.

1-140.   A-F.

1-141.   A-D.

1-142.   A.

1-143.   A, B.

1-144.   A.

1-145. A.
1-146. A.
1-147. A.
1-148. A-F
1-149. A.
1-150. F.
1-151. A.
1-152. A-D.
1-153. A.
1-154. A.
1-155. B.
1-156. C.
1-157. A,
1-158. A.
1-159. B.
1-160. A.
1-161. B.
1-162. A.
1-163. C.
1-164. A.
1-165. C.
1-166. A.
1-167. A.
1-168. A.
1-169.
    1.   C.
    2.   B.
    3.   A.
1-170. A-E.
1-171.
    1.   B.
    2.   A.
    3.   C.
1-172.
    1.   C.
    2.   B.
    3.   A.
1-173.
    1.   D.
    2.   B.
    3.   A, C, E.
1-174.
    1.   A.
    2.   B.
    3.   C, D.
1-175.
    1.   A.
    2.   A,
    3.   A, B.
1-176.
    1.   A.
    2.   A.
    3.   B.

4.	A.
5.	C.
1-177.	A.
1-178.	D.
1-179.	A.
1-180.	B.
1-181.	A.
1-182.	A.
1-183.	A.
1-184.	A-D.
1-185.	A.
1-186.	A.
1-187.	A-D.
1-188.	B.
1-189.	A.
1-190.	B, C.
1-191.	A-C.
1-192.	A-E.
1-193.	A, B.
1-194.	A.
1-195.	A.
1-196.	B.
1-197.	A.
1-198.	A-C.
1-199.	D.
1-200.	A.
1-201.	A.
1-202.	A.
1-203.	A-C.
1-204.	A-B.
1-205.	A.
1-206.	A-G.
1-207.	A.
1-208.	A-F.
1-209.	A.
1-210.	A.
1-211.	A.
1-212.	A-C.
1-213.	A.
1-214.	A.
1-215.	A.
1-216.	A-D.
1-217.	A.
1-218.	A.
1-219.	
1.	A, B, C, D.
2.	E, F, G, H.
3.	E, I-M.
1-220.	B, C.
1-221.	B, C, E.
1-222.	A.
1-223.	A.
1-224.	A.

1-225. A.
1-226. A-C.
1-227.
    1.   A, B, C.
    2.   D, E.
    3.   F, G.
1-228. A.
1-229. A-F.
1-230. A, B, E.
1-231. A.
1-232. A.
1-233. A.
1-234. A-C.
1-235. A
1-236. A-D.
1-237. A-G.
1-238.
    1.   PRE   A
    2.   SFD   B
    3.   DA   C
    4.   SA   C
    5.   L/T   D
    6.   D&P   E
    7.   FCS   F
1-239.
    1.   PRE   A
    2.   SFD   B
    3.   DA   C
    4.   SA   D
    5.   L/T   E
    6.   D&P   F
    7.   FCS   G
1-240. A.
1-241. A-C.
1-242.
    1.   Unicast   A, B, C.
    2.   Multicast   D, E.
    3.   Broadcast   F, G.
1-243. B, C.
1-244. A.
1-245. B, C.
1-246. A, C, D.
1-247. A, B.
1-248. A.
1-249. A.
1-250.
    1.   Directed Broadcast   A, B, C.
    2   Limited Broadcast   D, E, F, G.
1-251. A.
1-252. A.
1-253. A.
1-254.
    1.   MAC addresses   A.

2.	Burned-in address (BIA)	B.
3.	Universally administered addresses (UAA)	C.

1-255. A.
1-256. A-B, D-F, H-I.
1-257. A.
1-258. B.
1-259. B, C.
1-260. B.
1-261. B, C, E.
1-262. B. The first one is wrong since the MAC address can be used to direct data to group of hosts.
1-263. B, E.
1-264. A.
1-265. A.
1-266. A.
1-267. A, B.
1-268. B.
1-269. B. Length not origin.
1-270. A.
1-271. A.
1-272. A.
1-273. A.
1-274. B.
1-275. A.
1-276. D.
1-277. B.
1-278. A, D.
1-279. A.
1-280. A.
1-281. C, B, D, A.
1-282. A-H.
1-283. A.
1-284. A-F.
1-285. A, C.
1-286. A.
1-287. C.
1-288. A.
1-289. A.
1-290. A.
1-291. A-C.
1-292. A-D.
1-293. A.
1-294. A.
1-295. B.
1-296. A.
1-297. A-J.
1-298.

1.	Cat 1	A
2.	Cat 2	B
3.	Cat 3	C
4.	Cat 4	D
5.	Cat 5	E
6.	Cat 5e	F
7.	Cat 6	G

	8.	Cat 6a	H
	9.	Cat 7	I

1-299. A.
1-300. A-E.
1-301. A-G.
1-302. A.
1-303. A-E.
1-304. A.
1-305. A.
1-306. E.
1-307. A-F.
1-308.

	1,	Cat 1	F
	2	Cat 2	D
	3.	Cat 3	E
	4.	Cat 4	B
	5.	Cat 5	G
	6.	Cat 5e	C
	7.	Cat 6	A

1-309. A, B.
1-310. A, C.
1-311. C, F-H. Straight-through cables are used when connecting devices that use the opposite pairs of pins to transmit data.
1-312. A.

Answers to the Chapter 2 Learning Questions

2-1.   A. The DoD model is a concentrated version of the OSI model. It is comprised of four layers, instead of seven layers in the OSI model.

2-2.   D. DoD model is comprised of four layers, instead of seven layers in OSI model.

2-3.   A, B, C, D. DoD model is comprised of four layers. These are; the process/application layer, The Host-to-Host layer, The Internet layer and the Network access layer.

2-4.   A. A vast array of protocols combines at each layer of the DoD model to integrate the various activities and duties.

2-5.
   1.   A, B. All user-related functions are implemented in this layer.
   2.   C, D, E. This is an intermediate layer between the process/application layer and the internet layer.
   3.   F, G, H, I. All network communication related-functions are implemented in this layer.
   4.   J, K, L. All physical hardware related-functions are implemented in this layer.

2-6.   A, D, C. The top three layers in the OSI model correspond to process/application layer in the DoD model.

2-7.   D. The Transport layer in OSI model corresponds to Host-to-Host layer in the DoD model.

2-8.   E. The network layer in OSI model corresponds to Internet layer in the DoD model.

2-9.   F, G. The bottom two layers in OSI model correspond to Network access layer in the DoD model. The network access layer is responsible for putting frames on the wire and pulling frames off the wire.

2-10.   C. While both models are alike in design and concept and have similar functions in similar places, how those functions occur is different.

2-11.   A.

2-12.   A-E. There are many functions for this layer. The most common tasks are listed in this question.

2-13.   A-M. All these protocols/services are working in this layer. Most of them are user-oriented applications.

2-14.   A, B, C. These are the main Telnet features.

2-15.   A, B, C. Telnet is a text-mode virtual terminal, and it cannot give any GUI ability.

2-16.   A. It is mainly a terminal emulation to the remote server.

2-17.   A, B. All are true about SSH.

2-18.   B, A. Users begin a Telnet session by running the Telnet client software and then logging on to the Telnet server.

2-19.   A, B, C. Operating as a protocol, FTP is used by applications. As a program, it is employed by users to perform file tasks manually.

2-20.   A-D. These are the main FTP benefits.

2-21.   A, B, C. Remote files can be transferred easily with low-latency using FTP.

2-22.   A, B, C. FTP session begins by accessing the FTP server and then users are subject to an authenticated login that is probably secured with usernames and passwords implemented by system administrators to restrict access.

2-23.   A. Limited access into FTP server can be gained by logging using "anonymous" username.

2-24.   B. FTP cannot be used to execute remote files as programs if it is adopted as a protocol or as a program.

2-25.   A-D. TFTP is used for transferring public files.

2-26.   A. TFTP can do nothing but send and receive files.

2-27.   A-F. TFTP is used to download a new IOS (Internetworking Operating System) to CISCO routers.

2-28.   A-D. NFS is mainly used to provide file sharing between disparate file systems.

2-29.   A. NFS allows for a portion of the RAM on the NFS server machine to store NFS client files transparently.

2-30.   A. It is used for disparate file systems.

2-31.   A. Since NFS allows file sharing; it provides remote file access.

2-32.   A, B. SMTP uses a spooled, or queued, method of mail delivery on the internet.

2-33.   A-E. In this sequence, SMTP is working.

2-34.   C. SMTP is used to send messages.

2-35.   D. POP3 (Post Office Protocol version 3) is used to receive messages at the destination site.

2-36.   A. SMTP uses a spooled, or queued, method of mail delivery.

2-37.   C, A, B. POP3 is used by client e-mail applications for recovery of mail from a mail server.

2-38.   A, B. LPD is one of the Daemons in the server that provide printer sharing.

2-39.   B. LPR program is used to manage printer jobs.

2-40.   A. LPD is used as a background process to provide printer sharing.

2-41.   A, B. X-window server must be installed and configured first, and then X-window client can be defined.

2-42.   A. X window defines a protocol for the writing of GUI-based C/S applications.

2-43.   A-C. SNMP can be adopted by stand-alone devices, and it can be embedded with NOS.

2-44.   A-C. SNMP can be configured to prevent overloading the network.

2-45.   A. When all is well, SNMP receives something called a baseline. Which is a report delimiting the operational traits of a healthy network.

2-46.   B. When abnormal events occur, agents send a trap to the management station.

2-47.   A.

2-48.   A-D.

2-49.   A.

2-50.   A.

2-51.   A-C.

2-52.   A-C. It resolves thaartechnologies.com automatically to its unique IP address on the Internet.

2-53.   A, B, C. It mainly makes possible using names like www.thaartechnologies.com instead of using www.thaartechnologies.com IP address.

2-54.   A-C. MAC addresses are not used.

2-55.   B, C, A. A FQDN is a hierarchy that can logically locate a system based on its domain identifier.

2-56.   A.

2-57.   B. When **ip domain-name thaartechnologies.com** command is defined on the router, the suffix (thaartechnologies.com) will be appended to each request trying to access thaartechnologies.com domain.

2-58.   A-C. BootP stands for **Bootstrap Protocol**.

2-59.   A, B, D. Many benefits can be obtained by using BootP.

2-60.   A-C. Diskless workstation negotiates the server to find its IP address.

2-61.   B. BootP provides diskless workstation by its IP address.

2-62.   A-C. All these parameters can be provided by BootP server.

2-63.   B. Usually, the TFTP protocol is used for this purpose.

2-64.   A.

2-65.   A-E. DHCP has a great advantage in large networks (3000 users and more).

2-66.   A-F. There are a lot of information a DHCP server can provide to a host when the host is registering for an IP address with the DHCP server. However, DHCP server is not designed to provide Proxy information to a host.

2-67.   A-C. Host registers its MAC address in the DHCP server database.

2-68.   A-E. DHCP (dynamic BootP) =BootP (MAC addresses entered manually) + lot of information (Subnet mask, DNS, default gateway, WINS …etc.) – OS booting abilities.

2-69.   B. It provides IP address with a lot of information.

2-70.   A. All types of hardware can be used as a DHCP server, including CISCO routers.

2-71.   A.

2-72.   A, B, D, E.

2-73.   A.

2-74.   A.

2-75.   A.

2-76.   A-C.

2-77.

1.	Bandwidth	A
2.	Delay	A
3.	Jitter	A
4.	Loss	A

2-78.

1.	Bandwidth	B
2.	Delay	B
3.	Jitter	B
4.	Loss	A

2-79.

1.	Bandwidth	B/C
2.	Delay	A
3.	Jitter	A
4.	Loss	A

2-80.

1.	Bandwidth	B
2.	Delay	B
3.	Jitter	C
4.	Loss	C

2-81.

1.	Bandwidth	A/B
2.	Delay	B
3.	Jitter	C
4.	Loss	C

2-82.

1.	Bandwidth	B
2.	Delay	C
3.	Jitter	C
4.	Loss	C

2-83.

1.	Bandwidth	C
2.	Delay	C
3.	Jitter	C
4.	Loss	C

2-84. A-E. As soon as Host-to-host layer receives a data stream from upper-layer, it processes it and makes it ready for suitable transmission type.

2-85. A, B. Two protocols are implemented in Host-to-Host layer. These are TCP and UDP.

2-86. A-G. TCP is the core of TCP/IP protocol.

2-87. A-C. Applications used TCP to guarantee their data transmission.

2-88. B. Only reliable communication creates a virtual circuit before data transmission began.

2-89. A-E. Virtual circuit should be established before the sender starts sending data.

2-90. C, B, A. Before a transmitting host starts to send segments down the model, the sender's TCP protocol contacts the destination's TCP protocol to create a virtual circuit.

2-91. B. TCP can be considered as a block to a segment converter.

2-92. A. TCP receives a block of information.

2-93. A. TCP (on the sender site) numbers and sequences each segment before transmission to the destination site.

2-94. B-F. TCP is a full-duplex, connection-oriented, reliable, and accurate protocol.

2-95. A, E, F. A connection-oriented session creates a virtual circuit (call setup), transfers data, and then releases the virtual circuit (call termination).

2-96. A. TCP sets up a virtual circuit before transmitting any data. This creates a reliable session and it is known as a connection-oriented session.

2-97. D. The Transport layer creates virtual circuits between hosts before transmitting any data.

2-98. A. TCP (on the transmitting host) segments a data stream from upper layers and prepares it for the network layer. The network layer then routes the segments as packets through an internetwork. The packets are handed to the receiving host's Transport layer protocol, which rebuilds the data stream to hand to upper-layer applications or protocols.

2-99. A. TCP (on the receiving host) rebuilds the data stream to hand to upper-layer applications or protocols.

2-100.   A.

2-101.   A. From the number of fields in the header of TCP, it clears that TCP has many overheads.

2-102.   A-I. Application developers can use the UDP in place of TCP.

2-103.   A-D. It is a thin protocol as compared with TCP.

2-104.   A-C. It only segments the block of information, numbers these segments and send them down the model to the destination site.

2-105.   A. UDP breaks large blocks of information into segments.

2-106.   A-D.

2-107.   A. UDP receives information in block form.

2-108.   B. UDP does not create a virtual circuit.

2-109.   B. UDP only numbers the segments and not sequencing them at the sender host. UDP does not care in which order the segments arrive at the destination host. After numbers the segments, UDP sends them off and forgets about them. It does not follow through, check up on them, or even allow for an acknowledgment of safe arrival. Because of this, it is referred to as unreliable protocol.

2-110.   A. This is one reason for using UDP rather than TCP.

2-111.   B. UDP is an unreliable protocol. UDP sends segments down the model and forgets about them. It does not follow through, check up on them, or even allow for an acknowledgment of safe arrival.

2-112.   A, C. UDP is an unreliable, connectionless protocol. It adds a very low overhead as compared with TCP.

2-113.   B. UDP works at Host-to-Host Layer and does not create a virtual circuit.

2-114.   D. UDP uses unreliable, connectionless communication between hosts when transmitting data.

2-115.   A-J. These are the main differences between the two protocols. These differences must be taken in our account when choosing, which protocols are playing.

2-116.   A, B. Application developer uses TCP for reliability and UDP for faster transfers.

2-117.   A, B.

2-118.   C. VoIP is an example of the application that uses and must use TCP because of its sequencing.

2-119.   A. UDP (on the transmitting host) segments a data stream from upper layers and prepares it for the network layer. The network layer then routes the segments as packets through an internetwork. The packets are handed to the receiving host's Transport layer protocol, which rebuilds the data block to hand to upper-layer applications or protocols.

2-120.   A. UDP (on the receiving host) rebuilds the data block to hand to upper-layer applications or protocols.

2-121.   B. From the number of fields in the header of UDP, it clears that UDP has very low overheads as compared with TCP.

2-122.   A, B. Host-to-Host protocols must use port numbers to communicate with upper layers.

2-123.   B. Port numbers keep track of different conversations crossing the network simultaneously.

2-124.   A. Originating-source port numbers are dynamically assigned by the source host, which will be some number starting at 1024.

2-125.   A. Depending on the destination application, the destination port number will be assigned.

2-126.   A. 1023 and below are defined in RFC 1700, which discusses what is called well-known port numbers (ex: ftp: 21, telnet: 23, smtp: 25, dns: 53, tftp: 69, www: 80, POP3: 110 ...etc.).

2-127.   B. Numbers 1024 and above are used by the upper layer to set up sessions with other hosts.

2-128.   B. Numbers 1024 and above are used by TCP to use as source and destination addresses in the TCP segment.

2-129.   A. The source host makes up the source port for TCP/UDP segments.

2-130.   A. Echo process uses 7/TCP/UDP.

2-131.   D. Ftp process uses 21/TCP.

2-132.   D.

2-133.   A. Telnet process uses 23/TCP.

2-134.   B. SSH process uses 22/TCP

2-135.   B. SMTP process uses 25/TCP.

2-136.   B. Domain (DNS) process uses 53/TCP/UDP.

2-137.   C. Tftp process uses 69//UDP.

2-138.   B. Http (www) process uses 80/TCP.

2-139. D. POP3 process uses 110/UDP.
2-140. A. Nntp process uses 119/TCP/UDP.
2-141. B. News process uses 144/TCP/UDP.
2-142. C. Snmp process uses 161/UDP.
2-143. A. HHTPS process uses SSL with 443/TCP.
2-144. A. UDP is a connection network service at the Transport layer, and DHCP uses this connectionless service. It uses port 67 for server and port 68 for client.
2-145. A. UDP is a connection network service at the Transport layer, and BootP uses this connectionless service. It uses port 67 for server and port 68 for diskless workstation.
2-146. A. UDP is a connection network service at the Transport layer, and NFS uses this connectionless service at port number 2049.
2-147. A. UDP is a connection network service at the Transport layer, and RPC uses this connectionless service at port number 111.
2-148. A
2-149. A-C.
2-150. A, B.
2-151. A.
2-152. B.
2-153. A.
2-154. A-F.
2-155. A-D.
2-156. A.
2-157. D. PC1 should resend the TCP segment numbered 6000 since PC1 received an acknowledgment of 6000, which means that the TCP segment with sequence number 6000 was lost during transmission. Notice that, TCP uses a concept called the forward acknowledgment, in which the acknowledgment field in the header lists the next-expected byte, not the last-received byte.
2-158.

1.	Multiplexing using ports	A
2.	Error recovery (reliability)	B
3.	Flow control using windowing	C
4.	Connection establishment and termination	D
5.	Ordered data transfer and data segmentation	E

2-159. A-D. Internet layer's is responsible for routing, addressing, packaging, and providing a single network interface to the upper layers.
2-160. A-D. All network roads lead to Internet layer and of course to IP.
2-161. A-D. All these protocols are implemented in this layer.
2-162. A-C. To prevent these, IP provides routing and one single network interface for upper-layer protocols.
2-163. A-C. All are true for IP and more, it is simply the core of TCP/IP.
2-164. A-D. Routing and IP addressing are the major benefits for this protocol.
2-165. A-E. The complete IP description can be found in RFC 791.
2-166. A, D. IP is a connectionless protocol, which means that IP does not exchange control information (called a handshake) to establish an end-to-end connection before transmitting data to the destination host. IP relies on protocols in other layers to establish the connection if connection-oriented services are required. IP also relies on protocols in another layer to provide error detection and error recovery. Because it contains no error detection or recovery code, IP is sometimes called an unreliable protocol.
2-167. A, B. The Network number is the software, or logical address (the street). The Device ID is the hardware address (the mailbox).
2-168. B. Packets are generated by the IP in this layer from the Transport layer segments.
2-169. B. IP receives information from the Host-to-Host layer protocols in a segment form.
2-170. A. Source and destination IP addresses are added in the sender site by IP protocol.
2-171. C. Only IP in the model is dealing with such complex tasks like routing.

2-172.   C. Network layer adds IP source and IP destination to packets and dealing with routing.

2-173.   A. This is a software, or logical, address and contains valuable encoded information greatly simplifying the complex task of routing.

2-174.   A. IP (on the transmitting host) packets a segment from Host-to-Host layer and prepares it for the Network access layer.

2-175.   A. IP (on the receiving host) rebuilds the segments to hand to Transport layer protocols.

2-176.   C. IP treats with other protocols using Protocol number. The protocol number is important. If the header did not carry the protocol information for the next layer, IP would not know what to do with the data carried in the packet.

2-177.   A. It correctly depicts this relationship. IP can send the data to either TCP port 6 or UDP port 17 (both hex addresses).

2-178.   A-J. These are some of the popular protocols, which can be specified in the protocol field.

2-179.   C. IP is used to address hosts and route packets through the internetwork.

2-180.   A. IP uses protocol number 6 to communicate with TCP.

2-181.   C. IP uses protocol number 17 to communicate with UDP.

2-182.   A-E. ICMP works at the network layer, and it can be used by IP for many different services.

2-183.   B. ICMP messages are carried as IP datagrams.

2-184.   B. ICMP is a management protocol and messaging service provider for IP.

2-185.   C. ICMP at the network layer provides management and messaging services for IP.

2-186.   A, E. Many different kinds of routing failures can be reported via the ICMP frame Destination Unreachable (type 3). Masks can be found using the Address Mask Request and Reply ICMP frames (type 17, 18). TTL (Time to live) and Redirection exists at the Network layer (IP) rather than the Transport layer (TCP, UDP).

2-187.   D. ICMP is used to send redirects back to an originating router.

2-188.   A. ICMP is the protocol at the Network layer that is used to send echo requests and replies for PING utility.

2-189.   D. ICMP is the protocol at the Network layer is used to send messages back to an originating router.

2-190.   A-E. It is important for IP communication. It is used by IP to convert software addresses to hardware addresses.

2-191.   A-E. In this sequence ARP is working.

2-192.   A. It correctly depicts ARP operation.

2-193.   A, C. ARP resolves the IP addresses to the Ethernet addresses.

2-194.   A. The media access control (MAC) address or physical address can be found by ARP protocol at the Internet layer.

2-195.   A. ARP broadcasts are in the datagrams form.

2-196.   B. ARP (on the sender site) adds IP addresses of both source and destination hosts and only the MAC address of the source host before transmission the ARP broadcast packet on the local network. It uses 00: 00: 00: 00: 00: 00 as Target hardware address and FF: FF: FF: FF: FF: FF (Ethernet broadcast) as Destination address in Ethernet header.

2-197.   D. ARP provides "IP address → MAC address" mapping.

2-198.   C. Network layer maps "IP address → MAC address."

2-199.   A. MAC address of the destination host must be resolved before data are transmitted.

2-200.   D. ARP translates the software (IP) software (logical) address to the (MAC) hardware or physical address.

2-201.   A-D. It is important for IP communication. It is used by the IP protocol to convert hardware addresses to software addresses.

2-202.   A, B. It is a reveres to the ARP operation.

2-203.   A. It correctly depicts the RARP operation.

2-204.   B, A. ARP resolves the Ethernet addresses to IP addresses.

2-205.   B. The IP address for diskless workstations can be found by RARP.

2-206.   A. RARP broadcasts are in the datagrams form.

2-207.   B. RARP (on the diskless workstation site) sends a broadcast message to the RARP server contains its MAC address.

2-208. E. RARP provides a MAC address → IP address mapping.

2-209. C, G. Network layer maps the IP address → MAC address using RARP and Application layer using BootP.

2-210. A. Initially a diskless machine asking for its IP address

2-211. E. RARP translates hardware (MAC) or physical address to software (IP) address.

2-212. A, C. BootP is working in the Process/Application layer, layer and it uses RARP.

2-213. A. DHCP application uses RARP to map MAC address → IP address.

2-214. A-F. Proxy ARP is not really a separate protocol, it is a service run by routers (Servers).

2-215. A. It is a software numeric identifier assigned to each machine on an IP network. It identifies the location of a device on the network.

2-216. A-B. It uniquely identifies hosts on the Internetwork and makes them communicate.

2-217. A-D. MAC address is hard-coded on a network interface card (NIC). IP address can be assigned manually by administrator or automatically by DHCP.

2-218. B. A hardware address is 6 bytes long (48 bits).

2-219. A. A logical IP address (version 4) is 4 bytes long (32 bits).

2-220. A. IP address consists of 32 bits of information. These bits are divided into four sections, referred to as octets or bytes, each containing 1 byte (8 bits).

2-221. A-C. All these examples represent the same IP address. Although hexadecimal is not used as often as dotted-decimal or binary when IP addressing is discussed, hexadecimal can be found in some applications. Windows Registry uses hex to store machine's IP address.

2-222. A.

2-223. B. IP address is a 32-bit, structured, or hierarchical address.

2-224. A-D. The disadvantage of the flat addressing scheme relates to routing. If every address were unique, all routers on the Internet would need to store the address of every single machine on the Internet. This would make efficient routing impossible and routing tables very big.

2-225. A, B. An example of network address is 172.17 in the IP address 172.17.40.11.

2-226. A-C. An example of node address is 40.11 in the IP address 172.17.40.11.

2-227. A. The internetwork professionals create classes of networks based on network size.

2-228. C. Five network classes are available for dividing internetwork.

2-229. A-E. All these network classes are the valid.

2-230. A. The figure correctly depicts the network classes.

2-231. A. According to leading bits checking, the efficient routing is ensured. For example, since a router knows that a Class A network address always starts with a 0, the router might be able to send a packet on its way after reading only the first bit of its address.

2-232. A-E. Class A is used for very big networks like Internet. For calculating the maximum number of hosts per each Class A network, the first address (all hosts bits are OFF) and the last address (all hosts bits are ON) are not considered.

2-233. B. The range is 1-126.

2-234. A. Class A provides a maximum of only 2^24-2=16,777,214 host addresses per network ID.

2-235. B. Only, the first bit in the first octet must always be set to 0 or OFF.

2-236. A. In Class A, the first octet can be 126.

2-237. D. Class A general format is Network.Node.Node.Node.

2-238. A. Class A provides a maximum of only 126 network IDs.

2-239. B. It is invalid. It represents the address of network 126.

2-240. B. It is invalid. It represents the broadcast address of network 126.

2-241. F. Only 126 is Class A address.

2-242. A. For very large network, such as Internet, Class A is used.

2-243. A. Class A can contain 16,777,214 host addresses per network ID.

2-244. A. Class A provides a maximum of only 126 network IDs.

2-245. A-E. Class B is used for medium-sized to large-sized networks. For calculating the maximum number of hosts per each Class B network, the first address (all hosts bits are OFF) and the last address (all hosts bits are ON) are not considered.

2-246. D. The range is 128-191.

2-247.   B. Class B provides a maximum of only 65,534 host addresses per network ID.
2-248.   C. The first bit must always be ON and the second bit must always be OFF.
2-249.   B. In Class B, the first octet can be 172.
2-250.   C. Class B general format is Network.Network.Node.Node.
2-251.   B. Class B provides a maximum of only 16,384 network IDs.
2-252.   B. It is invalid. It represents the address of network 191.
2-253.   B. It is invalid. It represents the broadcast address of network 191.
2-254.   B-D. 128, 172, 191 are Class B addresses.
2-255.   B. For medium-sized to large-sized networks, Class B is used.
2-256.   B. Class B can contain 65,534 host addresses per network ID.
2-257.   B. Class B provides a maximum of only 16,384 network IDs.
2-258.   B. Any address with a first octet value between 128 and 191 is a class B network.
2-259.   A-E. Class C is used for small networks. For calculating the maximum number of hosts per each Class C network, the first address (all hosts bits are OFF) and the last address (all hosts bits are ON) are not considered.
2-260.   F. The range is 192-223.
2-261.   C. Class C provides a maximum of only 254 host addresses per network ID.
2-262.   E. The first and second bits must always be ON and the third bit must always be OFF.
2-263.   C. In Class C, the first octet can be 200.
2-264.   B. Class C general format is Network.Network.Network.Node.
2-265.   C. Class C provides a maximum of only 2,097,152 network IDs.
2-266.   B. It is invalid. It represents the address of network 194.
2-267.   B. It is invalid. It represents the broadcast address of network 194.
2-268.   A, C, E. 223, 192, 195 are Class C addresses.
2-269.   C. For small networks, Class C is used.
2-270.   C. Class C can contain 254 host addresses per network ID.
2-271.   C. Class C provides a maximum number of network IDs (2^21).
2-272.   A. Class A provides 2^24-2 hosts per each Network ID.
2-273.   C. Class C provides 2^21 different Network IDs.
2-274.   A. Class A provides 2^7-2=126 different Network IDs.
2-275.   C. Class C provides 2^8-2=254 different hosts per each Network ID.
2-276.   B. It is illegal IP address. It is reserved for loopback tests, and it cannot be used as Class A address or Class B address.
2-277.   The solution as follows:
   244   Class E.
   225   Class D.
   222   Class C.
   190   Class B.
   125   Class A.
2-278.   A, C, E. Class B address in a binary form always starts with 10 as the first two bits in the first octet. However, be sure to apply all the rules. For example, 01111111.10101010.10101010.10101010 starts with 0 but it's invalid Class A. It is only used for loopback purposes.
2-279.   A.
2-280.
   1.   IPv4   A, B, E, H.
   2.   IPv6   C, D, F, G, I.

Answers to the Chapter 3 Learning Questions

3-1.   B. By Subnetting, one large network is divided into many smaller, easy manageable, more efficient networks.

3-2.   A. For all Classes, Subnetting strategy can be implemented.

3-3.   A-F. The overall network cost is raised by adopting Subnetting strategy.

3-4.   B.

3-5.   A.

3-6.   B.

3-7.   B.

3-8.   A.

3-9.   A.

3-10. A.

3-11. A. By taking bits from the host portion of the IP address, and reserve them to define the subnet address.

3-12. A. The more subnets per network, the fewer bits available for defining hosts, the lowest number of host/subnet.

3-13. A, C. To calculate the best subnet mask and to find which IP address class to use, the number of hosts and subnets must be determined at first.

3-14. A-D. Subnet mask is the 32-bit value that allows the recipient of IP packets to distinguish the network ID portion of the IP address from the host ID portion of the IP address.

3-15. A. Default subnet mask is used. The 255.255.255.255 cannot be used. It is considered a broadcast address.

3-16. A. Using Default subnet mask means the network does not have a subnet.

3-17. B. 255.255.255.255 cannot be used. It is considered a broadcast address.

3-18. A-D. Default subnet masks cannot be changed. For example, subnet mask 255.255.0.0 cannot be used for Class C IP addresses.

3-19. C. A non-subnetted class 'C' network that use a default subnet mask has 8 bits available for host machines. Thus the total number of hosts that can be addressed on such a network is equal to 2^8; minus the network number (w.x.y.0.) and the broadcast address (w.x.y.255), for 254 hosts.

3-20. A-F. These points represent the valid subnet masks for class C IP addresses. Mask 255.255.255.255 is used for broadcast and mask 255.255.255.254 is invalid, because using one bit to define hosts is incorrect.

3-21. B. Using the mask 255.255.255.128 for Subnetting Class C IP addressing will create 2 subnets 0 and 128. The host 194.165.141.2 falls in the 0-subnet range. Therefore, the 128-bit must be 0 or OFF.

3-22. A. Using the mask 255.255.255.128 for Subnetting Class C IP addressing will create 2 subnets 0 and 128. The host 194.165.141.185 falls in the 128-subnet range. Therefore, the 128-bit must be 1 or ON.

3-23. B. First, start by using the 256 mask, which in this case is 256-252=4. The first subnet is 4; the second subnet is 8; the third subnet is 12. The host (196.100.100.10) must be in the 196.100.100.8 subnet; the broadcast address is 196.100.100.11 and the valid host range is 196.100.100.9- 196.100.100.10.

3-24. A. First, start by using the 256 mask, which in this case is 256-248=8. The first subnet is 8; the second subnet is 16. The host (196.100.100.13) must be in the 196.100.100.8 subnet; the broadcast address is 196.100.100.15 and the valid host range is 196.100.100.9- 196.100.100.14.

3-25. D. First, start by using the 256 mask, which in this case is 256-240=16. The first subnet is 16; the second subnet is 32. The host (196.100.100.20) must be in the 196.100.100.16 subnet; the broadcast address is 196.100.100.31 and the valid host range is 196.100.100.17-196.100.100.30.

3-26. A. First, start by using the 256 mask, which in this case is 256-224=32. The first subnet is 32; the second subnet is 64; the third subnet is 96. The host (196.100.100.115) must be in the 96 subnet; the broadcast address is 196.100.100.127 and the valid host range is 196.100.100.97- 196.100.100.126.

3-27. C. First, start by using the 256 mask, which in this case is 256-192=64. The first subnet is 64; the second subnet is 128. The host (190) must be in the 196.100.100 128 subnet; the broadcast address is 196.100.100.191 and the valid host range is 196.100.100.127-196.100.100.190.

3-28. A. The first subnet is 0; the second subnet is 128. The host (196.100.100.222) must be in the 128 subnet; the broadcast address is 196.100.100.255 and the valid host range is 196.100.100.129-196.100.100.254.

3-29. B. 255 is invalid. 252 gives 62 subnets. 248 gives 30 subnets. 240 gives 14 subnets. 240 is the most accurate.

3-30. A. First, start by using the 256 mask, which in this case is 256-252=4. The first subnet is 4; the second subnet is 8. The host (194.100.100.5) must be in the 194.100.100.4 subnet; the broadcast address is 194.100.100.7 and the valid host range is 194.100.100.5- 194.100.100.6.

3-31. D. The 192.100.188.170 /26 means that only 2-bits are used for Subnetting or the mask is 255.255.255.192. the valid host range is 192.100.188.129-190.

3-32. B. By applying the same principle, 192.100.188.23/30 will be the broadcast address for subnet 20.

3-33. C. 192.100.188.24 is the subnet address of an IP 192.100.188.30/29.

3-34. B. By applying, the above rules yield a subnet address of 193.250.12.0. However, closer inspection yields that there is only one subnet bit in this Class C address - therefore, this is an illegal address/mask pair. If the router is configured to accept **subnet-zero**, two subnets can be defined to this Class C IP address.

3-35. D. When using a notation like this 192.168.10.0/24, the 24 stand for the number of bits used for the network portion.

3-36. D. By applying the Simplified GSS rules, yield answer D is the correct.

3-37. A. 252 = 6 bits, the number of subnets = (2^6)-2 = 62, the remaining 2 bits allow for 2 hosts: (2^2)-2 = 2.

3-38. D. Mask 224 allows for 6 subnets and 30 hosts/subnet. However, mask 240 allows for 14 subnets and 14 hosts/subnet, which is the most suitable masking for this case.

3-39. A-N. These points represent the valid subnet masks for class B IP addresses. Mask 255.255.255.255 is used for broadcast and mask 255.255.255.254 is invalid, because using one bit to define hosts is incorrect.

3-40. C. The Class B network address has 16 bits available for hosts addressing. This means that up to 14 bits can be used for subnetting since at least 2 bits must be left for host addressing.

3-41. B. There are 14 different patterns can be used to subnet Class B. address. For more details, please, see Q3-32.

3-42. C, The process of subnetting a Class B network is the same as for a Class C, except that, there are more host bits available for masking.

3-43. A. For example, 64.**0** is a Class B subnet address, and 127.**255** its broadcast address. The valid hosts' range will be 64.1-127.254. This addition is only required, if the number of Subnetting bits less than 8.

3-44. A. The subnet is 172.17.10.0/25. Host range 172.17.10.1-126/25 and the broadcast address is 172.17.10.127/25.

3-45. B. The subnet is 172.17.10.64/26. Host range 172.17.10.65-126/26 and the broadcast address is 172.17.10.127/26.

3-46. C. The subnet is 172.17.10.32/27. Host range 172.17.10.33-62/27 and the broadcast address is 172.17.10.63/27.

3-47. D. The subnet is 172.17.10.32/28. Host range 172.17.10.33-46/28 and the broadcast address is 172.17.10.47/28.

3-48. B. The subnet is 172.17.10.8/29. Host range 172.17.10.9-14/29 and the broadcast address is 172.17.10.15/29.

3-49. C. The subnet is 172.17.10.16/30. Host range 172.17.10.17-18/30 and the broadcast address is 172.17.10.19/30.

3-50. B. 240.0 provides 4 masking bits. 2^4-2=14 subnets. Other subnets are unsuitable.

3-51. A. 30 masking bit or 255.252 subnet mask, so there are 14 subnetting bits. The S > 8, the same Class C subnetting rules is applied here. 256-252=4. The first subnet is 4 and the second subnet is 8. The host (100.5) must be in the 100.4 subnet; the broadcast address is 100.7 and the valid host range is 128.100.100.5-6/30.

3-52. A. 256-240=16. The first subnet is 16 and the second subnet is 32. The host (10.22) must be in the 10.16 subnet; the broadcast address is 10.31 and the valid host range is 172.16.10.17-30/28.

3-53. D. 256-255=1. The first subnet is 11 and the 17th subnet is 17. The subnet is 17.0; the broadcast address is 17.255 and the valid host range is 172.17.17.1-254/24.

3-54. B. A Class B network address is two bytes long, which means the host bits are two bytes long. The network address must be 172.17.0.0, which are all bits OFF. The broadcast address is all bits ON, or

172.17.255.255.

3-55. A. 256-128=128. Valid subnets are 17.0, 17.128 …etc.

3-56. D. It is invalid. 256-128=128. The first valid subnet is 0.128, with valid hosts range is 0.129-0.254 and broadcast address is 0.255. The subnet 0.0 should not contain a host 0.17.

3-57. D. When using a notation like this 172.17.17.17/22, the 22 stand for the number of bits used for the network portion. It can be rewritten into 255.255.252.0.

3-58. A. 256-192=64. 64.0 is the first subnet; 128.0 is the second subnet. The 126.255 host is in 64.0 subnet range, the broadcast address is 127.255, and valid host range is 64.1-127.254.

3-59. B. The 255.255.255.0 subnet mask is usually used to subnet Class B addresses into 254 subnets, with 254 hosts/subnet.

3-60. D. 255.128 is 9 subnetting bits. 2^9-2=510.

3-61. D. The most suitable masking for this case is a mask 240.0 that allows for 14 subnets and 4094 hosts/subnet. The valid host range is 16.1-31.254.

3-62. A. Using 248.0 masking yields 5 Subnetting bits and 11-bits for hosts. 2^5-2=30 subnets, 2^11-2=2046.

3-63. A. 256-224=32. The first subnet is 32.0; the second one is 64.0 and the third one is 96.0. Only host 63.51 uses the first subnet.

3-64. D. 256-248=8. Subnets are 8.0, 16.0, 24.0, 32.0, 40.0, 48.0, 56.0, 64.0, 72.0 …etc. The host 71.12 in 64.0 subnets. The broadcast address is 71.255 and valid host range 64.1-71.254.

3-65. C-G.

3-66. A, H.

3-67. A-V. These valid subnet masks can be used for class A IP addresses. Mask 255.255.255.255 is used for broadcast and mask 255.255.255.254 is invalid, because using one bit to define hosts is incorrect.

3-68. A. The Class A network address has 24 bits available for hosts addressing. This means that up to 22 bits can be used for subnetting since at least 2 bits must be left for host addressing.

3-69. A. There are 22 different patterns, which can be used to subnet Class A. address. For more details, please, see Q3-22.

3-70. B. The process of subnetting a Class A network is the same as for a Class B, except, there are more host bits available for masking.

3-71. A. For example, 64.**0.0** is a Class A subnet address, and 127.**255.255** its broadcast address. The valid hosts' range will be 64.0.1-127.255.254. This addition is only required, if the number of Subnetting bits less than 8.

3-72. B. 256-252=4. The first Subnet is 10.10.4, the second one is 10.10.8. The host 77.10.10.5 is in the 4 Subnet. The broadcast address is 77.10.10.7/30 and the valid host range is 77.10.10.5-6/30.

3-73. D. 256-240=16. The host 77.77.77.77 is in the 64 Subnet. The broadcast address is 77.77.77.79/28 and the valid host range is 77.77.77.65-78/28.

3-74. B. Since, 255.240.0.0 uses 4-bits for Subnetting, it can provide a maximum of 2^4-2=14 different subnets.

3-75. A. 256-248=8. The host 77.255.255.17 is in 16 Subnet. The broadcast address is 77.255.255.23/29 and the valid host range is 77.255.255.17-22/29.

3-76. C. 256-254=2. The Subnet 77.17.16.0/23 uses the broadcast address 77.17.17.255.

3-77. C. The default Subnet mask that Class A is used is 77.255.255.255.

3-78. C. Since, 255.240.0.0 uses 4-bits for Subnetting, it can provide a maximum of 2^4-2=14 different subnets.

3-79. C. Assuming a class A network, a Subnet mask of 255.248.0.0 uses five bits for subnets, which will be 32 unique combinations minus two equals 30 subnets.

3-80. A-B. All are true about VLSMs.

3-81. A, C. Yes, Classful routing protocols such as RIPv1 and IGRP do not have a field for subnet information, so the subnet information is dropped from these routing protocols. This means that if a router running RIPv1 has a subnet mask of a certain value; it assumes that all interfaces within the classful address space have the same subnet mask.

3-82. B, D. Classless routing protocols such as RIPv2, EGRP, and OSPF do have a field for subnet information, so the subnet information gets to advertise within these routing protocols. This means that if a router running RIPv2 has a subnet mask of a certain value; it does not assume that all interfaces within the classless address space have the same subnet mask.

3-83.   A. Classless routing protocols do support the advertisement of subnet information. Therefore, it is a possible to use VLSM with routing protocols such as RIPv2, EIGRP, or OSPF.

3-84.   B, D. Multicast Class D IP address cannot be used, therefore, answer A is invalid and answer C is actually a subnet broadcast address for subnet 99.100.153.0/26, and therefore, it cannot be used.

3-85.

1.	The use of 2^x-2 formula and avoiding the zero and broadcast subnets	A, C, E, G, I, K
2.	The use of 2^x formula with the zero and broadcast subnets	B, D, F, H, J, L

Answers to the Chapter 4 Learning Questions

4-1. A, B, C. The CISCO IOS is the kernel of CISCO routers and most CISCO switches.

4-2. B. CISCOFusion is proposed by CISCO to make all CISCO devices run the same OS. Most CISCO routers run the same IOS, but only about half of the switches currently run the CISCO IOS.

4-3. B. The IOS was created to deliver network services and applications. The CISCO IOS runs on most CISCO routers and on some CISCO Catalyst switches, like the CAT2.96K switch.

4-4. A-D. All networks OS facilities can be obtained by IOS and these are some functions of the IOS.

4-5. A, B, C. For example, A HyperTerminal Windows application can be used to access IOS through the console port of a Router. LAN Router interfaces can be used to access IOS using Telnet utility.

4-6. B. Access to the IOS command line is called an EXEC session. It is also called Command Line Interface (CLI).

4-7. A. The CISCO IOS runs on most CISCO routers and on some CISCO Catalyst switches, like the CAT2.06K switch.

4-8. A.

4-9. A, B, C. Connecting to a CISCO router is required for Configuring the router, Verifying the router configuration, and Checking statistics.

4-10. A, B, C. Any active interface can be used to connect a router and configure it.

4-11. A-F. Console port is used for configuring a router at the first time.

4-12. A-G. Auxiliary port is really the same as a console port and can be used as such. It also allows configuring modem commands.

4-13. A-D. Telnet is the most common way for router connection and configuration.

4-14. B. Auxiliary port allows configuring modem commands, which allows a modem to router connection. This provides dialing-up a remote router and configuring the router if it is down.

4-15. A, B, C. Several types of memories are used in CISCO devices.

4-16. A. Dynamic Random-Access Memory (DRAM) is using for both main system memory and shared memory. DRAM: needs refresh every ms, small chip, simple, cheap, easy to make, and hold = 4 times as much info a SRAM (Static RAM) hold.

4-17. B. Nonvolatile random-access memory (NVRAM) is used for storing configuration information.

4-18. C, D. Flash memory is used for running CISCO IOS software.

4-19. A. Running a Power-On Self Test (POST) is the First step.

4-20. B. Loading the CISCO IOS from Flash Memory is the second step.

4-21. C. Loading the Startup-config from NVRAM if it is found is the third step.

4-22. D. Entering the setup mode if no configuration is found in NVRAM is the fourth step.

4-23. B, A. setup mode is called automatically if no startup-config in NVRAM.

4-24. B. The CISCO IOS is loaded from Flash memory by default.

4-25. A, B. It is an easy Step-by-Step setup configuration tool.

4-26. A, C, D. The following command can be used to invoke the setup session: Router#**setup**.

4-27. A, B. Two options are available for using setup mode. These are; Basic Management and Extended Setup.

4-28. A. A basic Management option only gives enough configurations to allow connectivity to the router.

4-29. B. An extended setup option allows configuring some global parameters as well as interface configuration parameters.

4-30. A, B. Basic management setup configures only enough connectivity for management of the system; extended setup will allow configuring each interface on the system.

4-31. A-I. All these capabilities are supported by setup facility.

4-32. A. A bracket ([ ]) represents a default entry that will be accepted if you press the Enter key.

4-33. B. When '?' is entered a help can be obtained.

4-34. D. When Ctrl-C is pressed at any prompt, it tends to abort the configuration dialog.

4-35. C. For more details, see step 1 in configuration 4-2.

4-36. A. For more details, see step 2 in configuration 4-2.

4-37. B. The enable password is only used for pre-10.3 IOS versions.

4-38. A. The enabled secret password is the more secure ones since it is the only encrypted password by default. Answer D is not found.

4-39.   C. The VTY line password is used to secure the Telnet session in CISCO Router. If a password for the VTY lines is not set, you cannot by default Telnet into a Router.

4-40.   C. Class B network is 172.17.0.0, 8 subnet bits; mask is /24 or 255.255.255.0 masking is used.

4-41.   A. If you select 0, the configuration information you entered is not saved, and you return to the CLI mode.

4-42.   B. If you select 1, the configuration information you entered is not saved, and you return to the CISCO Router enable prompt (THAAR#). Type setup to return to the System Configuration dialog.

4-43.   C. If you select 2, the configuration is saved in NVRAM, and you are returned to the EXEC prompt (THAAR>).

4-44.   A, B. By answering **no** in step 1 in configuration 4-2 or selecting **0** in configuration 4-3.

4-45.   A.

4-46.   A.

4-47.   A, B, F.

4-48.   A, B, D. The password is required to invoke the user-mode if it is configured on Console or auxiliary ports or on VTY lines. Router configuration can only be changed from Privileged EXEC mode.

4-49.   C, E. The password is required after configuring the enabled secret password.

4-50.   B, E, G. The command **enable (en or ena)** will switch the router from user mode to privileged mode.

4-51.   A. The command **disable** will switch the router from privileged mode to user mode. However, Answers C and D can be used to logging out the Router from the privileged mode.

4-52.   C, D. The commands **logout** and **exit** will switch the router console OFF from both user mode and privileged mode.

4-53.   A. The command **disable** will switch the router from privileged EXEC mode to user mode.

4-54.   D. The command **enable (en)** will switch the router from user EXEC mode to privileged EXEC mode.

4-55.   B. It is Router> prompt.

4-56.   C. It is Router# prompt.

4-57.   C. The Router# **setup** is used to invoke the setup procedure.

4-58.   A. All commands in Global Configuration Mode have global effect.

4-59.   B. **config t** or configure terminal commands are used to change the running-config, which is the current configuration running in Dynamic RAM (DRAM).

4-60.   A. config mem or configure memory commands are used to change the startup-config, which is the stored configuration in NVRAM.

4-61.   B. The command **config t** will switch the router to global configuration mode.

4-62.   B. The command **config t** will change the running-config parameters.

4-63.   C, F. The command **config memory** or **config mem** will change the startup-config parameters. It is copies the running-config from DRAM to startup-config in NVRAM. This command is identical to **copy run start** command.

4-64.   B, E. The command **config network** or **config net** will change the router configuration parameters stored on a TFTP host. It copies the running-config from DRAM to a TFTP host. This command is identical to **copy run tftp** command.

4-65.   B, C, E. The command **int f0/0** will configure the fastethernet interface on the router. It is issued from Global Configuration mode.

4-66.   B, E. The command **int f0/0.1** will configure fastethernet Subinterface 1 on the router. It is issued from Global Configuration mode.

4-67.   B. The command **line console 0** will configure the console port parameters.

4-68.   C, E. The command **router rip** or **router ospf** will configure the routing protocols on a router

4-69.   D. This prompt must be shown in Global Configuration Mode.

4-70.   E. This prompt must be shown in Interface Configuration Mode.

4-71.   C. This prompt must be shown in Subinterface Configuration Mode.

4-72.   B. This prompt must be shown in Line Configuration Mode.

4-73.   D. This prompt must be shown in Router Configuration Mode.

4-74.   A, B, D. To exit to privileged EXEC mode, use the exit or end command.

4-75.   B, D. To exit to global configuration mode, use the exit command. To exit to privileged EXEC mode, use the exit command or press Ctrl-Z.

4-76.   A, B, D. To exit to global configuration mode, use the exit command. To exit to privileged EXEC mode, use the end command or press Ctrl-Z.

4-77.   A, B, D. To exit to global configuration mode, use the exit command. To exit to privileged EXEC mode, use the end command or press Ctrl-Z.

4-78.   A, B, D. To exit to global configuration mode, use the exit command. To exit to privileged EXEC mode, use the end command or press Ctrl-Z.

4-79.   B. The question mark.

4-80.   B. The question mark.

4-81.   C. The command + space + question mark.

4-82.   A. "% Incomplete command" is the error message that would appear.

4-83.   B. "% Invalid input detected at '^' marker" is the error message that would appear.

4-84.   C. "% Ambiguous command: "sh te"." is the error message that would appear.

4-85.   D. The editing command **Ctrl+B** will take the cursor back one character.

4-86.   A. The editing command **Ctrl+A** will take the cursor the cursor to the beginning of a line.

4-87.   E. The editing command **Ctrl+E** will take the cursor the cursor to the end of a line.

4-88.   C. The editing command **Ctrl+R** will redisplay a line.

4-89.   A. The editing command **Ctrl+U** will erase a line.

4-90.   B. The editing command **Esc+B** will move the cursor back one world.

4-91.   B. The editing command **Esc+F** will move the cursor forward one word.

4-92.   E. The editing command **Ctrl+W** will erase a word.

4-93.   C. The editing command **Ctrl+D** will delete a single character.

4-94.   C. The editing command **Ctrl+F** will move the cursor forward one character.

4-95.   B. The editing command **Backspace** will delete a single character.

4-96.   A. The editing command **Ctrl+Z** will end configuration mode and returns to EXEC.

4-97.   E. The editing command **Tab** will finish typing a command for you.

4-98.   C. The character $ indicates an automatic scrolling of long lines.

4-99.   A. The **show history** command lists the last commands entered on the Router. The default size for this command is 10.

4-100.   E. The **show terminal** command verifies the Router terminal configuration.

4-101.   E. The **show terminal** command verifies the Router terminal history size.

4-102.   C. The **terminal history size 30** set the Router terminal history size to 30. The maximum history size that can be set is 256.

4-103.   A, E. The editing command **Ctrl+P** and **UP arrow** will show the last or previous command entered.

4-104.   C, D. The editing command **Ctrl+N** and **DOWN arrow** will show next commands entered.

4-105.   C. The **no editing** command will turn OFF key sequences such as CTRL-B.

4-106.   A. The **show history** command will show the entries in the command history buffer.

4-107.   A, D. The **show version** command provides the system configuration information.

4-108.   A-L. All these parameters are provided by **sh version** command.

4-109.   C. Five passwords can be used to secure the CISCO Router.

4-110.   A-E. All these passwords are used to secure the CISCO Router.

4-111.   A, B. Enable and enable secret passwords are used to secure the Router privileged mode

4-112.   C, D, E. Console, auxiliary and telnet passwords are activated when the user mode. is accessed.

4-113.   A, B. Enable and enable secret passwords are used when the **enable** command is issued.

4-114.   D. Router(config)#**enable password thaar**.

4-115.   B. Router(config)#**enable secret altaiey.**

4-116.   C. From Global Configuration mode, the enable passwords can be set up on the Router.

4-117.   A, C. The enable secret is encrypted by default, and is superseded the enable password.

4-118.   A. The **line aux 0, login, password thaar** commands are used to configure the auxiliary line password on the Router.

4-119.   A, B. The **line con 0, login, password thaar** commands are used to configure the console line password on the Router.

4-120.   D. The **line vty 1, login, password thaar** commands are used to configure the Telnet password for only line 1.

4-121.   C. The user-mode passwords are set from line configuration mode. However, the line command is issued from global configuration mode.

4-122.   C. The **config t, line vty 0 4, no login** commands establish a Telnet access to the Router and without prompting for password.

4-123.   A. The **config t, line con 0, login, password thaar** command is used to configure the console port for access.

4-124.   A. The **config t, line aux 0, login, password thaar** command is used to configure the auxiliary port for access. There is only one auxiliary port so it is always aux 0.

4-125.   B. The **no login** command allows users to telnet into a Router and not be prompted with a user-mode password.

4-126.   A. The **logging synchronous** command stops console messages from writing over the command you are trying to type in.

4-127.   B. The **exec-timeout 0 1** command sets the console to time out after only one second.

4-128.   A. The **service password-encryption, line vty 0 4, login, password thaar** command encrypts the Telnet password on the Router.

4-129.   C. The command **line aux 0** will enter the auxiliary line configuration mode.

4-130.   B. The **sh run** or **show running-config** command shows and verifies the configured passwords on the Router.

4-131.   A. The **banner ?** command is used to list all types of banners, and then a particular type can be selected. Answer D is not completed. The rest are wrong answers.

4-132.   B. Four different types of banners can be defined.

4-133.   A, B, C, D. These are the four different banner types.

4-134.   A. The **banner motd ?** starts the configuration of this banner.

4-135.   B. The **banner login ?** starts the configuration of this banner.

4-136.   C. The **banner exec ?** starts the configuration of this banner.

4-137.   D. The **banner incoming ?** starts the configuration of this banner.

4-138.   B From global configuration mode, the banners can be configured.

4-139.   A. The **no banner motd** command deletes this banner completely from the Router.

4-140.   D. The **no banner exec** command deletes this banner completely from the Router.

4-141.   C. The **no banner incoming** command deletes this banner completely from the Router.

4-142.   B. The **no banner login** command deletes this banner completely from the Router.

4-143.   A. The **no exec-banner** command disables the EXEC banner on a particular line.

4-144.   A, B. The **no exec-banner** and **no motd-banner** commands disable the motd banner on a particular line.

4-145.   E. No way to disable it. It must be deleted completely from the Router.

4-146.   E. No way to disable it. It must be deleted completely from the Router.

4-147.   C. From line configuration mode, the banners can be disabled.

4-148.   A, B, C, D. All these statements are true about banners.

4-149.   B. The delimiting character can be any character of your choice --a pound sign (#) for example. It tells the Router when the message is done. The delimiting character must not be used in the message.

4-150.   A, B, D. all these forms can be used for configuring an Ethernet Router interface.

4-151.   A, B, C, D. all these forms can be used for configuring a fastethernet Router interface.

4-152.   B Router interfaces are selected from global configuration mode.

4-153.   C. Clock rates in bps.

4-154.   D. B/W in kbps.

4-155.   D. Serial interfaces parameters are configured from interface configuration mode.

4-156.   A, B, E. The Router(config-if)#**media-type 100BaseX** configures fastethernet interfaces.

4-157.   A. By default, all Router interfaces are shutdown.

4-158.   B. The Router(config-if)#**no shutdown** brings the Router interface up.

4-159.   A. The Router(config-if)#**shutdown** brings the Router interface down.

4-160.   A. The Router(config-if)#**ip address 172.17.17.17 255.255.255.0** sets an IP address on an interface.

4-161.   C. The Router(config-if)#**ip address 172.17.17.17 255.255.255.0 secondary** sets a secondary IP address on an interface.

4-162.   A. If an interface is shut down, the show interface command will show the interface as administratively shut down. It is possible no cable is attached, but this cannot be told from this message.

4-163.   C, D. The Router(config-if)#**no shut** command is used to bring an interface up.

4-164.   B. Different routers use different methods to choose interfaces used on a Router.

4-165.   A, B, C, D. Some of the configurations used to configure an interface are Network Layer addresses, Media-type, bandwidth, and other administrator commands.

4-166.   A, B, C. There are several syntaxes corresponding to different type of interfaces.

4-167.   A, B, C. The **sh run** and **sh int e0** commands are used to discover the interface status.

4-168.   B. The no clock rate command restores clock rate to its default values.

4-169.   B. The no bandwidth command restores bandwidth to its default values.

4-170.   A. The no ip address command removes and disables IP processing on a particular interface.

4-171.   A. The clock rate command is two words, and the speed of the line is in bps.

4-172.   A, B, C. In all these cases, the **no clock rate** command should be issued.

4-173.   A, C. On these interfaces, the **clock rate** command is issued.

4-174.   A, B. Bandwidth is used for calculating the best route.

4-175.   A. Every CISCO Router ship with a default serial link bandwidth of a T1, or 1.544Mbps.

4-176.   A, C, D. The bandwidth of a serial link is used by routing protocols such as IGRP, EIGRP, and OSPF to calculate the best cost to a remote network. The bandwidth setting of a serial link that using RIP routing is irrelevant since RIP uses hop count for calculating the best route.

4-177.   A. The Router(config-subif)# prompt indicates that the Router is in subinterface configuration mode. This mode is used to configure multiple logical interfaces on a single interface. The set of commands that are required to enter subinterface configuration mode is as follows:

Router>enable
Router#configure terminal
Router(config)#interface s1
Router(config-if)#interface s1.1
Router(config-subif)#

Entering the 'enable' command at the user mode prompt (Router>) "enables" privileged EXEC mode. Entering the 'configure terminal' command at the privileged mode prompt (Router#), places the Router in the global configuration mode. The 'interface serial1' command places the Router into the interface configuration mode. The 'interface s1.1' places the Router into subinterface configuration mode. The resulting prompt for the subinterface configuration mode is "Router(config-subif)#."

The Router(config-if)# prompt indicates that the Router is in interface configuration mode. This mode is used to configure physical-interface parameters. The set of commands that are required to enter interface configuration mode is as follows:

Router>enable
Router#configure terminal
Router(config)#interface s0
Router(config-if)#

The Router(config-router)# prompt indicates that the router is in router configuration mode. This mode is used to configure IP routing protocol parameters. The set of commands that are required to enter configuration mode is as follows:

Router>enable
Router#configure terminal
Router(config)#router rip
Router(config-router)#

The Router(config-controller)# prompt indicates that the router is in controller configuration mode. Channelized T1 is configured from the controller configuration mode. The set of commands that are required to enter the controller configuration mode are as follows:

Router>enable
Router#configure terminal
Router(config)#controller t1 0
Router(config-controller)#

4-178.   C, E.

4-179.   B. The hostname command is one word.

4-180.   A. The hostname setting is only locally significant.

4-181.   D. The command hostname, one word, is used to set the name of the Router.

4-182.   B. From global configuration mode, the Router name is set.

4-183.   A. The factory-assigned default host name is the router.

4-184.   A, B, C, D. The order of display at startup is the banner message-of-the-day (MOTD), login and password prompts, then EXEC banner, then hostname prompt.

4-185.   A, D. The global configuration command hostname or the Privileged EXEC setup command can be used to configure the router hostnames.

4-186.   A. The **config t, int e0, description my LAN** command is used to set the "my description" to an interface.

4-187.   A. The description setting is only locally significant.

4-188.   D. From line configuration mode, the Router description is set.

4-189.   A, B, C. All these commands are used to show the interface description.

4-190.   B. The **copy run start** command copies the current Router configuration to startup configuration file.

4-191.   D. The **copy run start** command copies the startup configuration file to current Router configuration.

4-192.   B. The **copy** command is issued from Privileged EXEC mode.

4-193.   B. The **sh run** command shows the content of running configuration file. If the contents of DRAM and NVRAM are identical, the **sh start** command can also be used.

4-194.   D. The **sh start** command shows the content of the startup configuration file. If the contents of DRAM and NVRAM are identical, the **sh run** command can also be used.

4-195.   B. The **copy** command is issued from Privileged EXEC mode.

4-196.   B. The **erase start** command deletes the content of the startup configuration file.

4-197.   B. The **erase** command is issued from Privileged EXEC mode.

4-198.   D. The **copy start run** command copies the NVRAM contents to DRAM.

4-199.   B. The **copy run start** command copies the DRAM contents to NVRAM.

4-200.   A, B. To enter setup mode, either type **setup** from privileged EXEC mode or erase the configuration stored in NVRAM and reboot the Router.

4-201.   A. The **copy run start** command copies the current config to NVRAM so that it will be used if the Router is restarted.

4-202.   B. The **erase start** command deletes the configuration stored in NVRAM.

4-203.   A-E. All these modes can be used to configure the router.

4-204.   B. The **show version** command verifies the hardware configuration of the Router.

4-205.   B, D. The **show cdp neighbor detail** or it is abbreviation finds the network layer addresses for the neighbor routers.

4-206.   B. The **show cdp neighbor detail** command is issued from Privileged EXEC mode.

4-207.   A. The **ping** utility checks the basic network connectivity.

4-208.   C. The **trace** utility discovers the path a packet takes as it traverses an internetwork.

4-209.   A, B, C, D. The **ping** utility is issued from Privileged EXEC mode, and it can be executed from any Router prompt.

4-210.   A, B, C, D. The **trace** utility is issued from Privileged EXEC mode, and it can be executed from any Router prompt.

4-211.   B. The **Telnet** utilities check the network connectivity. Telnet is the best utility, since it uses IP at the Network layer and TCP at the Transport layer to create a session with a remote host. If Telnet session is established with another device, the IP connectivity must be good. However, ping can also be used, but Telnet is the best.

4-212.   A, B. The **Telnet** utility is issued from Privileged EXEC mode, and it can be executed from any Router prompt.

4-213.   A, D. The **show interface** command verifies the network configuration of an interface. This command also verifies the configuration of the interface itself.

4-214.   C. The **show controllers** command verifies the physical configuration of an interface.

4-215.   D. The **clear counters e0** command clears the "show interface" counters of e0 interface.

4-216. A. The **sh controllers s 0** command shows if s0 interface needed to provide clocking.

4-217. A. The **sh controllers s 0** command shows if either a DTE or DCE cable is plugged into serial 0.

4-218. A. There is no problem on the interface. The interface is running.

4-219. B. If the line is UP and the protocol is DOWN, there is a clocking (keepalive) or framing issue. Check the keepalives on both ends to make sure they match; the clock rate is set, if needed; and the encapsulation type is the same on both ends.

4-220. C, D. When the line interface and protocol are DOWN, maybe there is a cable or interface problem. In addition, if one end is administratively shut down, then the remote end would show down and down. The no shutdown command will recover this problem.

4-221. E. **no shutdown** command must issue on the interface.

4-222. A, B. The **ping** and **trace** utilities can be used with different types of protocols such as TCP/IP, AppleTalk, DECnet. etc.

4-223. C. The **Telnet** utility can only be used with TCP/IP protocol.

4-224. A. The **Telnet** utilities check the network connectivity, Telnet is the best utility, since it uses IP at the Network layer and TCP at the Transport layer to create a session with a remote host. If Telnet session is established with another device, the IP connectivity must be good. However, ping can be used, but Telnet is the best.

4-225. A. At the Router prompt, there is no need to type telnet; just type a hostname or IP address, and the Router will assume that Telnet utility is required.

4-226. A. The first parameter refers to the physical layer, whereas the second one refers to the data link layer.

4-227. D. The **sh int s0** command shows the B/W of s0 interface.

4-228. D. The **sh int s0** command shows the MTU of s0 interface.

4-229. D. The **sh int s0** command shows the keepalive time of s0 interface.

4-230. A. The default value for s0 interface MTU parameter is 1500 bytes.

4-231. B. The default value for s0 interface B/W parameter is 1.544Mbps.

4-232. D. The default value for s0 interface keepalive time is 10 sec.

4-233. D. The default value for e0 interface B/W parameter is 10Mbps.

4-234. A, B. The **show controllers s0** command provides the physical interface and what type of serial connection the interface has. If it is a DCE, the clock rate should be set on that interface.

4-235. A. There is no problem. No shutdown command needs to be issued.

4-236. A. The EEPROM is a Flash memory. Flash is where the IOS is stored and loaded from by default. Show flash command will show the contents of flash memory. However, show version will show the version of IOS currently running. If only one IOS is in flash memory, then show version and show flash will always be the same.

4-237. B-G, E.

4-238. D.

4-239. A, C.

Answers to the Chapter 5 Learning Questions

5-1.   A. It is the process of moving packets from one network to another network and delivering the packets to hosts.

5-2.   A, B, C. By adding the routing software and suitable networks' interfaces, any automated machine can work as a Router.

5-3.   A, B, C, D. Routing process is the core of Router processes.

5-4.   A, B. The routing process can be either static or dynamic.

5-5.   A, B. Static routing is implemented and supported by administrator.

5-6.   C-G. Dynamic routing is implemented and supported by dynamic routing protocols, but it needs some administrator's interventions.

5-7.

1.	Step 1: Issuing the ping command.	A
2.	Step 2: Dotormining the destination Host B's Network.	B
3.	Step 3: Determining the R1 MAC address.	C
4.	Step 4: Completing the Packet.	D
5.	Step 5: Generating the frame by Host A.	E
6.	Step 6: Sending the frame.	F
7.	Step 7: Receiving data by R1.	G
8.	Step 8: Checking the destination MAC address.	H
9.	Step 9: Checking the Destination IP address.	I
10.	Step 10: Generating the frame by R1.	J
11.	Step 11: Replying to R1 broadcast.	K
12.	Step 12: Checking the IP address by Host B.	L
13.	Step 13: Generating the reply by Host B.	M

5-8.   A. If the network is much larger, the process would be the same, and with the packet simply going through more hops before it finds the destination host.

5-9.   A, D, E, F. In IP routing, the frame is replaced at each hop as the packet traverses the internetwork.

5-10.   A, C. The Source host would send a packet to the Router, only if the packet is destined to that Router or the packet is destined to remote network.

5-11.   A. With the help of the routing table, the Router will decide for which network the packet must be gone.

5-12.   A. The Router, by default, only knows about their directly connected networks.

5-13.   Rules 1-2 are implemented by the host, whereas rules 3-7 are implemented by the router.

5-14.   A.

5-15.   A. The **show ip route** command shows the IP routing table.

5-16.   B. Directly connected routes are identified in the routing table by a C.

5-17.   A. The Routers, by default, only know about their directly connected networks.

5-18.   D Configuring the routers interfaces make the routers to know about all directly connected networks.

5-19.   D. Directly connected networks have the highest administrative distance, or trustworthiness rating, of zero.

5-20.   B, C, D. Routes to remote networks can be added to the routing tables of the routers using the following routing methods: Static routing, default routing and dynamic routing.

5-21.   B. Static Routing is the process of an administrator manually adding routes in each router's routing table.

5-22.   A-D. These are the advantages of static routing process.

5-23.   A-D. These are the disadvantages of static routing process.

5-24.   D. Static routes default administrative distance is 1.

5-25.   C. Statically connected routes are identified in the routing table with an S.

5-26.   B, D, E. In static routes, a destination network and mask and either the next hop Router or the interface to that Router must be supplied; the administrative distance is optional.

5-27.   A. If a packet is received that is looking for a destination network that is not in the routing table, the Router will drop the packet.

5-28.   A. Static routes do not converge, and it must be updated by hand.

5-29.   D. Static routes are most believable by default.

5-30.   A, C, D. Static routes decrease network traffic by eliminating routing update traffic and increase security by limiting subnet access to only the subnets that want the routers to access.

5-31.   C. Exit interface uses in place of the next hop address if desired. It must be on a point-to-point link, such as WAN. This command does not work on a LAN, for example, Ethernet.

5-32.   E. The **permanent** command specifies that the route will not be removed from routing table, even if the interface shuts down.

5-33.   A, B. The route is automatically removed from the routing table in case of the interface shut down or in case of the Router cannot communicate to the next hop Router. However, the administrator can remove any route, using the no ip route command, but this is manually and not dynamically.

5-34.   D. The **ip route** command adds a static route to the routing table.

5-35.   A. The **no ip route** command removes a static route from the routing table.

5-36.   C. The Global configuration mode is used to define a static route using the **ip route** command.

5-37.   C. The Global configuration mode is used to remove a static route using the **no ip route** command.

5-38.   A. Static route is used to define routes remote networks.

5-39.   D. The **ip route 131.108.0.0 255.255.0.0 131.108.6.6** command routes the packets for network 131.108.0.0 to a Router at 131.108.6.6.

5-40.   A, B. To view the routing table, the **show running-config** or **show ip route** commands can be used.

5-41.   A. If one more route or another Router is added to the internetwork, all routers' routing tables must be updated by hand. This is maybe OK for a small network, but it is a big task for a large internetwork.

5-42.   A. By adding an administrative distance parameter to the end of a static route entry, the default administrative distance can be changed. As an example **ip route 172.18.20.0 255.255.255.0 172.18.30.2 175**.

5-43.   D. If the routes do not appear in the routing table, it is because the router cannot communicate to the configured next hop address. It is possible to use the **permanent** parameter to keep the route in the routing table, even if the next hop device cannot be contacted.

5-44.   E, D B, C. The static route is "S 172.18.80.0 [175/0] via 172.18.80.1."

5-45.   B, D.

5-46.   B, D. Machine A does not need to send an ARP broadcast looking for R1's MAC address, since the ping from Machine B to Machine A.

5-47.   B, D, F. HDLC, on the serial link, does not use MAC addresses.

5-48.   C, D. Default routing is used to send packets with a remote destination network not in the routing table to the next hop router. However, it can only be used on stub networks.

5-49.   C. Stub networks have only one connection to an internetwork. Default routes can only be set on a stub network, or network loops may occur.

5-50.   C. A default route can only be set on a stub network, which is a network with only one connection to the internetwork.

5-51.   A. Using all 0s in place of the network and mask IDs creates Default routes.

5-52.   A. An IP route with a wildcard of all zeroes for the destination network and subnet mask is used to create a default route.

5-53.   B. By default, default routes have an administrative distance of 1. The 175 represents an optional command that changes the default administrative distance.

5-54.   D. Default routes have an administrative distance of one by default.

5-55.   C. The **ip classless** command must be issued with default routing.

5-56.   A, B. To view the routing table, the **show running-config** or **show ip route** commands can be used.

5-57.   E. Default routes are identified in the routing table with an S*.

5-58.   A, B, D, E. In default routes, a destination network and mask using wildcards and either the next hop Router or interface to that Router must be supplied; the administrative distance is optional.

5-59.   B. If a packet is received that is looking for a destination network that is not in the routing table, the Router will drop the packet by default. However, if the router implements a default routing and the **ip classless** command is issued, the router will forward the packet on the default route.

5-60.   A, B, D. Default routes decrease network traffic by eliminating routing update traffic. It also decreases administration of routing tables since just one route entry can be used to represent many routes.

5-61. D. The **ip route** command defines a default route to the routing table.

5-62. A. The **no ip route** command removes a default route to the routing table.

5-63. C. The Global configuration mode is used to define a default route using the **ip route** command.

5-64. C. The Global configuration mode is used to remove a default route using the **no ip route** command.

5-65. A. Default route is used to implement routes to remote networks.

5-66. E, A, B, C. The default route is "S* 0.0.0.0/0 [175/0] 172.18.80.1".

5-67. C. The Router(config)# **ip route 0.0.0.0 0.0.0.0 172.17.100.10** command configures a default route on a router to go to 172.17.100.10.

5-68. A. RB and RA are not on the same network. "RB" interface "S0" is on network 172.15.0.0/28 with Range (172.15.0.0 - 172.15.0.15) and "RA" interface "S1" is on network 172.15.0.16/28 Range (172.15.0.16 - 172.15.0.31.)

5-69. A. It is the process of using protocols to find and update automatically routing tables on routers.

5-70. A-C. Dynamic routing is easier than static or default routing, but it uses at the expense of Router CPU processes and bandwidth on the network links.

5-71. D. Routing protocols create dynamic routes automatically.

5-72. A. A routing protocol defines the set of rules used by a Router when it communicates between neighbor routers.

5-73. B. Two types of routing protocols are used in the internetwork. These are; Interior Gateway Protocol (IGP) and Exterior Gateway Protocol (EGP). Open Shortest Path First (OSPF) is an example of an IGP. Border Gateway Protocol (BGP) is an example of an EGP.

5-74. A. IGP routing protocols are used to exchange routing information with routers in the same Autonomous System (AS).

5-75. B. EGP routing protocols are used to exchange routing information between Autonomous Systems (ASs).

5-76. A. It is a collection of networks under a common administrative domain.

5-77. A.

5-78. A-D. AD is used to measure the trustworthiness of routing information received on a Router from a neighbor Router. AD is an integer from 0 to 255, where 0 is the most trusted and 255 means no traffic (no trust) will be passed via this route.

5-79. A. Directly connected networks have the highest administrative distance, or trustworthiness rating, of zero. This is because the route will always use the interface connected to the network.

5-80. B. One is the default administrative distance for static routing.

5-81. B. One is the default administrative distance for default routing.

5-82. A. 100 is the default administrative distance for IGRP routing protocol.

5-83. E. 120 is the default administrative distance for RIP routing protocol.

5-84. A, F.

5-85. A. The administrative distance is used in routing to decide the trustworthiness of a route. 0 is the highest rating.

5-86. C. Directly connected networks have the highest administrative distance, or trustworthiness rating, of zero.

5-87. A, B, C. In this order, the router will use the two advertisements.

5-88. C. There are three types of routing protocols.

5-89. A, B, C. There are three types of routing protocols. These are; Distance Vector, Link State, and Hybrid.

5-90. A-D.

5-91. A, B.

5-92. A, B. The distance vector routing protocols use a distance to a remote network to find the best path. The route with the least number of hops to the destination network is determined to be the best route.

5-93. A.

5-94. A. Each time a packet goes through a Router, it is called a hop.

5-95. B, C. RIP, and IGRP are examples of distance vector routing protocols. OSPF is an example of link state routing protocol. EIGRP is an example of Hybrid routing protocols. RIP and IGRP send the entire routing table to directly connected neighbors.

5-96. A.

5-97. A-F. It is more complex than distance vector routing protocols, and it consumes more Router resources. However, it is used to exchange routing information in a larger internetwork.

5-98. A, B, C. Link state routing protocols creates three separate tables in each Router. As a result, they know more about the internetwork than any distance-vector routing protocol.

5-99. A. An example of an IP routing protocol that is completely Link State is OSPF. It uses only bandwidth as a way to determine the best path to a remote network.

5-100. A. Hybrid routing protocols use aspects of distance vector and Link State.

5-101. D. An example of a hybrid routing protocol is EIGRP.

5-102. A. Only distance vector routing protocol is required for CCENT test.

5-103. A, C. Distance Vector periodic updates are sent more frequent than Link state protocol updates. Link-state routing protocols are also known as Shortest Path First protocols.

5-104. A-F. Several types of metrics can be used by routing protocols to determine the best path to the destination network.

5-105. A-E.

5-106. A-C.

5-107. A.

5-108. A-D.

5-109. A.

5-110. A, B.

5-111. A.

5-112. A.

5-113. A, B.

5-114. A-D.

5-115. D.

5-116.

1.	RIPv1	D,F
2.	RIPv2	A,B,C,D,F,G,I,J
3.	EIGRP	A,B,C,E,F,G,H,I,J,K
4.	OSPF	A,B,C,E,G,I,J
5.	IS-IS	A,B,C,E,G,J

5-117. C. However, C, D, E protocols are considered capable of converging quickly.

5-118. A. This paragraph correctly depicts the distance-vector routing algorithm. Simply, this is called routing by rumor.

5-119. C. It is possible to have a network that has multiple links to the same remote network. If that is the case, the administrative distance is first checked.

5-120. B. In case of there are multiple links to the same remote network and the links have the same administrative distances, the distance vector algorithm uses another metrics to determine the best path to use to that remote network. RIP uses hop count as a metric for determining the best route.

5-121. A. RIP uses the only hop count as a metric for determining the best route to an internetwork.

5-122. A. If RIP finds more than one link to the same remote network with the same hop count; it will automatically perform a round-robin load balance between.

5-123. D. RIP can perform load balancing for up to six equal-cost links (four by default).

5-124. B. Distance vector uses primarily the lowest hop count to make routing decisions.

5-125. A. Distance-vector protocols, by definition, use metrics (distance) and next-hop data (vectors) to make forwarding decisions.

5-126. A-D. They are multiple RIP versions, such as version 1 and version 2.

5-127. B. RIP is only using hop count to determine the best way to a remote network, but is having a maximum allowable hop count of 15, meaning that 16 is considered unreachable.

5-128. A, D. These are the main differences between RIPv1 and RIPv2.

5-129. B. This is because RIPv2 does not send updates with subnet mask information in the internetwork.

5-130. B. This is because RIPv2 does send updates with subnet mask information in the internetwork.

5-131. B. Only RIPv2 is required for CCENT Test.

5-132. B. RIP uses the distance-vector routing algorithm and uses the only hop count as a metric to determine the best path to an internetwork.

5-133. D. RIP only uses the hop count to determine the best path to a remote network.

5-134. E. RIP, by default, is only configured to run 15 hops; 16 is deemed unreachable.

5-135. C. RIP has an administrative distance of 120 by default.

5-136. D. RIP version one uses a distance-vector algorithm that allows a maximum HOP count of 15. Any network that takes more than 15 hops to reach is considered unreachable.

5-137. A.

5-138. C. The global command **router rip** will turn the RIP routing on in the router. Then the **network** command needs to be configured to tell the RIP routing protocol, which network to advertise.

NOTE: The network command must also be issued to give the routing protocol permission to advertise the subnets connected to the router's neighbors.

The 'router rip' command selects RIP as the routing protocol from the global configuration mode. The network command from the router configuration mode is then used to assign an IP address to the network to which the router is connected.

To configure RIP on a router, which is directly connected to the 192.18.0.0 and 20.0.0.0 networks properly, issue the following commands:

Router(config)#router rip
Router(config-router)#network 20.0.0.0
Router(config-router)#network 192.18.0.0

The 'router rip' command enables RIP on the router. The 'network 20.0.0.0' and 'network 192.18.0.0' commands specify that these networks are directly connected to the router interfaces. Through routing updates, the router will learn the topology of the network.

5-139. E. The **network w.x.y.z** command is used to tell the RIP routing which network to advertise.

5-140. A. The **show ip route** command shows the IP routing table used by the router.

5-141. D. The **passive** command, short of **passive-interface**, stops regular updates from being sent out an interface. However, the interface can still receive updates.

5-142. B. The **show ip route** command, as well as **the show ip protocol**, can be used to verify RIP. Show protocol shows the routed protocols on the router, not the dynamic routing protocol.

5-143. A. The "R" means that the networks were added dynamically using the RIP routing protocol.

5-144. B, D, E. RIP routing must be turned on at first, and the network to be advertised must be specified.

5-145. D. In spite of, that RIP dynamic routing is easy to create and maintain it is consuming much of CPU process and bandwidth. It is also suffering from slow in convergence.

5-146. A. RIP routing has an administrative distance equal to 120 by default.

5-147. D. To turn OFF the RIP routing process, use the **no router rip** command.

5-148. A. To remove a network entry, use the **no network w.x.y.z** command.

5-149. A. The **config t, router rip, passive-interface serial 1** commands are used to stop a router from propagating RIP information out serial 1. However, answer D will stop the rip routing in the whole router.

5-150. C. From Global Configuration prompt, RIP routing can be turned OFF.

5-151. E. The Router(config-router)# prompt is used to remove a network entry from RIP routing.

5-152. B. Only, the new router must be enabled for RIP by hand.

5-153. D, C, A, E, B, F. The route will be shown as the following: "R   172.18.80.0   [175/15] via 172.18.80.1, FastEthernet0/0".

5-154. B. RIP is a distance vector protocol, whereas OSPF is a link state protocol. The difference between these IP routing protocols is the mechanism by which they operate, i. e., distance vector vs. link state.

5-155. A. The script **config t, router rip, network 10.0.0.0, network 172.16.0.0** enable networks 10.2.2.0 and 172.16.18.0 to run the RIP protocol.

5-156. A. It is brief the RIP routing.

5-157. A. RIP maintains only the best route to a destination.

5-158. A.

5-159. A-G. All these statements are true about RIP.

5-160. A-D. To use IGRP, all the routers must be CISCO routers in the network.

5-161. C. IGRP uses a maximum hop count of 255 with a default of 100.

5-162.   B. IGRP uses a maximum hop count of 255 with a default of 100.

5-163.   B. IGRP is a CISCO proprietary distance-vector routing protocol.

5-164.   B, C, D, G, H. IGRP uses a different metric from RIP. IGRP uses bandwidth and delay of the line by default as a metric for determining the best route to a network. This is called a composite metric. Load, reliability, and MTU can also be used, although they are not used by default.

5-165.   B. IGRP is a CISCO proprietary distance-vector routing protocol. This means that all routers must be CISCO routers to use IGRP in the network.

5-166.   B. The default administrative distance of IGRP is 100.

5-167.   C. The global command **router igrp** will turn the IGRP routing on in the router. Then the **network** command needs to be configured to tell the IGRP routing protocol, which network to advertise. However, the AS number must be added to **router igrp** command.

5-168.   E. The **network w.x.y.z** command is used to tell the IGRP routing which network to advertise.

5-169.   A. The **show ip route** command shows the IP routing table used by the router.

5-170.   B. The **show ip route** command, as well as **the show ip protocol**, can be used to verify IGRP. Show protocol shows the routed protocols on the router, not the dynamic routing protocol.

5-171.   A. The "I" means that the networks were added dynamically using the IGRP routing protocol.

5-172.   B, D, E, F. IGRP routing must be turned on at first, the AS number must be applied, and the network to be advertised must be specified.

5-173.   D, E. In spite of, that IGRP dynamic routing is easy to create and maintain like RIP, it consumes much of CPU process and bandwidth.

5-174.   C. IGRP routing has an administrative distance equal to 100 by default.

5-175.   D. To turn OFF the IGRP routing process, use the **no router igrp AS_number** command.

5-176.   A. To remove a network entry, use the **no network w.x.y.z** command.

5-177.   C. From Global Configuration prompt, IGRP routing can be turned OFF.

5-178.   E. The Router(config-router)# prompt is used to remove a network entry from IGRP routing.

5-179.   B. Only, the new router must be enabled for IGRP by hand.

5-180.   D, C, A, E, B, F. The route will be shown as the following: "I   172.18.80.0   [100/160876] via 172.18.80.1, FastEthernet0/0".

5-181.   A. IGRP will find the subnets and advertise them. Both RIP and IGRP are classful routing, which means that subnet mask information is not sent with the routing protocol updates.

5-182.   C. The config-router **passive-interface** command stops updates from being sent out an interface.

5-183.   A. IGRP, as well as EIGRP. Use bandwidth and delay of the line, by default, when making routing decisions.

5-184.   B. The **passive** command, short of **passive-interface**, stops regular updates from being sent out an interface. However, the interface can still receive updates.

5-185.   D. The **variance multiplier** command from router configuration prompt is used to control the load balancing between the best metric and the worst acceptable metric in IGRP routing.

5-186.   C, D. The **traffic-share balanced** command tells the IGRP routing protocol to share inversely proportional to the metrics, and the **traffic-share min** command tells the IGRP routing process to use routes that have only minimum costs.

5-187.   A, B. It creates routing areas. AS's are used with IGRP, EIGRP and OSPF.

5-188.   B, E. To control the set of interfaces that a router wants to exchange routing updates with, it is possible to disable the sending of routing updates on specified interfaces by configuring the **passive-interface** command. However, if an access-list is wrongly configured, the routes may be filtered from updates. Access lists filter network traffic by controlling whether routed packets are forwarded or blocked at the router's interfaces.

5-189.   A.

5-190.   A-D.

5-191.   A.

5-192.   A.

5-193.   A-C.

5-194.   A.

5-195.   A.

5-196. B, C. IP and the ARP protocols on a host are working together to determine what network this packet is destined for by calculating the binary multiplication of (the destination IP address * the source subnet mask) and (the source IP address * the source subnet mask). If both are equal, this means that the destination address is on the local network (the packet will be sent directly to that destination host); otherwise, the destination will be on the remote network. Therefore, R2 and Machine B are thinking that IP address 172.18.20.5 on the local network.

5-197. D. A host's pinging to its own IP address does not provide any indication, whether the subnet/LAN is working or not, because the Ping packet does not have to traverse the subnet. To prove the subnet works, at least a ping between the Machine B and default gateway (R2) must be succeeded, since this ping requires the packet to go from Machine B to the R2 over the subnet.

5-198. A, C, E.

5-199. A-F. All these commands can be used to verify and check the IP routing network configurations.

5-200. A-I, All these parameters can be presented by the **sh ip route** command.

5-201. D. The **sh ip route network_number** command shows the subnet mask of the route.

5-202. C. The **show protocols** command shows the routed protocols and the configured interfaces and addresses of each routed protocol.

5-203. B. The command **show protocols** show the IP address of the routers' interfaces.

5-204. A. The **sh protocol** command shows all configured interfaces even secondaries and subinterfaces.

5-205. E. The **show ip protocol** command will show the routing protocols configured on the Router, which displays the timers used by the routing protocol.

5-206. B. The command **show ip protocol** will show the configured routing protocols on the Router, which includes the timers. The broadcast frequency for IGRP is one of these timers.

5-207. D. The **sh ip protocol** command displays the parameters and the current state of the active routing protocol process on CISCO Router.

5-208. D. The **sh ip protocol** command shows the autonomous system value for IGRP. The **sh ip route** command does not show the autonomous system value for IGRP.

5-209. D, E. The **sh ip protocol** and **sh run** commands show both RIP and IGRP parameters if both are configured on the same router at the same time. Only IGRP is appeared in the routing table using the **sh ip route** command because of its lower AD.

5-210. B, D. All these commands can be used to verify that RIP is running on the router. RIP is not appeared in **sh ip route** if IGRP is configured.

5-211. D. The **show ip protocol** command is used to show the AD values for routing protocols.

5-212. A, C. The commands **show ip route** and **debug ip rip** are used to support and verify RIP networks.

5-213. A, C. The commands **show ip route** and **debug ip rip**, as well as **the show ip protocol**, can be used to verify RIP. **Show protocol** shows the routed protocols on the router, not the dynamic routing protocol.

5-214. C. The **debug ip rip** command shows the IP RIP routing updates as they are sent and received on the Router.

5-215. A, B, C, E. These commands can be used to stop the **debug ip rip** command.

5-216. A. It consumes much of router resources.

5-217. A. To receive the output of **debug ip rip** command, which is used to verify RIP routing through a Telnet session, the command **terminal monitor** should be issued first.

5-218. A. The **debug ip igrp** command checks IP IGRP running through the internetwork. This command contains two options **events** and **transactions**.

5-219. B. The **debug ip igrp events** command shows information about IP IGRP events through the internetwork.

5-220. B. The **debug ip igrp transactions** command shows message requests from neighbor routers asking for an update and the broadcasts sent from the Router towards that neighbor Router.

5-221. A, B, C, E. These commands can be used to stop the **debug ip igrp events** command.

5-222. A, B, C, E. These commands can be used to stop the **debug ip igrp transactions** command.

5-223. A. It consumes much of router resources.

5-224. B. It consumes much of router resources.

5-225. B, D. The **debug ip igrp events** EXEC command can be used to display summary information on IGRP routing messages that indicate the source and destination of each update, as well as the number of routes in each updates. Information about individual routes is not generated with this command. However, the **debug ip igrp transactions** EXEC command displays the source and destination of each update.

5-226. B. The **debug ip igrp events** EXEC command to display the number of routes in each updates.

5-227. B. The **debug ip igrp transactions** can flood the console and make the Router unusable. In this case, use **the debug ip igrp events** instead to display summary routing information.

5-228. D. The **debug ip igrp transactions** command shows the metric of routes in each IGRP updates.

Answers to the Chapter 6 Learning Questions

6-1.   B, A. Layer-2 Switching is Hardware based, which means it uses the MAC address (Layer-2 address) to filter the network.

6-2.   A. Switches use to build and maintain their filter table an Application-specific Integrated circuits (ASICs). ASICs can run up to Gigabit speeds with very low latency.

6-3.   B. Layer-2 switch is fast, because it looks at the frame's hardware address before deciding to either forward the frame or drop it.

6-4.   A, B, C, and D. Layer-2 switching provides Hardware-based bridging (MAC), wire speeds, Low latency and Low cost features.

6-5.   B. The switching process will be faster and so efficient (less error-prone than routing).

6-6.   A, B, and C. If VLANs are defined on the switch, Layer-2 switching can break up broadcast domains.

6-7.   E. This is one of the main factors for using the switch. The switch will give each station 10Mbps not like a hub.

6-8.   A. Yes, layer-2 switiohing network has the same problems as a bridged network.

6-9.   C. The right way to create Layer-2 switching is by correctly breaks up collision domains, so users should spend 80 percent of their time on the local segment as in bridging network. The rule is 80/20.

6-10.   A. Layer-2 switching networks break up collision domains but the network is still one large broadcast domain.

6-11.   D. Switches are used to separate (break up) collision domains.

6-12. A. Only one broadcast domain with 24 switches by default.

6-13. D. The switch breaks the network into 24 collision domains.

6-14.   A, B, D. Layer-2 switching problems are: Broadcast messages, Multicast messages, and slow convergence of spanning tree.

6-15.   B. Layer-2 switches cannot completely replace routers.

6-16.   B, C. To reduce the number of collisions on an Ethernet network while maintaining a single broadcast domain, either a switch or a bridge must be used. Switches and bridges actually create separate collision domains on each interface to which a network is connected. This allows several collision domains to exist while retaining a single broadcast domain.

6-17.   A. This paragraph correctly depicts the Ethernet network operations and shows how collisions can be occurred.

6-18.   A. This paragraph correctly depicts the broadcasts.

6-19.   A. This paragraph correctly depicts the routers.

6-20.   A. This paragraph correctly depicts the hubs.

6-21.   A-D.

6-22.   B, C, E. layer-2 switching functions are Address Learning, Forward/filter decisions and Loop avoidance.

6-23.   A. The MAC filtering table is empty when the switch is power ON.

6-24.   A. This is what the switch does when a new frame is received on the switch interface.

6-25.   B, C. Hubs forward all frames out all ports every time whereas Switches make a point-to-point connection, and the frames will only be forwarded between two devices.

6-26.   B. Switches forward all frames that have an unknown destination address. If a device answers the frame, the switch will update the MAC address table to reflect the location of the device.

6-27.   B. The switch will flood the network with the multicast frame looking for the devices.

6-28.   B. The switch will flood the network with the broadcast frame.

6-29.   B. Yes, the switch will flush the entries relating to Station 1 and Station 4 communication from the MAC database.

6-30.   B. Station 2 and Station 3 will completely not see all frames traversing between Station 1 and Station 4.

6-31.   C. The MAC address table contains a combination of INTERFACE NUMBER and STATION MAC ADDRESS that connected to the same switch port.

6-32. D. When a frame is received at a switch interface, the destination MAC address is compared to the forward/filter database.

6-33.   B. After the arrived frame is checked against the MAC database and the destination MAC address is found in the database, the switch does not transmit the frame out any interface except for the destination interface.

6-34. A. The switch does not transmit incoming frames with known destination MAC addresses out any interfaces except for the destination addresses. This preserves bandwidth on the other network segments, and it is called **frame filtering.**

6-35. C. The **frame filtering** feature is obtained since; the switch does not transmit incoming frames with known destination MAC addresses out any interfaces except for the destination addresses.

6-36. B. If the destination MAC address for the incoming frame, is not listed in the MAC database, then the frame is broadcasted out all active interfaces except the interface the frame was received on.

6-37. A. The switch updates the database with the device interface and starts a point-to-point communication between the two devices. The database contains a combination of the device MAC address and its interface.

6-38. C. The switch does neglect the frame, if no device answers the broadcast.

6-39. B. A use layer 2 addresses to forward frames, a router uses layer 3 addresses to route packets.

6-40. A, D. Redundant links are extremely helpful in network design and are used in switching network to help stop complete network failures if one link fails and to provide some kind of fault tolerance.

6-41. A. Redundant links are useful in switching network, but they cause problems in the network.

6-42. B, A. Loops can be occurred since the frames can be broadcasted down all redundant links simultaneously.

6-43. A, B, C, D. These are the problems of redundant links if a mechanism is not added to stop loops.

6-44. D. In the switched network with redundant links, Broadcast Storms occur when a frame is continually broadcasting through the internetwork Physical network.

6-45. A. In a switched network with redundant links and no loop avoidance schemes are provided multiple copies of the same frame can be received by Router A.

6-46. B. The switch cannot forward a frame because it is constantly updating the MAC database with source hardware address locations.

6-47. A. Thrashing the MAC table is occurred when the switches constantly updating the MAC filter table with source hardware address locations.

6-48. A, B. If multiple loops are generating throughout an internetwork, and the broadcast storm is occurred, the network would not be able to perform frame switching.

6-49. B, C. If multiple loops are generating throughout an internetwork, and the broadcast storm is occurred, the network would not be able to perform frame switching.

6-50. B. STP's main task is to stop network loops from occurring on the Layer-2 network (bridges or switches).

6-51. C. DEC (Digital Equipment Cooperation) was the original creator of STP. The IEEE created their own version of STP, which is called IEEE 802.1d.

6-52. B. All CISCO switches run the IEEE 802.1d version of STP, which is not compatible with the DEC version and there is no CISCO version for STP.

6-53. B. STP is used to prevent loops and ensures data flows through a single network path in a Catalyst switched network environment.

6-54. B, C, D. The Spanning Tree Algorithm is a requirement in the meshed switching network. It is used to stop network loops from occurring on the Layer-2 network, by monitoring the network, find all links, and make sure that loops do not occur by shutting down redundant links. So, STP is used mainly to discover a "loop free" topology and provide, as possible, a path between every pair of LAN's.

6-55. C. To stop network loops from occurring with redundant links, Layer-2 devices implement the STP.

6-56. A, B. STP monitors the network and finds all links and makes sure that loops do not occur by shutting down redundant links.

6-57. A. STP finds all links in the network, shuts down redundant links, and stops any network loops from occurring in the network. STP does this by electing a root bridge that will decide on the network topology.

6-58. C. There is only one Root Bridge in any given switched network.

6-59. A. There is only one Root Bridge in any given network.

6-60. D. Root Bridge ports are called designated ports.

6-61. B. The designated ports operate in Forwarding State.

6-62. C. Forwarding state ports can send and receive traffic.

6-63. C. In STP network, there is only one Root Bridge. Other switches are called nonroot bridges.

6-64. A, B. Nonroot bridges' ports can be categorized into root port (designated port) and nondesignated port.

6-65. B. Root port is selected using the Lowest cost rule (as determined by a link's bandwidth).

6-66. A. Root port in Nonroot bridges can send and receive traffic.

6-67. A. The nondesignated ports operate in Blocking State.

6-68. D. Blocking state ports cannot Send or receive traffic.

6-69. A. Nondesignated ports cannot Send or receive traffic.

6-70. B. Only two types of STP states can switch's ports be distinguished into.

6-71. A, B. Only two types of STP states can switch's ports be distinguished into. Either root bridges or Nonroot bridges.

6-72. B. Only two types of STP states can switch's ports be distinguished into, these are, designated (root) ports, and nondesignated.

6-73. B, C, D. Only two types of STP states can switch's ports be distinguished into. These are, root ports (designated ports), and nondesignated ports.

6-74. A. Yes, Switches and bridges exchange information between them using a special type of frames.

6-75. B. Switches/bridges exchange information between them using Bridge Protocol Data Units (BPDUs).

6-76. D. BPDUs are used to send configuration messages to neighboring switches, including the bridge IDs.

6-77. D. The bridge ID is sent via a multicast frame inside a BPDU updates.

6-78. A, B. Bridge ID is used to determine the root bridge and to determine the root port.

6-79. C, B, A. The Bridge ID is 8 bytes long and includes the Priority and the MAC address of the device.

6-80. A. The default priority on all devices running the IEEE STP is 32,768.

6-81. A, D. To determine the root bridge in the Layer-2 network, STP combines the priority and MAC address.

6-82. B. Root Bridge is selected using lowest Bridge ID, which is a combination from switch Priority and MAC address.

6-83. A. Switch A will be selected as a Root Bridge in STP network (Figure 6-5) since it has lowest MAC address. Remember that both switches have the same Priority.

6-84. C. BPDUs are sent out every two seconds by default.

6-85. C. The port with the lowest cost to the root bridge is the root port of the bridge.

6-86. B. Every two seconds, BPDUs are sent out from all active bridge ports by default.

6-87. A. Yes, to determine the port(s) that will be used to communicate with the Root Bridge, it must first find the path cost.

6-88. B, A. the port cost is an accumulated total path cost based on the bandwidth of the links.

6-89. C. For 10Gbps Ethernet network, the new IEEE typical cost path is (2) and the Original IEEE typical cost path is (1).

6-90. A. For 1Gbps Ethernet network, the new IEEE typical cost path is (4) and the Original IEEE typical cost path is (1).

6-91. B. For 100Mbps Ethernet network, the new IEEE typical cost path is (19) and the Original IEEE typical cost path is (10).

6-92. D. For 10Mbps Ethernet network, the new IEEE typical cost path is (100) and the Original IEEE typical cost path is (100).

6-93. B. The 2960 switches use the original IEEE 802.1d specifications.

6-94. A, D, E, F, and G. The five states are blocking, learning, listening, forwarding, and disabled.

6-95.

1. A. The switch ports in this state will not forward frames; listens to and receives BPDUs. All ports are in this state by default when the switch is powered up.

2. B. The switch ports in this state will listen to BPDU to make sure no loops occur on the network before passing data frames.

3. C. The switch ports in this state will learn MAC addresses and build a filter table but do not forward frames.

4. D. The switch ports in this state will send and receive all data on the bridged port.

5. E. The switches in this state (administratively) do not participate in the frame forwarding or STP. A port in the disabled state is virtually nonoperational.

6-96. E, F. Typical port states of a STP switch are blocking and Forwarding states.

6-97. A. A forwarding port has been determined to have the lowest cost to the root bridge.

6-98. A, B, C. If the network has a topology change because of a failed link or, even if the administrator adds a new switch to the network, the ports on a switch will be in learning and listening state.

6-99. D. Once a switch determines the best path to the Root Bridge, then all other ports will be in blocking state.

6-100. B. Blocked ports are still receiving BPDUs.

6-101. A. If a switch determines that a blocked port should now be the designated port, the port will go to listening state. It will check all BPDUs heard to make sure that it would not create a loop once the port goes to forwarding state.

6-102. A, C. In blocking state, the port forwards and receives no frames. This is used to stop network loops. However, the blocked port will listen for BPDUs received on the port.

6-103. F. All ports are in Blocking State by default when the switch is powered up.

6-104. A, D, F. In all these states, the ports are unable to send and receive data frames.

6-105. D, F. In all these states, the ports are able to listen and to receive BPDU's.

6-106. D. The switches in this state will listen to BPDU to make sure no loops occur on the network before passing data frames.

6-107. A. The ports in this state will learn MAC addresses and build a filter table but do not forward frames.

6-108. E. The ports in this state will send and receive all data on the bridged port.

6-109. A. Convergence is the time it takes a bridge in STP network to transition to either the forwarding or blocking states. It is important in STP network to make sure that all devices have the same database.

6-110. B. Convergence occurs when switches or bridges have transitioned to either the forwarding or blocking states.

6-111. A. YES, No data is forwarded during Convergence time.

6-112. C. Convergence is important in STP network to make sure that all devices have the same database.

6-113. A. The main problem with convergence is the time it takes for devices to update since all devices must be updated before data can be forwarded.

6-114. B. The update time takes 50 seconds to go from blocking to forwarding state. It is not recommended to change the default STP timers.

6-115. D. Forward delay is the time it takes to transition a port from listening to learning state or from learning to forwarding state.

6-116. C. 50 seconds is the default time for changing from blocking to forwarding state. This is to allow enough time for all switches to update their STP database.

6-117. A, B. the Latency for packet switching through the switch is depending on the chosen Switching mode.

6-118. B, C, D. The primary switching modes are Store, forward, cut-through, and FragmentFree.

6-119.

1. A. In store and forward mode, the complete data frame is received on the switch's buffer, a CRC is run, and then the destination address is looked up in the MAC filter table.

2. B. In cut-through mode, the switch only waits for the destination hardware address to be received and then looks up the destination address in the MAC filter table.

3. C. In FragmentFree mode (the default for the CAT2.96K switch), a switch checks the first 64 bytes of a frame for fragmentation (because of possible collisions) before forwarding the frame. Sometimes FragmentFree is referred to as a "modified cut-through."

6-120. B. Cut-through switching mode waits for the destination addresses and checks the filter table.

6-121. C. Store and forward run a CRC on every frame.

6-122. C. Store and forward has the highest latency of any LAN switch type.

6-123. B. Cut-through switching mode checks the hardware address before forwarding a frame

6-124. B. Cut-through switching mode has the lowest latency of any LAN switch type.

6-125. B. Cut-through switching mode switching mode has no error checking.

6-126. C. Store and forward switching mode filters all errors.

6-127. E. FragmentFree switching mode checks for collisions

6-128. E. The default LAN switch mode on a CAT2.96K switch is FragmentFree

6-129. A. The CAT2.96K switch can use the store-and-forward switching mode in addition to Fragment Free mode (default).

6-130. Figure 6-7-2 shows the different points where the switching mode takes place in the frame.

Figure 6-7-2 The Switching Modes Location on a MAC Data Frame

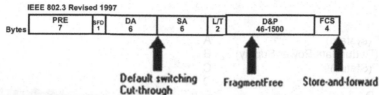

6-131. A, C. The CAT2.96K switch uses the store-and-forward switching mode and Fragment Free mode.

6-132. C. The store-and-forward switching mode checks the frame to see if it is too short (less than 64 bytes including the CRC), or if it is too long (more than 1518 bytes including the CRC). If the frame does not contain any errors, the LAN switch looks up the destination hardware address in its forwarding or switching table and determines the outgoing interface. It then forwards the frame toward its destination. This is the only mode on CAT5K switches.

6-133. A, B, C, D. these are the characteristics of the store-and-forward switching mode.

6-134. A. Some switches can be configured to perform cut-through switching on a per-port basis until a user-defined error threshold is reached. When errors reach to threshold point, the mode automatically change over to store-and-forward mode, so they will stop forwarding the errors. When the error rate on the port falls below the threshold, the port automatically changes back to cut-through mode.

6-135. E. FragmentFree switching mode looks at the first 64 bytes of a frame to make sure a collision has not occurred.

6-136. C. Store-and-forward has a variable latency time depending on the frame length. FragmentFree and cut through modes always read only a fixed amount of a frame, so they have fixed latency time. In store-and-forward mode, latency is measured by last-bit-received to first-bit-transmitted or LIFO. This does not include the time it makes to receive the entire packet, which can vary, according to packet size, from 65 microseconds to 1.3 milliseconds.

6-137. E. FragmentFree LAN switching mode keeps CRC errors to a minimum but still has a fixed latency rate. It checks into the data portion of the frame to make sure no fragmentation has occurred.

6-138. B, E. Store-and-forward has a variable latency time depending on the frame length. FragmentFree and cut through modes always read only a fixed amount of a frame, so they have fixed latency time.

6-139. A-D.

6-140. A-E.

6-141. A.

6-142. A-F

6-143. A.

6-144.

1.	Distribution	B.
2.	Access	A.
3.	Core	C.

6-145. A, C, F.

6-146. A.

6-147. A-C.

6-148. A, B.

6-149. A. Only power on the switch by connecting the power cable to the switch and a power outlet, and the switch will work.

6-150. A, B, C. connecting to switch's user interface is essential for doing crucial jobs.

6-151. A. Yes, this is TRUE.

6-152. A.

6-153. A.

6-154. A-E.

6-155. A.

6-156. A.

6-157. A.

6-158. B, A.

6-159.

1.	SYST (system)	A
2.	RPS (Redundant Power Supply)	B
3.	STAT (Status)	C
4.	DUPLX (duplex)	D
5.	SPEED	E

6-160. A-C.

6-161. A.

6-162. A.

6-163. A.

6-164. A-D.

6-165. A.

6-166. A.

6-167. A.

6-168. A, B, C. All these statements are true about CISCO CAT2.96K switch.

6-169. B.

6-170.

1.	Disabled	A
2.	Notconnect	B, C
3.	err-disabled	D
4.	connect	E

6-171.

1.	Disabled	A
2.	Notconnect	B, C
3.	err-disabled	D
4.	connect	E

6-172. A, B, D, F.

6-173. A, B, C. All these statements are true about CISCO CAT2.96K switch.

6-174. A.

6-175. A. SSH is the preferred method for remote login to switches and routers today.

6-176. A, B. SSH requires that the user supply both a username and password instead of just a password.

6-177. A, B. Two types of authentication can be used.

6-178. B. the **login local** subcommand defines the use of local usernames.

6-179. C. this command tells the switch to accept only ssh connections.

6-180. A. This command is used to tell the switch to generate a matched public and private key pair, as well as a shared encryption key.

6-181. A. This command is used to display a copy of the switch's key which is generated using the **crypto key generate rsa** command.

6-182. A. An interface can be configured to use duplex full by the **Switch(config-if)#duplex full** command.

6-183. B. An interface can be configured to use speed 100 by the **Switch(config-if)#speed 100** command.

6-184. A, B, C. The interface is in disable state.

6-185. A-E. The interface is in notconnect state.

6-186. A, B. The interface is in notconnect state.

6-187. A-C. The interface is in err-disabled state.

6-188. A-C. The interface is in connect state.

6-189. A, B. All these statements are true regarding this link.

6-190. A, B. The interface is configured with speed 100 & duplex full subcommands.

6-191. A. This statement is TRUE.

6-192. B, D.

6-193. A. Port security is an important tool to prevent some attacks.

6-194. A. The port should be an access port at first, which means that the port is not doing any VLAN trunking.

6-195. B. Secondly the port security feature should be enabled.

6-196. C, Thirdly, the actual MAC addresses of the devices allowed to use that port should be configured.

6-197. C. This command is used to configure the sticky learning on an interface.

6-198. A. This command is used to display the port security details on an interface 0/1.

6-199. A, B An interface in err-disabled state requires that manually **shutdown** the interface and then use the **no shutdown** command to recover the interface.

6-200. B, C In addition to these steps the port must be an access port at first.

6-201. C. This way is used to configure an interface.

6-202. D. From the Interface configuration mode, it is possible to configure interface properties.

6-203. A-E.

6-204. A.

6-205. A-C.

6-206. A, B.

6-207. A.

6-208. A, B.

6-209. A.

6-210. A-C.

6-211. A.

6-212.

1.	Excessive noise	A
2.	Collisions	B
3.	Late collisions	C

6-213.

1.	Excessive noise	A
2.	Collisions	B
3.	Late collisions	C

6-214. A. The first step is examining the switch LEDs combinations.

6-215. C. The CDP commands are used to verify CISCO networks.

6-216. A. This command is used to display the whole contents of the mac address table.

6-217. B. This command is used to display the dynamically learned mac addresses in the mac address table.

6-218. C. This command is used to display the statically configured mac addresses in the mac address table.

6-219. A, C. These commands can be used to display the MAC address table entries for MAC addresses configured by port security.

Answers to the Chapter 7 Learning Questions

7-1   C. The Random Access Memory (RAM) is a Volatile memory that can be read and written by a microprocessor.

7-2   A, C. The Static Random Access Memory (SRAM) retains its contents for as long as power is supplied. It does not require constant refreshing, like DRAM.

7-3   B, C, E. The Dynamic Random Access Memory (DRAM) stores information in capacitors that must be periodically refreshed. Delays can occur because they are inaccessible to the processor when refreshing their contents. However, they are less complex and have a greater capacity than SRAMs. It is used by CISCO Routers to store packet buffers and routing tables, along with the hardware addresses cache.

7-4   D, E. The NonVolatile Random Access Memory (NVRAM) retains its contents intact when a unit is powered OFF and it is used to hold the Router and Switch startup configuration.

7-5   A, B, C. The Read Only Memory (ROM) Chip used to boot and maintain the Router.

7-6   D. Electrically erasable programmable read-only memory (EPPROM) that can be erased using electrical signals applied to specific pins. It is the flash memory that used to hold the CISCO IOS.

7-7   A, D, E. Flash memory is an EEPROM chip used on the Router to hold the CISCO IOS.

7-8   B, A. Bootstrap is stored in the microcode of the ROM. It is used to bring a Router up during initializations. It will boot the Router and then load the IOS.

7-9   A, B. POST is stored in the microcode of the ROM. It is used to check the basic functionality of the Router hardware and determines which interfaces are present.

7-10   B, A. ROM monitor is stored in the microcode of the ROM. It is used for manufacturing testing and troubleshooting.

7-11   A, C, B. Mini-IOS is called the RXBOOT or bootloader by CISCO. The mini-IOS is a small IOS in ROM that can be used to bring up an interface and load IOS software into flash memory.

7-12   A, B. Configuration Register is used to control how the Router boot. The typical value of this register is 0x2102, which tells the Router to load the IOS from flash memory.

7-13   B, C. The CISCO IOS usually loaded from the flash memory, but it can also be run from RAM in some routers.

7-14   C. The **show version** command displays the value of the configuration register. The default value is 0x2102.

7-15   B. The device's startup-configuration is stored in NVRAM, and it is erased using **erase start** command.

7-16   A-E. RAM is used to hold packet buffers, routing tables, and the software and data structures that allow the Router to function. Running-config is stored in RAM, and the IOS can be run from RAM in some routers.

7-17   B. The flash memory is used to hold the CISCO IOS. It is a NVRAM, which it retains its contents when the device is reloaded and when the device is power OFF.

7-18   B. The RAM stores packet buffers and routing tables.

7-19   A, B, D, E. When the Router boots up, it performs a series of steps, called the boot sequence, to test the hardware and load the necessary software. The boot sequence consists of the following steps: POST step, Bootstrap step, IOS step and the setup step.

7-20   A. This step is repressible for testing the hardware to verify that all components of the device are operational and present.

7-21   B. This step is repressible for looking for and loading the CISCO IOS software.

7-22   C. This step is repressible for looking for a valid configuration file stored in NVRAM.

7-23   D. This step is repressible for operating the device either from setup mode or from the startup-config file.

7-24   A-C.

7-25   A.

7-26   A.

7-27   A. The 16-bit software register is found on all CISCO routers, which is written into NVRAM.

7-28   A, C. By default, the configuration register is set to load the CISCO IOS from flash memory and to look for and load the startup-config file from NVRAM.

7-29   D. The software configuration register is written into NVRAM.

7-30   A, B, C, D. The default configuration setting on CISCO Routers is 0x2102 (hexadecimal). This will make the Router to load the CISCO IOS from flash memory.

7-31   A. The values of the configuration register are used to determine how CISCO routers function during initializations.

7-32   C. The bits (0-3) are considered as the boot field.

7-33   C. The **sh ver** command displays the current configuration register.

7-34   C. The default value of the configuration register is 0x2102.

7-35   A, B, C, D. The **sh ver** command is issued from any Router prompt.

7-36   A, B, C, D. All these statements are true about default configuration register.

7-37

      A   Step2
      B   Step1
      C   Step3

7-38

    1.   boot system flash   C
    2.   boot system flash filename   B
    3.   boot system tftp filename 107.100.100.100   A

7-39   A, B, C. Changing the configuration register value provides the possibility to modify how the Router boots and runs.

7-40   A-H. All these operations can be implemented on the Router by modifying the configuration register.

7-41   A. The **config-register 0x2142** command sets the configuration register to new value.

7-42   B. From the global configuration mode, the **config-register** command is issued.

7-43   A, B. The 0x2102-0x210F values of the configuration register tell the router to boot the IOS from flash memory.

7-44   B. The configuration register is used to tell the Router how to load the IOS and configuration. The value 0x0101 tells the Router to boot from ROM.

7-45   A. Configuration register changes take effect only when the system reloads, such as when you issue a **reload** command from the console.

7-46   D. To invoke the ROM monitor mode, set the configuration register to 2100.

7-47   A, B. If the administrator in Privileged EXEC mode, he simply, can set a new password, or he can erase the configuration.

7-48   A. Password recovery can only be done from the console port on the Router.

7-49   A. By default, The router will look for and load a Router configuration stored in NVRAM (startup-config).

7-50   A. To recover a password, bit 6 must be turned ON; this will tell the router to ignore the NVRAM contents.

7-51   B. The configuration register value 0x2142 is used to recover a lost password since the bit 6 is turned ON.

7-52   A-I. All these steps are required for password recovery procedure and in the same order.

7-53   A.

7-54   B. Typically, the Ctrl+Break keyword is used to interrupt the Router normal booting when connecting through HyperTerminal.

7-55   A, B. To change the configuration register value out of the Router, the Router must be booted from ROM monitor.

7-56   C. The **confreg 0x2142** command from ROM monitor prompt prevents the Router from using the configuration in NVRAM next time booting.

7-57   C, D. Depending on the platform you have, i or reset commands can be used to initialize the Router from ROM monitor. The reload command is used from privileged EXEC configuration mode.

7-58   A. The **reload** command initializes the Router immediately from privileged EXEC mode.

7-59   D. The **reload in 10** command initializes the Router after 10 minutes from privileged EXEC mode.

7-60 B. The **reload at 13:00** command initializes the software on the Router at 1:00 p.m. today from privileged EXEC mode.

7-61 D. The **reload at 02:00 apr 10** command initializes the software on the Router on April 10 at 2:00 a.m. from privileged EXEC mode.

7-62 B. The **reload cancel** command cancels a pending reload from privileged EXEC mode.

7-63 C. The **confreg 0x2142** command is issued from ROM monitor prompt.

7-64 C. The **i** command is issued from ROM monitor prompt.

7-65 C. The **reset** command is issued from ROM monitor prompt.

7-66 B. The **reload** command is issued from Privileged EXEC mode.

7-67 A. To make a Router boot from ROM and skip NVRAM, just set the configuration register value to 0x2140.

7-68 C. The **reload** command halts the Router operations and does a complete restart of the Router.

7-69 A. The Router will boot the IOS stored in ROM.

7-70 A. To change the console line speed, bits 11 and 12 should be (0x0800-0x1000). This will tend that one of the 0x3 answers is correct. From table below, the 12 and 11 bits should be (10) for 1200-baud rate. This will tend that all 0x39 answers are wrong. Finally, to make the boot normally from NVRAM, answer A is the only correct. (See the table below for more information)

System Console Terminal Baud Rate Settings

Baud	Bit12	Bit11
9600	0	0
4800	0	1
1200	1	0
2400	1	1

7-71 A, H.

7-72 B.

7-73 C.

7-74 A, C.

7-75 A.

7-76 C, B, A. The flash memory should be verified before attempting to upgrade the CISCO IOS, to find if the Router flash memory has enough space to hold the new image or not.

7-77 B. The **show flash** command verifies the amount of the flash memory.

7-78 A-E. Flash memory related information is provided by **show flash** command.

7-79 B. The c3600 indicates the platform type.

7-80 D. The 11.2-18 indicates the CISCO revision number.

7-81 C, D. Both **sh flash** and **sh version** commands can display the current system image version.

7-82 B. From the privileged EXEC mode, the **show flash** command is issued.

7-83 E. Copies the IOS image in flash memory to tftp server.

7-84 A, C, D. Three information must be supplied by administrator. These are; The CISCO IOS image name to be copied; the address or name of remote tftp server; the destination file name.

7-85 B. The exclamation point (!) indicates that the copy process is taking place. Each exclamation point (!) indicates that ten packets have been transferred successfully.

7-86 D. The source CISCO IOS image name is the default name.

7-87 B. From the Privileged EXEC mode, the **copy flash tftp** command is issued.

7-88 A. It is recommended to check the network connectivity before **copy flash tftp** is issued. The **ping** utility can be used for this purpose.

7-89 A. Before **copy flash tftp** is issued, the TFTP host must have a default directory specified, or it will not work.

7-90 B. The **copy tftp flash** command restores the IOS image in flash memory from tftp server. Where the flash memory is the default location for the CISCO IOS in CISCO routers.

7-91 B. The **copy tftp flash** command upgrades the IOS image in flash memory from tftp server.

7-92   A, C, D, E. All these parameters must be supplied by administrator.

7-93   B. The exclamation point (!) indicates that the copy process is taking place. Each exclamation point (!) indicates that one UDP segment has been successfully transferred.

7-94   A. The "e" character indicates that the erase process is taking place to delete the contents of flash memory.

7-95   D. The source CISCO IOS image name is the default name.

7-96   B. From the Privileged EXEC mode, the **copy tftp flash** command is issued.

7-97   A. It is recommended to check the network connectivity before **copy tftp flash** is issued. The **ping** utility can be used for this purpose.

7-98   A. Before the **copy tftp flash** command is issued, the required file to be placed in flash memory should be placed in the default TFTP directory on the TFTP host.

7-99   A, D. You may need to restore the CISCO IOS to flash memory to replace an original file that has been damaged or to upgrade the IOS.

7-100   C. The **copy tftp flash** command requires two rebooting.

7-101   A, B. If the flash memory has no enough room or it is new, its contents will be erased.

7-102   A, B, C, D. All these confirmations must be supplied.

7-103   C. The **copy tftp flash** command prompts you three times for erasing the flash memory contents.

7-104   C. The **tftp-server system image-name** command configures a Router to become a TFTP server for a Router-system image that is run in flash.

7-105   A. The **boot system tftp [ios file name] [ip address of tftp host]** command tells a Router to run a CISCO IOS from a tftp host.

7-106   A.

7-107   A-F. All these commands will backup the Router configuration.

7-108   B. The **sh start** (**show startup-config**) command verifies the stored system configuration in NVRAM.

7-109   A. The **sh run** (**show running-config**) command verifies the system running configuration in DRAM.

7-110   B. The **copy run start** command stores the DRAM running configuration to NVRAM startup configuration.

7-111   C. The **copy run tftp** command backs up the DRAM running configuration to a TFTP host.

7-112   A. The **copy start run** command backs up the system configuration stored in NVRAM to DRAM.

7-113   B The **config mem** command is a pre-10.3 IOS command and restores the system configuration stored in NVRAM to DRAM. However, it is append the file in DRAM, not replace it.

7-114   E, F. The **copy tftp run** or **copy tftp start** commands restore the system configuration stored in a tftp.

7-115   A. The **config net** command is a pre-10.3 IOS command and restores the system configuration stored in a tftp host. Notice that, both **config net** and **config mem** commands append the running configuration in DRAM, not replace it.

7-116   D. The configuration file is an ASCII text file. This means that changes can be made on this file using any text editor before copying the configuration stored in a tftp host to DRAM or NVRAM.

7-117   A. The **erase start** command deletes the system startup configuration.

7-118   D. The **write mem** command is a pre-10.3 IOS command and backs up the system configuration stored in DRAM to NVRAM.

7-119   C. The **write net** command is a pre-10.3 IOS command and backs up the system configuration stored in DRAM to tftp.

7-120   A, C, D. A global parameter that can be configured on CISCO switches as well as Routers.

7-121   B, C, D. A global parameter that can be configured on CISCO switches as well as Routers.

7-122   C. The **sh cdp** command displays the cdp protocol timer information.

7-123   C. The **sh cdp** command displays the cdp protocol holdtime information.

7-124   A. The default value for cdp protocol timer information is 60 seconds.

7-125   C. The default value for cdp protocol holdtime information is 180 seconds.

7-126   C. To configure the cdp protocol timer information to be equal to 120 seconds, the following command is used: Router(config)#cdp timer 120.

7-127   D. To configure the cdp protocol holdtime information to be equal to 240 seconds, the following command is used: Router(config)#cdp holdtime 240.

7-128   B. The **show cdp** command must be issued from Privileged EXEC mode.

7-129   C. The **cdp timer 120** command must be issued from Global configuration mode.

7-130   C. The **cdp holdtime 240** command must be issued from Global configuration mode.

7-131   C. The **no cdp run** command must be issued from Global configuration mode.

7-132   D. The **no cdp run** command turns OFF completely the cdp protocol operations.

7-133   C. The command **cdp timer 120** changes the update frequency of CDP packets to 120 seconds.

7-134   C. The **show cdp neighbors** command shows information about directly connected devices.

7-135   B. The **sh cdp nei** command shows information about neighbor devices.

7-136   D. The **sh cdp nei detail** command shows detailed information about neighbor devices.

7-137   A. The **sh cdp entry *** command shows detailed information about neighbor devices like **sh cdp nei de** command.

7-138   B. The **sh cdp nei** command must be issued from Privileged EXEC mode.

7-139   B. The **sh cdp nei de** command must be issued from Privileged EXEC mode.

7-140   B. The **sh cdp entry *** command must be issued from Privileged EXEC mode.

7-141   A. It is important to remember that CDP packets are not passed through a CISCO switch, and only what is directly attached will be seen.

7-142   A, D. Both **sh cdp nei de** and **sh cdp entry *** commands show the IOS version of neighbor device.

7-143   B. R character refers to the Router device.

7-144   C. r character refers to the repeater device.

7-145   A. S character refers to the switch device.

7-146   C. B character refers to the Source Route Bridge device.

7-147   A. T character refers to the Trans Bridge device.

7-148   C. H character refers to Host device.

7-149   A. I character refers to IGMP device.

7-150   C, F, G, H, I, J. All these parameters are provided by the **sh cdp nei** command.

7-151   B, C. The **sh cdp entry *** and **sh cdp nei de** commands show the neighbor router's IP address from the Router prompt.

7-152   B, C, D. these commands show the hostname, local interface, platform, and remote port of a neighbor Router.

7-153   C, E-M. All these parameters are provided by the **sh cdp nei de** command.

7-154   A. The **sh cdp traffic** command shows information about interface traffic.

7-155   B. The **sh cdp traffic** command must be issued from Privileged EXEC mode.

7-156   A-H. All these parameters are provided by the **sh cdp traffic** command.

7-157   C. The **sh cdp int** command shows information about CDP status on Router interfaces or switch ports.

7-158   B. The **sh cdp int** command must be issued from Privileged EXEC mode.

7-159   A-D. All these parameters are provided by the **sh cdp int** command for each interface.

7-160   B. The **cdp enable** command enables CDP operations on Router interfaces or switch ports.

7-161   B. The **no cdp enable** command disables CDP operations on Router interfaces or switch ports.

7-162   D. The **cdp enable** command must be issued from Line interface mode.

7-163   D. The **no cdp enable** command must be issued from Line interface mode.

7-164   B. The **show cdp interface** command shows the status of interfaces enabled with CDP.

7-165   C. The **clear cdp table** command clears the CDP table where CISCO Router keeps information about neighboring devices.

7-166   B. The cdp is enabled by default on all interfaces and there is no requirement to configure IP or IPX protocols.

7-167   A.

7-168   A.

7-169   A-G. Telnet is the best utility for checking network connectivity, since it uses IP at the Network layer and TCP at the Transport layer to create a session with a remote host.

7-170   A-D. The CDP cannot be used for running programs.

7-171   C. VTY lines must be configured with **login** or **no login** commands before connection can be established.

7-172   B. VTY password alone is not sufficient to be able to configure remote devices. The enable password or enable secret passwords must be configured also.

7-173   A. Enable password or enable secret password must be configured to be able to access the enable mode of the remote router.

7-174   A. Telnet utility is used to access; to check and to configure remote, directly or indirectly connected devices.

7-175   A-E. All these commands can be used to terminate an active Telnet connection.

7-176   A. To keep open multiple Telnet sessions use the CTRL+SHIFT+6, then X keystroke combination.

7-177   A. It is possible to telnet into multiple devices simultaneously from the same device.

7-178   A. The enable mode password level 15 must be configured on the switch to be able to telnet into a **Switch1** switch.

7-179   B, C. The **sh sessions** command will show you the active connections made from your Router.

7-180   A, D. The asterisk (*) represents the last or current session.

7-181   C. To access the last session the **Enter** key must be pressed twice.

7-182   A. To access the session number five the **Enter** key must be pressed twice after the number 5.

7-183   A-F. The Conn, Host, Address, Byte, Idle, and Conn Name information are provided by **show session** command.

7-184   A. The **show users** command shows you the active consoles in use on your Routers.

7-185   A. The **show users** command shows you the active VTY ports in use on your Routers.

7-186   A, D. The asterisk (*) represents the last or current session.

7-187   A. The output shows that the VTY port 3 is being used.

7-188   A-E. All these parameters are provided by the **show users** command. If no user is listed in the user field, this means that no one is using the line. If an Idle value is found in the host field, this indicates no outgoing connection to a host. The location can be either the hard-wired location for the line or, if there is an incoming connection, the host the incoming connection is from.

7-189   A-D. All these types can appear in the **show users** command.

7-190   C. The **exit** command is used to terminate the Telnet switch session.

7-191   D. The **disconnect** command is used to clear a Telnet connection to a remote Router from your Router.

7-192   C. The **clear line #** command clears a VTY connection into your Router.

7-193   A. The **show users** command checks if any devices are attached to your Router.

7-194   A. The **ip host hostname ip_addresses** command builds a host table on your Router.

7-195   D. The **ip host zoo 172.17.17.10 172.17.17.20** command creates a host table entry for zoo, using ip addresses 172.17.17.10 and 172.17.17.20. The second IP address will only be tried if the first one does not work.

7-196   C. The **show hosts** or **show host** command shows the hostname resolved to the IP address on a Router.

7-197   C. From Global Configuration mode, the **ip host** command is issued.

7-198   A. This is one of the weaknesses for this command.

7-199   B. The **no ip host** command removes the name-to-address mapping.

7-200   A. The default port_number in **ip host** command is TCP port number 23. However, it is possible to create a session using Telnet with a different TCP port number.

7-201   C. It is possible to assign up to eight IP addresses to a hostname.

7-202   C. The **perm** in the Flag column means that the entry is manually configured.

7-203   B. The **temp** in the Flag column means that the entry is automatically resolved by DNS.

7-204   A. A DNS server should be used to resolve hostnames in the network containing many devices. It is difficult to create a host table in each device.

7-205   A-D. All these commands can test and verify the correct implementation on the CISCO Router.

7-206   C. The **show host** command shows the IP-address-to-hostname-resolution table.

7-207   D. The **ip host thaar 172.17.17.17** command resolves the name thaar to IP address 172.17.17.17.

7-208   A, B, C. These commands should be configured to make the DNS resolution works.

7-209   A. Anytime, a CISCO device receives a command it does not understand it tries to resolve this through DNS by default.

7-210   A-E. All these commands can be used to test or verify the correct implementation of the DNS resolution on your Router.

7-211   C. From Global Configuration mode, the **ip domain-lookup** command is issued.

7-212   C. From Global Configuration mode, the **ip name-server** command is issued.

7-213   C. From Global Configuration mode, the **ip domain-server** command is issued.

7-214   A. If the command **ip domain-name** is not configured with DNS name resolution, the FQDN must be used to access the network devices.

7-215   A. It is possible to enter the IP addresses of up to six servers.

7-216   B. The **ip name-server** command sets up a DNS server to resolve names on a CISCO Router.

Answers to the Chapter 8 Learning Questions

8-1 A.

8-2 A-G. All these statements are true about the WAN technologies.

8-3 A.

8-4 E, F.

8-5 A.

8-6 G.

8-7 A-E.

8-8 A-C.

8-9 A.

8-10   A.

8-11   A.

8-12   A.

8-13   A, E.

8-14
   1. Customer premise equipment (CPE) is equipment that has owned by the subscriber site and located on the subscriber's premises.

   2. The demarcation location is the spot where the service provider's responsibility ends and the CPE begins. It is generally a device in a telecommunications closet owned and installed by the telecommunications company (Telco).

   3. The local loop connects demarc to a CO of Telco.

   4. The Central office (CO) connects the customers to the provider's switching network.

   5. The toll network is a trunk line inside a WAN provider's network. This network is a collection of switches and facilities owned by the ISP.

8-15   A-D.

8-16   A.

8-17   A.

8-18   A.

8-19   A.

8-20   A.

8-21   C, B, A.

8-22   B. Serial WAN transmission requires serial WAN connectors.

8-23   A. Yes, it is correct.

8-24   A. It takes place one bit at a time over a single channel.

8-25   A-E. These types of WAN connections can be used by the service provider.

8-26   A. Serial transmissions are measured in frequency or cycles per second (hertz). The amount of data that can be carried within these frequencies is called bandwidth. Bandwidth is the amount of data in bits per second that the serial channel can carry.

8-27   A-F.

8-28   A.

8-29   A.

8-30   A.

8-31   A.

8-32   A.

8-33
   1. 1.544Mbps   C.
   2. 64 kbps   A.
   3. 2.048 Mbps   B.

8-34   A, B, C.

8-35   A-C.

8-36   A.

8-37   A-C. Yes, all these statements are true.

8-38   A. This paragraph correctly depicts Figure 8-4.

8-39   D.
8-40   A.
8-41   A.
8-42   A-E.
8-43   A.
8-44

1.	Dedicated link	A.
2.	Circuit-switched link	B.
3.	Packet-switched link	C. .
4.	Cell-switched link	D.

8-45   A-C. These are the types of WAN connections.
8-46   A, C, B. These are the right choices.
8-47   A, B, C. These are the right choices.
8-48   A, B, D, C. These are the right choices.
8-49   A. Figure 8-7-A represents a leased line WAN network type. Figure 8-7-B, represents a circuit switching WAN network type. Figure 8-7-C, represents a packet switching WAN network type.
8-50   A.
8-51

1.	Dedicated communication links	D.
2.	Circuit-switched communication links	C.
3.	Packet-switched communication links	B.
4.	Cell-switched communication links	A.

8-52   A, C, F-G.
8-53   A-C, E.
8-54   A, C, F, G.
8-55   A.
8-56   F.
8-57   A.
8-58   A. Yes, it is correct.
8-59   A.
8-60   A.
8-61   A.
8-62   A.
8-63   A-E. Each vendor's HDLC has a proprietary data field to support multiprotocol environments.
8-64   A, B. These are the differences between bit-oriented and byte oriented protocols.
8-65   A.
8-66   C. The address field is not really needed for Point-to-Point links, since there are only two known address and only one intended recipient at the other end. It used in the past years when the Telco sold multidrop circuits.
8-67   A-C, E.
8-68   A.
8-69   A. Yes, it is correct.
8-70   A-F. All these statements are true about PPP.
8-71   A-C. All these techniques are provided by the PPP.
8-72   A-D. These are the main components of the PPP.
8-73   A. EIA/TIA-232-C, V.24, V.35, and ISDN are Physical layer international standards for serial communication.
8-74   B. HDLC is a method for encapsulating datagrams over serial links.
8-75   C. LCP is a method of establishing, configuring, maintaining, and terminating the point-to-point connection.
8-76   D. NCP method of establishing and configuring different Network layer protocols.
8-77   A. Yes, it is correct.
8-78   A. Yes, it is correct.

8-79	A-C. These are the phases of the PPP session.
8-80	B, A, C. This is a Link establishment phase of the PPP session.
8-81	A, B. This is an Authentication phase of the PPP session.
8-82	B, C, D. This is a Network layer protocol phase of the PPP session.
8-83	A, B. These two methods can be used by PPP.
8-84	A, C. that is the Password Authentication Protocol (PAP) method.
8-85	A, B, C, D. That is the Challenge Handshake Authentication Protocol (CHAP).
8-86	A. Its right.
8-87	A.
8-88	A-E.
8-89	A.
8-90	A.
8-91	A-C.
8-92	A.
8-93	A.
8-94	A-H.
8-95	B.
8-96	A.
8-97	A.
8-98	A.
8-99	C.
8-100	A.
8-101	A. It is true.
8-102	A.
8-103	A.
8-104	A.
8-105	A-C.
8-106	A, D-F.
8-107	A-D.
8-108	A-D.
8-109	A.
8-110	A.
8-111	A.
8-112	A.
8-113	A.
8-114	A.
8-115	A.
8-116	A.
8-117	A.
8-118	A-D.
8-119	A.
8-120	A-C.
8-121	A.
8-122	A.
8-123	A.
8-124	A.
8-125	C.
8-126	A-D,
8-127	A.
8-128	A-C.
8-129	A-D.
8-130	A.
8-131	A.

8-132	B, D, F, G.
8-133	A, C.
8-134	A-C, F.
8-135	A.
8-136	A-F.
8-137	A.
8-138	A.
8-139	A-D.
8-140	A, B.
8-141	A, C.
8-142	A, B.
8-143	C.
8-144	C.
8-145	C.
8-146	B.
8-147	B.
8-148	A.
8-149	A.
8-150	A-D.
8-151	A, B.
8-152	A-D.
8-153	A.
8-154	A.
8-155	A, C, E.
8-156	A-D.
8-157	A-C. These are the main differences between circuit switching and packet switching services.
8-158	A.
8-159	A.
8-160	A.
8-161	A-D.
8-162	A.
8-163	A.
8-164	A.
8-165	A-C.
8-166	All points are in the correct order.
8-167	A.
8-168	A.
8-169	B.
8-170	C, D.
8-171	C, D.

8-172

1.	Router	A.
2.	Communication server	B.
3.	Modem	C.
4.	Other networking device	D.
5.	DSLAM	E.

8-173

1.	Inside interface	C.
2.	Outside interface	A.
3.	Static NAT	D.
4.	Dynamic NAT	F.
5.	Inside network	E.
6.	Outside global IP address	B.

8-174	C.
8-175	C.
8-176	C.
8-177	D.
8-178	B, D, F.
8-179	C.
8-180	D.
8-181	D.
8-182	D.
8-183	A, E.
8-184	A.
8-185	D-G.
8-186	A-C.
8-187	A.
8-188	A, C, E.

Answers to the Chapter 9 Learning Questions

9-1 A. Yes, this is TRUE.

9-2 A.

9-3 A. Yes, this paragraph correctly depicts Figure 9-2.

9-4 A. WLAN allowing communications to occur between wirelesses automated devices.

9-5 B. ELAN allowing communications to occur between wired automated devices.

9-6 C. WLAN defined by IEEE 802.11 family.

9-7 A. WLAN uses radiated energy waves, generally called radio waves, to transmit data.

9-8 B. WLAN waves overtake through space, so technically there is no need for any physical transmission medium.

9-9 B, D.

9-10

1, WLAN	A, C, E, G, I,
2. ELAN	B, D, Γ, II, J

9-11 A.

9-12 A.

9-13 A.

9-14 A.

9-15 A.

9-16 A-C.

9-17 A-D.

9-18 A-E. These are the IEEE standards for WLAN.

9-19 A-D. Four organizations have set or influence the standards used for WLANs today.

9-20 A.

9-21 C.

9-22 B.

9-23 A, C.

9-24 A.

9-25 B, E.

9-26 A. IEEE 802.11 is ratified in 1997.

9-27 B. IEEE 802.11a is ratified in 1999.

9-28 B. IEEE 802.11b is ratified in 1999.

9-29 C. IEEE 802.11g is ratified in 2003.

9-30 C.

9-31 A or B.

9-32 E.

9-33 E.

9-34 E.

9-35 E.

9-36 A or B.

9-37 F.

9-38 C.

9-39 C.

9-40 D or E.

9-41 E.

9-42 B.

9-43 E.

9-44 B.

9-45 D.

9-46 E.

9-47 B.

9-48 E.

9-49 C.

9-50 E.
9-51 B.
9-52 D.
9-53 B.
9-54 B.
9-55 B or D.
9-56 A.
9-57 B.
9-58 D.
9-59 C.
9-60 E.
9-61 B.
9-62 B.
9-63 B.
9-64 B.
9-65 B or D.
9-66 A.
9-67 B.
9-68 B.
9-69 C.
9-70 D.
9-71 B.
9-72 A.
9-73 C.
9-74 C.
9-75 D.
9-76 C, E.
9-77 A.
9-78 B, A, C, E, F, D.
9-79 A, C.
9-80 A.
9-81 A.
9-82 A.
9-83 B.
9-84 A.
9-85 A.
9-86 A.
9-87 B. WLANs transmit data at Layer 1 of the OSI model by sending and receiving radio waves.
9-88 A, B. The FCC defines two unlicensed frequency bands that can be used for WLAN transmission.
9-89 A, C, D, E. 802.11, 802.11b, 802.11g, and 802.11n WLANs use 2.4GHz frequency band.
9-90 B, E. 802.11a, 802.11n WLANs use 5GHz frequency band.
9-91 A.
9-92 A.
9-93 A.
9-94 A-C. These are the methods of encoding for WLANs.
9-95 A. It correctly depicts the FHSS modulation method.
9-96 A. It correctly depicts the DSSS modulation method.
9-97 A.
9-98 A.
9-99 A. It correctly depicts the OFDM modulation method.
9-100 A. 802.11 uses FHSS.
9-101 C-E.
9-102 B, D, E.

9-103 A, B.
9-104 A.
9-105 A.
9-106 A.
9-107 A, B. EIRP = The power of the signal as it leaves the antenna.
9-108 A. Yes, it is true.
9-109 A. Yes, it is true.
9-110 A. Yes, it is true.
9-111 A.
9-112 B. 3 nonoverlapping channels in IEEE 802.11b standard.
9-113 A. 12 nonoverlapping channels in IEEE 802.11a standard.
9-114 B. 3 nonoverlapping channels in IEEE 802.11g standard.
9-115 D.
9 116 C.
9-117 A. Yes, it is true.
9-118 A, B. To solve the above problems, an algorithm called carrier sense multiple access with collision avoidance (CSMA/CA) and acknowledgement mechanisms are used.
9-119 A.
9-120 A.
9-121 B. The AP can be connected to the wired Ethernet switch using straight through cables.
9-122 A.
9-123 A-E.
9-124 A.
9-125 A.
9-126 A.
9-127 A.
9-128 A.
9-129 A.
9-130 A.
9-131 A.
9-132 A-D.
9-133 A-I.
9-134 A, D.
9-135 B, D.
9-136 B.
9-137 C.
9-138 A-C.
9-139

1. CISCO Compatible Extensions	A
2. CISCO Secure Services Client	C
3. WZC/ZCF	B

Answers to the Chapter 10 Learning Questions

10-1 A-D.

10-2 A-F.

10-3 A.

10-4 C, B, A.

10-5 A. Yes, it is correct.

10-6 A-D.

10-7 A. Yes, it is correct.

10-8 A. Yes, it is correct.

10-9 A. Yes, it is correct.

10-10 A.

10-11 A, C, B. Anti-virus is one of the tools that can be used to enhance the security of the systems.

10-12 A.

10-13 A.

10-14 A, B. In this sequence, the paragraph should be completed.

10-15 A.

10-16 A-D.

10-17 A.

10-18 A-F.

10-19 A. Yes, it is correct.

10-20 A. Yes, it is correct.

10-21 A. Yes, it is correct.

10-22 A. Yes, it is correct.

10-23 A. Yes, it is correct.

10-24 A. Yes, it is correct.

10-25 A. Yes, it is correct.

10-26 A. Yes, it is correct.

10-27 A, B, C, D, E. The DMZ LAN is a place to put devices that need to be accessible by the internet.

10-28 A.

10-29 A-D.

10-30 A, B, C.

10-31 A-F. These problems can be prevented using CISCO ASA.

10-32

1. Anti-virus	A
2. Anti-spyware	B
3. Anti-spam	C
4. Anti-phishing	D
5. URL filtering	E
6. E-mail filtering	F

10-33 A. Yes, it is true.

10-34 A, B.

10-35 A, B, C.

10-36 B. IPS tools sit in the packets' forwarding path.

10-37 A. Yes, it is true.

10-38 A, B, C.

10-39 A. Yes, it is true.

10-40 A, B, C, D.

10-41 A.

10-42

1. War drivers	A
2. Hackers	B
3. Rogue AP	C
4. Employees	D

10-43 A. Yes, it is true.
10-44 A, B, C, D, E.
10-45 A, B, C.
10-46 A, B.
10-47 B. The solution is the use of authentication.
10-48 A. The solution is the use of encryption.
10-49 B. The solution is the use of authentication.
10-50 B, C. The solution is the use of authentication and IDS/SWAN.
10-51 C. The solution is the use of IDS/SWAN.
10-52 A. WEP is a WLAN security standard.
10-53 B. The interim CISCO solution is a WLAN security standard.
10-54 C. WPA is a WLAN security standard.
10-55 A. WPA2 is a WLAN security standard.
10-56 B. WEP is ratified in 1997.
10-57 C. The interim CISCO solution is ratified in 2001.
10-58 A. WPA is ratified in 2003.
10-59 B. WPA2 is ratified in 2005.
10-60 A. IEEE is ratified WEP.
10-61 C. CISCO is ratified the CISCO interim CISCO solution.
10-62 B. Wi-Fi is ratified WPA.
10-63 A. IEEE is ratified WPA2.
10-64 A. Yes, it is true.
10-65 A. Yes, it is true.
10-66 A. Yes, it is true.
10-67 A. Yes, it is correct.
10-68 A. Yes, it is correct.
10-69 A.
10-70 A-D.
10-71 A.
10-72 A.
10-73 A, B, C. These are the main features of CISCO security enhancements to WEP.
10-74 A. Yes, it is true.
10-75 A. Yes, it is true.
10-76 A, B, C. In this sequence, the paragraph should be completed.
10-77 A. Yes, it is true.
10-78 A, B, C, D. In this sequence, the paragraph should be completed.
10-79 A. Static key is used in WEP standard.
10-80 B. Dynamic key is used in CISCO WLAN Security standard.
10-81 C. Both static and dynamic keys are used in WPA standard.
10-82 C. Both static and dynamic keys are used in WPA2 standard.
10-83 A. It is Weak.
10-84 B. It is strong.
10-85 B. It is strong.
10-86 B. It is strong.
10-87 A. No user authentication is used in WEP standard.
10-88 B. 802.1x user authentication is used in CISCO WLAN Security standard.
10-89 B. 802.1x user authentication is used in WPA standard.
10-90 B. 802.1x user authentication is used in WPA2 standard.
10-91 A. The encryption in WEP standard is weak.
10-92 B. The encryption in CISCO WLAN Security standard is TKIP.
10-93 B. The encryption in WPA standard is TKIP.
10-94 C. The encryption in WPA2 standard is AES.

Index

M

N

O

S